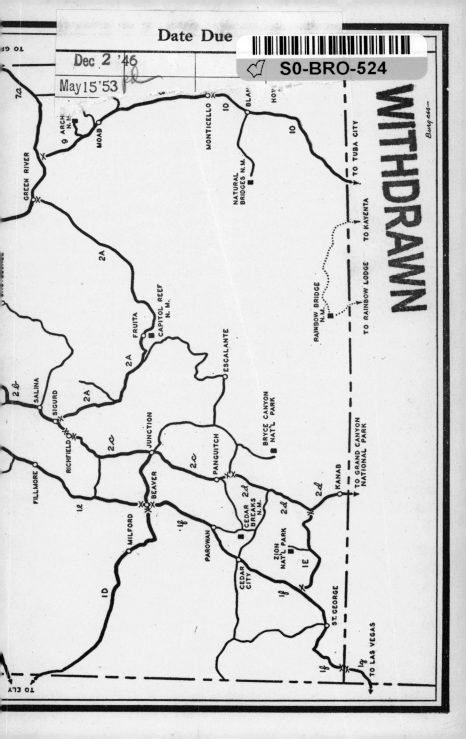

WITHDRAWN

Burgess—

TO CG

7a

9 ARCH N.M.

MOAB

GREEN RIVER

2A

2A

FRUITA   CAPITOL REEF N.M.

2A

SALINA   2b

SIGURD   2A

RICHFIELD   2c

2c

FILLMORE

MILFORD   BEAVER   JUNCTION

1c

1d

1c

PAROWAN   2c   PANGUITCH

CEDAR 2d BREAKS N.M.

CEDAR CITY

2d   2d   ZION NAT'L PARK

1c   1E

ST. GEORGE   1c   1c

TO LAS VEGAS

TO ELY

ESCALANTE

BRYCE CANYON NAT'L PARK

MONTICELLO   10

BLAN

HOV

NATURAL BRIDGES N.M.

10

TO TUBA CITY

TO KAYENTA

RAINBOW BRIDGE N.M.   TO RAINBOW LODGE

2d   KANAB

TO GRAND CANYON NATIONAL PARK

UTAH

A Guide to the State

UTAH

A GUIDE TO THE STATE

*Compiled by Workers of the Writers' Program
of the Work Projects Administration
for the State of Utah*

AMERICAN GUIDE SERIES

ILLUSTRATED

*Sponsored by the Utah State Institute of Fine Arts
Co-sponsored by the Salt Lake County Commission*

HASTINGS HOUSE · Publishers · NEW YORK

MCMXLV

FIRST PUBLISHED IN 1941
SECOND PRINTING, 1945

UTAH STATE INSTITUTE OF FINE ARTS

State-wide Sponsor of the Utah Writers' Project

FEDERAL WORKS AGENCY

JOHN M. CARMODY, *Administrator*

WORK PROJECTS ADMINISTRATION

HOWARD O. HUNTER, *Acting Commissioner*
FLORENCE KERR, *Assistant Commissioner*
DARRELL J. GREENWELL, *State Administrator*

 199

Foreword

Did you know that Theodore Roosevelt once took a bath beneath Rainbow Bridge; that Leland Stanford, when he swung on the "Golden Spike," missed; that Samuel Untermyer, trust-busting attorney, received the largest fee ever paid a lawyer for bringing about a merger of the Utah Copper Company with eastern interests; that Utah, a desert State, has a "sea serpent" story; that many of the "wisest" men a century ago predicted disaster for Mormon colonization of Utah under the direction of the Church President, Brigham Young?

Solid information interwoven with many a fascinating true story fills the pages of this book, written to make available to people without and within the State the facts about Utah—its places, its resources, its people. Complete coverage, accuracy, and readability was the three-fold goal. The large measure of success attained should make this book invaluable to schools, libraries, students, and casual readers alike.

Fully as significant, the Utah Guide supplies a glowing example of how reservoirs of unemployed labor and talent may be used to furnish the power for unique achievements that are valuable socially, artistically, and economically.

GAIL MARTIN
*Chairman, Utah State Institute
of Fine Arts*

June 1, 1940

Preface

When Lansford W. Hastings wrote his *Emigrant's Guide to Oregon
and California,* published at Cincinnati, Ohio, in 1845, urging use of
the "Hastings Cutoff" across the Salt Desert to California, he produced the first guide book to treat even partially the present area of
Utah. Hastings' book recommended a wagon route that could be
traversed with difficulty on horseback, but it led wagon travelers, such
as the Donner party, to tragedy. This guide to the Utah of 1941
is more conservative. One of a series prepared especially for automobile travelers on hard roads in the forty-eight States, it warns the
traveler of rough stretches, quicksands, and waterless deserts. Lesser-
known areas, reached only on shoe or saddle leather, are treated cautiously and factually, without the Hastings bravado.

The collective author has striven for accuracy, but in sifting thousands of facts from fifteen million words of field material, has no doubt
fallen short in many instances. Where error is observed, we should
appreciate substantiated corrections, looking toward the possibility of
a future edition. This book has, indeed, a collective author. Local,
county, State, and Federal agencies, transportation firms, commercial
associations, motor clubs, newspapers, travel agencies, and hundreds of
individuals have been of assistance in furnishing and checking material.
Educational institutions—the University of Utah, Utah State Agricultural College, Brigham Young University, and others—have helped
liberally in special fields. Librarians have been generous with their
facilities, including Alvin Smith, L. D. S. Church librarian; Miss Julia
T. Lynch, librarian, and Miss Johanna Sprague, former librarian, of
the Salt Lake City Public Library; and Professor Esther Nelson,
librarian of the University of Utah. Dozens of technical consultants
have given their time and special knowledge in reading and correcting
manuscript; space permits listing only a limited number of them in
the Appendices.

In preparation of the text, too, the author was collective. The
Utah Writers' Project takes pride in its cooperation with other projects:
The Utah Art Project prepared art work and maps; William Wallace

Ashby, Jr., executed the head pieces and Robert M. Jones the tail pieces. The Utah Historical Records Survey opened its files for much historical data, and aided the Writers' Project in preparation of the History essay, the Chronology, and the Selected Reading List. The Utah Adult Education Project provided the services of N. Field Winn for writing the articles on Geography and Climate, Geology, and Natural Resources and Conservation. Kenneth Borg, of the WPA Division of Operations, prepared the article on Irrigation.

Special thanks are due Mr. John M. Mills of Ogden and Mr. A. William Lund, assistant historian of the Church of Jesus Christ of Latter-day Saints, both of whom read the completed manuscript, corrected errors, and added essential material.

Maurice L. Howe, former State and regional director, and Charles K. Madsen, former State Supervisor, are responsible for gathering most of the factual matter presented in this book, and final work on the guide was done with the editorial co-operation of Darel McConkey of the WPA Writers' Program.

Population figures used are preliminary 1940 reports by the Census Bureau, subject to slight correction after issuance in 1941 of final figures.

DALE L. MORGAN
State Supervisor

Contents

	Page
FOREWORD, by Gail Martin	v
PREFACE	vii
GENERAL INFORMATION	xix
CALENDAR OF ANNUAL EVENTS	xxiii

Part I. Utah's Background

CONTEMPORARY SCENE	3
NATURAL SETTING	10
ARCHEOLOGY AND INDIANS	32
HISTORY	46
THE MORMON CHURCH	91
AGRICULTURE	98
IRRIGATION	105
INDUSTRY AND COMMERCE	112
MINING	119
TRANSPORTATION	126
EDUCATION	135
RECREATION	142
PRESS AND RADIO	149
THE ARTS	153

Part II. Bonneville Bench Cities

LOGAN	191
OGDEN	199
PROVO	215
SALT LAKE CITY	225

Part III. Highways and Dugways

Page

TOUR 1 (Preston, Idaho)—Logan—Ogden—Salt Lake City—Provo
—St. George—(Las Vegas, Nev.) [US 91] 271
Section a. Idaho Line to Logan 272
Section b. Logan to Ogden 275
Section c. Ogden to Salt Lake City 279
Section d. Salt Lake City to Spanish Fork . . . 284
Section e. Spanish Fork to Beaver 291
Section f. Beaver to Arizona Line 296
Section g. Arizona Line (through Arizona) to Nevada Line 309

TOUR 1A Ogden—Huntsville—Woodruff [State 39] 309

TOUR 1B Murray—Brighton [State 173, State 152, and Big Cottonwood Road] 313

TOUR 1C Junction with US 91—Midvale—Bingham—Utah Copper
Mine [State 48] 316

TOUR 1D Beaver—Milford—(Ely, Nev.) [State 21] 322

TOUR 1E Andersons Ranch—Zion Natl. Park—Mt. Carmel Junction
[State 15] 327

TOUR 2 (Montpelier, Idaho)—Salt Lake City—Spanish Fork—Kanab
—(Fredonia, Ariz.) [US 89] 329
Section a. Idaho Line to Spanish Fork 330
Section b. Spanish Fork to Richfield 333
Section c. Richfield to Junction with State 12 . . . 338
Section d. Junction with State 12 to Arizona Line . . 342

TOUR 2A Sigurd—Loa—Green River [State 24] 345

TOUR 3 (Malad, Idaho)—Plymouth—Junction with US 30 S [US 191] 351

TOUR 4 (Evanston, Wyo.)—Brigham—Tremonton—(Burley, Idaho)
[US 30 S] 353
Section a. Wyoming Line to Brigham 354
Section b. Brigham to Idaho Line 361

TOUR 5 Junction with US 30S—Coalville—Kamas—Provo [US 189] 366

TOUR 6 (Craig, Colo)—Salt Lake City—Wendover—(Elko, Nev.)
[US 40] 371
Section a. Colorado Line to Duchesne 371
Section b. Duchesne to Salt Lake City 377
Section c. Salt Lake City to Nevada Line 382

TOUR 6A Mills—Tooele—Junction with US 6 391

Page

TOUR 7   (Grand Junction, Colo.)—Price—Magna—(Elko, Nev.)
                    [US 50]   395
                    Section a. Colorado Line to Price   396
                    Section b. Price to the North Junction with US 91 . .   403
                    Section c. North Junction with US 91 to Nevada Line .   408

TOUR 8   Santaquin—Eureka—Delta—(Ely, Nev.) [US 6] . . .   410

TOUR 9   Crescent Junction—Moab—(Cortez, Colo.) [US 160] . .   422

TOUR 10   Monticello—Blanding—Mexican Hat—(Tuba City, Ariz.)
                    [State 47]   433

Part IV. Parks and Primitive Areas

ARCHES NATIONAL MONUMENT   449
BRYCE CANYON NATIONAL PARK   456
CAPITOL REEF NATIONAL MONUMENT   464
CEDAR BREAKS NATIONAL MONUMENT   471
DINOSAUR NATIONAL MONUMENT   475
GREAT SALT LAKE   480
HIGH UINTAS PRIMITIVE AREA   489
HOVENWEEP NATIONAL MONUMENT   496
NATURAL BRIDGES NATIONAL MONUMENT   501
RAINBOW BRIDGE NATIONAL MONUMENT   508
TIMPANOGOS CAVE NATIONAL MONUMENT   512
ZION NATIONAL PARK   520

Part V. Appendices

CHRONOLOGY   531
SELECTED READING LIST   538
LIST OF CONSULTANTS   552
INDEX   567

Illustrations

Page

THE SETTING I

Between 36 *and* 37

Zion National Park
  Courtesy Zion Easter Pageant Committees
Mountain Window, Zion-Mt. Carmel Highway
In the High Uintas—Hayden Peak (Right Center)
  Robert Davis: Utah Recreation Project, WPA
Brilliant-Hued Bryce Canyon
Goosenecks of the San Juan
  Bolton's Studio
Sipapu Natural Bridge—Natural Bridges National Monument
  Courtesy Department of the Interior
Rainbow Bridge
  Courtesy Gillham Advertising Co.

Mount Timpanogos
  Courtesy Chamber of Commerce, Provo
On the Toe of the Mountain—a Farm in Box Elder County
  Lee: F.S.A.
One of the Chain Lakes, Uinta Mountains
  Robert Davis
Colorado River, Near Rainbow Bridge
  Courtesy Norman Nevills
Great Salt Lake—Salt Evaporation Beds in Foreground
  Highton: F.W.A.
Boat Pier on Great Salt Lake, Near Salt Lake City
  Highton: F.W.A.

THE MORMONS

Between 98 *and* 99

The Temple, Salt Lake City
  Courtesy Gillham Advertising Agency
Mormon Tithing House, Salt Lake City (1869)
  Courtesy Union Pacific Railroad and Salt Lake Tribune
Brigham Young (c. 1850)
  Courtesy L.D.S. Church
Joseph Smith
  Courtesy L.D.S. Church
Mormon Tabernacle under Construction in the 1860's
  A C. R. Savage Photograph: Courtesy L.D.S. Church
Baptistry, Salt Lake Temple
  Copyright, 1940, by the Corporation of the President of the Church of Jesus Christ of Latter-day Saints. All rights reserved.

"This Is the Place" Monument, Salt Lake City
Sagebrush Desert, Box Elder County
  Lee: F.S.A.
Irrigated Land on the Outskirts of Logan
  Lee: F.S.A.
The Hamblin Home, Santa Clara, (c. 1870)
  Courtesy Nels Anderson
Jacob Hamblin, Mormon Missionary to the Indians
Logan Temple
  Courtesy Smith Printing Co.
Tabernacle, St. George
Lion House, Salt Lake City
  Courtesy Dale L. Morgan
Beehive House — The Brigham Young Mansion
  Highton: F.W.A.

Page

AGRICULTURE
Between 158 *and* 159

Dry Farm, Cache County
  Lee: F.S.A.
Highline Canal, Strawberry Valley
  Courtesy Department of the Interior
Farm Home, Centerville
  Lee H. Olsen
Mormon Hay Stacker
  Lee: F.S.A.
Wheat Harvest, Strawberry Valley
  Courtesy Department of the Interior
Mormon Farm Family
  Lee: F.S.A.
Guernsey Bull Owned by a Farm Cooperative
  Lee: F.S.A.

Sweet Corn
  Lee: F.S.A.
Sheep Camp, Beaver Creek
  Shipp: U. S. Forest Service
"Counted In" for Summer Pasture
  Clime: U. S. Forest Service
Draft Colts
  Lee: F.S.A.
Rodeo Stock
  Courtesy Salt Lake Tribune
Peach Orchard Cache County
  Lee: F.S.A.
Berry Pickers, Near Logan
  Lee: F.S.A.

INDUSTRY
Between 284 *and* 285

Copper Pit, Bingham Canyon
  Courtesy Utah Copper Co.
Ore Concentration Mill, Park City
  Courtesy Silver King Coalition Co.
Ore Train, Bingham Canyon
  Courtesy Utah Copper Co.
Smelter Smoke, Garfield
  Lee A. Olsen
Coal Miners, Columbia
  Courtesy Columbia Steel Co.
Coal Loader in a Carbon County Mine
  Courtesy Aberdeen Coal Co.
Steel Ingredients—Iron and Limestone
  Courtesy Columbia Steel Co.

Trucking Sugar Beets
  Courtesy Utah-Idaho Sugar Co.
Sugar in Storage
  Courtesy Utah-Idaho Sugar Co.
Canning—A Leading Utah Industry
In a Salt Lake City Brewery
  Courtesy Fisher Brewing Co.
Salt Piler, Near Salt Lake City
  Courtesy Royal Crystal Salt Co.
Plowing Salt
  Courtesy Royal Crystal Salt Co.

TOWN AND CITY
Between 314 *and* 315

Rotunda, State Capitol
  Courtesy Salt Lake Chamber of Commerce
State Capitol, Salt Lake City
  Highton: F.W.A.
Airview of Temple Square, Salt Lake City
  Courtesy Salt Lake Tribune

State Capitol
  Courtesy Salt Lake Chamber of Commerce
Utah State Agricultural College, Logan
  Courtesy Smith Printing Co.

Page

TOWN AND CITY—*continued*

High School Gymnasium, Spring-
ville
   Lee A. Olsen
Commencement Parade, Univer-
sity of Utah
   Courtesy University of Utah
Maeser Memorial Building, Brig-
ham Young University, Provo
   Lee A. Olsen

Downtown Ogden
   *Courtesy Ogden Chamber of
   Commerce*
Wendover, A Desert Town on the
Nevada Line
   Rothstein: F.S.A.
Main Street, Brigham City
   Lee: F.S.A.
Seagull Monument, Salt Lake City
   Highton: F.W.A.

THE SETTING II

Between 376 *and* 377

Taking Off at 9,000 Feet, Alta
Ski Run
   Lee A. Olsen
Forest Ranger on Mt. Timpanogos
Trail
   Shipp: U. S. Forest Service
Pack Trip in the High Uintas
   *Robert Davis: Utah Recrea-
   tion Project, WPA*
View Across the Wash in Capitol
Reef National Monument
   *Courtesy Utah Museum As-
   sociation*
Bridal Veil Falls, Provo Canyon
   *Courtesy Provo Chamber of
   Commerce*
In the American Fork Canyon,
Wasatch National Forest
   Courtesy U. S. Forest Service

White Water Fishing, Logan
Canyon
   Shaffer: U. S. Forest Service
Deer Hunters' Camp in Beaver
Canyon
   Koziol: U. S. Forest Service
Aspens on Boulder Plateau
   Swan: U. S. Forest Service
Buck and Fawn
   *Shipp and Parkinson: U. S.
   Forest Service*
Seagulls, Great Salt Lake
   *Courtesy Utah State Fish and
   Game Commission*
Boat Basin, Great Salt Lake
   Darel McConkey

YESTERDAYS

Between 438 *and* 439

Old Salt Palace, Salt Lake City
   Courtesy L. D. S. Church
Early Street Scene, Salt Lake City
   *A. C. R. Savage Photo: Cour-
   tesy L. D. S. Church*
Old Cove Fort
   *(Note remnants of rifleman's
   platform over gate.)*
Old Ranch House, Near Ibapah
   Lee A. Olsen
Empey House (c. 1855), Salt
Lake City
   Lee A. Olsen
Erastus Snow House (1875),
Santa Clara
Bauman Adobe House (1874),
Santa Clara

Ogden Canyon (c. 1870)
   *Courtesy U. S. Geological
   Survey*
Green River
   *Courtesy U. S. Geological
   Survey*
Quarrying Granite for the Mor-
mon Temple (c. 1871)
   *Courtesy U. S. Geological
   Survey*
Frisco, Utah's Richest Silver
Town, in the 1870's
"Butch" Cassidy (*Right*) and His
Gang in 1900
   *N. H. Rose Collection, San
   Antonio, Texas*

YESTERDAYS—*continued*

Meeting of the Trains at Promontory (1869)
A. C. R. Savage Photo

Pack-Mule Post to Boulder
Princess Alice (b. 1875)

INDIANS

Between 500 *and* 501

Making Navaho Bread
Charles Kelly
"Mastodon" Petroglyph, Near
Moab
Courtesy Frank Silvey
Rock Pictures, Natural Bridges
National Monument
Ruins of Prehistoric Houses, Hov-
enweep National Monument
Courtesy Norman Nevills
Poncho House, Southeastern Utah
Courtesy Norman Nevills
Navaholand—Monument Valley
Charles Kelly
Navaho Hogan
Roy and Brownie Adams
Navahos on the Move
Charles Kelly
Navaho Medicine Man in Cos-
tume
Roy and Brownie Adams

Painting by Gordon Cope of John
Duncan, Ute Chief
R. M. Jones
Ouray (*Center*) and Sub-chiefs
of the Southern Ute
Smithsonian Institution
Ute Indian (c. 1860)
*A. C. R. Savage Photograph:
Courtesy L. D. S. Church*
Ute Farmer
Courtesy U. S. Indian Service
Navaho Medicine Man with Sand
Painting Used in Healing Rites
Roy and Brownie Adams
Hogan on the Shivwit Reserva-
tion
Dr. D. E. Beck

Maps

	Page
TOUR KEY MAP	*front end paper*
TRANSPORTATION MAP	*back end paper*
LOGAN	195
OGDEN	209
PROVO	221
TEMPLE SQUARE AREA, SALT LAKE CITY	236
SALT LAKE CITY	252-253
UNIVERSITY OF UTAH	261
STATE MAP	555-566

General Information

Railroads: Denver & Rio Grande Western (D. & R. G. W.) R.R., Southern Pacific, Union Pacific (U. P.) R.R., Western Pacific R.R. Four electric lines furnish intrastate service.

Bus Lines: Burlington Trailways, Denver-Salt Lake-Pacific Trailways, Greyhound Lines, Overland Stages, Rio Grande Trailways, Santa Fe Trailways, Union Pacific Stages. Other lines provide intrastate service.

Air Lines: United Air Lines (transcontinental, New York City, Seattle, San Francisco), Western Air Express (Salt Lake City to Los Angeles and San Diego, and Salt Lake City to Yellowstone National Park in season).

Waterways: Boats are available at Moab for adventure trips on the Colorado River and at Mexican Hat for trips on the San Juan River. Boats for trips on Great Salt Lake are for hire at the boat pier near Garfield.

Highways: Nine Federal highways, more than 100 State roads. State police patrol main highways. No boundary inspection. State gasoline tax 4¢. Filling stations frequent on main-traveled roads, sometimes widely separated in desert areas. Advisable to carry extra water, oil, and gasoline on some roads (*inquire locally, and see Tours*). Free Road Maps issued annually by Utah State Road Commission and by oil companies.

Traffic Regulations: Maximum speed on State highways, 50 m.p.h.; highway signs indicate restricted speeds through cities, on mountain and canyon roads, in school zones and congested areas. Hand signals. Non-residents should register their cars with a State agency five days after entering the State; Utah license plates required after sixty days.

Accommodations: Larger cities and towns on main highways have adequate hotels and tourist camps. In isolated small communities, room and board can usually be obtained from local residents.

Climate and Equipment: In the mountains during summer months days are warm and nights cold. Rainstorms are frequent in higher mountain passes. Travel should not be attempted at high altitudes earlier than June or later than October. Main highways are usually clear of snow in winter, but may be temporarily blocked during severe snowstorms. Visitors should dress for warm weather in summer (but should remember the cowboy dictum that light clothes are not always cool clothes in the desert). Modified cowboy garb is recommended for roughing it in the mountains and deserts, "Levi's" (bibless overalls), denim shirt, broad hat, sun glasses, a bandanna to keep out the sand and protect the neck from sunburn, cowboy or laced boots (oxfords are sand-catchers and do not protect the ankles from cacti and snakes), a jacket, sweater, or light coat for cool evenings, and gloves to protect the hands in climbing rocks and rustling firewood. Rubber or cord soles are best for climbing over "slickrocks." Well-advised tenderfeet keep shirt collars buttoned and sleeves rolled down, for the desert and high mountain sun burns unmercifully. Slicker or slicker-type poncho helps in case of mountain rains. Equipment for extended horseback or pack trips normally furnished by commercial packers.

Photography: Clarity of atmosphere at high altitudes throughout Utah makes the light much more intense than in humid areas, and actinic values of light are much higher. Visitors to the State would be wise to use a light meter before each shot, translating the reading always on the side of the faster shutter speeds and tighter aperture—a good rule also for those who take photos by the "peep and snap" method. Light values vary enormously from full-lighted to shaded spots. Use yellow filter for cloud effects. Slower types of film apt to give best results. Odd-size photographic film and color film are more readily obtainable in larger population centers.

Recreation Areas: Utah has ten national forests, and parts of each are equipped with picnicking and camping facilities, including fire pits, picnic tables, safe water, and restrooms. Fires should be built only at designated places, within a ten-foot circle clear of inflammable material, and should be put *dead out* before leaving. Matches should be broken, with one finger on the burnt end, before they are thrown away. Cigarettes and pipe dregs should be stamped into humus-free soil. For other recreation grounds see *Recreation, and Parks and Primitive Areas.*

Fishing: Game fish are defined as trout, black bass, mountain herring, silver salmon, catfish, whitefish, crappie, and perch. Seven-inch limit on bass, trout, salmon and herring. Day's limit of ten pounds or thirty fish. Game fish season, usually June 15 through October, is proclaimed annually by State Fish and Game Commissioner. Resident license $2, non-resident license $3, required for game and common fish, which include carp, sucker, and chub (open season year round). Closed waters designated by signs. No fishing 9 P.M. to 4 A.M. Fishing on horseback is forbidden.

Hunting: Resident hunting license $3, combined hunting and fishing license $4; non-resident hunting (deer and bear excepted) and fishing license $10, bear and deer license $20; season for deer and game birds set by proclamation of Fish and Game Commissioner. Limited number of elk licenses issued each year. Federal duck stamps required for hunting waterfowl, season fixed by Federal government. Wild rabbits are fair game the year round, without license, but are apt to be diseased in summer. Seagulls are protected by State law. No open season on big-horn sheep, mountain goat, antelope, or moose, except by proclamation. Hunting from an airplane is forbidden.

Liquor Regulations: 3.2 per cent beer sold in public places, with or without meals, and on room-service order. Wines and liquors sold only at State stores, usually identifiable by frosted windows and venetian blinds, and at package agencies in privately operated business places (inquire locally). One-year liquor license, 50¢, obtainable at liquor stores.

Poisonous Plants: Three-leafed poison ivy, with foliage bearing an irritating oil, occurs throughout the State, except in deserts. If infected, wash exposed parts with strong soap and warm water; calamine lotion or sugar of lead are good counteractives after irritation sets in. Plant has seductively gorgeous foliage in fall. Lupine, growing on mountain slopes and foothills, has poisonous foliage; treat similarly to poison ivy. Stinging nettle, irritating but non-poisonous, occurs among thick growths in canyons and along rivers; sting is eased by vaseline or cold cream.

Poisonous Reptiles and Insects: Rattlesnakes, of the smaller varieties, range nearly all over the State. Wear high-top shoes or leggings for protection, use hands with care in climbing rocky places. Use tourniquet between bite and heart, releasing it occasionally to permit circulation; incise wound a quarter of an inch deep, suck out poison, but lips and mouth should be free of sores; pack incision with potassium permanganate crystals; give patient plenty of water, keep him warm and quiet; get a doctor.   Gila monster, with poisonous bite, found in lower parts of southern Utah; treatment same as for snake bite.   Scorpions occur in rocks and deserts; their sting has about the same intensity as that of a hornet and is treated the same way—with a pinch of wet soda or a dab of ammonia.   Tarantulas, huge black or brown spiders, occur in desert areas, but there is no record of anyone in Utah having been bitten by one.   Black widow spiders, identifiable by red hourglass on abdomen, have serious poison bite; put patient to bed, give copious quantities of non-spirituous fluids, treat wound with iodine, get a doctor. Wood ticks, flat, brown insects about a quarter of an inch long, are carriers of Rocky Mountain spotted fever, a disease with a high mortality rate.   Persons who frequent mountains, wooded sections, or even deserts should be inoculated against the fever (vaccination is provided by the U. S. Public Health Service).   Infection may result after a tick penetrates the skin and feeds two hours or longer.   Examine body frequently for ticks, remove those that have penetrated the skin with a steady straight pull, preferably with tweezers; outdoorsmen say a tick will back out of the skin if covered with a drop of turpentine or kerosene.   If head pulls off, open skin and remove it, treating wound with a good disinfectant.

Water: For complete safety, all questionable water should be boiled before use, to obviate typhoid infection or cramps, sometimes caused by alkali water when drunk by those not accustomed to it.

Calendar of Annual Events

January

First	at Ogden	Oratorio, *The Messiah*

March

No fixed date	at Salt Lake City	Annual Art Show, Utah State Institute of Fine Arts
No fixed date	at Brigham City	Box Elder County Poultry Day
No fixed date	at Beaver	Dairy Day

April

Week of sixth	at Salt Lake City	Annual Conference, L. D. S. Church
Last Friday and Saturday	at Provo	Invitational Track and Field Meet and Relay Carnival
Last Saturday	at Provo	Posture Parade of Utah High School Girls
All month	at Springville	National Art Exhibit
Easter	at Provo	Easter Service, Y Mountain
Easter	at Zion National Park	Easter Service and Pageant
No fixed date	at Ephraim	Rambouillet Day
No fixed date	at Whiterocks	Ute Indian Bear Dance

May

Early	at Spanish Fork	Utah Junior Livestock Show
Mid-month	at Brigham City	Dairy Day
Mid-month	at Logan	Livestock Exhibit and Horse Show

MAY—continued

Mid-month (two days)	at Richmond	Black and White (Holstein) Days
Last week	at Vernal	Uintah County Livestock Show
No fixed date	at Price	Intermountain Band Contest

JUNE

First week (two days)	at Salt Lake City	Intermountain Junior Fat Stock Show
Second week (three days)	at Pleasant Grove	Strawberry Day
Third week (two days)	at Tooele	Tunnel Days
Third week (one day)	at Providence	Strawberry Day
No fixed date	at Ogden	Ogden Horse Show
No fixed date	at North Ogden	Cherry Day
No fixed date	at Ephraim	Poultry Day

JULY

Fourth	at Provo	Fourth of July Celebration
Fourth	at Neola	Rodeo
Second week (three days)	at Price	Robbers Roost Roundup
Second week (three days)	at Nephi	Ute Stampede
No fixed date	at Aspen Grove	Timpanogos Community Hike
Twenty-fourth	Statewide	Pioneer Day
Week of twenty-fourth	at Salt Lake City	Covered Wagon Days
Week of twenty-fourth	at Salt Lake City	Oratorio, *Creation*
Week of twenty-fourth	at Ogden	Pioneer Days
No fixed date	at Manti	Sanpitch Powwow
No fixed date	at Whiterocks	Ute Indian Sun Dance
Last week	at American Fork	Poultry Day

AUGUST

First week	at Garfield	Utah Copper Field Day
First week	at Lewiston	Lewiston Race Meet and Stampede
Mid-month	in Central Utah towns	Black Hawk Celebration
Last week (three days)	at Fort Duchesne	Uintah Basin Industrial Convention and Indian Fair
No fixed date	at Garland	Wheat and Beet Day
Last week (three days)	at Payson	Onion Festival
Last week (three days)	at Salt Lake City	National Ram Sale
Last week	at Murray	Salt Lake County Fair

SEPTEMBER

First week	at Coalville	Summit County Fair
First week	at St. George	Dixie Roundup and Fruit Festival
First week (three days)	at Manti	Sanpete County Fair
First week (one day)	at Orem	Harvest Festival
Second week	at Ferron	Peach Day
Second week (three days)	at Midvale	Harvest Festival
Second week (two days)	at Brigham City	Peach Days
Second week (three days)	at Provo	Utah County Fair
Second week (three days)	at Logan	Cache County Fair
Second week (three days)	at Vernal	Vernal Rodeo
Third week (three days)	at Ogden	Ogden and Weber County Fair and Race Meet
Fourth week (three days)	at Price	Carbon County and Eastern Utah Fair
Fourth week (three days)	at Bingham	Galena Days Celebration
No fixed date	at Lehi	Community Day and Community Fair

SEPTEMBER—continued

No fixed date	at Kamas	Kamas Valley Fiesta
No fixed date	at Panguitch	Garfield County Fair and Race Meet
No fixed date	at Fountain Green	Lamb Day
No fixed date	at Beaver	Beaver County Fair
No fixed date	at Tremonton	Box Elder County Fair and Rodeo
No fixed date	at Moroni	Turkey Day
No fixed date	at Morgan	Morgan County Fair
No fixed date	at Fillmore or Deseret (alternately)	Millard County Fair
Last week	at Salt Lake City	Utah State Fair

OCTOBER

| Week of sixth | at Salt Lake City | Semi-annual Conference L. D. S. Church |
| Last week (two days) | at Huntington | Hereford Days |

NOVEMBER

Second week	at Ogden	Ogden Livestock Show
Thanksgiving week	Statewide	Celery Week
No fixed date	at Kanab	Horse Race Meet and Rodeo

DECEMBER

Mid-month	at Provo	Oratorio, *The Messiah*
Third week	at Ephraim	Oratorio, *The Messiah*
Last week	at Logan	Oratorio, *The Messiah*
Sunday after Christmas	at Salt Lake City	Oratorio, *The Messiah*

PART I
Utah's Background

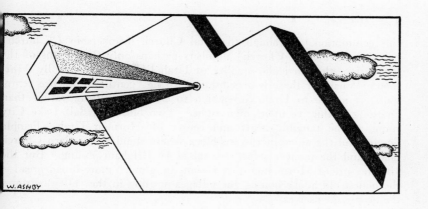

Contemporary Scene

THE Mormon habitat has always been a vortex of legend and lie. Even today, as the State settles down to gray hairs, there lingers something wonderful and outrageous about Utah, a flavor of the mysterious and strange. Many still journey to Utah to see a Mormon.

Even if there had been no background of Joseph Smith, Angel Moroni, and the Book of Mormon, Utahns would have been incomprehensible, misunderstood and lied about, because they set down in the book of Western history the most stubbornly cross-grained chapter it contains. All the conventions of Western life in Utah went haywire. Only late, and briefly, did Utahns turn feverish, like their neighbors, with get-rich-quickness. Wars of cattle baron and homesteader dissolved at Utah's borders, because farmers had come first to the creeks. Lynch law wandered into the bishops' courts to sit in the back pews and watch, bemused, the quiet sanity of theological justice. Immaculate woman and scarlet woman together lifted their petticoats to take flight before family migrations and polygamy. Utah has always had a way of doing things different. The rest of the country has never quite got over it.

Much of that pioneer distinctiveness survives in Utah life, although the forces of twentieth century civilization have shaped Utah into patterns of conformance, so that there are fewer outward stigmata to a Utahn, and somewhat less wild speculation about him. Most visitors now betray no disappointment at finding Mormons hornless.

"Utahn" is regarded as almost synonymous with "Mormon," although there have always been those who would quarrel fiercely with this assumption. Although the total Church membership ("Church" meaning always *the* Church) numbers perhaps only three-fifths of the population, the particular quality of Utah life is almost wholly Mormon. Whatever there is of substance to the "gentile" influence represents, if native to Utah, a reaction to Mormon culture rather than anything distinctive in its own right. Two blocks in Salt Lake City stand as the tangible heart and center of Mormon Utah—Temple Square and the adjacent eastern block where stand the modern Church offices and the pioneer structures raised by Brigham Young. But the vital texture of Mormon culture is something much more broadspread— the honest old adobe houses, the villages nestling in the valley bottoms, the people themselves.

Mormon Utah is primarily that fertile strip of occupied land, down through the north-central part of the State, lying at the foot of the Wasatch mountain rampart. Four-fifths of the population lives here, in towns that vary from metropolitan Salt Lake City to humble villages that are distinguishable as towns only by their general store and sturdy "meeting house." This densely populated area, said to sustain more persons to the acre than even crowded Japan, is the great monument to Mormon endeavor, although the log or adobe houses built by Utah's founding fathers rise from creek bottoms all over the State.

Even in this richest and oldest-settled area, the stamp of a pioneer culture is everywhere manifest. Grandsires built too sturdily, albeit of such building materials as wood and mud, for the pioneer period to have lost its substance. Even in Salt Lake City old adobe houses stand up indomitably to the years, the very earth of their dooryards seeming to have crumbled sooner. In smaller towns these houses retain their pioneer flavor of accomplishment; often they are still the best houses in town, despite modern structures of pressed brick, white-painted wood, or stone. There are few flourishes to such buildings. They stand upon the earth, compact and designed to live in, the bare high walls weathered native gray. Almost always these houses are shadowed by trees. If houses could not stand as monuments to a culture, trees, gardens, and sheer greenness could. The cities themselves, almost universally set four-square to the directions, reflect an ideal of spacious and noble planning. Exigencies of one kind and another have invaded the grand sweep of pioneer planning, but nothing is more quickly remarkable to visitors than the breadth and straightness of the streets, the width of the sidewalks, and the length of blocks in Utah cities. And all the cities are tree-grown, comfortable with homes and lawns and gardens and flowering shrubs.

Not in this greenest area but in the outlands most nearly survives the old Mormon society. Few "gentiles" have found that hard land to their liking; they have settled instead in the cities, and cast there the social and physical weight of their differentness. The Mormon "wards," or local congregations, in the rural villages comprise from ten to a hundred families living on terms of social intimacy unknown in the cities. Every man is every man's neighbor; all the children go to the same school; the families go together on Sunday to meeting, or to the canyons on outings. Perhaps the sons and daughters sing in the choir; certainly they go together to the dances, bazaars, and banquets held in the meeting house. Only the richer communities have church buildings sufficiently elaborate to boast chapel and "amusement hall" both; characteristically the meeting house serves all community purposes unless the school building is called into use. Until "gentile" accession to political power in the late eighties, the meeting house served also for school.

Always the most important person in the ward is the bishop. He may also be mayor or justice of the peace or some other officer of civil distinction, but to the people his authority stems first of all from his bishopric, because he there most nearly satisfies their daily needs. He may settle a dispute, officiate at a dance, preside at a marriage, or sign a "recommend" for a member planning temple work for his dead. On Sunday nights at Sacrament meeting, he has words of advice for the brethren, advice temporal as much as spiritual. The bishop is heart and center of a way of living, as close to the earth and the people as his grandfather, who may conceivably in his own time have served as bishop.

Something of this close-knit social fabric is common also to the cities, but the very size of the cities has broken down the completeness of intimacy. Schools are numerous, and school districts do not conform to ward boundaries; life is more complex generally; and "gentiles" live intermingled with Mormons. In the cities, indeed, "gentile" has become almost a word of lost significance, though in the outlying areas it is still a term of sharp differentiation. Yet Mormon feels closer to Mormon always, out of the long community of tradition, despite the forces of depression, and intermarriage, which have worked quietly to break down all distinctions among Utahns.

It is surprising how little of color survives out of the years of turmoil. The violent days of struggle between Mormon and anti-Mormon, polygamist and anti-polygamist, have faded almost to nothing. Polygamy has become almost legendary; the generation coming now of age marvels almost as greatly as outsiders that polygamy was once a part of the Utah way of life. There are a very few polygamists still alive, patriarchs looking back over the full years, but even among the Mormons there are few who number a polygamist among their acquaintances. In ordinary living, polygamy survives chiefly in a consciousness of relatives. Utah families are larger today than the national average—

larger than Utah's apparent capacity to retain the increase—but even monogamic families in times past ran to far greater size, and Utahns have relatives enough in the straight line of descent; the genealogical ramifications consequent upon polygamy—half-granduncles and grand-aunts, half second- third- fourth- and fifth-cousins—are such that the typical Utahn of old Mormon descent never inquires into the full extent of his relationships, content to stipulate vaguely that he may be distantly related to a tenth of the population of the State.

Mormons live perhaps more comfortably in Utah than non-Mormons, because the major pattern of the State's life is Mormon-made; Mormons are not, like "gentiles," under the necessity of challenging the structure of their social life. Probably in no other State is there so acute a religious consciousness as in Utah; there continues, not obviously, an undercurrent social antagonism that is, however, only a vestigial feeling out of the long warfare. Some of the anti-Church feeling derives also from the idealogical developments affecting other churches in other States, in the iconoclastic attitudes taken by the younger generation toward all churches and religions; if it is stronger here, the feeling grows out of greater helplessness toward a more strongly integrated church. The Church stands likewise as an embodiment of convention, in a time when convention and tradition are being broken upon the distress of American society; inevitably there are rebels to speak against it. For most Utahns, however, the Church contributes to a more comfortable life—it is itself a whole way of living.

The West, in popular argot, has always been radical—and Utah especially so. That is in part an Eastern egotism, which finds outrageous that which for excellently good reasons does not conform to the Eastern idea of how things should be done. But it is in the nature of Utah contrariety, perhaps a consequence in part of the strong New England breed which shaped Mormon beginnings, that Utahns in general are pronouncedly conservative, though lately consistent Democrats. In part this conservatism stems from the binding forces of Church convention and Church morality, and the homogeneity of the racial stock, which is not only more than 99 per cent white, but is almost wholly Anglo-Scandinavian; there has been no social conflict of racial groups to facilitate unrest. There is probably a greater emphasis upon the family in Utah than generally in the country; there is probably less drinking, less smoking, and perhaps less card-playing; certainly there is a greater disposition to stay put. Yet this conservatism certainly is not insularism. Probably there is a greater cosmopolitan leavening to Utah society, urban and rural, than anywhere in the country; there is hardly a village that does not contain one or more persons who have served upwards of two years as a Church missionary in distant lands—Europe, Africa, South America, Australia, or even Japan.

Utah's neighborliness is often remarked by visitors; here the years tell their own tale, for outlanders frequently, in early days, were viewed with a chill and suspicious eye. Utah socially is not large enough, or complex enough, to have mastered wholly the art of minding its own business—an art which can be carried to extremes. Many have settled in Utah for no other reason than this over-the-fence sort of friendliness, although there are those who have left the State in a wholehearted quest for more privacy. The State is also too close to its pioneer beginnings for the social amenities to come with entire grace. Art has been backward, and literature and music have been subordinated to religious ends. Education has been a pride of Utahns, who point to one of the highest literacy ratings in the country, but the State has not been sufficiently rich either economically or socially to attract from outside the mature, reflective minds that enrich popular living; indeed, Utah has lost many of its own sons and daughters to areas of greater opportunity. In a State where seven of twenty-nine counties lack a bank, eight a railroad, and several a telegraph line, it is inevitable that there should be some social lags.

Utah has its own characteristic symbolisms. Most omnipresent is the beehive. It occurs on the State seal, on the university seal, on the Beehive House in Salt Lake City, on the masthead of newspapers, on the Mormon-owned Hotel Utah in Salt Lake City, on top of policemen's call boxes, on every conceivable interior decoration, on places of business. Four names, drawn direct from Utah history, occur in probably every city of size in the State—there are Beehive laundries, Seagull loan companies, Deseret cafes, and Zion stores, or any imaginable reshuffling of the four. Book of Mormon names are widespread, both for places and persons. The State has towns named Deseret, Lehi, Manti, Moroni, and Nephi; Lehi, Moroni, and Nephi are still current as names of individuals, though now more rarely seen. Frequently occurring first names of historical significance are Orson, Heber, Parley, and Hyrum, though there are few Brighams in these latter years. Names of Biblical flavor are probably more numerous in Utah than anywhere outside tradition-bound New England, while Ute and Paiute place names also add their own distinctive flavor to the State.

Mormon Church conferences, the annual meeting in the spring, and the semi-annual conference in the fall, bring thousands of people from all over the State, and from many adjoining States, into Salt Lake City. The annual conference, normally including April 6, is, sartorially and socially, the Mormon Easter. There are more flower-trimmed hats, more pastel topcoats, at conference time than on Easter proper—and it nearly always rains. "Conference weather" is proverbial. In the 67-year period from 1874 to 1940, only once, 1916-1918, was there a period of successive conference weeks free of measurable precipitation, the average precipitation being about half an inch, although in 1929 there fell 15.4 inches of snow. In a desert State, "conference rains" are put up with gladly.

In Utahns there is universally a consciousness of the earth, in part because of the recency of its pioneering, but principally because Utah is an uncertainly subdued land, instinct with hardship. A Utahn who goes to New England or to Oregon looks at the broad rivers almost bitterly. It is unnatural that rivers should waste into the sea, just as it is unnatural that farmers should mature crops by rain alone. Rivers should be dammed at canyon mouths and their waters carried in canals to the thirsting land. Water in Utah is precious, savored as champagne might be in another land. Life does not come easy. Perhaps some of the especial flavor of Utah comes from this quality of things coming hard. Its beauty is not wholehearted; always there is something withheld. Utah's loveliness is a desert loveliness, unyielding and frequently sterile; its one sea, Great Salt Lake, is lethal and worthless. This kind of country does not appeal to everyone; some have fled it in hatred. Yet many Utahns have not really loved the land of their nativity until they have ventured into more prodigal areas, into the lush green Northwest, the fertile Middle West, or the granite-ribbed East.

The State is immense and varied, almost beyond belief. The band of irrigated green, west of the Wasatch Mountains, extends from north central Utah southward, curving gently west to a corner with Arizona and Nevada. West of this band is the gray-green Great Salt Lake, gray desert, and peaked mountains. Eastward is the red desert country of the Colorado Plateau, yellowing as it approaches the Uinta Mountains on the north, ever reddening as it extends southward and eastward to the Arizona and Colorado lines—a country of flat-topped mountains and violent color. These dessicated gray and red deserts, and these mountains, represent more than 90 per cent of Utah. The tremendous weight of the land lies upon everything. The mountains climb into the skies; the deserts ache with sheer empty immensity. Utah is many things at once: Utah is green-carpeted vales lying peacefully under the shadow of the Wasatch; Utah is a wide solitude of rolling dry valleys, with hills marching beyond hills to blue horizons; Utah is unearthly white desert; Utah is tall snow-crowned mountains; Utah is blue lakes; Utah is canyon and plateau wonderfully fragrant with pines.

Its aspect changes with the sharp progression of the seasons. Winter is a time of hibernation. In summer much of the State is bled by the sun to an inhospitable dun and gray. But in spring the flowering desert has a surpassing loveliness, and in autumn the canyons choke with color.

In Salt Lake City, in Ogden and Provo and Logan, the immensity of the State is circumscribed, and the world is as near as the front page of the daily newspapers. Yet the quiet hills bespeak something alien and impermanent to this urban reality of steel and stone, aspirin and cashiers' registers.   One can almost start out of a dream to see these things perished and the land returned to the hills—green-gray with sage or tawny with dry June grass under the blue-drifting smoke of Indian campfires.   Out in the desert the world changes; sheep and cattle graze in a land out of time and space, and even the radio in the sheepherder's wagon does not convince one that cities can exist in a world where the sun shines so brilliantly in the deep blue sky while the warm wind rustles in the sage.

In the red deserts are Utah's scenic and scientific marvels, its dinosaur bones, its cliff-dwellings, its multicolored canyons, its Indians, more natural arches and bridges than anybody knows—two more were discovered in 1940—its cow-country frontier, its vast tracts of unmapped, unexplored country.   Cárdenas discovered the canyon of the Colorado, but his reports use no single adjective of color.   Mormon pioneers, cowboys, and sheepherders have looked upon marvels of natural color to see them as "piles of rocks" that couldn't sprout a kernel or feed a beast.   Utah has been, historically, a detoured country; the Oregon Trail went north of it, other cross-country travel south of it.   Utah's deserts wait still, wrapped in multicolored serenity, for their full measure of appreciation.

It is fitting that the worthless dry deserts nevertheless should begin, profitably for Utah, to instill in popular consciousness some other definition of the State than Mormonism, for the richer land has been pressed almost to its uttermost by the Mormon struggle with the earth. Mormon enterprise was a powerful force that wrought greatly with a hostile environment; but Utah today is supported by its mines and its livestock far more importantly than by its farms, despite the national reputation of its celery and its fruit, and despite its alfalfa, wheat, sugar beets, and garden vegetables.   The fertility of the land has been outstripped by the fertility of the people.   The sons and daughters born so strangely stalwart from the loins of Eastern and European converts who left urban homes to wrestle with unfamiliar Utah deserts, today are migrating from the State, bringing their strength, their vigor, and their eager ambition to the great cities of either coast.   They go like a lifeblood, from wounds that Utah hopes one day to close.

Natural Setting

WEST of the Rockies, midway between Canada and Mexico, lies the State of Utah, a broad rectangular area from which a smaller rectangle in the northeastern corner has been cut away. The southeastern corner, where Utah, Colorado, Arizona, and New Mexico meet, is the only point in the United States at which four State boundaries are adjoined. Within an area of 84,990 square miles, 2,806 of which are water surface, Utah presents an irregular and diversified topography. Lofty mountains roll northward and eastward into Idaho, Wyoming, and Colorado; wide undulating plateaus sweep southward into Arizona; and vast unpeopled deserts of salt and alkali stretch westward across the Nevada line.

The Wasatch Mountains and continuing highlands extend north and south across the center of the State, dividing it roughly into two approximately equal sections. The loftiest summit in the Wasatch, Mount Timpanogos near Provo, reaches an elevation of 12,008 feet. Several other peaks in the vicinity have an altitude of more than 11,000 feet. The Wasatch Range terminates near central Utah, but the Sanpitch, Pahvant, and Tushar plateaus continue southward and merge at length into a broken table-land, which extends across the Arizona line. The Henry, La Sal, and Abajo mountains rise out of the southern plateau. In the Tushar Plateau near Beaver there are three 12,000-foot lava peaks. Extending eastward from the Wasatch Range, and covering most of northeastern Utah, are the Uinta Mountains, where Kings Peak, the highest point in the State, towers to an elevation of 13,498 feet. South of the Uinta Range is the Uintah Basin, an east-west valley bordered by sloping mesa lands.

Southeastern Utah is an immense broken plateau extending in a triangular form over nearly one-third of the State's surface. Most of this region is too rugged for agricultural use, and only a small part has enduring settlements. The *Deseret News* for September 11, 1861, describes the territory adjacent to the Green River as "one vast 'contiguity of waste' and measureably valuless, excepting for nomadic purposes, hunting grounds for Indians, and to hold the world together." Nevertheless, southeastern Utah is not completely valueless, for its streams have cut gorges hundreds of feet deep in the sandstone highlands, and the forces of erosion have strewn the plateaus with startling and fantastic geological formations. Certain groups of these natural marvels have become points of scenic interest, among them Capitol Reef, Arches, Natural Bridges, and Rainbow Bridge National Monuments.

The plateau region of south central Utah, near the Arizona line, is also replete with natural wonders, including Zion and Bryce Canyon National Parks, and Cedar Breaks National Monument. In Zion Canyon massive 3,000-foot cliffs rise perpendicularly on either side of the Virgin River. The Kolob Canyons of Zion National Monument are eight ravines cut into the plateaus north and west of Zion Park by tributaries of the same stream.

The Great Basin, which includes all of western Utah, is a huge depression enclosed by highlands and having no outlet to the sea. The western part of the Basin is characterized by arid valleys, extensive salt flats, and forbidding wastelands. In this region scattered mountain ranges rise like islands out of the flat, gray monotony of the surrounding country, and near the Nevada line a large area is included in the Great Salt Lake Desert. Depressions in the Basin are occupied by Utah Lake on the south and Great Salt Lake on the north. The former is the largest body of fresh water in the State, and the latter is the largest salt water body in the Western Hemisphere. Great Salt Lake is approximately 75 miles long and 50 miles wide. It has no outlet, but Utah Lake empties into Great Salt Lake by way of the Jordan River.

Utah drainage areas may be divided into three sections. The northwestern corner of the State drains through the Raft River country into the Snake River. The remaining drainage is divided between the Great Basin and the Colorado River system. Large areas in eastern Utah, together with most of the southern plateaus, drain through the Green River and other tributaries into the Colorado. Largest of these tributaries are the Fremont, San Juan, and Virgin rivers. Some streams, however, flow from eastern Utah or from the plateaus into the Great Basin. The most important stream flowing through the northeastern part of the State is Bear River, which originates on the north slope of the Uinta Mountains in Utah, flows across a corner of Wyom-

ing, back into Utah, then loops into Wyoming and Idaho before dis-
charging its waters into Great Salt Lake.   Many streams cut through
the Wasatch Mountains to find their way into Utah Lake or Great Salt
Lake.   Among these are the Weber, Ogden, Provo, and Spanish Fork
rivers.   The Sevier River flows out of the Panguitch Plateau, and disappears into the Sevier Desert, and the few small streams rising in the
western ranges run dry before they have progressed far across the floor
of the Great Basin.

An average elevation of approximately one mile above sea level is
the principal factor in determining Utah's temperate climate.   The
Santa Clara Valley and the Virgin River Valley, with an elevation of
2,700 feet, are known as Utah's Dixie.   Their winters are comparatively free from storm, and they have a semi-tropical climate and a
warm dry atmosphere.   In mountainous regions of the State the temperature is low in the winter and moderate in the summer.   In the
higher reaches of the Wasatch and Uinta mountains, particularly, the
summers are short and the winters cold and long.   The lowlands
adjacent to the mountains have a pleasant temperate climate, with only
a few extremely hot or cold days.   Temperatures in Salt Lake City
occasionally reach 100 degrees in midsummer and sometimes fall to
10 degrees below zero in winter.

Precipitation also is largely determined by the altitude.   The high
mountain ranges receive as much as forty inches per year, most of which
comes in the form of snow; the valleys near the mountains receive
about fifteen inches; and the desert regions are fortunate if they get
as much as five inches.   The Wasatch Mountains are responsible for
much of the precipitation on the arable land of the State.   Rain-bearing
clouds from the Pacific Ocean cross the hot deserts of the Great Basin,
and when they strike the cool mountain air, rain or snow falls upon
the western slopes of the Wasatch Range.   Because of the precipitation
in this section, a great agricultural belt paralleling the mountains has
been developed.

GEOLOGY

The man-made history of Utah is but a letter in the latest "syllable
of recorded time."   The geologic history of Utah is a story of mighty
rivers and deserts and mountains, of simple protoplasmic things in the
dark ooze of ancient seas, and of their struggle through millions of
years toward consciousness and light.   The geologist has divided the
story of the earth into five great chapters, and every chapter can be
read in the rock formations of Utah.   Some pages are missing, some
crumpled and torn; some words are blotted, some meanings obscure,
but on the whole the record is well preserved.

Scientists, through their study of the decomposition of radioactive minerals, calculate that the Archeozoic rocks, the most ancient formations in the world, are one billion, eight hundred fifty million years old. Archeozoic rocks, exposed by folding and faulting in the Wasatch Mountains, show no fossil trace of life. If life existed in Archeozoic time, the tremendous pressure of accumulating sediments has long ago obliterated its faintest impression.

During Proterozoic time (the second chapter) water covered the greater part of eastern Utah, and the first one-celled life forms that have been definitely recognized made their appearance. Proterozoic rocks are exposed in several places throughout the State—notably in the vicinity of Big Cottonwood Canyon, east of Salt Lake City, and in the desert ranges of the Great Basin, where faulting and erosion have stripped away the younger sediments.

Seas of the Paleozoic era advanced into Utah and retreated again many times, and each advancing sea brought with it strange new forms of life. At the beginning of the Paleozoic time the little crab-like trilobite, seldom more than three inches long, was the king of beasts. As the era lengthened into millions of years, gastropods, brachiopods, cephalopods, horn corals, and even higher types of fish appeared. Huge ferns and dense forest growths lined the waterways, and sprawling vertebrates swam in the oceans and crawled awkwardly on the shores. Exposure of Paleozoic rocks is widespread throughout Utah—particularly in the Wasatch, in the Uintas, in the basin ranges, and in the high plateaus of the south. Although vertebrate fossils of the Paleozoic era are comparatively rare in the State, there is an abundance of invertebrate forms. Fossilized trilobites may be found by the thousands near Antelope Springs west of Delta. Protruding from the canyon walls, or lying in the slide-rock of the Wasatch Range, there are many fossilized specimens of corals, sea lilies, snails, clams, mussels, and similar forms. Fossil shellfish are also numerous in the Uinta Mountains, in various parts of the Great Basin, and in south central Utah.

The major part of the Great Basin was above water in Mesozoic time, and the eroded sediments were carried east and south into what is now the plateau region. Mesozoic rocks, therefore, are confined largely to the eastern and southern parts of the State; buried within them is fossil evidence of the slow progression of life. In Mesozoic waters the shellfish continued to evolve; on Mesozoic landscapes lived the first dinosaurs, birds, and mammals, and the first hardwood trees. During this period in geologic history, large areas in northern Arizona and southern Utah were covered by flood plains upon which meandering rivers and streams left stranded a great number of logs. Later deposition covered them with mud and sand, and waters bearing silica, manganese, and iron filtered through the ancient flood plains and replaced the vegetable material of the tree trunks with stone. At Capitol Reef National Monument, Zion National Park, and near Escalante, Kanab, and St. George there is petrified wood estimated to be more than a hundred million years old.

Excavations in the Uintah Basin near Jensen since 1909 have uncovered a veritable graveyard of dinosaur bones, and the site has been set aside as a national monument. In this region long ago was a flood plain across which streams meandered. Upon the banks of these rivers and in the surrounding marshes the great reptiles lived. Some of them, preying upon smaller dinosaurs, became masters of their primitive world; others, feeding upon water plants, attained a length of a hundred feet and a weight of thirty-five or forty tons. When these mighty reptiles died, their carcasses were borne away by floods and deposited on a bar, where the drifting sediments, covering them hardened into stone. The Jensen quarry (*see Dinosaur National Monument*) has yielded hundreds of dinosaur bones. Among them are the back and leg bones of the herbivorous brontosaurus and diplodocus; the bones of a flesh-eating allosaurus; and the complete skeleton of an immense brontosaurus, a hundred feet long and twenty feet high.

Long after the dinosaurs were buried on the old river bar, masses of vegetable material accumulating on the margin of shallow seas were covered with sand and finally transformed by pressure into the extensive coal deposits of Carbon and Emery counties. Although no dinosaur bones have been found in this region, the sandstone above the coal beds still records the fact that no less than eight varieties of dinosaurs walked across the mud flats more than sixty million years ago. One huge beast left footprints which indicate that he took fifteen-foot strides, and another, apparently because he slipped in peaty mud, made an impression approximately four and a half feet long and two and a half feet across (*see Tour 7a*).

While the great reptiles were still living in some parts of the world, the region now known as Zion National Park was an arid waste or "fossil Sahara." There, sediments washed down from the mountains were blown by the wind into huge sand dunes. At the same time the desert plain was sinking gradually toward the bottom of a sea. After a long period, in which layers of limestone and shales were deposited above the sand, the area of deposition was again lifted above the water. Streams grinding down through the bedrock finally exposed the vermilion and white sandstones of Zion Canyon. The sandstone was laid down in the Mesozoic era; uplift and erosion, however, were products of a later time.

During the last period in the Mesozoic era the sea extended from the Gulf of Mexico to Alaska and from Ohio to central Utah. By the end of that period the sea had withdrawn, and lateral pressure from the west was folding the earth's crust into a system of mountains known as the ancestral Rockies. In following ages the pounding wind and rain and the abrasive action of streams reduced the ancestral mountains to a plain. By the middle of Cenozoic time the Cascade disturbance began, and vertical pressure under the present Rocky Mountain province resulted in elevation of the land and the consequent breaking and faulting of massive blocks of earth. The Cascade disturbance, together with the erosion that followed the lifting of land masses, created the Great Basin and the Rocky Mountain system, to which the Wasatch Range in Utah belongs.

The Wasatch Mountains extend from Collinston on the north to Nephi on the south, a distance of 150 miles. The Wasatch fault borders the west face of the range. North of Salt Lake City the fault scarp has been uncovered by the removal of sediments of comparatively late origin. In some places there are indications of recent movement on the fault; moreover, at some time within the past 500 years there has been a single abrupt movement of about sixty feet. The resultant earthquake must have been more severe than any recorded in historic time. Scattered along the entire length of the fault are warm mineral springs that bubble up to form steaming surface pools.

The latest chapter in the history of the earth began sixty million years ago with the advent of Cenozoic time. The Cenozoic era saw the development of mammals and higher plants, and, much later, the first appearance of man. In Utah, rock formations of this age are represented in the fresh-water deposits of Bryce Canyon and Cedar Breaks, in the sediments of streams and lakes, in the Wasatch conglomerate, in glacial debris, and in numerous lava flows.

In early Cenozoic time there were violent volcanic eruptions, resulting in deposition just north of the Salt Lake City boundary, near the State Capitol. About the same time there were intrusions of molten material in Big Cottonwood Canyon and near Park City, Bingham, and Alta. These masses cooled, and their mineral-bearing solutions formed valuable ore deposits. Numerous cinder cones preserve the record of volcanic activity near Zion and Bryce canyons. Lava beds, comparatively new in geologic history, cover portions of southern Utah, and there are several extinct volcanoes in this region. Outstanding among these is a crater twelve miles west of Fillmore (*see Tour 1e*) and several perfect volcanic cones with lava flows extending from them.

The long period of intermittent disturbances which marked the upper Cenozoic era determined many of the present topographic features of Utah. In what is now the Great Basin, block faulting gave rise to a series of north-south ranges; in northeastern Utah a single great fold already in existence was cut off by faulting to produce the Uinta Mountains. In the south, igneous intrusions lifted the strata into domes, and erosion weathered away the overlying rocks to develop the Henry and La Sal ranges.

Among the geologic phenomena of late Cenozoic times in the Great Basin, perhaps most interesting to the layman is the evidence that an ancient lake once covered the greater part of Utah and extended into Idaho and Nevada. This huge body of water, known to geologists as Lake Bonneville, is thought to have originated during the last ice age, more than fifty thousand years ago, and to have endured for about twenty-five thousand years. At its maximum the lake was 1,050 feet deep, 145 miles wide, and 346 miles long. Rolling hills, abrupt cliffs, and water-filled canyons formed an irregular shore line, and low mountains rising above the water studded the surface with islands. Contemporaneous with Lake Bonneville were more than seventy smaller lakes, which occupied minor depressions in the Great Basin.

Pre-Bonneville time was characterized by alternating lakes and deserts. The lake which immediately preceded Bonneville was probably little more than a brine pond in the midst of a vast wasteland. With the beginning of Bonneville time, however, the climate began to change. Cold wet years were more frequent, and evaporation was reduced. The level of the lake rose with the wet years, and though intermittent periods of drought prevented a constant rise, the trend was always upward. Approximately 1,000 feet above the present surface of Great Salt Lake the waters came to a halt and for a long time remained stationary. Pounding incessantly against their enclosing shores, the waves eventually carved out a shelf, in some places 1,500 feet wide. This shelf, known as the Bonneville Terrace, is today plainly visible on the north face of the Traverse Mountain about 18 miles south of Salt Lake City. It appears also on the north slope of the Oquirrh Range not far from Saltair, on Antelope Island, and on the mountains near Wendover.

The lake remained at the Bonneville level for a long time. Then, continuing its upward movement, the water reached Red Rock Pass in northern Cache Valley, and, through this lowest point in the rim of the basin, overflowed into the Snake and Columbia river systems. The Red Rock outlet carried the water through a loose gravel formation which was cut away so rapidly that within a comparatively few years the lake dropped 375 feet. When the outflowing water encountered a resistant limestone at the base of the gravel, the lake level again became constant and remained so until the Provo, largest of all Lake Bonneville terraces, was formed. Near Salt Lake City the Provo terrace appears at the foot of Ensign Peak and at Fort Douglas. Recognizable also in many other parts of the Great Basin, it stands in bold relief on the west side of the Wasatch and Oquirrh Mountains.

At the end of the Provo epoch the lake again resumed its downward course. After forming several intermediate terraces, the water dropped to a point approximately 300 feet above the present level of Great Salt Lake. Here for perhaps more than 1,000 years the waves ate into the jagged shoreline until they had produced the Stansbury Terrace, third in size and importance. In many places the record of the lake at the Stansbury level has been destroyed by erosion, but the terrace may still be seen from the Salt Lake-Ogden highway between the Municipal Baths and Becks Hot Springs (*see Tour 1c*). Between the Stansbury level and that of Great Salt Lake the waters of Bonneville left a great many small terraces, many of which appear today on the mountains at the north end of the present lake. More than fifty terraces, each recording a stage in the history of Lake Bonneville, have been recognized at various places within the Great Basin.

During the rise and fall of the ancient lake, streams flowing out of the mountains built deltas at the mouths of canyons. Many such deltas were formed while the lake stood at the Bonneville level, but nearly all of them were washed away and their sands and gravels reconsolidated into deltas on the Provo and other lower levels. Perhaps the most important remaining delta of the Bonneville stage is in Ogden Valley, where the village of Huntsville stands. At the Provo stage six major deltas—the Ogden, the Weber, the Logan, the Bear, the Provo, and the Sevier were built. In addition, many smaller deltas were scattered along the Wasatch from Santaquin to Brigham City. Much of the finest agricultural land in the State is of deltaic construction.

Sand and gravel bars formed by the action of longshore currents are further evidence of constructive forces at work in the old lake. Notable among these are the Stockton Bar at the north end of Rush Valley in Tooele County and the bar at Jordan Narrows near the Salt Lake-Utah County line. These embankments effectively separated Rush Lake and Utah Lake from the parent body of water. Rush, Utah, and Great Salt Lakes are thought to be present-day remnants of Lake Bonneville. Near Wendover, where Bonneville waters once covered the land, great flats extend westward into Nevada.

Although it is probable that Lake Bonneville teemed with fish and invertebrate forms, the only evidence of their existence is in the discovery of gastropods in lake deposits near the northwestern limits of Salt Lake City. The story of vertebrate life in the Bonneville area, however, is more nearly complete, for commercial removal of gravel along the base of the Wasatch Mountains has resulted in many enlightening discoveries. Along the shores of the old lake thousands of years ago roamed the hulking mammoth, the ponderous musk ox, and the predecessors of the modern camel and horse. Some of these creatures, attracted by water and abundant vegetation, wandered out on the deltas and sank in treacherous swamplands bordering the lake. Others were overcome by stronger beasts, and spring floods scattered their bones through gravel deposits at the water's edge. Although animals peculiar to glacial climates were common during the Provo stage of Bonneville history, they did not disappear entirely with the receding lake. In 1928 a post-Bonneville lava cave near Fillmore yielded the skull of a camel, apparently taken into the cave by some ancient carnivore.

At least twice during the latest ages of Cenozoic time ice accumulating in mountain basins scraped a path down Utah canyons. The southern plateaus record the story of slowly moving ice; the Uinta Mountains (see High Uintas Primitive Area) contain thousands of glacial lakes; and in the Wasatch Range there are perhaps fifty glaciated canyons, as well as numerous lakes, hanging valleys, and huge amphi-theater-like cirques. In Big Cottonwood Canyon the glacier moved down from the mountains, cutting a typical U-shaped path. Midway down the canyon, however, its progress was arrested by a narrowing channel and a mass of ice flowing in from the south. In Little Cotton-wood the ice flow extended the full length of the canyon and pushed far out into Lake Bonneville. In Bell Canyon, south of Little Cotton-wood, the shifting ice left well defined terminal and lateral moraines. All three canyons are strewn with the polished and grooved boulders characteristic of a glaciated landscape.

Wind and running water have played dominant roles in geologically recent times. Near Milford the prevailing winds have built sand dunes not unlike those of the Sahara Desert. The plateaus of southern Utah offer many amazing examples of the wearing away of stone by water and wind. Among these are narrow box-like canyons, natural bridges, massive archways, cathedrals, pedestals, and spires carved out of highly colored standstone.

PLANT LIFE

Utah, because of its irregular topography, has six plant zones, ranging upward from the Lower Sonoran, which covers the southern desert lowlands, to the Arctic, which extends above the timberline on the mountain summits. Between these, in ascending order, are the Upper Sonoran, the Transition, the Canadian, and the Hudsonian zones. Accompanying variations in temperature, altitude, and soil have encouraged the growth of nearly every type of plant ordinarily found between Alaska and Mexico. Botanists have recognized more than 4,000 species.

The Lower Sonoran zone in Utah is limited principally to the semi-tropical region of southwestern Utah, covering approximately 500 square miles adjacent to the Virgin River and its tributaries. Because figs, pomegranates, cotton, and similar crops can be successfully grown here, this region has become known as "Utah's Dixie." The natural flora includes creosote bushes, screwpod mesquite, and several species of cacti and sword plants. The screwpod mesquite is a peculiar shrub that grows in the dry, sandy soil of desert canyons. It bears numerous spirally-twisted pods containing ten to twenty beanlike seeds, from which the Indians formerly made a coarse grade of flour.

In this section also grows the strange Joshua tree, sometimes called Spanish dagger, an arborescent yucca found only in the southwestern part of the United States. The plant has an unusual tufted appearance, entirely different from that of any other tree or shrub in Utah. Its leaves, bristling on large, clumsy branches, are sharply pointed and bayonetlike. The biblical name, Joshua, was bestowed by Mormon pioneers, who likened the upturned limbs to arms lifted in prayer. The tree has an extensive root system that goes deep into the ground for water. It clings tenaciously to life, defying the hardships of storm and drought, and sometimes attains an age of 300 years. Its soft fibrous wood is heavy and full of moisture when green, but very light when dry; doctors find the wood useful in preparing splints and casts for setting broken bones. Indians used the coarse fibers for making baskets and sandals. Growing profusely along the lower streams and washes of southern Utah are dense thickets of tamarix, also called salt cedar, an odd shrubby plant with small scaly leaves and feathery pink flowers. Because of its value in water conservation, quantities of this plant have been transplanted to other sections of the State.

Nearly all of the Great Basin comes within the Upper Sonoran zone, of which the most characteristic plant is sagebrush. An excellent indicator of good soil, sagebrush grows best in fertile, well-drained ground, free from alkali. Much of Utah's prosperous agricultural belt, extending north-south along the foothills of the Wasatch Mountains, occupies land from which sagebrush has been cleared. In the alkaline soil of the lower desert areas, sagebrush gives way to shadscale, greasewood, and forage plants that provide winter range for sheep and cattle. Alfalfa and sugar beets, both alkali tolerants, are the crops most successfully grown in this type of soil. Certain extreme forms of saltbushes grow where alkali is too abundant to permit the growth of anything else.

Native trees of Utah nearly all grow in mountainous regions, ranging upward from the Upper Sonoran zone, and only about a score occur in considerable numbers. Among them is the blue spruce, a symmetrically shaped evergreen, blue-green in foliage, selected in 1933 as the State tree. It grows most commonly near mountain streams and lakes, at an altitude of approximately 8,000 feet. In swamplands it is often yellow-green and is sometimes called "water spruce." The wood is brittle and splinters too easily to make desirable timber, but it is popular as an ornamental tree. The Engelmann spruce, often miscalled "white pine," is a native of the high mountain regions and one of the small group of forest trees that survive near the timberline. It is an excellent timber tree, but frequently unprofitable for lumbering because of its inaccessible habitat.

Four species of pine are common in Utah. The ponderosa pine, generally known as yellow pine, grows in the mountains at the approximate level of the blue spruce. It is rapid-growing, attains a height of 100 to 150 feet, and is the most important source of pine lumber in the intermountain region. Closely associated with the ponderosa is the lodgepole pine, a tall slender tree used by the Indians in the construction of their lodges. From this custom it derived its most accepted name, though it has nearly a dozen others. Because this pine is long and straight, it is particularly adapted for telephone poles, house logs, mine props, and railroad ties. Its amazing aptitude for reseeding makes it a valuable asset in conservation and reforestation. The cones protect its seeds against forest fires, and thousands of sprouts quickly cover burnt areas, sometimes so densely as to result in overcrowding. The gnarled and stunted limber pine grows on rocky ridges and other inhospitable sites. This eccentric tree, which usually grows singly, is apparently equal to the conquest of the most miserly mountain soil, but its warped wood is of no commercial value. The piñon pine, small and round-topped, is found on hot dry foothills. Its gnarled wood is of little value, but the seeds are edible, and great quantities of "pine nuts" are gathered for the market, principally by Indians.

Three species of junipers, known locally as cedars, are found in Utah. The Rocky Mountain red cedar grows in scattered stands on rocky hillsides. It is generally too small and crooked for commercial use, though short lengths are sometimes sawed for cedar chests. One of these trees, the Juniper Jardine in Logan Canyon (*see Tour 2a*), has an estimated age of 3,000 years, and is said to be the oldest tree in the intermountain region. The One-seeded and Utah cedars grow, with the piñon pine, on hot dry foothills. The wood of the Utah cedar, by virtue of its resistance to decay, is much used for fence posts. The one-seed variety, so called because its cones contain only one seed each, is a multitopped tree with many trunks, none of them suitable for post wood.

Of the firs, the alpine and white are the only true varieties in the State. The alpine fir, known in Utah as "white balsam," is a native of mountain highlands. Its wood is used in rough construction work. The white fir, bearing the contradictory local name of "black balsam," is found at lower elevations. It yields a fair quality of tasteless and odorless wood, adapted for butter and cheese containers. Because of its accessibility, quantities of white fir are used for general farm purposes. The Douglas fir, locally called "red pine," is actually neither fir nor pine, but spruce. Botanists differentiate this variety from true firs because its cones fall from the tree whole. Although it does not attain as great size in Utah as in Washington and Oregon, the Douglas fir is one of the State's most valuable timber trees. Its strong tough wood is particularly useful for heavy construction.

One of the commonest mountain trees is the aspen, popularly called the "quaking asp"; the characteristic shimmering action of its leaves in the slightest movement of air is caused by the fact that aspen leaves have flat stems. Male and female flowers are borne on separate trees, and since female trees are rare, aspens seldom grow from seeds. New trees usually sprout from underground roots of older trees, hence aspens generally grow in dense groves. The trees, however, require plenty of light, for they cannot live even in their own shade. In Utah, the value of aspens is largely scenic, their slender white trunks adding an attractive touch in any season, and in autumn their golden foliage makes a bright splash on the landscape at altitudes around 7,000 feet. The wood is too soft for lumber, but is extensively used for fuel and miscellaneous farm purposes. Aspens also shelter young pines and firs, and pave the way for more valuable forests.

Growing along streams, from low to medium elevations, are several species of cottonwood. Like the aspen, they are members of the poplar family. The green of these trees was a welcome sight to early explorers, for it frequently marked the end of a weary desert journey. Great numbers have been transplanted from their native areas to near-by settlements, and many small communities are visible for miles because of green cottonwoods lining the streets. The planting of these trees has often been regretted by residents, who are annoyed by the silky-tufted seed carriers that get into their hair, on clothes, and in house screens. Attempts to uproot small cottonwoods from lawns usually result in the discovery of a network of roots extending from a tree across the fence. Probably the largest cottonwood tree in the State, more than eight feet in diameter, is at Moab (*see Tour 9*).

Bordering the canyon streams are a number of species of shrubs which ordinarily do not reach the size of trees. Among them are red birch, mountain alder, hawthorn, and several varieties of willows. The wood of the willows, being soft and flexible, is used by Indians in basket-weaving. Hillsides are covered with dense thickets of maple, scrub oak, chokecherry, service berry, and mountain mahogany. Also called "buck brush," the latter, related to the true mahogany, is of value as a browsing brush for deer, and straighter specimens were used by pioneers for cabinet work. Its wood is one of the few kinds that will not float. Of the maples, the dwarf is the commonest Utah species. This shrubby tree is an outstanding feature of the mountain scenery at all times, but particularly in the autumn, when the first touch of frost turns its foliage into a blaze of brilliant color. The big-tooth maple, a hardwood variety, grows to larger size, and in some of the national forests is more than a foot in diameter and more than fifty feet high. The box elder, for which one of the northern counties was named, is another variety of maple common along the water courses. The sweet sap of this tree was sometimes used for syrup in pioneer days, but it has an undesirable attraction for insects, especially a black-and-red-winged plant bug with the objectionable habit of wintering in houses. Chokecherry often forms extensive growths on canyon slopes. It has showy white flowers that bloom in May and June. The fruit is edible and quantities of it are gathered for jellies and wines. Service (or "sarvis") berries, which are also edible, are sometimes dried by the Indians and mixed with meat to make pemmican.

More than 4,000 kinds of smaller plants are represented in the State. In most sections many species grow together, but in certain areas a few varieties, or sometimes plants of a single species, usurp extensive tracts. This monopolizing characteristic is particularly notice-able during the flowering season when the blooms of certain plants form a blanket of color: the yellow of docks and dandelions, the blue of mertensia and lupine, or the pink of sweet-williams and wild roses.

Utah's floral emblem, the sego-lily, is common throughout the State. This plant, known also as Spanish mariposa (butterfly), is a west American bulbous herb with long-leaved, grayish green, grasslike foliage. It blooms in May and June, and has a flower consisting of three dainty white petals, delicately tinted with yellow, brown, and purple around the golden nectar glands. In southern Utah, possibly on account of some ingredient in the soil, the flower is frequently orchidlike in color. During periods of food shortage in early pioneer days, the bulb of the sego-lily was an important item of food. Friendly Indians explained that the sego roots were good to eat, and thereafter entire families were often busy digging on the hillsides, returning at night with buckets and sacks filled with bulbs.

In the blooming season, ranging from April to September, Utah's wild flowers offer a constantly changing display. Most of them grow in canyons and mountains. Indian paintbrush, however, grows in sagebrush country, where its spikes of bloom, in various shades of bright red or orange, are conspicuous against the background of gray vege-tation. The dogtooth violet, with its bright yellow flowers, grows in rich mountain soil, and is one of the first to appear after the snow melts. Then come the trumpet-shaped blossoms of blue or red pent-stemon, the grapelike purple clusters of monkshood, the delicate pink bells of mallow, the five-petaled flowers of pink or white geranium, the inverted blue blossoms of the shootingstar, the waxy red flowers of the prickly pear, the tiny white flowers of false Solomon's-seal, yellow clusters of Senecio and Oregon grape, pink sweetpeas and sweet-williams, small purple iris, blue and yellow violets, pale pink hollyhocks, scarlet monkeyflowers, and innumerable others. In autumn, dry pig-weeds and Russian thistles break away from their roots and become "tumbleweeds," rolled by the wind until they pile up against fences or other obstructions.

To early pioneers, the value of wild plants was more than esthetic. Dandelion roots and prickly pears were used in concocting home remedies. Cattails were dried and stuffed into cushions and mattresses. Dry weeds and bushes made serviceable brooms. Roots, berries, and leaves of various plants were ground and boiled for dyes. Dandelion leaves were eaten, as were thistle roots and sego-lily bulbs. Choke-cherries, service berries, wild currants, and berries from Oregon grape were made into jams and jellies. Chewing gum was prepared from milkweed juices, and in the spring the inner bark of cottonwood trees was sometimes scraped into a white pulpy mass which the early settlers called "cottonwood ice cream."

The pioneers, however, did not undervalue the beauty of plants. Nearly every home had its garden of flowers, some grown from seed carried across the plains, others transplanted from the mountains. Going to the canyons for wood, men frequently returned with a plant for the garden. Sometimes the watering of these gardens was a tiresome problem, many of the women finding it necessary to carry water from ditches and wells. Native and exotic trees were planted along the streets, and scattered Utah cities and towns soon gained the appearance of oases in the desert. Among the varieties introduced by the settlers were the American elm, umbrella elm, honey locust, black locust, sycamore, catalpa, acacia, ailanthus, horsechestnut, weeping willow, linden, hickory, mulberry, black walnut, and several species of poplar and maple.

Only three plants at all common in the State are poisonous to touch. These are poison ivy, poison oak, and stinging nettle (*Urtica*). Poison ivy and poison oak, both species of poison sumac, exude a volatile oil that causes painful inflammation of the skin. Poison ivy and poison oak grow throughout the State, principally on hillsides. The two species are characterized by leaflets in groups of three, glossy on top and fuzzy underneath. Poison ivy is a vinelike plant that spreads over the ground, while poison oak grows in the form of a bush or shrub, and has notched oaklike leaves that color attractively in autumn. Stinging nettle, which borders nearly every stream in the State, is similar in appearance to catnip, peppermint, and spearmint. Contact with it results in an unpleasant stinging sensation; the effect is painful, but usually of short duration and rarely serious.

ANIMAL LIFE

The mule deer, ranging principally in forest and mountain areas, is Utah's most numerous big game animal. Named for its mule-like ears, this creature is graceful and elusive, having choice meat and a magnificent head. According to the U. S. Forest Service census for the fiscal year 1939 there were 135,000 head of mule deer in the ten national forests, more than 28,000 having been killed during the eleven-day open season of October, 1938. These animals increase so rapidly, sometimes at the rate of 50,000 in a single year, that they constitute a problem to farmers all over the State. The State Planning Board advocates removal of submarginal grazing lands from the use of domestic animals to provide range for deer, which have high economic value; sale of hunting licenses, and the expenditures of some 36,000 hunters reach an impressive total each year.

The Utah Fish and Game Commission in 1939 reported four herds of pronghorn antelope in the State, totaling about 1,000, indicating that this fleet animal is on the increase. The herds range west of Great Salt Lake, in southwestern Utah, in the south central portion, and in the northeastern corner. The State has about 4,000 elk, most of them in Manti, Cache, Fishlake, and Uinta National Forests. Hunted to extinction early in the century and reintroduced in 1912, elk are increasing rapidly, and a few hundred special permits are issued for hunting them each year. The Forest Service game census lists 50 bighorn sheep, 30 in the La Sal Mountains and 20 in the Uintas. A small band of bighorns is also reported in Zion National Park and occasional flocks in the deep canyons of the Green, Colorado, and Virgin rivers. The State Fish and Game Commission enumerated 725 as of June, 1939. An occasional moose wanders into the State from the Jackson Hole country in Wyoming, apparently conscious of its complete protection by State law; two were reported in 1939, in the Bear Lake area. Utah has a buffalo herd on Antelope Island in Great Salt Lake, 28 animals in 1940, privately owned by the Island Improvement Company, with offices in Salt Lake City. This herd was used in filming buffalo-hunt sequences for the motion picture *Covered Wagon* in 1922.

The grizzly bear, the "Ole Ephraim" of the mountain men, is apparently extinct in the State. Private arsenals of "killb'ars" seem to have done for this most ferocious western animal. Utah once had a species of grizzly bear (*Ursus utahensis*) that has not been found elsewhere. It was identified from a skull in 1914 and no specimen has ever been seen alive. Black bears and their variants, brown and cinnamon bears, are considered pests. Game census figures in 1939 gave 600 bears in the national forests, 29 of which were killed in the same year. There are an estimated 550 mountain lions or panthers, 112 of them were killed or trapped by hunters in the year of the last census. Bobcats numbered 4,300, Canada lynx 125; both are hunted as predators. George E. Holman of the U. S. Biological Survey claims to have killed the last timber wolf in Utah, in 1935 or 1936. Since the extinction of the wolf, the coyote has spread into all sections of the State, and more than 6,000 are bagged by government hunters each year. Cunning and intelligent enough to merit their place in Indian mythology, they hold their own against traps, poison, and guns, and kill thousands of sheep, calves, and colts each year.

The most numerous fur-bearing animals are weasel, muskrat, beaver, badger, skunk, marten, fox, and ringtail cat. Under strict protection, beaver are on the increase, having been trapped almost to extinction in the early days. About 300 are planted on new streams annually. The badger is valued for its fur and for control of destructive rodents; shaving brushes made from badger fur are guaranteed for a lifetime. In addition to the common striped skunk, Utah has a spotted skunk (*Spilogale gracilis*), which first came to the notice of scientists in 1906; the animal described was taken near Provo. Comparatively plentiful, it measures about one foot long from nose tip to tail tip; it has four narrow white stripes running lengthwise along its back, which are broken across the hips by crossbars of black. Utah has three kinds of foxes, the red, the gray, and the desert swift fox. The gray fox (*Vulpes macroura*) was first described in 1852 from specimens taken in the Wasatch Mountains east of Great Salt Lake and purchased by Captain Howard Stansbury; it ranges through the mountains of Utah, Colorado, and Wyoming. Sporadic trapping of furbearers is carried on throughout rural sections, but most furs come from fifty fur farms in Utah.

In addition to jack rabbits, cottontails, and snowshoe rabbits at high altitudes, northern Utah is included in the range of the Idaho pygmy rabbit, a peculiar little animal with a small head, short broad ears, and a very short tail. It runs without leaping. The pygmy is seldom seen, since it feeds at night and hides by day. In 1905 the pika or rock rabbit (*Ochotona cimmamonea*) was found in the Beaver Mountains at an altitude of 10,000 feet and first described scientifically. This little rodent, only about five inches long, is nearest of kin to the rabbits. Grayish brown in color, it has no tail, and utters a peculiar bleat unlike that of any other animal. Living in the Uinta, Wasatch, La Sal, and Parowan mountains, it cuts and stores "hay" for the winter. Its Asiatic and African counterpart is the little hyrax, of an ancient order of ungulates related to the elephant.

Utah has a species of prairie dog (*Cynomys parvidens*) that is peculiar to the State. First introduced to science in 1905, when a specimen from Buckskin Valley was described, it ranges through the mountain valleys of the Sevier River in southern Utah. Like other animals of its kind, it lives in villages and subsists on vegetation. White-tailed prairie dogs are found in eastern and southeastern Utah, and the Zuñi prairie dog ranges southeast of the Colorado River.

Utah has many other kinds of rodents. The tree squirrel or chickaree is common throughout timbered regions. The flying squirrel, which glides through the air with the help of sailing membranes, inhabits dense coniferous forests of the Uinta and Wasatch ranges. The desert squirrel inhabits the sparsely vegetated Great Salt Lake desert. Several races of pocket gophers are common in fertile valleys and on mountain slopes to an elevation of 10,000 feet. Utah also has a plenitude of pack or trade rats, which visit houses and camps and carry off miscellaneous small articles, usually leaving some kind of token in exchange. Kangaroo rats, of several forms, have long hind legs for jumping and a long tail for balancing, with small forelegs and forefeet. Two species of marmots or groundhogs are common in the State. Foresters consider the porcupine a pest, because it often girdles trees. Many naturalists urge its preservation because it is the most feasible food animal for persons lost in the woods.

Ducks are the most numerous game birds in Utah, coming through the State on migratory bird flyways by the hundreds of thousands. Ten or more species of surface feeding ducks include the mallard, gadwall, baldpate, American pintail, three kinds of teal, the shoveller, and the wood duck. Diving ducks include the redhead, ring-necked, canvasback, greater scaup, American golden eye, Barrow golden eye, and buffle-head. Hybrids of the ring-necked pheasant have been introduced, and are the second most numerous among Utah's game birds; there is a short open season for pheasant hunting each fall. The 1939 U. S. Forest Service game census listed 13,800 sage hens in the ten national forests, 5,500 pine hens, and 4,800 ruffed grouse. The fool hen, which is nearing extinction in the State, numbered only 25. Quail, like grouse, are almost completely protected, open seasons being declared only by proclamation of the Utah Fish and Game Commission. There have been two open seasons since 1928.

Among the predatory birds, the golden eagle is the largest; it is common in outlying mountain areas. Hawks are numerous, and there are three or four kinds of owls, including the great horned owl, the western horned owl, and the western screech owl. The burrowing owl, slightly larger than a robin, is common throughout Utah in open flat country. They usually live in abandoned prairie dog holes, but occupy other burrows.

Four subspecies of birds were first described from Utah specimens, the Treganza heron, a resident of islands in Great Salt Lake; the Utah horned lark, a sweet songster; the Utah red-winged blackbird, quite common in the State; and the gray titmouse, a woodland songbird. A common songster in residential areas is the house finch. The magpie, a black and white bird, its feathers shining like gunmetal, is built on an airplane-like frame about twelve inches from beak to tail; it is common throughout the State, and has been known to attack blind or injured lambs and sheep. The cedar jay, or "camp robber," a noisy thief, lives in wooded mountain areas. Crows and vultures are common in the southern part of the State. The great blue heron, three feet high, is the tallest water bird in the Great Basin. The little marsh wren, in addition to its real nest fastened to tules in marshy places, builds three or more false nests to confuse its enemies. The seagull, a resident of islands in Great Salt Lake, is legally protected and held in reverence by the people of Utah because of its historic intervention against the crickets in 1848 (*see Salt Lake City*). One of the most appealing scenes in this high mountain country is to see a flock of seagulls, 800 miles from the nearest ocean, following plowmen in the spring, picking up insects from the furrow. In spite of local regard for them, gulls have been observed killing and eating young ducklings and pheasants, and have made inroads on cherries and other fruits. One of the largest, if not the largest, colonies of the great white pelican, a diminishing species, is on Gunnison and Bird islands in Great Salt Lake. They sometimes fly 100 miles or more from the rookery for their food.

Probably the most winning songster of all, a resident of canyons where swift water flows, is the water ouzel or dipper bird, which ranges throughout the Rocky Mountains. The ouzel is a gray robin-sized bird that builds its oven-shaped nest, where possible, behind a waterfall, and walks on the bottom of swift icy streams in search of food among submerged fungous growths. "In form," said the naturalist John Muir, "he is about as smoothly plump and compact as a pebble that has been whirled in a pot-hole," and as cheery a songster, even in midwinter, as any lark. The ouzel, not a web-footed bird, swims with its wings where the current is too swift for wading on the bottom.

There were eighteen native genera of fishes in Utah before the introduction of others by white men. The streams and lakes were filled with mountain or black spotted trout. Local isolation led to development of mutants, with variations in color and size. Bear Lake had a type of blue-nosed trout and Utah Lake another variety; both are almost extinct. Other native fishes are whitefish, suckers, chubs, minnows (Colorado River "minnows" sometimes weigh up to thirty pounds), bullheads, dace, and squawfish. Irrigation, diversion of water, drought, and excessive fishing greatly depleted native trout in Utah waters. About 1885, carp, catfish, and bass were introduced into streams and lakes. Yellow perch were introduced during 1930-31. Today there are thirteen State and Federal hatcheries rearing and distributing about ten million fish in Utah waters each year.

The sidewinder, a pygmy rattler that occurs in the southwestern part of the State, rarely attains a maximum length of two feet. The name well describes its odd sidewise progression. There are a few other types of rattlesnakes, the gopher snake, three species of garter snakes, and three types of whiptail or racer snakes. Lizards are common all over the State, the maximum in size being the rarely-found poisonous Gila monster. The desert horned toad, really a spiny lizard, is common. The desert tortoise, nine inches in length, is considered a delicacy by Mexicans and Indians. Among the amphibia, Utah has toads and frogs common to the Rocky Mountain region, and the tiger salamander or waterdog, three to ten inches long, in lowland marshes and high mountain ponds.

Of the insects, the so-called Mormon cricket is recalled for its terrible invasions, which are told in many old diaries and reminiscences, and occur frequently in contemporary prints. It has been variously called "the frightful bug," "the black Philistine," and "a cross between the spider and the buffalo." Incursions of crickets and grasshoppers clear the countryside of every green thing, and cars sometimes skid from the roads because of them. Utah also has the pestiferous mosquito, and the wood tick, dangerous as a carrier of Rocky Mountain spotted fever.

The ultra-briny waters of Great Salt Lake are inhabited only by the brine shrimp, a half-inch member of the crab family, and by the brine fly, which passes its larval stage in the lake. It is a small insect, similar in general to the housefly. The brine shrimp is a primitive form of crustacean, closest living kin to Cambrian fossil trilobites.

NATURAL RESOURCES AND CONSERVATION

Beavers and Indians were Utah's first conservationists. Most of the beaver were trapped out in the short heyday of the mountain men, between 1824 and 1840. About a hundred years later these rodent engineers were reintroduced, protected, and encouraged in their program of damming small streams, delaying runoff, building up the water table, and providing spawning pools for fish. Indians in the greater part of the Utah area had little to conserve, but where there was game to be hunted they took only such animals as they needed, and used every part of the animal for food, for thread, for implements, and for clothing.

The Mormon pioneers were behindhand only in point of time in the use of natural resources and their conservation. Choosing a land that nobody coveted so they would be free to develop their own religious and economic program, the Mormons on the first day of their arrival began to use soil and water, two prime Utah resources, to build a self-sufficient agricultural commonwealth. Timber was scarce, the nearest usable forests being up Big Cottonwood Canyon, whence a long, laborious haul was necessary by ox-team. It is not surprising, therefore, that they established rules limiting the use of green timber, the penalty for violation being "certain fines." In the spring of 1852 Elias Adams, possibly the first man in Utah to realize the value of water storage, built a dam about three miles east of Layton and filled it with water from Adams Canyon. In 1856 Brigham Young spoke of the desirability of a canal between Utah Lake and Salt Lake Valley; "when that work is accomplished," he said, "we shall continue our exertions until Provo river runs to this city." Such a canal was being built in 1940 (see Tour 5).

Water was the life blood of Utah in the early days, and it is still the most important natural resource. The average annual runoff within the State is 7,000,000 acre-feet; 10,750,000 acre-feet enter the State, while 15,750,000 acre-feet leave it. Approximately 5,000,000 acre-feet of runoff are lost because the water is not properly distributed to fertile areas. Since 1933 the Federal government has focused attention upon water resources. The diversion of water from worthless to rich lands, the development of ground-water sources, and the building of storage dams have all contributed to effective water conservation. Since 1930 the government has spent $26,000,000 for six major reclamation projects. The system of dams, aqueducts, and canals, scheduled for completion in the early 1940's, will benefit ten counties by providing water for more than 300,000 acres of land. Notable among these projects is the unfinished Deer Creek Dam in Provo Canyon (see Tour 5). At a cost of about $15,000,000 this dam will provide additional culinary water for Salt Lake City, Orem, and Provo, and will insure a permanent supply for irrigation. Moreover, the project will aid in flood control, prevent excess evaporation from Utah Lake, and utilize runoff from the east side of the Wasatch Range. The expenditure of private capital also is proving important in the state-wide program of water conservation. In the Oquirrh Mountains east of Tooele, for example, the million-dollar Elton Tunnel (see Tour 6a) now (1940) under construction will tap valuable ore bodies and yield irrigation water for large tracts of semi-arid land in Tooele Valley.

Closely associated with water resources is the development of hydroelectric power. Power for local needs is supplied by about sixty small electric plants scattered through industrial Utah. Developed power amounts to 227,864 horsepower. Undeveloped power is estimated at 800,000 horsepower. Most of the larger streams of the Great Basin have been utilized for the production of electricity, but nearly all of those in the Colorado and Green river systems are still untapped.

Nearly all of the arable land in Utah parallels mountain ranges bisecting the State from north to south. Here, with a rich soil, favorable climate, and successful conservation of water, farmers produce nearly every crop known to the temperate zone. The land in this area includes mountain, dry valley, and alkali soils. The mountain soil is loose, loamy, comparatively rich in organic matter, and poor in lime; the dry valley soil is rich in minerals and poor in lime. These two soils support nearly every important crop in the State. Mildly alkali soils produce sweet clover, alfalfa, and sugar beets, but strongly alkali regions remain as poor range or wasteland.

Much of Utah's land has been misused in late years. Faulty irrigation and lack of crop rotation have depleted the soil in some areas, and overgrazing has denuded once valuable range. Several minor catastrophes have been the inevitable result. "One of the notable examples of the dire results of overgrazing," says the *Deseret News* for December 16, 1939, "is to be found a short distance west of Salt Lake City, in the Grantsville area, where the drought years of the early 'thirties' produced a 'dust bowl' in Utah, a duplication on a smaller scale of the distressing conditions which almost completely ruined many entire communities in the Middle West. Wind storms sweeping over the barren ground took off the top soil and carried it miles away." In 1935 the U.S. Soil Conservation Service began a program of replanting, controlled grazing, and fire prevention. By the end of 1939 the land again supported a hardy growth of vegetation. A similar denuding of the land was responsible for disastrous floods of the 1920's, which took a toll of life and property in the vicinity of Farmington and Willard. Since that time, however, the Civilian Conservation Corps has built retaining walls, ditches, and terraces to prevent a recurrence of floods, and has engaged in reforestation to protect the watershed.

In many other sections of the State the Government has come to the aid of farmers and ranchers by restoring damaged watersheds, preventing floods, relocating farms, and managing range lands. Many grazing areas have been closed or controlled to restore them to reasonable forage production. As an added protection, stockmen have been instructed to keep animals constantly moving and to avoid allowing them to congregate too long at watering or bedding places. These measures have doubled forage production. Furthermore, at least two projects are taking land out of cultivation and restoring it to more economical use. The central Utah project is a controlled range, and the Widtsoe project involves range control and forestation.

Utah's national forests occupy 7,570,871 acres, and none of the twenty-nine counties is without some forest land. More than 75 per cent of the summer range and nearly all the important watersheds of the State are in national forests. Utah woodlands contain 5,000,000 board feet of saw timber, 10,000,000 cords of fuel timber, and 500,000,000 board feet suitable for posts and poles. Since much of the timber is far from markets, Utah imports 93 per cent of the lumber used for building. The annual cut of timber, 25,000,000 board feet, permits the forests to increase by 85,000,000 board feet every year. In addition to their commercial value, the timberlands, with their lakes and streams, are recreational assets enjoyed by thousands of sportsmen.

The national forests and other public lands of Utah support thousands of deer, elk, and bighorn sheep. Streams abound in fish, beaver, and muskrats. Marsh lands provide feeding and nesting grounds for great flocks of waterfowl. The Bear River Bird Refuge (*see Tour 1b*) is a giant project to insure good feeding grounds for waterfowl. About 1930, because many types of wild life were in danger of annihilation, Utah spent millions of dollars to establish refuges, preserves, and fish hatcheries. Game laws provide relatively short hunting and fishing seasons, and in many areas fish and game are protected the year round. Wild creatures are plentiful today, and the State receives substantial cash returns on fishing and hunting licenses, and on expenditures for food, recreation, and equipment.

Mineral resources, however, have contributed most of the wealth of Utah (*see Mining*).

Archeology and Indians

MANY centuries before the dawn of the Christian Era, roving bands of Old World hunters were already crossing the ice-bound waters of Bering Strait to the uninhabited North American continent. Some of these early groups undoubtedly reached the Southwest, for, in such localities as Folsom, New Mexico, Gypsum Cave, Nevada, and the Lindenmeier site in Colorado, their chipped points and other artifacts have been found in association with the bones of prehistoric bison, camels, sloths, mastodons, and other animals. These early comers did not possess a highly developed culture. They knew the arts of stone chipping and fire making and, possibly, used spears propelled by the *atlatl* (a notched stick used to increase the velocity of a hurled spear), employed bone awls for piercing and sewing skins, and owned domesticated dogs. They had no pottery or agriculture; nor did they, as far as is known, have any form of permanent habitation other than natural caves.

The earlier inhabitants of Utah were probably a group comparable in most respects with those whose artifacts are found in other parts of the Southwest. So far little information concerning them has come to light. Caves along the shore line of Great Salt Lake's predecessor, Lake Bonneville, have yielded objects the antiquity of which extends back several thousand years, although they were not necessarily left by the first human inhabitants of Utah. Flint points, knives, bone awls, and flint scrapers attest the presence of primitive hunters.

About the time of Christ, the inhabitants of the San Juan, Paria, Virgin, and Kanab river valleys began to raise corn. This marked the beginning of the long development of a culture known as the *Anasazi* (Navaho, the Ancients), which was distributed over northern Arizona and New Mexico, southwestern Colorado, southern Utah and Nevada, and southeastern California. The earlier phase of the Anasazi is called Basketmaker and the later Pueblo, which developed without a break into the period of the modern Pueblo peoples of Arizona and New Mexico.

The development of agriculture imposed a semi-sedentary mode of existence upon the people who practiced it. From this period of their history comes the first accurate knowledge of the dwellers of southern Utah and other parts of the San Juan basin. Permanent houses seem not yet to have come into use, but excavated in the floors of caves are found slab-lined bins, sometimes with a superstructure of pole and adobe construction. These apparently served as storage places for grain and occasionally as burial places for the dead. These people made coiled baskets, twined woven bags, ropes, woven sandals and robes, game snares, and long nets for catching small animals. The men probably wore small loin cloths while the women wore short apron-like skirts. Weapons were curved clubs, stone knives, and spears propelled by *atlatls*. The bow was unknown. Agriculture was carried on with wooden digging sticks. Pottery, in the form of crude, unfired, undecorated vessels reinforced with cedar bast (strong woody fiber obtained from tree bark), was attempted. This period was characterized by a rather simple culture. Although the Basketmakers understood agriculture, they still depended to a large extent upon wild vegetable foods and products of the chase. Virtually nothing is known of the inhabitants of central and northern Utah who were contemporaneous with the Basketmaker people.

As time passed the people of the Southwest improved their mode of life. The storage cists (used especially for sacred utensils) were enlarged and improved until they took the form of semi-subterranean dwelling places. These pit houses and slab houses, as they are called, were constructed in excavations from one to five feet in depth. Sometimes four posts were set up at some distance inside the pit and their tops connected by horizontal beams. Slanting walls of pole and adobe construction connected the beams with the periphery of the pit. The flat roof of the same construction was provided with a smoke hole which, in some houses, also served as an entrance. The completed dwelling, having perhaps also a side entrance, must have looked somewhat like a small mound of earth. In other types of house the roof was a simple cone of pole and adobe construction with the base extending to the edge of the pit. The other important development in this period, designated as Basketmaker III or as Modified Basketmaker, was in the ceramic arts. These were improved with the invention of fired pottery sometimes painted with crude black designs on a gray background.

The people of the Basketmaker culture complex were short in stature and slender in build, with rather delicate features and long narrow heads. The end of the Basketmaker periods saw the intrusion of a new physical type, a group with short, broad heads, artificially flattened behind. These newcomers, the Pueblo people, in time impressed their physical type upon the later cultures of southern Utah. They filtered into the Basketmaker territory in ever-increasing numbers until the older, long-headed strain ceased to exist. About the time of this amalgamation the bow and arrow and grooved axe came into use. Cotton (for woven clothing) and several new varieties of corn were introduced. The turkey was domesticated; turkey skin, cut into strips, was woven into robes. Pottery technique improved in style and execution. In addition to plain and black-on-white vessels, jars were made in a manner that gave a banded appearance to the neck of the finished product. The semi-subterranean dwelling had shallow pits with free-standing walls of pole and adobe construction. There is little evidence of this period in Utah. It is known as Pueblo I or Developmental Pueblo. It is best represented in Arizona, New Mexico, and Colorado, and probably dated from about 800 to 900 A.D., or a little later in southern Utah.

Intensive cultivation of corn, beans, and squash provided food in such vast amounts that the Pueblo people were able to build substantial permanent villages. They developed flat-roofed masonry houses containing several contiguous rooms, some of which were used for living quarters, while others provided storage space. They were usually laid out in the form of a rectangle partially enclosed. A central court containing a semi-subterranean room that preserved certain features of the old Basketmaker houses was the prototype of the modern Pueblo ceremonial chamber or *kiva* (assembly chamber built under or in the Pueblo houses and used for religious purposes). Pottery was made with black designs on a true white or red background. Cooking vessels were made with corrugated surfaces; structural coils of clay were pinched at intervals and not afterwards smoothed over. Crops were cultivated with simple agricultural tools, among which the digging stick was still the most important. This period, dating from about 900 to 1000 A.D., known as Pueblo II, is strongly represented in southern Utah. A general absence of Pueblo I indicates that the characteristic traits of this period were established in northern Arizona and later spread to southern Utah.

Somewhere around 1000 to 1100 A.D. there was a tendency on the part of dwellers in the small masonry houses of the San Juan valley to gather in large terraced pueblos of three or four stories. The dawn of the period known as Pueblo III or Great Pueblo produced large cliff dwellings similar to Mesa Verde's Cliff Palace in Colorado, great valley pueblos such as Pueblo Bonito in New Mexico, and large open-air villages in southeastern Utah. This concentration generated great cultural advances and specializations. Pottery was improved, each center producing a particular type. Fields were tilled, often at a distance from dwellings.

These Indian towns reached a cultural level unsurpassed at any other period in their history, and then, for some unaccountable reason (perhaps the increased pressure of nomadic peoples), were gradually abandoned. First the northern centers and later those of the south were deserted until by the end of Pueblo III, about 1300 A.D., the villages in the San Juan Valley and Utah in general were abandoned. The culture continued in other parts of the Southwest and passed through two subsequent periods: Pueblo IV or Regressive Pueblo, extending from 1300 to 1700 A.D.; and Pueblo V or Historic Pueblo, extending from 1700 A.D. to the present. The modern descendants of these people can be seen today at the Hopi towns in Arizona and Zuñi, Acomá, and the Rio Grande pueblos of New Mexico. It is possible to date these periods with some degree of exactness through study of the annual rings in timbers found within the ruins.

During the development of the Basketmaker-Pueblo sequence in southern Utah and adjoining States the larger part of Utah was inhabited by groups that lived in the northern hinterland of the progressive and comparatively highly cultured southern areas; from these they received their greatest stimulus. Since Basketmaker times cultural infiltrations have been diffused through central and northern Utah from the south. Certain ideas were more popular than others and moved more rapidly, producing strange combinations of comparatively recent traits practiced side by side with others that had been long discontinued in the focal area. This amalgamation of chronologically distinct southern traits, together with new adaptations and local inventions, produced a culture in Utah that can only be understood in terms of the Basketmaker-Pueblo sequence to the south.

The area in eastern Utah between the mouth of the San Juan River and the Uintah Basin acquired a culture that was basically Basketmaker but had such Pueblo ideas as the bow and arrow; at first, the people built shallow-pit lodges with pole and adobe roofs and a little later erected stone houses with free-standing walls. Cliff structures are common in this area, consisting mostly of small buildings on high ledges. Some are dwellings, while others are so small that they have given rise to the idea that they were inhabited by pygmies. Actually they were used as granaries. Truncated pyramidal pole and adobe structures have been found perched on high and narrow pinnacles many hundreds of feet above the valley floors. Similar dwellings are found near agricultural lands in the canyon bottoms, and slab-lined storage cists occur frequently.

The people to the west of the Wasatch Mountains and north of Provo depended to a great extent upon hunting. The common type of habitation was a pit-house somewhat like that of northeastern Utah and that used by the Pueblo I people of southwestern Colorado. Pottery was poorer than in most other areas and only a small portion of the food bowls were decorated. Western Utah south of Provo and north of the Colorado Plateau was characterized by a stronger agriculture complex than the northern country. The type dwelling was an adobe-walled structure, usually with two to twenty rooms, and was built somewhat after the manner of the Pueblo II masonry houses of southern Utah. Pottery was similar to that of the south, but had characteristics of its own. A large group was distributed about the shores of Great Salt Lake and somewhat to the south. They were a hunting and pottery-making people and preceded the Shoshoni, who occupied the area in historic times. It may be well to add that this area was never inhabited by pygmies, giants, Hebrews, Egyptians, or men associated with dinosaurs.

Petroglyphs and pictographs represent an important class of antiquities of wide distribution in Utah. The former are pecked or scratched on rock surfaces, and the latter are painted. An abundance of smooth stones in the mountains encouraged the development of these art forms. West of the Wasatch Mountains the designs usually consist of crude human figures, mountain sheep, deer, and various geometric figures. Throughout the Colorado drainage basin, especially near Vernal, there are groups of large ornamental figures, some pecked and others painted in red, yellow, brown, black, and white. Among them are the finest examples in the United States. It is generally agreed that the pictures had no significance as written symbols. A great many of them were, quite possibly, of a ceremonial nature, while others may have been inscribed for amusement. In a few cases there seems to have been an attempt to portray scenes of hunting, dancing, or war.

Aboriginal antiquities visible in Utah may be divided into two general classes: the minor elements of material culture, which can be viewed in museums; and the major antiquities, including cliff dwellings, mounds, glyphs, and other remains, which can only be seen *in situ*. Of the first class, Salt Lake City has the finest collections of archeological specimens in the State, on exhibition at the University of Utah and at the Latter-day Saints Church Museum in Temple Square. Smaller collections are at Brigham Young University, Provo; at Snow College, Ephraim; and at Zion National Park. The arid climate of the Southwest has preserved many elements of material culture, such as

The Setting I

Courtesy Zion Easter Pageant Committees

ZION NATIONAL PARK

MOUNTAIN WINDOW, ZION-MT. CARMEL HIGHWAY

Robert Davis: Utah Recreation Project, WPA

IN THE HIGH UINTAS—HAYDEN PEAK (*Right Center*)

BRILLIANT-HUED BRYCE CANYON

GOOSENECKS OF THE SAN JUAN

RAINBOW BRIDGE

SIPAPU NATURAL BRIDGE—NATURAL
BRIDGES NATIONAL MONUMENT

Courtesy Provo Chamber of Commerce

MOUNT TIMPANOGOS

ON THE TOE OF THE MOUNTAIN—A FARM IN BOX ELDER COUNTY

Lee: F. S. A.

ONE OF THE CHAIN LAKES, UINTA MOUNTAINS

COLORADO RIVER, NEAR RAINBOW BRIDGE

GREAT SALT LAKE—SALT EVAPORATION BEDS IN FOREGROUND

BOAT PIER ON GREAT SALT LAKE, NEAR SALT LAKE CITY

desiccated human remains, sandals, baskets, wooden implements, fur and feather blankets, corn, and other vegetable products. Beautiful examples of the ceramic wares of the ancient peoples are in great abundance, while the complete series of stone implements ranging from the largest *metates* (corn grinders) to the smallest arrow points illustrate the material equipment of every phase of life.

The best and most extensive major antiquities are concentrated in the southern part of the State, in regions closest to the focal area. However, a number of large and important groups of ruins are found farther north. Among these, perhaps, the structures in Nine Mile Canyon are most easily reached (*see Tour 7a*). Here, perched in every available crevice of the towering cliffs, are the most northerly examples of the cliff-dwelling type of architecture. Small, stone, tower-like structures occupy difficult ledges and commanding ridges. High above the canyon floor on the tops of narrow stone pinnacles are the remains of ancient living quarters. Numerous mounds on the canyon bottoms mark the sites of primitive villages. Practically every available rock surface is covered with examples of some of the finest glyphs in the West. Other important glyphs and masonry structures are near Vernal (*see Tour 6a*).

There are countless ruins in the southern and eastern counties, but the best examples are inaccessible except by pack train. The roads of this area are not of the best, but they are passable in all seasons and the available sites provide an excellent idea of the major antiquities of that part of Utah. Near Blanding, Bluff, and Mexican Hat (*see Tour 10*), are large clusters of cliff dwellings, and on the mesas many open-air masonry structures exist as mounds. There is, perhaps, more to be seen in this area than in any other part of the State. In the Hovenweep National Monument are several large groups of ruins of a specialized architectural type (*see Hovenweep National Monument*). East of Mexican Hat is a large cliff ruin known as Poncho House, interesting for its size and because it illustrates the Pueblo III type of cliff architecture. Other sites, reached by boat, are along the Colorado, Green, and San Juan rivers. Most of the remains that once existed in western Utah have been plowed under, and little of importance or interest survives in that section. A large cave on the western side of Promontory Point, on Great Salt Lake, was occupied by prehistoric peoples.

In visiting prehistoric sites the layman should remember that these ruins, often insignificant in appearance, represent valuable scientific material; any digging or disturbance of the site may cause irreparable loss to science. All archeological material in Utah is protected by State law and any excavation or other destruction by unauthorized persons entails a fine of $300, or six months in prison, or both. Antiquities on Federal property are protected by the Federal Antiquities Act of 1906, violation of which may result in a fine of $500, or ninety days in jail, or both. Serious students of archeology may obtain legal permission to conduct investigations in Utah through the Utah State Park Commission. Permission to investigate in national parks and monuments must be obtained from the Secretary of the Interior, and on national forest lands from the Secretary of Agriculture.

INDIANS

Utah Indians may be classified into three larger tribes: the Ute, the Paiute, and the Shoshoni, who include the Gosiute (or Goshute), though such a grouping is based only on similarities of language and culture and not on the existence of a central government or formal organization. In the early historic period the eastern and central portions of the State were claimed by eight bands of the Ute. Though they moved about to some extent, each occupied a fairly definite area. The Timpanoguts lived near Utah Lake; the Uintas and Kosunats in the Uintah Basin; the Yampas in the vicinity of the Green and Grand rivers; the Pahvants near Kanosh; the Seuvarits in Castle Valley; the San Pits in San Pete Valley; the Pavogogwunsings in Sevier County; and the Paiutes or Water Utes in southeastern San Juan County. Other bands of this group were found in an area extending east into Colorado and south into New Mexico. Eight bands of Paiute lived in the southwestern counties, including Beaver, Piute, Garfield, and southern San Juan. The Beaver band dwelt in southern Beaver and northern Iron counties; the Kaiparowits on and around the Kaiparowits Plateau; the Gunlock band in western Washington County; the Cedar in southeastern Iron County; the St. George band in southern Washington County; the Kaibab in southwestern Kane County; the Uinkaret in eastern Washington County; and the Panguitch in western Garfield and southern Piute Counties. There were other Paiute bands to the south and west. To the west and north of Utah Lake lay the Shoshoni country. At least four bands of Gosiutes lived at Deep Creek in western Juab County; at Skull Valley in central Tooele County; at Snake Creek in northwestern Millard County; and at Trout Creek in central Juab County. In western Box Elder County lived the Tubaduka (Pine Nut Eaters). To the east of these lived the Hukundukka and the Kamuduka (Jack Rabbit Eaters), while Cache and Rich Counties were occupied by the Pangwiduka (Fish Eaters). The Weber Utes lived on the east shore of Great Salt Lake. In addition to these permanent residents, bands of transient mounted Shoshoni from Idaho and Wyoming spent part of their time in northern Utah.

There was no great differentiation in mode of life among the Indians of Utah. Economic dependence was largely upon wild vegetable products and the smaller mammals. Except among the Ute and mounted Shoshoni larger animals were seldom hunted. Clothing was meager and poorly made in the southwest, but the Plains influence produced clothing of better quality in the north. Conical pole lodges covered with grass or brush were the usual type of dwelling, though skin tepees were in use among the Ute and mounted Shoshoni.

The greater part of the Utah Indian's time was spent in food-getting. The Ute, who obtained Spanish horses at a very early date, made good use of them in pursuing the buffalo which, before the nineteenth century, roamed as far west as northern California. Deer and antelope were lured or driven over precipices or into V-shaped enclosures where they were easily killed by arrows; antelope were also taken by "surrounds." Dogs were used, to some extent, by the Paiute for hunting deer and mountain sheep. Rabbits were driven into areas enclosed by long nets in which they became entangled. Several types of digging sticks were in use by the Paiute and Gosiutes for unearthing small rodents. Snares, including a type of deadfall, were also used. Although individual stalking with the bow and arrow was probably important, greater dependence was placed on traps, snares, and communal hunts. The sinew-backed bow, made of wood or mountain sheep horn, was perhaps the most effective weapon on the hunt. Ants and grasshoppers were a part of the Paiute and Shoshoni diet. Ants were obtained by scooping up the earth from ant hills and separating the ants from the earth by shaking in a basket somewhat after the manner of panning gold. Grasshoppers, driven into shallow pits, were gathered, dried, ground into meal, and used in a type of biscuit.

Although the western Utah bands depended to a very large extent on vegetable foods, agriculture is known to have been practiced by only one group, the Kaibab. Corn and squash were raised with the aid of irrigation. Even among this group, however, wild food products were the main staples. The leaves and stems of many plants were boiled and eaten. Various types of grass seeds were gathered and ground into meal on flat stones. Pine nuts, roasted for immediate use and stored raw for winter consumption, were an important article of diet. Annual expeditions into the hills were made by some groups to obtain great quantities of these nuts. Among the other plant products were sunflower seeds, sego-lily bulbs, camas roots, serviceberries, yucca pods, cactus pears, and arrowroot leaves. The various types of meal were made into porridges or mixed with dried berries and baked in ashes. The meat of the larger animals was broiled or cut into strips and dried. Small animals were baked in ashes in their own skins. Most boiling and cooking was in waterproof baskets with the aid of heated stones.

Perhaps the most universal article of clothing in Utah was the rabbitskin blanket, made of long strips of skin with the hair on. The strips were twisted into fur ropes, which were woven into a heavy blanket or cape. Robes of deer and elk skin were also used. Among all Shoshoni, a semi-tailored garment of Plains style was worn whenever materials for their manufacture were available. The men wore shirts and leggings, and ankle length dresses were worn by the women. In warm weather a breechclout or shredded bark kilt was the only garment of both sexes. Footgear was a hard-soled three-piece moccasin or a two-piece moccasin of knee or ankle length. A basketry hat was worn by Ute and Paiute women. Moccasins, when obtainable, and sandals of woven joss weed, were the common types of footwear. The most important garment of the Gosiutes was a rabbit-skin cape which was drawn about the neck with a cord. Moccasins and leggings were uncommon among them.

Dwellings were of poor quality. The Paiutes lived in lodges constructed on a framework of three cedar poles set up in tripod fashion. Two sides of this structure were covered with secondary poles and thatch, while the third, which always faced away from the prevailing winds, was left open. Villages were small and usually consisted of scattered dwellings. The Gosiutes were without lodges, in the strict sense of the word, but lived in circular windbreaks of brush without a roof. Perhaps the best habitations in Utah were the conical skin tepees of the Ute and mounted Shoshoni. Even these, however, were not as well made as the lodges of the Plains tribes to the east. They were constructed of ten to fifteen poles forming a cone about fifteen feet in height and thirteen or fourteen feet in diameter at the base. A skin cover was placed around this framework and staked to the ground, and a skin lining completed the structure. Among the Ute, a thatched dwelling of more or less rectangular outline was also used.

Basketry was an important minor industry. A great variety of forms were made by the coiled and the twined techniques. A pitch-covered bottle with a globular body and constricted neck was used for carrying liquids on long treks into the desert for wild seeds. Other forms were winnowing trays, conical burden baskets, and cradles.

It is not surprising that little information regarding the social organization and religion of the Utah Indians has survived. Scientific reconstruction began too late to provide a complete picture. However, certain determinations have been made which give an insight into their life. The foot Indians of western Utah seem to have lacked centralized authority: the concept of "chief" apparently developed after contact with the whites. The mounted Shoshoni, Ute, and probably some Paiute had strong native chiefs, and pre-white bands. The foot Shoshoni, Gosiute, and possibly a few groups of Ute and Paiute had no chiefs or bands whatsoever. The Paiute bands are known to have had leaders who directed the rabbit hunts, and the Gosiute and other Shoshoni had hunt and dance leaders and antelope charmers; in other activities these officers had no authority. In historic times, however, a number of Ute bands were united under the able chief, Ouray. Although the poorer, horseless groups of Shoshoni seem to have been without leaders, one of the transient mounted bands of Wyoming, which spent a part of its time in northern Utah, was governed by the noted Washakie. There was no type of clan organization. The only divisions among some were the family and village, and among others the band. Polygyny (the state of having several wives) was practiced by those economically capable of it and polyandry (the condition of having plural husbands) existed among some groups. In historic times the Ute carried on an extensive slave traffic. Children were obtained by barter or by force from poorer bands of Paiutes and exchanged with the Navahos and Mexicans to the south for blankets and other articles. Certain Paiute bands were almost depopulated by this traffic.

Religion in Utah was underlain by a general animistic belief in the spirit personalities of animals and plants. The Ute worshipped a bisexual deity, the He-She, represented by the sun; this power was the creator of all things. There were a number of animal gods, chief among them being Coyote. Many legends were associated with the feats of these creatures, and the Ute made every effort to win their favor. The religion of the Paiute and Shoshoni was probably very much like that of the Ute. The *shaman,* or medicine man, was an important personage. Perhaps his most important function was performed in the care of the sick, to whom he ministered by driving out the spirit-cause of the illness. Among the Ute and Paiute one type of "doctor" trusted entirely to the supernatural while another used physical restoratives.

Burial was usually in a rock crevice or excavation. The corpse, with a number of his personal possessions, was placed in the branch-covered grave over which a small cairn was sometimes raised. Funeral arrangements and ceremonial mourning were carried on by female relatives. Men did not even attend the funeral; their important function was to destroy the dead person's property. The Gosiute and other Shoshoni sometimes practiced a form of aquatic burial in which the corpse was placed in a spring and weighted down with stones; usually, however, the rock crevice was used.

The Bear Dance, held each April at Whiterocks, is perhaps most characteristic of the Ute. Men and women participate, and the dance, which lasts several days, is the occasion for much courting. The Back and Forth Dance, derived from the Bear Dance, was adopted by the Gosiute and other Shoshoni. The Ute Sun Dance, held in July at Whiterocks is an acquisition from the Plains by way of the Idaho and Wyoming Shoshoni. Its purpose is to acquire shamanistic powers, or relief from physical ills. The singing and dancing take place in a lodge consisting of a brush wall built around a central pole. The ceremony lasts four days, during which participants abstain from food and water and remain in the lodge. In former times the Ute had a number of other dances which provided a large part of their social- ized amusement. Among them were the Lame Dance, the Dragging Feet Dance, the Woman's Dance, the Double Dance, and others. Gambling games were a common form of recreation. Horse racing and other strenuous sports were engaged in by young men.

Most Utah Indians showed little of the warlike nature displayed by Plains tribes to the east. They were, to borrow Bernard DeVoto's characterization, "the technologically unemployed, victims of the com- petitive Indian society which had forced them to the badlands"; the density of population varied from one person to five square miles in the better hunting country east of the Wasatch Mountains to an extreme in the arid western deserts of one person to thirty-five square miles. Padre Escalante found them "gentle and affable," willing to receive his presents, and, so he thought, his preachings.

The attitude of the Mormons toward the Indians, or "Lamanites," was friendly. The Indians differentiated between "Mericats," or Americans, and "Mormonee," as Brigham Young shows in his letter of September 12, 1857, to Indian Commissioner James W. Denver: "Whenever the citizens of this Territory travel the roads, they are in the habit of giving the Indians food, tobacco and a few other presents." Among the things he "most respectfully suggested to be done" was "that travellers omit their infamous practice of shooting them down when they happen to see one." He added: "I have proven that it is far cheaper to feed and clothe the Indians than to fight them," which was a recapitulation of what he had written Commissioner Manypenny in April, 1856: "One fourth part of the money annually expended in fighting the Indians . . . rightly expended in peaceful operations, would not only leave thousands of Indians to cultivate the soil, cause them to raise their own subsistence, but maintain almost, if not entire peaceful relations with them."

The conflict between whites and Indians was not without "some show of justice" on the part of the Indians, as Brigham Young ad- mitted in his report to Commissioner Manypenny. The land was parceled out among the tribal groups long before white men came. There was a centuries-old ceremony involved in passing from the land of one group to that of another, as William R. Palmer points out in his article on Paiute government in the April, 1929, issue of the *Utah Historical Quarterly*. White men ignored this ritual, either because they had no knowledge of it or because they felt, in their superiority, no need to observe it. Mr. Palmer further shows, in his treatment of Paiute homelands, printed in the July, 1933, *Utah Historical Quarterly,* that the settlers of southern Utah occupied precisely the grounds set aside for various tribal units. There was not much economic land in Utah, and when one Indian group was forced out it had to enter the lands of another for subsistence. This caused conflict between groups, but they often joined against the common invader.

It is surprising on the whole that the history of Utah's Indian wars is not longer than it is. The killing of Captain J. W. Gunnison and members of his party by Pahvant Indians in 1853 was in retaliation for the fatal shooting of Chief Moshoquop's father by emigrants to California. The Walker War of 1853-54 was precipitated by the occupation of Indian lands by white people, and would probably have been more serious except for the restraining influence of the Ute war chief, Sowiette (*see Provo*). For years the killing of a number of white travelers at Mountain Meadows in 1857 was thought to be entirely the work of Paiute Indians, but subsequent evidence indicated that, though involved, they were not the instigators. A Mormon, John D. Lee, was executed in 1877, after conviction in a Federal court for his part in the crime (*see Tour 1f*). Shoshoni resistance to white settlement was crushed when six hundred Indians were surrounded and killed by Federal soldiers in January, 1863 (*see Tour 1a*). The Black Hawk War of 1865-68 (a Ute conflict, not to be confused with the Illinois Black Hawk War in 1827-31), was waged over the same question of white preemption of hunting grounds, and had the same sort of ending. In 1879 the Indian agent, N. C. Meeker, and others were killed at the White River Agency in western Colorado by Ute Indians who objected to maltreatment and to having soldiers on the reservation. The outbreak was quickly subdued, mainly because of the peaceful attitude of Chief Ouray, and the Utes were afterward moved to reservations (*see Tour 6a*). The three men who left Major J. W. Powell's Colorado River expedition in 1869 were killed by Shivwits Indians. There were Navaho raids in southwestern Utah in the sixties and seventies, and trouble with Paiutes and Utes in the San Juan area in the eighties and nineties (*see Tour 9*). As late as 1921 there was a lesser Paiute uprising in the San Juan country, which terminated when the leader, "Old Posey," was fatally wounded (*see Tour 10*). Between 1861, when the Uintah Basin was set aside for Indian use by President Lincoln, and 1929, when the Kanosh reservation was established, Indians within the State were settled on reservations.

Utah Indians have retained little of their original culture. At present (1940) they are engaged for the most part in agriculture and stock raising. They wear modern clothing and live in rural farmhouses comparable with those of white farmers in their districts. However, some native seed gathering is continued, the medicine man has by no means lost his influence, and native dances can be seen by white persons at one or two reservations upon payment of a small fee. Native handicrafts have been revived on most reservations through the encouragement of the Federal government and because of the current demand for hand-made goods.

1938 Statistics

Reservation	Location	Tribe	Approximate Population	Celebrations
Uintah-Ouray	Fort Duchesne, 23.7 m. W. and 1 m. S. of Vernal on State 88 (see Tour 6a).	Ute	1,304	Bear Dance—March Sun Dance—August Indian Fair and U.B.I.C.—August
Washakie (Non-governmental)	5.4 m. N. and 2.2 m. W. of Plymouth on an improved road (see Tour 3).	Shoshoni	132	
Skull Valley	23.6 m. S. and 2 m. W. of Timpie Junction on a dirt road (see Tour 6c).	Gosiute	38	
Goshute	52.5 m. S. of Wendover on a dirt road (see Tour 6c).	Gosiute	158	Bear Dance occasionally
Shivwits-Shebit	12.3 m. W. of St. George on US 91 (see Tour 1f).	Paiute	91	Mourning Ceremony occasionally
Navaho	79.3 m. S. of Monticello on State 47 (see Tour 10).	Navajo	306	
Kanosh	12.8 m. S. and 2 m. E. of Fillmore on a dirt road (see Tour 1e).	Paiute	4	
		Ute	20	
		Paiute	5	
Koosharem	2.9 m. S. and 0.6 m. W. of Koosharem on a dirt road (see Tour 2A).	Paiute	27	
Paiute	42.8 m. W. and 68.3 m. S. of Milford on a dirt road (see Tour 1D).	Paiute	21	
Gandy	15 m. N. of Robinsons Ranch on a dirt road (see Tour 8).	Ute	6	
Cedar City (Church Property)	Cedar City, Mormon Church Farm, on US 91 (see Tour 1f).	Paiute	29	
Allen Canyon	17 m. W. of Blanding, on State 95 (see Natural Bridges National Monument).	Ute	43	

W. ASHBY

History

THE blue waters of the Gulf of Mexico rippling above their
scuttled ships, the *conquistadores* of Hernando Cortez mounted
their horses and turned to the heights of Mexico. That was
in 1519. Twenty-one years later, and two thousand miles northwest,
a detachment of *conquistadores* stood on the brink of the Grand Canyon
of the Colorado. Led by Captain García López de Cárdenas, they
had reached this great river by a twenty-day march through the Painted
Desert of Arizona, and for several days had vainly sought a means of
descent down the precipitous canyon walls. The bright river five thousand feet below was unreachable, and their water ran low; at last
Cárdenas turned back toward Zuñi. The exact route followed by
Cárdenas is not clear, but some historians have held that the Spaniards
reached the Colorado somewhere on the southern rim of Glen Canyon,
a little northeast of the point where the river crosses into Arizona from
southern Utah. If their route has been correctly conjectured, they
were the first Europeans of record to enter the area now called Utah.
What is important, however, is not where Cárdenas went but what he
reported. By his verdict the northern desert lands were damned.
Although Coronado, Cárdenas' leader, remained at Zuñi almost another
year, he looked no more to the north, and no expedition of any importance entered Utah for 236 years.

Venturesome Spaniards before 1776 may have penetrated the canyons
of the Colorado; a 1642 inscription in Glen Canyon has yet to be
explained, and there are legends among the Indians at the mouth of
the Virgin River that their ancestors were forced by Spaniards to work
old lead mines in the vicinity; but it was the Escalante expedition of
1776 which first gave Europeans a true idea of the Utah region.

On July 29, 1776, when the ink was hardly dry on the American Declaration of Independence, Father Silvestre Vélez de Escalante and Father Francisco Atanasio Domínguez left Santa Fe, New Mexico, in search of a direct route to Monterey, California. Accompanied by a small party of Spanish soldiers and Indian retainers, the Franciscan priests made their way up through what is now western Colorado and turned west along the southern flank of the Uinta Mountains, entering the Utah region near the junction of White River with the present State line. They crossed the Green River, which they called the San Buenaventura, and pressed westward along the Duchesne and Strawberry rivers, emerging in September into Utah Valley, via Spanish Fork Canyon. They stayed three days with the timid and inoffensive "Yuta" Indians dwelling on the shores of the lake. Although told of a great salt lake to the north, they were insufficiently curious to investigate. Autumn was drawing on, and promising to return and establish a mission among the Yutas, the priests turned southward. Nowhere did they find word or sign of a promising route to California. In early October, encamped on Beaver River, they abandoned the effort to reach Monterey. Members of the party were so disaffected by this decision that another council was held, all to be bound by the solicited decision of God. "Concluding our prayers, we cast lots, and it came out in favor of Cosnina [New Mexico]. We all accepted this, thanks be to God, willingly and joyfully."

Crossing the Virgin River near the site of St. George, the Spaniards wandered for two weeks in the badlands to the east, seeking a place to cross the Colorado River. At last they located a ford, and by carving stone steps in the canyon walls, were enabled to cross at "Padre Creek," so named in 1937 when it was shown that Escalante had forded the river here rather than at the so-called Crossing of the Fathers a mile west. From this point on the Colorado, the fathers and their company proceeded directly to Zuñi and Santa Fe.

That Escalante, who had seen more of the Utah region, was more impressed than Cárdenas is evidenced by the increased Spanish interest following his return. Escalante observed a number of times in his journal that villages and towns could be supported by irrigation along streams, but no attempts at colonization were made, nor was the promised mission sent the Yutas. The international difficulties in which Spain was embroiled, and the Spanish tendency to recoil from the formidable Great Plains and their newly mounted Indians, discouraged formal efforts toward colonial expansion or governmental exploitation of the Utah area. But sanctioned and unsanctioned trading expeditions between Santa Fe and Utah Lake soon resulted in a well-defined route since known as "the Old Spanish Trail." This route seems at first to have followed that of Escalante, but variant roads presently were found to the south and the long northern trail through the Uintah Basin was less frequently used. The Indians of central Utah, through intercourse with Escalante's party and obscure expeditions such as that in 1805 of Manual Mestas and in 1813 of Mauricio Arze and Lagos García, picked up some smatterings of Christian belief, but also, and less reputably, acquired the idea of slave-trading; lesser tribes were subject to slaving raids by stronger neighbors, and, on occasion, sold their own children into slavery.

It was not Spanish intercourse in the south, however, but Anglo-American enterprise in the north, which opened the Utah region. Returning from their epochal trip to the Pacific in 1806, Lewis and Clark met fur traders pushing out of St. Louis in their track. John Jacob Astor established his unfortunate Astoria on the Columbia River in 1811-12. This venture may have resulted in the first white entrance into the Great Basin from the north, since four men, detached from the overland Astorian expedition in 1811, wandered hundreds of miles until meeting a return party of Astorians in 1812; they may have reached Bear River, and even Great Salt Lake.

Twelve years passed, while the fur trade prepared for its sudden ascent to the transmontane country. On the west the Hudson's Bay Company thrust eastward along the Columbia and Snake; on the east American trappers fought with Blackfeet and Aricaras on the Missouri, and then, headed by parties of General William H. Ashley, abandoned the Missouri for the broad highway of the Platte and Sweetwater, in 1823-24 penetrating to the lofty plains of Wyoming and, through South Pass, crossing the Continental Divide.

Ashley abandoned river transportation and permanent posts for horse-and-pack-train transportation, inaugurating annual rendezvous at designated points. Not a country of rivers, except for its turbulent mountain creeks and the appallingly-canyoned Green-Colorado, Utah could only have been looted of its furs by such a system. Ashley's men in the fall of 1824 came as far west as Cache Valley. Led by William Sublette, a party wintered on the Bear River, and wagers laid among the trappers resulted in the exploration by young Jim Bridger which ended in the discovery of Great Salt Lake (*see Great Salt Lake*). Bridger was barely in time for the honor; indeed, it is disputed whether Etienne Provot may not already have looked out upon the broad waters of the lake from the mouth of Weber Canyon, and claims have been made for Jedediah S. Smith and Peter Skene Ogden. Smith visited the Hudson's Bay post on Flathead Lake in Montana, pushing southward in late December in company with Ogden. They separated on the Bear River, Smith ascending and Ogden descending, the latter coming upon the lake in April to give his name to Ogdens Hole and Ogden River. Trappers converged on Great Salt Lake from the north and northeast, but were halted by forbidding deserts beyond the lake.

Ashley himself was hard upon the heels of his men; in April, 1825, he embarked on the "Spanish" (Green) River in a voyage of exploration almost as far as the present town of Greenriver (*see Tour 7a*), before turning back on horses purchased from the "Eutau" Indians. This canyon country Ashley found as appalling as Cárdenas had found that of the Colorado: "The river is bounded by lofty mountains heaped together in the greatest disorder, exhibiting a surface as barren as can be imagined." Returning, Ashley circled the Uintas (*see High Uintas Primitive Area*), on his way to the rendezvous up Henrys Fork (*see Tour 6a*). In 1826, Ashley sold out his interests to Jedediah S. Smith, William L. Sublette, and David E. Jackson.

A young man hardly past his twenty-eighth birthday, a Methodist Yankee reputed to carry rifle in one hand and Bible in the other, Smith at once set out with seventeen men on an expedition of discovery. By this time a party of trappers had gone around Great Salt Lake in skin boats, and the true character of the lake was known, but all the land to the south and southwest was *terra incognita*. Somewhere in those desert wastes was thought to rise a mighty river, the San Buenaventura, which presumably emptied into San Francisco Bay. The previous year Ashley, while on the Weber, had thought himself upon the headwaters of that fabled stream, and all the trappers must have been eager to find it. Smith pushed straight south, in the footsteps of Escalante, but, like Escalante, found no promise of a water-level route to California. Arriving at the Colorado, he turned west through the desert, reaching the San Gabriel Mission in November, 1826. He met with a cold reception, but was finally permitted to purchase supplies on condition that he return the way he came. He traveled inland only far enough to give the impression of compliance, then swung northward along the western flank of the Sierra Nevada Mountains. He wintered on the Stanislaus River and in the spring crossed the lofty Sierras. Smith's journey southeastward across central Nevada and the Salt Desert was one of great hardship (*see Tour 6c*).

He arrived at the Bear Lake rendezvous in July, being saluted by the wheeled cannon Ashley had sent to the trappers. Ten days later, with a company of eighteen men and two Indian women, he set out for southern California again. On crossing the Colorado River he was attacked by the Mohave Indians, losing ten men, the women, and most of his goods. After further difficulties with California authorities, he was enabled to purchase provisions and supplies and agreed to leave the country. He wintered with his men on the American River, so named from this circumstance, and the following spring, with eighteen men, made an extraordinarily difficult journey up the California and

Oregon coast. As he approached the Willamette Valley the Umpqua Indians fell on his party, and only three, including Smith, escaped the massacre. The survivors took refuge at Fort Vancouver. John B. McLoughlin of the Hudson's Bay Company recovered and purchased Smith's furs for $20,000. After wintering at Fort Vancouver, Smith turned eastward to rejoin his partners at Pierre's Hole in 1829. Smith and his partners sold out, in 1830, to James Bridger, Thomas Fitzpatrick, Milton G. Sublette, Henry Fraeb, and Baptiste Gervais. The young explorer, killed next year on the Cimarrón River, knew the Utah and adjacent area as no one else knew it for decades after him (*see Ogden*).

Envious of Ashley and his successors, the American Fur Company in 1830 extended its operations to the intermountain country, and competition between this firm, the already established Rocky Mountain Fur Company, and the powerful Hudson's Bay Company, for a decade was a wild, unscrupulous rivalry in which the Indians often were robbed and debauched by whisky. William Wolfskill, in 1830-31, leading a party of trappers out of Santa Fe, pushed the Spanish Trail on to southern California from central Utah; though his route was not followed too closely by subsequent trading expeditions, he showed that intercourse between the two Mexican outposts was feasible by the northern overland route. Trapping of beaver remained profitable only until 1840, when the bottom fell out of the market for beaver fur. From 1825 to 1840, yearly rendezvous of the mountain men were held at various points in Utah, Idaho, and Wyoming. Wild and uproarious celebrations, they were punctuated by wholehearted drunkenness and fights with fists, knife, and gun. With aching heads and empty pockets, company and free trappers annually left the gatherings, their hankering for "civilization" satisfied in a few riotous days.

In 1832 Captain B. L. E. Bonneville, on leave of absence from the United States army, came west with an expedition that has puzzled historians ever since. Whether his was a military reconnaissance under guise of a trapping expedition or a trapping expedition under guise of a military reconnaissance is still a subject for argument, although recent discovery of his muster rolls substantiates the idea of a military mission. He established "Fort Nonsense," as the trappers called it, on the Green River in Wyoming and in 1833 sent Joseph Reddeford Walker and others to California. Bonneville himself never entered Utah, though Walker circled the north shore of Great Salt Lake. Bonneville was fortunate in falling into the hands of a great writer, and, through the medium of Washington Irving's account of his travels, named Great Salt Lake for himself. History rejected that verdict, but the power of publicity is such that Bonneville's name subsequently was given the Pleistocene lake that had covered much of the Great Basin (*see Geology*).

Ashley sent a wheeled cannon to Bear Lake in 1827; Thomas Fitzpatrick took a wagon train to the Wind River Mountains in 1830; and Bonneville's wagons were brought across the Continental Divide in 1832 to Green River. It now became clear that the "boat" of the West was to be the "prairie schooner," drawn by horses, mules, or oxen. Dr. Marcus Whitman brought emigrant wagons to the Horse Creek, Wyoming, rendezvous of 1836. Obstinately determined to carry his wagons through to Oregon, Whitman had to abandon them west of Fort Hall, but the hour of the emigrant was at hand; in 1843 wagons traveled all the way to the Willamette Valley, and a year later climbed the passes of the Sierra Nevada and descended triumphantly into central California. The Oregon Trail, the "Great Medicine Road," was a highroad by 1840.

The trapping business was doomed. The few remaining trappers were settling down at isolated points in the mountains, or establishing fixed posts. As early as 1832 Antoine Robidoux built his fort in the Uintah Basin near the confluence of the Uinta and Duchesne rivers; five years later Philip Thompson and David Craig built "Fort Davy Crockett" in Browns Hole—this post was named for the famous Texan killed at the Alamo the previous year, but trappers more familiarly called it "Fort Misery" and described it as "the meanest fort in the West." The first fort west of the Wasatch Range was that erected by Miles Goodyear on the site of Ogden in 1844-45. Unlike Jim Bridger's famous establishment on Blacks Fork of the Green, built in 1842-43, these forts were off main emigrant routes. Before the establishment of Goodyear's Fort Buenaventura, emigrants and the path-marker for emigrants, John Charles Frémont, had already come into Utah. In the summer of 1841 the first emigrant train to California, the venturesome Bartleson-Bidwell party, left the Oregon Trail, circled Great Salt Lake to the north, and crossed the Salt Desert (*see Tour 6c*).

Frémont, en route to Oregon in the late summer of 1843, made a side trip into Great Salt Lake Valley from the north (*see Great Salt Lake*). Ignorant of the trappers who had circumnavigated the lake when he was a boy in knee-breeches, Frémont imagined himself the first to venture on the salt waters. Frémont was never the great discoverer he was called, for in his significant explorations he had been anticipated almost everywhere by the trappers, but he produced scientific reports and maps of the West at the moment that the rising tide of empire demanded them; the times and the man came together, and Frémont won a lasting reputation. He went on to Oregon and California, and in the spring of 1844 came up through Utah as far as Utah Lake. He thought it the southern extension of Great Salt Lake, and could

not imagine why it was fresh.   Thence he went east by way of Spanish
Fork Canyon, the Uintah Basin, and Browns Hole.   In 1845 he came
west again, passing around the southern shore of Great Salt Lake and
striking out across the Salt Desert to California, where he participated
in the "Bear Flag" rebellion.   The trail Kit Carson found for Frémont
across the Salt Desert contributed to one of the most tragic chapters in
American history, that of the Donner party (*see Tour 6c*).

As the dust settled into the wagon-tracks of the Donners, the first
era of white association with the Utah region was closed.   *Conquistadores, padres,* Indian traders, trappers, explorers, and Pacific emigrants
were transient shadows on the land.   The destiny of Utah lay in the
hands of a people who had never seen the country, and who, during
the winter of 1846, were encamped 12,000 strong at Council Bluffs
and along the Iowa plains, wretchedly waiting for spring.   After sixteen tumultuous years in the mid-western States, the Mormons were in
flight to the Rocky Mountains.

THE MORMON PIONEERS

The story of the Mormons is also the story of two great leaders.
Joseph Smith established the Church and its vital doctrines, and gathered
around him an extraordinary body of energetic and able men.   Brigham
Young was one of the greatest of these proselytes; after the death
of the prophet and founder, he held the membership together, successfully carried the Church to Utah, and in an extraordinary struggle
with a bitterly adverse environment accomplished the conquest of the
desert.

Smith was born in Sharon, Vermont, in 1805.   Ten years later
his father moved the family to Palmyra, on the New York frontier,
and four years later to Manchester, six miles south.   That much
about Smith is accepted, but practically everything else about him
has been for more than a century a subject of fiercest debate.   Few
men ever had such passionately devoted friends, or such bitterly antagon-
istic enemies.   Between the devotion and the enmity, the true stature of
Joseph Smith as a man has been slow to emerge.

Upper New York State at this time was roaring with religious
hysteria.   The whole Atlantic seaboard from 1790 had been convulsed
by the revivals of Methodist exhorters.   Congregations went virtually
mad; men barked like dogs, drowned out the preacher with their scream-
ing, or spoke ecstatically in tongues; orgiastic camp-meetings lasted for
days as men "got religion."   Herbert Asbury has observed that "all
the congregations were jerking, barking, jumping, hopping, dancing,
prancing, screeching, howling, writhing in fits and convulsions, falling
in cataleptic trances, and performing many other strange and holy

ntics." Religious feeling was a consuming flame which ate at the
whole frontier, but even the seaboard cities were not immune; Baltimore
in 1789 was shaken as by madness.   Even where religious excitement
did not take these violent forms, men pored over the Bible by day
and by night, seeking the ways of grace and salvation, and pondering
the imminence of the second coming of Christ.   Everywhere new
churches were springing up, and were splitting into sects and sub-
sects.   From this confusion, this nightmare of religious zeal, the
Church of Jesus Christ of Latter-day Saints, the Mormon Church,
merged on April 6, 1830.

The Mormon story of the origin of the Church is that the boy,
Joseph Smith, troubled by the welter of religious sects, was led in
1820 to inquire of God concerning the church he should join; in a
vision the Father and Son appeared to him and told him that all the
churches were wrong, and he must join none of them.   Subsequently
an angel of the Lord appeared to him several times, informed him that
he was to perform a great work, and that his name would be known
"for good and evil among all nations," and at last revealed to him
golden plates, an ancient record buried in the Hill Cumorah, which
he was to translate with the aid of the "Urim and Thummim."   In
1827 the plates were delivered to him, and for the next two years
he translated.   The Book of Mormon was published in March, 1830,
and formal organization of the Church in Fayette, New York, occurred
soon after.

Ever since, disbelievers have proposed other explanations.   It was
common at first to term Smith a rogue, charlatan, a shiftless money-
digger and a seer in peepstones, who encountered a Campbellite preacher
named Sidney Rigdon, and with him plagiarized a manuscript by Sol-
mon Spaulding, which had described ancient peoples in North America.
Joseph Smith and his "Gold Bible" were subjects for bitter derision.
Later the prevailing non-Mormon view of Smith changed, and he
was conceived to have been altogether sincere, but deceived by burning hallucinations; a still later view, advanced by Bernard DeVoto,
is that Smith was a paranoiac alternating between periods of sanity
and insanity, at the same time a man of great energy and spiritual
force.   The inability of non-Mormons to reach any settled conclusions
about Smith has confirmed the Church membership in its belief in him,
for the Church viewpoint from beginning to end has had the advantage of thorough consistency.   Here, however, it is not important
whether Joseph Smith was or was not a prophet of God; it is important that his followers believed him to be such, and they wrought
greatly in consequence of this belief.

In 1831, because of persecution in New York, the prophet moved
the Church to Kirtland, Ohio, previously a Campbellite stronghold;

whole congregations there came into the fold. The Church grew
amazingly. Missionaries "without purse or scrip" spread into the country, preaching and baptizing. Others heard the word, and sought
out Joseph Smith; such an one was Parley P. Pratt. The first temple
of the Church began to rise in Kirtland. In the summer of 1831
Joseph Smith visited the brethren in Jackson County, Missouri, and
felt Missouri was Zion; a revelation directed the faithful to assemble
in Zion, "the land of your inheritance, which is in the hands of
your enemies."

Alarmed Missourians found the "Saints" settling among them in
droves, with the prospect that more would follow. The two groups
mixed like fire and gasoline. The Missourians were hard individualists,
frontiersmen of slave-soil sympathies. The Mormons settled on the
land as solid social groups, announcing themselves as the chosen of
God arriving upon God's designated gathering place; they held to themselves, voted as a group, and sometimes talked unwisely of ultimately
possessing all Zion—Jackson County—"the earth and the fullness
thereof." Additionally, they came from free soil.

In July, 1833, amid scenes of rape and rapine, the Mormons were
driven from Jackson County; they settled in Clay County. But the
sympathies of Clay citizens soon soured; in 1836 the Mormons were
expelled again, into Daviess and Caldwell counties, where they founded
the towns of Far West and Adam-ondi-Ahman. "Persecution" and
"mobocrat," two burning words in Mormon history, were being graven
upon Mormon feeling. The Church in Kirtland likewise encountered
difficulties, for Joseph Smith, gathering around him in the Quorum
of the Twelve and the higher priesthood the men who later served
the Church so ably, was harassed by a lunatic fringe of charlatans,
adventurers, and zealots. Disaster for Kirtland came with the panic
of 1837; the city was caught in a fever of land speculation, and because of undercapitalization and embezzlement by its cashier, the
Mormon bank closed its doors.

Smith, Rigdon, and other Mormon leaders journeyed west, but
Missouri, where they arrived in March, was no sanctuary. Embittered people there listened avidly to counsel of resistance. In July,
1838, according to Hubert H. Bancroft, Sidney Rigdon delivered a
rousing sermon, in which he declared, "We take God to witness and
the holy angels to witness this day, that we warn all men, in the
name of Jesus Christ, to come on us no more forever. The man or
the set of men who attempt it, do it at the expense of their lives;
and that mob that comes on us to disturb us, there shall be between
us and them a war of extermination, for we will follow them till the
last drop of their blood is spilled, or else they will have to exterminate

s; for we will carry the war to their own houses, and their own families, and one party or the other shall be utterly destroyed."

The Missourians took Rigdon at his word. Mormons clashed in August with non-Mormons who sought to prevent them from voting at Gallatin. Minor in itself, this incident was a prelude to open combat. In October the two parties fought at Crooked River, and a week later a mob fell on the Mormons at Hauns Mill and massacred eighteen. The same day a mob-militia of 2,000 appeared before Far West, prepared to execute the order of Governor Lilburn W. Boggs that the Mormons be utterly exterminated or driven from the State. Joseph and Hyrum Smith, Sidney Rigdon, Lyman Wight, Parley P. Pratt, and other Mormon leaders were delivered into the hands of the mob-militia, and the expulsion of the people began on November 1. Smith lay in Missouri prisons until April, while the scattered members of the Church were led into Illinois by Brigham Young, who now began to demonstrate his great capacities for organization and leadership. At length escaping prison and rejoining his people, Joseph Smith designated Commerce, Illinois, as the gathering place for the inconquerable young Church.

The impoverished Mormon people found sympathy and a warm welcome in Illinois. But Illinois sympathy was not altogether altruistic: an increase of population seemed to promise an increase of business and a local remedy for the depression following the 1837 panic, and the numerically equal Whig and Democratic parties hoped to gain the Mormon vote. On the site of Commerce Joseph Smith set about building Nauvoo, "the Beautiful." He obtained a remarkable city charter from the legislature: Nauvoo was permitted to levy, collect and disburse taxes without reference to any authority except the city council; its courts were given exclusive jurisdiction over city affairs; more extraordinarily, the city was granted the right to raise and maintain an independent militia, the Nauvoo Legion; and a charter was granted the University of the City of Nauvoo, said to be the first municipal university in the United States.

Nauvoo rose amazingly; within five years it was the largest town in Illinois. But the causes which had operated to alienate the Missourians still were implicit in Mormon group relations. Again they had come as new settlers into an already occupied land; again they were coherent and powerful as a social group; again they alienated their fellows by their insistence that they were the chosen of God—the "saints" of the latter days. They began to be cordially hated by many, and lost the favor of both political parties by voting consistently for neither. There were new sources of irritation, too. "Mobbing and robbing" at the hands of the gentiles (non-Mormons) in Missouri had led some of the people to feel that reprisal at the expense of any

gentile was justified; and the urban growth of Nauvoo attracted un
savory characters, by no means averse to having their misdeeds assigne
to the Mormons. Rumors of adultery and polygamy overspread th
country. Relations between Mormons and non-Mormons grew steadil
worse. Mobs descended on outlying Mormon farms, killing an
mutilating Mormons and firing their houses and crops. The legislatur
began to consider repeal of the Nauvoo charter.

It had now become clear, with a prospect only of increasing vio
lence, that the Mormons would have to find a new land. As earl
as 1842 Joseph Smith had predicted that one day the Mormons woul
establish themselves in the Rocky Mountains and become a great an
mighty people; in February, 1844, Joseph "instructed the Twelv
Apostles to send out a delegation and investigate the locations of Cali
fornia and Oregon, and hunt out a good location, where we can remov
to after the Temple is completed, and where we can build a city in
day, and have a government of our own, get up into the mountains
where the Devil cannot dig us out, and live in a healthy climate, wher
we can live as old as we have mind to."

At the same time he resolved on a bolder step: he announced hi
candidacy for the Presidency of the United States. If he were success
ful, "the dominion of the Kingdom of God" would forthwith be estab
lished; if unsuccessful, the Mormons might turn westward, to Cali
fornia, Oregon, or Texas, and escape persecution. These plans were
shattered in June. Apostates from the Church published, in the
Nauvoo Expositor, charges about Smith and the leaders which were
regarded as libelous. The city council smashed the press as a nuisance
and the countryside was aroused. Imprisoned at Carthage under pledge
of protection, on the 27th of June Smith was shot dead with his brother
Hyrum, when a mob stormed the jail.

In August, 1844, Brigham Young, in his capacity as president
of the Quorum of the Twelve, was accorded leadership of the Church
it is said that he "spoke with the voice of Joseph," so that the mantle
of Joseph demonstrably had fallen upon him. Although not all Church
members were disposed to accept this leadership, and special dissenting
groups broke off, notably followers of James J. Strang, who later estab
lished the "Kingdom of Saint James" in the islands of Lake Michigan,
the greater part of the membership followed Young.

Brigham Young, the guiding genius of the Church in Utah, was born
in Whitingham, Vermont, in 1801. He joined Joseph Smith in 1832,
and was made a charter member of the Quorum of the Twelve in
1835. A man of enormous energy and great vision, he has come to be
recognized as one of the major figures in western history. No man
could have been found more brilliantly suited to the task of overseeing
the removal of the Mormons to a new land. In the autumn of 1845 he

nnounced that the following spring the Mormons would move from Nauvoo. In February, 1846, advance companies crossed the Mississippi.

Mormons on the Iowa plains made their way slowly westward, he advance companies building bridges and houses, and putting in crops or companies that followed. Captain James Allen arrived at Council Bluffs on July 1 with a Government proposal that 500 men be mustered nto a Mormon Battalion for service against Mexico. Although in ater years Battalion members were fond of referring to themselves s the "Ram in the Thicket," offered in sacrifice to save Israel, and Mormon leaders declared that the Government had "demanded" such battalion to test Mormon loyalty, it is now thought that the idea vas of Mormon origin. Brigham Young and the apostles in Iowa ctively aided in the recruiting, and the Battalion departed in July n an epochal 2,000-mile march to California (*see Salt Lake City*).

Before the Mormons settled into winter quarters in the fall of 846, the absolute necessity of a "gathering place for Israel" was demon-trated by the final expulsion of the Saints from Nauvoo. Difficulties here had been constant, and the city was definitely abandoned to the nti-Mormons after the pitched "Battle of Nauvoo" in September, vhen a small band of Mormons and "Jack Mormons" (gentile friends) allantly fought with a large force of anti-Mormons in defense of he city. From their winter quarters on the west bank of the Mis-ouri River near present Omaha, and pursuant to the "Will and Word f the Lord," vouchsafed Brigham Young as a revelation in January, 847, the Mormons dispatched an advance company of pioneers to find n the mountains an "abiding place for the Saints." In Mormon tradi-ion, Brigham Young knew from vision, before leaving Nauvoo, that he hould locate in Great Salt Lake Valley. Historically, his decision vas determined by reading the published reports of Frémont and other ravelers, and by special considerations affecting the Mormons as a roup. In Nauvoo he received letters, sometimes insolent, from other ntending migrants, warning him that the Mormons might expect rouble in California and Oregon; these must certainly have confirmed im in his conviction that the Saints must find a place where they vould be the first settlers, and where they would be privileged to say o later comers what had been so often said to them: "Get out!"

Oregon, already peopled by many emigrant Missourians, seems to ave attracted Young at no time; he gave some consideration to Van-ouver Island, more especially for the English emigrants; but it was he Great Basin, so named by Frémont, that seized upon his imagina-ion. As early as 1845 he had specifically mentioned Great Salt Lake Valley, the outstanding topographical feature of the Basin, and all hrough the early months of 1846 he talked about the Basin. Address-ng the Battalion prior to its departure, he informed them that the

Saints in all probability would locate in eastern California some 800 miles from the Pacific Coast; and to Colonel Thomas L. Kane he talked specifically of locating in Bear River Valley or Great Salt Lake Valley.

The general place of settlement had been determined sight unseen accordingly, only the specific locality remained a question mark as the pioneers rolled up the North Platte and thence along the Oregon Trail to the tune of "The Upper California, O, That's the Land For Me." In June the westbound Saints conferred with Jim Bridger and other mountain men, from whom they got discouraging reports, but the party pushed on from Fort Bridger in the tracks of the Donners, and into Salt Lake Valley. Orson Pratt and Erastus Snow, on July 21 1847, were first to enter; a small body arrived the next day, and the greater part of the company on the 23rd. Young, who had been ill with "mountain fever," entered the valley with the rear companies on July 24, which has since been "Pioneer Day," Utah's outstanding holiday.

Plowing began July 23, the day before Young's arrival, when the waters of City Creek were turned out of their bed to soften the land for plows. It was necessary to hasten if anything was to be grown this year, and a harvest would be important, for Parley P. Pratt and John Taylor were bringing westward more than 1,500 colonists who expected to winter in the valley. The original company, augmented at Fort Laramie by a few immigrant Saints from Mississippi, received further additions on July 29, when the rest of the Mississippi Saints and the sick detachment of the Mormon Battalion, which had wintered at Pueblo, arrived in the valley. Other Battalion members appeared from the west a few months later, having been mustered out in California on July 16, but the greater part of the Battalion stayed in California, and some members, working at Sutters Mill near the site of Sacramento, participated in the discovery of gold the next year. Notwithstanding the need for a harvest, exploring parties were dispatched north to Cache Valley, west to Tooele Valley and south to Utah Valley. Exploration, however, only served to convince the Mormons that they had already found their place of settlement. In August, Brigham Young and others turned back to their families at Winter Quarters, having, in George A. Smith's words, "broke, watered, planted, and sowed upwards of 100 acres with various kinds of seeds; nearly stockaded with adobies one public square (ten acres)," and built "one line of log cabins in stockade."

The colonists were not permitted to scatter out over the land. Co-operative practices and thinking, which had characterized Mormon life in the Midwest, had led to an emphasis upon the group, and the nature of that group life made possible exploitation of the arid lands and the creation of a desert civilization. As with all Mormon colonies

later years, the 1847 settlers gathered in a fort, not only for pro-
ction against Indians but because such a communal settlement allowed
or valid social life and religious activities. The settlers lived close
ogether, and went out to a distance to farm their lands. It is one
f the great triumphs of the Mormon Church that it not only surmounted the problems of an arid land, which forced settlers to scatter
idely over a large area, but made those problems of isolation and
remendous distances contribute to the power and coherence of its social
rganization.

The first laws in the region, issued as decrees by Brigham Young
n July 25, 1847, related to land ownership and conservation of re-
ources. Land, Young said, was neither to be bought nor sold; it was
o be apportioned to the settlers, and if they were to hold it, they
ust take industrious care of it. He also decreed community owner-
hip of water and timber resources. The Mormons, neither then
or thereafter, were much concerned with formal law; in general,
road principles were laid down, and the people were governed to a
onsiderable extent according to the moral codes and social relation-
hips developed within the Church.

Upon Young's departure for Winter Quarters, a president and
vo counselors, together with a "High Council" of twelve high priests,
ere nominated to administer the affairs of the "Stake of Zion" in the
alley. Major acts of the council were approved by congregational
oting. In general, local administration was by the bishops of the
everal wards, although, during the first year in Great Salt Lake
alley, the High Council served in virtually all capacities, legislative,
xecutive, and judicial. In later years the High Council served more
pecially as a court of appeal from decisions of the bishops' courts.
igh Council decisions could be overturned only by the Quorum of the
welve, the court of last resort. Since Brigham Young's time, the
resident of the Church has always been the senior apostle, and deci-
ons of the presidency have usually been synonymous with decisions
f the Twelve. No attempt was made until 1849 to establish a formal
vil government, though civil laws were passed by the High Council
December, 1847, with legislation against vagrancy, disorderliness,
eft and arson, adultery, and misconduct in general. There was
o need for civil government, since Church government was functioning
ffectively. The land they occupied still belonged to Mexico, and was
ot ceded to the United States until after signing of the treaty of
uadaloupe Hidalgo in 1848.

In accordance with instructions given by Young before his departure,
e High Council in November bought out Goodyear's interests on the
Veber River. When Young, who in December, 1847, had become
fficially designated as President of the Church, returned from Winter

Quarters in September, 1848, the Utah region lay ready for systemat
colonization. Already, indeed, Goodyear's property had become tran
formed to "Brownsville," and Peregrine Sessions had located the tow
of Bountiful.

Because their preoccupation with the desert was the outstandin
feature of their civilization for the next quarter of a century, it
important to realize the mood in which the Mormons migrated to Utal
The Church in the early years had a stirring millennial tone; to i
members the day of judgment seemed very imminent. In designatin
Missouri as Zion, Joseph Smith named a place of gathering for tl
faithful, and although he ridiculed the claims of Millerites, who pr
dicted the Second Advent for 1843 or 1844, and although he sa
on more than one occasion that many years would elapse before tl
maturing of this event, yet he anticipated the millennium at a relative
early date, once saying that if he lived to be eighty-five, he shoul
see "the face of the Son of Man."

The power and conviction of this belief, the deeply moving beli
of a people, may be heard in the hymns still sung by Mormon co
gregations:

> The Spirit of God like a fire . . . is burning!
> The latter day glory begins to come forth;
> The visions and blessings of old are returning!
> And angels are coming to visit the earth.
> We'll sing and we'll shout with the armies of heaven,
> Hosanna, hosanna to God and the Lamb!
> Let glory to them in the highest be given,
> Henceforth and forever; amen, and amen!

Because the Mormons looked to the afterlife more than to this lif
colonization of the desert was possible. "Faith through works" w
the keynote to Mormon living. Men starved on sego-lily bulbs ar
thistle greens, on hawks, owls, and crows, while they stayed stubborn
with the land. They were working out their salvation on eartl
They clung together because they had to; they succored one anoth
because they could depend only upon themselves. Not all of tl
Saints were saints; often there were rascals among them; often the
suspicion of the gentiles made them socially difficult; often as a peop
they were unbearably self-righteous. Had the Mormons aimed le
high, however, and achieved less greatly, their shortcomings wou
have been less emphasized.

Brigham Young's efficient colonization of the arid mountain va
leys was remarkable for its success and for the social discipline th
resulted in success. Church members were "called" as for a missio
Groups were carefully selected to include blacksmiths, tanners, mille
carpenters—perhaps also a doctor, though for the most part the fro

ier settlements depended upon midwives and amateur doctors. Everyone, actually or potentially, was a farmer. A president would be
named for the group, and on a designated date it would gather its
property into wagons and set out, perhaps to the valley of the Sevier,
perhaps to "Dixie," perhaps even to Idaho's Salmon River, or Nevada's
Carson Valley. Arriving on the site of settlement, sometimes selected
in advance by Brigham Young, as Fillmore was, the colonists would
build a fort, then irrigation ditches, fence farm lands, and raise
log or adobe houses. Major missions departed in midwinter, and
crops were put in as soon as spring opened. Often newly arrived immigrants were incorporated into such colonizing missions, but the backbone
was supplied by experienced settlers who had dwelt longer in Utah.
A man who had proved himself once might suddenly be called to for-
sake the few comforts he had wrested from the desert for a new struggle
with a barren untilled land. Sometimes he might feel that death was
preferable to another uprooting, but almost invariably the "called" man
obeyed, for he was contributing to the "upbuilding of the Kingdom";
he was laying up glories in heaven by his work on earth.

The late-sown crops of 1847 were scant, but the colonists planted
several thousand acres to wheat and corn. John Steele recorded in his
journal in the spring of 1848, "Our wheat, corn, beans and peas are
all up and looking grand and grass is 6 inches high. Sunday, June
4th, there is great excitement in camp. There has come a frost which
took beans, corn and wheat and nearly every thing, and to help make
the disaster complete the crickets came by the thousands of tons, and
the cry is now raised, 'we can not live here, away to California,' and
the faith of many were shaken, but . . . [the Battalion boys] almost to
a unit said God had sent us here, and here we were going to stay,
come weal come woe. This seemed to turn the tide of affairs in our
favor but times still looked very dark and hunger stared us in the face
at every step until about the 15th of July when we began to get some
new wheat which relieved us wonderfully, and we then thought of
beginning to live once more." The frost was forgotten, but the
crickets were remembered, because gulls came in flocks to gorge upon
them; the "miracle of the gulls," sent by God to succor the people,
has become a cherished part of Mormon folklore.

Crickets and late frosts were only a single feature of the Mormons'
environmental adjustment. Their first houses were built, on the advice
of Sam Brannan, after the California manner—flat-roofed adobe,—but
the water gathered on the roofs and reduced some of the houses to mud
puddles; then the Mormons built houses to withstand the storms. They
lived thousands of miles from manufacturers and supplies; what they
did not have, they went without or made themselves. Tanners made
shoes, shirts, and breeches along with harness and saddles; expeditions

were sent back along the emigrant trails to recover metal from discarded wagons, to be reworked into tools and plowshares; native clays were made into pottery; lumber, laboriously hauled from the canyons, was utilized for a thousand things, from wooden shoes to boats. Parley P. Pratt could write in his journal concerning 1848, "My family and myself, in common with many of the camp, suffered much for food. . . . I had ploughed and subdued land to the amount of near forty acres, and had cultivated the same in grain and vegetables. In this labor every woman and child in my family . . . had joined to help me. . . . Myself and some of them were compelled to go with bare feet for several months, reserving our Indian moccasins for extra occasions. We toiled hard and lived on a few greens and on thistle and other roots. We had sometimes a little flour and some cheese, and sometimes we were able to procure from our neighbors a little sour skimmed milk or buttermilk." But to his brother, Orson, then in England, he could write romantically, "All is quiet—stillness. No elections, no police reports, no murders, no wars, in our little world. . . . It is the dream of the poets actually fulfilled."

In December, 1848, the Mormons wrote a memorial to Congress for creation of a Territorial government. This memorial, bearing 2,270 signatures, and said to have been twenty-two feet long, was sent east the following May, but by that time the Mormons had undertaken to create a provisional government. A constitution was drafted in early March, and officers for the "State of Deseret" were elected in Great Salt Lake City. Brigham Young was named governor, Heber C. Kimball lieutenant-governor and justice of the supreme court, and Willard Richards secretary of State; the Mormons simply installed the First Presidency of the Church in the leading civil offices. The first session of the legislature was held in July, 1849, but no legislation was passed until the second session. The State of Deseret, named for a Book of Mormon word interpreted as meaning "honey bee," included within its proposed boundaries virtually all of what is now Utah and Nevada, the greater part of Arizona, and portions of Idaho, Wyoming, Colorado, Oregon, and New Mexico, as well as a strip of seacoast in Southern California near San Diego. One of the few physical reminders of the State of Deseret, in 1940, was an inscribed stone, donated by the provisional government, and still to be seen inside the Washington Monument in the Nation's capital.

The legislature sent east a delegate, Almon W. Babbitt, with a petition to Congress for admission as a State. Babbitt's application for a seat in the House was refused on the ground that seating him would be a quasi-recognition of Deseret. By July, 1850, a compromise committee headed by Henry Clay had drawn up a plan by which California was to be admitted as a State, and New Mexico and Utah admitted as Territories. Bitter argument between slavery and abolitionist partisans held up disposition of the territory acquired from Mexico and it was not until September, 1850, Congress having become frightened by the necessity of doing something, that proposals of the compromise committee were substantially adopted. The Mormon name of "Deseret" was held to be repulsive, and the territory was named Utah, to the chagrin of those who thought that "Utah" was descriptive only of a "dirty, insect-infested, grasshopper-eating tribe of Indians." The Territory of Utah extended north and south from the Oregon (now the Idaho) line to the New Mexico (now the Arizona) line, and east and west from the summit of the Rockies through what is now central Wyoming and Colorado to the Sierra Nevada Mountains.

The Mormons had fled from civilization, done with its abominations, but they had fled directly in the path of empire. In January, 1848, James W. Marshall picked up the first gold in Sutter's mill races. The first overland gold-seekers arrived in Great Salt Lake Valley in June, 1849. Almost all of them were in need of provisions and fresh horses when they arrived at the Mormon oasis. Many of them had brought stores of merchandise—clothing, tools, manufactured goods—which they sacrificed ruthlessly for fresh livestock and crops. Priceless goods were offered to amazed Mormons at far less than cost. The Lord had provided for His own.

But the Mormons must have agricultural self-sufficiency if they were to survive. Gold was a convenience, but food and livestock, iron and coal, were necessities. Moreover, Mormon isolation must be maintained. Young forbade prospecting for precious metals in Utah, and rebuked those who would have gone to dig gold in California. "Gold," he thundered from the pulpit, "is for paving streets. The business of a Saint is to stay at home and make his fields green." Members of the Church in California left the gold fields without regret. James S. Brown, the first to see Marshall's gold, returned to Zion in 1848 with other members of the Battalion. Just as he was preparing to leave, he located a rich find from which he washed out $49.50 in gold between 11 A. M. and sundown, but the next morning he left, never to see the spot again.

The "kingdom" began to build in Utah. Settlements spread down the mountain valleys south from Great Salt Lake City. Fort Utah was built near the site of Provo in 1849; the walls of Manti arose soon after in Sanpete Valley and by the end of 1850 George A. Smith was en route south to settle the Little Salt Lake Valley. But "building" did not proceed without harassment from without. In the summer of 1851 the officials named to Territorial office by President Fillmore appeared from the east. Fillmore had been gracious to the Mormons; he had named Young governor of the new Territory, and all the other officers were Mormon except four. These arrived to find that Young had completed a census of the Territory, apportioned representation for the Territorial legislature, and set a date for elections. The general assembly had formally dissolved the State of Deseret, and Young had assumed office as Territorial governor, upon receiving word of his nomination through eastern newspapers brought from California.

Unfortunately for the hope that the Mormons would get on amicably in their new relation to the United States, the gentile Federal officials were the first in a long line of scoundrels, fanatics, and well-meaning but ineffectual men who thoroughly exasperated the Mormons, who in turn thoroughly exasperated the rest of the nation. Invited to address the general conference of the Church in September, 1851, Associate Justice Perry D. Brocchus exhorted the Mormons to be true to the Government, and then alluded to the as yet officially unadmitted practice of polygamy, strongly admonishing the Mormon women to be virtuous. An uproar ensued. Brigham Young hushed the audience and turned on Brocchus. The United States Government had not, he said, earned the esteem of the Mormons when it stood idly by during the persecutions visited on the Mormons in Missouri and Illinois. It was an insult for such corrupt individuals as Brocchus to come before the Latter-day Saints as authorities on morality and virtue. "I love the constitution and government of the United States, but not the damned rascals that administer the government."

A further source of irritation soon appeared. Broughton D. Harris, secretary of the Territory, was dissatisfied because strict legal forms had not been followed in apportioning representation to the Territorial legislature. A new census should be taken, and everything done over. Brigham Young was not disposed to comply. Having completed a census of Utah's 11,380 inhabitants, he saw no need to do it over. Harris decided to return East with Brocchus. Lemuel G. Brandebury, chief justice of the courts, sided with Brocchus and Harris. Hastily the Territorial legislature was summoned, and an attempt was made by legal means to restrain Harris from leaving the Territory with its papers and funds. Brocchus and Brandebury, meeting as the supreme court despite the fact that no legal session could be held until the time and place was designated by Governor Young, sustained Harris, and the officials turned their backs on Utah, leaving the Saints to make what shift they could.

The Mormons were not dismayed. They had been getting along by themselves for four years. The legislature dispatched a memorial to Congress strongly protesting the action of the Federal officials, and declared the laws of the Provisional State of Deseret in effect wherever applicable and not in conflict with Federal territorial statutes. Congress was also memorialized for roads, railroads, and a magnetic telegraph.

Young named Willard Richards secretary *pro tem,* while the courts were sufficiently served by the Mormon justice, Zerubbabel Snow, who had refused to leave with Brandebury and Brocchus. The story goes that the runaway officers, reporting to Congress, undid themselves by asserting that "polygamy monopolized all the women, which made it very inconvenient" to live in Utah. In itself this first difficulty between Mormons and Federal officeholders was of no significance, but, as the first of a long series of troubles, it was an important indicator.

Before the next group of officeholders arrived, the Mormons had taken the plunge, and formally avowed the practice of polygamy as a fundamental tenet of Church doctrine. Polygamy was the pretext for all the varied dislikes and antagonisms the Saints aroused in the other citizens of the United States. More than any other feature of Mormon culture, polygamy has distinguished Utah and the Mormons in the public mind, and while it is no longer generally believed that the Mormons have horns and are practicing masters of the dark arts of seduction, Utahns are continually seized upon for information about polygamy.

The doctrine of polygamy (more correctly, polygyny, inasmuch as polygamy signifies "many marriages" rather than "many wives") seems first to have been put in written form in the revelation issued by Joseph Smith to Church members at Nauvoo in 1843. It is evident, however, as concluded by B. H. Roberts, distinguished Church historian, that the doctrine had been advanced in some form much earlier, perhaps as far back as 1831, in Kirtland. Persistent rumors of unorthodox marriage ideas and practices accompanied the Mormons throughout their migrations, and while these rumors were denied by Church authorities, there must, as Roberts notes, have been some basis for stories so persistent.

Joseph Smith seems to have lived in plural marriage from about 1841, and other leaders adopted the practice after issuance of the revelation in 1843, but the principle was not proclaimed to the world until 1852, at a special conference of the Church in Great Salt Lake City, when the Saints were solidly established in their mountain home. Many Mormon leaders shrank from it, and took plural wives only after earnest inquiry of God: polygamy was a stern ethic, the very guerdon of morality, not an easy flowering of sensuality. The question of *why* the Saints adopted polygamy, or "plural marriage," in Church terminology, is susceptible of as many explanations as there are viewpoints on Joseph Smith and the Church. The Church doctrine has been that plural marriage was divinely ordained, a higher order of marriage, as much advanced over monogamy as monogamy over celibacy. A man's wives and his children added to his glory in heaven, and they shared in that glory. Acceptance of plural marriage was thus, for Church members, an act of faith and belief, an essential expression of religious conviction.

Although individuals may now and then, in taking a new wife, have found as much encouragement in a pretty face as in religious conviction, it is important to emphasize that polygamy was never, for all the impact it made on American mores, an immoral institution. Moral standards were higher in polygamy than out, and adulterers were harshly dealt with by law. Mormons held that it was the right of every woman to be a wife and mother—indeed, in Mormon society a man could be compelled to marry a woman on her initiative—and a great many social evils were ascribed to the fact that many men refused their responsibilities, and women were reduced to celibacy and prostitution. The Saints inveighed against such social irresponsibles, and as fast as a Mormon could support a wife, he was urged to take one, sometimes to his discomfiture. Nevertheless, the number of polygamists among the Mormons has always been grossly overestimated : Levi Edgar Young, Church authority and Utah historian, places the figure at 3 per cent of marriageable adults, while Bernard DeVoto, critic of the Mormons, estimates it at perhaps 2 per cent.

Polygamy was a gathering storm, but for twenty years the Mormons occupied themselves with more immediate concerns. The dispossession of Indians from their lands inevitably led to embitterment among the aborigines, and though the Mormons endeavored to induce the Indians to settle down along with their white brothers, and were more humane than settlers elsewhere on the western frontier, the Indians were unable to adapt themselves at once to a new manner of living. The lands east of the Wasatch Mountains were at first ignored by the Mormons, and the economy of the Utes was not greatly disturbed, but the best lands of the Paiutes and Gosiutes were soon occupied by Mormon settlements. Indians were reduced to beggary or to intermittent theft and warfare. The important troubles of the white colonists, however, came at the hands of the powerful Utes, more particularly in the Walker War of 1853 and the Black Hawk War of 1865-68 (see Tour 2b). The earliest local difficulties of importance occurred in Utah Valley, in 1850, when a militia force, aided by Captain Howard Stansbury's men, routed Utes under Big Elk at Fort Utah (see Provo), but until 1853, Indian-white relations on the whole were peaceable.

The essential cause of the Walker War was the prohibition of Indian slave trade by the Mormon government, though the growing dissatisfaction of the Utes at white encroachment was also a factor. The Ute chief Walker (Wakara) had been friendly, and Manti was settled at his request. The Utes had been given to raiding lesser tribes and selling their captives in New Mexico. In 1852, the Territorial legislature passed a law designed to stop all traffic in Indian women and children. Enforcement of the law at the expense of white traders from New Mexico alienated Walker. In July, 1853, a raid on Springville initiated a series of attacks in Utah and Sanpete valleys, the Utes striking swiftly at the smaller settlements and retreating into the mountains after each attack. Previously, Young had advised that all settlements be fortified, and the outbreak of the Walker War led to general fortification throughout the Territory. The hostilities lasted only until spring. Twelve settlers were killed and a number wounded. Several hundred head of cattle and horses were stolen, but the greatest economic loss to the settlers consisted in the time lost in building forts and in the temporary abandonment of settlements. In May, 1854, to close hostilities, Young met Walker in a conclave on the Sevier River. Walker thereafter was friendly, and no more serious troubles were experienced until the Black Hawk outbreak of 1865.

A tragic event that accompanied the Indian difficulties of 1853 was the massacre of Captain John W. Gunnison and seven men, engaged in a Federal railroad survey. The murder of Gunnison near Sevier Lake was to revenge the killing of a Pahvant Indian by non-Mormon migrants a few days before. The Pahvants fell on Gunnison's party at dawn; four men escaped and reached the rest of Gunnison's command. Mutilated almost beyond recognition, the bodies were recovered by the Mormons, and conveyed to near-by towns for burial, the body of Gunnison being interred at Fillmore. Despite the fact that Gunnison's *History of the Mormons* (1852), had been criticized as being over-friendly to the Mormons, enemies of the Saints were quick to deduce that Gunnison had been slain by disguised Mormons or by Indians at Mormon instigation. This widely broadcast belief was not exploded for some years, despite explicit disavowals by Gunnison's second-in-command.

The constant slow irritations of Mormon-Federal relations, and the continued stream of anti-Mormon stories circulated in the East, determined President Pierce, in 1854, not to nominate Brigham Young as Governor of Utah Territory for a second term. Lieutenant Colonel E. J. Steptoe, who wintered at Great Salt Lake City in 1853-54, was chosen. Steptoe, however, declined the honor—the anti-Mormon story was that he had been neatly framed by Young with a variant of the "badger game"—and joined with the Mormons to petition the renomination of Young. Pierce acquiesced, and named the Mormon leader for a second term.

Events in Utah during the next three years piled upon one another kaleidoscopically. People continued to pour into the Territory, especially from Great Britain and the Scandinavian countries; in 1856, a census enumerated some 76,000 inhabitants, and while this was perhaps 36,000 too high, colonization of the arid mountain valleys was proceeding amazingly. The problem of raising sufficient food for such

a flood of immigration was not light, and there were grasshopper in
festations, commencing in 1854. The hoppers of that year laid thei
eggs by the millions, hatching out in such numbers in 1855 as t
threaten famine for the whole Mormon people. Crickets had almos
ceased to be a problem; irrigation ditches and other obstacles, with th
aid of bird predators, reduced their number. But winged grasshopper
blackened the sun at midday and filled the air with their raspin
flight. The winter of 1855-56 was exceptionally severe and increase
the suffering consequent upon crop losses.

To some Mormon leaders, the grasshopper infestation appeared i
the light of a rebuke from God for the wastefulness of the people
Many Church leaders commenced to feel that the Saints needed a re
ormation; they were losing sight of God. Additionally, as the Mor
mons proceeded with their conquest of the desert, non-Mormons wer
beginning to look on the Utah country with more favor, and wer
settling down among the Saints. The authorities had forebodings
The Saints should be made into a tighter group. Church leader
reinstituted the idea of "consecration of property," a socialistic pla
first experimentally tried in Missouri between 1831 and 1833. Devou
Saints "for and in consideration of good will" held toward the Church
deeded to it all their property, real and personal, amounting in som
cases to thousands of dollars. While no land titles had yet been grante
in the Utah area by the Federal government, it was thought that b
acting together through the Church, the Mormons would be in a posi
tion to defend themselves against an influx of gentiles.

The idea of "consecration" gained more currency after Septembe
1856, when the "Reformation," initiated by Jedediah M. Grant i
a speech at Kaysville, took fire among the people. Throughout th
Territory, the Saints confessed their sins and were rebaptized. Th
legislature of 1856-57, before being allowed by Heber C. Kimball t
proceed with legislation, went to the Endowment House to be baptize
for the remission of their sins. The emotions of the people were pr
foundly wrought upon; in some sections of Utah the emotional tensio
broke out into religious violence—and the Church ever since has had t
reckon, in books of anti-Mormons, with wild stories of blood atonemen

The feelings aroused by the Reformation were worked upon by othe
happenings of 1856-57. The anxious desire of many poorer Englis
converts to migrate to Zion induced Church authorities, in the autum
of 1855, to issue an epistle to the Saints: "The Lord, through h
prophet, says of the poor, 'Let them come on foot, with hand-carts o
wheelbarrows; let them gird up their loins, and walk through, an
nothing shall hinder them.'" But the thousand-mile trek across th
plains, pulling or pushing heavy hand-carts, the women, the aged, an
small children alike walking the entire distance, took a tragic tol

many immigrants were buried by the wayside, and the first year of the hand-cart migrations, 1856, was darkened when the Willie and Martin companies were caught by October snows along the Sweetwater River in Wyoming; many of them perished.

Mormon relations with the Federal government thoroughly disintegrated. A new attempt to obtain statehood in 1856 was fruitless. Almon W. Babbitt, Territorial secretary, was killed by Indians in Wyoming, and again Mormon critics were blackly positive that the sinister hand of the Saints was in the deed. The relations with the "foreign" judiciary continued to be cancerous. The Saints thoroughly resented being ruled by outsiders with whom they had nothing in common, and who too often revealed themselves as rascals. Nor were they always on their best behavior; in conflict with a group of Mormon lawyers, Justice George P. Stiles had his office raided and certain of his personal papers burned. Early in 1857 Stiles returned to Washington to report, in effect, that the Mormons were in a state of rebellion. W. W. Drummond, colleague of Stiles, was even more exasperating to the Saints; he refused to recognize the decision of the probate courts, which in Utah had an extraordinarily extended jurisdiction; he bluntly disposed of the whole body of Utah law as having been "founded in ignorance"; his despotic behavior on the bench looked no better to the Saints when it was discovered that he had abandoned his family in the East, and that the woman whom he had brought to Utah as his wife, and whom he was accustomed to seat beside him on the bench, was in fact a harlot. Returning east via California, Drummond reported that the Mormons regarded Brigham Young as sole authority in matters of government, and that they did not consider the laws of Congress binding; that the Church maintained a secret organization which took the lives and properties of those who questioned the authority of the Church; that Mormons had willfully burned the records of the Supreme Court; that Federal officials were daily subjected to public abuse and slander; that Young abused his privilege of pardon and was guilty of instructing juries whom and whom not to indict; that Gunnison had been killed by Indians at the instigation of the Church; and that Babbitt had been killed at the express order of Brigham Young.

In view of the fact that the Republican National Convention, as a part of its 1856 platform, had termed polygamy and slavery "the twin relics of barbarism," that the Democratic Stephen A. Douglas, once a Mormon friend, had denounced Mormonism as "the loathsome ulcer of the body politic," and that the authorities in Washington were anxious to divert public attention to something other than the continuous strife over slavery, such charges could not expect sober consideration and investigation. The Mormons were characterized as being in open rebellion; President Buchanan issued an order terminating

Brigham Young's governorship and directed General W. S. Harney to proceed to Utah with the Army of the West and put down the rebellion. The news reached Mormon leaders on July 24, 1857. On the invitation of Brigham Young, many of the people and most of the leaders were gathered at Silver Lake (Brighton) in Big Cottonwood Canyon for the tenth anniversary of the arrival of the pioneers in Salt Lake Valley. To this gathering the ominous news was brought. In 1847 Brigham Young had declared, "Give us ten years of peace and we will ask no odds of the United States." The ten years were up.

THE "UTAH WAR"

Young and the Saints unshrinkingly faced the prospect of conflict. For years they had felt that the forces of Satan would be unleashed upon the Lord's elect. With the crisis upon them they made preparations for defense. Brigham Young declared martial law in the Territory; to the Mormon colonies on the Salmon River, in Carson Valley and in Southern California, he issued orders to gather in Zion. The Utah militia, the Nauvoo Legion, began drilling, and Lot Smith, with a company of scouts, was ordered to the eastern plains to harass the Government columns. To Captain Van Vliet, who interviewed him in behalf of the army on September 8, 1857, Young said grimly, "We do not want to fight the United States, but if they drive us to it, we shall do the best we can; and I will tell you, as the Lord lives, we shall come off conquerors. . . . We have three years' provisions on hand, which we will cache, and then take to the mountains and bid defiance to all the powers of the government."

He was threatening a permanent guerilla warfare. That the threat was not an idle one is demonstrated by the success of Lot Smith, who had been dispatched to hamstring Government wagon trains. Smith burned almost all available forage between South Pass and Fort Bridger; he cut off the advance army supply trains and burned them; swinging behind the main column of the Utah Expedition, he burned several more supply trains. In his entire campaign less than fifty shots were fired, and not a single man was killed, but his tactics forced the Federal troops into winter quarters near Fort Bridger, 300 miles short of their objective. The precipitous walls of Echo Canyon were fortified by the Mormon troops, but it was lack of provisions and the onset of winter that enforced the decision to winter at Camp Scott on Black's Fork.

During September of this year, before the troops had settled down for the winter, the Mountain Meadows Massacre occurred in southern Utah (*see Tour 1f*). Fear and hatred aroused by the approach of the

roops was a major element contributing to the commission of that
rime.

General Harney, when ordered to Utah with his troops, had loudly
Ieclared, "I will winter in the valley or in hell." He wintered in
Kansas, and the command was given to Colonel (brevetted Brigadier
General) Albert Sidney Johnston, who later fought brilliantly for the
South. Johnston joined his troops in November, and with them eked
•ut a miserable winter near Fort Bridger, waiting for spring. But
he tide of affairs had now taken another direction in the East. Captain
Van Vliet reached Washington in November with his report of the
nterview with Brigham Young, and of the Mormon "scorched earth"
»olicy. This, with an outbreak of scandal in connection with army
ontracts, gave public opinion a new perspective on affairs in Utah.
The whole idea of the Utah Expedition began to be sharply criticized in
he press, where it was frequently termed "Buchanan's Blunder."
Several million dollars had been and were being expended, and more
ober consideration was given to just what was being accomplished
it all this expense.

With an acute sense of political timing, Colonel Thomas L. Kane,
ι Philadelphian who time and again had proved himself a staunch
Mormon friend, interviewed Buchanan about a possible solution of the
Jtah difficulty; Buchanan evidently made no official commitments, but
Kane packed his bags and departed for Utah via Panama and southern
California. He arrived in Great Salt Lake City in February, 1858, and
.fter conferring with the Mormon authorities, made a difficult journey
o Camp Scott, where he arrived March 12. Johnston received him
oldly, but Alfred Cumming, named the previous July to succeed Young
is governor, gave him a gracious reception, and was so impressed with
iim and his pacific proposals that he agreed to accompany Kane back
o Great Salt Lake City. They arrived in April.

Brigham Young had declared in June, 1853, "I am and will be gov-
:rnor, and no power can hinder it until the Lord Almighty says,
Brigham, you need not be governor any longer.'" Acting on that as-
umption, and over his signature as governor, he had in September,
857, issued a proclamation forbidding the army to enter the territory,
ınd had advised their commander that the troops might remain only
f their arms and accouterments were delivered over to the Mormon
quartermaster general for safekeeping. The Lord Almighty, apparently,
ıad spoken to him, for he received Cumming with official deference.
But if Cumming was governor in name, Brigham remained governor in
'act, and however Federal officials might come and go, to the end of
iis life Brigham Young's was the word by which the Mormons were
guided. Young had, Cumming discovered, no faith in the troops and
iew officials. Despite his pledges of protection, the dismayed governor

found the Mormons busy with preparations to flee the troops, and little disposed to give ear to reassurances. The idea of fighting the army had been given over, but now it had been determined that the people would enter upon a new migration. It was not exactly clear where they would go—rumors of Sonora and the South Sea islands were most current among the people; only Young knew that he had sent out an exploring expedition which he hoped would locate, somewhere in the desert wilds south of Great Salt Lake Valley, new oases where the Mormons might live in peace.

In late April and early May, the people began an active exodus. All the settlements north of Utah Valley, where they gathered, were abandoned; there remained behind only a few men in each settlement, to fire the houses and crops if the exodus should definitely be decided upon. Dismayed, Cumming watched the progress of "The Move." But from Brigham Young he won the assurance that if the troops did not molest the people, nor settle near them, the thirty thousand would return. Cumming went back to Camp Scott in mid-May to report that the Mormons acknowledged his authority, and that many stories circulated about them were false. A few days after his arrival peace commissioners arrived from the East, bearing a proclamation of pardon which President Buchanan, bowing to the change in popular clamor, had issued on April 6. The commissioners and Cumming went to Great Salt Lake City, where they conferred with Young, Heber C. Kimball, and Daniel H. Wells, the first presidency of the Church. The Mormons were offended at being "pardoned" for "rebellion" they declined to admit, but granted that they had burned army supply trains and stampeded army cattle; for these acts they accepted the pardon. They also declared their desire to live in peace under the constitution and laws of the United States. This constituted sufficient compromise, and Johnston was notified of the successful outcome of negotiations. Johnston replied with a proclamation assuring the Mormons that all would be protected in person, rights, and the peaceful pursuit of their vocations. This proclamation was published with a declaration from Cumming that Federal and Territorial laws were to be strictly obeyed. Johnston left Camp Scott with his troops, and late in June marched through the silent, deserted streets of Great Salt Lake City. He crossed the Jordan River, marched south, and located west of Utah Lake in Cedar Valley. The Mormons waited upon events a few days, but since the soldiery showed itself pacific turned their faces homeward in July.

Establishment of troops at Camp Floyd was, for the Mormons, a mixed evil. The camp-followers of Johnston's army transplanted themselves to Great Salt Lake City, and flourished like the green bay tree. Gambling, theft, drunkenness, and murder signalized the arrival of civilization among the Saints; the principal thoroughfare in the Mormon capital became known as Whisky Street, and the oldest profession took root for the first time. Yet farmers were able to sell surplus foodstuffs and livestock at prices previously undreamed of, while manufactured goods of all kinds fell into their hands at absurdly low prices. Eastern speculators and contractors had licked up the greater part of the rich gravy attending the Utah Expedition, but the scattered drops that fell in Utah amazed the people. The army remained in Utah three years, until the outbreak of the Civil War— it was said that Southerners in Washington had much to do with this disposition of able Union troops—and through most of those years there was imminent possibility of clashes between troops and people, each holding the other in contempt. Establishment of *Valley Tan,* first gentile newspaper in Utah, in 1858, did nothing to cement relations, since frontier editors had vigorous ideas as to how newspapers should be run.

The position of Governor Cumming was wholly unenviable. He was handicapped by his status as the resented successor of Brigham Young, and by the attitude of the judiciary, which thoroughly antagonized the people—a gift the judiciary always seemed to possess. Judge Charles E. Sinclair opened his court at Great Salt Lake City with the announcement to the grand jury that he could not take judicial cognizance of the presidential pardon, and strongly recommending that body to give close attention to the crime of treason; Judge John Cradlebaugh, presiding at Provo, opened his session with 100 troops in attendance "to take care of the prisoners and to preserve the peace." When Provo citizens protested, Cradlebaugh summoned eight more companies. Governor Cumming, to whom appeal was carried, requested Johnston to remove the troops; Johnston refused, and the question of authority was not settled until the U. S. Attorney General formally delegated to the governor power over all ordinary troop dispositions. Like other judges who came to Utah, Cradlebaugh was thoroughly sincere and fanatically devoted to his duty, but also like his fellows, he had little social insight and no social sense of humor, and a talent for putting his worst foot forward. His arrogance completely nullified his usefulness. His grand jury refused to find indictments according to instructions, especially refusing to accept his suggestion that the authorities of the Mormon Church, to whom they looked for temporal and spiritual guidance, be indicted for the Mountain Meadows Massacre. Enraged, Cradlebaugh discharged the jury and proceeded south to look into the massacre. Although he obtained some evidence, and the names of the principal white participants, the guilty fled to the hills and Cradlebaugh accomplished nothing.

The arrival of Johnston's Army was significant of the breakdown of

Mormon isolation. However the Saints had kept to themselves with the statement that "we are a peculiar people," their location athwart the highroads of American empire made inevitable constant adjustments to the current of American life. The soldiery was followed by the Pony Express, which began operations through Great Salt Lake City in April, 1860. Two stage lines had preceded the wild-riding horsemen, but neither had succeeded in maintaining anything like a schedule, especially in winter. The Pony Express brought Great Salt Lake City within seven days of the national capital, with semi-weekly service; the riders were hip-hurrahed east and west until completion of the Overland Telegraph in October, 1861.

"The Move" had thoroughly shaken up the people; some remained in the south, while those who returned to their homes in the north sometimes were accompanied by southern settlers. Utah's population was forever in a state of ferment, men migrating or being "called" constantly from one part of the Territory to another, so that they had roots in many places and knew many people; a thoroughly homogeneous culture resulted from this constant intermixing of the settlers, who were further confirmed in their identity with the Church by continual service in its behalf.

Following the "Move," Cache Valley and Provo Valley were settled in part during 1859, and the following year the settlements were more firmly established. Sanpete Valley was more completely settled, and the Church turned its eyes definitely toward Utah's Dixie, emigration pouring into that southern country in 1861-62. In 1863-64 Sevier and Circle valleys were settled, and the towns of Richfield, Salina, Monroe, Marysvale, Circleville, and Panguitch were founded. Almost immediately thereafter, Charles Coulson Rich led a company of settlers north to the Bear Lake Valley. By the end of the Civil War all of the principal valleys west of the Wasatch Mountains had been colonized, and the Church was spreading into Idaho and Arizona. An attempt to settle the Uintah Basin was defeated through an adverse report by scouts (*see Natural Setting*) and through use of the region as an Indian reservation. The desolate lands east of the Colorado and Green rivers were not attractive to colonists so long as less arid lands were unoccupied.

This intensification of colonization was accompanied by a paring of Utah to its present-day dimensions. In 1861, after years of agitation, citizens of western Utah succeeded in persuading Congress to organize the Territory of Nevada, and all of Utah west of 116 degrees west longitude was lost to the new Territory. By a somewhat disgraceful political deal Nevada was made a State soon after its creation as a Territory; Utah lost two more degrees of longitude to Nevada, in 1862 and 1866. At the same time lands were carved off on the east, the creation of Colorado Territory in 1861 cutting off all the country between the summits of the Rockies and 109 degrees west of Greenwich. The final slice of Utah was taken in 1868, to complete the rectangle created as Wyoming. Though Utah in later years argued for more territory, notably for the "Arizona strip" north of the Grand Canyon of the Colorado, the boundaries of 1868 were not again altered.

The Civil War impacted spectacularly upon Mormon society. Here was fulfillment of the prophecy made by Joseph Smith in 1832, that civil war should break out in South Carolina, and that war should be poured out upon all nations. Surely the day of the Lord was at hand. Hardly three weeks before the attack on Fort Sumter in 1861, Brigham Young declared to a congregation in Great Salt Lake City, "The whole government is gone; it is as weak as water. I heard Joseph Smith say, nearly thirty years ago, 'They shall have mobbings to their heart's content, if they do not redress the wrongs of the Latter-day Saints.' Mobs will not decrease, but will increase until the whole Government becomes a mob and eventually it will be State against State, city against city, neighborhood against neighborhood, Methodist against Methodist, and so on. It will be Christian against Christian and man against man; and those who will not take up the sword against their neighbors, must needs flee to Zion." To the Latter-day Saints, the Mormons were convinced, the world must turn for guidance. All that was good in the government of the United States should live in them and because of them. "We shall never secede from the Constitution of the United States," Heber C. Kimball, Young's first counselor, promised in an address on April 6, 1861. "We shall not stop on the way of progress, but we shall make preparations for future events. The south will secede from the north, and the north will secede from us, and God will make the people free as fast as we are able to bear it."

Those "preparations for future events" took active shape next year. The Saints drew up their third constitution for a "State of Deseret," elected a governor (Brigham Young) and a legislature, and dispatched to Congress a memorial seeking admission to the Union. Congress, instead, passed a new law aimed directly at the practice of polygamy, and the Federal government so far suspected Utah's loyalty as to detail Colonel Patrick Edward Connor, with 300 California-Nevada volunteers, to duty in Utah. Vowing that he should subdue the obstreperous Mormons though all hell yawned, the fire-eating Connor crossed the Jordan River in October, and established his camp on the bench above Great Salt Lake City, his cannon within range of Brigham Young's residence.

The legislature of the "State of Deseret" met in January despite failure of Congress to recognize the Mormon State; the members met this and every succeeding year until 1870, a total of nine sessions, yearly passing, for the State of Deseret, the same legislation they had passed while sitting as the Territorial legislature, so that, in Brigham Young's words, "everything [might] be in readiness when Congress [should] recognize our State organization, and to save confusion and trouble when the transition from a territorial condition to that of a state [should] have been fully accomplished." Privately the legislature and the Mormons generally conceived that they sat as the Kingdom of God. The "ghost government" of Deseret persisted through nine years as an ideal, at once pitiful and inspiring, tragic and ridiculous. The Saints' eyes were fixed on heaven, but during the nine years the government lasted, things were happening on the earth.

Many terrestrial things happened because of the Irishman, Connor, whose military activities were confined to massacring the Shoshones at Bear River in 1863 (see Tour 1a), to fighting the Sioux at Tongue River, Montana, and to minor skirmishes with Indians who harassed the mail and stage routes through western Utah. But Connor was a man of parts, with social and economic ideas. He disliked Mormon authoritarianism, and sought some means of inducing sufficient gentile migration into Utah to equalize or dominate the vote. Agriculture was no solution; the Mormons already held virtually all the land which would offer a living, as well as much that would not. In the mining industry, however, he saw potentialities. The Church had stifled mining initiative except in the development of iron, lead, and coal deposits. Precious metals lay untouched—if they could be found. Connor gave his men leave to prospect the hills, organized the first mining district in the Territory in 1863, and wrote its mining code. Personally he never benefited from his exertions, but he earned his reputation as the father of Utah mining. His efforts to stimulate the mining industry bore no real fruit until the seventies; meanwhile the Mormons spoke sarcastically of the "poor, miserable Diggers" inhabiting the bench above the Mormon capital. But gentile business men took firmer root in Great Salt Lake City.

The Ute Black Hawk War, Utah's last major Indian conflict, broke out in 1865, and until 1868 intermittent, desperate warfare was carried on between marauding Utes and the settlers of central Utah. More than fifty Mormon settlers were slain, and immense quantities of livestock lost, while many of the southern settlements for a time were abandoned. Economic losses of the settlers were estimated in excess of a million dollars, but despite the fact that the militia served for more than two years without pay, Congress declined to reimburse Utah settlers. The Utes finally quieted down, the greater part of the tribe not having participated in the war, and were settled, for the most part, on the reservation in the Uintah Basin.

On May 10, 1869, the transcontinental railroad was completed at

Promontory (*see Transportation*). This railroad had been dreamed about in 1850, and as early as 1852 the Mormons had memorialized Congress for its construction. The United States government for almost a decade kept surveying parties in the field, with the new emphasis on communication with California, but until outbreak of the Civil War there was no active progress. In 1862 Lincoln authorized the construction of a transcontinental railroad, and the following year work was launched by the Union Pacific and Central Pacific companies. The enterprise slowly gathered momentum, and by 1868 the two companies had graded into Utah. The Union Pacific built its grades down Echo and Weber Canyons to Ogden, and thence around the northern end of Great Salt Lake, but Ogden subsequently was made the junction city. When it became apparent that the transcontinental road would miss Great Salt Lake City (renamed Salt Lake City in 1868), Brigham Young organized a company to build a trunk line between the Mormon capital and Ogden, the last rail of the Utah Central being placed at Salt Lake City on January 10, 1870.

The immediate effect of the railroad was to break down once and forever the physical isolation of the Mormons, but the destruction of isolation in space promptly led to a new stress on isolation in spirit. The nature of the Mormon group life gave shape to the economic struggle. The ideal of co-operation, as also of consecration of property for co-operative ends, had become ingrained in Utah life. As the railroad neared Utah in 1868, Mormon leaders, in recognition of the success of co-operative stores, tanneries, and mills, organized a major commercial concern, Zion's Co-operative Mercantile Institution, more familiarly called ZCMI. Pressure was immediate upon gentile entrepreneurs, for the Saints were expected to trade with their own store rather than with outsiders, who were regarded as mere profiteers. Monetary exchange was always scarce in Utah, and barter and scrip were too common to be remarked; Mormon leaders had no desire to see the Saints placed under the economic thumb of gentile merchants. ZCMI virtually drove those merchants to the wall; they were saved only by completion of the railroad, which enabled them to compete on even terms with ZCMI. Although no all-seeing eye of God, or legend "Holiness to the Lord," was engraved over their doors, a bargain is a bargain, and the gentiles survived the lean months until the mining industry awoke at the magic touch of rail transportation.

The Church now had to contend with a revolt in its ranks, of fateful social and political implications. Schisms before 1869 were not new to Brigham Young, though the removal to Utah had stilled many disruptive movements; in 1852 the public announcement of polygamy caused an uninfluential and unfruitful schism led by Gladden Bishop; a more spectacular apostasy was that of the Morrisites in 1861-62.

The Godbeite rebellion of 1867-69 was a more formidable development. At the heart of the movement were the wealthy and influential William S. Godbe and Elias L. T. Harrison, who in 1869 were expelled from the Church for advocating, among other things, development of the mining industry. Essentially the conflict was between first and second generations in the Church, a struggle between the philosophy of aloofness and that of fraternization with gentiles; more directly, the established Church authority was challenged in its right to speak solely for the Mormon people—the Godbeites did not question Mormon doctrine, and even declared their course sanctioned by heavenly beings.

In the religious field the "New Movement" amounted to nothing, but a coalition of Godbeites with followers of Colonel (now General) Connor led to organization of the Liberal Party. At its first organization in 1870 at Corinne (*see Tour 4b*), the Liberal Party was primarily a reform organization, but extremist elements subsequently gained full control, and when the Godbeites withdrew, the Liberal Party became bitterly anti-Mormon, its voice for many years being the *Salt Lake Tribune*. Previously no political parties had existed in Utah, candidates for public office being named by Church leaders and "sustained" by the populace in periodical plebiscites. The Mormon organization now, however, assumed the name of People's Party and rolled up its sleeves. The political situation was complicated by the fact that the Mormons were under assault from without, and struggles within the Territory echoed thunderously in anti-Mormon activity outside. Except for local Liberal successes in the mining camps, and such freak developments as establishment of the "Free Republic of Tooele," as the Liberals called their 1874-78 Tooele County regime, the People's Party controlled Utah until the catastrophic eighties.

THE ISSUE OVER POLYGAMY

The struggle over polygamy took particular shape after 1870. Previously it had been a moral more than a political issue, and except for the dead-letter Anti-Polygamy Act of 1862, the Saints had been pretty much left to themselves. Moral indignation in the East unquestionably influenced the refusal of Congress to admit Deseret into the Union, the niggardly appropriations by Congress for the Territory, and perhaps the disposal of land, no land titles in Utah being granted by the Federal government until 1869; up to that time the Mormons had the status of squatters. President Ulysses S. Grant gave polygamy its political aspect. With his accession to the presidency in 1869 the battle lines were clearly drawn: polygamy was to be crushed. Two bills to that end were introduced into Congress in 1869-70. In substance they would have abolished trial by jury in cases arising under the 1862 law, transferred appointment of Territorial officers to the governor, made the governor auditor of Church funds and properties, given the judiciary right to seize any building for its needs, and transferred direction of jails and prisons from the legislature to the governor. Both bills were voted down by Southern legislators, who had tasted carpet-bag rule, but they are significant of the thinking Washington did about Utah during the next two decades. The Federal government was searching for political expedients to get at polygamy and the Mormons.

In Utah the new campaign against polygamy was inaugurated spectacularly in 1870 by a debate between the Reverend J. P. Newman, chaplain of the U. S. Senate, and Orson Pratt, Mormon scientist and philosopher. Held in the Tabernacle, the debate on Biblical sanction of polygamy attracted thousands and was publicized all over the nation; no formal decision was made, except in the national press, which concluded that Newman had been technically bested but was nevertheless right: Bible or no Bible, polygamy was not to be tolerated in American society. The spiritual fire the Saints had carried to the war against the deserts now availed them little. They had been rooted in Utah for more than twenty years. A generation had grown up which "knew not Joseph"; another migration to escape persecution would not be easy. The Church considered removal to Mexico before the conflict was over, but the membership was too firmly rooted for flight. The Mormons had to stand their ground and fight persecution with the spiritless weapons of the law.

The Mormons had troubles with Federal governors, but their desperate struggles were with the judiciary. One of the most formidable Federal judges was James B. McKean, a Grant appointee of 1871. McKean was exemplary in his private life, a fine scholar, and a man of high principles. His principles, however, he was willing to sacrifice for the ends to be attained. He set aside the Territorial law governing selection of jurors by lot from the taxpayers' lists, and transferred selection to the U. S. marshal. With the handpicked grand jury thus obtained, he set about scuttling the Mormons. A Salt Lake City alderman and his officers were arraigned before McKean for destroying the stock of the Engelbrecht Liquor Store, which had violated the city license ordinance. A decision was rendered against the city, with damages in excess of $50,000. By one slender thread the whole Mormon resistance hung: damages above $50,000 could be appealed to the U. S. Supreme Court. Had McKean limited the amount to $49,999.99, the Mormons would have been utterly without recourse before the arbitrary dicta of his court. Carried to the Supreme Court, the decision in the Englebrecht case was unanimously overturned in 1873, and all indictments made by McKean's juries were ordered quashed.

The Mormons might well be thankful for the Supreme Court, for

McKean had shown every intention of making a frontal assault upon Mormon authority. In 1871, his grand jury had indicted Brigham Young for "lewd and lascivious cohabitation," McKean flatly declaring, "The case at the bar is called the people versus Brigham Young, [but] its real title is Federal Authority versus Polygamic Theocracy." This case dragged on but came to nothing; General Connor had by this time so far come to respect Young as to offer bail for him. McKean's willingness to sacrifice strict legality for anti-Mormon ends is evidenced by his decision in 1873 when Ann Eliza Webb Young, who later wrote *Wife No. 19,* sued for divorce and alimony. The Federal government did not acknowledge the validity of polygamic marriage, and there could be no civil divorce where there had been no civil marriage, least of all any alimony; notwithstanding these contradictions, McKean assessed Young with court and lawyer fees and ordered him to pay alimony at the rate of $500 per month. When Young refused to pay and appealed the case, McKean found him in contempt of court, fined him, and imprisoned him for twenty-four hours. The case was, after several years, decided in Young's favor.

McKean was replaced in 1875, but he had given the Mormons a frightening view of their helplessness before autocratically inclined Federal officers. The fourth effort, in 1872, to attain statehood was a desperate reaction to oppressive Federal administration. The Saints believed polygamy only an expedient by which they were subjected to a religious crusade; polygamy, they argued, was an exercise of religious worship with which the Federal government could not, under the Constitution, interfere. Moreover, the Mormons contended that "a territorial or colonial system, under which a government is provided by a remote power and without the consent of the governed, is inherently oppressive and anti-republican." Congress thought otherwise. The memorial for State government was ignored, and the Poland Act of 1874 voided the extended jurisdiction of the Mormon probate courts, where polygamists previously had been assured a sympathetic hearing at the hands of fellow religionists. The courts thus were given over completely to the Federal judiciary, and effective prosecution of polygamists was made possible.

This attack from without, together with the success of Mormon co-operatives, and perhaps the depression following the panic of 1873, was influential in the effort of 1874 to reestablish the United Order. Principles of "consecration" and of "stewardship" had characterized Mormon social thinking since 1831. After a series of revelations issued by Joseph Smith, Church members had lived for a time in what was variously known as the "United Firm," "Order of Enoch," or "United Order." The Order, according to Joseph Geddes, was a Mormon attempt to redefine the relation of the individual to property, and was socialistic in nature. The earth was considered the Lord's; the people were stewards only over their possessions, which were to be known as stewardships or inheritances. Those who had surplus property, more than required to provide a frugal living for the family, were to consecrate it by deed to the Church, to benefit the poor. Surplus production beyond family needs was to be turned over to the bishop's storehouse. The bishop was to apportion inheritances among the people on three bases, equal according to their families, circumstances, and wants and needs. Those who left the Church kept the inheritances deeded to them, but did not receive back the surplus. In other respects, business relations were to be carried on in the usual manner, and the virtues of simplicity, frugality, cleanliness, industry, and honesty were stressed.

"The Order of Enoch" was disrupted in Missouri when the Mormons were expelled from Jackson County in 1833 and no direct effort was made to reestablish it until 1874, though co-operative thinking, with the principles of consecration, strongly conditioned Mormon social life through the intervening thirty years. The lesser law of tithing to a considerable extent replaced that of consecration. Church members had always anticipated restoration of the Order, and since conditions in Utah appeared to necessitate reintegration of Mormon society in the face of gentile infiltration and attack, the "United Order of Zion" was established in 1874.

The United Order was an effort by a local group to attain self-sufficiency and a favorable balance of trade. If the Saints lived frugally, bought nothing from without, and produced an exportable surplus, they might, in Brigham Young's view, become a rich people. Moreover, by uniting their individual means, the Saints might evade mortgaging themselves to outside capital. The United Order was also a religious reaffirmation. Applicants for membership frequently were required to renew their covenants by baptism, and religion strongly influenced all that was done, not alone by such famous Orders as that at Orderville (*see Tour 2d*) but in northern Utah, where little was accomplished temporally. Although there were outstanding local successes, notably at Orderville, Glendale, Richfield, and Brigham City, the United Order as a whole hardly survived its first year. In none of the urban centers was anything at all accomplished. Southern Utah was the field of principal success; previously agricultural communities built tanneries, shoe and hat factories, and cotton and woolen mills, but these enterprises for the most part collapsed with collapse of the Orders. The Church finally terminated the existence of surviving Orders. Social and economic pressure from without and reluctant co-operation from within were probably factors in ending the experiment. Ultimate re-establishment of the United Order is still taught as an essential Church doctrine, but the date is placed in some indefinite future when the people shall have proved themselves worthy.

Brigham Young hardly outlived the United Order—many Church members thought the Order could have succeeded had he lived. On August 29, 1877, in the Lion House in Salt Lake City, he breathed his last. The Saints were stunned and the entire nation took note of the death. For thirty-three years he had been the Mormon colossus, a giant who bestrode the Mormon universe and who symbolized Mormonism for the world. The Lion of the Lord had led the Saints to an empire, built it with them, fought for it with them. By some he had been hated; by more he had been loved. Thousands of his people he knew and called by name. So dominant a figure had he been that many believed Mormonism must collapse with his death.

With Young the Church lost its last great personal leader, but if there was no dominant personality to succeed him, there were able men trained in a hard school of experience, who have led the Church since 1877. Congress periodically rumbling its dissatisfaction over polygamy, Young's death was followed by an "apostolic interregnum" of three years and the accession of John Taylor to the presidency of the Church. The people in Utah were occupied with economic concerns—with dry-farming possibilities, with mining, and with the growth of the livestock industry. Political battles between Liberal and People's parties grew yearly more spectacular.

Struggle in the eighties centered fiercely and conclusively about polygamy, which was in actuality the lever, not the object to be moved. Enemies of the Mormons wanted primarily to shatter the temporal power of the Church, to break down its economic, social, and political domination of Utah. Prelude to the combat was the dispute over the office of delegate to Congress, fought out on the floor of the House between 1880 and 1882 by George Q. Cannon, Mormon incumbent, and Allan G. Campbell, gentile contestant. Cannon had won the election by an overwhelming majority, but Governor Eli Murray had certified Campbell on the ground that Cannon was not a citizen. Campbell was not admitted, and Cannon was rendered ineligible by passage of the Edmunds Bill in 1882.

This new act was designated to implement the Anti-Polygamy Act of 1862 and the Poland Act of 1874. It defined polygamy as a felony, punishable by fine not exceeding $500, and by imprisonment not exceeding five years. To evade the difficulty of proving Church marriages, it defined polygamous living (unlawful cohabitation, within or without the marriage relation, with more than one woman) as a misdemeanor, punishable by a fine not exceeding $300, by imprisonment not exceeding six months, or both. It excluded all found guilty of either offense from the right to vote and hold office. It declared vacant all elective and registration offices in Utah, providing for a commission of five men to supervise registration of voters, conduct of elections, eligibility of voters, counting of votes, and issuance of certificates to elected candidates. Between 1882 and 1884 the Utah Commission disfranchised some 12,000 voters, utilizing a test oath which required the prospective voter to swear that he was not a polygamist, bigamist, or guilty of unlawful cohabitation, or in sympathy with these practices. The people of Utah made another effort for statehood in 1882, the first under the name of Utah, but the effort was fruitless.

Chief Justice Charles S. Zane, arriving in 1884, convicted Rudger Clawson, subsequently a member of the Quorum of the Twelve, of polygamy under the Edmunds Act, and sentenced him to four years in the penitentiary. The appeal to the Supreme Court was lost. With this case under their belts, Federal authorities began intensive prosecutions. Mormons were peremptorily excused from jury service if they declined to deny the doctrine of polygamy; wives and minors were permitted, even forced, to testify against husbands and fathers. Prosecution centered about the misdemeanor clause of the Edmunds Act. Federal officials devised a system of indictment for separate offenses, so that sentences might be pyramided even to life imprisonment. The Mormons had to give up all they had stood by for forty years, all the sternly held religious beliefs of four decades, their wives and their children to whom they were bound by all the ties of tenderness and love, or take refuge in flight and risk imprisonment if caught.

Six terrible years ensued for the polygamists. Church leaders almost uniformly had embraced polygamy as a test of their faith. The most prominent leaders were forced into hiding. Brandishing warrants, United States deputies broke into homes at the dead of night on "polyg hunts." It went hard with the "cohabs" who were caught. Popular feeling was exemplified in Salt Lake City on July 4, 1885, when flags were flown at half mast until raised by angered gentile mobs; in Provo the *Enquirer* carried a large cut of a coffin inscribed "Independence Day, Died July 4th, 1885." But the true meaning of this period is written in the journals of the humble. "The hounds of hell were laying in wate for me," wrote one hunted polygamist, and again, in despair, "How long will the Lord allow these wicked reches to gain power over us?" Another prayed God to move the heart of the President of the United States. Imprisoned men were considered martyrs, and often were met by the town band upon their release, and parties were held in their honor. Congress put even more savage teeth in the laws against polygamists with the Edmunds-Tucker Act of 1887: the L. D. S. Church was disincorporated and most of its property confiscated; female suffrage was abolished; the Perpetual Emigration Company was abolished; the Utah Commission was continued in office, and a test oath was required of citizens who would vote, hold elective office, or serve on juries. The Church was already in financial stress; this last blow all but bankrupted it. Congress was memorialized again in 1887 for a State government, the proposed constitution expressly prohibiting polygamy, but Congress had no intention of giving up its power over Utah while the struggle over polygamy endured, and the warfare continued until 1890.

By that year the leadership of the Church once again had changed hands, John Taylor having died while in hiding in 1887. Acting for the Church, the new president, Wilford Woodruff, in September, 1890, published in the *Deseret News* a manifesto advising all members of the Church to abstain from the practice of polygamy. In October the manifesto was ratified at a general conference, and the Saints officially abandoned polygamy as an essential Church doctrine. This crucial decision was not taken without bitterness among the Church membership, or skepticism among the gentiles. Many of those who had suffered for polygamy doubted the power of man to set aside the decree of God, and in the ensuing fifty years there have been undercurrents, always diminishing, of polygamic thinking in Church ranks. Many gentiles were unable to conceive that Mormonism in a few decades would become as wholly monogamic as Methodism; in their view the Church had made a shabby deal to save itself from extermination. Chief Justice Zane, however, accepted the pronouncement of Woodruff at face value. Further punitive legislation pending in Congress was abandoned, and the President of the United States, after a period of waiting, pardoned all polygamists, and restored their civil rights.

Developments within the Territory gave promise, between 1887 and 1890, of better days for Utah. Gentile business men began to desert the radical anti-Mormons. The Mormon People's Party, in 1889 offered four places on its Salt Lake City ticket to prominent gentiles in a gesture of reconciliation, and the fusionist party easily carried the election. In Salt Lake City, a Chamber of Commerce was organized which made a point of ignoring creedal differences. The immediate effect of the capitulation to Federal pressure was to deliver populous centers, politically, into gentile hands. The Liberals carried Ogden in 1889, and next year took Salt Lake City. They embarked on a program of spending for municipal improvements. The People's Party officeholders had tended to over-conservatism in expenditures for public improvements; the Liberals had less hesitancy about bonding cities for waterworks, sewers, and other appurtenances of urban civilization. The Liberal ascendancy also bore fruit in the schools, an 1890 act of the Territorial legislature establishing public schools throughout the Territory for the first time. Centralization of education on a non-sectarian basis emphasized the separation of church and State.

As though to offer an earnest proof of their continued sincerity, the Mormons abandoned the People's Party, Church leaders advising the people, in 1891, to affiliate with the Democratic and Republican parties. Reluctant to abandon its hard-won victory, and perhaps distrustful of Mormon trickery, the Liberal party maintained its organization two years longer.

Joseph L. Rawlins, elected to Congress in 1892, introduced an enabling act for Utah, and a bill providing for the return of escheated Mormon Church property. Both bills carried; Caleb W. West, governor during the last phase of the polygamy struggle, recommended statehood in his annual report for 1893. The Enabling Act was signed by President Cleveland the following July.

UTAH AS A STATE

Utah's seventh constitutional convention met in Salt Lake City in March, 1895. Real debate ensued only on two points. The long quarrel over female suffrage ended with giving the vote to women— an unusual concession at that time. The second dealt with polygamy. The Enabling Act explicitly required that polygamous marriage should be forever prohibited, but the problem arose as to whether those who had already contracted polygamous marriage should be permitted to continue living in polygamy, or whether polygamous living itself should be prohibited. The more humane alternative was adopted. The constitution was ratified by the people of Utah in the autumn of 1895, when State officers were elected, headed by Heber M. Wells, first Governor of the State of Utah. On January 4, 1896, President Cleveland proclaimed Utah as the 45th State of the Union, and two days later its officers were inaugurated.

Spectacular conflicts with the rest of the nation, meantime, had tended to obscure the social and economic development of the Utah area. Completion of the transcontinental railroad in 1869 revolutionized Utah economically. Prices of manufactured goods fell, and those of agricultural products rose greatly; the railroad had much to do with the failure of the United Order in 1874; it doomed irrigation-raised cotton in "Dixie," and discouraged native manufactures (*see Industry and Commerce*). Opening of the mines, however, was contingent on transportation, and boom developments in the Wasatch, Oquirrh, Tintic, and other areas (*see Mining*) owed much to the railroads. In turn, opening of mines was influential in expansion of the railroads through central and southern Utah. The Utah Central, completed between Ogden and Salt Lake City in 1870, was extended south under the name of the Utah Southern in 1871; by 1880 tracks were laid as far south as Milford. The Utah Southern and Utah Southern Extension roads were acquired in 1900 by the San Pedro, Los Angeles & Salt Lake route, which in 1905 completed its line to southern California, and in 1921 was incorporated into the Union Pacific system. Between 1881 and 1883 the Denver & Rio Grande Western graded west into Utah from Colorado; by 1883 it had 386 miles of narrow-gauge road in Utah. In 1890 this company changed to standard gauge, and an affiliate, the Western Pacific, in 1908-10 built a road to San Francisco from Salt Lake City. Construction of the D. & R. G. W. coincided with the first real development of country east of the Wasatch Mountains. The railroad ran through the richest coal sector in Utah, and exploitation of the Carbon-Emery mines followed quickly.

The railroads were built just as western livestock began to acquire importance. Mormon pioneers had brought livestock of every kind, but their ideas on animal husbandry were those of the East and Midwest. Environmental conditions led to changed handling of herds, from farm to range technique, but the real stimulus for livestock in the West followed introduction of Texas ranching practices on the Wyoming plains. Construction of railroads and the spread of great herds into the desert adjacent to the Colorado River made raising of sheep and cattle an important factor in Utah economy. The dying glow of the frontier lit eastern and southern Utah through the final years of the century. Activities of outlaw gangs in Browns Hole, in the Uintah Basin, and near Robbers Roost set a romantic stamp upon American life; many "Western" novels have had Utah locales. Indians ceased to be a problem after the Black Hawk war, though existence of the Uintah reservation, largest in Utah, prevented development of the Uintah Basin until it was opened for settlement in 1905.

"Utah" and "Mormon" have been considered almost synonymous, but other religious denominations came to Utah at an early date, and the moral outrage of many of these denominations in connection with polygamy had much to do with the crystallization of American public opinion against polygamy. Utah was never a fertile proselyting ground for other creeds, and the Mormons have maintained a complete grip on the religious life of the area. The first non-Mormon denomination was the Congregationalist, which organized a church in Salt Lake City in 1865. Roman Catholic work began in 1866, but owes its position as second-ranking Utah denomination principally to the work of Father Lawrence Scanlan, who came to Utah in 1873. Jewish services were first held in 1866. Episcopalians held their first services in 1867. Presbyterians organized in Corinne in 1870, Methodists organizing in Salt Lake City the same year. The Baptists came in 1871. Lutherans organized in 1882, Disciples of Christ in 1890, Unitarians and Christian Scientists in 1891. The Seventh-day Adventist, Bible Student, Buddhist, Greek Orthodox, Gospel Mission, Nazarene, Pentecostal, and Spiritualist denominations are among those established later. In 1940 there were approximately 730 active church congregations in Utah, of which approximately 575 were Mormon. Congregationalists, Catholics, Episcopalians, and Presbyterians took an active interest in education, conceiving the schools as the best means of attacking intrenched Mormonism, and established many schools throughout Utah in pre-statehood days (see Education). In 1940, however, only the Catholic church maintained a parochial school system.

Masonry in Utah merits attention because of a long-standing controversy between the Mormon Church and Freemasonry. Masons contend that certain Mormon rites are of Masonic origin, dating from Nauvoo, when Joseph Smith and other prominent Mormons were Masons. The first Masonic lodge in the Territory was organized at Camp Floyd in 1859 by officers of Johnston's army, but the first native lodge was established in Salt Lake City in 1865. Masons were influential in opening a free public library in Salt Lake City, and its fine western Americana collection has grown from the nucleus they provided. Mormons and Masons have maintained a mutual aloofness to modern times.

The Spanish-American War, which broke out in 1898, demonstrated the changes in popular Utah feeling since the Civil War. The Mormons took no part in the internecine conflict, but for the war with Spain Utah supplied three batteries of light artillery and two troops of cavalry, volunteers seeing active service in Cuba and the Philippines.

Three major echoes of the long struggle with the United States featured the next dozen years. Brigham H. Roberts, a ranking Mormon and a polygamist, was elected to Congress in 1898. His opponents made campaign issues of his Church connections, and his participation in polygamy, and a petition protesting his seating, signed by upwards of a million citizens, was sent to Congress. The House voted not to admit him, necessitating a special election in 1900, when he was succeeded by William H. King, who later was elected to the Senate and until 1940 was senior senator from Utah. Democrats dominated early elections, but in 1900 the Republicans carried the general election and assumed a dominance virtually unbroken, despite several Democratic governors, until the Roosevelt upheaval of 1932, when the State became decisively Democratic. Reed Smoot, an apostle of the Church, was elected to the Senate in 1903, and another violent struggle began. Smoot fought almost four years for his seat, and won, serving until 1932, and becoming dean of the Senate.

The Smoot case reverberated locally and nationally. Locally a new anti-Mormon party was organized in 1904. The central plank of the "American Party" was unalterable opposition to Mormon ecclesiasticism in politics, and a determination to break the Mormon influence over the public schools. The American Party carried Salt Lake City in 1905 and 1907, but after a decisive Salt Lake City beating in 1911 disappeared from the political scene. Of more consequence to the Church was the muckraking period in American journalism, which swung into full stride at the time of the Smoot hearings. For a number of years national magazines depicted Mormons as polygamous, treasonable, and alien, and as a monstrous oligarchy sucking at the financial life blood of the West. Much damage was done the Church by this onslaught.

The rapprochement of Mormon Utah and Gentile United States was sealed by the World War. Utah supplied 21,000 men and millions of dollars for the prosecution of the war. The 362nd Infantry of the "Wild West Division," recruited principally in Utah, engaged in the St. Mihiel and Meuse-Argonne drives, and was conspicuous in other actions. Seven hundred sixty Utah men died in service, and nearly every town in the State has its memorial to the war dead.

The course of Utah history since the World War has little relation to the violent years which gave Utah a history wholly unlike that of other States. Developments in Utah, socially and economically, have been nearer the American norm, as instanced by the fact that Utah, though Mormon-dominated, gave prohibition its death blow in 1933 when the State was thirty-sixth to pass the repeal amendment. Outside capital has taken more interest in Utah since resolution of the polygamy struggle in 1890. Development of open-cut copper mining at Bingham (see Tour 1C), beginning in 1907, has been the most productive enterprise of the kind. All readily arable land was preempted before 1900, but development of dry-farming practices after 1870 and construction of large irrigation works after 1900 added new acres to cultivation (see Agriculture and Irrigation). Perfection of sugar refining processes made sugar beet production a major enterprise for Utah farmers, and influenced Utah opinion with respect to cane sugar areas— Cuba, Hawaii, Puerto Rico, the Philippines. Agriculture has been influenced by highway developments, which have enabled outlying Utah areas, by trucking, to compete in Pacific Coast markets. The post-war mining and manufacturing boom swept Utah along, though agriculture was handicapped by drouth and uncertain markets, while urban areas drew the rural population. The farmers, in the 1920's, organized associations for disseminating information and for co-operative marketing, and initiated the Utah Farm Bureau.

The depression bore severely upon Utah. Collapse of the mining industry, the backbone of Utah economy, was especially serious. During the early years of the depression, one person out of every four in the State received relief. This high percentage of unemployed fluctuated with business revivals and recessions, but remained fairly constant through the years 1933-40. Self-help efforts like the National Development Association, which preceded direct Federal welfare, accomplished little. The Church Welfare program, initiated by the Mormon Church to aid needy members, has proved of local utility and has won considerable publicity but has accomplished nothing toward solving the larger problems of labor and relief. It is no longer possible, as in Brigham Young's day, to spread out into new lands, since remaining open land is submarginal, and irrigation costs are out of all proportion to the returns brought by crops in open market. Nor, in the intricately developed capitalistic business economy, is it usually possible for individuals or groups to create a business with shoestring capital.

The difficulties faced by Utah are not to be minimized. High freight rates and distance from markets preclude extensive development of manufacturing enterprises, and expansion of agricultural and livestock production and small farms are also a limiting influence. Although labor has had to contend with criminal syndicalism laws and a Mormon Church tendency to frown upon union affiliation by its members, Utah has been progressive in social legislation, including eight-hour, child labor, minimum wage-and-hour for women, workmen's compensation, workmen's lien, unemployment insurance, old age assistance, social security assistance, and workmen's safety appliance laws. The cost of such a program, however, adds to production costs and further handicaps businesses predicated upon a desert civilization. In consequence, Utah has tended to high tariff viewpoints in its legislative thinking.

Utah's adjustment to a troubled national economy is further complicated by the birth rate. Like Idaho, and for much the same reason— Mormon emphasis upon the family—Utah has a birth rate out of all proportion to its capacity to absorb the increase. Children are reared to a high standard of living, and the money spent on education is lost in a migration of youth to areas of greater economic opportunity, particularly to Pacific and Atlantic Coast cities.

The growing emphasis upon tourism in America has Utah's hearty approval. Chamber of Commerce activities center more upon attraction of tourists than upon encouragement of business in competition with that already established. It is ironic that Utahns of today are so interested in publicizing their spectacularly eroded wastelands—lands on which utilitarian grandparents looked with embittered eyes for their worthlessness. But tourism, for all its cash-crop importance, is a parasitic industry, dependent upon the economic well-being of the rest of the country. The State Planning Board concludes that Utah will have to find means of support for a decreasing number of young people and an increasing number of older people, that it must support its natural increase of population, that the youthful population must be influenced to remain in the State. This must be done by careful and thorough exploitation of mining, agriculture, manufacturing, and recreation, with final emphasis on quality rather than on quantity production.   Utah, in Lincoln's phrase, "is a storehouse of riches for the nation," but somehow the storehouse must maintain itself until such time as its stored riches shall come into demand.

The Mormon Church

THE Church of Jesus Christ of Latter-day Saints, generally known as the Mormon Church, taking its popular name from the Book of Mormon character who abridged the records of the Nephites, was formally established in 1830, in Seneca County, New York, by Joseph Smith (*see History*). Joseph's function, as purportedly revealed to him by God, was to restore the original Christian church in "these latter days"—to return to mankind the true gospel in which they could live and achieve salvation during the "last dispensation." To many outsiders, the closely knit spiritual fabric of Mormonism is the most impressive thing about it.

Mormon doctrine is based on the Bible, the Book of Mormon, the *Doctrine and Covenants,* and the *Pearl of Great Price.* The Book of Mormon is chiefly a history of ancient peoples. The *Doctrine and Covenants* is a compilation of the revelations received by Joseph Smith and others. These revelations laid down one by one nearly every article of faith and creed that the Mormons live by. The *Articles of Faith,* a condensation of Mormon gospel which Joseph wrote in answer to a request from a gentile, give Mormonism in a nutshell. Abridged, they are as follows: Mormons believe in God, in Jesus, and in the Holy Ghost; they believe that man will be punished for his own sins and not for Adam's; that mankind can be saved through the atonement of Christ and by obedience to the gospel. The gospel includes chiefly a belief in repentance, in baptism, and in the laying on of hands for the gift of the Holy Ghost. Mormons believe in the same organization that existed in the "primitive church": namely, in apostles, prophets, pastors, etc.; they believe in the gift of tongues, in prophecy, spiritual healing, visions; they believe the Bible to be (so far as it is translated correctly) the word of God, and the Book of Mormon also; they believe in the literal gathering of Israel, in the restoration of the Ten Tribes, in the building of Zion upon this continent, and in the reigning of Jesus personally upon this planet for a thousand years. Perhaps their most famous article of faith is the thirteenth: "We believe in being honest, true, chaste, benevolent, virtuous, and in doing good to all men; indeed we may say that we follow the admonition of Paul: 'We believe all things, we hope all things,' we have endured many things, and hope to be able to endure all things. If there is anything virtuous, lovely, or of good report or praiseworthy we seek after these things." The *Pearl of Great Price,* purporting to be a translation of certain writings of Moses and Abraham, is a practical day-by-day guide to healthful and righteous living.

On the whole, Mormon doctrine is simple and practical. It believes in baptism by complete immersion for the remission of sins; in righteousness, which under some of the leaders approached the sternness and self-denial taught by the famous New England divines; in serious contemplation of this life as a preparation for the next; and above all in the holiness of the human body as an instrument created and endowed by God. It was this reverence for the human body that produced the "Word of Wisdom"—those stern prohibitions against the use of alcohol, tea, coffee, tobacco, and all foods, beverages and habits which impair efficiency and health. For the gentile—a word used by Mormons to designate all non-Mormons—nothing in Mormonism is more striking than the emphasis placed on health, and on the saint's duty to keep his body and mind healthy and clean. In Mormonism cleanliness has always been and still is next to godliness—and when their doctrine speaks of cleanliness, it means inside and outside.

A striking expression of Mormon faith, with all the literary compactness and patriarchal feeling of Old Testament Scripture, is the prayer delivered by George Washington Brimhall, Mormon pioneer, at Spanish Fork in 1873:

> Thou didst bring us up into this desert land by the hand of Thy servant Brigham, and didst bless it. Thou didst bless the mountains with snow, the air with health and the land with fertility, our spirits with wisdom, our arms with strength, and our bodies with the power of increase. Thou didst turn back the power of the enemy, and hast withheld the devouring cricket and grasshopper. The desert has yielded its fruits and furnished us food. We have beaten our sword into pruning hooks. Thou hast checked the savage in his corner, and made treaties of peace. Thou hast taken his poisoned arrow and placed it in the quiver. . . .

It is interesting to note the Mormon explanation of the origin of the American Indian and the Negro. The Indian, according to the Book of Mormon, is the Lamanite, descended from an intelligent people of the white tribe of Joseph, who were led by the Prophet Lehi from

Jerusalem to the western hemisphere in 600 B. C.; Laman, a son of Lehi, rebelled against his father and his brother, Nephi. In regard to the Negro, they are the posterity of Cain, and are black because Cain killed Abel. It must be observed, however, that Mormons believe human spirits lived before coming to this planet, and that all spirits are pure; there is, therefore, a chance for the redemption of all the children of Adam excepting the sons of perdition. A number of Negroes have joined the Church, but they are not allowed the privilege of temple rites, or to hold the benefits of the priesthood. There is no discrimination against members of any other race.

Marriage under Mormonism is a most sacred institution, and divorce is not common among the orthodox members. When a couple is married in a Mormon temple, it is not merely "until death do you part," but for time and eternity. To Mormons, adultery is a sin practically as abhorrent as murder, and for this reason infidelity is the only ground, except murder and extreme cruelty, for a Church divorce. The civil courts recognize other justifiable grounds.

Children are christened in the Church when a few weeks old; at the age of eight the child is baptized, and is usually confirmed as a member the next day. At the age of twelve boys enter the priesthood— but priesthood in Mormonism does not mean what it means in other churches. The highest members in Mormonism are not distinguished by official robes or gowns; it is a democratic church in this, that even the humblest lay member has the privilege of priesthood, and in dress is indistinguishable from his apostles and prophet.

The priesthood is an avenue of spiritual authority, with many temporal obligations. The Aaronic Priesthood, embracing deacons, teachers, and priests, is concerned chiefly with temporal welfare. The Melchizedek Priesthood, embracing elders, seventies, and high priests, is concerned chiefly with spiritual welfare. The temporal and the spiritual, however, are closely integrated and mutually supporting. Boys 12 to 15 years of age may be designated as "deacons." These lads are given the task of passing sacrament (bread and water) in church, in gathering offerings from homes, and of assisting as ushers. Between the ages of 15 and 17 they advance to "teachers," and visit homes to give religious instruction and to report needs. At 18 they became priests and may then bless the sacrament, perform baptisms, and accept work as missionaries. After the age of 19 a man is eligible to the Melchizedek Priesthood in which the younger members give unction to the sick, or baptize converts and the young; serve as missionaries; ordain officeholders in the lower priesthood; and anoint ill persons with consecrated oil. Certain groups of male adults are known as "seventies" or as "minute men": they serve in the mission field and teach the gospel at home and abroad. Thus, deacons become teachers, teachers become priests, priests become elders, elders become members of the seventies, and the seventies advance to high priests. Women never hold a priesthood, but share in the blessings of priesthood with their husbands.

The highest order of the Church consists of the president and his two counsellors who with him constitute the first presidency; the twelve apostles, vacancies in the quorum of which are filled by the president, approved by a conference of the membership; and seven men who comprise the First Council of Seventy. The senior member and the president of the Twelve has always been elected to succeed a deceased president. The president of the Church has always been also the working head of many divisions, both religious and temporal, including such secular activities as mines, factories, banks, hotels, irrigation projects, mercantile establishments, insurance companies, railroads, and many others. The present incumbent, Heber J. Grant, was at one time president or director of many institutions in Utah. The Church is in possession of and actively directs several large financial institutions.

Geographically, the Church is organized into wards, each consisting usually of from 200 to 1,200 persons within a convenient boundary. Each of these ecclesiastical units has a bishop and two counsellors, the three together being known as a bishopric. There are 531 wards in Utah, and about 1,120 throughout the world. The wards in turn are grouped into 129 larger geographic divisions known as stakes, each of which has a president and two counsellors. The bishop, appointed to an indefinite term by the Church presidency, vaguely resembles a pastor or minister in other denominations; but he has no special training in theology, receives no salary, and does little preaching. A bishop in his profession or vocation may be a lawyer, banker, doctor, farmer, or even a mechanic or a clerk. In each stake there is an average of ten wards. The president and his two counsellors are known as the stake presidency, but the president also has a "high council" of twelve men who are chosen to act with him in a judicial capacity. A rather small community may comprise one stake of from six to ten wards, some of which extend into the agricultural area roundabout. Often the stake is geographically coextensive with a county, but in sparsely populated regions it may cover several counties. Stake conferences are held quarterly in ward chapels, or in the stake tabernacle if it is prosperous enough to have one. Ecclesiastic courts survive from early times, when they were sometimes the only courts in pioneer communities. Disputes are still occasionally settled by Church officials in rural settlements.

The Mormon Church has seven temples, but others are being built or have been planned. The largest and most impressive is, of course, that in Salt Lake City. In Utah there are also temples in Logan,

St. George, and in Manti. The other three are in Mesa, Arizona, in Cardston, Alberta, Canada, and on the Hawaiian Island of Oahu, a few miles from Honolulu. There is a male president of each temple, and many persons to assist those who enter to accept the rites. Mormonism emphasizes the advisability of "temple work"—and in consequence many persons assist in the temples; their services are given without pay. Non-Mormons are not admitted to temples. Mormons perform many vicarious ceremonies in their temples. Ancestors, for instance, can be saved in the "highest kingdom of God" through vicarious baptisms and marriages in their behalf, though they retain the privilege of accepting or rejecting the gospel when it is presented to them in the hereafter. Vicarious marriages can be performed for deceased relatives who were not married under the "celestial order." Those without the time to engage in these rites may hire temple attendants to serve as proxies.

The Church has a large and smoothly functioning missionary system, and annually about 500 missionaries are sent to all parts of the world. Fare thereto and maintenance costs are paid by the missionary or by relatives, but if at the end of his service he is honorably released, the Church pays his fare home. The usual period of service in an English-speaking country is two years; in one where a language must be learned, the time is customarily six months longer. Very devout Mormons sometimes fulfill several missions. Women are rarely sent on missions abroad, but serve chiefly in the United States, Mexico, and Canada. It is against the rules for a missionary to marry while in the field, but a married man or woman who receives the "call" may take his mate with him.

Finally, in the matter of organization, the Church holds two conferences annually in Salt Lake City. These huge meetings are chiefly for the purpose of sustaining the leaders in office, of detailing activities and statistics of the past half-year, and of outlining proposals for the half-year to follow. One conference, called the annual, is held during a period including a Sunday and the 6th of April, the latter date being the anniversary of the founding of the Church, as well as, in Mormon belief, the anniversary of the birth of Jesus. The semi-annual conference occurs during the first week of October.

Mormonism has always strongly emphasized charitable organizations and social life and the Church has several institutions that work towards these ends. With the Mormon ward meeting house is also usually a recreational hall, used variously as gymnasium, dance floor, and theater. Chapel meetings are held Sunday morning and evening, and various priesthood quorums and other groups meet at different times for an hour or two on Sunday. Dances, basketball games, motion pictures, and amateur theatricals are given on week nights in the recreation hall.

Outstanding among charitable organizations is the National Women's Relief Society. In operation since 1842, it is the oldest auxiliary in the Church, and is thought to be the oldest continuously operating organization for women in the United States. Each ward has a branch of the Society and is a charter member of the National Council of Women, national and international in its scope. Local meetings are held weekly.

The L. D. S. Sunday School Union, largest auxiliary in the Church, has a membership of 362,000. The Mutual Improvement Association has charge of amusements and entertainments. The Boy Scouts and Bee Hive Girls (Camp Fire Girls) are included in this group, but children under twelve are enrolled in the Primary organization, a form of kindergarten that teaches games, dancing, story-telling, and singing. This auxiliary, sponsoring amusements for children, has a membership of 115,900.

The Church maintains a genealogical library at 80 North Main St., Salt Lake City. Study groups under the general name of Genealogical Society are organized in nearly every ward. The function of these groups is to trace ancestry and family trees so that vicarious baptisms and marriages can be performed for deceased relatives. Members of families may be "sealed together to make a unit in the Kingdom of God." Mormons believe in three degrees of glory in the next life— the telestial, terrestrial, and celestial, the last of which can be gained only through merit and the appropriate ceremonies.

All auxiliary organizations maintain general boards with presidents and counselors in each stake and in each of the mission headquarters.

The Church maintains its own department of education, for spiritual instruction. Brigham Young University, at Provo, Utah, now (1940) in its sixty-third year, with an enrollment of more than 2,000 students, is Church-owned and -operated. The Church also maintains seminaries where theology is taught to high school and college students, who are granted permission to attend theological lectures when not busy with their regular classwork. These seminaries are near public schools, but under the law may not occupy public school property. Utah statutes allow no religious training in public schools, but do permit all sects to maintain parochial schools.

The Church has a number of publications, most important of which is the *Deseret News,* an evening paper (no Sunday edition) printed in Salt Lake City; it was established as a weekly in 1850. Monthly magazines under the auspices of Church organizations are published in Salt Lake City, in the eastern United States, in England, and elsewhere throughout the world. The Church also maintains several hospitals, among which are the Latter-day Saints Hospital and the Children's Hospital in Salt Lake City, the Dee Hospital in Ogden, and the Latter-day Saints Hospital in Idaho Falls, Idaho. These are modern institutions, open to persons of all creeds.

It is to be expected that so experimental a people would have given some thought to the matter of recreation and amusement. Nothing today is more characteristic of the Mormons than their love of dancing, singing, dramatics, and social get-togethers. Many of the wards and all of the stakes have excellent choirs, and the 300-voice group that sings with the famous pipe organ each Sunday in the Salt Lake Tabernacle is nationally known. Most Mormons learn to dance at a very early age. It is not unusual in remote agricultural areas to see on the wardhouse floor tots under the age of five, some of whom dance gravely with one another, and some with adults. Most Mormon children dance well before they are fifteen. Many oldsters dance as long as they are able to walk.

The Church is supported by tithing. Members are supposed to contribute one-tenth of their gross income and to give additional money (or labor) for the construction of ward halls, or for the maintenance of buildings and the poor. Orthodox members fast on the first Sunday of each month and give to the Church the equivalent of food saved. The local bishop receives a small allowance for his services in collecting tithes and offerings and keeping records, but his counsellors are not paid, nor are the other local officials. High officials of the Church receive salaries and traveling expenses. There is no collection of money at services, nor is it usual for local bishops or stake or temple officials to charge a fee for the marriage ceremony. There is no charge for funeral services: members of the ward give their time in the speaking, singing, and praying. Missionaries, ward workers, and others who call to give advice, instruction, or assistance, tender their services free.

Today the Church claims a membership of 760,000, most of whom are in Utah and adjacent States, though there are branches throughout the world. In the beginning Utah was all Mormon and it is still preponderantly so, more than two-thirds of the population being members of the Church. L. D. S. officials estimate that about 50 per cent of Salt Lake City is non-Mormon, and that the State is about 70 per cent Mormon. Southeastern Idaho and parts of Colorado, Arizona, and California are strongly Mormon. The Church maintains missions in the United States, Canada, Mexico, Europe, Asia, Africa, and in many of the islands of the seas. There are Mormon churches in all the larger cities in the United States.

Agriculture

SYMBOLICALLY, the first act of the Mormon pioneers, when they entered Great Salt Lake Valley in 1847, was to plow the soil. When plowshares broke in the sun-baked earth, the settlers flooded the land with water from City Creek. The next day they planted potatoes. That was the first farming by white men in Utah. The system of Mormon settlement, in agricultural villages and communities, brought farmers in from their acres each evening, where they could "swap" experiences and theories with their neighbors. This system has not materially changed; Utah farmers in 1940 are still preeminently village dwellers, with social, economic, and religious life centered around communities. There are some 30,000 farms in Utah, about half of which are in the six counties adjacent to Salt Lake City. Because of this concentration, in reach of electrical lines, Utah is fifth in the nation in percentage of farm homes wired for electricity.

Of the total area of the State, only 3.3 per cent is tilled land, and about 1 per cent is dry-farmed. Much more land could be farmed if water were available. Most of the irrigable land was under cultivation at the close of the nineteenth century, and the farms, never large, have since been subdivided among large families. Third and fourth generations today face the problem of making a small farm of 20 acres or less support a family.

Utah soil, like that of other arid States, is exceptionally rich in plant foods—there has never been abundant water to carry away the minerals necessary for plant growth. Some Utah soils are 60 per cent limestone, and with limited rainfall and careful irrigation may never require additional lime. Large phosphate deposits exist in the mountains of northern Utah, and soils derived from weathering of

The Mormons

THE TEMPLE, SALT LAKE CITY

Courtesy Union Pacific Railroad and Salt Lake Tribu...

MORMON TITHING HOUSE, SALT LAKE CITY (1869)

BRIGHAM YOUNG (c. 1850)   JOSEPH SMITH

Courtesy L. D. S. Church

A C. R. Savage Photograph: Courtesy L. D. S. Church

MORMON TABERNACLE UNDER CONSTRUCTION IN THE 1860'S

BAPTISTRY, SALT LAKE TEMPLE

"THIS IS THE PLACE" MONUMENT, SALT LAKE CITY

Here, in 1847, Brigham Young made his
decision to settle in Salt Lake Valley.

Lee: F. S. A.

SAGEBRUSH DESERT, BOX ELDER COUNTY

Over country similar to this Brigham Young looked when he announced the end of the Mormon hegira. The accompanying picture shows how his people "made the desert to blossom."

IRRIGATED LAND ON THE OUTSKIRTS OF LOGAN

Lee: F. S. A.

THE HAMBLIN HOME, SANTA CLARA (c. 1870)

JACOB HAMBLIN,
MORMON MISSIONARY
TO THE INDIANS

Courtesy Smith Printing Co.

LOGAN TEMPLE

TABERNACLE,
ST. GEORGE

LION HOUSE, SALT LAKE CITY

This "house of twenty gables," now a social center, was once the home of Brigham Young and some of his wives.

BEEHIVE HOUSE—THE BRIGHAM YOUNG MANSION

Highton: F. W. A.

these mountains have half again as much phosphorus as is found in the average crust of the earth. In a few cases excessive irrigation has flushed out the plant foods, and in others has brought alkali salts to the surface, after which cultivation is impossible. Robert Stewart, professor of Chemistry at the Utah State Agricultural College, in 1913 reported the following yields per acre at the Greenville Experiment Station Farm: 82 bushels of oats, 50.4 bushels of wheat, 262.3 bushels of potatoes, and 21.8 tons of sugar beets. "The yields of oats, wheat and potatoes are eight year averages, and have been obtained upon the soil which has been cropped continuously for over fifty years so far as is known without the addition of any plant food or barnyard manure. . . . In the eastern sections of the United States, during a corresponding period of time, the yield of potatoes has only been 83.8 bushels per acre."

The *Utah Farmer* in 1935 issued a report showing the superior production of irrigated Utah soils per acre over the average for the United States, as follows: Utah sugar beets 11.2 tons as compared with the national average of 10.2 tons, Utah wheat (all kinds) 29 bushels as compared with 12.7 bushels average, oats 34.1 bushels as against 29.6 bushels, barley 32.3 bushels compared with 22.8, potatoes 150 bushels as against 109.3 bushels, and 2.22 tons of tame hay per acre compared with the average of 1.32 tons per acre.

In the peak year of 1925, Utah's cash income from agriculture was $64,000,000; in 1938 it dropped to $45,168,000. In an effort to increase their income, farmers tend to seek scientific help, and endeavor to produce more readily marketable crops on their small acreages of irrigable land. Since the turn of the century, diversified farming— intensive gardening of small tracts, poultry raising, and the growing of a few hogs, sheep, and turkeys on every farm—has been encouraged, in order to bring in a well-spaced income throughout the year.

The poultry industry contributes about one million dollars a month to Utah's agricultural income. Sugar beets provide a cash income averaging five millions a year. Turkeys bring in more than a quarter of a million dollars annually. Horticulture produces annually an average of two and one half millions, while commercial crops for canning, such as peas, tomatoes, beans, and corn, together with celery, onions, and other truck products add another million dollars to the total. Hay, including alfalfa and wild hay, leads all field crops, followed by oats, barley, rye, and other grains. Utah livestock consumes 70 per cent of all farm products, the major one of which is hay. The growing of fruits and vegetables, of exceptional quality from rich soil in the State, has declined since about 1925, when refrigerator transportation brought cheaper products from outside. It was then impossible to realize premium prices for luscious native-grown fruits and out-of-season vegetables. An attempt is being made, through co-operative marketing with neighboring States, to restore the demand for these products. Utah farmers also keep a hopeful eye on the price of silver, an increase in which brings greater consumption of farm products.

Statistics for 1935 show a favorable percentage of farm tenantry in Utah—14.9 per cent as compared with the average of 42.1 per cent for the United States. Secure in their ownership, farmers have been scarcely conscious of a growing danger. When they were forced to operate at a loss because of lost markets, lowered prices, and other economic conditions, they began to live on credit. In 1910 the recorded mortgage indebtedness of all Utah farms was $7,500,000 while in 1940 it was $45,000,000. Unless the mortgages are paid it is impossible to estimate what the future percentage of tenant farms will be.

Because approximately 85 per cent of Mormon Church members in the State are farmers, the L.D.S. welfare program, begun in 1938, is essentially agricultural. The five-point Church plan urges a new spirit in the conservation of resources, the growing of more profitable crops, co-operative practices in production and marketing of crops, ownership of farms and help for those about to lose them, and more attractiveness in farm life. Working with the Utah State Agricultural College Extension Service, the Church considers specific problems in each area, giving suggested solutions.

L. M. Winsor, now (1940) civil engineer for the U. S. Biological Survey, was the first county agricultural agent in any northern or western State. In 1912, after Mr. Winsor had been working for about a year with the extension division of the Agricultural College, he was called to Washington to explain to the Secretary of Agriculture what type of work he was doing. Mr. Winsor explained that he was a farm adviser, a "common carrier of ideas," riding from farm to farm on horseback through three eastern counties, helping farmers with their difficulties and trying to find solutions for their problems, using the facilities of the college whenever he needed them. He did important pioneer work in the agricultural extension field, finding that his most successful method of reaching the people was through the Church.

Since 1920 the farmers have organized several groups for co-operative marketing, the most active and successful being the Northwestern Turkey Growers, the Utah Wool Growers, the Utah Horse and Cattle Growers, the Utah Poultry Producers Co-operative, the Sugar Beet Growers, and the Utah Dairymen. These groups co-operate in the production and marketing of standardized quality products.

Sugar beets are one of Utah's major crops, taking a normal place in crop rotation and promoting soil fertility. Shallow-rooted plants which exhaust the upper soil levels, are rotated with sugar beets, which draw from lower levels. Beets are resistant to alkali, and certain alkali lands have been reclaimed by their culture. It is estimated that beets in rotation increase wheat production of the same soil by 15 per cent, and other crops by 10 per cent. The long roots of the sugar beet drive down six or seven feet into the earth, creating a useful disturbance of the lower soil. When the beet is pulled up the small roots remain in the soil, contributing to its fertility. The tops are plowed under, or fed to animals, which provide fertilizer in the form of manure. Sugar beets were introduced into Utah from France by John Taylor, then a Mormon missionary, in 1852.

Dry farming, commonly practiced throughout the arid West, began in Utah in 1863. "A group of Utah farmers," says *Bulletin 282* of the Utah Agricultural Experiment Station, "found their farm lands, which had for years been irrigated with water from Malad Creek near Bear River City, so impregnated with alkali that growth of crops was impossible. In desperation they plowed and seeded the dry land above the canal. The ripened dry-farm grain which they harvested in the fall . . . was almost as much a gift of heaven to these transplanted, old-world Mormon converts as manna to the children of Israel." For years after this successful if somewhat desperate experiment, many doubted that crops could be grown without irrigation. David Broadhead, who owned a farm near Nephi, testified in court in the middle 1880's that "of course wheat can be raised without irrigation," and was indicted for perjury. Broadhead went back to his farm, hung up a sign, "PERJURY FARM," and for many years was one of the biggest growers of dry-land wheat in the State.

Successful dry-farm land must have a natural rainfall in excess of 10 inches per year, which produces an average yield of about 20 bushels of wheat per acre. Utah sows about 200,000 acres of dry land to wheat each year. Barley, oats, seed alfalfa, rye and potatoes are other successful dry-farm crops. San Juan County, in southeastern Utah, raises dry-land corn and beans. Good practice in dry farming is to use two years' moisture to produce one crop. During the vacant year the land is summer-fallowed and cultivated to keep down weeds and conserve moisture. During the years between 1912 and 1921 everybody went "dry farm," with land selling for as much as $60 an acre. With two years' cultivation the land yielded 35 bushels per acre of high grade wheat. This was probably the peak in dry farming, and lower prices for wheat, coupled with occasional crop failures, have since made it a precarious method of making a living.

Livestock is a $40,000,000 industry in Utah, in spite of the fact that it does not operate at maximum efficiency.

For range improvement, Utah has a Desert Range Experiment Station in the southwestern part of the State, and constant studies have been made by the U. S. Grazing Service and the U. S. Forest Service.

Reseeding, seed collecting, and experiments have aided materially in range revegetation. Water developments include the maintenance of wells and springs, the building of reservoirs, ditches, and dams, and facilities for transporting and storing water. For herd improvement, ranchers have organized bull associations for the introduction of better strains of stock.

Cattle in Utah, range and milk cows, totaled 432,000 in 1940, with a capital value of more than sixteen million dollars. The U. S. Forest Service has granted permits for the grazing of 108,515 head for this year. The rest will be fed or pastured on farms, or grazed on private range, and the public domain. Cattle are admitted to the forests in May or June. Locally this is called "putting the cows on the mountain," where they graze until the latter part of October. Then they are "brought off the mountain" and "finished up" for shipment by grazing on cut-over grain and alfalfa fields, or fed during the winter.

For the spring and fall roundups, boys and men gather from small farms and ranches. They wear "Levi's" (bibless overalls), 69-cent shirts, big stetsons, and cowboy boots, all bought for service. Chaps are worn only when working in brush. In the spring they work at assembling the herds, branding and ear-marking. If the drive is a long one, a commissary wagon, or more frequently a truck, is the basis for their camps and the center of operations while on the trail. At the fall roundup, the cattle are fat, full of life, and reluctant to leave their good forage. Roping and hard riding are then taken as a part of the day's work. At night, when the cows are bedded down, there are songs and stories around the camp fire. Some of the old-timers, still able to attend the roundup, remember the old West; their reminiscences and tall tales· are unexcelled. Cowboy characters used by Zane Grey and other authors still live in the southern and southeastern parts of the State, and Utah cowboys have guided exploring expeditions into unsurveyed regions. Their names crop up in travel books, and in scientific papers.

Horses are on the wane in Utah. They have been replaced by machinery in the dry-farm areas, and in many cultivated districts groups of farmers buy tractors and power machinery to be used in common. The tendency, however, is to have better breeds of horses. Some wonderful draft animals are shown at State and county fairs, and wealthy people breed saddle horses that are of kin to Man o' War and other great racers.

In pioneer days the light, sure-footed Indian pony was favored for this country. They could exist on the scant desert forage, go without water, climb like a goat, and endure things that would have killed heavier horses. The accepted theory is that the Indian horses were descended from animals that escaped from early Spanish explorers. The breed degenerated, producing "hammerheads" and "broomtails," but occasionally, in the wild herds, there is a throw-back with the build, spirit, speed, and bearing of the pure-blood Arabian. Zane Grey's *Wildfire* was a story of such a Utah horse. The animals have been relentlessly hunted, to rid the range of unprofitable stock, and it is seldom today that bands of wild horses can be seen, but there are still a few.

Sheep graze over much desert and semi-arid land that will not support cattle. The State ranks fifth in the nation in the production of wool, the 1938 clip, according to the U. S. Department of Agriculture, having a value of $3,783,000. Utah's high altitudes and cool summer nights provide good conditions for wool growing. There were, in 1940, a total of 2,554,000 sheep in the State, almost two million of which are grazed on privately owned land or public domain. The Forest Service issued permits in 1940 for grazing 682,025 head of sheep and goats. At lower altitudes sheep are admitted to the forests between the middle and the last of May, and at higher altitudes until July. They start toward winter grazing on the deserts and on the islands of Great Salt Lake between the end of September and the middle of October. Sheep are herded by horsemen, assisted by trained sheep dogs. In rough country the dog's feet get sore, and he hops up behind his master and rests his feet with a horseback ride. Utah farmers and Indians clipped 45,000 goats in 1939, which yielded 212,000 pounds of mohair. At Jericho the Union Pacific Railroad has large shearing sheds and corrals, which are leased to the wool growers forming the Jericho Wool Pool, one of the largest in the West. The sheds are equipped to shear forty to fifty thousand sheep in a twenty-day season.

Glynn Bennion, of the L. D. S. Historian's Office in Salt Lake City, in a manuscript paper credits the Mormon pioneers with an important part in the evolution of range practices in the West: "Mormon pioneers came, as did all other first settlers of the west, from well-watered regions where each farmer might keep a few sheep on the thick, ever-growing grass of a small enclosed pasture. But when these men came into the deserts of the Great Basin where the forage growing on one square mile might not equal what one acre in Ohio can produce, they had to learn, in the interest of labor economy at least, new ways of gathering that sparse growth. In the new land the sheep had to wander far to get enough to eat, through a rough terrain which was and still is alive with bears, coyotes and cats." Required to range outward from the near-by forage preempted by milk cows and draft beasts, he shows, a few herders protected the flocks of several owners, and the compact sheep-camp wagon evolved as a movable "home on the range."

Turkeys are herded in Utah, and the flocks are called "herds." The State has high altitudes, cool nights, and cold fall weather before the holiday season, a suitable set of conditions to prepare the meat course for Thanksgiving dinners. Turkeys are herded on range land almost in the same manner as sheep but for a different reason. Sheep are herded to find forage, but turkeys are fed specially prepared foods all the time they are on the range.

The range method is used because of the difficulty in raising young turkeys, the necessity for sanitation and clean ground, exercise during the growing period, and well-developed feathers during the finishing period. Incubated poults, or day-old turkey chicks, are purchased in quantity, put through a brooder, and enter the pens when they are about six weeks old. Soon after, usually about May, they are put into herds of from 1,500 to 3,000 and headed for the foothills and bench-lands. A well-equipped "sheep" camp is the center of operations, with additional wagons for grain and feed. Racks or roosts are mounted on the running gears of wagons, not enough for all the turkeys, but to serve as a gathering place for the "herd" at night. Utensils, feed racks, and watering troughs are kept spotlessly clean, and the camp moves to clean ground every two weeks. Intelligent, well-trained turkey dogs keep the birds together during the day, start them towards the bedding grounds in the evening, and guard them from attack by predators at night. A good turkey dog, when the herd is crossing a road, splits the flock for cars to pass through. In case of cricket invasions, turkey herds are sometimes moved up to feed on the insects.

Irrigation

UTAH land is valuable mainly in relation to its irrigation water. It is not easy to place a monetary value on water in an arid State, but the following calculation gives a rough idea: The U. S. Bureau of Reclamation has spent some $15,000,000 in construction of irrigation works, making available 200,000 acre-feet of water at an average rate of $75 per acre-foot (the amount of water needed to cover an acre of ground a foot deep). The assessed value of Utah's real property in 1938 was $121,272,248, probably about half its worth. Since this figure includes $20,000,000 worth of water it is evident that land without water is of little value in Utah.

All natural streams flow along courses offering the steepest immediate descent. To divert water from streams to the higher adjacent land, interference with the natural watercourse is necessary. Storage dams impound a considerable volume of water, so that the stream flow at high stages can be held back for later use. Diversion dams raise the water surface a small distance above the diverting channel. Irrigation is the process of spreading delivered water over farm land sown to crops. The streams are divided into small parts so they convey water to the entire irrigated area in nearly uniform quantities, but great care is required to prevent erosion. Levees are sometimes used to hold water in shallow pools until it sinks into the dry soil. In Utah's arid climate the irrigation water required for a growing season varies from a few inches to a few feet in depth over the irrigated area, divided into a number of applications, depending on the character of the soil, the kind of crop, and the weather. Use of three to four acre-feet per acre per annum is common. More than a little art is required on the part of the farmer to insure a uniform distribution of water, and to prevent erosion and water wastage.

It was fortunate for the pioneers that a large preponderance of lands made irrigable by their diversion dams and primitive works were arable lands. Early diversion dams were usually simple and small, built of rocks, logs, and brush. As arable lands below the old lower works were appropriated, new works were begun at higher places. The result was, and is, a system of roughly parallel canals diverting water from a mountain stream, and serving irrigation water to lands between canals.

Irrigation works built at higher elevations along a stream are more expensive than lower works, requiring more elaborate dams and diverting channels built of reinforced concrete, stone masonry, and timber. The "highline" canal is frequently excavated through rock, and requires tunnels, flumes, syphons, aqueducts, and open concrete-lined channels. Storage dams and highline canals are almost exclusively a twentieth-century development, necessary for the irrigation of lands otherwise impossible to serve. Such projects are so expensive that they require subsidy or financial credit as a rule.

The most important storage facilities in Utah are natural lakes—Utah Lake and Bear Lake. These lakes as water sources have had an obvious effect on the growth of Utah's population and its agricultural and industrial economy in a concentrated area. The leading man-made storage facilities, in a descending order of importance, are the Strawberry Valley, Consolidated-Sevier, Echo, Piute, and Scofield reservoirs. These storage dams, with the lakes, account for about 75 per cent of the total in the State. Of the 1,375,000 acres of land normally irrigated in Utah (about 5 per cent of the total area), 500,000 acres were under irrigation by 1903. Of the 875,000 acres brought under irrigation subsequently, between 50,000 and 75,000 acres are not irrigated in years of subnormal water supply. A *Report on Proposed Reservoirs in Utah,* issued in 1935 by the Utah Emergency Relief Administration, catalogues the more important undeveloped storage sites capable of serving a vast acreage.

It is reasonably certain that the Mormon pioneers knew something about irrigation. Ancient Babylon flourished with the help of irrigation farming, by diverting waters from the Tigris and Euphrates rivers. Irrigation had been practiced successfully in Egypt, India, Spain, and Italy. The Spanish *padres* used it at San Diego, San Jose, and Los Angeles, California, in the eighteenth century, and Spanish and Mexican settlers of the Rio Grande Valley had built canals of considerable size by 1842, which were still in use as late as 1920. Knowing they were moving into an arid land, Mormon leaders must have acquired some of the necessary background for diverting water to agricultural use.

In any event they lost no time, upon their arrival in Salt Lake Valley, in starting a program of irrigation (*see History*). Co-operative effort was the foundation of early Mormon enterprises, of which irrigation, in an arid land, was of prime importance. Irrigation in the West was not a new institution initiated by the Mormons, but it was first established by them as the basis for extensive colonization, and they were the first to formulate rules, regulations, and laws governing the use of water for irrigation. In this respect they had little enough precedent to lead them, except for such Old World irrigation rules as they might have known, and the "Doctrine of Riparian Rights" (that the body of water on the land belongs to the landowner), an established and undisputed principle in the humid East; it was not, however, easy to see how any adaptation of this doctrine could be used in a country where the problem was essentially one of bringing water to the lands instead of taking care of water on the lands or draining it away from them.

The period from 1847 to 1852 was one of orientation. They were otherwise busy at the same time, satisfying the immediate physical necessities of food, shelter, clothing, providing walls against possible Indian attack, dealing with Indian thieves of their livestock, exploring the country. Contemporary with abatement of immediate necessities through community effort, individual, partnership, and community enterprises were undertaken. The canal, above all things, was understood to be a community problem. It very soon became the practice, when several colonies or individuals settled along a stream and planned the use of a single canal to serve them all, that everyone should work on the ditch to the lands of the first settlers. An accounting would then be made of work done by each colony, the water divided on that basis, and the first colony would cease work on the joint project. At the lands of second, third, and subsequent colonies, other accountings would be made, and it would finally fall upon the last colony to complete the job. The fruits of this system were put to immediate and co-operative uses. As soon as water was available for the first lands, they were placed under cultivation to provide bread for the coming winter and seed for the next growing season, both of which were shared with colonists on whose lands the water arrived too late for a crop.

Lands thus laboriously subdued by the Mormon pioneers had a peculiar legal status, being part of the vast territory acquired by the United States from Mexico in the war of 1846, and without civil government until 1850. As trespassers in the eyes of the Indians and mere squatters in the eyes of the Federal government, the settlers had difficulty to induce Congress to extend Federal land laws to the Territory and extinguish the rights of the Indians. In the absence of Congressional enactment, the Territorial legislature in 1852 gave county courts control over all water privileges, on the theory that the Territory owned the waters within its boundaries in so far as they were not inter-state streams, and had the right to regulate their use. The Church had held from the beginning that the right to use water in the Territory was the right only to use it beneficially, and this doctrine was con-sistently confirmed by the county courts.

As soon as self-preservation was reasonably assured, the pioneers ex-panded to localities where good land and water were available together. This program continued until most of the lands that could be brought under irrigation had been claimed, and their water uses had been con-firmed by the county courts. About 100 irrigation districts were or-ganized under the Territorial law of 1865. Because land and water were both available in the early years, there was little trafficking in either. Meantime, county courts and boards of county selectmen did not permit the transfer of water rights, or even a piece of land, from one individual to another without their consent, nor without cogent evidence that such transfers would be beneficial to the individuals, lands, and waters involved, and without injury to others.

Not until 1869, when a Federal land office was opened in Utah, was it possible to homestead a piece of land under Federal law. In the interim non-Mormons could not speculate in lands because there were no Federal laws permitting a patent, and the Church would not tolerate land speculation, allowing members land only to the extent of their needs, usually twenty to forty acres each. When the land office opened, many claimants were usually in joint possession of a single quarter-section (160 acres) of irrigated land, but without title to it. The custom adopted, by Church members, was then for one claimant to file application with the U. S. Land Office for a full homestead, and, when patent had issued, to convey by deed the various parcels in the homestead to others holding interest in it by mutual agreement or by ecclesiastical allotment. Where this system was not followed, there was an inviting opportunity for land-jumpers, who could file, under Federal law, on an entire quarter-section of arable ground. Land-jumping was mainly done by non-Mormons, but the practice in-cluded some Church members. The Church system of occupying land operated to keep farms at their previous size, twenty to forty acres each, particularly on the established irrigation systems. This limitation of farm sizes left lands under irrigation and canal capacities open for settlement by newcomers, who usually subdued more ground and pro-duced more irrigation facilities than they individually acquired. Those who came after could then buy water rights with their labor. The system operated in favor of rapid colonization, and prevented large indi-vidual holdings of land and water.

Before 1880, water rights were appurtenant to the land, but the

Territorial legislature in that year enacted a law that made them personal property. Borrowers could then pledge water rights to secure loans, meantime paying taxes on real property, while lenders, paying little or no taxes, exacted interest from landholding borrowers. Cooperative irrigation partnerships and community canals were incorporated as stock companies, facilitating free traffic in water rights. The law opened the way for private capital to try venturesome irrigation schemes, most of which failed or needed refinancing. There was uncontrolled speculation in lands and water, resulting in great losses to bondholders. An outstanding example of this type of manipulation was the Bear River Canal, which cost more than one and a quarter million dollars, and sold for $125,000 at a bankruptcy sale; the canal company was forced into insolvency when land owners delayed purchase of water rights until they could be bought cheaply.

The law of 1880 brought Utah to the nadir of its fortunes so far as water rights were concerned, and represented a complete reversal of the original law of 1852, under which water was public property, to be distributed by grants. Under the enactment of 1880 the Territory was stripped of its ownership of water, and could only regulate the various irrigators and act as a judge in cases of controversy. Under the law, new appropriators of water had no way of knowing, until after their irrigation works were built, that they would be protected in court. The harvest of this law was over-appropriation of streams, irrigation works rendered worthless because there was not enough water to satisfy all claims, and a great expenditure of money for legal processes. The law of 1880 was amended in 1884, providing "That no tax created or payable by this act shall be or create a lien upon the land." By this amendment, taxes were made a lien upon water rights. Voting on irrigation matters was done on a per capita basis within irrigation districts until 1892. By this time so much financial inequality had been established between various water users that the law was amended to place voting on a basis of acres irrigated. The irrigation districts operating under the law of 1880 were reestablished as stock companies, in which water was again bought and sold as private property.

The enabling act admitting Utah to statehood in 1896 bequeathed 500,000 acres of land to the State, to be selected under direction of the Secretary of the Interior from unappropriated lands and sold, the proceeds to be used for building permanent reservoirs. The land sold slowly, and payments were slow. The State legislature maneuvered the reservoir fund into liquidity by purchasing its warrants with land board funds. Two dams, the Piute and the Hatchtown, were built with part of the money. The Hatchtown Dam, with a capacity of 13,500 acre-feet, designed to irrigate 6,000 acres of land, was completed in 1908. It washed out six years later, causing a loss of $178,000 to the State, and a great loss to farmers. The Piute Dam, designed to impound 93,000 acre-feet of water and irrigate 35,000 acres of land, was nearly finished when the Hatchtown dam was destroyed. These two projects cost $1,640,000 to build.

With passage of the National Reclamation Act in 1902, and State legislation in 1903, the swing back to the intent of the Territorial law of 1852 was almost complete. Both new acts confirmed beneficial use of water, and the Reclamation Act required the appurtenance of land and water; both discountenanced speculation, monopoly, and the Doctrine of Riparian Rights. With reclamation funds available from the sale of western lands, amounting to several millions of dollars annually, the first adequate financial aid for storage projects was in sight.

The Act, however, was not altogether streamlined. Projects were selected by the Secretary of the Interior, who, to prevent speculation, withdrew all affected public lands from entry before investigating the feasibility of a project. When a plan was pronounced practicable, the lands were thrown open for entry. It was sometimes years before the water got to the land, but the homesteader, under laws requiring strict residence, was forced to live on the land without water. This procedure was very soon corrected, by withholding entry until a short time before water was available, but in the meantime several crops of poor farmers were starved off their homesteads before water arrived. Applications for farm units under reclamation projects were made a part of the applications to purchase irrigation water; under this arrangement land and water were not available for separate speculation. Ownership of land by an individual was restricted to a farm unit of a quarter-section or less, and the right to use water could not exceed beneficial use.

The State law of 1903 was drawn to define existing rights and to control acquisition of new rights. It vests ownership of water in the State, and places the State engineer in charge of forcing an orderly definition of existing rights through the courts. At the time the law was passed, many Utah streams had been over-appropriated, and the State was faced with the problem of obtaining supplemental water for lands only partially irrigated. An act for organizing irrigation districts was passed in 1909 and later amended. Subsequent legislation has progressed along lines calculated to interest the Federal Bureau of Reclamation, and legislative enactments are for the most part compatible with the Federal program. Where there are existing water rights, not under irrigation districts or Reclamation projects, there is still a certain antipathy against abolition of the right to deal in water as personal property, there is the possibility of maladministration by the State engineer in allocating water, and there is still the old States rights attitude of decrying too firm direction from Washington.

In summary, the history of Utah irrigation reveals five years, from 1847 to 1852, devoted by the Mormon pioneers to orientation and finding criteria upon which to base a doctrine of land and water use; twenty-eight years, from 1852 to 1880, of integrated co-operation in land and water use, with legislation directed to its firm establishment; twenty-two years, from 1880 to 1902, of unwise legislation and speculation in water as personal property; and thirty-eight years, from 1902 to 1940, of retrenchment and return to the original Mormon doctrine of beneficial water use. The indication was, in 1940, that many more years may elapse before the post-1880 renaissance is complete.

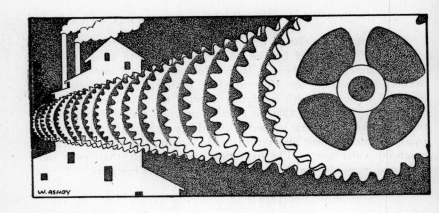

W. ASHBY

Industry and Commerce

GRISTMILLS and sawmills were Utah's first industrial "plants." They appeared rapidly, though not without a certain deliberate orderliness, following arrival of the Mormons in 1847, and tanneries, carding, spinning, and weaving mills followed close behind. The first sawmills were "hand powered," consisting of two men and a whipsaw, with plenty of sawdust raining down on the man in the "pit," but in 1848 water-driven saws were operating on Mill Creek in Salt Lake Valley and in Bingham Canyon. In the same year two gristmills were built on City Creek, and the following year a public carding machine began operating on Mill Creek. These infant industries were, however, subsidiary to farming in a Mormon community that stressed agricultural self-sufficiency. They were developed to serve specific needs, and the man who operated a mill was usually a farmer too.

Captain Howard Stansbury found in 1850 that the Mormons had a woolen factory, a pottery, and plans for a beet sugar factory, and adds that it was their policy "to provide for their own wants by their own skill . . . and to dispense, as much as possible, with the products of the labour of others." How well they succeeded is attested by a list of prizes granted by the Deseret Agricultural Society in 1860 for home-produced plows, cultivators, drills, rakes, shovels, washing machines, spinning wheels, reapers, threshers, corn shellers, steam engines, lathes, well pumps, shoes, saddles, harnesses, wool and cotton fabrics of all kinds, furniture, rifles (made from crowbars), revolving pistols, knives, wrought nails, glassware, wine, soap, landscapes and bird's-eye views of Salt Lake City, transparent blinds, and sculpture. (The saints already had a crude reduction plant and foundry at Cedar City and a lead smelter at Minersville.) Such a list of local production for a colony just thirteen years removed from its beginnings in a desert wilderness is impressive. The products had a certain rugged crudity, for they were designed to fill an immediate and functional need rather than a polished and decorative niche. Flour from the early gristmills, for example, had about the texture of corn meal, but was not wanting in nutrition value. Leather made in Salt Lake Valley, one traveler noted, compared favorably with the product of English tanneries; it came to be known as "valley tan" in distinction to imported stocks, and the expression was for a time applied to all home products. The label fell into disrepute after its application to "home grown" whisky, which Mark Twain said was "made of imported fire and brimstone."

An accurate estimate of the cash volume of pioneer industry in Utah is difficult, because almost all commercial transactions were conducted by barter, by the due-bill system, or with script issued by the Mormon tithing house. H. H. Bancroft in his *History of Utah* estimates that the entire cash capital of the Mormons in Utah in 1848 did not exceed $3,000. The merchants Livingston and Kinkead, who opened the first store in Great Salt Lake City in 1849, expected it would take five years to dispose of a $20,000 stock. Some cash income from forage, horses, cattle, and farm produce, was created by passage through Utah of gold seekers and colonists to the Pacific Coast but in general they, as the Mormons, came west with equipment, not money. Great Salt Lake City issued script and attempted to mint gold coins in 1849, but abandoned both projects when it was discovered that script was discounted and the coins had too much gold in them. In one sense the Mormons were fortunate: a man might make his farm yield all he needed to eat, and he could "swap cabbages for yarn" at the local carding mill, or establish credits at the tithing house and draw on them as he needed. Tithing was paid in produce too, and a well-to-do farmer might have an abundance of home-made comforts, but he might conduct his business for a twelve month without a dollar passing through his strong box. Such lean cash reserves as the Mormons possessed could not long survive if they were invested in imported "luxuries" such as sugar at forty cents to a dollar a pound and calico at seventy-five cents a yard. Accordingly, Brigham Young and other Mormon leaders kept a weather eye on imports, and tried to reduce them by establishment of home manufactures. Pack and wagon-freight exports to adjoining territories were also encouraged.

The presence of Johnston's Army at Camp Floyd during the years 1858 and 1859, and troops quartered at Fort Douglas after 1863, gave Utah settlers their first substantial market. Products were sold high and bought low from the government, and for a time things "prospered exceedingly." Completion of the transcontinental railway in 1869 was hailed as a kind of final bulwark to prosperity. The firm of Hooper, Eldridge, and Company, Utah's first financial house, opened its doors the same year and matured two years later into the Bank of Deseret, with a capital of $100,000 and Brigham Young as president. Walker Brothers bank incorporated the next year, and within ten years the Territory had twelve private and five national banks with an aggregate exchange business between twelve and fifteen millions of dollars. The railroad was, however, not an unmixed commercial blessing. It gave Utah an outlet for low-grade ores, for beef, and for wool, but destroyed many small industrial enterprises; eastern manufacturers could put their goods on Utah markets more cheaply than they could be produced at home. The ideal of self-sufficient isolation, which the Saints very nearly achieved, slid away along the shining rails. Imports increased 800 per cent, and so also did exports. In 1870 Utah was buying farm machinery, dry goods, clothing, groceries, lumber and other building materials, and leather goods; it was selling gold, silver, lead, copper, beef, wool, hides, pelts, furs, and tallow. The business of tanning, because it had to import extracts of tanbark, was replaced by the shipment of hides; the silk, linen, and cotton industries were driven into bankruptcy before they had well started; Utah timber, in many cases too remote to be profitably cut, was replaced with outside stock; iron foundries, for which high hopes had been entertained, met lethal competition in eastern machine factories.

Between 1870 and 1890, Utah industry marked time. Industrial beginnings were made in the period, but Utahns had not the necessary capital to develop them, and Mormon-Federal antagonism in polygamy and other matters made eastern capital wary. Outside pressure on Mormon tenets, together with the demonstrated success of co-operative stores and social thinking that stressed isolation and self-sufficiency, induced establishment of the United Order (*see History* and *Tour 2d*). Members pooled their resources and labor, and received what they needed in return. Industries that had been broken by competition with eastern companies were revived in miniature. The Order, however, was of brief duration. Meanwhile, mining (*see Mining*) as a source of income to the Territory was making giant strides.

Twentieth-century industrial Utah began taking definite shape about 1888. Nationwide indignation over the institution of polygamy had spent its fury, the manifesto which abolished it was just around the corner, and a coalition of gentile and Mormon merchants had already formed the Salt Lake Chamber of Commerce to break the paralysis that had settled on Utah trade. Companies at Ogden, Salt Lake City, and Provo began production of hydroelectric power during the decade 1880-90. Finally, after publication of the Woodruff Manifesto in 1890 and the subsequent return of escheated Church property, the Mormons, who then comprised some 80 per cent of the total population, settled themselves to develop what they had.

Canning, a logical process for a region blessed with prolific truck-garden soil and distant markets, began in 1886, when a man and his wife hand-soldered and -packed tomatoes and fruits in a home plant at Ogden. New companies added peas, beans, beets, pickles, sauerkraut, fruits, catsup, and milk to the list of canned foods, and by 1932 about 20,000 acres were devoted to canning crops. By 1937 the industry was the State's fourth most important, with an annual pack worth seven million dollars. Beet sugar manufacture, first attempted in 1853 on Temple Block, Great Salt Lake City, and the subject of much subsequent experiment, was not commercially successful until 1890, when a plant was opened at Lehi. The industry had sixteen major factories in 1940, with a combined annual production of about ten million dollars worth of sugar. A generous portion of Utah-manu-factured sugar is converted into candy. In 1937 there were sixteen candy factories in the State, with a combined output worth $2,800,000. Utah began commercial export of salt from Great Salt Lake in 1899, a business simplified by the great quantity of available salt, and by the relative simplicity of extraction from brine by evaporation (*see Tour 6c*). The annual export since 1930 has been consistently in excess of 80,000 tons.

Flour milling assumed commercial significance about 1890, when the practice of grading wheat was introduced. In the following decade the development of dry-farm wheat provided Utah millers with raw material to make flour for export. Utah in 1940 had sixty-five flour mills in operation, with a combined output of about $12,000,000 worth of flour and $3,000,000 worth of livestock feeds. As a kind of step-child to flour milling, baking grew into economic significance after 1910, and was, in 1940, the State's seventh ranking industry, with an annual output valued at $5,000,000. The high percentage of European-born people in Utah probably accounts for the popularity of bakery prod-ucts; in this respect Utah departs from the home-baking norm of other States. The textile industry has perhaps undergone more vicissitudes than any other single field of Utah manufacture. The urgent pioneer need for clothing led to an expansion of textile manufacture that could not, as a profit and loss business, survive. Silk, cotton, and flax processing were almost completely abandoned by Utah mills after 1880. The climate was not well suited to growth of raw materials, and the textile industry in New England could put finished goods on the Utah market more cheaply than Utah plants. Wool, however, offered possibilities and after 1890 was Utah's major textile. The Provo Woolen Mills, founded in 1858, was for many years the largest maker of woolen fabrics west of the Mississippi. The industry suffered heavily in the early depression years after 1929, and many of the mills, including the Provo company, closed and did not reopen. After 1935, a few new mills and several old ones opened or expanded, and by 1937 there were thirty-four in the State, with an aggregate annual output of clothing, blankets, and other woolen fabrics worth $3,800,000, a figure which has continued to 1940 with but small variation.

Cheap and fast motor-truck transportation opened Pacific Coast markets to Utah dairymen and poultrymen during the 1920's. About 1924 they began the practice of co-operative marketing, and since that date have steadily pushed to the front of the State's agricultural industries. In 1939 their aggregate income was more than five million dollars, and, as a subsidiary to the dairy industry, the business of condensing milk produced an annual pack worth an additional three millions. The Sego milk plant at Smithfield (*see Tour 1a*) is one of the Nation's largest. The meat-packing industry began modestly with smoked bacon in 1860, and, encouraged by improved refrigeration after 1900, was in 1939 Utah's sixth most important industry, with an annual pack worth between eight and nine million dollars. Manufacture of machinery and printing were Utah's eleventh and twelfth ranking industries in 1939, with products for the year valued at $1,857,000 and $1,543,000 respectively.

Smelting, Utah's single most important industry, has made its major development since 1910. Between 1870 and 1900, the richest mines operated their own stamp mills and shipped concentrated ores out of the State for reduction. After 1910, with adequate and inexpensive power available, and large reserves of coal and fluxing material near at hand, smelters were built in Salt Lake Valley and at Tooele, and the mines sold their products in Utah. The tremendous demands for non-ferrous raw metals made by the United States and foreign powers during the World War of 1914-18 launched the industry on a period of development which culminated in the peak year of 1929, when Utah's mineral production was valued at $112,989,000. In the depression years that succeeded 1929, smelting was hit harder than any of Utah's industries. In 1939, non-ferrous metals smelted in Utah were valued at only $19,780,000. Iron reduction, though not nearly so important to the State as other metal products, may offer more promise for the future. Until 1924, when the Columbia Steel Corporation first operated its blast furnace at Ironton, the hematite deposits of southern Utah had been allowed to rest undisturbed after initial attempts by the Mormons in 1852 to establish a foundry at Cedar City. Ample reserves of coking coal are available in Carbon County and all necessary fluxing materials have been found within easy distance of Ironton. Utah ranked fifteenth among iron-producing States from 1930 to 1940.

The whole picture of industry in Utah for the decade after 1929, and prospects for the decades after 1940, is at once encouraging and discouraging. During the depression decade of 1930, mining and agriculture were both retarded, mining from production of 48 per cent of the State's annual wealth to about 24 per cent; agriculture from 17.22 per cent to about 13 per cent. Manufacturing, however, increased steadily. In 1929 it produced 21.94 per cent of the State's income, in 1940 very nearly 40 per cent. However, this impressive gain in relative importance came not from expansion alone, but primarily from tremendous declines in agriculture and mining, for the cumulative value of industrial products had not in 1940 climbed back to those of 1929. Since 1935, however, Utah industry, in spite of fluctuations, has steadily increased the volume and value of its output. The twelve biggest producing industries were, in order of their importance: smelting, grain milling, dairying, canning (which has made the single most rapid advance since 1929), sugar refining, meat packing, baking, livestock feed, textile-making, candy-making, machinery, and printing, exclusive of newspapers. Of these, manufactures based on farm produce, such as canning, meat packing, sugar refining, and grain milling have restricted and not too distant limits beyond which they cannot expand unless more desert land can be reclaimed. The possibility for expanding the smelting industry into fabrication of finished products is confronted with twin bugbears—distance from and high freight rates to the large consuming centers, and competition with already established factories. Less than 1 per cent of the metals produced by Utah mines and smelters is converted within the State to finished products.

In its social aspects the prospect of Utah industry in 1940 was even less encouraging. Studies made by the Utah State Planning Board in 1937 led that body to conclude that employment, including employment in industry, increased at a much slower rate than the increase of population, and wages paid per capita in Utah are about 60 per cent lower than the national average. Studies made in 1935 by Lowery Nelson and T. David Hettig for the Federal Emergency Relief Administration, revealed that Utah's rural population lost more heavily than the rural population of any other State during the gala years after 1920. In 1935, however, they found that the population shift was moving heavily the other way. This population shuttle actually represents a section of people who have no place either in urban or rural sections. Consequently, Nelson and Hettig conclude the population must either reach a plateau, or new economic resources and new industries must be found. One of the white hopes of Utahns during the years after 1920 has been the possibility of developing the immense recreational areas of the State into an industry serving tourists. Zion National Park, established late in 1919, Bryce in 1928, and the national monuments established in southern Utah since 1920, have induced the people of Utah to pay close attention to this resource. However, the total dependence of a tourist industry on the economic welfare of the Nation at large does not make it a substantial investment for a large number of people.

W. ASHBY

Mining

UTAH in 1938 ranked fifteenth in the production of metals in the United States and 'fourth among the western States. Behind that bald statement lies nearly eighty years of adventure, romance, tragedy, bitterness, poverty, sudden wealth, and equally sudden failure. Hidden behind Utah's production of 20 per cent of the nation's copper is the story of "Colonel" Wall's faith, and "Colonel" Jackling's tenaciousness. The dislike of a military colonel—P. E. Connor—for the Mormons, plus his insatiable curiosity, is responsible for Utah mining 18 per cent of the nation's lead, and 10 per cent of its gold and silver. Thousands of others have contributed toward the $2,112,-340,000 worth of non-ferrous metals recovered since mining began in 1864. The industry has grown into a $65,000,000-a-year business, accounting for 40 per cent of the State's income. Fifty-four per cent of the population in Utah is directly or indirectly dependent upon the mining industry. The State has all the generally known metallic minerals and an undetermined but large variety of non-metallics. In 1939, according to the preliminary report of the U. S. Bureau of Mines, the mines of Utah yielded 341,040,000 pounds of copper; 10,574,987 ounces of silver; 276,060 ounces of gold, 130,826,000 pounds of lead, and 66,714,000 pounds of zinc.

Exploitation of mineral resources in Utah is governed primarily by transportation costs and the accessibility of minable property. Most of the commercial ores are found in lode or bedded deposits, and, in the case of metallic ores, are frequently of a complex or refractory nature, requiring elaborate equipment for concentration and separation. In general, minerals and ores are shipped as raw or semi-finished materials to refining and manufacturing centers outside the State. Copper, lead, silver, zinc, and gold are, in the order named, the most important metals produced in Utah, and are responsible for 95 per cent of the State's mining income. Other metallic ores exist and are sporadically worked, but price, demand, and the difficulty of competing with mines equally rich and more fortuitously located have rendered them commercially unimportant.

Development of mining in the early days was deliberately retarded by the Mormon Church. Its leaders, fresh from gentile persecutions in the East and Middle West, sought to create in Utah an inland agricultural empire, isolated, self-sustaining, and dominated by members of their creed. They discouraged prospecting because they feared a mineral strike would divert people from agriculture, threaten the stability of the economy they were creating, breed restless characters, and bring an influx of undesirable non-Mormons. Orson F. Whitney stated their position in the 1860's when he said, "Who wishes to see Deseret, peaceful Deseret, the home of a people who fled for religious freedom and quiet to these mountain solitudes, converted into a rollicking, roaring mining camp? Not the Latter Day Saints!"

The Mormons knew of metalliferous ores in the area. Reduction of galena, a lead mineral, for bullets before 1850 is mentioned in several old diaries and journals from southern Utah. When news reached Brigham Young of the approach of Johnston's army in 1858, he sent Isaac Grundy to Beaver County, there to erect a small furnace and convert galena into bullion for Great Salt Lake City. Lead thus processed was molded into bullets for the arsenal. Grundy was Utah's first metallurgist. The lead deposit (*see Tour 1D*) became known as the Rollins mine (later the Lincoln Silver mine), and is said to be the oldest in the State. After the departure of Johnston's army, the plant was used to manufacture farming implements, when supplies and Indians would permit. These developments, however, were obviously related to frontier demand and to the needs of the self-sustaining Mormon State.

Mining, as an industry developed independently of Mormon political philosophy and agricultural economy, received its first impetus from Colonel (later General) Patrick E. Connor, the perverse and violently anti-Mormon commander of Federal troops dispatched to Great Salt Lake City in 1862. Connor reputedly would praise anything the Mormons contemned, or contemn what they praised, and his attitude toward mining was no exception. His men, most of whom had been recruited from California gold fields, needed little encouragement to go prospecting, and Connor granted them generous leave. Their searches resulted in a series of important strikes.

Although Tom and Sanford Bingham, ranchers, really discovered (in 1850) the first ore in the district which bears their name, credit for opening the district in 1863 has been given to George Ogilvie, an apostate Mormon who was logging in Bingham Canyon. Ogilvie kicked up a piece of ore, and knowing of Connor's interest in mining, took the sample to him. Connor had the specimen assayed, and, finding it rich in lead and silver, successfully encouraged development of the canyon (*see Tour 1C*). The ensuing history of Bingham Canyon is, in essence, the history of mining in Utah. The rich silver-lead ores were worked profitably in spite of inadequate transportation and expensive supplies. It was not until 1870, when Salt Lake City was joined to the transcontinental railway by the Utah Central Railroad, that development of the lode deposits was begun on a large scale. Rich veins of silver, lead, and copper ore were put into immediate production, and low-grade ores made Bingham famous.

Recognition of the value of low-grade ores came about mainly through Colonel Enos A. Wall, who went to Bingham in the mid-1890's. Other miners scoffed at "Wall's Rocks," but the colonel went on experimenting, and getting financial backing. Two young engineers, Daniel C. Jackling and Robert C. Gemmell, sent to investigate the property, completed their report in 1899—the first comprehensive analysis of a mining enterprise based on the treatment of low-grade ores. Jackling, convinced that there was great wealth in recovering low-grade copper, bought an interest in the Wall property. *The Engineering and Mining Journal,* with the most pious intentions, warned investors against "Jackling's Wildcat." His idea was to apply mass-production methods to mining, plus improved metallurgy. The present (1940) concentration plants have a combined capacity of 80,000 tons of ore a day. The mine, the open-cut Utah Copper Mine (*see Tour 1C*), has set an example for the development of low-grade copper ore bodies throughout the world and has produced more than six billion pounds of copper, with gold, silver, and molybdenum as by-products, the whole valued at $1,214,449,000.

Three of Colonel Connor's men wandered into the Park City district (*see Tour 6b*) in 1869 and stumbled upon the ore body which became the Flagstaff mine. Big capital became interested with the discovery of the Ontario by Rector Steen in 1872. The commercial ores of the Park City Mining District, mainly silver ore, silver-lead ore, and zinc-lead ore, with small amounts of gold and copper, extend from the surface to a depth of 2,000 feet. There are twelve large mines in the vicinity of Park City, with 500 miles of underground workings, and a total output from 1870 to 1939 of $321,729,000 worth of non-ferrous metals.

About the early history of the Tintic district in Juab and Utah counties, one of the rich silver areas of the United States, little is known. The most accepted story is that of the discovery made by George Rust, who was herding cattle in the district in 1869. The area belonged to Tintic, a Ute chief, who was, no doubt, one of the first billionaires in the West, but he never knew it. His favorite campsite was later occupied by the Centennial-Eureka Mine, which produced more than $15,000,000 worth of minerals. Development of the district (*see Tour 8*) has been characterized by slow, steady, and unpublicized growth. The ores contain, chiefly, silver, lead, gold, zinc and copper, with small amounts of bismuth and manganese. The Tintic District from 1869 to 1939 produced metals with a gross combined value of $367,883,000, and its mines have not approached depletion.

Soldier-prospectors were first to discover ore in Little Cottonwood Canyon, 20 miles southeast of Salt Lake City. In 1869, J. B. Woodman uncovered the vein of the Emma mine, and the boom town of Alta came into hectic existence. Where now (1940) only a handful of people live, 8,000 persons worked, fought, drank, bled, and died (*see Tour 1d*). Today, the original vein of the Emma is exhausted, but during its short span of life, $35,000,000 worth of ore containing gold, silver, copper, lead, and zinc was shipped from Alta to the smelters.

Coincident with Woodman's discovery, Arie Pinedo, a Bavarian, located a gold-bearing claim in Tooele County. He called his find Mercur, for the streaks of mercury sulphide associated with the gold ores (*see Tour 6A*). The ore assayed $30 to $40 per ton in gold, but it was impossible to make complete recovery by pan amalgamation, the most advanced method of extraction at that date. Not until the 1890's, when the cyanide leaching process was applied to Mercur ores, did the camp come into its own. The town by 1912 had a population of 12,000, but the original deposits were worked out, fires gutted the camp, and by 1925 Mercur was little more than a memory. In 1934 mining and milling were rejuvenated at Mercur, and four years later the Camp Floyd (Mercur) District produced 23,001 ounces of gold, more than half its production in 1909.

Hundreds of claims, located south of Little Cottonwood Canyon, were organized in 1871 into the American Fork Mining District. Silver Reef (*see Tour 1f*) was created in the 1870's after discovery of the amazing fact, not known before, that silver could occur in sandstone. Popularity of the district lasted ten years, until lowered silver prices shut down the mines. In its short career, Silver Reef produced ore valued at $10,500,000.

Other discoveries gave every county at least one mine, and made it necessary to identify 135 mining districts. Many of the districts were short-lived and are today marked only by decaying ghost towns and memories of dividends, but others are increasing their production.

At least three areas, Bingham, Tintic, and Park City, are large producers of copper ore, lead ore, and zinc-lead ore. Mines in the Iron Mountains near Cedar City produce iron ore that is reduced to pig iron at Ironton. The deposits contain an estimated 160,000,000 tons of 57 per cent ore in sight, with probabilities of vast deposits to be uncovered. They have been worked on a small scale by the open-pit method, but the Ironton plant has a limited capacity and no successful method of competing with eastern iron mines has been devised.

An alunite deposit near Marysvale, with 16,000,000 tons of ore above the creek level, and with an estimated 4,400,000 tons for every 100 feet in depth, is being exploited as a source of metallic aluminum, with potash as a by-product. One deposit produced potash during the World War. Until 1939 foreign market prices had retarded the development of this property. The San Rafael Mountain region produces radioactive minerals containing uranium and vanadium, and the Little Grande district farther north has workable deposits of manganese. Along the Colorado and Green rivers are large deposits of sand and gravel containing gold. The metal is so fine that most efforts to recover it have failed—expensively. As long as human practice depends rather on hope than precedent, however, these experiments with river sands will probably continue. Other metals, such as antimony, cadmium, and arsenic are recovered at the various smelters. The sulphide of molybdenum is separated from copper ore, and small amounts of platinum, palladium, osmium, and iridium are recovered from copper bullion.

Utah has had no adequate survey of its non-metallic resources. Attention has been concentrated on metallic products because they have had ready markets and because the profits were immediate and large; whereas, with the exception of fuels, the value of non-metals has been largely potential. Most of them have been restricted to local consumption or have been forced to await the researches of industrial chemists to create external markets. Systematic prospecting for nonmetals in Utah was, until after the World War, a thing unknown. However, increasing demands for soil correctives, mordants, dyes, medicines, road surfacing, and the raw materials for a myriad of synthetic fabrications are rapidly injecting order into the search for extractable non-metallic minerals. Results of surveys since 1920, conducted by private and public agencies, are favorable enough to warrant prediction by many experts that the future of mining in the State rests with this field.

Indians revealed to the earliest Mormon emigrants outcroppings of mysterious and devil-inhabited "rocks that burn." The Mormons recognized the rock to be coal, drove shafts into the mountains at Wales and Clear Creek, and soon after their Zion became the Territory of Utah, established a thriving coal industry. Subsequent surveys reveal that beds of coal from eight to seventeen feet thick underlie one-sixth of the State's area—a quantity sufficient to supply the needs of the entire world for 250 years. Although 98 per cent of the coal is produced in the Carbon-Emery Coal Fields, mining operations extend throughout eastern Utah. The average annual production for the State, including coking and non-coking varieties, is about 5,000,000 tons. The coal is predominantly high-grade bituminous, low in moisture, ash, and sulphur, highly volatile, and varying from friable to blocky in structure. One mine near Zion National Park produces cannel coal, a hydrocarbon used in drugs, dyes, and perfumes. A near-by mine produces jet, a semi-precious black stone used for ornamental purposes.

Dome formations and oil seeps occur with tantalizing frequency throughout the State, but despite widespread drilling, very few, if any, wells produce petroleum in commercial quantities, and only a few produce any oil whatever. According to geologists, the extensive oil shales of the Uintah Basin were laid down as a result of vegetable deposition in ancient Lake Uinta (*see Tour 6a*). The shales, which the U. S. Geological Survey estimates may ultimately produce from 60 to 80 billion barrels of oil, can be excavated by power shovel and processed to remove petroleum, but at present (1940) it is unprofitable to produce oil in this manner in competition with more accessible crude oils. Petroleum residues—elaterite, ozokerite, and gilsonite—which resemble tar except that they are harder and more glossy in their natural state, are mined in the Uintah Basin and shipped to manufacturers of varnishes, insulations, acid-proof paints, mineral rubber, plastics, and water-proofing compounds. The same area also yields a natural rock asphalt that can be applied to roads without processing.

Near Rozel, north of Great Salt Lake, are deposits of natural asphaltum that seep up from the bed of Great Salt Lake. A market is assured when production can be stepped up to a commercial level, for the asphaltum contains an exactly requisite amount of sulphides for production of rubber tires. This brown material also contains "ichthyol," a medicinal preparation used externally, in Webster's clarifying phrase, "as an alteratent and discutient." The Indians first discovered the medicinal properties of the asphaltum, but they have steadfastly refused to disclose its location despite a $50,000 reward. The asphaltum "seeps," with a potential value of millions, were known for sixty years, and the sticky, tar-like substance could be had for the taking. The land, however, has been leased for miles in every direction, and three companies in 1940 were operating wells in the district. Trestles run out into the lake, and the shore is dotted with rigs, storehouses, and camps. One well produces, every sixteen hours, a

500-pound barrel of asphalt valued at $90 a ton. The temperature, thought to approximate 132 degrees at the bottom of the well, is sufficiently warm for the liquid to flow to the top. As it rises in the pipe, the temperature drops, and the fluid becomes sluggish and flows thickly from the pipe. Newer wells have a dead-air space between the casing and the well pipe which acts as a non-conductor of heat and permits a more ready flow of liquid asphalt. The asphaltum deposits at Rozel are said to carry a higher percentage of gum asphalt than any other deposit known. The pure liquid is 54 per cent gum and is exceptionally suited to the rejuvenation of old rubber and the manufacturing of paints, lacquers, and medicines.

Salt reserves in Utah, with no appreciable difficulty, could supply the world for a thousand years. Great Salt Lake alone contains more than six billion tons of salines in solution, and the adjacent desert contains many billions more. Common table salt of low iodine content predominates, though magnesium chloride, sodium sulphate, and such derivatives as caustic soda, chlorine gas, hydrochloric acid, soda ash, and sodium bicarbonate can be produced. Rock salt of high iodine content is mined in Juab, Sanpete, and Sevier counties, and, with the addition of sulphur, it is converted into blocks for livestock. Sulphur occurs in several localities, but the deposit at Sulphurdale in Beaver County is the only one being exploited. The sulphur is mined by power shovel and used in its crude state as a soil corrective, or processed and sold as flowers of sulphur. Utah silica, until recently, has been used in limited quantities for smelter flux and for the fabrication of refractories. Tests indicate, however, that one variety of silica found in Utah possesses advantages for the manufacture of glassware. It melts at a low temperature, requires only three-fourths the usual proportion of soda-ash flux, and contains a small percentage of titanium oxide, which facilitates control of color in glass.

Sand, gravel, and rocks suitable for building purposes are accessible in all sections of the State. Whole mountains of gypsum occur at Nephi and Sigurd, which are worked for local and out-of-State consumption.

Semiprecious gems occur in several localities in Utah, ordinarily in association with lava beds. Precise information concerning gem mines is unavailable because of the secrecy with which gem miners traditionally surround their operations. Agate, chalcedony, jasper, azurite, malachite, garnet, opal, obsidian, rock crystal, and topaz are mined sporadically in various districts. Amatrice, a matrix stone resembling turquoise, is mined regularly in Utah and, so far as is known, nowhere else in the world.

Transportation

STREAMS and rivers were Utah's first trailmakers. Unimportant in themselves for navigation, they carved valleys that were used by the buffalo, possibly America's greatest road engineer, as avenues for herd migration. Early Utah Indians followed the buffalo, a source of food and shelter as well as a trail-blazer. Before white men introduced horses, the Indians traveled on bare or moccasined feet, and women were the usual beasts of burden. Some Indians, east and north of the Wasatch Range, tied their belongings together and secured the bundle to two poles, which were fastened at one end to a dog and left to drag on the ground at the other. With this crude device, known as a travois, the load was pulled along the trails that were ultimately followed by railroads and automobile roads. Father Escalante, who brought a pack train through Utah in 1776, is the first known traveler to use horses in the present State. Ashley's cannon (*see History*) was, ironically, the first vehicle to leave the print of wheels on Utah land.

The first pioneer wagon caravan to cross Utah was the Bartleson-Bidwell train of 1841 (*see History*). Six years later, thousands of Mormon pioneers began the long trek westward into Utah. They traveled in covered wagons and kept accurate accounts of their journey. On May 8, William Clayton wrote in his journal, "I have counted the revolutions of a wagon wheel in order to get the exact distance we have traveled. The reason why I have taken this method which is somewhat tedious, is because there is generally a difference of two, and sometimes four, miles in a day's travel between my estimation and that of some others, and they have all thought I underrated it." From

Orson Pratt's journal comes a further account of this pioneer attempt to make an accurate determination of distance. On May 12 he wrote, "William Clayton, with the assistance of Appleton Harmon, a mechanic, has constructed a machine and to-day attached it to a wagon, to indicate the number of miles traveled. It is constructed upon the principle of the endless screw. By the mile machine we came this forenoon about six miles. . . ." The wooden "mile machine" is on display in the L. D. S. Museum at Salt Lake City.

As a result of unprecedented demand for supplies and military stores during the gold rush of 1849-50, overland freighting companies were organized. Although Utah men engaged in the freighting business, the most important firm of the 1850's was that of Russell, Majors, and Waddell, whose principal office was in Leavenworth, Kansas. At one time this company owned 75,000 oxen and more than 6,000 prairie schooners. The freight caravans usually consisted of about twenty-five wagons, each wagon drawn by six yoke of oxen and carrying approximately 5,000 pounds. "Each wagon is marked with a name, as in the case of ships," observed the Jesuit Father De Smet, "and these names serve to furnish amusement to the passer-by, the caprices of the captains in this respect having imposed upon the wagons such names as the *Constitution,* the *President,* the *Great Republic,* the *King of Bavaria, Lola Montes, Louis Napoleon, Dan O'Connell, Old Kentuck.* On the plains, the wagoner assumes the style of 'captain,' being placed in command of his wagon and twelve oxen. The master-wagoner is admiral of this little land fleet; he has control of twenty-six captains and 312 oxen. At a distance the white awnings of the wagons have the effect of a fleet of vessels with all canvas spread."

Passenger service, however, was slow, cumbersome, and erratic. Travelers who came by ox team required several months to cross the plains, and mail to the frontier grew old in transit. Utah, created a Territory in 1850, did not receive full details until January of the following year. By 1851, however, stage coaches were making regular trips from Independence and St. Joseph to Great Salt Lake City, and soon afterward to Sacramento. The stage coaches, light vehicles drawn by six fast horses, accommodated fourteen passengers, with mail, express, and about twenty-five pounds of baggage for each person. To insure speed, horses were changed frequently at stations along the route. At first thirty days were necessary for the journey from St. Joseph to Great Salt Lake City, but ultimately the time was reduced to eighteen days. Coach fare varied from $150 to $180, and during the Civil War it reached an all-time high of $350. While the overland coaches were operating in the country west of the Missouri River, smaller stage lines were carrying passengers, mail, and express between scattered towns in Utah. The necessity for travel within the Territory resulted in the building of roads, bridges, and ferries, nearly all maintained by tolls.

A great many Mormon immigrants, however, were too poor to travel by wagon train or stagecoach. Church authorities devised a new plan for migration, by hand-carts. Every traveler was limited to seventeen pounds of luggage, and every able-bodied person was expected to pull a hand-cart. The plan went into effect in the spring of 1856. Between then and 1861 nearly 4,000 persons crossed the plains with the hand-cart companies (*see Salt Lake City*).

In 1860 the freighting firm of Russell, Majors, and Waddell organized the Pony Express to carry mail from St. Joseph to Sacramento. The firm provided 500 fast horses and employed more than 200 men. Stations were established at intervals, and 80 of the lightest men were selected as riders. The first rider left Sacramento on April 3, and arrived in Salt Lake City on April 7, where he met another rider who arrived six days after leaving St. Joseph. The route through Utah from east to west, entered through Echo and Weber Canyons, ran southwest to Salt Lake City, thence skirted the southern end of Great Salt Lake and the Salt Desert, reaching the Nevada line west of present Ibapah. The Pony Express continued to carry the mail until 1861, when the Overland Telegraph provided faster and more effective communication. In 1867 the Deseret Telegraph Company began operating a line between Great Salt Lake City and St. George, and later in the same year the service was extended into Idaho. The company operated independently until it was absorbed by Western Union in 1900.

For many years residents of the Great Basin had discussed the feasibility of a railroad, and in 1852 the Territorial legislature approved a memorial to Congress asking for the establishment of rail service. On May 10, 1869, the golden spike ceremony marking completion of the road was held at Promontory (*see Tour 4b*). That cold, sunny May day closed a spectacular chapter in American history. The Forty-Niners who crossed the continent the hard way, on foot, or horseback, astride tough, stringy mules, or behind the powerful shoulders of yoked oxen, set up an immediate clamor for a railroad. To that "golden-browed" demand the Federal government hearkened as it never had to the importunities of Asa Whitney, who between 1840 and 1850 haunted Washington with his plans for a Pacific railroad. Surveying parties were dispatched into the field, and the American West for a decade was criss-crossed by the tireless feet of topographical engineers. More than a commercial convenience, the Pacific Railroad was regarded as a military necessity, to bind the Pacific Coast to the Union. Construction work was kept at a standstill until outbreak of the Civil War by quarrels over the respective advantages of northern and southern routes, but Congress, in July, 1862, passed the Pacific Railroad Act, authorizing the Forty-Second Parallel route, to be subsidized by the Federal government. Builders were promised a right of way through the public domain; cash subsidies of $16,000 a mile on the plains and from $32,000 to $48,000 a mile through the mountains; free use of building materials from public lands; and every alternate, odd-numbered section of public land, checker-board fashion for 20 miles back on each side of the tracks.

The Union Pacific, in the East, and the Central Pacific, in California, organized to undertake the work. The C. P. bogged down in a morass of small difficulties and snaked its way eastward only by such stratagems as "moving" the Sierra Nevada twenty-five miles west to hasten the increase in bonus, while the U. P. drove a few rails west of Omaha and discontentedly wasted the months in search of more thorough ways to milk Congress. Despite new railroad legislation, the Pacific Railroad until 1866 dragged out a miserable visionary existence. In that year, however, the U. P. rails began to move. Location parties, with a wary eye for Sioux scalp-hunters, marked the path, followed quickly by brawny construction gangs, which graded a hundred miles or more at a crack. Transportation problems were enormous. Supplies for a force amounting sometimes to 10,000 animals and as many humans had to be brought all the way from Omaha. In *How We Built the Union Pacific,* Major General Grenville Dodge recalls, "To supply one mile of track with material and supplies required about forty cars, as rails, ties, bridgings, fastenings, all railroad supplies, fuel for locomotives and trains, and supplies for men and animals for the entire work had to be transported from the Missouri River." Dodge saved the U. P. from financial disaster in 1867 by getting his rails west to Cheyenne, beyond which the cash subsidy rose from $16,000 to $48,000 a mile. By winter of the next year, rails were being laid into Utah.

The railroads were racing for wealth. In 1862 Congress had fixed the junction point at the California State line; in 1864 the junction was moved 150 miles east; in 1866, getting the spirit of the thing, Congress provided that the railroads might build until they met. Cash subsidies for every completed mile of track were an immediate windfall, and the land grants were of incalculable value. The Union Pacific graded as far west as Humboldt Wells, in central Nevada, while the Central Pacific graded as far east as Echo, Utah. At many points the two grades ran side by side. The U. P.'s unruly Irishmen scowled upon the moon-faced, slant-eyed coolies the C. P. had imported from China, and riotous skull-cracking set in. The Chinese were slight, but built like whipcord steel, with a wholesome knack for pickhandle free-for-alls. To vary the monotony, the Irishmen commenced firing their blasts without warning the lean yellow men on the adjacent C. P. grade; the poker-faced Chinese buried the remnants with due respect for the souls of the departed, and blasted a dozen Irishmen into eternity. This fun was too strenuous, and ceased by mutual consent. Meanwhile the tracklayers stormed on, east and west. Through the early spring of 1869, it began to look as though the Union Pacific had settled upon San Francisco as its terminus, while the Central Pacific seemed enamored of the Missouri River. Congress settled the argument in April, fixing Promontory as the point of junction. Tracklaying was finished May 2, and the stage was set for driving the final spikes. Special trains set out from east and west; the first, from California, arrived May 7 to find that the ceremony must be delayed some days; the dignitaries frowned out the train windows upon Promontory, "drenched and forlorn in a driving rain, its sodden streets an extensive mudhole, colored bunting hanging limp and dripping across the facades of its wooden shacks." Held up by floods, the U. P. special train did not arrive until Monday, May 10.

The time was not passed in idle waiting. Both the Central Pacific and the Union Pacific, as Oscar Lewis relates with gusto in *The Big Four,* "recognized that the company building a siding at Promontory would have an advantage in the future control of the settlement. . . . A hundred miles back, a [Central Pacific] work-train had been made up, loaded with men and materials; only the storm delayed execution of the coup. Sunday night the rain ceased and the sky cleared. The Central construction train moved from the rear, timed to reach Promontory at daybreak. It arrived on schedule—and was greeted by derisive shouts from Casement's Irish track-layers. They had been working all night; the Union Pacific siding was completed."

For hours, in an icy wind, the celebrants waited. Two magnificent special trains were to have arrived from east and west to touch iron noses. Instead, battered construction trains rolled in loaded to bursting with pop-eyed graders, track-layers, and teamsters. The morning went by; noon passed, and the early afternoon hours—where was the Union Pacific special? Strong words began to pass among the onlookers. At last the screech of the Union Pacific whistle was heard, and the special rolled into Promontory to the sound of ironical cheers. Out of it piled U. P. officials and guests, several companies of the 21st Infantry, and the Camp Douglas regimental band. The soldiers were mustered as police to force some semblance of order upon the crowd. A more motley five hundred than the Golden Spike audience could hardly have been gathered. Shoulder to shoulder stood "Irish and Chinese laborers, teamsters, cooks, engineers, train crews, officials, guests, and parties of excursionists from California and Salt Lake City." There was also a generous admixture of strumpets, saloon-keepers, and gamblers, who did not get into the history books. Mormon representatives included John Sharp, C. R. Savage (the pioneer photographer whose picture of the meeting of the trains has been reproduced in history books throughout the country), E. T. Benson, Robert T. Burton, and T. B. H. Stenhouse, the latter there to report the affair quite inaccurately for his *Salt Lake Daily Telegraph,* which had just been transplanted to Ogden. Brigham Young had sent his regrets.

Special ties and spikes had been prepared for the ceremony. A Nevada representative presented a silver spike; from Arizona came a spike "ribbed with iron, clad in silver, and crowned with gold"; from Idaho and Montana, spikes of gold and silver. Most important of the ceremonial spikes was the "gold spike"—in reality not one spike but two, presented by David Hewes of San Francisco. While a nation listened, the telegraph operator tapped out the tale of proceedings. "We have got done praying," he presently reported; "the spike is about to be presented." For an hour spikes were presented and received while the crowd shifted from one collective foot to the other. The spike driving, into a polished tie of California laurel, commenced at last. Lest the spikes be flattened out by some honest blow, holes had been bored to receive the fabulous nails; for almost an hour distinguished guests hammered away with a silver maul. Finally the gold spike was placed, a telegraph line attached to it, and another to the silver hammer, so that the actual blows might ring out telegraphically to the nation. California's Governor Leland Stanford raised his hammer and swung a mighty blow. He missed the spike entirely, but the telegraph operator, a man of practical foresight, simulated the blow with his key and let tumult loose upon the cities of the country; fire bells, cannon, and factory whistles joined with shouting human voices to signalize the linkage of a continent. At Promontory the two locomotives gingerly nosed their cowcatchers together. To the world the telegrapher tapped out a lean and beautiful message:

> The last rail is laid.
> The last spike is driven.
> The Pacific railroad is finished.

Stanford, Dodge, and the other dignitaries clambered into the Central Pacific special trains where, as Dodge records, "many speeches were made."

Behind the Union Pacific engine at Promontory lay 1,085.5 miles of track; behind the Central Pacific "iron horse" lay 690 miles. To bring its rails from Omaha to Promontory had cost the Union Pacific $90,000,000; with much the harder job in crossing the Sierras, it had cost the Central Pacific $75,000,000 to come from Sacramento to the junction. Promontory was unequal to the responsibility of adding up $165,000,000 of railroad construction work, and the junction was soon moved to Ogden. Promontory was maintained as a railroad siding, but water had to be brought from Ogden or Corinne, and the town crumbled. Dry farming and successful artesian wells dug in the last years of the century revivified the region, but completion of the Lucin Cutoff across Great Salt Lake in 1903 robbed the town almost completely of its railroad importance. The Southern Pacific, successor to the C. P., for many years ran a weekly train along the old Golden Spike route, more to keep the route alive for military reasons than for profit, but in April, 1940, the railroad company announced abandonment of regularly scheduled train service, and the historic steel highway was to be used only for carload freight service on Wednesdays, when the service was requested by shippers. The gray glory of the past alone remains to vivify the windy summit on the Promontory Range.

Brigham Young, disappointed when he learned that the two railroads forming the transcontinental line would not meet in Salt Lake City, set out to build branch roads within the State. The Utah Central Railway from Salt Lake City to Ogden was completed in 1870, the Utah Southern from Salt Lake City to Draper in 1871 (and an extension south to Milford by 1880), and the Utah Northern from Ogden to Logan in 1873 and to Silver Bow, Montana, in 1880. The Utah Central and Utah Northern now form part of the Oregon Short Line (affiliated with Union Pacific), which connects Salt Lake City with Montana points.

Although the first railroads served large areas in Utah, the mountainous regions were still dependent upon more primitive transportation. About 1869, ore produced by the Emma Mine at Alta was "rawhided" to the mouth of Little Cottonwood Canyon. The process of "rawhiding" consisted of loading ore into green skins and using horses to drag it down to the nearest road, where it could be transferred to ox-drawn wagons and hauled to the railroad terminal at Ogden.

The development of mining, however, soon resulted in the extension of rail service to the mountains. One of the first ore-hauling lines was completed in 1880, when the Utah Eastern Railway established a line from Coalville to Park City. In 1883 the Denver and Rio Grande began operating between Salt Lake City and Grand Junction, Colorado; in 1903 the Southern Pacific built the Lucin Cutoff (*see Great Salt Lake*) across Great Salt Lake; and in 1905 southern California was linked to Utah by the San Pedro, Los Angeles, and Salt Lake Railroad. In 1940 Utah was served by four major railway systems: the Union Pacific, the Southern Pacific, the Western Pacific, and the Denver & Rio Grande Western. Branch lines serve local needs and operate as parts of the larger systems. Electric railways appeared in Utah toward the close of the nineteenth century, and there were, in 1940, four interurban lines operating in the central and northern parts of the State.

From Salt Lake City electric trains travel northward to Ogden, Logan, and Preston, Idaho; southward to Provo and Payson; and westward to Magna and Garfield.

Since 1900, when the first gasoline automobile in Utah bumped over the rough roads between Ogden and Salt Lake City, there has been increasing emphasis on highway building and improvements. A concrete road, the first of its kind in the State, was built from Tremonton to Garland in 1912; it was eight feet wide and three miles long. What might be termed the first modern highway in Utah was the Salt Lake City to Ogden road, portions of which were paved in 1915 by convict labor. The highway across the Salt Desert, built in 1925, used a new principle in highway engineering (*see Tour 6c*). In 1940, six Federal highways traversed the State, and a network of graded roads gave access to small towns and recreation areas. As an outgrowth of highway improvement, truck and bus transportation developed rapidly in Utah. In 1910 trucks began hauling goods to and from mountainous districts not served by rail. A decade later many of the mining companies were transporting ore in fleets of large trucks. About 1913 the moving and transfer companies were born, and in a few years were offering serious competition to the railroads. In addition to motorized freight service, Utah has a network of bus lines providing transportation to every important town in the State. Because of great distances to be covered, Utah ranks high among western States in ownership of passenger automobiles.

With the advent of the airplane, the Salt Lake airport assumed a focal position as the chief junction point in the intermountain area. In 1920, when travel by air was in its infancy, the Federal government routed its first national airmail line through Salt Lake City. Commercial planes began to transport passengers to and from Utah in 1926, and by 1940 the business had grown to a schedule of thirty planes a day. Airlines operate in five directions out of the Salt Lake airport, Utah's only commercial terminal, which handles the seventh largest number of passengers in the country. The third largest volume of airmail, popularly used in the West because of the great distances, is handled at the same important airline junction. Emergency landing fields and beacon lights have increased the safety of the airways, but the mountainous topography of Utah is still a hazard to flying. In 1937 a giant airliner crashed in the mountains east of Salt Lake City, killing crew and passengers. The accident occurred in such a remote area that plane and victims were not found for several months, and Salt Lake City newspapers reported recovery of the bodies by "pigeon express," using carrier pigeons. As a result of this disaster, and another that happened about the same time as the wrecked ship was found, the Civil Aeronautics Authority ruled that no pilot should fly lower than his mountain-top visibility. The airlines voluntarily increased flight levels to give pilots a 3,000-foot margin of safety in flying over peaks on the Salt Lake run, and lines operating into Utah participated with others the country over in a non-fatality year in 1939.

Water transportation has never been important in arid Utah, but its history is peculiar. Attempts have been made to operate freight and passenger boats on Great Salt Lake, but its heavy, briny waters usually pound boats to pieces (*see Great Salt Lake*). It has been traversed by explorers in bull boats and by Frémont's patent rubber boat, but it remains a unique and intractable body of water, traveled by a relatively few pleasure craft and by the small, businesslike motorboats of the Lucin Cutoff safety patrol. Utah's rivers do not lend themselves to navigation, but many explorers, scientists, and thrill-seekers have journeyed down the swift, canyon-walled Green and Colorado rivers (*see Tour 7a*). Tourist adventure trips are possible on these rivers and on the San Juan (*see Tour 10*).

Utah's transportation, in the main, has followed the norm for many western States, from buffalo trail to concrete highway and hitch-hiker, from dog travois to silver mainliner. The State has witnessed the advent of pipe lines as a means of subterranean transportation for water, gas, and oil, and in 1940 was considering the same method of moving coal, ground dust-fine and suspended in liquid to give it motility. It could then be sold as pulverized fuel or briquetted into popular sizes. The State has had one ingenious transport development that may be unique, the dog-powered "houndmotive"—a dog hitched to a railroad handcar—which developed as a result of isolation, plus a railroad (*see Great Salt Lake*). However, there are still vast areas in the State, with long distances between water, that can be reached only on horse-back or with a pack train, the same method used by Escalante.

Education

APEAKED military tent was Utah's first schoolhouse, and Mary J. Dilworth, 17, a Mormon of Quaker descent, the first teacher of a day school that opened in October, 1847, some three months after the vanguard of Mormon emigrants pitched camp in Salt Lake Valley. She had thirty scholars of assorted ages, a Noah Webster speller, half a dozen Lindly Murray readers, one arithmetic book, and a Bible. The following spring, Hannah Holbrook opened a similar school somewhere near the site of Bountiful, and though they are but indifferently recorded, other schools appeared in almost all of the settlements during the next two years. They seem to have been run on a haphazard basis, whenever the exigencies of plowing, weather, and house building would permit. Miss Dilworth, Utah's first schoolmistress, apparently had accomplishments in fields other than pedagogics, for her name, after the season of 1847, disappears from the roster of Utah teachers (*see Tour 1A*).

In 1850, the *Deseret News* announced with considerable pride that "Elder Woodruff has arrived with two tons of school books," and in the same year the legislative assembly of the Provisional State of Deseret empowered the city councils of the already numerous Mormon settlements to "establish, support, and regulate" common schools. This law, ratified without change by the Territorial legislature, seems to have been tentatively aimed at a free school system supported by local tax levies, and many villages did, in the first flush of civic pride, attempt to support their schools wholly by tax. Ogden, for example, voted such a tax, but the assessor and collector reported at the end of 1852 that the city had been unable to collect the money, "owing to the scarcity of it." Other communities found themselves in the same predicament, and, for a time at least, the public school system of Utah was forced to operate on a tuition basis. It was not until 1866 that the first free school was established at American Fork. The villagers in most cases had no more money for tuitions than for taxes, and early teachers were more accustomed to trundle wages home in barrows than to carry them in their pockets. Nevertheless, a schoolhouse was usually among the first considerations of new communities, and the legislature passed compulsory attendance laws as early as 1852. Minor apprentices must be sent to school at least three months out of the year, and this was also the case for indentured Indians between the ages of seven and sixteen.

The legislature of 1850 passed also an ordinance incorporating the "University of Deseret," and placed control of it in the hands of a chancellor and board of twelve regents. A month after passage of the act, the board of regents solemnly announced to:

PATRONS OF LEARNING:
The citizens of the State of Deseret have established a University at Great Salt Lake City. . . . It . . . will teach all nations all useful arts and sciences . . . instruction by means of lectures or otherwise will be brought to the level of the laboring classes. . . . It is neither arrogant nor extravagant to say that this institution is forthwith prepared to teach more living languages classically, than any other University on the face of the earth . . . as to the matter of dead languages, we leave them mostly to the dead. Facilities for acquiring intelligence from every portion of the globe will be more perfectly secured to this institution than to any other of our acquaintence. Correspondence will be kept up with persons in the service of the University, living at London, Edinburgh, Paris, Rome, Copenhagen and Calcutta.
Whatever is valuable in the laws and usages of nations . . . diversified languages . . . practical mechanism . . . fabrics of governments . . . physical laws . . . will be copiously poured into the lap of this institution.

This paragon of universities opened in the parlor of John Pack's adobe cabin, November, 1850, under the name of Parent School. The *Deseret News* for the same month said that the object of the school was "to qualify teachers for the district or ward schools." Hubert H. Bancroft, in his *History of Utah,* takes the name literally and says that it was for the heads of families, which may have been the case for there is a legend among Utah historians that Brigham Young himself registered for classes. The prophet's position was, as always, a practical one. He wished to see a uniform and efficient system of common schools, and afterward to talk about higher education. The legislature of 1851 appropriated $5,000 for the university—from an empty treasury—hopefully memorialized Congress for a like sum in 1854, and became discouraged. The Parent School was abandoned in 1855, and the university was suffered to lapse into nominal existence until 1867. Common schools (which loosely comprised the grammar grades) were more fortunate. By 1854, there were 226 of them in Utah Territory, about 13,000 scholars, and three hundred-odd teachers, not a few of whom were of the Ichabod Crane stamp. The *Deseret News* (still championing the cause of education) in that year observed that it was "high time to turn a little attention, and means towards hiring good teachers at fair salaries and prompt pay." Five years later, Richard F. Burton observed in *City of the Saints* that "A certain difficulty exists in finding instructors," and that to turn schoolmaster was "about equivalent to coming upon the parish." Kate B. Carter, in *Frontier Schools and Schoolmasters,* adds that those "who were physically unable to do heavy work were engaged to teach." The *News* undertook a persistent campaign to rectify the evils arising from such principles of selection. The editors had no objection to "a teacher using a portion of his leisure time at a party or a dance, or other innocent amusement," but felt that he should retire before 10 P.M., and that he should spend the major portion of his leisure "posting up." The legislature of 1855 authorized the university chancellor and board of regents to appoint a superintendent of public schools "to ensure a uniformity of books, subjects, and system of school government," and at the same time empowered county courts to appoint "three competent men" to determine qualifications of teachers within their precincts. The long distances between Mormon villages and their consequent autonomy virtually nullified these ordinances. It was not until 1876 that all counties could report a board of examiners, and not until 1919 that a State board had power enough to extend uniform educational practices throughout the public school system.

In outlying regions, school seldom "kept" more than six months of the year, and three months would probably come closer to the average. During the first three decades after settlement of Utah, the city council of many a town went on record as being unalterably opposed to "female" teachers. One Mr. Chadwick, pioneer schoolmaster of Eureka, "always carried a six shooter in his pocket when in the school room," according to I. E. Diehl's manuscript, *Tintic.* The ubiquitous Burton owned Mormon education to be "peculiar. . . . At fifteen a boy can use a whip, an axe, or a hoe—he does not like the plow—to perfection. He sits a bare-backed horse like a Centaur, handles his bowie-knife skillfully, never misses a mark with his revolver. . . . With regards to book-work, there is no difficulty to obtain in Great Salt Lake City that 'mediocrity of knowledge between learning and ignorance' which distinguished the grammar schools of the Western Islands in the days of Samuel Johnson. . . . Everyone learns to read and write," though the Mormons had discovered that "the time of school drudgery may profitably be abridged. A boy, they say, will learn all that his memory can carry during three hours of book-work, and the rest had far better he spent in air, exercise, and handicraft." Burton concludes that the purpose behind Mormon education was "to rear a swarm of healthy working bees. The social hive has as yet no room for drones, book-worms, and gentlemen."

Public school support until 1874 came wholly from local taxes—"local" being almost universally coextensive with "town"—and from tuitions, but between 1874 and 1878, the legislature made regular appropriations of lump sums to be apportioned on a school-age per capita basis among the various districts, and in 1878 inaugurated a Territorial tax for a permanent school fund. Generous land grants, both Territorial and Federal, had been made for the public school system between 1850 and 1870, but it was not until after 1870 that title to Utah lands began to be granted. The meager income obtained from taxing a people without any cash, and from tuitions paid in produce, besides barely affording to support a teacher for three or four months at best, would not permit construction of schoolhouses unless they served as community meeting places. The Territorial superintendent of common schools reported in 1857 that there were "log school houses in most of the settlements, most of which had slab seats, some of which had very long legs, doing a double duty among the rising and risen generations." The ward or community chapel of the Mormon Church frequently served as a school on weekdays, a town hall on election days, and a meeting house on Sundays. The quality of instruction in such schools, plus the inadvertent creeping in of doctrine in communities where the school and the Church were scarcely to be distinguished, led in the 1870's to establishment of a number of denominational schools. Completion of the transcontinental railway in 1869 brought to Utah a substantial non-Mormon population which was in no way disposed to have its children reared in "Mormon dominated" schools. Moreover, Mormon-Gentile antagonism was rapidly approaching crescendo, and there were those among the critics of Mormonism who felt that the most effective method of undermining the Mormon position was through education. Denominational schools grew so rapidly that in 1888 the Territorial commissioner of schools reported (almost with alarm) a total of 99 such institutions, of which but six were Mormon. In 1894 there were 113 of them; the Mormons in the meantime "having bestirred themselves," had 26, the Congregationalists 33, the Presbyterians 33, and the Methodists 21, the rest being distributed among Catholics, Lutherans, Baptists, and Episcopalians.

Many private schools had appeared during the earliest days, especially in Salt Lake City. As early as 1852 the Polysophical Society offered high school courses, with gymnastics and military training for young men and music and drawing for young ladies. Orson Pratt's Science School was especially remarkable because it taught college courses. Such schools were in the main ephemeral, seldom lasting more than a year or two, while the denominational schools of the 1870's and 1880's were established on a more or less permanent basis. Moreover, the denominational schools had nine- and ten-month school terms, and the best instruction they could obtain. They began at common school levels, but soon pushed into preparatory school work, and were undoubtedly instrumental in forcing development of colleges. The public school system had not, as late as 1884, any high schools. The Territorial superintendent of common schools, in that year, reported "an apparent necessity of schools of a grade between the district schools and the University," and the legislature gave districts having more than 1,200 population powers to establish "a graded school, or a graded department within a school . . . in which pupils may be instructed in higher branches of education than those usually taught in the common school."

Whether the denominational schools had a direct bearing on Utah colleges or not, the University of Deseret was revived in 1867 and placed under Dr. John R. Park two years later. In 1869 Dr. Park established a normal department and a training school and though until 1890 most of the University students were on high school levels, the schools of law, medicine, education, and mining followed rapidly. In 1892, the name was changed to University of Utah and in 1900 the institution was moved to its present site on the broad East Bench of Salt Lake City. In 1875, the Mormon Church "called" Dr. Karl G. Maeser to establish Brigham Young Academy (renamed Brigham Young University in 1903) at Provo. The school originally granted teachers' certificates for one year's work, later gave two-year normal certificates and the degree of Bachelor of Pedagogy on completion of four years' work. In the 1890's, William K. Reid of Sanpete reported that his county had a "great many very good teachers and a few bad ones." Most of the early teachers were graduates of Brigham Young Academy or the University of Utah. Utah was turning out its own teachers. In 1875, also, the Presbyterian Church founded the Salt Lake Collegiate Institute, which subsequently became Westminster College, and in the same year the Catholic Church established Saint Mary's Academy in Salt Lake City. In the 1880's the Mormon Church founded Brigham Young College at Logan. In the midst of all this college-making, the Morrill Act of 1862 bore fruit, and the Utah State Agricultural College was established at Logan as a land-grant school.

The presence of many institutions of higher learning seems to have had a reciprocal effect on the lower levels. The comprehensive school law of 1890 made all common schools free. No official provision was made for a Territory-wide system of preparatory schools, but the cities of Salt Lake and Ogden had high schools already, and the towns of

Nephi and Eureka followed in 1894-95. The constitutional convention of 1895 engaged itself with a prolonged quibble over the status of high schools. Dr. Maeser, delegate from Provo, headed a bloc that wished, in the interest of common schools, to exclude high schools from participating in the State school fund. There were not, at that late date, sufficient funds in many districts to maintain free common schools more than six months out of the year. Free high school advocates, however, won a partial battle. Districts which already had them (Salt Lake City and Ogden) were permitted to retain them. Elsewhere they were to be established and supported wholly by local tax, if at all, in spite of the eloquence of Mr. Thurman, delegate from Provo, who argued that "the time may come that we will find we have reached that degree of perfection or advancement that the children everywhere in the Territory at 16 will be out of the common school, or ready to advance."

In 1910 the State legislature voted a special tax for support of high schools, and the following year authorized counties to "consolidate" for high school purposes. In 1930, encouraged by a generous State fund and by consolidation of districts, the high school system could show an enrollment of almost 81 per cent of high school-age students, as against a national average of 57.3 per cent. Breakdown of secondary education into a junior-senior high school organization began somewhat timidly in 1908. Ogden's school superintendent, John M. Mills, was already convinced of the superiority of the junior-senior division, and when circumstances presented him with an assistant superintendent having no duties, an empty schoolhouse, and over-crowded grammar schools, he withdrew his eighth grades from the grammar schools, placed them in the empty building under supervision of his assistant, and gave his invention the name "Sub-High School." The following year he added the seventh grade and in 1915 the ninth grade. In 1918, Ogden's board of education succeeded in ousting Mills but not his system. Since 1925, the 6-3-3 plan of lower education increased in favor, until in 1930 many districts employed it.

Except for a brief "reaction against reactionism" in the universities during the decade before the World War and an occasional flare-up of sectarian antagonism, the progress of education in Utah has been consistent since 1910. Three professors resigned in 1911 from the faculty of Brigham Young University because they could not "conscientiously restrict" their teachings as their trustees requested, and a few years later the University of Utah precipitated a near-Nationwide scandal when seventeen members of the faculty resigned in protest of the dismissal of three professors whose only crime was, according to the American Association of University Professors, to have been moderately outspoken. Continued pressure brought passage of a law in 1921 which (exhaustively) declared that "no atheistic, infidel, sectarian, religious, or denominational doctrines" are to be taught in Utah's public schools. Since 1922, the Mormon policy has been to withdraw from the field of secondary and grammar school institutions. The present policy of the Mormon Church is to establish "seminaries" adjacent to high school campuses, where Mormon theology may be taught. The two universities, together with the Agricultural College, offer the degrees of Master of Arts and Master of Science. The universities are supplemented by five State and two private junior colleges, Branch Agricultural College at Cedar City, Carbon Junior College at Price, Snow College at Ephraim, Weber College at Ogden, Dixie College at St. George (the last three were turned over gratis to the public school system by the Mormon Church during the 1930's), the Catholic St. Mary of the Wasatch, and the Presbyterian Westminster College. Custodial schools for deaf, blind, feeble-minded, and delinquent minors have been established since the turn of the century. In 1940, the Utah State Art Center, co-operating with the Exceptional Child Guidance Group of Utah, inaugurated art classes for spastic children, pioneering in the use of painting as a therapeutic aid to children who suffer from faulty muscular co-ordination. The Adult Education Project of the Work Projects Administration had in 1940 some 56,000 on its rolls, and was doing valuable work with its Americanization courses for aliens seeking citizenship. In 1930, the State legislature established an equalization fund which in 1940 had done much toward standardization of public schools. The act specifies that the "sum of $5 per census-child shall be raised annually" to equalize the costs of education throughout the State—which is to say, if a district is poor and cannot of its own accord maintain schools as good as those of a better-to-do district, it may draw from the equalization fund. The uniform school fund, set aside by the legislature in 1937 and 1939, further equalizes educational opportunity in the State.

𐐢𐐇𐐝𐐤 III.

Page from Deseret Second Reader, Used in Utah Schools Before the Railroad Broke Down Mormon Isolation

𐐜 𐐔𐐯𐑅𐐨𐑉𐐯𐐻 𐐰𐑊𐑁𐐩𐐺𐐯𐐻.

Long Sounds.			Letter.	Name.	Sound.
Letter.	**Name.**	**Sound.**	𐐑	p	
𐐀	e	as in *e*at.	𐐒	b	
𐐁	a	" *a*te.	𐐓	t	
𐐂	ah	" *a*rt.	𐐔	d	
𐐃	aw	" *au*ght.	𐐕	che	as in *chee*se.
𐐄	o	" *o*at.	𐐖	g	
𐐅	oo	" *oo*ze.	𐐗	k	
Short Sounds of the above.			𐐘	ga	as in *ga*te.
𐐆		as in *i*t.	𐐙	f	
𐐇		" *e*t.	𐐚	v	
𐐈		" *a*t.	𐐛	eth	as in *th*igh.
𐐉		" *o*t.	𐐜	the	" *th*y
𐐊		" *u*t.	𐐝	s	
𐐋		" b*oo*k.	𐐞	z	
Double Sounds.			𐐟	esh	as in fle*sh*.
𐐌	i	as in *i*ce.	𐐠	zhe	" vi*s*ion.
𐐍	ow	" *ow*l.	𐐡	ur	" b*ur*n.
𐐏	ye		𐐢	l	
𐐎	woo		𐐣	m	
𐐐	h		𐐤	n	
			𐐥	eng	as in le*ng*th.

Deseret Alphabet, Compiled by Mormon Scholars in the 1850's

Recreation

U TAH people are said to be the greatest campers and picnickers in the world. Nearly every family has a smoke-blackened coffee pot and skillet, a brace of wire grills, a set of oversize spoons. and tinware suited to rough usage and large helpings in the open. The geographic basis for this proclivity is easy to find. Utah is an arid State, and nearly everybody, whether a city or rural dweller, lives at the mouth of a canyon, from which the family-size or city-size water supply is obtained. On hot summer evenings or weekends it is customary to toss a camp or picnic outfit in the family car and go where canyon breezes blow, or where increased altitude provides relief from the heat. The ten national forests and the eleven national parks and monuments provide recreation for residents mainly in proportion to their distance from populous centers, though more distant areas have a way of achieving popularity for hunting and fishing.

The Wasatch National Forest, being nearest to Salt Lake City, draws most visitors—in the neighborhood of 200,000 every year. About 150,000 of these are picnickers, spending only a day at a time; most of the remainder are weekend campers. The forest is also popular as a summer home site, and for fishing and winter sports. The four widespread units of Fishlake National Forest attract more than 110,000 visitors per year, and serve the recreational uses of a considerable population in southern Utah. As the name indicates, it is the most popular fishing area, and has the greatest number of hotel and resort guests. Cache National Forest, checkered about the northern end of Utah's population axis, draws more than 75,000 visitors yearly, and has the largest concentration of summer cottages. Minidoka National Forest, in the northwestern corner of the State, has only 600 or 700 visitors a year, most of them hunters.

Away from the cluster of communities that line the central axis of the State, Utah is still essentially frontier—with, perhaps, the rough edges knocked off, the old pony trails sometimes widened into dubious roads, and an occasional iron-lidded stove competing with Indian fire pits. The best sports the State offers are of the frontier breed, the kind that "take a good eye and make a flat belly." Hunting and fishing of one kind or another extend throughout the year and account for about 65 per cent of the money spent for recreation in Utah; winter sports, skiing, skating, and tobogganing last from November to May; water sports are best in the summer and fall, though some, such as the descent of the Colorado River, may be engaged in during the winter months; trips into the mountains, whether by car, pack train, or afoot, may be undertaken from April to November without serious discomfort; trips into the desert regions are possible at any time, but are most comfortable in the spring or fall. Water should be carried where camping on the desert is contemplated.

The major cities all have golf courses, tennis courts, swimming pools, tournaments, and the other adjuncts of cosmopolitan recreation, and there are few places in the State where there is not a quiet hotel, lodge, or private home that will "take in" guests who want to live in the tranquillity of the rural West for a week or two. Utah, Bear and Great Salt Lake have bathing beaches and boat moorings; there are skiing facilities in the mountains adjacent to Salt Lake City, Ogden, Logan, and Provo; and there are picnic grounds with pure water supplies in most of the canyons that can be reached by car.

Although the tourist is no novelty in Utah, recreation as a significant economic factor is a comparatively recent development. The Utah State Planning Board estimates that from a nominal figure in 1900 the income from recreational traffic has grown to $12,000,000 annually, an advance due mainly to the building of good roads into and through the State and the establishment of national parks and monuments in the scenic and recreational regions. Bryce Canyon and Zion National Parks are best known and most visited, both by residents and visitors.

Hunting: With more than eight million acres of forest reserve and many millions more of near-wilderness rich in game, Utah offers excellent opportunities to those who vacation with a gun. The variety of game ranges from elk to squirrel, with many species of pest and predatory animals. Both hunters and game are protected by regulations, game laws are simple, and the expense of licenses and special fees is not exorbitant. Those who have tried all the State has to offer agree that top hunting is for the big mule deer which abound from one end of Utah to the other in such numbers that stockmen periodically accuse them of depleting the range. Deer hunters generally form parties of from six to ten men, complete with pup tents and beer, and drive or pack into the hunting areas for a week of shooting and yarning. A visiting hunter is generally welcome into one of these companies, and if he joins one is almost assured a chance at his buck; guides and pack outfits can be hired in villages adjacent to the hunting regions. Many towns, as Beaver in southern Utah, stage an all-night shindig the night before the season opens, whence hunters are reputed to proceed tenderly into the canyons for a day or two of recuperation. Deer are plentiful along the whole course of the Uinta, Wasatch, Pahvant, Tushar, Pine Valley, Abajo, and Blue mountains, and in the plateau area of Powell National Forest. In the northern part of the State the deer are larger, in the southern, smaller but more numerous. If the season opens early, the best hunting is high, near timber line; if fall snows have begun, in the canyons and valleys. It is estimated that hunters spend an average of about $50 for every deer taken in Utah.

Elk are fairly numerous in the mountains as far south as Salina, and may be hunted at irregular seasons by obtaining a special license from the Fish and Game Commission in the State Capitol. The number of elk licenses is limited; if the number of applications exceeds it, licenses are awarded by lot. The big fellows dress as high as 600 pounds and their meat surpasses venison, and some say beef, both in texture and flavor. The average cost of elk meat to Utah hunters runs around $6 a pound. Cinnamon bears are common in all the high mountain ranges, and since they are classed as predatory, may be hunted at any time, though the pelts are best in the late fall, before hibernation. The meat is edible, but old-timers, at the prospect of a bear steak, quote the frontier recipe: "Take two pounds of meat from the rump, boil three days in a deep kettle with the head of an axe, and, then, throw away the meat and eat the axe."

The mountain lion is, next to the coyote, the most common of the larger predatory animals in Utah. They are seldom seen unless started by a pack of trained lion dogs (see *Tour 2b*). The coyote, the predator of the west and the wise old man of Indian mythology, is fair game any time, and harder to hit than any other western animal. Their dun color and smooth stride make them almost invisible against desert brush and the undergrowth of forests, and their cunning enables them to travel all day within a few yards of a hunter without once intruding into his vision. Among the lesser animals, jack rabbits, badgers, wood-chuck, and gophers are numerous, but are suitable only for "potting," and are not classed as game. Bobcats, mink, muskrats, and beaver are more easily trapped than hunted. Antelope and bighorn sheep are still occasionally found, but they are protected at all times.

The best duck hunting is in the marshes that border the lakes and major rivers, especially those on the northern and eastern shores of Great Salt Lake. Bear River Migratory Bird Refuge is on two of the main duck flyways, and the public shooting grounds adjacent to the refuge yield limit bags. The public shooting grounds in Millard County and on the Green River near Jensen are equally popular with hunters, but being distant from the center of population are less frequented. The duck season is controlled by the Federal government, and it is necessary to have a Federal duck stamp in addition to the regular license. Ringnecked pheasants, introduced into Utah about 1918 and very popular with hunters, have thrived in spite of heavy winters. They are protected by a very short open season, and occur in the greatest numbers in farming districts of central Utah. Good quail hunting is confined to Washington County and the Uintah Basin. Sage hen, ruffed grouse, and pine hen, have steadily lost ground as civilization encroached on their breeding and feeding grounds; they are protected the year round.

Fishing: Despite water shortage caused by the diversion of streams for irrigation and hydroelectric power, Utah has an annual trout catch in excess of 200,000 pounds. Fifty thousand fishermen take an average of four pounds each, and it is estimated that each angler spends $15 in the effort, which places the cost of game fish at $3.75 per pound. Native and brook trout are plentiful in the remote lakes and headwaters; rainbows, German browns, and mountain herring are more frequently found in stocked waters; catfish, carp, and suckers are common wherever streams enter the lower valleys. The San Juan, Green, and Colorado teem with catfish and a species of whitefish, locally called "minnows," that attain weights up to thirty pounds. Fly fishing is popular, though the heavy undergrowth along many of the streams makes casting difficult. Lake trolling with fifty yards of light line and a small spinner is top sport when the two-pounders bite. In northern Utah, Strawberry Reservoir, Moon Lake, and Mirror Lake are favorite trout waters. In the High Uintas Primitive Area, the Grandaddy Lakes and some 700 unnamed lakes and ponds afford excellent opportunities for creel limits to fishermen who do not mind a short hike or a pack trip. No roads have been or will be built into this area, and many of the lakes and streams have been fished only a few times. The Weber River is renowned for its occasional "big ones," though the world record German brown trout, a twenty-five pound veteran, was taken from Logan River. Provo River, from the mouth of Provo Canyon to its headwaters in the Uintas, is the most frequently fished stream in the State. Within the forest reserves, almost any of the myriad small streams will yield trout from eight to fourteen inches long.

In the southern part of the State, Fish Lake, Puffer Lake, Panguitch Lake, Navaho Lake, Pine Valley Reservoir, and the ponds of Thousand Lake Mountain are the most popular waters. The head-waters of the Sevier River, though difficult to reach, make fine stream fishing. The streams draining into the Colorado River are usually too muddy for trout, but they yield good catches of catfish and whitefish. The increased interest in fishing among Utah sportsmen has made neces-sary a rigid control of all waters. However, the creel and cumulative limits are generous and the season on game fish is a long one, usually from June through October. Specific dates and special regulations are printed on licenses or are posted on waters affected by them.

Winter Sports: Utah's winter lasts all year in many of the high *ranges.* Mount Timpanogos has a "glacier" that never thaws, and elsewhere in the State there are perpetual snows that can be used in a pinch for skiing and tobogganing. Normally, the season lasts from November to May for skiing, skating, and tobogganing; bobsled parties, traditional to rural America, begin whenever the farmers exchange wheels for runners on their wagons and hayracks. Though skiing in Utah has been on an organized basis only since 1925 and the develop-ment of ski areas has been slight, the mountains from the north to the south boundary are admirably suited to the sport. The winter climate is dry, with a preponderance of clear days; "powder snow" is the rule rather than the exception above the 7,000-foot level, where the best ski trails and facilities are found; and the improved ski areas are easily reached by car or bus. Alta, Brighton, and Park City, in the mountains one hour east of Salt Lake City, reached by different roads, are con-nected by a network of ski trails, cleared and widened at the turns. Brighton and Park City offer overnight accommodations, Alta has a Forest Service lodge. The Alta chair lift attains a vertical altitude of 700 feet above the lower terminal, carrying skiers to the crest of a ridge, from which there are runs for any degree of skill. Ecker hill ski jump, in the Park City area, 310 feet from take-off to dip, with a slope of 58 degrees, is one of the largest in the nation, and has been used several times for national championships. Brighton is the special haven of those who take their skiing comfortably, with fireplace gossip and an occasional skating party on Silver Lake. Tony Grove near Logan, Farm Creek Mountain near Duchesne, Polehaven near Manti, and Horseshoe Mountain and Taylor Field near Ephraim, are regions with minor improvements. Information concerning snow conditions should be obtained in the nearest town before visiting them.

Boating: The western terrain is full of abrupt changes and the rivers that flow through it usually foam down between navigable stretches in cataracts where no boat could survive. The lakes are gen-erally small and frequented by fishermen rather than yachtsmen. How-ever, since the introduction of outboard motors and portable boats,

manna to the fishermen with a taste for trolling, the number of boats
in the State has multiplied many times. There are as yet no organized
outboard regattas, but sail and speed boat races are held each July
on Pine View Reservoir, in Ogden Canyon. Most of the sailing in
Utah is done by members of the Salt Lake Yacht Club, which dubs
itself the "saltiest on earth." The problem of attaining speed through
the dense waters of Great Salt Lake has encouraged development of
shell-draft centerboard sloops, which are raced at regattas sponsored
by the club. Completion of the Salt Lake Yacht Basin in 1939, with
slips to accommodate fifty boats, and all necessary facilities for launching
and maintaining them, and the possibilities for cruising on Great Salt
Lake, indicate that yachting is taking its place with other Utah sports.
Perhaps the best the State can offer boatmen is descent of the Colorado,
Green, and San Juan rivers. Since the 1870's, when Major John
Wesley Powell explored the Colorado from an armchair on the bow
deck of a flatboat, ambitious rivermen have been attempting to go him
one better (*see Tour 7a*). All three rivers have long smooth passages
through canyons and valleys whose only entrance is by the waterway,
a strange land and one worth visiting. Boat trips are run on charter
out of Moab, Bluff, and Mexican Hat (*see Tours 9 and 10*). Longer
downstream voyages are in the nature of expeditions and are usually
planned months ahead.

Hiking: The westerner, normally, walks to get somewhere that he
cannot get in an automobile or on horseback. Hiking for its own sake,
for the sheer animal pleasure of good condition and brisk exercise, is
not an easy thing for him to comprehend. But tourists and those
Utahns who are confined to cities have adopted the old Indian foot-
trails, or made new ones, as the best way to see the country intimately,
and as the only way to visit some regions. There are a few organized
hikes, the most notable being the ascent of Mount Timpanogos, which
is made by hundreds of people every July. Participants assemble at
Aspen Grove, high on the mountain, for ceremonies and a night's rest
before ascending the peak the next morning. Climbs up Mount Nebo
and the peaks about Brighton, though not so well known or attended
by so much ceremony as the Timpanogos hike, are popular with parties.
Within the national forests well-marked trails are provided for an
hour's hike or pack trips of two or three weeks' duration, and guides,
though convenient, are seldom necessary. Trips into the High Uintas
Primitive Area and the Badlands of the Colorado Plateau, however,
should never be undertaken by visitors without guides. Spectacular
or difficult hikes are rarely undertaken, though there are many peaks
in Utah above 11,000 feet that have not been scaled and many more
that have been conquered only a few times.

Riding and Packing: In Utah any trail too narrow for cars serves as a bridle path; to the old-timer any surface that will offer traction to a "broomtail," a diminutive, goat-footed desert pony, is a "hoss trail." Horsemen may ride for an hour or for weeks; may seek mountain scenery, or desert; may follow foolproof roads, or plunge into a wilderness with guides and a string of pack horses. The preferred saddle is the western, with a sturdy horn, large swells, and a deep cantle; they are more comfortable when the going is tough. Horses for short rides may be hired at renting academies in the larger cities, and in the less populous regions at a few dude ranches. Much of the State is accessible only to horsemen, as for example Rainbow Natural Bridge and the Kaiparowitz Plateau country. Other regions, where the roads are too rough for extended driving and the distance between water too great for hiking, are best seen from horseback. Pack trip expenses average about $2 per day per horse and $5 a day for a guide. Independents often buy horses for long trips. Mustangs, "Indian broke," that is to say with the surface orneriness knocked off, cost about $15, cowponies from $40 to $100, and burros may be had for the taking.

Press and Radio

ON June 15, 1850, under the motto "Truth and Liberty," the *Deseret News* proposed "to publish a small weekly sheet, as large as our local circumstances will permit." Local circumstances permitted a sheet about 7½ by 10 inches that cost $2.50 for six months, "invariably in advance." The paper was printed on a Ramage hand press, which Scipio Africanus Kenner, in *Utah As It Is,* says was "but little larger than a clothes wringer." Kenner adds that the Deseret News Building was "as easy to get on top of as into." The first issue was a newsy little morsel; it contained, besides its prospectus and divers sermons, an account of a fire in San Francisco, a commentary on the proceedings of Congress for the previous February, and well chosen bits of local news. Four months after these beginnings, the *News* sent out a desperate appeal for rags—its paper was exhausted and shipments from the Missouri were slow; however, no more than a few issues were skipped, and the subscribers, most of whom had paid with promissory notes or farm produce, remained loyal.

In 1858, *Kirk Anderson's Valley Tan,* published in Great Salt Lake City, but intended for consumption at Camp Floyd, entered the field as competitor to the *News*. Anderson was the first of a long series of anti-Mormon editors in Utah, and he regularly graced his editorial columns with such headings as "Complicity of Mormon Officials" and "An Incredible Catalog of Crime." There was some muttering among the brethren on the *News* concerning an editor who needed a detachment of the United States Army to back up his editorial policy, but no open violence. J. Cecil Alter, in *Early Utah Journalism,* published by the Utah State Historical Society, observes that "if the 'Danites' had been as vigilant and as efficient as Editor Anderson claimed

them to be, he would not have lasted through the first two issues."
In May of 1859, Anderson discreetly announced his departure after he
had gone, and his paper, with the name shortened to *Valley Tan,* after
"using up" half a dozen editors during the next six months, came into
the hands of one S. DeWolfe, who promptly announced that conservatism was at an end. Alter suggests that he was probably glad "when
the paper gave out" early in 1860. Kenner, in a delayed obituary,
attributes *Valley Tan*'s demise to its being "unable to exude its virus
as fast as the same was generated."

These two papers set the tempo for the next fifty years in Utah
journalism. The major papers of Utah Territory either stood vigor-
ously for or against Mormonism, and those hardy idealists who announced themselves "independent" either got off the fence or were
squeezed to death. Occasionally a paper managed to survive for a
time on an open editorial policy, but statistics show that eight newspapers "succumbed to the inevitable" for every one that was in existence
in 1940. Salt Lake City received the name "Journalistic Cemetery,"
and pessimistic editors more than once called Ogden the "Graveyard
of Western Journalism." Language was vigorous, because, as Alter
observes, editors usually "laid all the cards on the table so as to leave
their hands . . . free for more persuasive arguments!" The citizenry
at large retaliated as best they could. In 1879 Editor A. E. Howard
of the *Central Utah Press* ran in his best pica "This thing is becoming
awful. Nearly every newspaperman in the Territory during the past
year has received a terrible thrashing." Howard could think of only
three editors who, because of superior size and armament, had not been
visited by the vengeance of irate citizens.

The *Mountaineer,* which Sir Richard F. Burton said was considered "rather a secular paper" because it followed the motto "Do what
is right, let the consequences follow," lasted from 1859 to 1861, and
was succeeded by the *Vedette* in 1863 as chief gentile organ. When
the *Mormon Tribune* began publication at Salt Lake City in 1870,
the *Vedette* had been "extinct" for several years. In 1871, the *Deseret
News* noted that the *Tribune* had dropped Mormon "from the title as
well as from friendly consideration," and the two papers continued to
be the spearheads of an unpleasant editorial war until after the turn of
the century. A journalistic convention of the day was that the beginning and end of a newspaper be acknowledged, but there were no strings
on the character of the acknowledgement. In 1880 the *Deseret News*
noted the birth of the *Silver Reef Miner* at Leeds with high compli-
ments; the *Tribune* said merely, "Silver Reef Miner has been patted
on the head by Granny, who regards it as full in the faith." Until
1900, almost every paper that began and ended was patted on the
head by one of these two papers.

Outside of Salt Lake City, journalistic activity began somewhat late, but soon made up for lost time. The editor of *Our Dixie Times* announced his paper as the only one in Utah outside of the capital city in 1868—and in the same issue bemoaned postponement of his next issue until the mud dried on the California road. T. B. H. Stenhouse moved the *Salt Lake Telegraph and Commercial Advertiser* to Ogden in 1869, at the time the transcontinental railway came through; however, he returned to Salt Lake City the same year—a circumstance perhaps encouraged by injudicious retention of "Salt Lake" in the title of his paper. In the same year, James H. Beadle, one of the strongest-voiced early anti-Mormon editors, started the *Utah Reporter* at Corinne. Beadle was "terribly beaten" late in 1869 and in December announced that he had "left the Territory for his health." He returned the following year, but his second tenure was no longer than the first, and the tender condition of his health did not warrant a third appearance. His *Utah Reporter,* however, was a pioneer gentile paper, and the first daily in Utah outside of Salt Lake City. In 1870, the *Ogden Junction* appeared under the editorship of Charles W. Penrose, who in later years became editor of the *Deseret News.* About 1877 Penrose enlarged his staff with Scipio Africanus Kenner ("one of Brigham's greatest and smoothest liars," according to the *Salt Lake Tribune,* but nevertheless one of Utah's outstanding journalists). In the small city of Beaver, there began about 1873 a succession of newspapers, which led Alter to conclude that "more first class, two fisted, paying newspapers have flourished and died with their boots on in Beaver than in many other cities several times the size." The *Salt Lake Tribune* that year acknowledges "semi-occasional" receipt of the *Beaver Enterprise* and adds that it was a "fossil concern, muzzled by the priesthood." Almost all Utah towns of the 1870's and 1880's had more newspapers than they could support, and their journalistic history is an impossible tangle of editorial alignments and ownerships. Where no type was available, they were often issued as pen-and-ink manuscript, as the *Manti Herald,* the *Sanpitcher* of Mount Pleasant, and the *American Fork Gazette.* When paper was lacking the editors set up crude mills to convert rags— often the paper was so dark that the print could scarcely be read— or printed on wrapping paper.

Of the 585 papers which have appeared at one time or another in Utah very few have persisted. Salt Lake City had five energetic dailies in 1885; in 1940, though the population was five times as great, it had but three that were widely read. Ayer (1940) lists a total of sixty-five newspapers for the State, seven of them dailies. The *Deseret News* and the *Salt Lake Tribune,* the latter partly merged with the *Telegram* in 1928, have persisted long enough to see the old enmities buried. They are the most prominent papers in Utah, with the *Ogden*

Standard-Examiner and the *Provo Herald* modest seconds. The *Park City Record,* whose masthead has carried "S. L. Raddon, Editor," for fifty years, has set some kind of record for continuous service—though the *Provo Enquirer* in 1877 remarked pessimistically that the paper "had the Mormon rabies bad." In 1940, most of the towns of 2,000 and over had at least a weekly, though most of the weekly editors were still riding that antiquated pun "weakly"—and they apparently meant it. To explain the paucity of papers in towns of lesser population, there is a comment often made to country editors by reluctant subscribers— "You ask us for the news, then you print it and ask us to buy it."

Of the numerous Utah periodicals, the *Improvement Era, Instructor,* and *Relief Society Magazine,* published by the Mormon Church, and the *Utah Magazine* and *Rocky Mountain Review* are the most widely read. The Church magazines have a large circulation among out-of-State Mormons; the *Review* is a literary quarterly; the *Utah Magazine* is devoted mainly to articles on contemporary Utah.

Radio: There were eight radio stations in the State in 1940, of which three were in Salt Lake City. KSL, the first station in the State, made its initial broadcast in 1921; KDYL followed in 1922. KSL is the most powerful station in Utah. KLO, at Ogden, was broadcasting as early as 1924; KEUB, at Price, in 1936; KSUB, at Cedar City, in 1937; KVNU, at Logan, in 1938; KUTA, in Salt Lake City, in 1938; and KOVO, in Provo, in 1939. All eight stations are well patron-ized—the *Radio Guide* for 1940 lists Utah as having 90 radios for every 100 families.

The Arts

THE literature of Utah, like that of other frontier States, is marked rather by volume than by literary distinction, and is valuable chiefly as a part of the historical record of a time and an area. The published accounts of early explorers, trappers, scouts, leaders of Government expeditions, and homeseekers who crossed the Great Plains in covered wagons have the vividness of untutored and experimental writing. They are supplemented by a vast store of unpublished material, chiefly letters and diaries, that completed, if somewhat crudely, the impressive picture of a desert region transformed into a fertile land. Consciously literary pioneer works—whether poetry, fiction, biography, history, or literary criticism—were a curious mixture of old traditions and new and vigorous forces. The verse of Parley Pratt, one of the early Mormon apostles, for instance, is an imitation of Pope mingled with the spirit of the early West.

There is a more important, and too infrequently emphasized, aspect of the early literature of Utah and other western States. Life on physical frontiers has always been hard and earnest. There is little time or place for social amenities and cultural refinements. It is not surprising, therefore, and it is perhaps inevitable, that the children and grandchildren of pioneers should react against the lives of their forebears. On the physical frontier there is too much hardship, too much hunger and cold, for its offspring to remember it with kindness. They have almost invariably tried to shut it out, to remember only that which is pleasant to remember. And so the stories and verse about it are for the most part stories and poems about clouds and sunsets and peaks, lucid streams and burgeoned shrubs, golden valleys and tapestried skies. There are stories and poems about men compounded almost entirely of courage and tenderness, women of patience and vision, and children of wide-eyed and appealing wonder. Almost never is there a description of the shacks and huts and cabins in which pioneers lived; of the crude tools with which they labored; of the galling physical and emotional hardships which they endured.

In 1776 Silvestre Vélez de Escalante, a Catholic priest, made an exploratory journey from Santa Fe toward Monterey, crossing through the region that was to become Utah. His accurate observations, recorded in his diary, are of value as the impressions of the first white man to enter the region. Some fifty years later, fur traders and trappers, following buffalo trails through the Rockies, added their casual journals to the knowledge of this little-known land. The "experiences" of James Beckwourth in the 1820's found their way into book form as *The Life and Adventures of James P. Beckwourth*. In the next two decades, the personal journals of Osborne Russell, Jedediah Strong Smith, James Clyman, and Peter Skene Ogden were set down and eventually published.

Washington Irving's *Adventures of Captain Bonneville* (1837), based on the unpublished journals of an explorer, made up in popular interest what it lacked in historical accuracy. Widely and eagerly read a short time later were the reports of John Charles Frémont, who visited Great Salt Lake on his way to the Pacific Coast in 1843. Thousands of copies of his report of this expedition of 1843-44 were absorbed by a public intensely curious about the Salt Lake region. In the fifties S. N. Carvalho made capital of this widespread interest in *Incidents of Travel and Adventure in the Far West with Colonel Frémont*. Not so well known are the Government report of Captain Howard Stansbury and the *History of the Mormons* by Lieutenant J. W. Gunnison. Among the most interesting of the explorers' accounts were those of Major J. W. Powell and F. S. Dellenbaugh, who between 1869 and 1873 made several hazardous boat journeys down the Colorado. Powell, who led the expeditions, tells his dramatic and popular story in *First Through the Grand Canyon;* the result of Dellenbaugh's experience and research was *The Romance of the Colorado River*. Among the finest of government reports are those of Clarence Edward Dutton, which have literary values rarely found in government annals.

Pioneer ways and hardships are reported in such books as the *Autobiography of Parley P. Pratt,* an early Mormon leader; *Life of a Pioneer,* by James S. Brown, a California gold-seeker; *Reminiscences of Alexander Toponce,* by an early-day freighter of that name; *Forty Years Among the Indians,* by Daniel W. Jones; *The White Indian Boy* (or *Uncle Nick Among the Shoshones*), by E. N. Wilson and Howard R. Driggs; and *Pioneering the West,* by Howard R. Egan.

After the coming of the Mormons in 1847, writing in the Territory was for many years chiefly theological. The Latter-day Saints brought with them the Book of Mormon, published in New York in 1830, and supplemented it later with the *Doctrine and Covenants,* a compilation of the revelations of Joseph Smith and his successors, and *The Pearl of Great Price,* comprising the "Book of Moses" and the "Book of Abraham," both translated by Joseph. The *Journal of Discourses* in twenty-six volumes consists of sermons by Brigham Young and other leaders. Parley and Orson Pratt, two early apostles, wrote widely on theological and scientific subjects; and among the writings of later apostles *The House of the Lord* and *The Vitality of Mormonism* by Dr. James E. Talmage, *Rational Theology* by Dr. John A. Widtsoe, and *The Progress of Man* by Joseph F. Smith have been popular within the Church. A history of the Church in six volumes has been published by Brigham H. Roberts, one of the most prolific writers among the Mormons; and many have written hymns relating to aspects of Mormon history and faith (*see Music.*)

Among biographies of Church leaders by Mormons, George Q. Cannon's *Life of Joseph Smith,* John Henry Evans' *Joseph Smith: An American Prophet,* and Preston Nibley's life of Brigham Young are notable. John Henry Evans' *Charles Coulson Rich,* the *Life Story of Brigham Young* by Susa Young Gates and Leah Widtsoe and, more lately, *One Who Was Valiant* (Brigham Young) by Clarissa Young Spencer and Mabel Harmer, caused much comment because of their discussions of Mormon family life. A significant biography by a non-Mormon is M. R. Werner's *Brigham Young.* Mormon theological writing of recent times has often been an attempt to reconcile science and Mormonism and to ameliorate the continued bitterness and skepticism of many non-Mormons.

It was inevitable that "exposures" of Mormonism should be written. Though all of them doubtless contain some truth, it is nevertheless true that all of them were largely motivated by rancor and hatred and in consequence gave a distorted picture of the events chronicled. The first of these, E. D. Howe's *Mormonism Unveiled,* published at Painesville, Ohio, in 1834, furnished material for anti-Mormon attacks since that time. There are several such books by embittered apostates, notably another *Mormonism Unveiled,* including "The Life and Confessions of John D. Lee," by William W. Bishop, Lee's attorney, William H. Hickman's *Brigham's Destroying Angel,* and Ann Eliza Young's *Wife No. 19.* Lee was executed for his part in the Mountain Meadows Massacre and furnished Bishop material for his book while awaiting death; Hickman was arrested for murder in his old age and wrote his book while in jail; Ann Eliza Young was the only one of Brigham Young's wives who sued him for divorce.

Among the books about the Mormons by non-Mormons, it is to be doubted if there has been an unbiased one. Sir Richard Francis Burton's *City of the Saints* was the work of a man who brought a background of world travel to Utah; but even such a man, armed with the experiences of an eventful month among the Mormons, could not write a thoroughly impartial book. Hubert H. Bancroft's history is inaccurate in detail; on the other hand, Colonel Thomas L. Kane's *Sketches* declare the anger and concern of one of the most, faithful friends Mormonism ever had. Many of the accounts by persons friendly toward Mormonism are impelled more by sympathy than by scholarship. Even more recent books like *Holy Murder* by Charles Kelly and Hoffman Birney (1934), which purport to be fair and scholarly, try to prove their charges by quoting from such bitter apostates as John Bennett and T. B. H. Stenhouse. It can still be said of books about the Mormons that those by Mormons themselves are too apologetic or naive or dogmatic; and that those by non-Mormons depend too much on old and discredited assertions. One of the best books on Mormonism by a writer of Mormon origin is Professor E. E. Ericksen's doctoral thesis on *The Psychological and Ethical Aspects of Mormon Group Life.*

The materials of Mormonism offer a fertile and dramatic field to the novelist. Harry Leon Wilson used Mormon background in *Lions of the Lord,* and Arthur Conan Doyle in his Sherlock Holmes story, *A Study in Scarlet.* N. S. Parker in *Hell and Hallelujah,* and Susan Ertz in *The Proselyte* have used Mormon materials, and Frank G. Robertson in *The Rocky Road to Jericho* used the great trek across the Plains. Among novels with a Utah setting are Lela Horne Richards' *Poplars Across the Moon,* Jeremiah Stokes' *The Soul's Fire,* Bernard De Voto's *The Crooked Mile,* and Zane Grey's *Riders of the Purple Sage.* Maurine Whipple in 1938 was awarded a Houghton Mifflin Fellowship to complete her novel, *The Giant Joshua,* a story of three generations of Mormons in southern Utah. One of the more spectacular studies of Mormonism is Vardis Fisher's 1939-40 Harper prize novel, *Children of God,* which starts with Joseph Smith's youth and carries the story to 1890. Jean (Florence Maw) Woodman's *Glory Spent* (1940), an honest and simple first novel of modern Utah by a graduate of Brigham Young University, anticipates the novels which may be expected of Utah writers. Encouragement to a native literature has been extended since 1935 by the *Rocky Mountain Review* (formerly the *Intermountain Review of Speech and Literature*), a "little magazine" published quarterly at Cedar City by Ray B. West and Grant H. Redford of the Branch Agricultural College.

Of native Utah writers, Bernard DeVoto, born in Ogden in 1897, is probably best known. He followed *The Crooked Mile* with two other tales of the West: *The Chariot of Fire* (1926) and *The House of Sun-Goes-Down* (1928). In 1930 he published an annotated edition (without index) of *The Life and Adventures of James P. Beckwourth;* in 1932, *Mark Twain's America,* an attempt to demolish a theory advanced by Van Wyck Brooks; and has since published *Forays and Rebuttals,* which includes an essay on the Mormons. DeVoto has been a vigorous and sometimes a bitter critic of his native State.

Other nationally known Utah writers include Whit Burnett, editor of *Story;* Harold Ross, editor of the *New Yorker;* Wallace Stegner, an Iowan educated at the University of Utah and later a teacher there, who won the Little, Brown and Company novelette contest (1936-37) with *Remembering Laughter;* and George Dixon Snell, whose early work has shown much promise. His *The Great Adam* is a realistic novel with an Idaho background; his second, *Root, Hog and Die,* deals with early Mormonism; and his third book treats of the Manly expedition. Nym Wales (Helen Foster), a University of Utah graduate who traveled in China with her husband, Edgar Snow, wrote *Inside Red China. A Woman's Place,* by Harriet McQuarrie Odlum, is the autobiography of a valiant woman who went from a southern Utah town to the direction of an important New York business institution. Bill Haywood, famous as an IWW radical, who published his *Autobiography* in 1929, was of Utah birth. Brewster Ghiselin is the author of numerous short stories and poems. Utah's best known poet is Phyllis McGinley, whose trenchantly satiric volumes are in the vein of Dorothy Parker. Orson F. Whitney was a pioneer poet whose best effort was *Elias, an Epic of the Ages,* and Mrs. Lula Richards Greene published (1904) a book of Mormon poetry titled *Branches that Run Over the Wall.*

Among the many writers of short stories are Olive Woolley Burt and Edwin Herron; and among playwrights are Orestes Utah Bean, who produced the popular *Corianton,* based on the Book of Mormon; Prof. W. F. Hansen, whose all-Indian opera, *The Sun Dance,* has appeared on Broadway; Milton Royle, who is known for *The Squaw Man, These are My People,* and *The Struggle Everlasting;* and Channing Pollock, who has produced many plays. Otto Harbach, author of popular musical comedies, formerly lived in Salt Lake City.

Of Utah writers outside the categories of fiction and verse, perhaps none is more significant than Charles Kelly, whose hobby is digging into old sources and publishing the results himself. His *Salt Desert Trails, Old Greenwood, Outlaw Trail,* and *Miles Goodyear* (in collaboration with Maurice L. Howe) are excellent combinations of scholarship and historical gossip. Other notable volumes in this and allied fields are U. S. Senator E. D. Thomas' *Chinese Political Thought;* former U. S. Senator Frank J. Cannon's *Utah Under the Prophet;* Levi Edgar Young's *The Founding of Utah;* Dr. Leland H. Creer's

Utah and the Nation; and A. L. Neff's *History of Utah.* Scientific and professional books written by Utah schoolmen are numerous. Typical among them is Professor B. Roland Lewis' two-volume *Shakespeare Documents.*

Many other writers, not named here, have achieved a degree of success in various fields.

THE CRAFTS

The desert fringes along the Wasatch Mountains and the mesa lands of Utah's southeast fostered one primitive culture and laid the groundwork for a second before white men ever reached the Americas. The older people, best known to moderns as Cliff Dwellers, raised many of their crafts to an amazing efficiency. They were skilled basketmakers, a relic perhaps of nomadic days, employing a wide variety of shapes and sizes, from shallow meal dishes to full-bellied, small-necked *ollas* three feet in diameter, decorated with designs woven into the yellow basketwork with black withes. At the height of their development they became equally skilled potters, transferring the old basket shapes and designs to the clay. The earliest pots were decorated with incised patterns that seem to be an attempt to reproduce the texture of their baskets; indeed, some archeologists have suggested that their first pots were produced accidentally when they attempted to make their baskets watertight by lining them with clay. The lining fell away when it dried, and the basketmaker turned potter. In its maturity the craft produced exquisite results: hollow figurines, stocky amphoras, storage jars four feet in diameter, cups, dippers, dishes—smoothed, ornamented with designs in red and black against pale grey clay, and surfaced with a kind of glaze known as "slick." The traditional designs, though apparently drawn freehand, retained the geometric character imposed on baskets by the weaving process, though many new elements, such as spirals, were added. In the finest pots the design covered the entire surface, inside and out. The Archeological Museum of the University of Utah possesses an excellent collection of Cliff Dweller pottery that includes several figurine jugs with the sex carefully indicated, dippers with long handles, and even flutes of baked clay.

These same people were indefatiguable muralists. The flat places on the cliffs near their communities and the walls of their *kivas* (underground ceremonial chambers) were decorated with markings that range from elaborate paintings of ceremonial scenes to crude drawings scratched in the rock with a sharp stone. The pigments used in the paintings were the reds and blacks of their pottery, and the designs and representations have the same geometric formality. Occasionally, where the cliff permitted, as the one between Thompsons and Sego on State 94

Agriculture

Lee: F. S. A.

DRY FARM, CACHE COUNTY

HIGHLINE CANAL, STRAWBERRY VALLEY

Courtesy Department of the Interior

Lee H. Olse

FARM HOME, CENTERVILLE

Lee: F. S. A.

MORMON HAY STACKER

WHEAT HARVEST, STRAWBERRY VALLEY

Courtesy Department of the Interior

MORMON FARM FAMILY

Lee: F.S.A.

GUERNSEY BULL OWNED BY A FARM COOPERATIVE

Lee: F.S.A.

Lee: *F.S.A.*

SWEET CORN

SHEEP CAMP, BEAVER CREEK

"COUNTED IN" FOR SUMMER PASTURE

DRAFT COLTS

RODEO STOCK

Lee: F.S.A.

PEACH ORCHARD, CACHE COUNTY

BERRY PICKERS, NEAR LOGAN

Lee: F.S.A.

(*see Tour 7a*), the paintings attained heroic proportions, depicting cos-
umed tribal dignitaries with hour-glass figures and triangular heads.
Petroglyphs, or designs and symbols scratched or pecked into the stone,
are more common and generally more accessible than paintings, and
hey are more diverse in subject matter. An unusual collection of
petroglyphs lines the upper campus walk at Brigham Young University,
Provo. Nine Mile Canyon, northeast of Price, is studded with petroglyphs (*see Tour 7a*).

The Cliff Dwellers possessed other decorative crafts: etched bone,
bead necklaces, shell ornaments, carved wood, reed mats with woven
patterns and fringed ends; but they are neither so numerous nor so
spectacular as their pottery and rock designs. Cliff Dweller relics are
now possessions of the Federal government and may not be disturbed—
an injunction made necessary by wholesale lootings of dwellings and the
activities of tourists and natives who have been constrained to add ini-
ials or bullet pocks to an otherwise perfect mural. However, the
refuse heaps invariably found beneath cliff dwellings contain many rare
shards that may be taken, and an occasional bit of mat, or a fragment
of worked wood.

The prehistoric culture terminated abruptly about 1400 A.D., and
he people who produced it were displaced by the nomadic ancestors of
he modern Navaho and Shoshone Indians. The crafts of these tribes
were addressed to portable objects, painted hides for tepees, quill-worked
buckskins, feather ornaments, and, after the whites came, beaded shirts
and moccasins. In 1864 the Navahos were rounded up by a de-
achment of the United States Army under Christopher "Kit" Carson
and driven into a species of Babylonian captivity in New Mexico.
There they learned the two crafts for which they are chiefly known:
rugmaking and silversmithing. Their rugs, spun tediously from raw
wool on hand spindles and woven on primitive looms, are known
oday wherever rugs are sold. Less known is the Navaho custom
of leaving a break in the pattern through which the evil spirits may
escape. The designs for the rugs are taken from sand paintings, an
art peculiar to the Navahos and quite unknown outside their reserva-
ions. The paintings are made freehand by pouring vari-colored sands
on a smooth piece of ground, and, since they bear religious significance,
are made and destroyed while the sun is up. The designs are traditional
and are carried in the heads of the medicine men who reproduce them,
each one for a distinct purpose. The more elaborate designs contain
formalized figures of men and animals, desert plants, together with conventional signs such as the zigzag lightning line and the swastika, their
symbol of friendship. (In February, 1940, a council of Navaho chiefs
decided to ban the swastika, feeling that its employment by Nazi Germany had irrevocably damaged the original meaning for them.) Navaho

silver work has, since 1910, grown into a flourishing business. Their turquoise-set rings, bracelets, necklaces, and brooches appear everywhere on jewelry counters, but in Navaholand a man takes his greatest pride in the silver buttons that line his clothes from moccasin to headdress and in belts heavily studded with etched conchas. In the old days ornaments were hammered from dollars and dimes, but Federal laws regulating defacement of coins has led them to substitute bar and slug silver. This concession has not altered the methods of the craft; pieces are still pounded out with a small hammer and a piece of rail. The old formalized designs have been augmented by new ones, and the range of items produced has been extended to include such un-Indian items as cigarette trays.

The Ute and Washakie Indians have gradually abandoned their native crafts except beadwork, and each year there is less and less of that. Their main production is beaded leather belts, amulets, purses, gauntlets, moccasins, sheaths, and gadgets to catch the tourist's eye.

The cowboys who moved up the Chisolm trail to Dodge City in the 1870's and spread out fanwise through the West, had a passion for flamboyant dress, but they were restrained from too complete indulgence by the exigencies of "cow punchin'." They selected their leather for hard wear, feathers were out of the question, and beads wore none too well. But there were calico shirts enough among them, and brass tacks in their gun butts; to which they added a taste, learned from *vaqueros* below the Rio Grande, for hammered silver plates on their saddles, conchas for chaperejos, shanks for spurs, bits, buckles, and even buttons of dimes in the Navaho fashion. Skirts, cantle, *tapideros,* and sometimes the swells of their saddles were stamped with relief or intaglio designs. The most prevalent motifs, prompted by a lonely and womanless existence, were erotic or were drawn from the cowboy's background of range, broncs, and longhorns. Spur shanks were lovingly pounded into ladies' legs of indescribable perfection and headstalls were fastened with little silver buffalo skulls. Cattle brands, originally done freehand with a running iron, are worthy of special study as a contribution to native design.

In the valleys below Moab, in the San Rafael Swell, and on the Wahweep, a few cowhands carry on, though they mutter prophetically about Argentine beef while they work over a bit of leather. Buck Lee (who will not confess that his name is William), co-owner of the W-Bar-L Ranch south of Bluff and cowboy craftsman par excellence, still turns out stamped leather of his own designing that has the old arrogant flavor of the "free life."

For the Mormon colonists, the rigors of pioneer life and their isolation west of the Plains and Rockies, left them little time to practice crafts and gave but meager opportunity to import them. They were

ager enough to recreate the Victorian comforts they had left behind
n their eastern homes, but bullhide and buckskin could not be tailored
and a bottle of indigo dye was worth twice its weight in silver. How-
ver, such difficulties were almost routine to a people who had been
orced three times to emigrate into frontier country. They furnished
huts and adobe houses with crude but efficient furniture, spun wild
cotton, made sun-dried pottery, salvaged scrap iron for tools, and
embroidered "GOD BLESS OUR HAPPY HOME" on discarded
bits of cloth if a bit of yarn could be filched from the homemade looms.

The colonists attempted cotton-growing in Salt Lake Valley; they
ate no mutton in order to conserve their wool, and suffered no scrap
of cloth that might be worked into a hooked rug or a quilt to be discarded. Lacking dyes they learned to extract red from wild rose pods
and madder plants, yellow from rabbit brush, and black from oak chips
and iron; and having no commercial fixatives they used urine—an
odorous business according to those who remember the process, but the
dyes stuck. Quilting bees were regular affairs, and the production of
mottoed samplers grew to large proportions. In 1868 Octovius Ursenbeck imported silkworms from France and Brigham Young urged his
people to plant mulberry trees. The venture eventually failed, because
the railroads brought Oriental silks, which could be purchased cheaper
than home goods, but there is scarcely a town in the south of Utah
that has not its avenues of mulberry. Daughters of Utah Pioneers
museums throughout the State contain many fine and curious examples
of early textiles, from homespun woolens to elaborate silken drapes,
many of which have been reproduced by WPA artists for the Index of
American Design. Two of the Index plates were displayed in Chicago
in 1939: a memorial embroidery of the martyrdom of Joseph Smith,
designed by Martha Taylor Cheyney in 1847, and a quilt block of
anonymous production. Others have been shown in New York and
Los Angeles. In 1869, the St. George newspaper carried the advertisement:

I am now prepared to supply the public with all kinds of
CROCKERY WARE . . .
John Eardly

Unornamented pottery jugs and crocks were produced in every
quarter of the early Territory—a modern Utah grandmother's pickle
and cookie jars are very apt to be one of them, standing with unassum-
ing and sturdy utility on a shelf otherwise filled with machine-made
crockery. In Salt Lake City glass not unlike modern Mexican ware
was blown into dishes, bottles, and such curiosa as canes and paper-
weights. Glass blowing was discontinued about 1880, when it became

possible to ship by train, for known Utah sands were unsuited to th
manufacture of fine glassware.

The earliest woodwork in Utah, chairs hacked from a single sectio
of log, bole tables, and whittled bootjacks often have, in their enforce
simplicity, a charm never quite recaptured by later and better equippe
artisans. Brigham Young's bootjack, on display in the Capitol Museun
was cast from Utah copper; it was given national publicity followin
its "discovery" by the Index of American Design, in the July, 1938
issue of *House and Garden*. About 1885, the Mormon Churc
employed William Bell, cabinetmaker, and Ralph Ramsay, carver, t
"embellish" official buildings. Several of their "embellishments,
straightforward cabinets, day desks, intricately carved hall trees, an
whatnots, are in the Capitol Museum; others are still in use in th
Lion and Beehive Houses. Brigham Young, who seems to have ha
a hand in nearly everything, left an excellently designed settle an
several smaller pieces in the Lion House. Laurentius Dahlquist's muc
prized cabinets and panel-work for the Gardo House have long sinc
disappeared into private collections, but his furnitures and decoration
for the Salt Lake Temple were still intact there in 1940. At Provo
Anders Frederik Ahlander, pioneer carriage maker, established a reputa
tion for carved woodwork that well outlasted his death in 1921. Joh
Hendrickson, also of Provo, was, during the period from 1870 to abou
1910, one of the best known potters in the intermountain region. Hi
kiln, between Provo and Utah Lake, remained in 1940 as a muc
dilapidated but respected relic of fine craftsmanship; his stoneware an
pottery are to be found in many old Utah homes. Public and privat
museums have in their comprehensive collections many other product
of early Utah craftsmanship, but the best way to see craftsworks is t
find them in their natural surroundings, in the old homes of adob
and cut stone scattered from one end of the State to the other, wher
many a rare and unsuspected gem still serves the needs of hospitality.

Mormon handicraft shops sell contemporary home crafts, includin
especially good quilts after the old patterns, braided and woven rug
and lacework. Since 1930, copper crafts, which have been encourage
by such sponsors as Mrs. Arthur L. Beeley of Salt Lake City, who ha
profitably introduced them into NYA activities, have been a conspicu
ous attraction in handicraft shops. Trading posts with authenti
Indian goods are found mostly in southeastern Utah.

PAINTING AND SCULPTURE

Perhaps the nearest approach to a graphic art in the early day
of Utah was the work of a hardy band of photographers who undertoo
to supply the curious East with views of the Plains, Rocky Mountains

Mormons, Indians, and whatever else that was strange or romantic in
the West. Apparently the first man to lug daguerreotype equipment
into Utah Territory was M. Cannon, who had a photographic gallery
in Salt Lake City as early as 1850. The original plates made by
John Wesley Jones, who daguerreotyped his way from Missouri to
California after 1851, have all been lost, but several pencil sketches
made from them, including a view of Great Salt Lake City in 1853,
have been preserved in eastern museums. Jones was closely followed
by S. N. Carvalho and C. C. Mills, both significant figures in the
history of American photography, and in 1860 by C. R. Savage. Savage
obviated the difficulties of transporting the heavy equipment of the day
(a photographer's outfit during the 1850's weighed something more
than 200 pounds) by setting up a gallery in Great Salt Lake City,
which he used as a base for forays into the mountains and Indian
country. His pictures are rated as classic by collectors, and his most
widely known photograph, the meeting of the east and west trains at
Promontory in 1869, which marked completion of the transcontinental
railway, has been reproduced in half the books of American history.
During the 1870's E. O. Beaman, Clement Powell, and Jack Hillers,
photographers to one or another of Major John Wesley Powell's
Colorado River expeditions, made a fine collection of photographs, some
of which were published in 1939 by the Smithsonian Institution. The
work of these men was augmented, especially during the 1860's, by
itinerant water-colorists, who left innumerable stilted profile portraits
to the ultimate limbo of Mormon attics and bookstalls, as well as a
motley of tin and brass novelties (early peddlers of art in the West
usually had a varied stock).

The beginnings of painting and sculpture proper in Utah are identified with the Mormon building program. By 1855 Brigham Young
was recommending that foreign missionaries address special emphasis to
conversion of skilled artisans and architects. In 1855, William Ward,
though an architect by profession, completed the lion couchant that
still crouches over the portico of the Lion House in Salt Lake City,
and about the same time C. C. A. Christensen, a Danish convert, painted
panoramic views of incidents and places along the trail from Nauvoo
to Great Salt Lake City. Between 1860 and 1863, three painters,
George Martin Ottinger (1833-1917), Daniel Weggeland (1829-
1918), and John Tullidge (1826-99), were brought to Utah and employed at painting scenery for the Salt Lake Theater, and later, murals
for the ceremonial chambers of Mormon temples. These three men,
though they came from New England, Norway, and England, respectively, had all matured in the same general tradition. Ottinger received
his scant instruction under teachers imbued with the precepts of the
Hudson River School of Landscape. His work is labored, literal, and

usually quite static, but his enthusiasm for legendary subjects (drawn from the Book of Mormon and from the fabulous histories of the Incas current in his day) keeps local interest in him fresh and usually stirs the curiosity of those who have not known his paintings before. His two contemporaries, though they had not Ottinger's literary interest, were perhaps more competent craftsmen. Both were literalists in the manner of the painters of the Dusseldorf Academy in Germany, though neither studied outside his native country. Since 1900, interest in Tullidge's work has almost disappeared; Weggeland's low-keyed landscapes have, on the other hand, gained in popularity. Weggeland, Tullidge, and Ottinger banded together in 1863 and organized the Deseret Academy of Fine Arts, the first such school in the West; they were forced by a lack of paying students to close their doors within a few months. Weggeland, reporting the enterprise in a letter home, said that he could occasionally dispose of a painting or a lesson for a few home-knit socks or a basket of onions, but that without his commissions for the Salt Lake Theater he would never have been able to pay his rent.

Alfred Lambourne (1850-1926), who shares the position of first home-trained painter with H. L. S. Culmer, came to Utah from Missouri in 1856. He studied with Weggeland and Tullidge, graduated to scene painting for the Salt Lake Theater, and near the middle of his life abandoned painting for a literary career. During his short period of production he devoted himself almost exclusively to painting pictures of the Wasatch Mountains and Great Salt Lake, two segments of the Utah scene for which he had a passion. Culmer (1854-1914) was a businessman to whom painting was a Sunday avocation, yet with the assistance of Lambourne he became one of the best known of Utah's painters. He fell early under the influence of Thomas Moran, and in his mature work adopted a frankly imitative style. Moran painted several pictures in Utah, most of which now hang in the Library of Congress, Washington, D. C. While he was in the Territory Moran exhibited his work in Salt Lake City, where Culmer made his acquaintance. Culmer followed Moran in his taste for grandiose subject and for large picture sizes. His copy of Moran's *Shoshone Falls* is as spirited as the original, though the luminosity which marked the master's painting is lacking in the pupil's. Works of all these early men, together with paintings by Phineas Young and Ralph Ramsay, lesser known painters, may be seen in the State Capitol, in the Mormon Church Museum, and in the University of Utah galleries, in Salt Lake City.

Painters of this early period were hampered by a lack of organized exhibits and public interest. Paintings were normally shown in jewelers' shops, department stores, and recreation halls, where space was restricted and the lighting poor. About 1869, the Deseret Agricultural and Manufacturing Society, forerunner of the State Fair, was persuaded to exhibit and to award medals for paintings as well as Durham bulls, insuring at least one comprehensive annual show. In the 1870's the universities began to include art instruction in their courses; previously the Salt Lake Polysophical Society announced classes in drawing "for young ladies," declining to make such provision for young men. In general the people of the Territory were too engrossed in the endless struggle with their lands to give the arts more than a cursory (and somewhat suspicious) glance.

John Hafen (1856-1910), regarded by many as Utah's finest landscapist, came to the Territory from Switzerland in 1860. He studied under Weggeland and Ottinger, and in 1890 was sent abroad by the Mormon Church to prepare himself for commissions in Mormon temples. In France, Hafen came under the influence of Corot, with whom he was already identified by disposition, and there perfected the sensitive approach to nature which is characteristic of his work. Though today his paintings command higher prices than those of any other Utah artist, he never managed during his lifetime to throw off the restraints of poverty. His work was, in the words of one who knew him, "too chaste, too subtle, too delicate in the manipulation of values to suit a western audience whose inclination ran to spectacular subject and photographic likeness." Almost every major collection of paintings in the State boasts a Hafen, the most comprehensive group being in the Springville Museum, which owns *The Quaking Aspens,* considered by Hafen his best work.

Donald Beauregard (1885-1914), noted for his scenes of Indian life, died while painting murals depicting the life of Saint Francis in the Santa Fe (New Mexico) Museum. John W. Clawson (1858-1936), who made his home alternately in California and Utah, was known throughout the intermountain region for his richly colored portraits, several of which hang in the collection of Brigham Young University and in the Capitol. Lawrence Squires (1887-1928), remembered for his etchings as well as his paintings, Mary Teasdale (1863-1937), the first Utah woman to be accepted in the Paris Spring Salon, and E. H. Eastmond (1876-1936), former head of the Brigham Young University art department and a sensitive master of the monotype, are some of the lesser known Utah artists who have died in recent years. John B. Fairbanks (1855-1940), though he is well loved for his glowing harvestscapes, has been sometimes eclipsed by the achievements of his two sons, Avard, sculptor, and J. Leo, painter. Edwin Evans, who accompanied Hafen to France, though he does not exhibit as often as in former years, is active yet. Evans, soon after his return from Europe during the nineties, organized the art department of the University

of Utah, and continued as its head for twenty-five years. He was per
haps the first teacher in Utah to break with the methods of the Aca
démie Julian and insist that his students be allowed to develop natur
ally.   His own painting derives its chief charm from solid space an
form relationships as well as rich and varied textural effects.

Almost all Utah painters of the three decades after 1890 followe
the precedent of these men, and went to Paris, or at least imitated th
spirit of French landscape.   James T. Harwood and Cyrus E. Dalli
preceded Hafen to France by about two years.   Between 1890 an
1910 they were followed by Mary Teasdale, Rose Hartwell, Le
Greene Richards, Alma B. Wright, Bent F. Larson, and Mahonr
Young.   Harwood, teacher directly or indirectly to many of Utah'
finest painters, died in 1940 at the age of eighty.   From 1905 h
exhibited regularly at the Paris Spring Salon, was a contributor t
many American shows, and he was known on the Continent as on
of the most adept moderns in colored etching.   His *Preparation fo*
the Dinner, which hangs at the University of Utah, is a represen
tative early piece; in his late years he adopted the pointellistic brush
technique of the impressionists without the pure palette, which im
parted to his landscapes an atmospheric quality much prized by hi
buyers.   Richards, though he painted the murals for the Utah Stat
Capitol, will probably be best remembered for his portraits, several o
which hang in the Capitol gallery.   His *Portrait of a Violinist,* in th
collection of Brigham Young University, is generally conceded to be hi
best work.   Larson, in 1940 head of the Brigham Young University ar
department, is one of the most thoughtful craftsmen among Utah
painters.   His earlier landscapes in oil, usually low in key and quite
subtle, strongly reflect his French masters; his pictures of western life
produced since 1930 are more boldly painted.   Le Conte Stewart, hea
of the University of Utah art department in 1940 and the first o
Utah's recognized painters to turn his back uncompromisingly on senti
mental landscape, belongs in point of time, though he has steadfastly
refused to study in any but American schools, with these painters
Ranch Kimball, businessman and painter, whose *Man Manicures Moun-*
tains was hung in the National Exhibition of American Art; Mabel
Frazer, of the University of Utah Art Department, winner of several
awards; Waldo Midgley, known for his water colors and portraits, are
other Utah painters who have broken with tradition and adventured in
new fields.   Dean Fausett, brother of Lynn—both sons of pionee
parents in the Carbon County coal fields—has won national recognition
as a muralist.   Other artists, who attained prominence in the period
before and after the World War are Cornelius and Rose Howard Salis
bury, Orson D. Campbell, Florence Ware, Caroline Parry, Joseph

A. F. Everett, Milton Wassmer, Henri Moser, and John H. Stansfield.

In point of excellence, it is probably in the field of plastic art that Utah has contributed most. Mahonri Young, a grandson of Brigham Young, fellow of the Arts and Letters Society and of the National Academy, and the only Utah artist to be dignified by a paragraph in the *Encyclopedia Britannica,* is among the most prominent of contemporary American sculptors. His earliest aspirations were directed toward painting rather than modeling. *The Blacksmiths,* in the State Capitol collection, painted near the beginning of his career, shows even then the strong feeling for structural solidity that has characterized his mature work in the round. His sculpture is realistic, and, though not imitative, is somewhat in the manner of Meunier, the Belgian. One critic has said that had Meunier lived after Young, Young would have received the greater acclaim. Young, though he has maintained his studio in New York City for many years, has returned to Utah at intervals to execute commissions, among them the Sea Gull Monument, whose four plaques are among the best reliefs in America, and the excellent life-size statues of Joseph and Hyrum Smith, all in Temple Square, Salt Lake City. In 1939 Young was commissioned to design and execute an ambitious monument to the Mormon pioneers of 1847, to be placed at the mouth of Emigration Canyon, overlooking Salt Lake City. Three of Young's Salt Lake students have achieved national prominence as commercial artists: William Crawford of Provo (who signs himself Galbreith), illustrator for the *New Yorker, Esquire,* and other magazines; Hal Burrows, illustrator of the former *Life* and *Judge;* and John Held, Jr., creator of the now passé flapper girl cartoons.

Cyrus E. Dallin, best known for his often-reproduced Indian equestrian statues, *The Appeal to the Great Spirit, The Medicine Man,* and *The Signal of Peace,* was born in Springville, Utah, and did his first modeling there with coarse native clays. In 1882, in competition with many of the finest sculptors in America, he was commissioned to execute the statue of Paul Revere (which in January, 1940, was finally approved by the city council of Boston), and has made his home in Massachusetts since that time. His work, realistic and usually meticulously finished, has often been criticized for sentimentality; however, his enthusiasm for native subjects, especially the Indian, has not been without influence in the contemporary tendency of American artists to depict American topics. The best known of his statues in Utah are the *Pioneer Mother,* a bust, in the city park of his birthplace, and the original plaster cast of Massasoit in the Capitol rotunda—the bronze Massasoit stands on Coles Hill, Massachusetts, overlooking Plymouth Bay. Avard Fairbanks received his preliminary instruction from his father, John B. Fairbanks, and while still very young was granted a special scholarship to the Art Student League in New York City as a reward for his group study, *Fighting Panthers*. He entered the Ecole des Beaux Arts at seventeen, and was in 1940 professor of sculpture at the University of Michigan. The only pieces by Fairbanks accessible to the public in Utah are in the Springville Art Gallery. Other contemporary Utah sculptors of prominence are Millard F. Malin, whose best-known work, the Sugarhouse Monument in Salt Lake City, has received much comment for the structural honesty of its two heroic figures; Torlief Knaphus, executor of the Constitution Monument in Salt Lake City, the Hill Cumorah Monument (a Mormon shrine) in New York State, and the hand-cart pioneer group in the L. D. S. Museum at Salt Lake City; and Maurice Brooks, best known for his portrait busts.

Utah, always conservative, has been slow to accept the more extreme forms of contemporary art. The buying public, those who purchase paintings for home and office, have a strong preference for conventional portrait and realistic landscape, and the public agencies have been, in general, content to echo this taste. Artists who remain in the State conform to the public standards. At the Utah State Agricultural College in Logan, a small group led by Professor Calvin Fletcher has been experimenting since about 1930 with cubistic forms, bringing Mrs. Irene Fletcher, George Smith Dibble, Mary Farnham, and H. Reuben Reynolds, into prominence. Appointment of Maud Hardman as supervisor of art in the Salt Lake City schools in 1938 exerted an important influence toward greater progressivism in art. The jury for the annual exhibition of the Utah State Institute of Fine Arts in 1940 turned *volte face* on its former practices and selected, for national purchase awards, works by Henry N. Rasmusen and Roy Butcher, both young painters who lean strongly toward modern tendencies. Rasmusen's *How Hard the Furrow* bears kinship to the *American Gothic* of Grant Wood in use of subject material; Butcher's *Jerry Gang* is a sweeping landscape centered on a group of severely simplified workmen.

There are several important collections of paintings in Utah: that of the Springville Art Association, the state-owned collections in the Capitol, those of Brigham Young and Utah universities. The museum at Springville (*see Tour 1d*), the only building in Utah designed for and devoted exclusively to the hanging of paintings, originated as a movement among the students of Springville High School. Beginning with a gift painting from John Hafen, the students of this little town of 3,700 have assembled by gifts and purchases, through an annual spring salon, a collection valued in 1940 at $150,000. In 1937, the Works Progress Administration, co-operating with the School District and civic agencies, erected the museum building.

The paintings in the Capitol comprise four State-owned collections:

Prize paintings purchased by the State Fair Association, paintings given to the State by individuals and through the Federal art agencies, portraits of governors, and the Alice Art Collection. This last is named for Alice Merrill Horne, who introduced the bill creating the Utah Art Institute in the Utah Legislature of 1899 and who served as first chairman of the institute board. Much of the State's early sponsorship of art in Utah is directly attributable to Mrs. Horne, and the collection assembled by the institute with small yearly appropriations granted it in the legislature was designated by Mrs. Horne's first name.

Since the World War, many local organizations have promoted interest in the plastic arts. The annual show at Springville, attracting exhibits from the country at large, has been a potent factor. The Art Barn, in Salt Lake City, has maintained galleries and classrooms since 1933, and has brought many meritorious traveling exhibits to Utah. Creation of the WPA Art Project in 1935 enabled young and progressive artists to remain in the State, and, under the leadership of State Director Elzy J. Bird, has given widespread stimulus to art in Utah, through its exhibits and the painting of murals for communities that could not otherwise have afforded them. The State legislature in 1937 passed a bill reorganizing the Utah Art Institute, changing its name to the Utah State Institute of Fine Arts, enlarging the board to represent all the arts, authorizing it to do business as a corporation, and permitting co-operation with the Federal government.

Soon after, under the leadership of Chairman Gail Martin, a movement was organized to create a Utah State Art Center in co-operation with the WPA Art Program. Governor Henry H. Blood, a lifetime patron of the arts, allocated $5,000 of State funds to the Art Center, and the public was given the benefit of further cultural opportunities through State and Federal co-operation. Donald B. Goodall, director of the Art Center, reported that at the end of the first year (November, 1939), more than 75,000 persons had visited the galleries and attended lectures, musicales, and forums, while 2,000 students had enrolled in art classes. Branch centers were launched by the Utah Art Project at Provo, Helper, and Price. The center at Helper set a national record when, in a mining community of 2,700 people, 3,000 attended the opening exhibit in a ten-day period.

Artists of the Utah Art Project have done notable work for the program and in their own right. Director Bird's *Takin' Five,* a water color exhibited at the New York World's Fair in 1939, drew favorable comment from eastern critics. Lynn Fausett, president of the Art Students' League from 1931 to 1936, completed large murals for the University of Wyoming, for the Price, Utah, Civic Auditorium, and for the Ely, Nevada, High School. Gordon Cope painted the official portrait of Governor Blood and Indian portraits at the State Capitol. Notable work has also been done by William J. Parkinson, Howell Rosenbaum, W. H. Shurtliff, Paul Smith, and others.

MUSIC

The Shoshoni remember a time when the whole earth was covered with water and everything perished except two birds that held to the sky with their beaks. One was the tiny bird that builds its nest in the shape of a water jar; the other was gray with a large beak and tail. The black waters rose steadily beneath them, and the large bird, being a coward in his heart, began to cry so loud he was in danger of losing his hold; the little bird clung valiantly and whispered words of encouragement. When the waters receded, both were saved. The children of the small bird are the songsters of today, while those of the larger, because he showed fear, have no song, only cries. The Shoshoni say, some men can sing, some cannot; but the man with a sweet voice has the courage in him of the tiny bird that builds its nest in the shape of a water jar.

The music of the Indian is scarcely known outside his race, perhaps because, like the tiny bird, his songs have no scale, no recognizable key, because his melancholy quarter-tones are alien to white ears, because his melodies and harmonies seem no more than intricate obligatos of rhythm, and because, finally, he sings for the sheer joy of singing. Since 1930, belated interest in Indian culture has brought about some curious attempts to document his songs, generally with indifferent success. The best of such works, as George W. Cronyn's *Path on the Rainbow,* capture something of the subject and the imagery, but the singing itself defies notation, and no stage directions have yet made tangible the Indian's background of desert and mountain. The Shoshoni of Utah, the Utes, Gosiutes, and Paiutes, are shy and ordinarily do not sing in the presence of strangers but at Whiterocks and at Fort Duchesne in the Uintah Basin twice each year there are traditional ceremonies that white people may see, may sometimes even join. These, the Sun Dance at Whiterocks and the Bear Dance at the fort (*see Tour 6a*), have what the books about them do not, the whole picture of costume, desert, dancing, song set to drums with deer-hide heads, and the unblushing sincerity of men performing songs as old as their tribes.

With the Mormons, in the days of the settlement of Utah, when pioneers sang to keep their courage up, music played a more important part in community cultural life than any other art. It was a humble music, inclined to hymns, ballads, sentimental songs, reels, and, where instruments were available, to martial airs; but it was a folk music gathered, as were the rank and file of the Church, from every State in the

Union and from half the countries of Europe. The Mormons played or sang with very little restraint; indeed, their authorities encouraged them to do so and the Church sponsored secular singing and dancing— they had no dour Puritan taste for rote singing nor terror of mixed dancing. "There were musical instruments," says Bancroft, "in every company of Mormons that crossed the plains." And, however remote, there was rarely a community that grew up in the days of the Territory that did not boast, besides its choir, a quadrille band or "squeeze box" and fiddles—in prosperous sections the band would include a bass viol, clarinet, flute, and trombone, but no drums. In outlying towns the quadrille bands persisted until the widespread advent of radio, when they were gradually replaced by small "woefully rhythmical" jazz bands. Many of the old players remain, however, who remember that once a single fiddle could keep the light-footed colonists in rapid motion a whole night through, but they have fallen into disrepute, and play no more.

In the cattle country, cowboy ballads, cow lullabies, and trail songs continue to be the cowhands' chief relief from loneliness. The immemorial right of balladists to add new verses to an old song is much honored among them, and the stranger lucky enough to be "out" during a roundup is sure to hear additions, both bawdy and decorous, to such favorites as "Chisolm Trail," "Cowboy Jack," and "Bury Me Not on the Lone Prairie." In the sheep country there is seldom a camp that has not at least one instrumentalist. Banjos, harmonicas, and guitars are the preferred instruments.

Mormon religious music lies mainly in the province of hymns, and though the Mormons borrowed heavily from the hymnal literature of other denominations, they themselves composed many excellent works. However, in keeping with their self-reliance and the objectivity of their religious views, much of their hymn book does not, in a strict sense, belong to the genre at all, being odes to the Great Basin Zion, exhortations to courage, or snatches of doctrine put to music. Charles W. Penrose, one of the most celebrated Mormon composers, scarcely paused in his enthusiasm for the western mountains, as in his "O Ye Mountains High":

> O ye mountains high
> Where the clear blue sky
> Arches over the vale of the free
> Where the pure breezes blow
> And the clear streamlets flow
> All my fond hopes are centered in thee.

The most lofty of all Mormon hymns, "O My Father," by Eliza R. Snow, breaks its high tone of nostalgia for God to assert the peculiar Mormon doctrine of a heavenly mother. Moreover, purely secular songs written to commemorate important events were scarcely distinguished by the devout from the contents of their hymn book. There were songs (sometimes serious, frequently satiric, and occasionally almost ribald) to celebrate a convert from Sweden or the planting of mulberry trees in the southern colonies, to "josh" sheep skinners, or to lampoon turncoats who deserted the army to marry Mormon girls. Sometimes there is a curious admixture of hymn and folk music, as in the following verse and chorus of "The Hand-cart Song":

> Ye saints that dwell on Europe's shore
> Prepare yourselves with many more
> To leave behind your native land,
> For sure God's judgment is at hand.
> Prepare to cross the stormy main
> Before you to this valley gain
> And with the faithful make a start
> To cross the plains with other hand-carts.
>
> Some must push and some must pull
> As we go marching up the hill,
> As merrily on the way we go
> Until we reach the valley, oh!

Perhaps most moving of all the Mormon hymns is William Clayton's "Come, Come Ye Saints," written to the tune of an old English hymn, "All is Well," to inspirit the Saints during the weary crossing of the plains:

> Come, come ye Saints, no toil nor labor fear.
> But with joy wend your way;
> Tho' hard to you this journey may appear,
> Grace shall be as your day.
> 'Tis better far for us to strive
> Our useless cares from us to drive;
> Do this, and joy your hearts will swell—
> All is well! All is well!

> * * * * * * * * *

> We'll find the place which God for us prepared,
> Far away in the West;
> Where none shall come to hurt or make afraid;
> There the Saints will be blessed.
> We'll make the air with music ring—
> Shout praises to our God and King;
> Above the rest these words we'll tell—
> All is well! All is well!

The beginnings of more serious music in Utah are rooted in the Salt Lake Musical and Dramatic Association and the Salt Lake Tabernacle Choir, both organized in the early 1850's at the express order of Brigham Young. Out of the former grew the Salt Lake Theater, which in its heyday between 1870 and 1900 billed the finest musical artists in America, and maintained its own company of "command" performers (it was Young's custom to "call" singers as well as settlers) who produced light operas not markedly inferior to those of visiting professional companies.

Any history of formal music in Utah begins with the organization of the Tabernacle Choir. During its first years, the choir is said to have sung "very prettily" accompanied by a small pedal organ. In 1867, the Church installed in the Tabernacle the organ, which with additions and improvements has become the noble instrument of today. The quality of the Tabernacle Choir was immeasurably improved when President Young appointed Professor George E. P. Careless, director. Professor Careless, a vigorous and progressive leader, believed music should rise above creed, race, or politics. He was perhaps the first leader to attempt to bridge the gap between Mormon and gentile through music. Besides directing the Salt Lake Theater Orchestra, Professor Careless organized a chorus and instrumental group to give the first production in the Intermountain West, on June 3, 1875, of Handel's *Messiah* at the pioneer playhouse.

Professor T. Radcliffe, organist at the First Congregational Church, first produced Haydn's oratorio, *The Creation,* May 10, 1881, at the Salt Lake Theater. Oratorio singing in Utah received much of its impetus from the organization of the Salt Lake Oratorio Society in 1913 by Squire Coop, then head of the music department of the University of Utah. Each year, the *Messiah* is given during the Christmas holidays at the Tabernacle. In Ogden, a similar work has been done by Lester G. Hinchcliff, a former pupil of Squire Coop, as director of the Ogden Oratorio Society. The leadership and burning enthusiasm of Evan Stephens, who organized the Salt Lake Choral Society, in 1889, shortly thereafter becoming Tabernacle Choir director, had a quickening effect upon music. Under his direction, the choir reached new levels of excellence, winning much renown on tours of American music centers, and receiving second prize at the Chicago World's Fair in 1893. Evan Stephens is also ranked among the Church's favorite composers of hymns, anthems, and cantatas. Ebenezer Beesley, an early leader in Church music, is another composer of solid attainments in Utah music. The hymn "Come Thou Glorious Day of Promise" by A. C. Smyth is admired for its solid English style. Maintenance of the organ and subsidy of music by the Church has resulted in the development of several organists, who have gained national recognition: John J. McClellan, who died in 1925, and two of his former pupils, Alexander Schreiner, present (1940) Tabernacle organist, and Winslow Cheney, now of New York City.

During its long service on behalf of music, the Tabernacle Choir, none of whose singers are paid, has had five directors: Charles J. Thomas, Professor Careless, Evan Stephens, Anthony C. Lund, and

J. Spencer Cornwall, director since 1935. Organists include Joseph J. Daynes, John J. McClellan, Edward P. Kimball, Tracy Y. Cannon, and the present organists, Frank W. Asper, Alexander Schreiner, and Wade N. Stephens. Joseph Ballantyne, former director of the Ogden Tabernacle Choir, did much to build up the reputation of the Ogden group. In August, 1929, the Tabernacle Choir at Salt Lake City, augmented to 325 voices, embarked upon a weekly broadcasting program which has carried its music and that of the organ to millions of listeners.

Having no subsidy to depend upon—as Church music has had continuously—the career of symphonic music has been studded by a few peaks and many depressions. The first symphonic group, the Salt Lake Symphony Orchestra, was organized in 1892 by Anton Pedersen, director. Arthur Shepherd became director in 1902, and continued in this position for several years, during which he raised the performance of orchestral music to a high level. The orchestra discontinued its performances when he left the State for a career that led later to international recognition as a composer. He twice won Society of American Composers' awards for musical compositions, was for several years assistant conductor of the Cleveland Symphony Orchestra, and is now (1940) head of the music department of Western Reserve University, Cleveland. In 1912, the symphony was revived as the Salt Lake Philharmonic Orchestra, with Anton Pederson directing. The first concert was given in 1914. Two weeks later, the director died, and his son, Arthur Pedersen Freber, was elected to fill the vacancy. In 1924, the Philarmonic Orchestra, directed by Charles Shepherd, was replaced by the Salt Lake Symphony Orchestra. This group, under Mr. Shepherd's leadership, played but two seasons, disbanding in 1925.

Two grandchildren of President Brigham Young—Emma Lucy and B. Cecil Gates—pioneered the cause of opera in Utah. Between the years 1918 and 1923, they organized, managed, directed and took leading roles in Lucy Gates Grand Opera Company productions. Emma Lucy Gates (now Mrs. A. E. Bowen), coloratura soprano, had received intensive training in Germany, where she sang leading roles in the Royal German Opera before the World War. Her brother, B. Cecil Gates, had studied conducting. Though having achieved marked artistic and popular success, the Lucy Gates Grand Opera Company had to cease activity, and its founders assumed a sizeable deficit. Between productions, Emma Lucy Gates carried on with her concert and stage career, touring America. Her brother, B. Cecil Gates, since has composed a number of widely sung anthems, cantatas, and songs.

In 1929 the last stronghold of opera and legitimate stage in Utah, the Salt Lake Theater, was razed. Development of talking pictures caused theater orchestras to disband. Musicians had to leave the State for employment or seek other occupations. The cultural program of the Works Progress Administration and organization of the Utah WPA Orchestra of thirty to forty musicians in 1935 under the direction of Reginald Beales alleviated this condition and brought substantial programs to a new audience of 50,000 school children, besides many others who never before had heard symphonic music. Concert audiences have increased by leaps and bounds since 1930. More amateur orchestras and bands exist in Utah than ever before. The achievements of the Brigham Young University orchestra at Provo, under the direction of Professor LeRoy J. Robertson, winner of the Society of American Composers' award, have earned the acclaim of professional musicians. The State's three universities and the McCune School of Music and Fine Arts (owned and operated by the Church) stress the importance of music; through their work with bands and orchestras, they are building audiences for the future. The Church Music Committee's program, under the direction of Tracy Y. Cannon, is providing a service, unique in the annals of American music, by holding Church music institutes and training annually several thousand amateur organists and choristers.

Walter Welti, choral director, and N. W. Christiansen, instrumentalist, both of the Utah State Agricultural College, together with Dr. Lorin F. Wheelwright, supervisor of music in the Salt Lake City public schools, Mark Robinson, Ogden school music supervisor, and Professor Thomas Giles, head of the University of Utah music department, direct musical activities at focal population points. Professor William F. Hanson of Brigham Young University, composer of Indian operas, has had one of his works produced in New York by John T. Hand, a Utah tenor of wide stage experience engaged (1940) in light opera production on Broadway. Like nearly every other State, Utah has more talent than it can employ on a professional basis. Happily, some progress is being made toward giving the State's artists better opportunities for development. Student orchestras are using local artists as soloists. The Utah WPA Orchestra gives "opportunity" programs at the Utah Art Center in Salt Lake City, in order that young singers and instrumentalists may have the experience of working and performing with a symphonic group. Work is being done to establish a permanent symphony orchestra. Using the WPA Orchestra as a nucleus, augmented by other professional musicians, the Utah State Symphony Orchestra Association, a department of the Utah State Institute of Fine Arts, gave its first concert May 8, 1940, with Hans Heniot, young American, as guest conductor. Artistic and financial outcome of this first venture give rise to the hope that Utah may at last possess a symphony orchestra.

THE THEATER

The first play produced in Utah was either *Robert Macaire* or *The Triumph of Innocence*. It was presented "with the aid of a little home-made scenery, a brass band, and considerable fanfare" in the old Bowery on Temple Square by the Musical and Dramatic Association. The year was 1851; the Salt Lake colony was four years old. Two years later the pioneer stock company changed its name to Deseret Dramatic Association—having dispensed with the band by this time—and the following year moved its homemade scenery into Social Hall. The Hall was less commodious than the Bowery, but more comfortable, and it had a permanent stage; besides the Bowery was little more than an oversized *cabaña,* erected to serve as a temporary meeting place for the earliest settlers. The Dramatic Association opened in its new quarters with *Don Caesar de Bazan,* an immediate success and a great favorite with Utah audiences for many years thereafter. Scripts were rare, but there was a goodly sprinkling of Elizabethan and early Victorian drama in the meager libraries of the settlers, and the Social Hall players, nothing daunted by the difficulties of *Othello* or *Damon and Pythias,* followed their "initial triumph" with the best they could get their hands on. The limited repertoire was no serious drawback; Alfred Lambourne in his memoir of the Salt Lake Theater said that early Utah audiences did not go to the theater to see a new play, anyway, ". . . but to see some new actor or actress in the old parts."

In 1858, Sergeant R. C. White organized a dramatic company among the soldiers stationed at Camp Floyd and built a theater there of "pine boards and canvas—principally canvas." His scenery was painted with beet juice, mustard, and other commissary delicacies, and, since the camp's women were few in number and mostly had talents other than dramatic, he secured the services of Mrs. Tuckett, the most accomplished of the Social Hall leading ladies. White's methods in gaining Mrs. Tuckett for his own troupe were not entirely above question; moreover, her absence severely crippled the Social Hall players—J. S. Lindsay in *The Mormons and the Theater* says that only "light plays were produced at Social Hall during the next two years." These considerations, together with the universal distaste with which Mormons regarded the presence of Federal troops in Utah, gave White's theater little patronage outside the personnel of the camp, and it was abandoned when the troops were called east at the beginning of the Civil War. The Mechanics Dramatic Association, organized by "Phil" Margetts at Great Salt Lake City, had a more permanent influence. The association began producing plays in 1859 at Bowring's Theater—which is to say, in the unfinished living room of Harry Bowring's home, but the first theater to be designated as such in Utah. The playhouse was intimate, about 18 by 40 feet, of which the stage occupied one third—the families of Brigham Young and Heber C. Kimball (about 90 in all) filled it to capacity. After attending a performance at this theater in 1860 Young announced his intention of building a "real one." Shortly thereafter Bowring's living room was reconverted to its original purpose. Social Hall, after a somewhat checkered career as library, gymnasium, and restaurant, enjoyed a brief resurgence of pioneer splendor between 1918 and 1921, when the University of Utah used it as a Little Theater, and was razed in 1922.

Brigham Young's "real one," the Salt Lake Theater, was begun in 1861 and dedicated to use (after the custom of the Mormons) the following year. From 1862 until 1928 the record of this playhouse was almost the whole history of the theater in Utah. Makeshift theaters, and, later, "opera houses" (the term was applied indiscriminately to ramshackle false fronts, converted public buildings, and the gory show palaces of the 1890's) appeared here and there through the Territory. The Amateur Dramatic Association of Provo purchased $275 worth of scenery from the Camp Floyd Theater in 1861, and, according to report, put it to good use. In his *Zealots of Zion* Hoffman Birney says: "Parowan was the scene of the first theatrical performance, south of Provo. An audience of more than two hundred witnessed the staging of . . . *Slasher and Crasher* and *The Village Lawyer*." He adds: "Admission was twenty-five cents, but the total cash receipts were only $6.75, 'the large number of deadheads being due to the fact that each performer was entitled to have his friends admitted free. . . .'" During the 1870's and 1880's Ogden was proud of its opera house, and the mushroom city of Corinne boasted one of the most gaudy stages west of the Mississippi. However, all these enterprises suffered from amateurism, from transience, and from modest income. The Salt Lake Theater alone remained a regular playhouse with professional standards.

The Salt Lake Theater building was, at the time of its construction, and for many years thereafter, the most imposing structure in the Territory. Both the Church and Young's private exchequer were at low points, but the theater was a community enterprise and laborers worked for tickets, for orders on the Tithing House, and often for nothing at all. Hiram B. Clawson, later manager of the theater, purchased some $40,000 worth of building materials from Camp Floyd for a tenth its original cost—a circumstance which led George D. Pyper to conclude in his *Romance of an Old Playhouse* that ". . . one would almost be led to believe that Johnston's Army was sent to Utah to assist the Saints in their recreational activities." The theater was opened to the public March 8, 1862, with a doubleheader, *Pride of the Market* and *State Secrets*. The precedent set then was rigidly followed for many years—a performance at the theater consisted of a drama and a farce separated by an olio. Many Utahns came great distances to attend and they would have their fill of play-acting before returning to the outlands. Young's personal distaste for tragedy, though he did not specifically forbid it, generally inclined the management to present "drama, melo-drama, and farce," excepting, of course, the great Elizabethan tragedies. Prices were: "parquette, 75¢, galleries, 50¢, babes in arms, $10, all firearms to be checked [the honor system was employed here] with the nearest usher."

The stock company of the new theater was that of Social Hall. They were unpaid in the early days, were later given pro-rata the proceeds of two annual benefit performances, and, in the late 1870's, were put on a definite wage scale. Performers were often "called," much as missionaries and settlers were. Nellie Colebrook was requisitioned with the following note:

Dear Brother and Sister Colebrook:
    Would you allow your daughter Nellie to act upon the stage. It would very much please me.

                                        Your Brother
                                        Brigham Young

Pyper says that Nellie subsequently ". . . became very well known and greatly loved in her stage career." While the theater was under construction, Young repeatedly expressed his determination to circumvent the lax morality which crept into theaters elsewhere. In the spring of 1862 Thomas A. Lyne, a gentile actor known to the Mormons from their Illinois days (Young himself had played High Priest to Lyne's *Pizarro* there), opened an engagement in the Salt Lake Theater. Supported by the stock company, he played *Virginius, Othello, Richelieu, Richard, William Tell,* and a number of farces and lesser dramas. Lyne was succeeded by Mr. and Mrs. Seldon Irvin in 1863, and by Julia Dean Hayne in 1865. During Miss Hayne's engagement, the first competitor for the Salt Lake Theater opened in Great Salt Lake City. It was called "The Academy of Music," and was a product of the joint efforts of Miss Hayne's former manager and the actor Lyne. It was built in thirty days, had as many successful nights, and closed its doors before the year was out.

"There was," says Alfred Lambourne in his memoir of the Salt Lake Theater, "a peculiar bond between those who acted on the stage, and those who comprised their audience. All were friends. . . . They would meet in daily labor, they would dance together . . . or listen to the same sermon on the coming Sunday." Pyper says that Heber J. Grant, who in 1940 was President of the Mormon Church, made his first and only appearance on the stage of the theater as a pickaninny in *Uncle Tom's Cabin;* Heber M. Wells, later governor of Utah, was noted for his Grimaldi in *The Life of an Actress;* and Orson F. Whitney, historian, was a favorite with Salt Lake audiences in the 1870's. The audience, moreover, seemed to feel a keen sense of partnership in the theater. It was Brigham Young's custom to make thorough inspections at regular intervals, and, says Lambourne, "woe betide him who had left a job bidden undone." Pyper, after he became manager in 1898, attempted to replace a favorite curtain. He confesses: "Only when it actually became thread-bare and the stage lights could be seen through its worn fabric would the public permit me to junk it."

About 1880 complete companies began to be booked from New York agents. The stock company was abandoned, and the big names in American theater of the time began to appear regularly on the Salt Lake Theater billboards. The Home Dramatic Club, organized in 1880 at Salt Lake City, in a period of fourteen and a half years presented about forty-five plays. Tony Pastor, the pioneer of vaudeville, played the theater in 1876 with his variety show. He had been preceded by P. T. Barnum, and an occasional performer such as Professor Simmons, "Great, Weird, Wondrous, and Invincibly Incomprehensible . . . Basiliconthamaturgist." However, the variety show never gained a substantial hold on Salt Lake Theater clientele, though vaudeville enjoyed a pre-war vogue in Utah as elsewhere. According to Pyper, the booking facilities were well-nigh perfect after 1891— which is to say that home productions had been pushed completely into the background. The Walker Opera House, built in 1882, crippled the Salt Lake Theater for a time by securing superior bookings. However, the theater's managers "persuaded" booking agencies to divide evenly between the two theaters, and in 1891 the opera house burned down.

Since the World War, the egregious cinema has steadily driven Utah's legitimate theaters toward insolvency. The Salt Lake Theater ceased yielding adequate profits about 1925, and three years later was razed to make way for a telephone exchange. Legitimate theatrical activity has shifted to little theater groups, to high schools and colleges, and to occasional road shows. Greek theaters and natural amphitheaters have appeared here and there in the State since 1900, but the climate of Utah precludes a wide development of such theaters and the pageantry that is usually identified with them, though the Zion Canyon Easter Pageant, a passion play modeled on that of Oberammergau, had by 1940 become traditional.

Utah has contributed to modern drama playwrights Channing Pollock and Edwin Milton Royle and librettist Otto Harbach, who have, however, achieved their successes outside the State. The actress Maude

Adams belongs more completely to Utah. Her mother, Annie Adams Kiskadden, was a popular leading lady in the 1870's at the Salt Lake Theater, and Maude was sometimes permitted to sleep backstage in an old, wide-board rocking cradle, while her mother played. During an entr'acte of *The Lost Child,* the baby normally used in the play became ill, or fell into a fit of crying (raconteurs of the incident are not in harmony on this point), and Maude, aged seven months, played her first role as substitute for an infant supernumerary. She returned about six years later with her mother in *The Stepmother, Little Susie,* and *A Woman of the People,* scored her first solo success at the age of nine with an intermission song, "The Yaller Girl Who Winked at Me," and played the Salt Lake Theater as a leading lady in her own right at the age of twenty. Thereafter she went on to acquire an international reputation. Her old cradle is carefully preserved in the Capitol Museum, together with posters advertising *Peter Pan,* the role which some say will be remembered longer than the old Salt Lake Theater.

ARCHITECTURE

Sir Richard Burton wrote in 1860, "An American artist might extract from such scenery as . . . Echo Kanyon, a system of architecture as original and as national as Egypt ever borrowed from her sandstone ledges or the North of Europe from the solemn depths of her fir forests." Sir Richard had not traveled southward through Utah into the Colorado drainage, where a western river had carved a sheerwalled Nile Valley, and a squat, dusky folk had in prehistoric times captured some similarity to a portion of the gloomy magnificence of Egypt's Middle Kingdom. These American primitives appeared first in Utah along the western slopes of the Wasatch Mountains as ingenious troglodytes, having learned that a pit with a brush and sod roof could be more conveniently located than caves. About 1000 A. D. they began moving by slow migrations into the mesa country of the southeast, their houses steadily acquiring height until a small man might stand on the packed topsoil with his thatched, mud-plastered roof head-high and anchored to thick walls of rock and patted clay. As their houses grew more difficult to build and rebuild they sought increasingly to situate them in invulnerable positions, on the tops of the hills, against the bases of cliffs where attack could come from one side only, and finally in the immense caves and fissures that pock the mesa faces of the Colorado Plateau, acquiring thereby their name "Cliff-Dwellers." In the relative security of their cliff caves, sometimes as much as five lariat lengths from the top or from the jumble of talus at the bottom, their builders were restrained only by limited mechanics and availability of materials. At Hovenweep National

Monument the cliff buildings have as many as four stories with window-less facades eight or ten rooms wide; elsewhere single rooms were built one above another into a square tower, or joined one to the other in a haphazard pattern over the whole of the cave floor.

Since the cliff communities were built with no preconceived plan (the usual procedure was apparently to build a unit adequate to house a family or clan, and afterward to tack on additions as the prosperity and increase of the inhabitants demanded), cliff dwellings from a distance often give the impression of an orderly jumble of planes characteristic of cubistic paintings or the horizontal stepped-back construction of Spanish Colonial and much modern architecture. Internally they are less imposing. The rooms, built to accommodate a small people, seldom have a maximum dimension exceeding ten feet and never headroom for a Caucasian. Those on the first story are floored with smooth stone or a flinty mixture of clay and refuse, and raftered with stripped cedar logs overlain by a matwork of branches to hold the clay for the flood above. The walls, of rock, with clay mortar and an outside plaster of sunbaked clay (often still fingermarked), are usually ponderous things, as much as four feet thick; they are broken only by pinched entrances and an occasional smoke-hole. There are no passageways, rooms are continuous and are reached through the rooms adjacent to them—a piece of practical designing that eliminated many partitioning walls. They still dug pits as their ancestors had, but for storage purposes and (clinging, one presumes, to religious usages older than themselves) for the performance of certain ceremonies. These latter, the ceremonial chambers or *kivas,* were always built in pit form, perfectly circular, from eight to twelve feet deep, their plastered walls inscribed with incised symbols. They were entered through a square aperture in the roof and contained nothing but small fire-blackened altars.

Though from their size some of the Cliff-Dweller communities must have had thousands of inhabitants, they seem to have fallen prey to nomads who swept down on them about 1400 A. D., driving them, according to Navaho legend, into the waters of the Colorado River, where they became *pishlakai,* or fish-people. The conquerors, having strong religious taboos against desecration or even habitations of houses of the dead, left the cliff dwellings untouched (a respect lacking in the white wanderers who have visited them since), and passed on to their descendants, the Navahos, a strong prejudice against eating fish from the Colorado. The modern inheritors of the mesa country have profited nothing from the examples left them. The Navahos build a kind of fixed tepee, called *hogan,* of cedar posts set in the ground, brought together at the top, and made weathertight with a thatchwork of mud and twigs. The desert winds, in their ceaseless moving of sands, cover them sometimes until they are indistinguishable from the mounds that accrete about sagebrush and chaparral. For summer the Navaho builds a bower of cedar posts with a thatched roof. The Utes, Paiutes, and Gosiutes made tepees of skins once, but since the 1920's they have been content with mail-order tents and government-built houses.

Miles Goodyear, trader to the Indians, built a cabin of logs and a stockade on the present site of Ogden about 1844. The log-cabin architectural tradition, brought west from the rainy eastern frontier by Mormon pioneers in 1847, very early encountered proponents of the adobe house. The first of these was Sam Brannan, who had lately passed through California; he said 'dobe houses could be built, and well in a week. Necessity for immediate housing, and the relative availability of materials, led to a wedding of the two structural forms in the original Pioneer Fort, constructed of adobe and logs. Soil for adobe bricks existed everywhere, but green fir timber had to be hauled tediously from distant canyons.

A majority of colonists turned to "mud 'n' straw," moulded in bricks a foot and a half long, hardened in the sun, and laid in walls two or three feet thick. It was not always a happy material. Consider the plaint of the old-timer from St. George, whose house "riz right up outa the mud she stood on, 'n' when it rained, oozed right back down again." But, with a proper mixture of straw, or manure, if straw were lacking, and adequate drying and a bit of "fixin' " now and then when the bricks were in place, it could be made to endure indefinitely. The earliest homes built of it were rectangular, two small rooms long. If a man found time, the house might boast a porch across the front and a timber lean-to aft. The cornice was narrow and simple in outline, and the roof was quite flat. The rectangular plan was retained in later 'dobe homes (they were easiest and cheapest to construct and simplest to heat), but with four or six rooms on the first floor, and a dormer-windowed second story added. Roofs, except the makeshifts of the first season in a settlement, were usually common gable and shingled. The floors were, as often as not, the dirt the house was built over.

Though the Mormons turned to adobe as a grim necessity, and not without protest, it has splendid building properties. Adobe clay, with its straw-formed cavities, is a good insulator, and the blocks, though not as durable as modern fired bricks, are easier to make and with care will last about as long. In Utah many builders, capitalizing on the post-World War growth of interest in the California ranchero houses, have reintroduced it in home construction, protecting the walls with a coat of stucco or plaster. Adobe, indeed, has one quality that should rank it high in the estimation of modern architects—it cannot be worked into anything but what it was intended for; it will build a straight wall only. Comparing its qualities with log or frame, the visitor to Utah looks in vain for a pioneer cabin of logs, unless under a canopy, as the specimens in Ogden, and Temple Square and Liberty Park in Salt Lake City; whereas there are pioneer-built 'dobe houses, in constant use, in half the towns of the State.

About 1853, Brigham Young let contracts for an official residence for the Mormon Church president, a Church Office, and a private residence, all to be built in Great Salt Lake City on what is now South Temple Street. They were designed by William Ward and Truman O. Angell, the first practicing architects in the Territory, excepting of course, Young himself, who in his capacity of final authority for all things Mormon, had some positive (and workable) notions of his own about construction. They were built of the ubiquitous adobe, laid in walls three feet thick over foundations of hewn stone, the interiors whitewashed and the exteriors plastered. The rectangular Lion House, broken only by its twenty gables and a small square portico, is a replica of a home Young had seen in New England. He reproduced it completely, including the carved stone lion couchant over the doorway. The official residence (Beehive House), somewhat more elaborate than the Lion House, is closely identified with New England Colonial Houses, with its wide square-columned porch all the way across the front. Its square cupola belongs to the New England coastal genre called "widow's watch," from which anxious eyes were turned to sea. The Church Office, sandwiched between the other two, and connected to them as an afterthought, is less imposing, though it does boast the first mezzanine balcony built in the West. The three together strike a quiet Old World note among the office and apartment buildings that surround them, and inside, soundproofed as they are by thick walls, there survives a Victorian dignity. The walls and doorways are paneled with free-carved pine; the staircases ascend ornately into dim upper floors exactly as they did when Brigham entertained in the old days; and though the fireplaces have been converted to gas, the large mantle-pieces have not been touched since they were put in.

The Salt Lake Temple, which took forty years to complete, was also commissioned to Angell early in the 1850's; and in 1863 William Folsom and Henry Grow began to build a tabernacle with a seating capacity of five thousand. Folsom and Grow raised an egg-shaped dome above a series of stone buttresses, using rawhide and thole pins in lieu of nails. Grow was a bridge builder, and he constructed the Tabernacle on the Remington principle of arched supports. The resultant building has been variously described, by Kipling (fresh from India) as a "shingled fraud," by J. A. Hester as "absolutely unique and a most wonderful structure," and by an anonymous Englishman as "astonishin'." In 1940 it had served for more than seven decades as the principal gathering place for the Mormon Church. After his success in designing the Tabernacle, Folsom was given commissions for the Manti and St. George temples. They are modeled on the temple the Mormons were forced to abandon in Kirtland, Ohio, which in turn was an enlarged version of the typical New England "meeting house." They are rectangular in plan, with pyramidal-roofed square bell towers at the front. Construction was of stone, vermilion-hued sandstone in St. George and limestone at Manti, which was quarried by the crudest of methods. The blocks were cut along natural cleavages by the Egyptian method of drilling holes into which pegs were driven and wetted, the stone splitting when the pegs swelled. The temple at Logan, designed by Angell, though of the same basic design, has from the darkness of its stone and its octagonal corner towers the gloomy aspect of a Norman castle. Of all their buildings, however, the Mormons take greatest pride in the Salt Lake Temple, built tediously and carefully of native granite. Though sternly rectangular in plan as the others, its east and west ends are heightened by a system of ascending pyramidal towers, which, if not strictly Gothic, give much the same impression of vertical aspiration as the products of Gothic architects. Among the lesser buildings belonging to the early period of Utah architecture, the tabernacles at Logan and Brigham City, and the chapels built in almost every community, possess the naive charm of straightforward building with native materials, though many an architect attempting to classify them has been obliged to use the unacademic expression "Mormonesque." The Old State House at Fillmore, in design, consisted of an elaborate system of wings about a central Moorish dome, but limitation of the Territorial treasury reduced the actual building to one austere wing. Of the low-walled forts that in early days were everywhere in the Territory, the best remaining examples are the crumbling mud walls of Fort Deseret (see Tour 8), and the perfectly preserved Cove Fort (see Tour 1e), whose houses have but three walls, the fourth being the fort wall itself.

The penetration of Utah by railroads in 1869, with the attendant mine boom, had a profound effect on the whole social structure of the Territory, an effect that was nowhere more marked than in its architecture. Between 1847 and 1870, homes had gradually grown more spacious, more comfortable, without, however, altering the basic design or freeing them from the pioneer simplicities. In many towns, such as Pleasant Grove, commodious old dormitories rear themselves somewhat grimly above the more modest dwellings, with unadorned entrances in the exact middle of the front, windows broken into small panes (since it was easier to freight small sizes of glass by wagon), and interiors of unfinished pine. If an occasional home had a bit of scrollwork about the porch or stoop, or a patch of paneling carved freehand inside, it was simply done. The railroad altered all that. The anonymous author of *Art in Utah,* published in twelve immense folio volumes in Chicago (1896), said: "The air had cleared wonderfully in Utah. . . . The house of adobe has become but a relic of the past; it is superseded by the artistic home of pressed brick or stone." Utah was within seven days of the Atlantic seaboard, freight rates were shattered, and the people of the Great Basin had nothing to restrain them from imitating an East which was, in its turn, imitating with all its might the gaudy extravagances of the Second French Empire. Mansard roofs replaced the honest gable; cornices and porches were larded with floriated machine-cut brackets; turrets, towers, and bay windows broke the old rectangularity. By 1880 the moneyed portion of Utah had entered fully into the rococo age of "Victorian-Gothic and mail order house gingerbread." The residential districts of Salt Lake City, Ogden, Logan, and Provo were still, in 1940, tolerably well supplied with these pretentious and complicated houses. Commercial and public architecture was generally more restrained. The tabernacles of Ogden and Provo, the Brigham Young University Administration Building, and the Utah State Agricultural College Administration Building, though they have the broken facade, the towers, and the turrets of the times, have retreated into ivy coverings, and groves of trees have grown high about them. The Cathedral of the Madeleine in Salt Lake City (built much later, however) is an excellent example of a more primitive Gothic style, as are the First Methodist Episcopal and First Presbyterian churches. Business districts of the larger towns sported an occasional turret, but in general the Gothic influence was minimal.

In the 1890's Richardsonian Romanesque was introduced into Utah in the Salt Lake City and County Building. The plan for this structure was an adaptation of London Town Hall, a complex of pillared upper-story windows, corner towers, pinnacles, arches, pilasters, erected in gray standstone. The venerable old building was almost shaken apart during the gentle earthquake of 1934, but it was reinforced, its east and west halves bolted together, and continued in 1940 staunchly to serve as the outstanding example of Romanesque in Utah. The Dooly Building in Salt Lake City, built by Richardson, was still in service as a suitable business structure in 1940. The Governor's Mansion in Salt Lake City is the best example of elaborate Romanesque in residence construction.

After 1900, Utah followed the rest of the Nation in a return to "classic architecture"—a renaissance expressed principally in public buildings such as the State Capitol, the City and County Building at Provo, and the Maeser Memorial Building at Brigham Young University. The Hotel Utah in Salt Lake City, built in 1911, is of the ornate French-Classical style. Residence design wandered timidly from mild Gothic to Georgian Colonial, exhibiting the general taste for classicism in an occasional home, as the lovely Peyton residence in Salt Lake City, or creating designs garnered from the whole background of Utah architecture, as the old David Eccles home in Ogden. About 1900, home builders discovered the bungalow. This squat hand-me-down from Nepal and Bombay neither fitted the Utah terrain nor adequately met the needs of Utah people, yet it completely dominated small residence architecture in the State until the late 1920's. Examples of it, in its worst and best forms, appear in every community.

Since the depression began in 1929 there seems to have been a revival of Colonial straightforwardness. The direct design of industrial buildings, office buildings, and apartment houses, having crept into schools, government buildings, and even into churches, has its counterpart in a residence architecture more fitted than the Gothic, the Romanesque, or the East Indian to the simplicities of the Utah landscape. The cottage, as well as the less extreme forms of California and modified New England Colonial houses, have appeared since 1935 with increasing frequency. The Ogden City and County Building in an admirable adaptation of stepped back skyscraper structure to the modest needs of a western community. The administration building at the Salt Lake City airport, though built on lines characteristic of modern aviation centers, has a disappointing interior plan; it is as crowded as a bus station, and has little of the spacious, high-altitude design that air travelers have come to expect from terminals elsewhere. Mormon and other church chapels constructed since 1930 have incorporated the block forms and horizontal movement of concrete and steel construction, though they have been content to do without the more extreme styles that have attached themselves to this material. The Community Center of Ephraim, completed in 1939, is an unusually charming adaptation of the New England Colonial. It is built of a native oolitic limestone which, though quite soft and easily workable in the quarry, becomes almost granite hard with exposure to the air. In the mining towns Utah's rare indulgence in the old "false front" commercial buildings (commercial meaning "saloon, brothel, and gambling palace") can still be seen. Copperton, in Bingham Canyon, is a livable "company town," planned by post-war architects. Two of its houses are experiments in the use of copper in home construction; the roof, walls, and partitions are of sheet copper.

The English artist, J. A. Hester, as early as 1914 commented on the growing originality of Church design in Utah, observing that it tended to do away with ornament and curves, depending on nice balances of flat areas for its effect. He concluded that this architecture "may in time absorb the rest and be a determining factor in the one great style that will undoubtedly arise in time from the chaos that now reigns" in America. Yet no Utah architect has, as Burton suggested, "extracted from such scenery" as exists here an original system of architecture. No one has drawn the design for a building from the stepped mesas, or for a bridge from the immense wind- and water-hewn arches of Utah's southeast.

PART II

Bonneville Bench Cities

PLATE II

Bonneville Beach Cities

Utah's principal cities are all built on terraces, or "benches" of prehistoric Lake Bonneville, a vast body of water that once covered most of western Utah and extended into Idaho and Nevada. Deltas deposited by rivers flowing into this gigantic lake were carved into relatively flat shelves by the action of shore waves. The larger lake cut an outlet through the mountains at its northern end and drained out through the Snake River country about 25,000 years ago, this sudden recession of the waters exposing the highest of the benches. After Snake drainage ceased, successive periods of recession left other old terraces standing high and dry above the bed of Great Salt Lake, which is a remnant of the ancient water body.

Logan

Railroad Stations: Union Pacific Depot, 600 W. Center St., for Union Pacific R.R.; Interurban Depot, 65 S. Main St., for Utah-Idaho Central R.R.
Bus Stations: Hotel Eccles, Center and Main Sts., for Union Pacific Stages, and Bear Lake Stages; Interurban Depot, 65 S. Main St., for Utah-Idaho Central Bus.
Airport: Municipal Airport, 4.5 *m.* NW. on US 91; no scheduled service.
Taxis: 15¢ 1 to 6 blocks, 25¢ 6 to 16 blocks.
Traffic Regulations: Speed limit 25 m.p.h.; no U turns; right turn permitted against red light after full stop.

Accommodations: Five hotels; tourist camps.

Information Service: Chamber of Commerce, 41 S. Main St.

Hospitals: William Budge Memorial Hospital, 3rd East and 2nd North Sts., 86 beds; Cache County General Hospital, 55 N. 1st East St., 46 beds.

Motion Picture Houses: Five.
Radio Station: KVNU (1230 k.c.).
Golf: Logan Golf and Country Club, 2 m. E. on US 89, 9 holes, greens fee 35¢. Open to public weekdays.
Tennis: Courts at Agricultural College, 4th North and 7th East Sts.; Central Park, 1st South and 3rd East Sts.; Logan High School, 160 W. 1st South St.; Adams Field, 5th North and 4th East Sts.
Football: Utah State Agricultural College Stadium, 7th North and 8th East Sts., Mountain States Conference.
Skating: Logan Skating Rink, 1st East and Center Sts.
Swimming: Central Park, wading pool, free; Logana Plunge, 1.5 *m.* NW. of Logan, fees 25¢, 35¢.
Fishing and Hunting: Trout fishing on Logan River and Blacksmith Fork; elk and deer hunting in highlands bordering Logan Canyon.

Annual Events: Cache County Fair, Fairgrounds, Sept. Founder's Day, Utah State Agricultural College, March.

LOGAN (4,535 alt., 11,875 pop.), on the east side of fertile Cache (pronounced Cash) Valley, for which it is the trading center, between two ranges of the Wasatch Mountains, is built on the lowland and terraces of a north-reaching arm of prehistoric Lake Bonneville. It lies to the north of the Logan River, near the point where that stream issues from Logan Canyon in the nearby range to the east, and is 20 miles south of the Idaho line.

Visible for miles from any approach in the valley, the Mormon Temple, with its twin gray towers, stands on an eastern terrace overlooking the tree-grown city. The square gray belfry of the Mormon Tabernacle rises above the trees in the downtown area; and to the northeast, on a mountainside campus, is the bell tower of the main building of Utah State Agricultural College. Westward and northward from the city are irrigated fields of sugar beets, peas, and grain, laid out like checker squares, and the western range of the Wasatch in the background. Logan Peak, almost due east of the city, rises to an altitude of 9,713 feet. The mountains on both sides of Cache Valley are tinted with the new green of foliage in spring, while snow is still on the high peaks. In autumn the maples on the foothills turn crimson, and, after the first touch of frost, the aspen groves make bright splashes of yellow against the green firs of the higher mountains.

The city is a pleasant residential community, its streets lined with trees. Lawns are numerous, and are kept green in summer by frequent watering. Nearly every home has a vegetable and flower garden in back, and many residents of the city have prosperous farms in Cache Valley, a few miles out of town. Families are large, and so are individual incomes, as revealed by a survey of the State Planning Board in 1936. The people are mostly of English or Scandinavian extraction, and a goodly number are foreign-born. Few of their native customs survive. A few Japanese live in the vicinity and work farms in the valley. Olive-green uniforms of U. S. forest rangers are not uncommon on Logan streets, for the city is headquarters of the Cache National Forest. The Cache County Fair, held in September, is typical of all county fairs. It includes prize animals, handicrafts, produce, and industrial displays. A carnival with the usual devices is always present. Farmers gather before the displays and argue about crops and cattle. Their wives gossip by the needlework and canning exhibits and children trudge wearily at their sides. The business district, large for a city of its size, is restricted to Main and First West Streets. Logan's industries—a sugar beet factory, pea canneries, textile mills, candy factories, milk condenseries, and others—are for the most part in the western and southern part of the city, convenient to the railroad.

The first white men to visit the region, in 1824, were American beaver trappers, who *cached* or hid their furs in present Cache Valley (*see Tour 1a*). Because there were numerous bison and other game in "Willow Valley," as the trappers called it, they used the area as winter quarters. In the summer of 1847, Brigham Young, always eager to bring more land under Mormon control, dispatched an exploration party to determine the valley's resources.   The party returned in autumn with reports of abundant water, timber, and tillable lands.   No attempt was made to colonize until 1855, when grass shortage in Salt Lake Valley influenced a company of eight men to drive their livestock north.   They established a ranch at Wellsville, near the present site of Logan, and by autumn had driven several thousand head of horses and cattle into the valley, constructed log cabins and corrals, and prepared for permanent residence.

In 1857 the Federal government sent an army to Utah under Colonel Albert Sidney Johnston.   The Mormons, fearing that the persecutions which had driven them from the East were to be resumed in the West, made a general exodus from the northern part of Utah (*see History*).   The valley, however, was permanently resettled in the spring of 1859, lands apportioned by lot, and the site of Logan surveyed.   The settlement was named for Ephraim Logan, an early trapper.   Shoshone Indians, aroused by the influx of white men with plows and fences, were by this time covertly hostile.   For protection against them, the homes were built in a double line, forming a fort-like enclosure.   A militia was organized "to be ready for instant service," but was strictly enjoined to give the Indians no cause for offense.   The aborigines, deprived of hunting, fishing, and adequate camping ground, were already too deeply disturbed to be reconciled.   They harassed the settlers with petty thievery and occasional attacks on isolated farms.   In 1863 hostilities culminated in an engagement (*see Tour 1a*) at the junction of Bear River and Battle Creek in Idaho just north of the Utah line.

In 1859 the Mormons scraped a shallow irrigation canal from Logan River to farms in the town and made plans for irrigation of the valley.   In the same year James Ellis and Benjamin Williams established the first sawmill, with a hand-operated whipsaw.   During the succeeding decades, water power replaced hand labor, and sawmills, carding mills, and flour mills were built along the banks of streams. Hezekiah Thatcher opened a retail store for business, and Thomas Weir and Joel Ricks began tanning leather for "harness, saddles, shoes, britches, and shirts."   The city was granted a charter and incorporated in 1866.   The following year, telegraphic communications with Salt Lake City were completed.

In the early seventies, a watchmaker named Growe published a folio newspaper—half in Danish and half in English—and another watchmaker introduced photography.   The public school was moved from its log cabins to a new stone building; the Episcopalians established a grammar school, the Presbyterians an academy, and the Mormons a college.   The United Order, established by the Mormons in various parts of Utah and Arizona, as a communal form of living, was instituted in Logan about 1875.   Harvests and produce were distributed on a basis of the amount of work contributed.   The plan failed in a decade.

Mrs. Lydia Hamp Baker, whose family came to Logan from England in 1877, recalls in an interview that "the town was mostly willows in the early days." She worked at her trade of boot-closing, or sewing boot and shoe uppers by hand. The settlers slept in four-poster cord beds, with rope stretched on the frame in lieu of springs. They burned willows for fuel, carried water from irrigation ditches for home use, and farmed exclusively with hand tools. Meat was scarce, and neighbors gave their peelings and table leavings to help fatten the nearest pig; when it was butchered they received "pig fry" for their investment—liver, fat, and a little pork. Indians begged from house to house, carrying their bundles of biscuits, sugar, and scraps to wigwams in the willows.

Completion of the Utah Northern Railroad from Ogden in 1874 gave Logan the outlet necessary for the development of native resources. But this advantage was mitigated by lack of capital and by Brigham Young's predilection for the fruits of the soil. Timber and farm produce were almost the sole exports of Logan for many years. Factories in and about the city were introduced for the most part after the turn of the century. A municipal electric plant was put into operation in 1903-04. It is estimated that the lower rates result in an annual saving of $50,000 for local users of electricity, as compared to the average for the State.

Logan is the home of Lieutenant Russell Maughan, who made the first dawn-to-dusk flight from New York to San Francisco in 1924, requiring 21 hours for the trip. His grandfather, Peter Maughan, was one of the original settlers of this area in 1859, taking six days to journey by ox-team from Salt Lake City to Logan. Marriner S. Eccles, chairman of the board of governors of the Federal Reserve Board since 1934, is a native of Logan, and William M. Jardine, Secretary of Agriculture 1925-29, and envoy to Egypt 1930-33, taught at Utah State Agricultural College from 1904 to 1906.

POINTS OF INTEREST

1. MORMON TABERNACLE (*open during services*), Main and Center Sts., a cupola-crowned structure of gray limestone, is an excellent example of early Mormon architecture. The building, started in 1865, was razed and begun again in the following year when discrepancies were found in the plans. The completed building, with a seating capacity of 2,000 and a pipe organ, was dedicated thirteen years later.

2. LOGAN TEMPLE (*grounds open*), 1st North and 2nd East Sts., is maintained by the Latter-day Saints (Mormon) Church for the administration of sacred ordinances, and is not open to the general public. The building, a grim castellated structure with octagonal corner towers surmounted by cupolas and massive buttresses, commands the city from the crest of an abrupt promontory two blocks east of Main Street. The walls, of rough-hewn limestone, are unrelieved by ornamentation, except mouldings of light sandstone at the story levels and on the cornices. Fenestration is simple, and the end towers, 170 feet high, are capped with unornamented cupolas. The level grounds

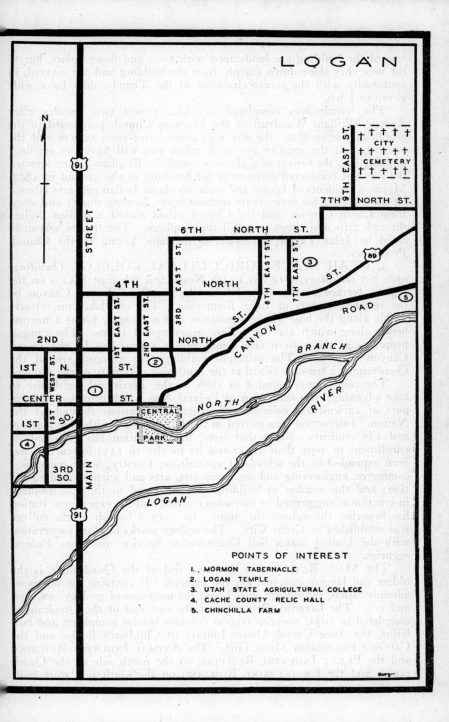

LOGAN

CITY CEMETERY

9TH EAST ST.

7TH
NORTH ST.

6TH   NORTH   ST.

91

STREET

89

4TH   NORTH

3RD EAST ST.

6TH EAST ST.

7TH EAST ST.

CANYON   ROAD

5

2ND   NORTH

1ST EAST ST.

2ND EAST ST.

2

BRANCH

1ST   N.

NORTH

CANYON

RIVER

1ST

1ST WEST ST.

CENTER   ST.

1

NORTH

1ST SO.

CENTRAL
PARK

LOGAN

MAIN

4

3RD
SO.

91

LOGAN

Burg—

POINTS OF INTEREST

1. MORMON TABERNACLE
2. LOGAN TEMPLE
3. UTAH STATE AGRICULTURAL COLLEGE
4. CACHE COUNTY RELIC HALL
5. CHINCHILLA FARM

east of the building are landscaped with trees and flower plots, but to the west they slope down sharply from the building and are covered, in conformity with the severe character of the Temple, only by a wide sweep of lawn.

The temple was completed in 1884, almost two decades after Apostle William Woodruff of the Mormon Church prophesied to the people of Logan that "the day will come, after your fathers and the prophets and the apostles are dead, when you will have the privilege of going into the towers of a glorious temple." Brigham Young selected the site and conducted ceremonies for breaking of the ground in 1877. Mormon residents of Logan and some Shoshone Indian converts labored on the building for seven years without wage, hauling timber and stone from Logan Canyon, and the Church raised almost a million dollars through gifts and tithes to fulfill the prophecy. The temple was dedicated by John Taylor, successor to Brigham Young in the Church Presidency.

3. UTAH STATE AGRICULTURAL COLLEGE (*buildings open 9-5 weekdays, 9-12 Sat.*), 4th North and 7th East Sts., is on the highest terrace of the delta left at the mouth of Logan Canyon by the receding waters of Lake Bonneville. The old lake line, clearly visible along the base of the mountains east of Logan, forms a narrow bench along which are the college experimental farms. The campus proper is at the eastern city limits and is approached by the Logan Canyon highway. The principal buildings are grouped around the Quadrangle, a ten-acre sward at the southwest extremity of the campus.

The college was founded in 1888 by the Territorial legislature to take advantage of a succession of Federal Acts which provided for support of agricultural colleges and experiment stations throughout the Nation. Instruction was started in the fall of 1890, with nine teachers and 135 students. Since that time, the institution has increased its enrollment to more than 3,300 and its faculty to 125; instruction has been expanded by the schools of agriculture, forestry, home economics, commerce, engineering and mechanic arts, arts and sciences, and education; and the number of buildings has increased to thirty. Resident instruction is augmented by extension courses, and the experiment station has branches throughout the State. In 1913 a branch of the college was established at Cedar City. The college works in close cooperation with the United States Soil Conservation Service and other Federal agencies.

The MAIN BUILDING at the west end of the Quadrangle is the oldest and largest structure on the campus. It contains the offices of administration, the college chapel, and the museums of geology, zoology, and art. The LIBRARY BUILDING at the east end of the Quadrangle, completed in 1931, contains 60,000 volumes besides pamphlets and bulletins, the Anne Carrol Moore Library of Children's Books, and the Carnegie Foundation Music Gift. The ANIMAL INDUSTRY BUILDING and the PLANT INDUSTRY BUILDING on the north side of the Quadrangle and the ENGINEERING BUILDING on the south side were built during the World War to serve as barracks and arsenals. At the termination of the war they were converted into classrooms and laboratories. The HOME ECONOMICS AND COMMONS BUILDING, adjacent to the Engineering Building on the south side of the Quadrangle, was completed in 1935 and contains student offices, recreational rooms, and the cafeteria, in addition to classrooms.

North of the Quadrangle are the barns, used for the study of housing and feeding livestock. The STADIUM, three blocks north of the Main Building, utilizes the slope of a hill to support its bleachers and is used for football games and track and field meets of the Mountain States Conference.

4. CACHE COUNTY RELIC HALL (*admission by appointment with Daughters of Utah Pioneers*), 1st West and 1st South Sts., a stone building, contains a collection of pioneer tools, farm implements, art, and furniture. The hall, a reminder of the days of "brick barns and frame houses," was erected as a stable and carriage house by Hezekiah Thatcher in 1861. He transferred it to the old Brigham Young College in the 1870's to be used for classrooms, and that organization, when dissolved in 1927, gave it to the Daughters of Utah Pioneers.

5. The CHINCHILLA FARM (*open 9-4 weekdays*), 1052 Canyon Road, has ten chinchillas, each pair worth $3,200. The chinchilla is a bunchy little rodent, smaller than a cottontail, and resembling a rabbit more than a squirrel. "It has a sweet face," Ernie Pyle, Scripps-Howard's "roving reporter" wrote in 1939, "and whiskers stick out on each side of its mouth at least three inches. It sits humped up, it hops, and its fur is a kind of gray blue." The fur, extremely popular in more expensive circles around the turn of the century, is the reason for propagating these animals. It is estimated by dealers to be next in value to that of the platinum fox. Chinchilla pelts in 1940 were worth about $150 each, and about 100 are required to make a chinchilla coat. There are seventeen such coats in existence. The price is $17,000 each.

The animals are housed in wire pens with wooden floors, each pen having a box for a nest. The pairs mate for life, and produce two or three young about every eight months. "A chinchilla's gestation period is 111 days," says Ernie Pyle, "which, in case you're interested, is three days longer than a lion." A constant temperature of about 70 degrees is maintained in the pens. Though worth actually twice their weight in gold, chinchillas are very inexpensive to feed. They hold strictly to a vegetarian diet, eating lettuce, carrots, grit similar to that fed to chickens, and pablum, a cereal food usually given to babies. The grocery bill is about $3.50 per animal per year.

The chinchilla is said to have been originally a low altitude animal, inhabiting the Pacific coast of South America. They were so fiercely hunted, more than a million pelts having been shipped from South America in 1900, that they retreated to the high Andes for self-preservation. They were almost exterminated by 1918, when South

American governments put a ban on shipment of their fur. M. F. Chapman, American mining engineer, began in 1917 to purchase live chinchillas from Indian trappers. By 1920 he had eleven, and started to bring them down the mountains by such slow degrees, to accustom them to the change in elevation, that it was three years before he got to the seashore. In 1923 he arrived with the animals at his home near Los Angeles. That was the beginning of the chinchilla fur farm business in America, which is still controlled by Chapman's family. The animals are raised on thirty-odd farms in the United States, of which the Logan farm is one. Eventually it is hoped to raise enough furs to reopen the market, but a sufficient supply is not expected before 1945.

POINTS OF INTEREST IN ENVIRONS

Smithfield, largest pea cannery in the West, 7.5 *m.;* Clarkston, grave of Martin Harris, one of Three Witnesses to Golden Plates of the Book of Mormon, 25.6 *m.* (*see Tour 1a*). Bear River Migratory Bird Refuge, 42 *m.* (*see Tour 1b*). Logan Canyon, trout fishing, elk and deer hunting in season, campsites, 2.5 *m.;* Juniper Jardine, Logan Canyon, 15 *m.* (*see Tour 2a*). Bear Lake, 40 *m.* (*see Tour 2a*).

Ogden

Railroad Stations: Ogden Union Passenger Depot, Wall Ave. and 25th St., for Union Pacific R.R.; Denver & Rio Grande Western R.R.; and Southern Pacific R.R. Interurban Terminal Depot, 258 24th St., for Bamberger Electric R.R., and Utah & Idaho Central R.R.
Bus Station: Union Bus Depot, 25th St. and Grand Ave. for Union Pacific Stages, Inc., Interurban Terminal Depot, 258 24th St., for Bamberger and Utah-Idaho Central Busses.
Airport: 2 *m.* S. of city on US 30S; no scheduled service.
Taxis: Zone fare system, 15¢ and up.
City Busses: Fare 5¢; weekly pass $1.
Traffic Regulations: Traffic semaphores in business district; 2-hr. parking in downtown section 9-6 weekdays. No U-turns in business district; right turn on red light after full stop.
Street Order: Wall Ave., running north and south, forms the E. boundary of the R.R. yards which occupy the extreme western part of the city. Streets parallel to Wall Ave. eastward are named for presidents of the United States. Beginning several blocks S. of the N. City limits, the streets running east and west are named 1st St., 2nd St., etc.

Accommodations: Fifteen hotels; tourist camps.

Information Service: Chamber of Commerce, 2510 Washington Blvd., in Hotel Ben Lomond.

Hospital: Thomas D. Dee Memorial Hospital, 2440 Harrison Ave., 240 beds.

Radio Station: KLO (1430 kc.).
Motion Picture Houses: Five.
Golf: Ogden Municipal Golf Course, 1300 Valley Drive; 9 holes, greens fee. Ogden Golf and Country Club, 4200 Washington Blvd., open upon introduction by members, or to members of the Western Golf Association.
Tennis: Double courts at Monroe, Liberty, and Lester Parks and Pingree and Central Jr. High Schools; single courts at Lorin Farr Park, Weber Jr. College, and the Lincoln, Madison, Washington Jr. High, and Grant Schools.
Softball: Lorin Farr Park, Canyon Rd. between Monroe and Quincy Aves.; Five Points, 4th St. and Lincoln Ave.; Beckers Field, 20th St. and Lincoln Ave.
Swimming: Patio Springs, 12.1 *m.* E. on side road from State 39; Utah Hot Springs, 10 *m.* N. on US 91; Weber Gymnasium, 550 25th St.; Washington Junior High School; Lorin Farr Park, Canyon Rd. between Monroe and Quincy Aves.
Skiing: Skiing with tows at Snow Basin, 18 *m.* E. of city.
Skating: Pine View Dam, 8.5 *m.* E. on State 39; the Old Mill, 12th St. and Canyon Rd.; John Affleck Park; El Monte Springs, Ogden Canyon E of city.
Riding: Wasatch Riding Academy, 4102 Adams Ave.
Hiking: Jump-Off Canyon, E. of city limits at 2nd St.; Taylor's Canyon and trail to Malan's Heights, 6,000 ft. elevation, E. from 25th or 26th Sts., and to Mt. Ogden, 9,574 ft. elevation; Waterfall Canyon E. of city limits at 30th St.; Limestone Cave, NE. of city in unnamed canyon (*guide necessary*).
Hunting and Fishing: The area from Weber Canyon S. to North Ogden Canyon (13 miles) and from the east city limits eastward across the Wasatch

Range to Mountain Green and Ogden Valley (10 miles) is a State game preserve (*fishing permitted, firearms forbidden*). Elsewhere in season waterfowl, pheasants, deer, and rabbits may be hunted. Numerous streams and reservoirs afford trout fishing.

Trapshooting: Ogden Gun Club, 4200 Washington Blvd.   Open to public. No fees.

Rifle Range: E. of city limits and N. of 23rd St.   Open to public.

Annual Events: Free public oratorio, *The Messiah,* Ogden Tabernacle, New Year's Day; Jollification of Weber County Fish and Game Protective Ass'n., April; Loyalty Day, street parade of 10,000 school children, last week in May; Pioneer Days, week of July 24; Ogden Livestock Show, 6 days in early November.

OGDEN (4,299 alt., 43,719 pop.), second largest city in Utah, is the principal railway center of the intermountain region. Though east of the dividing line between Mountain and Pacific time, the city is, in railway practice, the place to reset watches. Travelers going west retard timepieces one hour to Pacific time at this point. Those going east advance their watches one hour. The city is built on the deltas of Ogden and Weber (pronounced Wee-ber) rivers, where these two streams once emptied into prehistoric Lake Bonneville. Although most of their water is diverted into storage reservoirs and canals, some continues down the channels to Great Salt Lake, about fifteen miles due west. East of the city looms the massive bulk of the Wasatch Range, cut by Ogden and Weber canyons. Mount Ogden, immediately east, and Ben Lomond, several miles north of the city, are topped with snow about eight months of the year. In autumn the mountain slopes are splashed with the brilliant foliage of the scrub oak, maple, aspen, service berry, hawthorn and chokecherry, interspersed with evergreens. Extensive areas of prosperous farmland merge with the city on the outskirts.

The most marked feature of Ogden is the broad, straight vista of Washington Boulevard, main thoroughfare, north and south. The city's wide streets (planned in true Mormon geometrical style on the four cardinal directions) are bordered by poplar trees, box elder, elm and cottonwood. The residential section is on the east and the industrial area on the west. Within the original townsite (bounded by 21st Street, Wall Avenue, 28th Street, and Madison Avenue) the business and older residential district has structures characteristic of Ogden as fort, village, town and city. Some of the older homes are the former dwellings of polygamous families, distinguished by several entrances and family divisions; in some instances they have been converted into apartment houses. A few homes still display the ornate jigsaw woodwork of the Victorian period. Outside this area, the bungalow, English Colonial, and more modern types of residence predominate. In the vicinity of Marilyn Drive, extending to the foothills of Mount Ogden, are newer and more costly dwellings forming the more exclusive residential area.

Nearly 98 per cent of the population is white. In early years Mormonism attracted many emigrants from England and northern Europe.

Later, the industrial and agricultural growth of the region brought small groups of Mexicans, Japanese, Negroes, Chinese, Italians, and Greeks, most of whom are engaged in railroad and farm work. Since Ogden was made the division headquarters for railroad dining cars, the inflow of Negroes has been more noticeable. About 500 (1940) live in the city and 60 per cent own their homes.

The dominant church is that of the Latter-day Saints, but other religious denominations, including Catholic, Protestant, Jewish, and Buddhist adherents, are well represented. Many business, fraternal, and charitable organizations draw membership from all sects; Ogden was one of the first Utah cities to overcome antipathy between Mormons and non-Mormons.

Throughout most of the year the life of the city is marked by no greater excitement than the arrival of tourists for winter sports or the livestock show, or of summer vacationists heading for the national park and forest areas. Late in July, however, the city undergoes a transformation, for on the 24th of that month the annual Pioneer Days, commemorating the arrival of the Mormon settlers in 1847, is celebrated. Rodeos, pageants, and parades recreate in colorful manner the atmosphere of the Old West, and the festivities last a week.

Shoshonean tribes lived in this region until after the arrival of trappers in the early 1820's. In summer the various bands moved into the mountains, even venturing into Wyoming and Montana to hunt bison. In autumn and winter the Indians established themselves near Great Salt Lake, while some groups traveled a hundred miles west to the pine nut country for the fall harvest. As late as the 1880's there was an abundance of fish in the mountain streams, waterfowl in the marshes, sage-grouse and rabbits in the foothills, and deer, elk, bighorn sheep, and other game animals in the mountains.

After the coming of white men, the site of Ogden and its vicinity was an important rendezvous and wintering place for fur traders and trappers over a period of six or seven years. As such it was a focal point for explorations, and for trade rivalry between American fur companies and the British Hudson's Bay Company, with headquarters at Fort Vancouver, Washington. Peter Skene Ogden (1794-1854), who was a brigade leader for the Hudson's Bay Company, was in northern Utah as early as 1825. That company held absolute dominion over the rich Oregon country, which, by agreement between the two governments, was under "joint occupancy" by British and Americans after 1818. Invasion by American settlers was out of question so far as the British could see, for the high mountain passes between the Missouri and Columbia river headwaters, discovered by Lewis and Clark in 1805, were impracticable for wagon travel. To this geographic barrier was added the enmity of the Blackfoot Indians, with whom Captain Lewis's party had hostilities on the return trip in 1806. Attempts to trap and trade in the Blackfoot country after 1806 had ended in disaster.

Jedediah Smith's—or Thomas Fitzpatrick's—traverse of South

Pass in the spring of 1824, however, opened a feasible way, far south of Blackfoot country, through which General William H. Ashley's fur men poured in great numbers. Among them was Étienne Provot, for whom Provo is named, who camped on or near the site of Ogden in the winter of 1824-25. Another party of trappers, probably under the leadership of William Sublette, spent the same winter in Cache Valley, and from this camp young Jim Bridger discovered Great Salt Lake (*see Great Salt Lake*). While trapping beaver streams in the Great Basin that winter, the mountaineers took particular note of westward-flowing rivers, hoping to find the legendary Buenaventura River, which was said to flow into the Pacific Ocean through San Francisco Bay. Jedediah Smith, meantime, visited a Hudson's Bay Company fort on the upper Columbia River in the fall of 1824, and saw the advantage of a river outlet to the Pacific. The first summer rendezvous, or trade gathering, west of the Rocky Mountains was held on Henrys Fork of the Green River (*see Tour 6a*). Here occurred an instance of rivalry between American and English fur traders that threatened to have international consequences.

The trappers spent the winter of 1825-26 at the present site of Ogden, living in skin tents. Many of them had taken Indian wives, and they settled down, "healthy as bears," to a winter of eating, sleeping, yarn-spinning, and contests of strength. More than a thousand Shoshone Indians came down and camped around them. "They were perfectly friendly," James Beckwourth, the mulatto trader, recalls, "and we apprehended no danger from their proximity. It appears that this was their usual resort for spending the winter." Bannock Indians raided the camp one night and stole eighty horses, but they were pursued by fifty men led by Thomas Fitzpatrick and James Bridger. In a daring raid on the Indian camp the white men recovered all their horses and collected forty others by way of interest. Early in the spring four men, one of whom was James Clyman, set out in bullboats to "circumambulate" Great Salt Lake, to find beaver streams, and to determine whether it was an arm of the Pacific (*see Great Salt Lake*).

The summer rendezvous of 1826 on the site of Ogden was a gala affair, after the arrival of General Ashley from St. Louis with 100 well-laden pack animals. Jim Beckwourth preserves a picture of the scene: "It may well be supposed that the arrival of such a vast amount of luxuries from the East did not pass off without a general celebration. Mirth, songs, dancing, shouting, trading, running, jumping, singing, racing, target shooting, yarns, frolic, with all sorts of extravagances that white men or Indians could invent, were freely indulged in. The unpacking of the *medicine water* contributed not a little to the heightening of our festivities." At that rendezvous General Ashley sold out his interests to Jedediah S. Smith, David E. Jackson (for whom Jackson's Hole, Wyoming, was named), and William L. Sublette.

Meantime the trappers sent to explore Great Salt Lake had returned with the news that it had no outlet and was a total loss as beaver country. Jedediah Smith, now a partner, was free to seek the fabled

Buenaventura River or some other water outlet to the Pacific. Following the rendezvous he started out with seventeen American and French companions—and one Negro—on the first Anglo-Saxon overland journey to California. The following winter the trappers spent on the site of Ogden, and the summer, or trade, rendezvous of 1827 was held on Bear Lake, near present Laketown (*see Tour 2a*). Here Smith rejoined them, having made the first crossing of the Great Salt Desert (*see Tour 6c*). Following the rendezvous he started his second trip to California, a disastrous journey in which he lost all but two of his men and ended by throwing himself on the mercy of Dr. John McLoughlin, factor of the Hudson's Bay post at Fort Vancouver, after making the first overland journey north from southern California through Oregon. The magnanimous but practical Dr. McLoughlin salvaged his furs, which had been stolen by the Indians, and gave him a London draft for $20,000. As a result of this treatment Smith agreed thereafter to confine his activities to places east of the Great Divide. Following the winter of 1828-29, the Americans moved eastward and three succeeding summer gatherings were held in the Wind River and Powder River country of present Wyoming.

As the fur trade declined and the trappers showed a disposition to settle down, the site of Ogden continued to be an occasional camping place for Indians and trappers, until the arrival of Miles Goodyear (1817-49), a native of Connecticut, who built a cabin here in 1844 or 1845. He was the earliest white settler in Ogden, and probably the first in Utah to plant a garden. Coming west from present Kansas with the Whitman party in 1836, he assisted in pioneering an untried wagon road as far as Fort Hall, Idaho, out of which he worked as hunter, trapper, and trader until he had gained sufficient experience to open a trading post of his own. To the original cabin, intended for the use of Goodyear, his Indian wife, and their two children, was added a stockade for livestock and other cabins for his partners, one of whom was Jim Baker, noted mountain man. The arrival of the Mormons in 1847 induced him to sell out, claiming that he held a Mexican grant; existence of such a grant has not been found, but the Mormons probably considered it worth about $2,000 to establish a clear title to all the Utah region.

As for Goodyear, neighbors forty miles away at Great Salt Lake City made things too crowded, and he was glad to dispose of his "property."

The purchase was made under the direction of the Mormon Church by Captain James Brown of the Mormon Battalion, who moved his family into the fort and with the aid of his sons planted five bushels of seed wheat and half a bushel of seed corn, brought from California. Butter and cheese made from the milk of cows and goats purchased from Goodyear gave rise to Ogden's first industry. Other settlers were permitted to possess, without payment, as much land as they could put under immediate cultivation, and in proportion to the size of the family.

Goodyear revisited his old home only once thereafter. He went to California, bought a large herd of horses, and in 1848 drove them east to Fort Leavenworth, Kansas, hoping to sell them at a profit. The market was bad. He turned around and drove them back to California the following year, hitting the gold rush at the right time to market his horseflesh at a handsome profit. On the return trip westward he stopped off at his old place to celebrate July 4 in approved trapper style. His exploit of driving a herd of horses four thousand miles to find a profitable market still stands, even in the annals of mountain men. Goodyear died (1849) in the California gold fields.

Brigham Young came to the settlement of Brownsville, so named from Captain Brown's occupancy, late in 1849, and climbed a near-by hill "to view out a location for a town." The following year the townsite was surveyed and 100 families were sent by the Church leader to settle here. Flood waters washed away part of the cultivated land, Indian trouble grew out of the killing of friendly Chief Terikee, and cholera killed nearly thirty people. In spite of these tribulations the people established schools, held religious meetings, and Ogden (named for Peter Skene Ogden) became the seat of Weber county, one of the original six in the State. With the increase of settlers, irrigation facilities required expansion, and a seven-mile canal, bringing water from the Weber River at Riverdale, was started in 1852. Greater protection from Indians was also needed, and in 1853-54 walls were built or started around Ogden, Bingham's Fort, and Mound Fort, all in the present Ogden area.

The growing season of 1855 and the ensuing "Hard Winter" brought severe trials to the settlers. Grasshoppers partially destroyed the crops. Drouth and early frosts all but completed the devastation. During the winter heavy snows buried grazing lands, causing the starvation of beef cattle, horses, and sheep. Snowbound and unable to get firewood from the canyons, the people were forced to burn their fences. Arrival of destitute emigrants depleted meager food supplies. By the spring of 1856 local people were reduced to eating sego, thistle, and other wild roots. Late that year, according to a portion of the journal of Lewis W. Shurtliff, printed in the January, 1932, issue of the *Utah Historical Quarterly,* "All the little forts around were vieing with each other in growth, each ambitious to become the central city. President Brigham Young, looking into the situation, advised all to move into Ogden. 'Here,' he said, 'a large city will be built up, and railroads will make it a city of importance.' "

Ogden men were mustered into service during the so-called Echo Canyon War in 1857 (*see History*) and assisted in guarding Echo and Weber canyons against the entry of Colonel Albert Sidney Johnston's troops. The following spring, after crops had been planted, Ogden people packed all their movable possessions into wagons and started south. Most of them camped along the Provo Bottoms. A few men were left in the settlement to burn homes, orchards, and fields should the army molest anything. They returned to Ogden following

Governor Cumming's proclamation of amnesty, and found their untilled crops ready for harvest.

Much of the development of Ogden was due to the energy of Lorin Farr, a Vermonter converted to Mormonism at the age of 11. He arrived in Ogden in 1850, formed a city government in 1851, and became the first mayor, a position he held for twenty-two years. He built a gristmill, which included a sawmill operated by water power. Among other activities he was president of the Weber Stake; superintendent of grading for new railroads; represented the county in the Territorial legislature for thirty years; organized the militia; and was president of the first library association. In accordance with Mormon doctrines of the time, Farr married six times, and five of his wives bore him 36 sons and daughters. His direct descendants numbered nearly 400 in 1940.

The most significant event in the history of Ogden was the coming of the railroad. In March, 1869, the first train steamed into the city. A brass band welcomed its arrival, a parade was hastily organized, and speakers depicted the glories to follow. There are residents still living (1940) who recall the afternoon when the entire populace gathered around in Sunday finery to see the iron monster. Suddenly the engineer blew the whistle, yanked a steam valve, and announced he was going "to turn the train around." A wild scramble for safety ensued and many ran pell-mell through a near-by slough in their fright, ruining their Sunday clothes. Some terrified children were not found until evening. Brigham Young sent two men to Ogden with printing presses of the *Salt Lake Daily Telegraph,* and the first issue appeared May 11, 1869, the morning after the driving of the Golden Spike at Promontory. The life of the enterprise was short, for Ogden people resented a Salt Lake City name on a local paper.

In 1870, the year the Utah Central Railroad was completed to Salt Lake City, census returns showed that Ogden had doubled its previous decennial population of 1,463. Most of the newcomers were non-Mormons, and there quickly developed, in the early newspapers, and in the battle for political control of the city, a marked bitterness between Mormons and "gentiles." The Mormon Church, which had acquired the site of Ogden from Miles Goodyear, resented possible control by rough people brought in by the railroad.

Branch railroad lines were built in the seventies and eighties, connecting the transcontinental system with other settlements in Utah, Idaho, and Montana. During the last third of the nineteenth century Ogden was an outfitting point for trappers and hunters going north to Idaho and Montana, and for railroad workers constructing new lines into the mountain States. The saloons and gambling halls were typical of a frontier town. By 1880 the population had doubled again, bringing more non-Mormon settlers, and the acrimonious feeling between Church members and gentiles was reflected in the plain-spoken press of the period; at least one editor was tarred and feathered for his reportorial temerity.

A familiar figure on the streets of Ogden in the 1870's and 1880's was Tom Cahoon, conductor on the passenger train from Ogden to Green River, Wyoming. While working on the railroad crossing the plains in the 1860's he was wounded at Plum Creek, Nebraska, when Indians attacked the train, and "had his hair lifted" while still alive. Always well-dressed and gallant, he kept his hat tilted to cover the place where his scalp used to be. He left the railroad company and planted an orchard on the foothills east of the city.

Meantime business and commercial activities were developing, and a series of setbacks pointed the way to further municipal advancement. Serious fires in 1873, 1879, and 1881 accented the need for adequate fire protection. A smallpox epidemic in the late 1870's showed the want of an adequate health service. Lynching of a Japanese in 1884 indicated that better police protection was required.

Between 1880 and 1900, Ogden boomed. Electrical service was extended to homes and factories; the telephone system, one of the first in the West, was established; the canning industry began; and a clothing factory was opened. An electric street railway system was installed, replacing horse-drawn cars. An attempt was made to start an iron factory with ore taken from the mountains east of Willard, but the furnace and the venture blew up simultaneously. The census of 1900 gave Ogden a population of 16,313.

In the early years of the twentieth century civic improvements were numerous and the feeling between Mormons and non-Mormons gradually improved. The first curb and gutter district was created, the streets were paved by modern methods, and the city at last realized its ambition for an adequate hospital. The building of the Southern Pacific Railroad across Great Salt Lake—a cutoff that shortened the distance to the Pacific coast by forty miles—was a major activity for Ogden from 1900 to 1904. John M. Mills, superintendent of schools, established the junior high school here in 1908 (*see Education*). This system, first called the "sub-high," had been advocated in the East but was not in operation at the time. An important development was the establishment of Ogden, on July 1, 1908, as Headquarters of Region Four of the U. S. Forest Service.

In 1912 Ogden changed from the council to the commission form of government. The waterworks system was purchased, the supply pipe line of which had been laid in 1891. William Bostaph, city engineer, proposed an artesian waterworks system in 1913. The following year artesian wells were drilled in Ogden Valley, which supplied the city with thirteen million gallons of water daily. The wells were submerged under forty feet of water in the lake formed by Pine View Dam, completed in 1937, but the water is piped from the wells to the city, untouched by lake water. In 1918 a branch office of the U. S. Bureau of Public Roads was established in Ogden and the era of important work on highways was inaugurated. Natural gas from Baxter Basin, 300 miles distant, was piped into homes and factories during 1929.

Ogden is one of the largest distribution points for manufacturing, milling, canning, livestock, and agriculture in the intermountain West; it ranks third in the Nation in the number of sheep received in its yards, and eleventh in cattle. The Union Stockyards is the largest shipping point for sheep and cattle west of Denver. More than 100 industrial plants employ in excess of 4,000 persons and the volume of business exceeds $38,000,000 annually.

Among the citizens of Ogden who have gained national or international repute are the brothers, John Moses and Jonathan Edmund Browning, inventors of improved automatic firearms. Frank J. Cannon, son of George Quayle Cannon, Mormon apostle and Territorial delegate, was an editor of the *Ogden Standard* in the nineties. Elected as the first United States Senator after statehood (1896) Cannon, a Democrat, was known as Utah's "Silver Senator" because of his advocacy of "free" silver coinage. Having taken issue with certain policies of the Mormon Church at the time of the Senate trial for seating Senator Reed Smoot, he renounced his allegiance to the Church and published two controversial books, *Utah Under the Prophet,* and *Brigham Young and His Mormon Empire.* William Hope (Coin) Harvey, another advocate of free coinage of silver and credited with having brought this issue to the attention of William Jennings Bryan, was an Ogden business man during the late 1880's and early 1890's. Marriner S. Eccles, financier and prominent "New Dealer," governor of the Federal Reserve Board, is a resident of Ogden. Robert H. Hinckley, another prominent "New Dealer" resident of Ogden, was appointed Assistant Secretary of Commerce in 1940. Bernard DeVoto, writer and literary critic, born and raised in Ogden, used the city as his locale in a novel, *The Crooked Mile* (1924). Moroni Olsen, stage and screen actor, Gean Greenwell, baritone and Metropolitan Opera singer, and Phyllis McGinley, writer of satirical poetry that has received national attention, are from Ogden. Coleman Cox, author of *May Be So,* was a reporter on the *Ogden Standard* in the early 1900's. Another staff man for that paper was Cuthbert L. Olsen, who in 1940 became Governor of California. The seven children of Edwin F. Tout are well known in theatrical and musical circles, Nannie, Margaret, "Romaine," and Hazel "Dawn," being the most prominent. Solon Hannibal Borglum, sculptor, was born in Ogden.

Harman Peery, Ogden's "Cowboy Mayor" from 1934 to 1939, attracted national notice through the press. Late in 1934 he was presented with a pinto pony by the management of the Ogden Union Stockyards; a few days later he accepted the challenge of the Evanston, Wyoming, fire chief to run a race. The contest seems never to have been staged. Early the following year he challenged members of the Byrd Antarctic Expedition to a beard-growing contest, results to be decided at the time of Ogden's Pioneer Days celebration. In October, 1935, to lower gasoline prices in the city, he inaugurated a four-day "gasoline war," selling motor fuel at fire station pumps; city sale was resumed in December because of a price differential between Ogden and Salt Lake City. In November of the same year he waged a losing battle to take the local bus system under municipal management. Early in 1936 he offered free marriages to local couples and near the end of the year cabled the abdicating King Edward VIII of England (later the Duke of Windsor) and Wallis Warfield Simpson that he would give them a free wedding and a trip through the national parks. In 1938 he led fruitless battles for municipal light and power.

POINTS OF INTEREST

1. CITY HALL PARK, Washington Ave. between 25th and 26th Sts., extending to Grant Ave., covers an area of ten acres almost in the heart of the city. The mansarded old City Hall, built in 1888 and "decorated" with neon lights, was superseded in 1940 by a ten-story modern setback structure designed by Leslie S. Hodgson. This distinctive City and County Building was erected with and from PWA funds. In the northeastern section of the park is the JEDEDIAH STRONG SMITH MONUMENT, a granite shaft erected by the Utah Pioneer Trails and Landmarks Association to commemorate one of the West's outstanding explorers (*see History*).

The CARNEGIE FREE LIBRARY (*open 11-9 weekdays, reference dept. open 2-6 Sun.*), in the southeastern end of the park, was opened in 1903. This dignified white sandstone structure, neo-classic in style, with colonnaded entrance loggia, was the first building in Utah used exclusively as a library. Its shelves contain almost 50,000 volumes, and borrowers' cards in use represent about 60 per cent of Ogden's residents. The library has an excellent collection of western Americana, purchased with the $10,000 "Golden Spike" fund, donated by the Southern Pacific and Union Pacific railroads on the fiftieth anniversary of the Golden Spike ceremony (*see Transportation*).

2. The BROOM HOTEL, 376 25th St., constructed in 1882, was at the time considered the finest establishment between Omaha and San Francisco. The ground floor was modernized early in 1940 for commercial uses. John Broom, a Mormon convert from England, was an early pioneer who settled on a bit of high land near Marriott, known as Broom's Bench. He began to make money, at first by salvaging iron from abandoned wagons along the emigrant trails. In 1857 the Mormon militia, while resisting the entrance of Colonel Johnston's troops into Utah, burned a number of supply trains of the U. S. Army in Wyoming. Iron was then very scarce in Utah and Broom gathered many tons, brought it to Ogden, and sold it for 50¢ a pound. Wagon tires were cut into hand-wrought square nails, which brought a premium in the growing community. Properly tempered, crowbars could be bored for musket barrels, and band iron, while not as good as Damascus steel, served to make sabers for the Mormon militia. Broom also put up large quantities of hay, and when the transcontinental railroad came through Ogden he found a ready sale for hay and farm produce at high prices. In 1869 he invested heavily in profitable real estate. After spending several years in San Francisco, Broom returned to

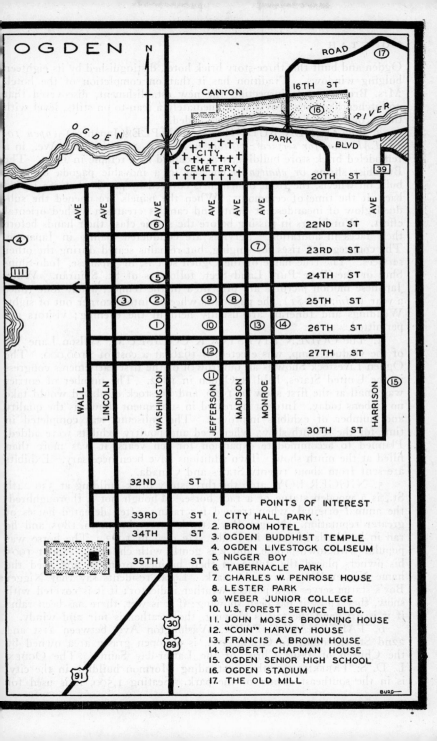

OGDEN

N

ROAD

CANYON — 16TH ST

OGDEN

RIVER

PARK — BLVD

† CITY † 20TH ST
† CEMETERY †

22ND ST

23RD ST

24TH ST

25TH ST

26TH ST

27TH ST

30TH ST

WALL AVE
LINCOLN AVE
WASHINGTON AVE
JEFFERSON AVE
MADISON AVE
MONROE AVE
HARRISON AVE

32ND ST

33RD ST

34TH ST

35TH ST

POINTS OF INTEREST

1. CITY HALL PARK
2. BROOM HOTEL
3. OGDEN BUDDHIST TEMPLE
4. OGDEN LIVESTOCK COLISEUM
5. NIGGER BOY
6. TABERNACLE PARK
7. CHARLES W. PENROSE HOUSE
8. LESTER PARK
9. WEBER JUNIOR COLLEGE
10. U.S. FOREST SERVICE BLDG.
11. JOHN MOSES BROWNING HOUSE
12. "COIN" HARVEY HOUSE
13. FRANCIS A. BROWN HOUSE
14. ROBERT CHAPMAN HOUSE
15. OGDEN SENIOR HIGH SCHOOL
16. OGDEN STADIUM
17. THE OLD MILL

BURG

Ogden and built this three-story brick hotel, distinguished by its eighteen bulging windows. Tradition has it that on completion of the hotel, Mrs. Broom, while inspecting the new establishment, discovered that no kitchen had been provided; immediately a lean-to on stilts, level with the second-floor banquet hall, was added.

3. The OGDEN BUDDHIST TEMPLE (Japanese) (*open 10-11 A.M. Sun. for services; visitors welcome*), 2456 Lincoln Ave., in a remodeled brick store building, was occupied as a temple in 1937. The Buddhist shrine or *chaitya* is encased in a movable pagoda or *tope,* built on wheels, the front of which is covered by panels that are folded back at the time of ceremony. When the panels are opened the subdued glow of incandescent lights and candles creates a hushed oriental effect. Worshipers in passing before the shrine clasp their hands before their faces in adoration. Services are conducted mainly in Japanese. The congregation rises for singing, but remains seated during the other services. The true name of the Ogden sect is, in Japanese, Jodo-Shin-Shu, or the True Pure Land Sect, followers of St. Shinran. When Japanese motion pictures are presented in the temple, about four times a year (*adm. 75¢-$1*), the pagoda is wheeled into a corner out of sight. Weddings and funerals are usually held in the evening; visitors are permitted.

4. The OGDEN LIVESTOCK COLISEUM, Wilson Lane W. of the viaduct ramp, was erected in 1926 at a cost of $100,000. The Ogden Livestock Show is an outgrowth of the first cattlemen's congress in the United States, held at Ogden in 1892. The number of entries was small at the first show in 1920, and livestock displayed would take no ribbons today. Interest increased in subsequent shows as the quality and number of exhibits improved. The coliseum was completed in time for the seventh show, when seed and poultry exhibits were added. Planned to accommodate expansion for ten years, it was more than filled at the ninth show. Two additions have been necessary. Exhibits are sent from about twenty States and Canada.

5. NIGGER BOY, atop the three-story brick building at 336 24th St., is a wooden statue of a race horse. Though not a thoroughbred, the animal original, when trained for racing, often defeated horses of greater reputation. Nigger Boy's track career began in 1895 and he ran in hundreds of races in Utah. He died in 1912. The horse was popular with townspeople, and was gentle with children. About 1905 his owners placed the statue on their business property and used the name Nigger Boy as a trade mark. Local residents say that Nigger Boy's statue serves as a perfect weather indicator: if it is covered with snow, they know it has been snowing; if it is wet, there has been rain; if it is dry, and the tail is blowing, the weather is fair and windy.

6. TABERNACLE PARK, Washington Ave. between 21st and 22nd St. extending to Grant Ave., is an open grassy area owned by the Church of Jesus Christ of the Latter-day Saints. The OGDEN L. D. S. TABERNACLE, the outstanding Mormon building in the city, is in the southeast corner of the park. Seating 1,500, it is used for

religious services, conferences, and conventions of the Church, and for cultural gatherings. North of the Ward Amusement Hall and the chapel is the STAKE RELIEF SOCIETY BUILDING (*open, caretaker 2147 Grant Ave.*). Daughters of Utah Pioneers have a two-room collection of pioneer relics on display.

At the rear of the Relief Society Building is the MILES MORRIS GOODYEAR CABIN (*not open*), a crude pioneer structure built of cottonwood logs in 1844 or 1845. Protected by a canopy and fenced in with wire, it is the oldest remaining building erected by white men in Utah. The cabin was originally part of a group making up Goodyear's Fort Buenaventura on the banks of the Weber River, southwest of the railroad station. It has been moved several times, and was placed here by the Daughters of Utah Pioneers in 1928. A new roof and foundation logs have been provided, but otherwise it stands as Goodyear built it. In the northeastern section is the LORIN FARR MONUMENT, a granite block with a bronze bust of Farr and a bronze plaque detailing his services as Ogden's first mayor. The monument faces the homes of his first and second plural wives.

7. The CHARLES W. PENROSE HOUSE (*private*), 2236 Madison Ave., is a whitewashed adobe house, in the front yard of which are lilac bushes more than fifty years old. Penrose was an apostle of the Mormon Church, a composer of hymns, and one of the editors of the *Ogden Junction*. The house was built by Robert Chapman in the sixties.

8. In the northwest corner of LESTER PARK, Madison Ave. between 24th and 25th Sts., extending to Jefferson Ave., is the PIERRE JEAN DE SMET MONUMENT, a granite shaft dedicated to the noted Catholic missionary, who is thought to have visited Salt Lake Valley in 1841.

9. WEBER JUNIOR COLLEGE, 2445 Jefferson Ave., was founded by the L. D. S. Church as the Weber Stake Academy in 1889. In 1916 it became a normal college and in 1922 a junior college. In 1933 the school passed into the hands of the State as a gift from the Church. The LOUIS FREDERICK MOENCH BUILDING houses the lecture rooms, laboratories, library, reading rooms, auditorium, and cafeteria. The building, named for an early-day educator in Ogden, has accommodations for 1,000 students. With a faculty of 30, the average enrollment is 700 students; the college awards the degree of Associate of Arts on completion of two years' work. The WEBER GYMNASIUM (*open weekdays 10-9*), 550 25th St., a modern brick structure costing $300,000, was dedicated in 1925. Although it is now a part of the school, the public is privileged to take membership and use the recreational facilities.

10. The U. S. FOREST SERVICE BUILDING, 507 25th St., a modern structure designed by Leslie S. Hodgson, is constructed of gray granite, brick, and terra cotta. The entrance has white bronze doors and the lobby is finished in golden Utah travertine. As headquarters for Region 4, forest research work is carried on from this

building in Utah, Nevada, southern Idaho, and western Wyoming. Here, too, is one of the twelve experiment stations conducted by the Forest Service.

11. The JOHN MOSES BROWNING HOUSE (*private*), 505 27th St., is a two-story brick and red stone building with large plate glass windows. A wrought-iron fence encloses a well-kept lawn and grounds. John Moses Browning (1854-1926), was born in Ogden, the son of Jonathan Browning, an ingenious mechanic and gunsmith, who had three wives. At Nauvoo, Illinois, he built many of the wagons used by the Mormons to cross the plains. By the time John was 19, he had made several guns from odds and ends of material in his father's blacksmith shop. Later, he and his brothers, Matt and Jonathan Edmund, patented many inventions for automatic firearms, most of which were purchased by Winchester. All of the Colt automatic pistols and other automatic shotguns and rifles are Browning inventions. For his services in developing Belgian firearms, King Albert of Belgium bestowed upon him the decoration of Knight of the Order of Leopold. Upon his death in Belgium, in 1926, a U. S. military escort accompanied the body to his home. His brother, Jonathan Edmund, died in 1939.

12. The WILLIAM HOPE (COIN) HARVEY HOUSE (*private*), 2671 Jefferson Ave., is an old-fashioned, rambling frame cottage, with a gabled roof. In front, a red sandstone coping gives it an air of past elegance. Colonel Harvey, by all odds the most picturesque and original character of Ogden's "Golden Age"—the late 1880's and early 1890's—came to Ogden from West Virginia in 1888, opened a law office, and promoted a real estate subdivision. He was also interested in extensive farm properties and started to build a showy residence on the east slope of Little Mountain. Early in 1890 he began promoting a carnival for Ogden modeled after the Mardi Gras of New Orleans. The carnival, however, was a financial failure, and since Harvey had assumed all obligations, the affair cost him his fortune and his properties.

Despite the setback Harvey remained in Ogden, and when the La Plata mining excitement broke out in the nineties at a boom town 38 miles northeast, he sent out special articles to dailies all over the country advertising Ogden as a coming mining center, a hope never realized. Harvey was one of the first to recognize the advantage of making Ogden a livestock center. Harvey went to Chicago to edit a magazine advocating free silver, and in due time his friends in Ogden received copies of the magazine, *Coin,* from which he received the nickname of "Coin" Harvey. He later lived in Monte Ne, Arkansas, and built a tower to house objects and writings for archeologists 20,000 years hence. In 1932 Harvey—still vigorous at 80—ran for President of the United States on an independent ticket. He wrote a book, *Paul's School of Statesmanship.* He died in Arkansas in 1936.

13. The FRANCIS A. BROWN HOUSE (*private*), 2506 Madison Ave., a white-plastered adobe structure built in 1870, sits in grounds planted with locust and mulberry trees. In the early days members of

the family experimented with raising silkworms and the second floor was the site of Ogden's silkworm industry. The venture was never a success. Francis A. Brown, an early-day school teacher, came to Ogden in 1856, became a prominent Church worker, and served as a bishop for many years.

14. The ROBERT CHAPMAN HOUSE (*private*), 2554 Monroe Ave., of pioneer adobe construction, probably is the oldest building in Ogden occupied solely as a home since pioneer days. Robert C. Chapman, a Mormon pioneer born in Norfolk, England, came to Ogden in 1855, where he built several adobe houses, many of which are still standing.

15. The OGDEN SENIOR HIGH SCHOOL, Harrison Ave. and 28th St., a four-story steel and concrete building designed by Leslie S. Hodgson, was erected in 1937 from funds partially supplied by the Public Works Administration. A notable example of modern architecture, it is designed on a U-shaped plan and constructed of brick with terra cotta trim. The massive buttressed exterior, with its setback wings, is marked by a pattern of vertical lines formed by the channeled treatment of the fenestration. The interior is featured by tile partitions, metal trim, and acoustic plaster. The auditorium seats 2,200.

16. OGDEN STADIUM, Canyon Rd. and 16th St., is the scene of the annual Pioneer Days rodeo, held since 1934. Steel and concrete stands on the north and south sides of the stadium accommodate the crowds that witness the rodeos, pageants, parades, and carnivals. Residents of the community don the garb of prospectors, trappers, and cowboys, and Shoshone and Ute Indians are brought to Ogden for the occasion. The Ogden Horse Show is held during the celebration.

17. The OLD MILL (*open daily 10 A.M.-12 P.M.*), 12th St. and Canyon Rd., is the gristmill built by Lorin Farr in 1849. The original millstones are still on the premises, adjoining the mill race. The building is used as a dance hall and restaurant.

MOUNT OGDEN (*firearms prohibited*), 7 m. E. on a foot trail up Taylor Canyon, E. from 25th or 26th Sts., is the highest point (9,575 alt.) on the Wasatch Mountains between Ogden and Weber canyons. From its summit Colorado can be seen to the southeast, Wyoming to the east, Idaho to the north, and Nevada to the west. Great Salt Lake, with its islands and gleaming white salt beds, spreads out to the west, and range upon range of mountains are visible in every direction. The mountain was known as Observatory Peak until the late 1920's, the Federal government having used it as a triangulation point during the eighties while surveying the mountains of this area. Heliograph beams were flashed 130 miles to Pilot Peak, Nevada, and to other peaks in adjoining States to assist in mapping.

POINTS OF INTEREST IN ENVIRONS

Utah Hot Springs, 9.2 *m;* Bear River Migratory Bird Refuge, 37.7 *m.* (*see Tour 1b*). Lagoon, 21.2 *m.* (*see Tour 1c*). Ogden Canyon, 3.3 *m;* Pine View Dam, 8.5 *m.;* Monte Cristo Recreation Grounds, 43.6 *m.* (*see Tour 1A*). Weber Canyon, 8 *m.;* Como Springs, 27 *m.* (*see Tour 4a*). Lucin Cutoff, 15m. (*see Great Salt Lake*).

Provo

Railroad Stations: Union Railroad Depot, 6th South and 3rd West Sts., for Union Pacific R.R., and Denver and Rio Grande Western R.R.; Orem Depot, 95 West Center St., for Salt Lake and Utah Ry. (electric interurban).
Bus Stations: Orem Depot, 95 West Center St., for Burlington Trailways, Rio Grande Trailways and Salt Lake and Utah Ry. bus line; Union Pacific Station, 99 N. 1st West St., for Union Pacific Stages, and Santa Fe Trail Transportation Co.
Airport: Training airport, 2 *m.* W. of business district on Center St.
Taxis: Fare 25¢ and up.
Traffic Regulations: Standard traffic lights in business district; R. turn against red light permitted after full stop. Two-hour parking limit in business district.
Street Order: All streets are numbered from intersection of Center St. (running east-west) and University Ave. (running north-south). Streets east are named 1st East, 2nd East, etc., and streets west, south, and north are similarly named.

Accommodations: Four hotels; tourist camps.

Information Service: Chamber of Commerce, 234 West Center St.

Motion Picture Houses: Four.
Radio Station: KOVO (1240 k.c.).
Golf: Municipal Golf Course, 8th South St. and University Ave., 9 holes, greens fee.
Tennis: Brigham Young University (upper campus), 8th North and 2nd East Sts., 12 courts; Sowiette Park, 5th West and 5th North Sts., 6 courts; Soldiers Memorial Park, 8th East and Center Sts., 2 courts.
Swimming: Sowiette Park 5th West and 4th North Sts., open-air pool, cold water, no fee; Saratoga Springs, 24.2 *m.*, W. side of Utah Lake, warm water, adm. 25¢.; Park Ro Sha, 5 *m.* S. on Highway 91.
Baseball: Timpanogos Park, 4th West and 5th North Sts., Utah Industrial League (semi-professional), and American Legion League (amateur).
Skating: Utah Lake.
Skiing: Vivian Park in Provo Canyon, Aspen Grove, and Hobble Creek Canyon.
Fishing and Hunting: Trout fishing in Provo River and other near-by streams; duck hunting on Utah Lake; pheasant hunting in lowlands; deer hunting in near-by mountains and canyons.

Annual Events: Sunrise Services, Y Mountain, east of Provo, Easter Sunday; Brigham Young University Annual Invitational Relay Carnival, late April; Posture Parade of Utah High School Girls, last Saturday in April; Pioneer Day Celebration, parade and rodeo, July 24; Mount Timpanogos Community Hike, late July; Utah County Fair, Oct.; Community Christmas Celebration, Dec.

PROVO (4,549 alt., 18,129 pop.), Utah's third largest city, is built on a wide terrace or bench level of prehistoric Lake Bonneville, along the south bank of the Provo River in Utah Valley. The city huddles at the base of the precipitous Wasatch Range, the western face of

215

which is an almost perpendicular fault scarp. Provo Peak, rising to an altitude of 11,054 feet due east of the city, extends sharply above the jagged ridge of the Wasatch Range. On the base of the peak, about 2,000 feet above the upper level of the city, is the white block-letter "Y," 300 feet tall, which is newly whitewashed each year by freshmen of Brigham Young University. Northward there rises the long bulk of Mount Timpanogos, 12,008 feet high. The Provo area slopes gently westward, and beyond the city limits are farmlands and pastures, and broad, fresh-water Utah Lake, which can be seen only from the upper streets of the city. Across the lake rises the low range of the Lake Mountains, and other mountains are visible in every direction.

The town centers about the intersection of University Avenue and Center Street. Within a four-block radius are the principal stores and most of the public buildings, mainly two- and three-story structures of the architectural style popular soon after the turn of the century. Outside the business district the streets are bordered by the trees and lawns of modest brick homes. To the northeast is the sharp rise of University Hill, with the brick and graystone buildings and landscaped grounds of Brigham Young University, one of the State's three major educational institutions.

Like other Mormon-built towns, Provo has wide streets laid out in the four cardinal compass directions. There is a profusion of shade trees, mostly Lombardy and Carolina poplars, Norway maple, box elder, elm, and walnut. In the residential sections the houses are set well back in spacious green lawns, which must be watered every day; and in the backyards there are usually vegetable and flower gardens. The city is large enough to have its share of modern conveniences, yet small enough to retain an old-fashioned neighborliness. Provo is the commercial hub of a normally prosperous agricultural region, and railroad shops, warehouses, packing plants, lumber and coal yards line the railroad tracks. Although many local people are associated with commercial, industrial, and educational enterprises, a goodly portion of the population consists of retired farming people.

Two Spanish priests, Francisco Silvestre Vélez de Escalante and Francisco Atanasio Domínguez, were probably the first white men to visit Utah Valley. Exploring the region for a more direct route from Santa Fe to the Catholic mission at Monterey, California, the two priests and a party of seven men arrived at the shore of Utah Lake in September, 1776. They "ascended a low hill and beheld the lake and extended valley of Nuestra Señora de la Merced de los Timpanogotzis, as we called it . . . surrounded by the peaks of the Sierra." Provo River, Escalante recorded, "runs through large plains of good land for planting . . . plenty . . . if irrigated, for two and even three large villages." In 1825, Étienne Provot, a young French-Canadian for whom the city and river were named, explored the valley with a party of trappers employed by General William H. Ashley of St. Louis.

On July 27, 1847, three days after the arrival of the main body of Mormon pioneers in Salt Lake Valley, Orson Pratt led a small party southward, climbed a ridge of the Oquirrh Mountains, and obtained a view of Utah Valley. On the same day L. B. Myers "returned from Eutaw Lake," according to the *Journal History* of the L. D. S. Church. He reports ". . . that on the east side of it is plenty of timber, which might easily be floated down" the Jordan River to Great Salt Lake City. Jesse C. Little and others, making a further reconnaissance in early August, "reported that there was a fine country east of that lake and that the land there was well adapted for cultivation."

In March, 1849, John S. Higbee, at the head of thirty families, took wagons, horses, cattle, farming implements, and household equipment, and left Great Salt Lake City to establish a Mormon colony on the Provo River. The place chosen was a favorite Indian fishing ground, where the Utes held a fish carnival at the time of the spring spawning. Within a few miles of their goal the settlers were confronted by a band of Ute Indians. After solemnly promising not to drive the Indians from their lands, they were allowed to continue. Fording Provo River, the settlers established themselves on the south bank. Farming and building were begun and within a few weeks they had constructed a fort, plowed 225 acres of land, and planted rye, wheat, and corn.

A month before the first settlement, a company of militiamen from Great Salt Lake City defeated a Ute band at Battle Creek (near the site of Pleasant Grove) in the first conflict between Mormons and the Indians of Utah. Settlers at Fort Utah experienced little serious difficulty with the Utes until after August, when a native was slain in a dispute over a shirt. Relations then grew steadily worse, but Brigham Young held that the settlers were to blame. Not until February, 1850, would he agree to strong measures. With the approval of Captain Howard Stansbury, Government surveyor, he then dispatched two companies of militia from Great Salt Lake City, which were joined at Fort Utah by local infantry. A last attempt at peaceful settlement failed when, during a parley with Chief Ope-Carry, a band of warriors led by Chief Big Elk opened fire on the whites. The soldiers retaliated, but the Indians, barricading themselves in an abandoned log house and the bed of the Provo River, withstood the attack for two days before they retreated. During the pursuit of the hostile band one white man and a number of Indians were killed, including Big Elk; after a final skirmish near Table Mountain, at the south end of Utah Lake, the surviving Indians agreed to a peace. Thereafter, the whites were not molested, and by the fall of 1851 most of the settlers had built homes outside the fort.

In 1849 Samuel Clark established the community's first tannery and John Blackburn erected the first sawmill, a crude, hand-operated affair that was soon replaced by a water-driven mill. Two large canals, diverting water from Provo River, were dug for irrigation. That same year the first gristmill was built, and in 1851 a carding mill was put in operation. Eighteen months after the settlement of Provo, officials of the Mormon Church assumed jurisdiction in religious and political affairs, but in 1851 a city charter was granted by the Provisional State of Deseret, vesting authority in a council consisting of a mayor, four aldermen, and nine councilors. The first school was held in a fort cabin, and in 1855 the Mormon Church built a two-story adobe seminary. By 1861 each of the five Church wards had a small schoolhouse. School equipment was crude; textbooks were of many varieties; slates were used because of a shortage of paper; and a switch was the standard disciplinary implement.

In 1858 the population of Provo was temporarily increased by the arrival of 30,000 Mormons from Great Salt Lake City and other northern Utah settlements, who feared the advance of Colonel Albert Sidney Johnston's army (*see History*). When the Federal force molested no property, Brigham Young announced that he was preparing to return to Great Salt Lake City. Within a few hours all of the settlers had begun their homeward journey.

The Utah Southern Railroad, now a part of the Union Pacific System, was completed from Salt Lake City to Provo in 1873. The Utah and Pleasant Valley Railroad, built by Milan Packard to transport coal from the mines near Scofield, was extended north from Springville to Provo in 1878. It was known as the "Calico Road" because the workmen who graded the roadbed were paid mainly in general merchandise from Packard's store in Springville. In 1881 The Calico Road was sold to the predecessor of the Denver & Rio Grande Western Railroad, and Provo obtained its first trunk line service. Completion of the railroad gave new impetus to the city's industrial growth, and was followed by installation of the city's first electric service (1890) and a waterworks system (1892). Culturally and commercially, the town forged steadily ahead. In 1912 the city adopted its present mayor-commissioner form of government. In 1914 an interurban electric railroad was built from Salt Lake City to Provo, and blast furnaces, foundries, flour mills, brick yards, and other industrial plants have made Provo an important manufacturing center. After an involved fight, Provo authorities in 1939 instituted a municipal power plant which it was expected would contribute to the city's industrial growth. The city is headquarters for the Uinta National Forest, which occupies more than 900,000 acres east of the city.

Provo has produced one outstanding present-day inventor, Dr. Harvey Fletcher, acoustical engineer, and was the home of another, Philo Farnsworth. Dr. Fletcher, who has been called the "patron saint of the hard of hearing," was born here in 1884. He was graduated from Brigham Young University in 1907, and took postgraduate work at the University of Chicago, where he earned a reputation as an outstanding physicist. He returned to his alma mater as the head of the physics department, but resigned in 1916 to accept a position in the Bell Telephone Laboratories, in New York, where he has been since. Dr. Fletcher invented the audiophone, and several other standard instruments which have aided many partially deaf persons, and perfected the audiometer, an instrument to measure the audibility of sounds. He received the Louis Edward Levy medal in 1924 for accomplishments in the physical measurement of sound, and was president of the Acoustical Society of America and of the American Federation of Hard of Hearing in 1929 and 1930. He lives (1940) on Long Island, New York.

Philo T. Farnsworth, television inventor, a former resident of Provo, was declared by *America's Young Men,* a biographical almanac, to be one of the "ten outstanding young men of 1939." Born at Beaver, Utah, in 1906, he determined at the age of·six to become an inventor; by that time he knew how to operate and repair a tiny dynamo and electric motor, the former generating current when attached to his mother's sewing machine. When he was twelve his family moved in wagons to a ranch near Rigby, Idaho, where he kept a power plant, power hoists, and a variety of farm machinery running smoothly. The family moved to Provo in 1923, and he entered Brigham Young University as a special student. By 1924, when he was eighteen years old, Farnsworth had worked out the fundamental concept of television. The following year, when his father died and he was forced to leave school, he opened a radio shop in Salt Lake City, which failed. In 1926 he went to San Francisco as a research scholar and eight years later gave the first public demonstration of television at Franklin Institute, Philadelphia. He now (1940) lives in Philadelphia, where he is research director of the company bearing his name.

POINTS OF INTEREST

1. BRIGHAM YOUNG UNIVERSITY (*all buildings open 9-5 weekdays, 9-12 Sat.*), owned and operated by the Latter-day Saints (Mormon) Church, has two campuses, five minutes walk apart. The Lower Campus, University Ave. and 5th North St., occupies a city block in the residential district and consists of four ivy-covered buildings surrounded by trees. The Upper Campus, 8th North and 2nd East Sts., occupies the benchland known as University Hill, and is taken up by the newer buildings and stadium.

The school was founded in 1875 by Brigham Young as Brigham Young Academy, its original objective being to supply trained teachers for the public schools. Dr. Karl G. Maeser, a Salt Lake City teacher and former German schoolmaster, began an experimental term with twenty-nine pupils in 1876. The first full term began the following August with a student body of only twelve, but the enrollment increased so rapidly that by 1883 two additions had been made to the original building. The academy was destroyed by fire in 1884, and temporary quarters were used for eight years. Early in 1892, with 500 pupils enrolled, first classes were held in the Education Building. The name was changed to Brigham Young University in 1903. Its average enrollment, non-sectarian, is 2,800 students. Bachelor's and master's degrees are offered in the colleges of applied science, arts and science, commerce, education, and fine arts. The Alpine Summer School, established as a branch of the university in 1923, is conducted at Aspen Grove near the summit of Mount Timpanogos (*see Timpanogos Cave National Monument*). Among the more prominent alumni are George Sutherland, retired associate justice of the United States Supreme Court; Reed Smoot, former dean of the United States Senate; and William H. King, United States Senator.

Lower Campus

The EDUCATION BUILDING, oldest of the group, was erected in 1891 and still bears the inscription "Brigham Young Academy." It stands between two other buildings, College Hall and the Arts Building, to which it is connected by arcades. COLLEGE HALL, built in 1898, contains the University Chapel and the schools of music and dramatics. The ARTS BUILDING, erected in 1904, is used by Brigham Young High School and the department of domestic science. The TRAINING SCHOOL, completed in 1902, provides accommodations for elementary grade classes taught by students in education, and houses the men's gymnasium.

Upper Campus

The MAESER MEMORIAL BUILDING, named for the first instructor and completed in 1911, contains administrative offices and an auditorium seating 400. The HEBER J. GRANT LIBRARY, constructed in 1925 and named for the President of the Mormon Church, contains approximately 105,000 volumes of old and recent works, and more than 50,000 pamphlets and bulletins. The collection includes several valuable sets of books, among which are twenty-four volumes of the rare Ante-Nicene Christian Library, and an eight-volume set of Foxe's *Acts and Monuments,* printed in 1559. In the GEORGE H. BRIMHALL BUILDING, named for a former president, are museum collections including the geological exhibit of mineral samples from mining districts throughout the world; the entomological exhibit of more than 190,000 specimens; the comprehensive zoological collection of fishes, amphibians, reptiles, mammals, and birds of this region; an archeological exhibit embracing several cases of Utah Indian artifacts, together with collections from South America and islands of the Pacific. The university also owns an art collection of 300 pictures by early and contemporary artists, which are exhibited in classrooms, halls, and offices. The STADIUM, used for football games and track and field meets of the Mountain States Conference, is modeled after the Greek amphitheater. Accommodating approximately 5,000 persons, the stadium seats follow the contour of University Hill. Here the school holds the Annual Invitation Relay Carnival, which, from the standpoint of participation, is the largest athletic event in the Rocky Mountain region. A $200,000 religious education building is (1940) in process of construction.

2. SOWIETTE PARK, 5th West and 5th North Sts., on the site of the second fort built at Provo, was named for the principal war chief of the Utes, who tried to protect the settlers from the warlike followers

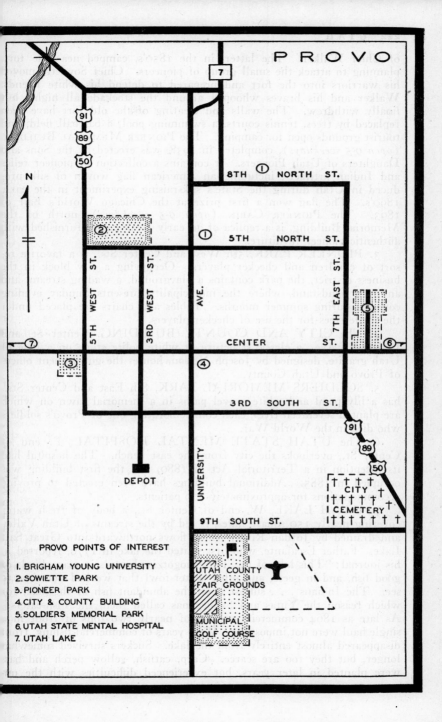

PROVO

N

8TH ① NORTH ST.

① 5TH NORTH ST.

CENTER ST.

3RD SOUTH ST.

DEPOT

9TH SOUTH ST.

CITY CEMETERY

UTAH COUNTY FAIR GROUNDS

MUNICIPAL GOLF COURSE

PROVO POINTS OF INTEREST

1. BRIGHAM YOUNG UNIVERSITY
2. SOWIETTE PARK
3. PIONEER PARK
4. CITY & COUNTY BUILDING
5. SOLDIERS MEMORIAL PARK
6. UTAH STATE MENTAL HOSPITAL
7. UTAH LAKE

of Chief Walker. The latter, in the 1850's, camped near the fort, planning to attack the small group of pioneers. Chief Sowiette moved his warriors into the fort and prepared to defend his white friends. Walker and his braves whooped around the stockade all night, but finally withdrew. The walls and clearing of the old fort have been replaced by trees, tennis courts, a swimming pool, a baseball field, and tourist grounds open for camping. The PIONEER MEMORIAL BUILDING (*open 9-5 weekdays*), completed in 1938, was erected by the Sons and Daughters of Utah Pioneers. It contains a collection of pioneer relics and Indian artifacts, including an American flag woven of silk produced in Utah during the State's silk-raising experiment in the early 1890's. The flag won a first prize at the Chicago World's Fair of 1893. The PIONEER CABIN (*open 9-5 weekdays*), north of the Memorial Building, is a replica of an early Utah cabin, furnished with authentic pioneer furniture.

3. PIONEER PARK, 5th West and Center Sts., is a favorite resort of children and checker players. Occupying a city block in the business district, the park contains a playground, a wading stream, and an open bandstand, where the municipality presents Sunday evening concerts during summer months. Tables and chairs are placed under the shade trees for the use of checker players.

4. The CITY AND COUNTY BUILDING, Center St. and University Ave., a classic structure of white oolite stone on a base of Utah granite, designed by Joseph Nelson, houses the government offices of Provo and Utah County.

5. SOLDIERS MEMORIAL PARK, 8th East and Center Sts., has a lily pond and white gravel paths in a memorial lawn on which are planted seventeen trees, each commemorating one of Provo's soldiers who died in the World War.

6. The UTAH STATE MENTAL HOSPITAL, E. end of Center St., overlooks the city from the east bench. The hospital had its inception in a Territorial Act of 1880, and the first building was occupied in 1885. Additional buildings have been erected to provide accommodations for approximately 800 patients.

7. UTAH LAKE, W. end of Center St., a body of fresh water covering nearly 150 square miles, is fed by the streams of Utah Valley and drained by Jordan River, which flows northward into Great Salt Lake. Father Escalante, who first visited the lake in 1776, reported in his journal: "This lake of the Timpanogotzis abounds in many kinds of good fish, and in geese, and other water-fowl that we had not time to see. The Indians . . . subsist upon the abundant fish of the lake, for which reason the Yutas and Sabueganas called them the Fish-eaters." As late as 1864 commercial catches of nearly two tons of trout in a single haul were not impossible. With years of commercial fishing, trout disappeared almost entirely from the lake. Suckers survived somewhat longer, but they too are scarce. Carp, catfish, yellow perch and bass were planted in later years, but experienced difficulties with the un-

table lake levels. In 1940 there was hope that bass fishing would again become important.

The Jordan River, principal source of irrigation water for the farms of a large portion of Salt Lake County, originates at Utah Lake, and the concept that it would serve as a reservoir led to an inter-county legal controversy that lasted for more than twenty-five years. In 1872 Salt Lake County built a dam in the river eight miles north of the lake, to facilitate the diversion of water for irrigation, and for the storage of winter inflow. The year following, because of heavy snows melting in the mountains, the lake level became so high that landowners on the border of the lake, in Utah County, objected seriously to flooding of their property. During the wet winter of 1873-74 "the head gates washed out being helped by persons unknown," and it was not till the spring of 1875 that the dam was rebuilt. Trouble was more or less continuous until 1884, when Utah County filed suit for damages against Salt Lake City and four canal companies, then owners of the dam. Before the case came to trial, officials of the Mormon Church persuaded the litigants to arbitrate. John Taylor, President of the L.D.S. Church, and his first councilor, George Quayle Cannon, presided. Damages of $8,000 were awarded Utah County farmers, in addition to which the Church donated 3,000 bushels of wheat for those who had lost their crop on account of high water, to assist the canal companies, and to aid the poor along some of the canals. Another phase of the arbitration was to agree on a "compromise level," which fixed a high-water point in the lake above which the water could not be raised by artificial means.

Between 1888 and 1890 the city and the canal companies dredged the lake and river and constructed a new dam. Their dredging operations lowered the river bed two feet, but they claimed the right to establish the sill of the dam at the height of the old river level. This led to another legal battle in 1896, which ended in fixing high water at the old "compromise level" of 1884. The level is still in force, having been recognized in several adjudications since. Despite the fact that the lake has risen three and a half feet above compromise point since 1922, and had fallen as much as twelve feet below, the old controversy has not been resumed. Pumps were installed in 1902, and a steel and concrete dam was erected in 1914, its sill and openings exactly at "compromise level."

Since 1931 all the water taken from the lake has been pumped. In 1935, when the level was pumped down to twelve feet below compromise point, leaving a mudhole with less than a foot of water at the deepest places, and nearly all the fish died, pessimists predicted that the lake would never come back. During the three ensuing winters, however, the lake gained steadily, till the water stood only four and a half feet below compromise point, and stored 400,000 acre-feet of water. At compromise level it holds 830,000 acre-feet. On May 1, 1940, the lake level was four and a half feet "below compromise." At that time a major legal battle was being waged, involving water rights valued at millions of dollars, which indirectly concerns Utah Lake. The courts

had been asked to decide whether a junior right, held on water tributary to Utah Lake, had superior force over rights owned by prior user
drawing water directly from the lake.

The canal system using Utah Lake water furnishes irrigation fo
about 60,000 acres of land, and supplemental waters for an additiona
acreage. The Jordan River supplies water for three flour-milling an
power companies, for condenser purposes at the Jordan steam plant o
the Utah Power and Light Company, for smelting at Midvale, and fo
the operation of ore-concentrating plants at Magna and Garfield.

Heavy use of the lake for irrigation purposes has made it difficul
to develop adequately recreational facilities, but the rise in the lake leve
since 1935 has permitted some progress to be made in restoring its im
portance to fishermen, while Provo City has taken considerable interes
in developing boating facilities, a boat harbor at the mouth of th
Provo River being of particular utility for recreationists. In 194
Mayor Mark Anderson of Provo was endeavoring to promote plan
by which the lake level should not be permitted to fall under a certai
depth, so that long-range plans for recreation might be carried throug

POINTS OF INTEREST IN ENVIRONS

State Fish and Game Farm, 5 *m.;* Springville Art Gallery, 6.3 *m.;* America
Fork Canyon, 28 *m.* (*see Tour 1d*). Provo Canyon, 6.6 *m.;* Bridal Veil Fall
9.6 *m.;* Deer Creek Reservoir, 17.6 *m.* (*see Tour 5*). Midway Hot Pots, 27*m*
(*see Tour 6b*). Timpanogos Cave, 30 *m.;* Aspen Grove, 43.1 *m.;* Mount Tim
panogos, 48.1 *m.* (*see Timpanogos Cave National Monument*).

Salt Lake City

Railroad Stations: South Temple and 3rd West Sts. for Union Pacific R.R., 3rd South and Rio Grande Sts. for Denver & Rio Grande Western R.R. and Western Pacific R.R.; 107 W. South Temple St. for Bamberger Electric R.R. and Salt Lake & Utah (electric) R.R.; 1055 W. North Temple for Salt Lake-Garfield and Western (electric) R.R.

Bus Stations: Union Bus Depot, 77 W. South Temple St., for Union Pacific Stages, Interstate Transit Lines, Pacific Greyhound Lines, Santa Fe Trailways, Salt Lake-Tooele Stage Line, Rio Grande Motor Ways, Lewis Bros. Stages, Salt Lake-Coalville Stage Lines, Salt Lake Transit Lines, and Bingham Stage Line. Salt Lake Bus Depot, 60 E. 2nd South St. for Burlington Tailways, Rio Grande Trailways, Denver-Salt Lake-Pacific Trailways, Santa Fe Trailways, Lewis Transportation Stages, and Bingham Stage Lines.

Airports: 3 *m.* W. on US 40 for United Air Lines and Western Air Express. Taxi fare $1 for one or two persons, 50¢ per person extra; time 20 minutes.

Local Busses and Streetcars: Fare 10¢, three tokens 25¢, weekly passes $1.25 to $1.75.

Taxis: Zone system, fare 25¢ and up.

Sightseeing Busses: Gray Line Motor Tours, 29 W. South Temple St.; Utah Motor Tours, 59 W. South Temple St.

Traffic Regulations: Right turn against red light following full stop and hand signal. Maximum speed limit within city 30 m.p.h. Parking in business district (do not block gutter) governed by parking meters: 1¢ for 12 minutes, 2¢ for 24 minutes, 5¢ for an hour, two nickels for two hours.

Accommodations: 24 hotels, 38 tourist camps.

Information Service: Chamber of Commerce, SE. corner Main and 2nd South Sts.; Utah State Automobile Association, 30 E. 4th South St.; American Express Tourist Bureau, 24 W. 2nd South St.; Hotel Utah, NE. corner Main and E. South Temple Sts.; Newhouse Hotel, 4th South and Main Sts.; American Automobile Association, 911 S. State St.; Tribune-Telegram Information Bureau, 143 S. Main St.

Street Order and Numbering: All streets run north-south or east-west, and most principal streets are numbered according to their direction and distance from SE. corner of Temple Square. Thus, the street bordering Temple Square on the south side is South Temple St., the parallel street one block S. is 1st South St., and so on. Streets N. and W. of Temple Square are similarly named. Street bordering E. side of Temple Square, however, is Main St., next parallel street is State St., next is 2nd East St., and so on. South Temple St. divides intersecting streets into N. and S. segments, Main St. divides intersecting streets into E. and W. segments.

Motion Picture Houses: 17, vaudeville at one, occasional road shows at others.

Golf: Forest Dale, 2375 S. 9th East St., 9 holes; Nibley Park, 2700 S. 7th East St., 9 holes; Bonneville Park, 21st East St. and Yale Ave., 9 holes. Greens fees.

Swimming: Wasatch Springs Plunge, sulphur water, 840 North 2nd West St.; Beck's Hot Springs, sulphur water, 4 *m.* N. on US 91; Saltair Beach, Great Salt Lake, 13.8 *m.* W. on US 40; Sunset Beach, Great Salt Lake, 14.5 *m.* W. on US 40; Black Rock Resort, Great Salt Lake, 15.1 *m.* W. on US 40; Lagoon, fresh water, 17 *m.* N. on US 91.

Tennis: 40 free public courts, 29 lighted for night play; players may use any unoccupied court without an attendant, but must take turn at courts where attendant is in charge.

Baseball: Community Park, 1301 S. West Temple St., for games of Salt Lake "Bees," Pioneer League (Utah and Idaho teams); Municipal Park, amateur leagues.

Fishing and Hunting: Fishing in near-by canyon streams; duck hunting on flats W. of city and sloughs adjacent to Great Salt Lake, 15 *m.* W. on US 40; pheasant hunting in lowlands.

Winter Sports: Ice skating at Liberty Park, 6th East and 9th South Sts.; skiing at Alta, 26 *m.* SE. on US 50-91 and county road up Little Cottonwood Canyon.

College Sports: Football, basketball, and track at University of Utah, 2nd South and University Sts., and Westminster College, 1840 S. 13th East Sts.

Libraries: Salt Lake City Public Library, 15 S. State St., which has five branches; University of Utah Library, 2nd South and University Sts.; L. D. S. Church Historian's Library, 47 E. South Temple St.

Hospitals: Latter-day Saints Hospital, 8th Ave. and C St.; St. Mark's Hospital, 2nd West and 7th North Sts.; Holy Cross Hospital, 1045 E. 1st South St.; Salt Lake County General Hospital, 21st South and State Sts.; Emergency Hospital, 105 S. State St.; Ninth East Emergency Hospital, 153 S. 9th East St.; Mountain View Sanatorium, 57 S. 8th East St.; Primary Children's Hospital, 44 W. North Temple St.; Veterans' Hospital, 12th Ave. and F. St.; Shriners' Hospital for Crippled Children, 851 N. 2nd West St.

Radio Stations: KSL (1160 kc.); KDYL (1320 kc.); KUTA (1500 kc.).

Annual Events: Annual conference of Mormon Church, early April; Covered Wagon Days, three days including July 24; Utah State Fair, late Sept.; semi-annual conference of Mormon Church, early Oct.; Oratorio *Messiah,* first Sunday after Christmas.

SALT LAKE CITY (4,266 alt., 150,021 pop.), capital of Utah and of the Mormon Church, is a city of broad tree-lined streets—the first of many Utah towns laid out by the Mormons foursquare with the compass—built on the benches of ancient Lake Bonneville in a sheltered angle of the Wasatch Mountains on the east and on a spur extending from them on the north. Mountains can be seen in every direction— the rugged Wasatch Range to the east and southeast, the more rounded hills of the spur on the north, capped by Ensign Peak, the angular masses of the Oquirrh and Stansbury ranges to the southwest, and the lesser range of Antelope Island, in Great Salt Lake, on the west. The white glare of salt beds and the reflected light from Great Salt Lake rise in the west and southwest, though neither can be seen except from more elevated portions of the city. The Jordan River, a small and tortuous but economically important stream, winds through the western part of the city. A number of canyons open from mountains to the north and east, providing the city with water and offering access to skiing grounds in winter and to fishing, hunting, hiking, riding, camping, and picnicking areas in other seasons.

From most approaches the copper-domed State Capitol, rising from the elevated North Bench, is the most conspicuous building in Salt Lake City. South of it, and lower down, is the six-spired Temple of the Church of Jesus Christ of Latter-day Saints, within the seclusion of high-walled Temple Square. From the southeast corner of this square pivots the numbering and nomenclature of the city's streets. Southward from this corner extends South Main Street, through the principal business center of the Great Basin. Blocklike business buildings rise on either side. The shop-fronts are modern, with abundant plate glass, and the exceptionally wide sidewalks are none too roomy for Saturday shopping crowds. Automatic police whistles, mounted on poles at downtown corners, signal for changes in traffic. West of Temple Square is the warehouse, railroad, and industrial area.

East of Main Street the city is primarily residential, its skyline accented by the tall tower of the Romanesque City and County Building and by the twin towers of the Roman Catholic Cathedral of the Madeleine. Wide streets extend eastward from the downtown area to the white and yellow buildings of the University of Utah, and beyond, on East Bench, to the military reservation of Fort Douglas. A few miles south of the city limits is the suburb of Murray. Pretentious residential areas climb the benches to the east and northeast, limited only by the height to which municipal water can be piped. North of South Temple Street the long city blocks are broken up into the smaller squares of the "Avenues" and lettered cross-streets, which cling to the hill-flanks; the more fashionable residential area however, is East Bench.

The capital of an arid State, Salt Lake City presents the paradox of an exceptionally well-watered municipality. Water runs in its gutters, and an ordinance keeps parked cars the width of a street-sweeper's broom from the curb. Drinking fountains bubble day and night. Salt Lake lawns are exceptionally well-flowered and well-turfed, and it is often necessary to detour exuberant sprinkler systems. Another paradox for a town 800 miles inland is the sight of gulls flying over the city.

At night, electric lights give the city a different garb. The capitol dome is sometimes floodlighted, and the Temple spires are illuminated with golden glows. Southward on Main Street from the huge orange beehive atop the Hotel Utah, there is a display of neon in every color of the spectrum. Eastward, on top of a mountain, an airway beacon flashes. From Wasatch Boulevard, on North Bench, there is a view of the city at night that reveals its huge light-sprinkled area, some eight miles square, and the double line of yellow sodium lights on South State Street. The city's curfew is a stentorian whistle blown at about 10 P. M.

Visitors are usually taken up City Creek Canyon and around Wasatch Boulevard for the best view of the valley. Sloping southward, the city spreads fanwise on the benches and valley floor. In the foreground is the Capitol and the Temple, the business district, and State Street cleaving the city in a straight line from the Capitol for twelve miles. Beyond, the residential areas spread outward, accented by occasional factories, until, thinning at the outskirts, homes give way to valley bottom and lifting brown hills, patterned with scores of farms. On the east stretches the Wasatch Range, its rugged heights in an upward crescendo to the 11,491 feet of Twin Peaks, blocking the horizon twenty miles to the south. Westward, in a north-south tangent twenty to thirty miles away, the Oquirrh Range stabs the sky. In the foothills and canyons of this range mushrooms of smoke ascend from the smelters at Magna and Garfield. To the west, in the valley, are the burnished stripes of irrigation canals, the crossed runways of the airport, and the waters of Great Salt Lake, obstructed from full view by the mountainous slopes of Antelope Island.

Architecturally, Salt Lake City traces the periods of its growth. The transitions are not obvious, but the southward and eastward expansion of the city is marked by changing architectural thought. Log houses are preserved in Temple Square and in Liberty Park. Adobe houses exist in many an odd corner of the city, but principally in the first-settled north and west sections. Placed farther back than many of newer houses, they come suddenly upon the observer, with their simple lines and diminutive but pleasing proportions. Mining money put up extravagant Victorian castles, of which there are many in the city, particularly on the hill between Temple Square and the Capitol. An astonishing number of these houses have been made over into mortuaries—a fitting destiny—but most of them are rooming houses. The city spread southward in the midst of another architectural evolution, and beyond Ninth South Street many an avenue might aptly be named "Bungalow Boulevard." Norman, English Colonial, Spanish Mission, New England Colonial, and other types occur in various additions, especially on the fashionable East Bench. Restricted areas opened during the 1930's reflect the trend toward modern architecture. The old adobes, meantime, are coming into renovated popularity. The style in public buildings, excepting those of the Church, follows that of most American cities (*see Architecture*).

Salt Lake City, as a center of municipal, county, State, and Federal governmental activities, and as Utah's chief religious and educational center, has probably more brief cases per capita than any other city in the State. In spite of these habiliments of importance, however, the tempo is relatively unhurried, with time enough to chat beside the parking meters about crops and precipitation, Church news and the price of copper, and to read the news bulletins in front of newspaper offices. Men's headgear runs more to the stetson than in the East, and a cowboy in a ten-gallon hat, copper-riveted "Levi's," and high-heeled boots arouses no comment. The population of Salt Lake City is predominantly Anglo-Saxon and Scandinavian, with occasional Chinese, Japanese, and Filipinos. Negroes are rare, probably less than one per cent of the total, and Indians seldom get into the city.

Temple Square is the center of tourist activities—it accommodated 406,132 visitors in 1939—and the streets around it are reserved during the tourist season for automobiles with foreign licenses. Bus tour barkers congregate on near-by corners, in front of souvenir shops, trading and handicraft houses, and camera equipment stores. Temple

Square is also the hub of Salt Lake City's principal gatherings, the spring and fall conferences of the L. D. S. Church, when the city is so crowded that private homes are brought into requisition to supply the need for lodgings. During the State Fair in autumn there is a succession of traffic jams between the downtown area and the fair grounds. Covered Wagon Day, July 24, attracts thousands of people for the annual parade, pageant, and rodeo. The percentage of hotel guests checking out in the evening to make the westward desert crossing at night, or checking in during the morning hours following an all-night drive is probably higher than in most other cities.

The history of Salt Lake City is almost inseparable from that of Utah, the city having been the capital in turn of the State of Deseret, Territory of Utah, and State of Utah, except between 1851 and 1856, when Fillmore was a theoretical capital, and 1858, when Parowan was likewise honored. The major part of the city's story, consequently, is that of the State (*see History*).

Regardless of whether Jim Bridger ever said he would give $1,000 for the first grain, or ear, or bushel, of corn produced in Great Salt Lake Valley, the story exemplifies the attitude of the mountain men toward this area. They entered it from the north in 1824 and for some years General Ashley's beaver hunters overran the region. Their thinking, however, did not run to agriculture, irrigation, or city sites. Not all early travelers were so single-minded. Rufus B. Sage, who passed this way in 1842, felt that, "taken as a whole, the vicinity of the Great Salt Lake holds out strong inducements to settlers, and is capable of sustaining . . . a dense population."

Brigham Young, however, was not looking for a land flowing with milk and honey. When Sam Brannan urged him to go on to California, the Church leader said, according to John R. Young, in the *Utah Historical Quarterly* for July, 1930, "Brannan, if there is a place on this earth that nobody else wants, that's the place I am hunting for." In the eyes of some of his followers, he had found it. To George Washington Brimhall and to Gilbert Belnap, both of whom came in 1850, the valley seemed "as nude of a wardrobe as the Indians themselves," and "a vast desert whose dry and parched soil seemed to bid defiance to the husbandman."

Soon after entering this "extensive scenery," the vanguard of the pioneers, on July 23, 1847, began to plow, "and the same afternoon built a dam to irrigate the soil." The following day Brigham Young came behind the main body of the pioneers: 143 men, 3 women, 2 children, 70 wagons, 1 boat, 1 cannon, 93 horses, 52 mules, 66 oxen, and 19 cows. Among the men were Green Flake, Hark Lay, and Oscar Crosby, "colored servants." Three days later, on the Sabbath, Orson Pratt preached a sermon; his text was, "O Zion, that bringest good tidings, get thee up into the high mountains!"

Four days after their arrival, according to Wilford Woodruff's journal, Young called a council of the Quorum of the Twelve, and they "walked from the north camp to about the centre between the two creeks, when President Young waved his hand and said: 'Here is the forty acres for the Temple. The city can be laid out perfectly square. . . .' " The quorum then decided that the blocks would contain ten acres each, that the streets would be 132 feet wide, and the sidewalks twenty feet wide. The following Sunday the first Bowery was built in Temple Square, and the next day Orson Pratt "commenced laying out the city, beginning with the Temple block."

The winter of 1847-48 was mild, but attended with sufficient inconveniences. "Conditions within the fort," relates Charles Coulson Rich, "were especially bad when it rained. For, the roofs having been made with too little slant, small streams of thin mud trickled down upon those underneath, and it so happened that, on such occasions, the only protection was the hoisted umbrella. . . . And there were the bugs and mice. . . ." Provisions were scanty, and some of the settlers, such as Priddy Meeks, went up into the high mountains for game (see *High Uintas Primitive Area*). Amenzo Baker dug thistle roots to feed the family, and his father made molasses from cornstalks. The growing season of 1848 gave promise of sufficient crops, and more emigrants came, but frost, drought, and the cricket plague nearly destroyed growing things. The coming of the gulls, since regarded as providential, saved enough of the crops for the settlers to eke out the hard winter of 1848-49.

The balance of Great Basin wild life was upset by the arrival of the pioneers, and a "competitive vermin hunt" was organized. "Articles of agreement between Captains John D. Lee and John Pack" open with the provision for a "social dinner to be given by the losers." The score was kept in "raven equivalents," as follows: "The right wing of a raven counting one, a hawk or owl two, the wings of an eagle five, the skin of a minx or pole cat five, the skin of a wolf, fox, wild cat, or catamount ten, the pelt of a bear or panther, fifty." The final count showed 14,367 "raven equivalents" turned in, John D. Lee's company of 37 hunters winning over John Pack's 47 hunters by "2543 ravens majority for Lee."

By the time Captain Howard Stansbury came to the Great Basin to survey Great Salt Lake in 1849, he found that "A city has been laid out upon a magnificent scale, being nearly four miles in length and three in breadth. . . . Through the city itself flows an unfailing stream of pure, sweet water, which by an ingenious mode of irrigation, is made to traverse each side of every street . . . spreading life, verdure and beauty over what was heretofore a barren waste."

The city was under ecclesiastical rule until 1851, when "Great Salt Lake City" was incorporated by the "Provisional State of Deseret."

Brigham Young, with characteristic energy and leadership, authorized construction of a wall around the city and around Temple Square, partly as protection from the Indians and partly as a work-relief project. The Temple foundation was started in 1853, and there was almost constant activity within Temple Square in succeeding years. Meantime, the California gold rush brought emigrants through Great Salt Lake

City, and though the Mormons for the most part kept strictly to agriculture, trade with emigrants brought them a measure of prosperity. One transaction by Zodak Knapp Judd serves to present the picture: "I traded them two horses, for which I received three yoke of cattle, a good wagon, a sheet iron stove, a dozen shirts, a good silver watch and nearly a half barrel of pork and some mechanical tools."

From the time of its settlement an air of the incredible has attended Salt Lake City, and travelers have forever been coming to see for themselves "the New Jerusalem," "the Utah Zion," "the City of the Saints." In all but a handful of the books written on Utah and the Mormons during the first thirty years of the city's existence, the Mormon capital *was* Utah, a way of thinking not yet entirely disposed of.

During the so-called Utah War of 1857-58 (*see History*), when the United States Government declared "a state of substantial rebellion" in Utah, the people of Great Salt Lake City joined a general movement southward. When the troops came through the city that summer day in 1858, as recorded by an army correspondent, "the utter silence of the streets was broken only by the music of the military bands, the monotonous tramp of the regiments, and the rattle of the baggage wagons." George "Beefsteak" Harrison, a cook with Johnston's army, "said that Salt Lake was still as a cemetery when they marched in. He saw only two people, a man riding a sorrel mule and an old lady who peeped out of a window blind at the troops."

Following the "Utah War," there ensued a period of lawlessness when the army's camp followers settled in the city. T. B. H. Stenhouse recorded that during a part of 1859 there was a murder every week. Mormon people kept away from "Whisky Street" and attended to their own business, but Brigham Young's house was strictly guarded, day and night. Gradually a lucrative trade grew up between the city and Camp Floyd, but the soldiery was always resented.

Great Salt Lake City became a Pony Express post in 1860, when the first riders came in from Sacramento and St. Joseph. Upon completion of the Pacific Telegraph line to Great Salt Lake City in 1861 Brigham Young sent the first eastbound message to Cleveland. The Nevada-California Volunteers, under the leadership of Colonel P. E. Connor, marched through the city in 1862, surprised to find women and children out to greet them; they had heard rumors of rebellion in Utah. In 1863, following the passage of Federal anti-polygamy laws, there were persistent rumors that Colonel Connor's soldiers would take Brigham Young prisoner. A telescope was mounted on the Beehive House to watch the movements at Camp Douglas, and more than once the militia assembled around the Young residence to protect the Church President. When a cannon boomed from Fort Douglas one midnight there was a hurried Mormon mobilization, but no armed conflict followed. It was later learned that the cannon shot was to salute the news that Colonel Connor had been brevetted a brigadier-general.

Meantime, work was begun on the Tabernacle in 1864, and relations continued poor between townspeople and soldiers. The following Fourth of July, however, they united in a joint celebration of the second inauguration of Abraham Lincoln and of Union successes in the Civil War. Two months later city and camp joined in mourning the assassination of President Lincoln.

The 1870's and early 1880's were railroad years, in the course of which Salt Lake City (the "Great" was dropped in 1868) was connected by rail to cities in each of the four cardinal directions. Following completion of the transcontinental railway through Ogden and north of Great Salt Lake in 1869 (*See Transportation*), Young began construction of the Utah Central Railroad, connecting Salt Lake City with Ogden. Early in 1870, in Salt Lake City, Young drove the "last spike," bearing a beehive emblem, the inscription "Holiness to the Lord," and the initials U.C.R.R., with a hammer similarly decorated. The Utah-organized Utah Southern was completed from Salt Lake City to Provo in 1873, and the Utah Southern Extension reached Milford and Frisco in 1880. The city acquired connections with Logan upon completion of the Utah Northern to Logan and Pocatello, Idaho, in 1874, and to Montana points in later years. Connections were made with Denver and other eastern points over the Denver & Rio Grande Western by 1886. In subsequent years other rail connections have been completed.

Meantime, the Salt Lake Theater was opened in 1862, and took its place as the leading theatrical center of the intermountain West. The Tabernacle was sufficiently completed to house the annual conference of the Mormon Church in 1867. Musical history was made in 1875, when Handel's *Messiah* was presented in the Salt Lake Theater. Building progressed meantime on the Temple, its granite walls gradually rising tier after tier, and Temple Square was a scene of constant industry. Consternation was created in 1870 when two boys, practicing with a rifle, blew up the arsenal on the present site of the State Capitol, breaking nearly every window in the city; long queues of people formed outside establishments selling window glass, and there were gruesome descriptions of finding parts of the boys' bodies.

The death of Brigham Young in 1877 was a shocking event that drew 25,000 people to view the body of the great Church leader as it lay in state in the flower-decked Tabernacle. Music played on the Tabernacle organ included *Brigham Young's Funeral March,* composed for the occasion by Joseph J. Daynes. The funeral address, by Daniel H. Wells, occupied probably less than a minute. "I have no desire or wish to multiply words," he said, "feeling that it is rather a time to mourn. Goodbye, Brother Brigham, until the morning of the resurrection day. . . ."

Young's death occurred just as political battles, initiated in 1870 by the formation of a non-Mormon Liberal Party, took on greater heat. For all their strenuous efforts, however, the Liberals could not carry the city until 1890, when the "manifesto" disavowing polygamy in the

Church ended the warfare in city and Territory over that issue (*see History*).

Building of the Temple, which had been slow up to 1873, when a branch railroad line was run into Little Cottonwood Canyon to facilitate the moving of granite blocks, was speeded thereafter, and the capstone was placed at the time of the annual Church conference in 1892. Andrew Jenson, Assistant Church Historian, writing in the *Utah Magazine* for September, 1936, relates that "over 40,000 people gathered within the confines of Temple Block, while other thousands, unable to find a place in the great square stood in the street or looked down from roofs or windows of adjoining buildings. This was the largest assembly of people ever known in Utah up to that time." Dedication, pending completion of the interior, was deferred to the following year.

Utah marked its semi-centennial, or "Golden Jubilee," with five days of celebration in the summer of 1897, opening with the unveiling of the Brigham Young Monument at Main and South Temple Streets. There was a "Children's Day" parade of 10,000 youngsters on floats drawn by Shetland ponies; as the children passed the monument they threw flowers on it until the base was covered with "a confused heap of colors." More than 700 pioneers were presented with badges, and the Jubilee closed with "a display of pyrotechnics from Capitol Hill."

The Salt Palace, built in 1899 on Ninth South Street, was covered with rock salt and illuminated at night with hundreds of electric lights. A saucer-shaped bicycle track was, at the time, probably the fastest in the country, and world's records were established on it. Barney Oldfield was one of the early competitors. The Salt Palace burned in 1910.

In the closing decades of the nineteenth century and those opening the twentieth, Salt Lake City began to assume its present character. Electric trolleys were installed, Eagle Gate was taken down and erected again at a higher level, the Capitol was built, and many of the present business buildings were erected. Up to 1928 streetcars served the city's transportation needs, and in that year the first trolley bus was installed. During the 1930's streetcars were gradually displaced by trolley and gasoline busses, and the last streetcar line is to be abolished in 1941. Since 1930 the city has concentrated on prevention of automobile accidents; a white flag flies from a downtown building on accident-free days, a black flag on days of fatalities.

Salt Lake City experienced a mild but frightening earthquake in 1934, when a block of land in Hansel Valley (*see Tour 4b*), north of Great Salt Lake, dropped seventeen inches. The first shock was at about eight o'clock in the morning, and, the *Salt Lake Tribune* reported, "Beds, chairs and tables were rocked, chandeliers were broken, plaster was jarred loose, and a few buildings were cracked. At the first disturbance, residents just arising fled from their homes partly clad." The first shock was followed by three others of less intensity. Schools were closed, and employees were sent out of the City and

County Building. The aftermath of the 'quake, harvested in subsequent years, has been a series of doors awry on their hinges, windows that open only with prying, and winter zephyrs dancing through cracks around the wall openings.

A long-standing tradition in Salt Lake City, that a new mayor is ushered into office every four years or less, was maintained in 1939 when Ab Jenkins, Utah's noted racing driver, was elected mayor in what was regarded as a political upset.

In the spring of 1940 the U. S. Bureau of the Census reported a 7 per cent gain in the city's population since 1930.

POINTS OF INTEREST

1. TEMPLE SQUARE (*open 9-8:30 daily, summer; 8-5:30 daily, winter; no smoking; free guide service, no tips*), main entrance W. South Temple St. between Main and West Temple Sts., the heart of Mormonism and the most-visited point of interest in Utah, is a ten-acre city block enclosed by a fifteen-foot wall. The grounds are landscaped with trees, shrubs, winding walks, flower beds in geometric patterns, and a velvety green lawn. Two greenhouses in the northwest corner and one north of the Temple provide flowers for the numerous beds and borders. The square is dominated by the six-spired Temple of the Church of Jesus Christ of Latter-day Saints, on the east side, but the turtle-backed Tabernacle, just west, attracts scarcely less attention because of its strange design. Other structures, monuments, and collections present a cross-section of pioneer and present-day Mormon life and beliefs.

A. The GREAT SALT LAKE BASE AND MERIDIAN STONE, without the wall at the southeast corner of the square, was fixed on the spot designated by Orson Pratt in 1847; when he began the original survey of Great Salt Lake City. Inside the wall, about fifty feet northwest, is a sandstone marker indicating the U. S. meridian line established by the U. S. Coast and Geodetic Survey in 1869.

B. The BUST OF CHARLES R. SAVAGE at the curb just south of the meridian marker, is a combined monument to Old Folks Day, June 21, and to its founder, Charles R. Savage, noted early-day photographer. A bronze bust of Savage, by Gilbert Riswold, stands atop a six-foot pink granite base with drinking fountains on each side.

C. The BUREAU OF INFORMATION AND MUSEUM, just inside the south entrance, is a long two-story white brick building with a Doric entrance. On each side of the entrance steps are stones bearing Indian petroglyphs.

Centering the first floor hall is Torlief Knaphus' *Hand-cart Family,* a bronze group portraying a man pulling a hand-cart, a woman pushing on one side, and a little boy pushing from behind. On the cart are a baby girl and the family's possessions. This group memorializes the Mormon hand-cart migration from the Missouri Valley to Utah between 1856 and 1861, when nearly 4,000 persons crossed the plains by this primitive method.

Visitors are assigned to missionary-guides in this building, which has a lounge for tourists. Books on Mormon theology can be purchased here, and post cards can be written on Brigham Young's octagonal wooden desk. Relics having importance in the history of the Church include a brick from the temple at Nauvoo and the "million-dollar bell" that once tolled from the Nauvoo temple. Personal relics of Church leaders include locks of Joseph Smith's and Brigham Young's hair, and various articles of their clothing. Oil paintings portray miraculous scenes from Mormon theology and history, and there are portraits of Church Presidents.

Relics of the migration and of early pioneer life are plentiful. The wooden-cogged "roadometer" used to measure mileages on the trek across the Great Plains, is shown in a glass case (*see Transportation*). A battered plowshare is inscribed as having plowed the first half-acre in Salt Lake Valley, in July, 1847. A dog-hair cloak recalls a time when clothing materials were so scarce in the valley that dogs had to be shorn. Pioneer furniture, much of it crude and simple, makes up a goodly portion of the first-floor display. There are spinning wheels, pioneer cradles, musical instruments brought across the plains, Brigham Young's safe bearing the inscription "Holiness to the Lord," early presses upon which the *Deseret News* was first printed, pioneer tools, and a great variety of other memorabilia.

The second floor, west room, is the Indian room. Some of the early Mormon homes were built on old Indian sites, and a portion of this collection came from excavations for pioneer homes. There are, however, accessions presented by present-day archeologists. Many of the best-preserved artifacts are from the San Juan country, including mummies, effigy jars, dippers, *ollas,* baskets, bags of dogskin and woven cotton, and a great variety of pipes. Displays in the eastern portion of the second floor were mostly collected by missionaries from nearly every part of the world.

D. The OLDEST HOUSE IN SALT LAKE CITY, a log cabin protected by an iron fence and wooden canopy, is in the southeast corner of the square. Built by Osmyn Deuel in 1847 near present-day Pioneer Park, it is placarded as the house occupied as winter quarters by Captain Howard Stansbury, U. S. Army engineer, during his survey of Great Salt Lake in 1849-50. Stansbury, however, describes his "weary and monotonous quarters" as "a small unfurnished house of unburnt brick or adobe, unplastered, and roofed with boards loosely nailed over, which, every time it stormed, admitted so much water as called into requisition all the pans and buckets in the establishment." The door of the cabin stands open, and visitors can see the oddly angled adobe brick fireplace inside.

E. The THREE WITNESSES MONUMENT, northwest of the cabin, is a rectangular gray granite block with bronze bas-relief likenesses of the three men, Oliver Cowdery, David Whitmer, and

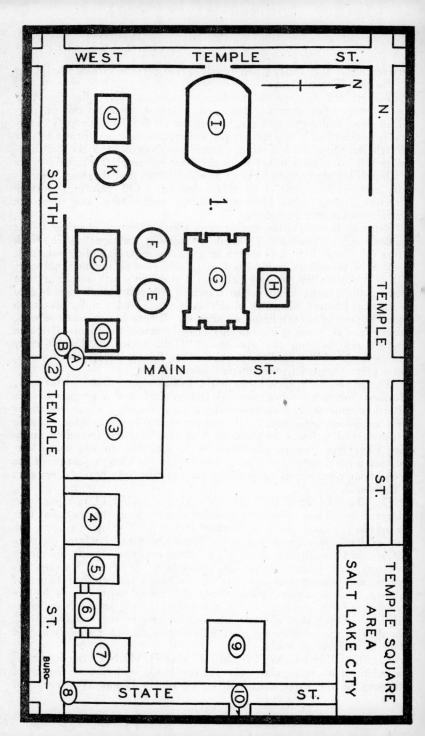

Martin Harris, who testified that an angel showed them the golden plates from which the Book of Mormon was translated. The monument, sculptured in 1926, is the work of Avard Fairbanks.

F. The STATUES OF JOSEPH AND HYRUM SMITH, life-size bronze likenesses of the Mormon prophet and his brother, mounted on square pedestals of Utah granite, are west of the Three Witnesses Monument, on opposite sides of the walk. Both statues were executed by Mahonri Young, grandson of Brigham Young. The prophet and his brother were martyred at Carthage, Illinois, in 1844.

G. The TEMPLE (*not open to non-Mormons*), facing east from the east-central section of the square, is a monumental six-spired gray granite edifice, representing more the inspiration and theologic functionalism of its founders than any one architectural style. The building is 186½ feet long and 99 feet wide, with walls 167½ feet high. The east center tower rises 210 feet, capped by the shining, trumpet-bearing statue of the angel Moroni. The statue, of hammered copper covered with gold leaf, is the work of Cyrus E. Dallin, Utah-born sculptor. It is anchored by a pendulous iron rod, extending into the spire beneath, where it is heavily weighted, allowing free movement of the figure in high winds. The six spires, three on the east and three on the west, with their varying heights, represent the two high priesthoods of the Church. Those on the east signify the higher Melchizedek Priesthood, and those on the west, the highest rising 204 feet, symbolize the Aaronic Priesthood, each with its presidency and two counselors.

At the feet of the buttresses are the "Earth Stones," each bearing bas-relief carvings of the globe. "Moon Stones," depicting the moon in various phases, are on the face of buttresses about midway up the main wall. "Sun Stones," each with its halo of rays, are similarly placed near the top of the main wall. Other symbolic decorations include starred keystones over the round-arched stained-glass windows along the side; the clasped hands, the "all-seeing eye," and carven scrolls with the

---

TEMPLE SQUARE AREA. Points of Interest

1. Temple Square
   A. Great Salt Lake Base and Meridian Stone
   B. Bust of Charles R. Savage
   C. Bureau of Information and Museum
   D. Oldest house in Salt Lake City
   E. Three Witnesses Monument
   F. Statues of Joseph and Hyrum Smith
   G. The Temple
   H. Temple Annex
   I. The Tabernacle
   J. Assembly Hall
   K. Seagull Monument
2. Brigham Young Monument
3. Hotel Utah
4. L. D. S. Church Office
5. Lion House
6. Brigham Young's Office
7. Beehive House
8. Eagle Gate
9. Mormon Missionary Home

inscription, "I am the Alpha and Omega," as decorations on end windows.   High on the east facade is a tall arched niche with a gilded inscription, giving the inclusive dates, 1853-93, of the Temple's construction.   The corresponding space on the west facade is occupied by seven stars in the form of the Great Dipper.   Far up, flanking the central eastern tower, are cloud-and-rain symbols, fitting emblems for a temple in the desert.   A battlemented parapet surmounts the walls, and the three major towers at each end rise from a mass of spires, turrets, pinnacles and finials, where pigeons nest and fly about, casting quick dark shadows on the clean gray granite.   The six spires, softly lighted at night, are a landmark of the city.

There are two large recessed portals at either end, seldom used except for high Church officials or for special ceremonies.   The heavy oaken doors each have three medallions, centered by the ubiquitous beehive.   An iron fence surrounds the building, preventing a nearer approach than twenty or thirty feet by any but Church members.   The Temple is used exclusively by members of the Church for such religious rites as baptismals for the living and the dead, sealing ceremonies, and for marriages (*see The Mormon Church*).

Construction of this $3,500,000 edifice was envisioned before the Mormon exodus from Missouri in 1846-47.   Its plan was conceived by Brigham Young, and the details were worked out by Truman O. Angell, Church architect.   Ground was broken in 1853 and the first cornerstone was laid that year.   Work was suspended in 1857, before the advent of General Johnston's army; Mormon workmen refilled the foundation and the grounds resembled a plowed field when the soldiery arrived.   Some of the great stones were hauled, one at a time, by four-yoke ox-teams, from Little Cottonwood Canyon, 26 miles south.   After the arrival of the railroad, a spur was built into the canyon in 1873.   The walls were twenty feet high when Brigham Young died in 1877.   Construction was completed and the Temple dedicated in 1893, forty years to a day after it was begun.

For a short time following the dedication the public was admitted to the richly appointed interior, but the building was soon closed to all except Church members.   *The House of the Lord,* by James E. Talmage, a Church publication with photographic illustrations, printed in 1912, and *The Great Temple,* by D. M. McAllister, published in 1914, describe the interior.   Both are available through the L. D. S. Bureau of Information and through libraries.

H. The TEMPLE ANNEX (*not open to non-Mormons*), immediately north of the Temple, is an ivory-painted Moorish-type building of oolitic limestone with a cylindrically vaulted roof, the four lunettes decorated with round-arched stained glass windows.   This is the usual entry to the Temple, with which it is connected by a ninety-foot passage.

I. The TABERNACLE (*open when accompanied by guide*), centering the west section of the block, a mammoth oval auditorium seating 5,000, 250 feet long and 150 feet wide, resembles the gray back of a huge tortoise. Unique and severe in design, it is a pioneer among structures employing the self-supported, vaulted type of roof, which was designed as an ellipsoid with a focal point at either end; this, together with the unbroken inner ceiling surface, accounts for the unusual acoustics of the building. A pin dropped at either focal point, when the building is vacant, can be heard at the opposite end, more than 200 feet away. Forty-four gray-painted buttresses of red sandstone mark the circumference of the building. Upon them rest giant wooden arches, ten feet thick, making a span of 150 feet, 70 feet high at the center. The timbers, still in perfect condition—the building was begun in 1864—are braced with lattice-like cross-members, fastened with wooden thole pins and rawhide thongs, since reinforced by nails. A gallery, thirty feet wide, extends around three sides of the interior. Of offset construction, separate from the Tabernacle walls, it is supported by columns, and there is a space of two and a half feet between gallery and wall.

The TABERNACLE ORGAN, at the west end, is known the country over through Columbia broadcasts every Sunday, with the 300-voice Tabernacle Choir. A mammoth structure, it has 6,868 pipes, varying in length from five-eighths of an inch to thirty-two feet. Four motors drive centrifugal blowers to provide wind pressure, which is distributed to the pipes through air chests. A celestial or echo organ, operated from the console, is under the floor at the opposite end of the building. Free organ recitals are given weekdays (*children under 12 not admitted*), the doors opening at 11:50 A. M. to receive the audience, and closing promptly at 12:10 P. M. To prevent untoward sound or interruptions they remain closed throughout the recital, which ends at 12:45 P. M. The program ordinarily includes a number of classical compositions and one of the favorite Mormon hymns. Sunday broadcast concerts are held from 10:30 to 11 A. M., and visitors gather at the Bureau of Information at 10:15.

The design of the Tabernacle is attributable to Brigham Young, and the plans were drawn and the building erected under the supervision of William H. Folsom and Henry Grow, a Pennsylvania bridge-builder, who employed the Remington lattice-truss method by which suspension bridges of the sixties were built. The original organ, begun in 1866, was built by Joseph H. Ridges, an Austrian immigrant, who used timber from the hills around Parowan, 300 miles south. Boiled buffalo and cattle hides provided glue for the pipes. Improvements have enormously changed the character of Ridges' first organ, but many of the pioneer pipes are still in use.

Spring and fall conferences of the L. D. S. Church are held in this auditorium, and it is the scene of many civic and patriotic gatherings. Nationally known symphony orchestras, instrumentalists, and singers have appeared here. At least one musician, Leopold Stokowski, is quoted as saying he thought the acoustics unsuited to the symphony.

J. The ASSEMBLY HALL (*open when accompanied by guide*), in the southwest corner of the square, is a rough gray granite structure with white wooden spires thrusting above its gray slate roof; the auditorium seats 2,000. Services held in this building, in contrast to those in the inviolable Temple, are open to the public. It is, from time to time, devoted to social and intellectual as well as religious uses, and during weekday noon hours it serves as a free nursery for children under twelve while their parents are attending Tabernacle organ recitals.

K. The SEAGULL MONUMENT, east of the Assembly Hall, surrounded by a granite-rimmed pool, is a memorial to the gulls for saving crops of the pioneers during the cricket invasion of 1848. Mounted on a square granite base is a sixteen-foot Doric column, surmounted by a sphere upon which two gilded seagulls are alighting. Four excellent high-relief bronzes decorate the sides of the square base. The north plaque gives the name of the monument and shows two gulls in flight. That on the east presents a pioneer camp scene, with the head of an ox extending around the corner of the granite—a pleasing bit of sculptural unorthodoxy. The south plaque shows the advent of the gulls, and that on the west shows the subsequent harvest. The plaques are considered by many to constitute the best work of the Utah-born sculptor, Mahonri Young, who designed the memorial.

The story of opportune help by seagulls from the islands of Great Salt Lake is one of Utah's most favorite oft-told tales. Some consider the incident to have been a miracle. Priddy Meeks, a pioneer who was on the ground, tells the story in his autobiography, a copy of which is in possession of the Utah State Historical Society:

> Now everything did look gloomy, our provisions giving out and the crickets eating up what little we had growing, and we a thousand miles away from supplies. When Sunday come we had a meeting. Apostle Rich stood in an open wagon and preached out of doors. . . .
> At that instant I heard the voice of fowels flying over head that I was not acquainted with. I looked up and saw a flock of seven gulls. In a few minutes there was another larger flock passed over. They came faster and more of them until the heavens were darkened with them and they would eat crickets and throw them up again. A little before sundown they left for Salt Lake, for they roosted on sandbar a little after sunrise. In the morning they came back again and continued that course until they had devoured the crickets and then left Sinedie and never returned. I guess this circumstance changed our feeling considerable for the better.

2. The BRIGHAM YOUNG MONUMENT, centering the intersection of Main and South Temple Sts., is a heroic bronze figure of the Church leader, on a granite base. Seated at the base is the bronze figure of an Indian facing east, while the figure of a bearded trapper, in a similar pose, faces west. On the south face is a bronze bas-relief of a pioneer man, woman, and child. Another plaque, on the north face, lists the pioneers and equipment making up the main body of Mormon pioneers who arrived in Salt Lake Valley on July 24, 1847. The twenty-five-foot monument, unveiled during the Utah Jubilee in 1897, was executed by Cyrus E. Dallin, Utah-born sculptor.

3. The HOTEL UTAH, NE. corner Main and South Temple Sts., a ten-story hostelry of white terra-cotta brick, erected in 1911, is owned by the Mormon Church. The ornate French Renaissance building is lavishly decorated with figure carvings and scrollwork, and its ornate cupola is topped with the State emblem, the beehive. The emblem is lighted with neon at night and is one of the most outstanding objects on the Salt Lake City skyline. A roof garden affords a widespread view of Great Salt Lake Valley.

4. The LATTER-DAY SAINTS CHURCH OFFICE BUILDING (*open 9-4 weekdays, summer; 9-5, winter; guides*), 47 E. South Temple St., is a granite structure of Greek Revival design, with fluted Ionic columns extending through the full height of its four stories. Completed in 1917, the building houses the offices of Mormon Church leaders, and the CHURCH HISTORIAN'S OFFICE AND LIBRARY, on the third floor, the richest repository of original source material in the State. In addition to ecclesiastical records of the Church since its founding in 1830, the library has a priceless collection of pioneer documents and diaries giving detailed contemporaneous accounts of the exploration and settlement of the State.

5. The LION HOUSE (*open 10-5 daily, summer; 10-10 daily, winter; guides*), 63 E. South Temple St., is a two-story cement-covered adobe structure with small-paned windows, green shutters, tall gray chimneys, and a gray tile roof. East and west exposures are topped with ten steep-roofed gables. The house is named for the carved stone lion, executed by William Ward, pioneer craftsman, over the first floor portico, and is used as a social center and banquet hall by L. D. S. Church organizations. This building, because it housed some of Brigham Young's wives, has always been an object of great curiosity to visitors, who have often stood outside and counted the gables, in the belief that each gable represented a wife's apartment. Brigham Young, who is credited by some authorities with twenty-six wives, offered no assistance in this guessing game. On the contrary, he seemed to take particular delight in keeping curious persons in suspense. Concerning family trips into the country, he once said, "You know what they say about me in the east; should I take my ninety wives and their children, with carriages and wagons enough to convey them, it would make such a vacuum here, and so many others would wish to go, that there would be no Salt Lake City. I think I will take a few of them, but I dare not take the whole, for if I did they would then know how many wives I have got, and that would not do."

Sir Richard F. Burton, who visited Great Salt Lake City in 1860, was one of those who looked with great inquisitiveness at this building, with "a small acute ogive or gable" over each upper window. "It was finished in 1845 [1856], and is tenanted by the 'plurality wives' and their families, who each have a bed-room, sitting-room, and closet, simply and similarly furnished. There is a Moslem air of retirement about the . . . House; the face of woman is rarely seen at the window, and her voice is never heard from without."

The first floor interior, remaining much as it was originally, has a suite of sitting rooms on the west side. Beveled window casements, set in the thick adobe walls, are of paneled mountain mahogany, and the mantels are of simple design. Original furnishings, including a settle designed and made by Brigham Young, occupy the west rooms, and there is an excellent oil portrait of the Church leader. The floors are of the original wide boards, fastened with hand-made iron nails.

Centrally situated on the east side is the BRIGHAM YOUNG MUSEUM (*open by permission*), containing numerous memorabilia of the Church President, assembled in the room in which he died. Centered on an octagonal mountain mahogany table is a six-inch "Joslin's Terrestrial Globe," printed in Boston in 1854, which must have afforded Brigham Young considerable amusement for its geographic errors: it shows "Lake Salado" connected by a river with Monterey, California, and "Lake Timpanogos" joined by an uncertain river, tentatively dotted, with San Francisco Bay. A glass case on the west side of the room displays numerous personal effects, including a set of hinged ivory toothpicks, a walking stick graduated for various measurements, a pair of field glasses, a bracelet made from Sutters Fort gold, delicate brass scales for weighing gold dust, monogrammed dishes and glassware, generously sized silverware, and a number of photographic portraits, including a daguerreotype in a bullet-punctured frame, reminiscent of an attempt on the Church leader's life. Another group includes clothing used by Brigham Young's wives and daughters. A japanned old-style Remington typewriter, still in working condition, and a mechanical music case indicate Brigham's Jefferson-like interest in gadgets. A pair of blue sun-glasses, with side pieces, startlingly like those worn by the motorist of 1940, are included in the collection. Original straight wooden chairs, cut and curved for an astonishing degree of comfort, are included in the collection, as well as the Church President's old green cloak and tall hat. In a small adjoining room is a rocker with padded wings, in which, Brigham's granddaughters remember, the Church leader took naps in his latter years. In the same room is a framed group of photographs showing twenty-one of Brigham's wives.

A gently sloping straight stairway, simply neweled and banistered, leads to the second floor, from which nearly all the partitions have been removed to convert it into a spacious banquet hall. The lines of the "ogives or gables" are carried indoors by intersection planes over each of the twenty narrow windows. Apartments of the "plurality wives" are preserved only in present-day restrooms, each about ten feet square, with a closet.

In the basement, now used as a cafeteria, foundation stonework can still be seen, and layers of adobe brick. This part of the house was originally used as a dining room and kitchen, presided over by one of Brigham's childless wives, and for storage purposes.

The keeping of law and order in such a household as this must have been one of the Mormon leader's major projects. All reports indicate that he ruled his family with the same firm hand as he did his followers.

He rose every morning at seven o'clock, went to his office next door, and spent the morning administering Church matters. At two o'clock he had dinner with his family at the Lion House, in the room now used as a cafeteria. Picnics and outings were usually planned at this time, including gay rides in the *Julia Dean Haynes,* a bobsled named for the noted actress. He maintained a sort of gymnasium for his children, using the equivalent of a present-day medicine ball for exercise. Good posture was encouraged among his daughters by making them wear wooden yokes to keep their shoulders back. In the afternoon he visited his wives individually, and at seven o'clock rang the prayer bell, calling his fifty-six children and their mothers into the room now used as a sitting room. Here, too, were held the family councils, including "juvenile court," at which differences between children were adjusted by the father-judge. The family then retired, if no social events were planned for the evening, the women with small children to bedrooms on the first floor, those with older children to the twenty bedrooms on the second floor. A daughter, Clarissa Young Spencer, has written charmingly of life in the Lion House in *One Who Was Valiant.*

Brigham Young encouraged his wives and children to develop their talents. Eliza R. Snow, "The Sweet Singer of Israel," widow of Joseph Smith and later sealed to Brigham Young, was an accomplished poetess and author of the Mormon hymn, "O My Father." One of his wives taught all the children until he established a private school for them. Others sewed, made hooked rugs, knitted, wove, and made laces. Wives waited on tables, laundered, cleaned, and contributed their various talents to the self-sufficient household. Although he did not discourage young men courting his older daughters—most of Brigham's children were daughters—he insisted on a bright lamp in the parlor on calling nights. If the suitors overstayed the hour of ten, the Mormon leader would appear in the parlor, his arms full of hats, and ask each young man to identify his own.

6. BRIGHAM YOUNG'S OFFICE (*open 9-4 daily*), 67 E. South Temple St., entered from the Lion House, is a small two-story adobe between the Lion and Beehive Houses. Designed by Truman O. Angell and built in 1852, it has a square-columned one-story portico surmounted by iron grillwork, small-paned windows, and a gray slate roof. The original pine desk remains, and there are closets and built-in pigeonholes for the keeping of records. A steep stairway behind a closet leads to the oval mezzanine, said to be the first in the West. The building is used today mainly as a conference room for Church organizations.

7. The BEEHIVE HOUSE (*open 9-4 weekdays; guides*) 75 E. South Temple St., is a two-story buff adobe structure with a square-columned two-story porch, a green roof, and tall gray chimneys. Designed by Truman O. Angell and built in 1855, the Beehive House, more than any of the early Mormon residences, has an aura of gracious mid-nineteenth-century living. In its exterior design the house has a certain New England solidity, yet there is a Victorian air about it,

probably encouraged by iron parapet railings and by the wood-railed eastern-seaboard "widow's watch." Far from the seacoast, where anxiety for those at sea produced a watchtower on nearly every house, the Mormon architect adapted the tower to enclose Utah's symbol of diligence. The surmounting flagpole further marks it as a house of consequence.

Entrance is through massive carved doors with opaque glass panels, originally "Dutch doors," top and bottom halves swinging separately. The cast iron doorknob is decorated with the figure of a bee, and the door plate has a beehive motif.

The interior effect is one of depth, space, and manor-house hospitality. A long hallway runs back from the entrance, and west of it is a spacious high-ceiled room, close to Brigham Young's office, in which he probably received Church and Territorial committees and held conferences. In this room, as elsewhere in the house, the thick adobe walls, can be noted, with each casement beveled and paneled to give an effect of greater light and space inside. The mantelpiece is surmounted by a scrollwork beehive, and the window frames are carved, each differently. A spacious bedroom adjoins, on the same side of the house, furnished with a burled four-poster bed and other objects in keeping with the period of occupancy. East of the hallway is a long suite of rooms that could be opened for almost the full depth of the house, to accommodate family or social gatherings of great size. There are mirrors, silver chandeliers, beveled wall-openings admitting a flood of light, and old-fashioned furniture.

The paneled hallway and staircases reveal the ingenuity of early carvers, who carried their patterns up with the stairs, moved out to greet the landings, and swept on to higher levels. Even on planes beneath the stairs they paneled with the same care and carved freehand with the same originality. Each newel post is separately and ornately carved, each with different motifs; one, on the second floor, uses an early railroad train in a design. Three stairways are embellished in like manner, each leading to second floor and attic. On the second floor are spacious bedrooms with four-poster beds and oil paintings.

After the death of Brigham Young in 1877 the house was occupied by Church presidents until 1918, when it was made into a home for out-of-town young women who work or attend school in Salt Lake City. It was chosen in 1934 by the Historic American Buildings Survey as a structure worthy of preservation in its present condition.

8. EAGLE GATE, spanning N. State St. at E. South Temple St., designates the former entrance to the private property of Brigham Young. A copper-plated wood-carved eagle, its outspread wings measuring sixteen feet, is perched on a beehive, and the whole motif is held up by curved iron supports on square stone posts. The eagle was modeled on an actual specimen, killed in City Creek Canyon, and carved by Ralph Ramsay. The gate was erected in 1859 and for many years served as the only entrance to City Creek Canyon. Not everybody has liked the emblem and the gate. Sir Richard F. Burton,

who visited the city the year after it was put up, describes it as "a huge vulturine eagle, perched, with wings outspread, neck bended as if snuffing the breeze of carrion from afar, and talons clinging upon a yellow bee-hive;—a most uncomfortable and unnatural position for the poor animal. The device is doubtless highly symbolical, emblematical, typical,—in fact, everything but appropriate and commonsensical." With the arrival of electric streetcars in the 1880's, the gate was removed, but in 1891 it was rebuilt at a greater height and width to accommodate trolley cars, and the original wooden emblem was electroplated. A model of the gate was displayed at the Chicago World's Fair in 1893. Though some local people object to it as a traffic hazard, Eagle Gate is one of Utah's most widely known and most photographed landmarks.

9. The MORMON MISSIONARY HOME (*open 8-7 daily*), 31 N. State St., a two-story red brick building with a white porch, operates a two-weeks preparatory school for outgoing Mormon missionaries. They are trained in proper conduct, the choice of associates, personal appearance, punctuality, and other personal virtues. Prospective missionaries, averaging twenty-one years of age, are instructed in the Mormon gospel, church organization, languages, singing, genealogy, priesthood and auxiliary work, gymnastics, and standard church works. This and the adjoining houses, dedicated to their present purpose in 1925, accommodate ninety people.

10. BRIGHAM YOUNG CEMETERY (*open on application to Mormon Church Bureau of Information; guides*), 1st Ave. between N. State and A Sts., is a green-lawned area surrounded by an iron fence. In the southeast corner, surrounded by an iron fence overgrown with vines, is the grave of Brigham Young (1801-77), President of the Church of Jesus Christ of Latter-day Saints from 1847 to the time of his death. Recumbent white marble tombstones mark the graves of three of his wives and of several of his children. A city ordinance prevented burial of the remainder of his family in this plot.

(Out Wasatch Boulevard)

11. The STATE CAPITOL (*open 8-5:30 Mon.-Fri., 8-5 Sat., Sun.; guide*), N. end of N State St., a classically styled four-story edifice built on the lines of the National Capitol, stands on a bench of the Wasatch foothills at the northern rim of the city, its magisterial air emphasized by the 300-foot elevation above the valley floor; it can be seen in the distance from nearly every approach to the city. The building, of Corinthian lineage, was designed by Richard K. A. Kletting, Salt Lake City architect. Though capped by the usual dome, it is articulated with spacious simplicity. Following the structural precedent of two wings, one for each branch of a bicameral legislature, it departs from the precedent in placing the House of Representatives in the west wing, the Senate in the north center, and the State Supreme Court in the east wing. Built of Utah granite on a rectangular plan, it

is 404 feet long, 240 feet wide, and 285 feet high at the tip of the dome, which is covered with Utah copper. The south facade is broken only at the center by the customary monumental entrance leading up to a well-proportioned Corinthian portico.

The forty-acre grounds, grass-carpeted and planted with trees and shrubs, crown Capitol Hill. North of the building are an ample parking ground, a rock garden and pool, and stone benches. Southeast of the capitol, on the grounds, is the MORMON BATTALION MONUMENT, the work of Gilbert Griswold, Chicago sculptor, erected in 1927 to perpetuate the memory of Mormons who fought for the United States in the Mexican War of 1846. A mass of rose-pink granite, roughly triangular in shape, the memorial is centered by the heroic bronze figure of a Battalion infantryman; from the prow of stone behind and above him emerges a symbolical woman's figure. In the concave sides of the granite mass, front and back, are high reliefs depicting scenes in the life of the Battalion. Paid at the rate of $12.50 per man per month, they received about $75,000; the monument was erected at a cost of $200,000.

The Mormon Battalion was a body of 536 officers and men; the roster is usually extended to include thirty-six women. Between Santa Fe, New Mexico, and San Diego, California, they averaged almost 13 miles per day on an 85-day march that covered 1,125 miles, the longest sustained march ever made by an infantry detachment of the U. S. Army. Only once, on the San Pedro River, did they engage in armed conflict, at the so-called Battle of the Bulls. Part of the Battalion remained in San Diego from January to July, 1847, when 81 men reenlisted and 240 started for Great Salt Lake City. They passed the site of the Donner encampment (see Tour 6c) and found portions of unburied bodies. Informed by messengers from Brigham Young that food conditions were not favorable in Salt Lake Valley, about half of the detachment turned back and were employed in California that winter; a few found work at Sutter's Mill, where they participated in the discovery of gold in California (see Tour 1f). Gradually, most of the Battalion personnel, including those who had reenlisted, rejoined the Mormons in Utah. In addition to their great trek, unguided, across a forbidding section of the Southwest, they are credited with holding California garrisons to good effect, with building roads and digging wells on their route, and with the introduction of new plants from New Mexico and California—California peas, club-head and "Taos" wheat, which, as a cross, was the principal seed wheat in Utah for years after their return.

Until 1912, when ground was broken for the present Capitol, the legislature and high court of Utah had an orphaned existence. Meeting in the old Council House in Great Salt Lake City, the first Territorial legislature of 1851 picked Fillmore as a central situation for the State capital. Truman O. Angell, Church architect, designed a three-winged, acorn-domed State House, the completed south wing of which was first occupied by the legislature in the session of 1855-56.

The building was never finished, though the one wing still stands in Fillmore (*see Tour 1e*). Finding the new capital too far removed from the center of population, the same legislature returned the government to Great Salt Lake City. It came back in the midst of a Church "reformation" movement. Members of both houses were called into joint session, as recorded in the journal of Isaac C. Haight, and made "to repent of all their sins and be baptized for remission of same before any business could be done . . . and all the members . . . were baptized in the font, and were confirmed and all were made to rejoice with joy and gladness unspeakable." Several subsequent legislatures trekked to Fillmore, 150 miles away, to fulfill legal requirements, but immediately adjourned to Great Salt Lake City. Sessions continued in the Council House until it burned in 1883, and one session was held in Social Hall. There was agitation for the erection of a capitol during the last years of Territorial government, but the legislature continued to meet in the Old Courthouse until completion of the City and County Building in 1894, when it was occupied as capitol. Finally, in 1912, when $1,500,000 had been collected from inheritance taxes, authorization was given to start the building. The cornerstone was laid by Governor William Spry in 1914, and the edifice was completed the following year at a cost of $2,739,528.54.

The interior of the building is laid out with a spacious and rectangular dignity, departing from the usual formula of a rotunda under the dome; the plan conforms to this tradition only to the extent of a circle of opaque glass set in the floor, upon which is centered the bronze-painted plaster cast replica of Cyrus E. Dallin's heroic *Massasoit*, mounted on a marble-painted wooden base; the bronze original looks out over Plymouth Bay, Massachusetts. The story is that the Utah sculptor used the torso of a Negro wrestler and the head of an Indian woman in composing his statue of the great chief of the Wampanoags. Some say that the Capitol was built around *Massasoit*; at any rate the tall magnificent figure dominates the view from any point within the three-story rectangular hall, whether seen from the main (or second) floor, from the marble-banistered stairs that sweep up at each end, or from the mezzanine-like third and fourth floors. The hall is flanked with smooth monolithic columns of gray Georgia marble, with Ionic capitals. The walls of the main floor are paneled with quartered marble, and guides point out such configurations as "the Persian rug," "the butterfly," "the hourglass," "the yawning lion," and "heels of two socks together," while "Santa Claus" is seen peering down from a column. A wall niche northwest of- *Massasoit* contains a marble bust of Emmeline B. Wells (1828-1921), woman suffragist, poetess, and editor; the bust was executed by Cyrus E. Dallin in 1928.

In the pendentives, or arched triangles leading up to the dome, are four murals depicting phases in Utah's early history—the march of Father Escalante in 1776, in the southwest pendentive; Peter Skene Ogden, Hudson's Bay Company trader, in the northeast; John C. Frémont at Great Salt Lake in the northwest; and Brigham Young with an ox-drawn covered wagon, in the southeast. Examination of the latter reveals that the oxen have no ears. The mural group, and the cycloramic historical mural inside the base of the dome, were designed by Lee Greene Richards, who was assisted by Henry Rasmusen, Gordon Cope, and Waldo Midgley. When the murals were mounted in 1934, and the scaffolding taken down, it was discovered that a paint-stained cloth had been left on a shelf at the base of the dome. Gordon Pope, armed with a long fishing rod, spent the greater part of a day at casting before the undecorative object was landed. The interior of the dome, 165 feet above the floor at its highest point, is decorated with a skyscape, and from its center hangs a 6,000-pound chandelier on a 7,000-pound chain. Giant semi-circular murals at each end of the long hall were done by Girard Hale and Richard White in 1917. The west mural depicts the arid Great Salt Lake Valley as it looked to the pioneers in 1847, and that on the east shows the green and fertile valley after it was cultivated by early settlers.

The GOLD ROOM (*opened for display by guide*), southwest of the main hall, is the governor's reception room, in which Presidents and royal visitors have been received. It is a long rectangular room with a vaulted ceiling, liberally decorated with yellow metal. Capitol guides take pleasure in listing foreign-made furniture and decorations including the 1,350-pound seamless chenille rug measuring twenty-two by forty-eight feet, the French tapestries, the handmade lace curtains, the rich drapes, the cut-glass chandeliers, the beveled mirrors with gold-leafed frames, the long Circassian walnut table. A painting in the center of the ceiling, by Louis Schettle of New York, is called *Children at Play*.

The skylit HOUSE OF REPRESENTATIVES opens off the end of the stairway leading to the third floor at the west end of the building. It is reminiscent of the House in the National Capitol, with its clock-and flag-surmounted dais, but is built on a smaller scale, and the desks of the sixty members are in close-crowded rows.

Millard F. Malin's marble BUST OF UNCA SAM stands on the south side of the doorway to the House of Representatives. Unca Sam (Red Sam) was a White River Ute Indian whose age, at the time of his death in 1939, was estimated to be from 107 to 127 years old. "At any rate," says Malin, "Unca Sam grew up during the heyday of the fur trade, and was hunting buffalo when the first white settlers piloted their covered wagons into the Rocky Mountain region." Following the Meeker massacre in Colorado in 1879, Unca Sam was a member of the peace mission sent to Washington to patch up relations between his people and the Government. Moved thereafter to the Uintah Reservation he lived as a reservation Indian for about fifty years before he was chosen as Malin's model at Whiterocks in 1934. "It was hard to keep the ancient Indian in pose," says the sculptor in an account specially prepared for the Utah Guide; "he was so interested in watching the artists at work. His face was an intricate study, a marvelous network of wrinkles."

A companion piece, on the north side of the doorway, is the BUST OF JOHN DUNCAN, also by Malin. Duncan, a chief of the Utes who is (1940) in his eighties, can remember the passing of Mormon hand-cart brigades in 1856-61. "His strong-boned face and figure were a delight to the artists," Malin says.

The SENATE CHAMBER, on the north central side of the main hall, is similar in plan to the House, except that it is less crowded in accommodating twenty-odd senators.

The UTAH SUPREME COURT CHAMBER, at the east end of the second floor, has a subdued atmosphere, accented by its dark blue rug and rich walnut furnishings. Behind the chairs of the five supreme court justices hangs H. L. A. Culmer's oil painting of the Augusta (now Sipapu) Natural Bridge.

The UTAH STATE ART COLLECTION, arranged around the mezzanine hall on all four sides of the third and fourth floors, is in reality a number of collections. Murals and governors' portraits belong to the Capitol and are under the care of the secretary of State. The Alice Art Collection, named for Alice Merrill Horne, who introduced the bill creating the Utah Art Institute in 1899, is under the care of the Utah State Institute of Fine Arts, and represents accessions purchased with annual appropriations ranging from $100 to $2,000. The Utah State Fair Collection, administered by the Utah State Fair Association, is made up of prize paintings exhibited at the fair. Art work by the Federal Emergency Relief Administration and by the Public Works of Art Project was presented to the State by the Federal government. Printed keys, for identification of pictures, hang on both floors.

On the third floor, turning right (east) from the elevator, is Rockwell Kent's *Dennis,* painted in 1916 and acquired by the State in 1935 because Kent disremembered the known and rhymed fact that November hath but thirty days. He was scheduled to lecture on the last day of November, 1934, and his audience waited for hours. When he appeared the next day—"November 31st"—Kent showed his contriteness by giving the State one of his pictures. At the north end of the east hall is Gordon Cope's portrait of John Duncan, Ute Indian chief, made in 1935; it shows the old Indian wearing a war bonnet, which is the way John Duncan wanted Gordon Cope to paint him. In the south hall, just west of Room 320, is another portrait, showing the chief in profile, wearing long braids and a ten-gallon hat with a vividly colored band. This was the way Gordon Cope wanted to paint John Duncan. In the north hall is a Rubens, copied by Avard Fairbanks; examination reveals a patch three inches square (by Henry Rasmusen), repairing damage done by gallery visitors to the nude figure of an infant. Many paintings by early and contemporary artists are included in the collections.

RELIC HALL, the museum of the Daughters of Utah Pioneers, is in the southeast portion of the first or ground floor. Its exhibits, in glass cases and on walls, present an excellent cross-section of the life of the Mormon pioneers. A case of coins and money includes early Mormon media of exchange such as a ten-cent tithing script and a fifty-cent "bill" issued by the Manti United Order. A case of women's dresses includes silk and wool garments made and worn by Utah women, and there are pioneer watches, spectacles, fans, fire-place bellows, and rugs. A display on the south side of the building, in a simulated log cabin interior, includes Maude Adams' cradle (*see Theater*), a branding iron, and an intricately carved wooden hall tree made by Ralph Ramsay. A large case contains the wagon in which Brigham Young came over the plains, ox yokes, the skull of a buffalo, and a kettle used by General Johnston's army. In a special case are possessions of Brigham Young, including his carpetbag, his Panama hat, the dental forceps with which he pulled his children's teeth, and his much-publicized home-made copper bootjack, made about 1870. There are displays of early militia equipment, Salt Lake Theater costumes, dresses and handicrafts, old surgical instruments, and pitchers made by James Eardley, early St. George potter. The works of Ralph Ramsay, indefatigable pioneer woodcarver, include a rejected model for Eagle Gate and an ornately carved bedstead upon which the craftsman worked from 1860 to 1898.

Wall and display cases covering most of the remainder of the first floor include dioramas, displays and color transparencies of Utah industries, agricultural products, and scenery. In the west hall is a huge block of Utah coal measuring five by five by ten feet and weighing 20,900 pounds and a model of the old State house at Fillmore, and in the east hall is the cast of an enormous dinosaur footprint. The San Juan County case displays Buck Lee's colorfully and artistically hand-tooled cowboy saddle. Also in the east hall is a bronze-painted plaster cast of Cyrus E. Dallin's *Signal of Peace,* one of his many Indian equestrian sculptures. The story is that Dallin loaned the cast for the Utah Jubilee celebration in 1897, with the understanding that it would be destroyed after the celebration. The cast was moved from the City and County Building, then in use as the State capitol, to its present place in 1915. About ten years later, according to the story, Dallin found the cast in the capitol and belabored it furiously with his cane, breaking it, as he thought, beyond repair. However, capitol employees replaced the fragments and glued the fractures, painting them over with bronze paint. Damage done by the angry sculptor can still be seen.

12. MEMORY GROVE PARK, a tastefully landscaped area on both sides of Canyon Rd. in City Creek Canyon below the Capitol, is dedicated to Utah soldiers who lost their lives in the World War. The landscaped area has terraced lawns with native stone retaining walls, against which flowers bloom in spring and summer. On the east side of Canyon Road is a white marble pergola commemorating the 760 Utah soldiers who died in the war. Near the north end of the park is a memorial shaft erected by the 145th Artillery. The area west of the road is centered by MEMORIAL HOUSE, a long stucco colonial-

type building with green shutters and seven round-topped dormers. Development of the park began in 1923.

13. The U. S. VETERANS HOSPITAL (*visiting hours 2-4 Sun., Tue., Thu.*), Wasatch Blvd. (11th Ave.) on a line with E St. extended, is a massive red brick structure of Georgian Colonial design, with a five-story central section and four-story wings. It occupies a landscaped tract of twenty-seven acres high on a terrace of ancient Lake Bonneville, and there is an extensive view of the city from the grounds.

14. CITY CEMETERY, main entrance NE. corner 4th Ave. and N St., a monument-dotted hillside area of 267 acres, is truly a city of the dead, with marked streets and avenues. Tastefully planted, mainly with evergreens, the cemetery is a haven for birds during inclement months. Bevies of California quail, their topknots bobbing, wander through the grounds, and the trees provide choir-room for hundreds of songbirds. Used as a burial ground since 1848, the area contains the graves of several Mormon Church Presidents, including those of Wilford Woodruff, Anthon Lund, and Joseph F. Smith. Burial plats of polygamous families are often fenced, with a large monument to the head of the house and lesser monuments to the various wives. The "STRANGER'S PLAT," NE. corner of 5th Ave. and Main St. within the cemetery, is an open area containing the unmarked graves of wanderers. Adjoining the municipally-managed burial grounds are a Roman Catholic cemetery, three Jewish cemeteries, and a cemetery for Japanese Buddhists.

SALT LAKE CITY. Points of Interest

1-9 (See Temple Square Area)
10. Brigham Young Cemetery
11. State Capitol
12. Memory Grove Park
13. U. S. Veterans Hospital
14. City Cemetery
15. Fort Douglas
16. Hogle Gardens Zoo
17. "This Is The Place" Monument
18. St. Mary of the Wasatch
19. Empey House
20. Cathedral of the Madeleine
21. Governor's Mansion
22. Masonic Temple
23. George H. Dern House
24. Art Barn
25. University Ward Chapel
26. University of Utah
27. Pony Express Monument
28. Site of Social Hall
29. Utah Art Center
30. Site of Salt Lake Theatre
31. City and County Building
32. St. Mark's Episcopal Cathedral
33. First Congregational Church
34. Ambassador Hotel
35. Liberty Park
36. Westminster College
37. Utah State Prison
38. Pioneer Park
39. Utah State Fairgrounds
40. Salt Lake City Airport

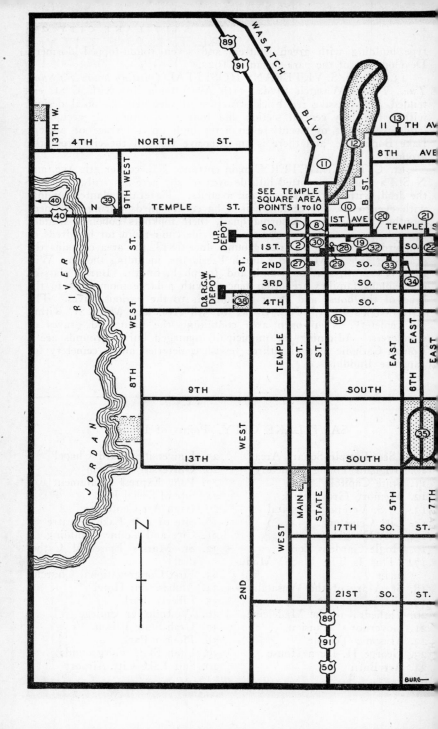

SALT LAKE CITY

15. FORT DOUGLAS (*open; guides for groups on application*), main entrance Fort Douglas Blvd. and Gibbon St., occupies a 9,000-acre reservation on East Bench. Resembling a small town, the fort has 170 buildings. Until late 1940 it was regimental post of command for the 38th U. S. Infantry; the ROCK OF THE MARNE MONUMENT, at Fort Douglas Blvd. and Soldiers' Circle, is dedicated to that regiment. In the autumn of 1940 the 38th Infantry was replaced by the 5th Air Base Group, the 7th Bombardment Group, and the 88th Reconnaissance Squadron, G.H.Q. Air Force. In addition to the Air Corps troops are Medical, Quartermaster, Ordnance, Finance, and Signal units, totalling at the end of 1940 approximately 2,800 enlisted men and 250 officers. The 20th Wing headquarters were also to be established at Fort Douglas in the near future. The aviation units operate from the Salt Lake Airport Lease, immediately north of commercial properties at the Salt Lake Municipal Airport, and barracks in 1940 were under construction at the airport to accommodate there approximately 1,000 officers and enlisted men. Areas in the Salt Desert set aside for bombardment purposes (*see Tour 6c*) were to be utilized by these forces. Fort Douglas—originally Camp Douglas—was founded in 1862 by Colonel Patrick E. Connor; the fort cemetery has monuments to Connor, to his California-Nevada Volunteers, and to twenty-one German prisoners who died here during the World War. Red Butte Canyon, which furnishes the water supply for Fort Douglas, is closed to the public.

16. HOGLE GARDENS ZOO (*open daylight hours; adm. free*), 2600 Sunnyside Ave., occupies a forty-seven-acre plot at the mouth of Emigration Canyon. The principal resident of the gray brick main building is Princess Alice, a 9,000-pound elephant, born in 1875. Alice made elephant history by giving birth to the first baby elephant ever bred and born in America, at Salinas, California, in 1912. Gene Fowler, in his book *Timber Line,* devotes an entire chapter to "The Royal Family"—Princess Alice, her gloomy husband Snyder, and their four ill-fated offspring. Alice's first-born, Baby Hutch, Fowler writes "was twenty-four inches high and thirty-six from tip to tail and had an orphans'-home personality"; Alice tried to crush him, and he lived only two months. When Tambon, her second calf (named for Harry Tammen and Fred Bonfils, owners of *The Denver Post* and co-owners of the Sells-Floto Circus), was born in Denver in 1914, Alice was attended by an obstetrician, a surgeon, a stomach specialist, a practicing physician, and two veterinarians; Tambon lived less than a month, dying of the same intestinal ailment that took Baby Hutch. Little Miracle, the third bull calf, born in 1916, lived five months.

In 1917, it was decided that Alice no longer was fit for show purposes. Tammen offered her to the school children of Salt Lake City, who were asked to contribute dimes [$3,200 worth] toward the purchase. And so she was exiled to the Utah Siberia, and there gave birth in 1918 to the fourth son," Prince Utah, the only elephant ever born on Utah soil. This fourth crown prince of the elephant

"Royal Family" lived eleven months. He was stuffed following his demise, and is stored in the basement of the L. D. S. Museum in Temple Square, no longer in condition for display. "Dutch" Schieder, Alice's trainer in the circus, came with her to Salt Lake City, and during her more docile days in Liberty Park he would put her through a routine of tricks on Sundays and holidays. Occasionally a lucky child would be given a ride on Alice's head, and there was hardly ever a time when Schieder could walk through the tangle of importunate kids that surrounded him when he appeared; but then, there are grown-ups even today who stand in awe of a man who can operate an elephant.

In the mid-1920's, in the fall of the year, Alice was put to work moving a wooden shed in Liberty Park. She was probably cold, and wasn't in a very good temper. Hitched to the shed, she pulled it out through the trees, bumping first one and then another, leaving a Samson-like trail of debris behind. As her burden lightened, she headed for the warmth of the barn. Somebody waved at her to stop, which Alice had no intention of doing. She went on a trip up Parley's Canyon, lightly brushing off a residential porch or two on the way. She was brought back in a truck. Not long after this incident Alice went on a hunger strike when the city commissioners suspended her trainer. For several days she would neither eat nor drink, and resumed her diet only after "Dutch" Schieder came back to take care of her. Alice had one more ride in a truck, in 1931, when she was moved from Liberty Park to her present quarters, provided by Mr. and Mrs. James A. Hogle of Salt Lake City. She didn't like either ride. A somber and historic character, Alice is chained much of the time, and weaves ceaselessly back and forth, her swinging trunk describing an arc on the concrete floor.

Other occupants of Alice's apartment house include leopards, lions, a wildcat, and monkeys. In summer the monkeys are put outdoors on a moat-surrounded island west of the main building. The zoo has a pond where waterfowl swim; screened pens housing birds and animals indigenous to Utah; a llama in a half-screened octagonal house belonging to the Victorian bandstand school of architecture (WARNING: the llama has the distasteful habit of snorting on visitors when he feels his privacy is invaded); and a pint-size pasture in which a lone buffalo lives on good terms with two white billy goats.

17. The "THIS IS THE PLACE" MONUMENT, a few hundred yards north of Hogle Gardens Zoo on a dirt road, is a simple square granite shaft with a buffalo skull carved in bas-relief near the top. It marks the spot where Wilford Woodruff's light spring wagon was turned around after it emerged from Emigration Canyon on July 24, 1847, permitting Brigham Young to look out across Great Salt Lake Valley. "It is enough. This is the right place, drive on," he is credited with saying. The monument stands on an uninhabited spot, overgrown with scrub oak, on an old terrace of ancient Lake Bonneville,

and it is possible to observe the geographic outlines of what Brigham Young saw, changed now by irrigation and the building of a city.

A more pretentious memorial is planned for this place, to be unveiled during the Utah centennial celebration in 1947. The commission was awarded in 1939 to Mahonri Young, sculptor and grandson of Brigham Young.

18. ST. MARY OF THE WASATCH (*open 3-6 weekdays; 2-6 Sun.*), East Bench and 13th South St., a large four-story red brick building, housing a Roman Catholic school for girls, occupies a 420-acre tract at the foot of the Wasatch Mountains. The school, founded in 1875 by the Sisters of the Holy Cross, confers Bachelor of Arts and Bachelor of Science degrees for majors in twenty-one curricula. The institution owns the Madeline collection of paintings and the Don Maguire anthropological collection.

(*East South Temple to University*)

19. The EMPEY HOUSE (*private*), 180 E. South Temple St., is a two-story buff adobe dwelling with a pine tree beside it, accenting its Gothic architecture. Steep green-roofed gables give the house a Continental air, and second-story Gothic windows lend height to a cottage-sized dwelling. Two of the three red brick chimneys are octagonal, the same shape as a bee cell, and a diamond window in the north facade contains a stained glass representation of a beehive. A mansard portico, bay windows, and an oddly-angled little porch give the house a touch of Victorian elegance. Within the thick adobe walls, window casements are beveled, and there is a flood of light from outdoors. The first floor bay window lights a high-ceiled sitting room with a fireplace and well-designed mantelpiece. A graciously curved hall stair ascends to the second floor. There, surprisingly, the Gothic windows light a single corner room, windows and gables giving the ceilings intersecting planes that carry the Gothic motif indoors. Another spacious bedroom is lighted by the bay window on the east. The stained glass in the diamond window is exceptionally rich, with its golden beehive in the center, delicately-tinted sego-liles on one side, and ripened fruit on the other.

The house was designed by Truman O. Angell, architect of the Mormon Temple, and was built, probably about 1855, by Brigham Young for Ann Eliza Webb Young, the only one of his wives who ever sued the Church leader for divorce. In her bitterly anti-Mormon book, *Wife No. 19,* she remarks that "Visitors to Salt Lake City are always to see 'Ann Eliza's house,' and . . . Taking a view of it from the street, it was an exceedingly pretty cottage, with an air of cosiness about it. . . . Inside . . . to my bitter disappointment, the only stairs in the house ascended from the parlor!"

After Ann Eliza's departure, the house was occupied by Bishop Nelson P. Empey, who married a daughter of Brigham Young. Following the death of his first wife, Bishop Empey married again, and the house is still (1940) occupied by his widow. Bishop Empey was a member of the Territorial committee to the Chicago World's Fair in 1893, and the house was remodeled the following year. The spirit of Angell's design was followed with great fidelity. A porch on the northeast corner was converted into a room, the stair was built from the north entrance, removing the abomination of a stairway through the parlor, the west slope of the north gable was raised to its present level, and the diamond window was placed in the new wall-space. The stained glass beehive, made under the supervision of James Ferguson, a son-in-law of Brigham Young, was used in the Utah building at the Chicago fair.

20. The CATHEDRAL OF THE MADELEINE (*open 9-6 weekdays; 6:30 A. M.-7 P. M. Sun.*), NE. corner E. South Temple and B Sts., a Roman Catholic edifice of brownish-gray sandstone in the Roman Gothic style, was built in 1900. Its ornate twin towers, decorated with gargoyles and inhabited by birds, are a landmark on the Salt Lake City skyline. Its full-toned bells ring frequently in the course of the day. A large rose window in the facade sheds a dim light into the nave, and decorated columns reach upward in the interior to vaulted arches high above. A series of richly colored stained glass windows was done by the House of Zetter, Royal Bavarian Institute, Munich.

21. The GOVERNOR'S MANSION (*private*), 603 E. South Temple St., a three-story building of cream-colored oolitic limestone, is a residence of French Renaissance design, with corner towers, a vivid green roof, and tall white chimneys. Built in 1904, it was presented to the State in 1939 by Mrs. Jennie J. Kearns, widow of U. S. Senator Thomas Kearns. It was first occupied as an official residence by Governor Henry H. Blood.

The life of Thomas Kearns provides Utah with one of its outstanding success stories. Born in Ontario, Canada, in 1862, of Irish immigrant parents, Thomas left school before he was seventeen years old. Mining camps drew him irresistibly; he was a freighter during the Black Hills gold rush of 1879, freighted and mined at Tombstone, Arizona, and took a job shoveling ore at Park City in 1883. For seven years he worked as a laborer, prospecting on the side. While timbering a tunnel in the Woodside mine he observed that the main ore vein led toward the undeveloped Mayflower property. A lease was taken on the mine, and it produced $1,600,000 worth of silver before it was worked out. Kearns entered politics as a member of the Park City council in 1892, but in 1901 was elected to the U. S. Senate; in the same year he acquired ownership of the *Salt Lake Tribune*. He died in 1918.

22. The MASONIC TEMPLE (*open 9-4 weekdays*), 650 E. South Temple St., a four-story gray brick building, decorated in the Egyptian style, was dedicated in 1927. Four principal chambers—the Gothic Room, the Egyptian Room, the Moorish Room, and the Colonial

Room—are used for ceremonies. The Colonial Room is a replica of the George Washington Lodge Room at Alexandria, Virginia.

23. The GEORGE H. DERN HOUSE (*private*), 715 E. South Temple St., home of the Secretary of War in President Franklin D. Roosevelt's cabinet, is a three-story gray frame structure of ornate Victorian architecture. George Henry Dern was born in Nebraska, of German parents, in 1872. He came to Utah in 1894, and took a position as bookkeeper at Mercur. By 1902, he had advanced to the general managership of the Consolidated Mercur Gold Mines Company. While he was general manager of the Tintic Milling Company, 1915 to 1919, in co-operation with T. P. Holt and W. C. Christensen, he assisted in developing the Hold-Dern ore roasting process, which has since been widely used. Dern was elected to the State senate in 1914 and in 1918, and was elected governor in 1924 and 1928. While governor he met Franklin D. Roosevelt, then governor of New York State. He was appointed Secretary of War in Roosevelt's cabinet in 1933, and held that position till his death in Washington in 1936.

24. The ART BARN (*open 10-10 daily*), 54 Finch Lane, a two-story white frame building with yellow trim and a red roof, was opened in 1933 for current exhibitions of contemporary art. The only permanent item in the Art Barn collection is an oil portrait of Maude Adams, in her celebrated role as Peter Pan, by Sigismund de Ivanowski. The League of Utah Writers, the Barnacles, an organization of short story writers, and the Photographic Club, meet here, and the Art Barn conducts a school of fine arts.

25. The UNIVERSITY WARD CHAPEL (*open 9-5 weekdays, 9-9 Sun.*), 160 University St., a Mormon religious center for university students and residents of the university area, is an L-shaped modern building of cast stone, two stories high in front and three in back, decorated with yellow, tan, and brown terra-cotta. Above the entrance, as in an arched one-story proscenium, is a vividly colored tile mosaic of Christ teaching in the mountains.

26. The UNIVERSITY OF UTAH, main entrance University and 2nd South Sts., Utah's leading educational institution, is grouped about a tree-planted U-shaped campus, on one of the terraces of old Lake Bonneville. The oval park, faced by eight buildings, is bisected by a walk, the eastern third of which is known as "Hello Walk," where students are required by custom to speak to everyone they meet. A "no smoking zone" includes most of the buildings and their immediate environs.

There is a mountain view in nearly every direction from the campus, and probably the best silhouette of Salt Lake City's skyline, outlined against Great Salt Lake and the Oquirrh Range. To the north, against a foothill of the Wasatch Range, is a concrete-block "U," 100 feet high and 90 feet wide. Each spring university freshmen whitewash the emblem, and there is a tug o' war between freshmen and sophomores. Another student custom is the so-called log-rolling. On the eve of the "big" football game of the year with the Utah Aggies, freshmen are required to spend the night collecting logs for the "victory" bonfire following the game. A gun is fired at six o'clock the next morning, and sophomores rush at the freshman-guarded logs. The rules of the game are that if one sophomore touches one log, the sophs win the log-rolling. Only once, in 1929, were the freshmen victorious. They kidnaped sophomores, made them bury the logs, then built a bonfire over the interred firewood.

The university has 153-acre grounds, an enrollment of about 4,000 exclusive of extension and summer students, and a faculty of 275; it is administered by a president and fourteen regents appointed by the governor. Bachelor's degrees are conferred in the schools of arts and sciences, education, mines, engineering, medicine, law, and business, and master's degrees in all schools except those of law and medicine. The institution was established as the University of Deseret by the Provisional State of Deseret in 1850, and the first classes were held that year. It was chartered the following year but classes were suspended from 1851 to 1867 for want of funds. The university was reestablished as a commercial academy in 1867, and two years later it was reorganized by Dr. John R. Park, and normal, classical, and scientific curricula were introduced. The university was empowered to confer degrees in 1884, and engineering courses were inaugurated in 1891-92. The name was changed to the University of Utah in 1892, and the itinerant university settled on the present site in 1900. The school of mines was established by legislative enactment in 1901. Other schools, buildings, and grounds have been added in subsequent years, as increased enrollment and a broadening educational program demanded.

A. The LIBRARY (*open schooldays 8 A. M.-10 P. M. Mon.-Fri., 8-5 Sat.; vacation, 8:30-5 Mon.-Fri., 8:30-1 Sat.; public use of library confined to those with Library cards*), SW. point of the U-shaped parkway, is a square three-story structure of buff cast-stone, built in 1935, housing the largest academic library in the State—more than 142,000 bound volumes and 36,000 pamphlets. Periodical and reference rooms are on the second floor, and the Edward Rosenbaum Memorial Library is on the third floor. The University Press, in the basement, issues the *Utah Chronicle,* a weekly newspaper edited by students; the quarterly *Utah Humbug,* a student-edited humor magazine; *The Pen,* a literary magazine, issued quarterly; the biological series of the *University of Utah Bulletin,* published every two months; bulletins on economics and research; and the yearbook, *The Utonian.*

B. The WILLIAM M. STEWART BUILDING (1918), behind the Library, is the center of teacher-training activities. The William M. Stewart School, with classes from kindergarten to ninth grade, is maintained for demonstration, experiment, and practical training.

C. The INDUSTRIAL EDUCATION BUILDING, on the south side of the U, is a three-story buff brick structure housing the departments of economics, home economics, and business.

D. The MEDICAL BUILDING, behind the Industrial Education Building, housing the school of medicine, has a pathological museum with specimens contributed by Utah physicians.

E. The BIOLOGY BUILDING, on the southeast curve of the U, a three-story buff brick structure, houses a ZOOLOGICAL MUSEUM (*open by permission*) on the second floor, with mounted specimens of birds and animals native to the Great Basin. The HERBARIUM, in the same building, has a collection of more than 10,000 mounted specimens of Utah flowering plants. The University Biological Survey publishes results of its studies in the biological series of the *University of Utah Bulletin*. The department of biology also maintains a Vivarium, where living plant and animal specimens can be studied.

F. Directly south of the Biology Building is the STADIUM, largest in the State, seating 20,000. Football games and track meets of the Mountain States Conference are held here.

G. The GYMNASIUM, back of the Biology Building, has separate playing floors for men and women, and a swimming pool. The Field House, south of the Gymnasium, provides facilities for indoor football, basketball, and track.

H. The GEOLOGY BUILDING, a two-story buff brick structure erected in 1918, southeast of the Biology Building, houses the GEOLOGICAL AND MINERALOGICAL MUSEUM (*open 1-2 Mon., Wed.; 11-3 Tue., Thur., Fri.*). The exhibits, in a high-ceiled, well-lighted room, center around the mounted skeleton of an allosaurus, a toothy carnivorous dinosaur thirty feet long and about twelve feet high, that lived in eastern Utah about 100 million years ago. Bone remnants of the giant brontosaurus, a heavy-bodied, goose-necked vegetarian monster 100 feet long and 20 feet high, include a hind leg eleven feet long and a section of seven vertebrae, six feet long. Dinosaur spine scales measure two or more feet across. The museum also has a number of dinosaur tracks dating from the "Age of Reptiles" in Utah. A collection of fossil turtles includes one from Myton, in the Uintah Basin. Pleistocene or "Ice Age" remains of Utah animals are plentiful.

UNIVERSITY OF UTAH. Points of Interest

A. The Library
B. William M. Stewart Building
C. Industrial Education Building
D. Medical Building
E. Biology Building
F. The Stadium
G. Gymnasium
H. Geology Building
I. John R. Park Memorial Building

J. Mechanical, Metallurgy, and Mining Buildings
K. Liberal Arts Building
L. Physical Science Building
M. Engineering Building
N. Astronomical Observatory
O. Kingsbury Hall
P. Student Union Building
Q. Music Building

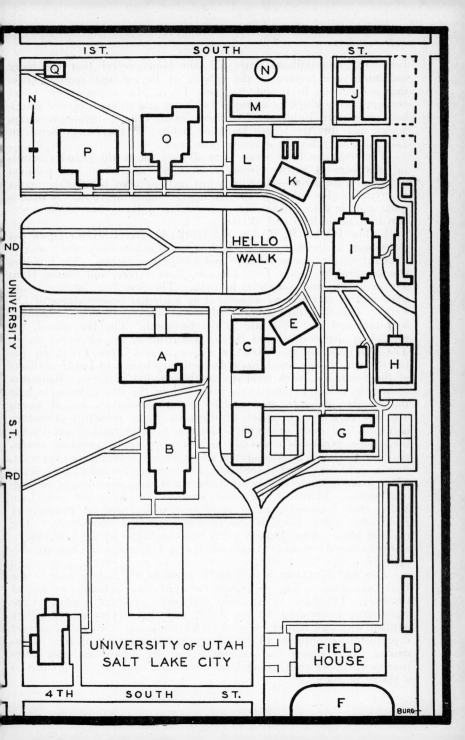

Less than two millions years old, the bones reveal that the hairy mammoth once roamed in the vicinity of Payson and Spanish Fork, that a mastodon lived and died near Provo, that a prehistoric camel was apparently killed by an early flesh-eater and its skull carried into a lava cave near Fillmore, that musk oxen, camels, mountain sheep, horses, and Ice Age felines had their habitat on the North Bench of Salt Lake City 60,000 or more years ago.

The collection of minerals from all over the world includes beautiful specimens of petrified wood from Utah, and a cut and polished section of a meteorite—gleaming white metallic alloy bearing the marks of crystallization—that fell in Duchesne County in 1896. A plaster relief map, in color, measuring about twelve by thirty feet, shows a section of Utah, Idaho and Wyoming.

I. The JOHN R. PARK MEMORIAL BUILDING (*open 9-5 weekdays*), at the east end of the campus, is a four-story white marble structure with monumental steps and a tall Ionic portico. The building was designed by Lewis Telle Cannon, John Fetzer, and Ramm Hansen, architects, and completed in 1914. The first floor interior is finished in gray marble, and is centered by a life-size bronze statue of Dr. Park. The first floor is devoted to administrative offices, and the bookstore and post office are in the basement. The law school, the psychology department, and the art department, are on upper floors. The ARCHEOLOGICAL MUSEUM (*open 8:30-5 Mon.-Fri.*), on the fourth floor, though small, has a distinctive collection of Indian artifacts of the Southwest, with emphasis on those found in Utah. Remnants of ancient cultures, remarkably preserved in the dry climate, include Basketmaker mummies, mat sandals, buckskin moccasins, bits of woven material, ears of corn, *atlatls* or throwing sticks, remnants of feather garments, and many other physical traces of Basketmaker and Pueblo life. Less perishable materials include arrowheads, grinding stones, skulls, and pottery. Among the effigy pottery is a prairie dog vase, convincingly done, duck-shaped pots, and human figurines of both sexes. Mugs made by early Pueblo people bear a striking resemblance to German steins. Many of the Utah artifacts are from the San Juan Valley, but some were taken from prehistoric caves on Promontory Point, the Black Rock bathing beach area, and Wendover. The museum has a case of Donner party relics gathered on the Salt Desert, and primitive Mexican artifacts collected by University of Utah archeologists.

The ART GALLERY is in a skylit room on the fourth floor of the Park Building. The collection of pictures includes works by Ottinger, Tullidge, Weggeland, and other pioneer artists. Canvases hang three deep on the walls, and the center of the gallery is filled with cast masterworks of Greek sculpture. Studios of the art department are adjacent to the gallery, and students set up their paint-daubed easels among the statuary. The art department also offers courses in copper craft, using Utah's principal metallurgical product as a plastic medium.

J. North of the Park Building are the MECHANICAL, METAL-LURGY, and MINING BUILDINGS, in that order; this is the physical center for significant classwork, laboratory testing, and experiments on mine and metallurgy problems. The U. S. Bureau of Mines occupies a building northeast of the campus. The Utah Engineering Experiment Station, which operates in connection with the school of mines and engineering, conducts research in mine problems of the State, including those related to agriculture, and publishes reports on original investigations. The station has a number of specialized laboratories, and maintains a technical library of several thousand volumes. In university coal research laboratories a study is made on the best utilization of Utah coals, and there is continuous research on the potential use of oil shales. The UNIVERSITY MINE, excavated on the grounds of the Mining Building, is a 350-foot tunnel of standard dimensions where students consider representative problems of mine timbering, ventilation, lighting, and blasting.

K. The LIBERAL ARTS BUILDING (1900), a three-story buff brick structure on the northeast curve of the campus U, is devoted to offices, classrooms, and the Phonetics Laboratory, for the study of speech problems. The Speech Science Laboratory in the same building is used in studies of radio speech.

L. The PHYSICAL SCIENCE BUILDING (1900), on the north side of the campus, is occupied by the departments of physics and chemistry.

M. The ENGINEERING BUILDING, behind the Physical Science Building, is occupied by the departments of civil, mechanical, and electrical engineering. Civil engineering courses include a consideration of irrigation problems peculiar to the State, and there are mechanical engineering courses for the study of automobile, airplane, and Diesel engines. Electrical courses include a study of telephone and radio engineering.

N. The ASTRONOMICAL OBSERVATORY (*open to public 7:30-9:30 P. M. Tues., autumn and spring quarters, if sky is clear; free*), behind the Engineering Building, is a small two-story buff brick building topped by a red dome, housing a nine-inch refracting telescope, a three-inch telescope, and other astronomical and mathematical equipment.

O. KINGSBURY HALL, fronting on the campus parkway just west of the Physical Science Building, is a tan three-story structure, built in 1930. Decorated after the Egyptian manner, it houses speech department classrooms and an auditorium seating 2,000.

P. The STUDENT UNION BUILDING, at the northwest segment of the campus U, a light gray structure erected in 1931, is a center for student activities. A self-governing body, the Associated Students, is active in athletics, journalism, debating, dramatics, and music.

Q. The MUSIC BUILDING, a small one-story structure situated at a good acoustical distance behind the student social center, is in the northwest corner of the campus. Music instruction includes band, orchestra, string quartet, chorus, and glee club courses.

(Downtown and Southeast)

27. The PONY EXPRESS MONUMENT, in front of 147 S. Main St., is a seven-foot granite marker commemorating the inauguration of Pony Express service between St. Joseph, Missouri, and Sacramento, California, in 1860. Bronze medallions of a Pony Express rider were executed by A. Phimister Proctor; the monument was erected in 1931.

28. The SITE OF SOCIAL HALL, S. State St. and Motor Ave., is marked by a granite shaft bearing a bronze bas-relief of the old Social Hall, built by the Mormons in 1853. From that time until 1922, when it was razed, the hall was a center of Mormon social life in Salt Lake City. Frequent balls were held here, which were attended by Brigham Young and his wives. Ten-dollar tickets entitled the bearer to bring one wife, but additional wives were admitted for $2 each.

29. The UTAH ART CENTER (*open 8:30 A. M.-9:30 P. M. weekdays, 2-9:30 Sun.; adm. free*), 59 S. State St., is a three-story brick building with a white painted front, green doors, a green balcony, and a green tile roof.

The Art Center has five galleries where exhibits of arts and crafts are held; most exhibitions are those circulated by the WPA Art Program. The center has about 200 visitors daily. Offices of the Utah Art Project and of the Art Center, are on the first floor. The project and the center provide free public classes in arts and crafts; in 1938-39, 21,000 students were enrolled. Since opening in 1938 the center has done pioneer work in training physically handicapped children to coordinate their movements while expressing themselves through painting and design.

On the second floor are offices of the Utah Music Project and of the Utah Writers' Project. In the auditorium on the same floor, are held "opportunity concerts," at which talented young musicians appear in public with the WPA Symphony Orchestra. On the third floor are offices of the Utah Historical Records Survey.

30. SITE OF THE SALT LAKE THEATER, NW. corner S. State and 1st South Sts., is occupied by a business building. The theater, suggested by Brigham Young and seating 1,500, was the largest building in western America at the time of its construction in 1862. For many years it provided the only theatricals of importance in the West (*see Theater*). The building was razed in 1928.

31. The CITY AND COUNTY BUILDING (*open 9-5 weekdays, 9-1 Sat.*), 4th South and S. State Sts., thrusts its sandstone clock tower far above the five stories used for administrative offices of the two local governments. It is one of the outstanding landmarks on the Salt Lake City skyline. The Richardsonian Romanesque building was com-

pleted in 1894, and served as Territorial and State capitol until completion of the present State house in 1915.

32. ST. MARK'S EPISCOPAL CATHEDRAL (*open 9-9 weekdays*), 225 E. 1st South St., is a brown sandstone Gothic structure, designed by Hobart B. Upjohn. Built on a cruciform plan, the edifice has a rose window over the simple arched entrance, and is surmounted by an iron-braced bell gable. The cornerstone was laid in 1870.

33. The FIRST CONGREGATIONAL CHURCH (*open on application to minister*), 402 E. 1st South St., a gray stone Gothic building, was erected in 1891 on the site where the first non-Mormon church services (1865) were held in Salt Lake City.

34. The AMBASSADOR HOTEL, 145 S. 5th East St., is a large white stucco structure with a six-story central section and five-story wings. The building was erected under a Congressional grant in 1889 to house women and children who would abandon polygamy. Mormon women held indignation meetings, and the story goes that only three took advantage of the offer. The project was soon abandoned, and it is further related that Mormon Church members purchased the building at a fraction of its cost, remodeled it, and opened it as a hotel.

35. LIBERTY PARK (*open daily 7 A. M.-12:30 A. M.*), main entrance 6th East and 9th South Sts., a level tree-planted municipal recreation area four blocks long and two blocks wide, is popular as a picnic and reunion ground. On the west side of Sixth East Street, within the park, is the ISAAC CHASE HOUSE (*private*), a two-story yellow adobe building erected in 1852.

SALT LAKE CITY RELIC HALL (*open on application to Daughters of Utah Pioneers*) is housed in the old Chase Mill, a gable-roofed gray adobe building near the center of the park. Chase, who transported the millstones and irons across the plains by ox-team, built the mill in 1852. Free flour from this mill saved many lives in a famine winter of the fifties. Just north of the mill, under a canopy, is "one of the first log cabins built in Utah," erected in 1847.

East of Sixth East Street is a bandstand where free concerts are presented in summer, and a small lake where boats can be rented. Opposite the lake are TRACY'S AVIARIES, where various types of birds are displayed. The aviaries were presented in 1938 by Mr. and Mrs. Russell L. Tracy of Salt Lake City. Among the aviaries are a pool for seals and wire pens for kangaroos. In the spring of 1940, city policemen shot a beaver that had wandered into the park and was cutting down trees. The park also has an aquarium, swimming pools, a playground, a merry-go-round, picnic areas, and tennis and horseshoe courts.

36. WESTMINSTER COLLEGE (*open 9-5 Mon.-Fri., 9-12 Sat.*), 1840 S. 13th East St., is the only Protestant co-educational college in Utah. A four-year Presbyterian junior college, it includes two years of high school and two years of college work. The landscaped forty-acre campus is centered by the four-story red brick Converse Hall, housing administrative offices and classrooms. Westminster is an out-

growth of the Salt Lake Collegiate Institute, an evangelical school established by the First Presbyterian Church in 1875.

37. UTAH STATE PRISON (*open 9:30-11, 1:30-3 Mon.-Fri., 9:30-11 A. M. Sat., 1:30-3 Sun.; adm. 25¢*), 1400 E. 21st South St., occupies seven acres within an eighteen-foot red sandstone wall on the foothills of the Wasatch Range. Within the walls are a clothing factory where prison uniforms are made, and a factory that produces automobile license plates and State road signs. A new prison is being constructed (1940) at the southern end of Salt Lake Valley. Utah is the only State that gives condemned men a choice between death by hanging or before a firing squad. Most prisoners prefer the firing squad, but one obstinate convict in 1912 elected to be hanged because "hanging is more expensive to the state."

Probably the first electro-cardiograph record ever made of a man's heart action while he was being executed, was taken here in 1938, when John Deering paid the penalty for murder before a firing squad. Electrodes fastened to Deering's wrists registered his pulse-beat. Though apparently unconcerned, his heart beat at the rate of 180 times per minute shortly before he was shot; the heart of a man doing violent exercise seldom beats faster than 120 times per minute, and the prison physician said he would have died even had no bullet been fired. His heart stopped 15.6 seconds after it was pierced by the bullet.

(West Side)

38. PIONEER PARK, 3rd South and 2nd West Sts., is the landscaped one-block area upon which Mormon settlers first built a fort and living quarters. Brigham Young laid the foundation in August, 1847, and seventeen log and adobe houses were built during the winter of 1847-48. The first school in Utah was established in a tent on this site. Mary Jane Dilworth was the teacher, and her original class consisted of nine Mormon children. The area was made a public park in 1898, and the level grounds are equipped for the recreational needs of the city's industrial section.

39. The UTAH STATE FAIRGROUNDS (*open 10-10 during fair week; adm. varies annually*), NW. corner 9th West and W. North Temple Sts., is a seventy-acre tract surrounded by a high fence and studded with exhibit buildings. The main entrance is on 9th West Street. Rising high above the other buildings, and extending across a double line of exhibit structures, is the COLOSSEUM, a huge oval-shaped structure with "Utah State Fair" painted in black letters on its red roof; this building is used for horse shows, usually three evenings during fair week. On the north side of the grounds is the STADIUM, where races are run on a half-mile dirt track, where circuses and rodeos are held. There are corrals and chutes where the animal performers are penned, and the bucking stock is released through red and white double gates directly in front of the canopied concrete bleachers.

40. The SALT LAKE CITY MUNICIPAL AIRPORT, 2450 W. North Temple St., occupies a thousand floor-level acres criss-crossed with broad concrete runways, on the edge of glistening salt flats. As the only terminal of importance in the Great Basin, the Salt Lake port receives and dispatches thirty silvery "mainliners" daily in five directions—southwest to Los Angeles, west to San Francisco, northwest to Seattle, north to Yellowstone National Park and Montana points, east to Chicago and the Atlantic coast. It ranks third in the nation in the volume of airmail handled and seventh in number of transport passengers—88,656 in 1939—and is a center for local sightseeing and charter trips to the national parks. Speedy private planes and grasshopper-shaped "flivver" ships are quartered in hangars here.

The ADMINISTRATION BUILDING, a concrete structure of modern architecture, has a central two-story section and short one-story wings. An outer promenade atop the wings provides a vantage from which the setting and traffic of an aviation center can be viewed. The long runways reach across the salt flats in distance-dimmed perspective, and above, in every direction, are mountains.

POINTS OF INTEREST IN ENVIRONS

Little Cottonwood Canyon, 31.2 *m.* (*see Tour 1c*). Big Cotton Canyon, 22.2 *m.* (*see Tour 1B*). Bingham Canyon, open-cut copper mine, 28 *m.* (*see Tour 1C*). Salt Factory 11.1 *m.;* Great Salt Lake Yacht Club, 14.8*m.;* Bonneville Speedway, 114.9 *m.* (*see Tour 6c*). Magna, 17.7 *m.,* and Garfield, 21.4 *m.,* smelting towns (*see Tour 7c*). Great Salt Lake, 13.8 *m.* (*see Great Salt Lake*).

PART III

Highways and Dugways

The word "dugway" is of Mormon vintage, coined originally to designate a species of road which consisted essentially of a deep rut scraped into the face of a hill. A wagon with its upper wheels sunk to the hub in this rut, and with a spare team pulling uphill to keep it from tipping, could "go up, down, or around almost any hill with a pitch less than 90 degrees." In later times the word has come to mean any road excavated around the side of a mountain.

Tour 1

(Preston, Idaho)—Logan—Ogden—Salt Lake City—Provo—Fillmore
—Cedar City—St. George—(Las Vegas, Nevada); US 91.
Idaho Line to Arizona Line and through Arizona to Nevada Line,
471.2 *m.*

Union Pacific R.R. parallels route between Idaho Line and Nephi; Utah-
Idaho Central R.R. between Idaho Line and Ogden; Bamberger Electric R.R.
between Ogden and Salt Lake City; Salt Lake and Utah R.R. between Salt
Lake City and Payson.
Roadbed mostly concrete between Idaho Line and Nephi; asphalt and oil-
surfaced between Nephi and Arizona Line. Open all year, though winter
drivers should observe caution in Sardine Canyon between Brigham City and
Logan, and at Point of the Mountain between Crescent and Lehi.
Accommodations at short intervals in northern section of route, in larger
towns of southern section.

US 91, passing through the State's principal centers and intersected
by all major roads, is Utah's arterial highway. Along its curved and
undulating reaches transcontinental busses zoom, huge Diesel trailer-
trucks roar by with their cargoes, and the license tags of many States
pass in a colored blur. Between towns, hay-racks make their plodding
way, and battered, red-dusted sedans sag under loads of family and
farm supplies. For pleasure-seekers, US 91 is a favored route to the
recreation and scenic areas of the intermountain States and to southern
Pacific beaches.

For almost its entire length in Utah, the highway follows the eastern
margin of the Great Basin, the vast bowl between the Rockies and the
Sierra Nevadas. The road crosses the Utah-Idaho Line near the
extreme northeast tip of prehistoric Lake Bonneville (*see Geology*) and
proceeds along the still-visible eastern shoreline of the lake until it
strikes over the Pine Valley Mountains in southwest Utah. There the
road follows the lower contour of Utah's "Dixie," which slopes off
to the Colorado River drainage. Between the Idaho Line and Nephi,
the mountain rampart on the east is formed by the rugged Bear River
and Wasatch ranges; south of Nephi it is made up of shorter ranges,
the Sanpitch, Valley, Pavant, Tushar, and others. Lower mountains
jut up to the west, with far-reaching views between.

Along the northern half of the route, where most of the major
cities and town lie in prosperous valleys, the road swings past Great
Salt and Utah lakes, the State's largest bodies of water. Industrial
centers, mainly of this area, include railroad shops, flour mills, canneries, packing plants, oil refineries, freight and stock yards. South of

Nephi, the towns are small and lonely. Life here is dwarfed by the red and gray desert; the land is arid, winters are bitter, summers hot and dusty. Extinct volcanoes, lava outcroppings, and sculptured sandstone mesas give fantastic credence to the patience of prehistoric earth-building and earth-wrecking. Cut-offs from the southern section of the route enter the scenic areas of "Zion's" and "Bryce's," as Utah's national parks are locally called, Cedar Breaks, and Capitol Reef. Cowpuncher-farmers raise corn and alfalfa in the spring months and "punch" cows the rest of the year. Sandblasted, sun-scorched countenances are surmounted by "five-gallon" stetsons and "Levi"-sheathed extremities are encased in cowboy boots. On Sundays the "Levi's" generally give way to catalogue-fitted mail order suits. Occasional Indians appear in towns, the men wearing "Levi's," moccasins, and "ten-gallon" hats, the women clad in "mother hubbards" obscured by blankets.

Section a. IDAHO LINE to LOGAN; 18.9 m., US 91

Passing through mountain-bordered Cache Valley, US 91 traverses an area of Iowa-like fertility, noted chiefly for its dairy cattle, sugar beets, and peas. Industries are mainly those related to farming. Green alfalfa and sugar-beet fields checkerboard the landscape between towns. Well-kept farm buildings mark this as one of the most productive regions in the State.

Sartorial demands of beaver-hatted eastern dandies brought the first white men into Cache Valley in 1824 (see History)—buckskin-clad trappers seeking new streams for beaver pelts. Because their number included a fair proportion of French-Canadian voyageurs, the Canuck name for fur deposits, or caches, was soon attached to the valley. James P. Beckwourth, a mulatto trapper, tells of caching seventy-five packs of beaver skins in 1825: "While digging a cache in the bank, the earth caved in, killing two of our party, who were Canadians." Beckwourth took as a "servant" the Indian widow of one. "She was of light complexion, smart, trim, and active, and never tired in her efforts to please me." Caches are described by the historian J. Cecil Alter as "juglike holes, cisterns or caverns . . . dug deep in the earth, each holding a ton or more of property. Lined with leaves and branches and covered securely against rain, the goods remained in perfect state until called for."

US 91 crosses the IDAHO LINE, 0 m., 8 miles south of Preston, Idaho (see Idaho Guide).

The gray stone BEAR RIVER BATTLE MONUMENT (R), 1.1 m., commemorates the last major Indian battle in the vicinity of northern Utah, in January 1863. Colonel Patrick E. Connor, stationed at Fort Douglas with his California Nevada volunteers, mobilized 300 men to put an end to Indian troubles in the area. It was sub-zero weather, deep snows submerged the trails, and seventy soldiers were disabled by frozen feet. The Indian camp was in a gorge twenty feet deep and forty feet wide. "I ordered the flanking party," Colonel Connor reported, "to advance down the ravine upon either side, which gave us the advantage of an enfilading fire and caused some of the Indians to give way and run toward the north end of the ravine. At this point I had a company stationed who shot them as they ran out. . . . Few tried to escape, however, but continued fighting with unyielding obstinacy. . . . The most of those who did escape from the ravine were afterwards shot in attempting to swim the river." Firing ceased in four hours. Federal losses were 14 killed, 49 wounded.

Accounts of native casualties vary. "We found 224 bodies on the field," Colonel Connor officially reported. A Cache Valley settler, William G. Smith, later said: "Instead of offering the Indians a chance to surrender, and be taken peaceably, General Connor issued a very cruel order to his men—'Take no prisoners, fight to the death; nits breed lice.'" Colonel Connor paid handsome tribute to his troops for their intrepidity and fortitude. Two months later he was brevetted a brigadier-general.

At WEBSTER JUNCTION, 1.5 *m.,* is the junction with State 61.

Right on State 61 to LEWISTON, 2.4 *m.* (4,505 alt., 1,804 pop.), a prosperous farm and dairy community reclaimed from a desert. Platted on blocks one mile square when the townsite was settled in 1870, it has the largest spread of any incorporated city of equal population, covering twenty-four square miles. The principal crops are alfalfa, sugar beets, wheat, barley, potatoes, tomatoes, oats, and hay. Dairying and livestock feeding are companion industries, utilizing farm and mill by-products. A sugar factory, built in 1905, can grind 1,600 tons of beets daily, and during "campaign," after the harvest, employs nearly 500 workers.

The site was chosen by a scouting party, after most of the desirable locations in the valley had been taken up. In the early years of the settlement, winter snows were deep and heavily crusted, summers were so dry that seed sometimes blew away with the soil, July frosts killed the wheat for three consecutive years, and in 1879 grasshoppers devoured all the crops. Settlers dug a small ditch from near-by Worm Creek in 1873, and a year later excavated a canal from the Cub River. The Lewiston-Bear Lake Irrigation Company was organized in 1915 to draw water from the Bear River. Four pumps lift the water eighty-six feet and divert it to the Cub River system, which waters 29,000 acres in Lewiston and southern Idaho.

An annual "Race and Stampede" celebration is held in August in a city-built stadium, complete with chutes for rodeo riding and a fast track.

RICHMOND, 5.3 *m.* (4,608 alt., 1,130 pop.), in the Bear River Range, is a Mormon farm community settled in frontier days. Older houses stand in a close-knit group around the parked city square (L), with its red-painted brick tabernacle. Farms lay on the slopes and valley floor, and, behind tree-shaded dwellings, are barns, corrals, and farm machinery. Dairying and cattle-breeding are the principal industries. Holstein cows, brought here in 1904, thrived so well that Richmond has won recognition as Utah's Holstein center. During "Black and White Days," held annually in May, local breeders of blooded stock vie for ribbons and cash awards. Originated in 1913, the Richmond Holstein show was reputedly the first in the country. The 1940 exhibition was subsidized to the extent of $1,000 by the State legislature. The town's two creameries, each of which handled 30,000 to 40,000 pounds of milk daily in 1902, were absorbed by the Utah Condensed Milk Company in 1904. The enterprise was reorganized in 1920 as the Sego Milk Products Company. Marriner Eccles, "New Deal" chairman of the Federal Reserve Board during Franklin D. Roosevelt's administration, is (1940) president of the company. With 96 per cent of its area under irrigated cultivation, Richmond produces grains, beets, and peas.

John Bair, operator of a ferry on Bear River, scouted the valley in 1855, but Agrippa Cooper was the first settler in present Richmond. Pleased with the lush grasses and adequate water, settlers built scattered log cabins, dugouts, and a log fort in 1859. A ditch was dug from a near-by stream and a dam placed in another to provide irrigation for the first year. The settlers built shingle, grist, carding, and molasses mills, and a horsepower sawmill was erected in 1860. A threshing machine with maple-wood cogs and cylinder was assembled, and Thomas Griffin, pioneer mechanic, constructed the first miniature steam engine in the State. Mrs. Julia Wright Petty, member of a Richmond pioneer family, has left recollections of early life in the community: "We had to raise everything we ate except sugar. We made our own soap and candles, cured meat, poured bullets, spun yarn and were self-supporting." Mrs. Petty's husband "earned five dollars for locating the Indians and giving the information to General Connor's soldiers in 1863, when the whites massacred the Indians in Cache Valley" (*see above*).

The brick SEGO MILK PRODUCTS PLANT (*open 9-12 work-days; guide*), in Richmond, a landmark because of its high smokestack, was erected in 1904.

Right from Richmond on State 170, graveled, to TRENTON, 7.3 *m.* (4,461 alt., 553 pop.), amidst rolling grain fields, with a grain elevator as a badge of agricultural importance. Scarcity of timber accounts for the pioneer stone houses, many of which, erected by Andrew McCombs, still stand. Trenton had many trials to obtain sufficient irrigation water. A small ditch dug in 1872 was inadequate and artesian wells struck more gas than water. In 1898 construction was finally begun on the West Cache Canal, completed in 1940. Flood waters washed out the banks, but the canal now waters 22,000 acres of surrounding land.

CLARKSTON, 12.8 *m.* (4,930 alt., 578 pop.), set against a background of towering peaks and green canyons, is a center for one of the chief dry-farming areas in Utah. A complete crop failure has never been reported; yields of thirty to forty bushels of hard wheat per acre are common, and those of fifty bushels are not unusual. Dairying and cattle and poultry raising are principal sources of income. All-year pasturage is obtained by alternate grazing of bottom lands, foothills, and mountains. Indian John, a Shoshone under-chief, claimed all the land west of Bear River, including Clarkston. In payment for its preemption he demanded 150 beef cattle and a ton of flour, but finally accepted "a few beeves and several hundred pounds of flour." Right from Clarkston on a graveled road to the junction, 0.7 *m.*, with a dirt road; R. on the dirt road to a small cemetery (R), 1 *m.*, in which a granite shaft marks the GRAVE OF MARTIN HARRIS, one of the three witnesses to the authenticity of the Book of Mormon (*see The Mormon Church*).

SMITHFIELD, 11.4 *m.* (4,595 alt., 2,461 pop.), on the foot-ills of the timbered Bear River Range (L), is the focal point of a diversified farming area. Peas and sugar beets, dairying and stock-raising, are important. There are two flour mills, a large canning plant, a brick and tile factory, and a cold storage and locker plant.

Right from Smithfield, on graveled State 142, to NEWTON, 9.5 *m.* (4,525 alt., 549 pop.), a mountain-walled agricultural community; R. from Newton on a graded dirt road (*sometimes closed in winter*) to NEWTON DAM, 3.5 *m.*, 58 feet high and 127 feet across, which was completed in 1886.
At 18.1 *m.* is the junction with US 89 (*see Tour 2a*).

The CALIFORNIA PACKING CORPORATION CANNERY (R), 12.3 *m.* (*open workdays in season*) is one of the leading pea canning plants in the State. It has canned as many as 25,738 cases in a sixteen-hour run, and handles the yield of 2,500 acres.

At 14.1 *m.* on US 91, is the junction with a gravel and a concrete road.

1. Right on the gravel road to BENSON, 5.8 *m.* (4,417 alt., 279 pop.), a farm community bordering the Bear River. Sugar beets are an important source of income, one of the first thirty-ton per acre crops in Cache Valley having been grown here. The area is known for its fine draft horses.

2. Left on the concrete road to HYDE PARK, 0.6 *m.* (4,449 alt., 696 pop.), birthplace of George Thomas, president of the University of Utah (1940) and author in the fields of economics, government, and irrigation.

At 18.4 *m.*, on US 91, is the north junction (L) with US 89 (*see Tour 2a*) which unites briefly with the main route; at 18.7 *m.* is the south junction (R) with US 89.
LOGAN, 18.9 *m.* (4,535 alt., 11,875 pop.) (*see Logan*).

Section b. LOGAN to OGDEN; 47.7 m., US 91

Between LOGAN, 0 *m.*, and Ogden, US 91 traverses the southern end of Cache Valley, climbs over the Wasatch Mountains through Sardine Canyon, and parallels Great Salt Lake through busy farming communities along the west slopes of the Wasatch Range.
At 1 *m.* is the north junction of US 91 with State 101, an oiled and concrete road known as the Hyrum Loop.

Left on State 101 to the junction, 0.9 *m.*, with a concrete road; L. on the concrete road to PROVIDENCE, 0.6 *m.* (4,600 alt., 1,111 pop.), an agricultural and commercial center, populated chiefly by Mormons of German and Swiss origin. Its tree-shaded streets run diagonally to the cardinal directions, an arrangement unusual in Utah. Pioneer structures of log or adobe are still standing. Berries and fruits are important local crops and dry-farm wheat is grown on the slopes. During Strawberry Day, in June, strawberries are served free. The PROVIDENCE LIMESTONE QUARRY (*open workdays June to November*), in Providence Canyon, has a yearly output of 30,000 tons of crushed limestone used in purification of beet juice for sugar making. The rock assays 97 per cent calcium.

At 2.9 *m.* on State 101 is the junction with an oiled road; L. on this roa to MILLVILLE, 0.5 *m.* (4,542 alt., 403 pop.), a farming community settled 1859. A Virginian pioneer named Edwards made beds, chairs with rawhid bottoms, stools, and other furniture, some of which is still in use. The talente joiner, with the aid of a small molasses mill and a distillery, also made potent beverage called "Valley Tan," which made "Edwards' place" a have for the thirsty in the early days.

At 5.9 *m.,* where State 101 turns R. sharply, is the junction with a grade dirt road and with State 163.

1. Left on the dirt road to the mouth, 1 *m.,* of BLACKSMITH FORK CAN YON (*campgrounds, fishing, deer and elk hunting*), traversed by trout-stocke Blacksmith Fork Creek. At various points in the creek and its tributarie are "petrified" beaver dams, covered with a calcareous substance carried i the water.

At 21 *m.* is the junction with a dirt road which runs between Round Valle (*see Tour 2a*), and State 39 (*see Tour 1A*).

2. Left (straight ahead) from State 101 on State 163, graveled, to PARA DISE, 4.5 *m.* (4,860 alt., 500 pop.), a farm community on the east bank o the Little Bear River.

AVON, 8 *m.* (4,950 alt., 110 pop.), is an agricultural town named fo Avon, England, birthplace of Shakespeare. Avon is at the southern terminu of State 163 and the northern terminus of a county road; south (straigh ahead) the county road runs through a mountainous area, to the junctior 13.3 *m.,* with State 162 (*see Tour 1A*).

HYRUM, 6.8 *m.* (4,706 alt., 1,874 pop.), on State 101, built on a plateau has a municipal light plant and several industrial establishments. The com munity, settled in 1860, was named for Hyrum Smith, brother of the founde of the Mormon Church. An engineer's error compelled the colonists to surve their own irrigation canal from the Bear River, nine miles distant. The; began digging late in the season, when the growing crops were in urgen need of water and, on bread and water rations, completed the nine-mil ditch in twenty-one days. For equipment they had eight shovels, a few wor spades, some home-made plows, and a contrivance made of two split log fastened together at one end to form a wedge. This "go-devil," drawn b oxen along the bottom of the ditch, pushed the dirt aside and simplifie shoveling.

At 7.7 *m.* is the junction with a gravel-surfaced road; L. on this road to th HYRUM DAM AND RESERVOIR, 0.7 *m.,* designed to furnish water for 10,000 acre of farmland. The earth-fill and concrete structure, a U. S. Bureau of Re clamation project, 540 feet across the top and 101 feet high, was completec in 1935. When filled to capacity, the reservoir contains 18,000 acre-feet o water.

At 10.6 *m.* is the southern junction of State 101 with US 91.

Between the two junctions with State 101, US 91 threads a patch work of cultivated fields.

At 7.6 *m.* is the southern junction with State 101 (*see above*).

WELLSVILLE, 8.7 *m.* (4,495 alt., 1,401 pop.), a dairying and diversified farming center, has dwellings that are eloquent of pioneer days. Farms hug the slopes of Wellsville Cone and Willard Peak which loom (R) above the community.

Wellsville is at the junction with graveled State 164, through Mendon to US 89 (*see Tour 2a*).

South of Wellsville the highway runs through a posted area indi cating the 5,500-acre WELLSVILLE GROUSE REFUGE, largely on private lands set aside for the perpetuation of Columbian sharptail

rouse. The bird is almost extinct in Utah, but the refuge preserves
several bunch-grass "islands," its native habitat.

Between Wellsville and Mantua, US 91 traverses SARDINE
CANYON, a precipitously-walled pass over the shoulder of Mount
Pisgah (7,144 alt.). The road twists through sandstone outcroppings
and thick groves of scrub oak, maple, and aspen, which in the fall are
ablaze with color. The 5,500-foot summit is crossed by a dugway
about half-way up the canyon wall. Pioneers named the canyon for
a small trout, called "sardine."

MANTUA, 21.5 m. (5,175 alt., 314 pop.), a farming town in a
meadowed valley encircled by mountains, was founded in 1863 as a
flax-raising center. The linen-producing venture lasted only a few
years.

At 22.4 m. is the entrance (L) to BOX ELDER COUNTY
PARK (*camp and picnic grounds*) in Box Elder Canyon, a short ravine
shaded by groves of box elder, cottonwood, maple, birch, and willow.
The steep slope of Reservoir Hill (L), at the canyon mouth, is used
for motorcycle hill-climbs.

BRIGHAM CITY, 26 m. (4,439 alt., 5,643 pop.) on a fan-shaped
alluvial delta at the base of lofty mountains, is the seat of Box Elder
County, and a manufacturing and agricultural center. The district
is particularly noted for its peaches, introduced in 1855. Peach Day,
a two-day festival in September, draws many visitors. Spreading syca-
mores border the streets, while hundreds of locust trees planted throughout the city furnish blossoms for local bee swarms.

Settled in 1851 as Box Elder, the town was renamed in 1856 for
Brigham Young, who made his last public address here in 1877. When,
in 1858, M. L. Ensign was called on a mission to England, leaving
the family with only twenty pounds of flour, Mrs. Ensign was not
dismayed: "After my husband left, an Indian came to me with a nice
buffalo robe, which he wanted to trade . . . for old clothes and a brass
kettle. Soon thereafter another Indian traded me a pony for the robe.
I sold the pony for a yoke of small oxen and 300 pounds of flour.
Immigrants came along and traded me a yoke of large oxen, which
were very poor, for my oxen, which were fat. The poor oxen soon
became fat on our meadows, and I sold them for $110 in cash, thus . . .
from a few old clothes and a brass kettle I soon realized $110 in cash
and 300 pounds of flour." The co-operative Brigham City Mercantile
and Manufacturing Association, organized in 1864 by Lorenzo Snow,
former Church President, issued scrip called "Home-D" as a medium
of exchange. A fine of $10,000, imposed for printing illegal money
was later refunded.

Brigham is at the north junctions with US 30S (*see Tour 4a*),
and US 89 (*see Tour 2a*), which unite with US 91 for 23.1 miles.

Right from Brigham on a dirt road which traverses a region of flats
and salt marshes rimming Great Salt Lake to the 64,200-acre BEAR RIVER
MIGRATORY BIRD REFUGE, 15 m. (*open 9-5, all visitors required to
register and check firearms; hunting, fishing; no gasoline available*), which

occupies a land and water area around the mouth of Bear River at a
avian crossroads of two of the continent's major migratory waterfowl flyway
The river's delta and its spreading swamps have long been a natural feedin
ground for millions of birds that pause here on their flights from Alaska
South America or to and from the Mississippi Valley. In pioneer days water
fowl were so thick they blackened the sky. Commercial hunters of th
nineties sold teal for $1 a dozen, mallard for $1.50 a dozen. George Muelle
Salt Lake City sportsman, recalls in the *Salt Lake Tribune* for April 21, 194
that in 1894 he met a disconsolate hunter who "only got 325" in a day
bombardment. The drouth years around 1930 brought on an epidemic
botulinus poisoning, or western duck disease, and thousands of birds died. I
1940, miles of green tules and aquatic feeding growths, stretched away in
the blue distance. On the gigantic "birdport" squadrons of waterfowl, of 2c
recorded species, alight and take off in aerial symphonies of movemen
Among rare species that visit here are the black or glossy ibis, similar to th
bird worshiped by ancient Egyptians; the trumpeter swan; snowy egret
nearly exterminated in the mauve decade for feminine plumage; the snow
heron; and the marbled godwit. Swans are more numerous on the refuge tha
at any other known place on the continent.

Created in 1928 by Congress and placed under jurisdiction of the U.
Biological Survey, the cost of the refuge by 1938 was $750,000. Much of th
construction has been done by the CCC. In 1929, an extensive canal syste
was dug and overflow gates installed. A 20-mile dike was built around th
outer rim of the swamp to impound the fresh waters of Bear River and kee
out saline waters of Great Salt Lake. To the main bulkhead were attache
four cross-dikes, dividing the 50,000-acre water area into five units. At th
spillways, egrets, terns, and pelicans gather to fish for suckers, chubs, car
and minnows. Besides feeding and nesting grounds, the sanctuary has a
administration building, research laboratory, power and filtration plant, servi
building, garage, duck hospital, and two residences. A 100-foot trussed-ste
observation tower affords a view, through field glasses, of the entire area.

Before the area was improved, millions of waterfowl died here of botulis
a ptomaine-like disease that took an annual toll second only to that of huntin
It is caused by an organism coming from alkaline soil. Infected fowls di
within a few days unless treated. The hospital, with its receiving war
pens, and convalescent pond, treats bird patients by injection of distilled wate
into the stomach; a high percentage of birds are cured. Efforts are mad
to control the disease by regulating the temperature, degree of alkalinit
and air content of the water.

The program at the refuge includes a study of bird-feeding habits, intr
duction of food plants, and an annual waterfowl census. Tiny aluminu
bands are placed on the legs of birds to check the extent of migration. Perso
killing or capturing a banded bird are requested to report the date, place, an
number of the band to the U. S. Biological Survey. Hunting in season
permitted in designated areas on 40 per cent of the refuge.

The exclusive "million-dollar" BEAR RIVER GUN CLUB, 17.5 m. (*private*
was organized in the early 1900's by wealthy sportsmen. Owning a fence
18,000-acre tract which includes a 6,000-acre lake, the club has a $75,00
clubhouse, roads, canals and a 3.5-mile dike.

PERRY, 29.5 m. (4,358 alt., 386 pop.), is the center for fruit an
vegetable farms along the highway. The town was flooded in 189
when the irrigation dam gave way up Three Mile Canyon.

WILLARD, 33.4 m. (4,266 alt., 543 pop.) is set against a ga
in the Wasatch, through which floods have poured several times. Si
covers the foundations of some houses so they appear to rest direct
on the ground. Rock and adobe dwellings of frontier simplicity remai

from early years, built shortly after the town was settled in 1851. Willard was the home of Evan Stephens, noted Mormon hymnist.

UTAH HOT SPRINGS, 38.5 m. (*open 9 A.M.-midnight; swimming, children 20¢, adults 35¢; hot pools 50¢*), has outdoor and indoor pools, whose waters, containing iron and salts, are said to have curative properties. The springs, flowing at a temperature of 144 degrees, and at the rate of 750,000 gallons a day, are cooled for use in the resort.

At 38.8 m. is the north junction with a paved alternate route.

Left on the alternate route to NORTH OGDEN, 4 m., (4,275 alt., 682 pop.), an agricultural suburb of Ogden. The granite PETER SKENE OGDEN MONUMENT, in North Ogden, east of the highway, commemorates the fur trader's entrance into the valley in the 1820's (*see History*). From the summit of BEN LOMOND (9,717 alt.), reached by foot-trails, in view northeast of North Ogden, can be seen a great vista of sky-brushed mountains and deep-cut valleys, and the silvered reaches of Great Salt Lake.

At 7.3 m. on the alternate route is the south junction with US 91.

On US 91 south of the north junction with the alternate route, the great gash of Ogden Canyon (*see Tour 1A*) is visible (L).

At 45 m. is the south junction of US 91 with the paved alternate route (*see above*).

OGDEN, 47.7 m. (4,299 alt., 43,719 pop.) (*see Ogden*).

Ogden is at the junction with State 39 (*see Tour 1A*) and State 38.

Right on State 38, paved, to the junction, 3.7 m., with asphalt State 37; R. here to HOOPER, 7 m. (4,240 alt., 1,020 pop.) a farm community founded in 1867.

West of Hooper, on the lakeshore is the State-owned OGDEN BAY MIGRATORY BIRD REFUGE AND HUNTING GROUNDS, a Joint State, Federal, and Civilian Conservation Corps project.

At 6 m. on State 38 is the junction with US 91 (*see Tour 1c*).

Section c.   OGDEN to SALT LAKE CITY; 37 m., US 91

The highway runs through the fertile, sloping lake shore region between the towering Wasatch Mountains (L) and Great Salt Lake (R). Towns along the route are supported largely by surrounding fruit and vegetable farms, which provide raw materials for numerous canning plants. Cherry and peach orchards border the road, tinting the landscape in spring with waves of pink and white blossoms. Above the lower mountain slopes lies a crinkled band of snow, ever narrowing before the advancing season, to finally disappear and leave the summits a bare bluish-gray. As summer wears on, dying June grass spreads a tawny cloak over the foothills. Great Salt Lake, which is sighted at intervals, has a dull gray look by day. In the evening, however, the briny waste comes alive with colors struck off by richly-colored sunsets.

South of OGDEN, 0 m., is the southern junction, 1.4 m., with US 30S (*see Tour 4a*) and US 89 (*see Tour 2a*), which unite northward with US 91 for 23.1 miles.

At 3.1 m., the road crosses a curving viaduct over mainline railroad tracks that parallel the broad, shallow Weber River. Left of the viaduct, out of sight behind cottonwood trees on a bend of the river, is Utah's largest hobo jungle. "Bo's" gather here in spring and fall, and between trains "work" the neighborhood for the "makin's" of their "mulligan" stew. The population of the tin-shacked jungle mounts at time to nearly 200.

At 5.5 *m.* is the southern junction (R) with State 38 (*see Tour 1b*).

SUNSET, 6.9 *m.* (204 pop.), was named for its commanding view of sunsets over Great Salt Lake.

The OGDEN ORDNANCE DEPOT, 7.9 *m.* (*administration section open by permit from gatekeeper*), occupying a 2,200-acre area (L), is the only U. S. Army munitions station in the West. Besides shell and bomb loading equipment, it has storage facilities for 36,000,000 pounds of munitions. Among the stores are airplane bombs containing 1,000 pounds of high explosive. The walled depot has about 400 buildings, of which 350 are igloo-type ammunition magazines. Anti-explosion precautions include the use of sparkless tools made of copper alloyed with beryllium, and the vacuum-cleaning of factory buildings to remove explosive dust. Reconstruction and improvement of the arsenal up to 1940 involved the expenditure of more than a million dollars of WPA funds, and the employment of as many as 1,350 WPA workers at one time. In 1940 HILL FIELD was being developed here as a major army air base.

CLEARFIELD, 9.2 *m.* (4,487 alt., 799 pop.), is centered by a block of business houses on a half-crescent bend in the highway. Irrigated alfalfa fields and acres of forage crop land (L) crowd the highway and press close to the business district. Dirt roads branch off to residences, which are a half-block to two blocks apart. When a fire in 1926 destroyed one of Clearfield's canning plants, firemen were subjected to a bombardment of exploding cans of beets, peas, string beans, and apricots.

The red brick UTAH CANNING PLANT (R), 9.5 *m.* (*open workdays in season*), is the summer employment center for many of the town's younger women. Tomatoes—and other vegetables and fruits—are packed not later than one day after picking. The tomatoes are mechanically washed, then fall on an inspection belt, from which those showing mold or decay are discarded. Jets of live steam play upon them in a scalder, until, by a slight finger pressure, the skin slips from the fruit. Girls core and peel them by hand, and they are placed in an automatic filling machine, which fills each can with the specified amount of juice and tomatoes. The cans are then inspected and pass into the "exhaust box," where they are heated and automatically sealed. The pack is run into the automatic cooker where it remains for nine minutes, and is given fifteen hours for cooling before shipment. Labeling and casing are done by machines, and the labels are customarily put on upside down, so the housewife can have a shiny, dust-free top to open.

At 11.3 *m.* is the junction with graveled State 108.

Right on State 108 to SYRACUSE, 3.3 *m.* (4,241 alt., 890 pop.), a farming community on the shore of Great Salt Lake.

LAYTON, 14.2 *m.* (4,356 alt., 597 pop.), is the center of an upland agricultural area in which there is considerable dry farming. In addition to its stores and business houses, the town has a sugar factory, canning and packing plants, coal and lumber yards, and a flour mill.

When John Thornley, in an early attempt at dry farming, planted grain on Sand Ridge east of the village in the spring of 1869, neighbors questioned his sanity. One declared that without irrigation he could not raise enough to "feed a goose." Nevertheless other settlers followed his example, planting corn, wheat, and alfalfa on the ridge, which is still extensively farmed without irrigation. The original water storage reservoir, begun in Layton in 1852 by Elias Adams, was built up by a "ground sluicing" device, or ditch, running through a deposit of sand and clay to the top of the dam. In a few years the water dropped enough silt to raise the dam to the required height.

The FRANK ADAMS HOME AND MUSEUM (*open by appointment*), in Layton, was built of 100,000 vari-colored rocks collected over a ten-year period in thirteen foreign countries and twenty States. One stone is from St. Joseph's workshop, the scene of Christ's boyhood labors, another is from Christ's tomb, and a number are from the Dead Sea and Bethlehem. War relics, old books, journals, and diaries, are displayed in the museum.

The DELL ADAMS COLLECTION (*open by appointment*), in Layton, consists of 600 stuffed animals and birds, Indian-made saddles, guns from three American wars, and other articles.

KAYSVILLE, 16.6 *m.* (4,294 alt., 992 pop.) is midway on the plain between the foothills of the Wasatch and the shore of Great Salt Lake. The land surrounding the city is checkered with productive farms and truck gardens. For protection against spring frosts, young tomato plants are shielded with white paper cones, row on row against the dark soil. Kaysville is the birthplace of Henry H. Blood, governor, of Utah in 1940, and a former stake president in the Mormon Church. Dr. Sumner Gleason, 79 years old in 1939 when he left for the East, had lived here since 1885. He was the county school doctor and a man of wide interests and attainments. He introduced loganberries to Utah, developed the Gleason Early Elberta peach, and a bantam sweet corn with more kernels and rows than any other variety.

Eight years after its founding, in 1858, settlers proposed the town be named Freedom. When the suggestion was taken to Brigham Young, he asked bluntly, "When did Kay's Ward get its freedom?" The change was not made. In 1887, in the midst of the rapidly climaxing drive against the doctrine and practice of polygamy (*see History*), John Taylor, third President of the Mormon Church, went into hiding in Kaysville, where he "died in exile," a fugitive from prosecution under the Edmunds Law.

The remodeled white adobe BLOOD FAMILY RESIDENCE (*private*), in Kaysville, retains the simplicity and fine proportion characteristic of early Utah architecture. Built about 1851, its stuccoed fifteen-inch adobe walls are intact except for a few alterations in wall-openings. The front porch was added in 1867, when the building was acquired by William Blood, father of the governor. The rough stone rear wing was built in 1938.

Left on US 91-Alt, asphalt, to the junction, 1.5 *m.*, with an improved dirt road; L. on the dirt road through tree-clad Farmington Canyon. The road climbs, by switchbacks, to the top of Bountiful Peak, from which there is a view westward of Great Salt Lake Valley. FARMINGTON, 2.8 *m.* (4,261 alt., 1,339 pop.) on US Alt. 91, at the base of the Wasatch Mountains, is the seat of Davis County. The city, with wide, tree-shaded streets, is noted as Utah's "Gretna Green," being a popular place for marriages. In former years it was a well-patronized divorce "mill." Of 165 divorces granted during ten months of 1877, 112 were sought by husbands.

A sidelight on labor conditions of the 1870's is provided by Mrs. Arvilla Burk Earl, who, as a girl, operated the first hosiery machine in the town for "$1.50 per week . . . and often we worked from early in the morning until ten or eleven o'clock at night. After the sox were knit we had to wash them and get them ready for . . . the Z.C.M.I. store in Salt Lake City the next morning."

The DAUGHTERS OF UTAH PIONEERS CHAPTER HOUSE (*open*), on the courthouse grounds, is commemorative of pioneer days in the settlement. The restored two-room log structure was once occupied by Charles W. Penrose, composer of Mormon hymns. Pioneer memorabilia are on view within. An inscribed monument marks the LOT SMITH GRAVE, in Farmington cemetery. Smith, a major in the Mormon militia, is said to have been the only man ever known to hold back the U. S. Army without killing a man. During the "Utah War" (*see History*) in 1857, with forty men he outflanked the army's main forces in Wyoming, and burned supply wagons far in the rear. Smith was killed by Indians at Tuba City, Arizona, in 1892. He had eight wives, two of whom were still living in 1939. Between Farmington and Centerville (*see below*), huge boulders by the roadside and a half-buried house are reminders of disastrous floods that raced down five canyons in the area in 1923, taking seven lives, and again in 1930, causing damage in excess of a million dollars. Spewing mud, debris and rocks weighing up to 300 tons each, the outpour blocked the highways and a railroad, smashed homes, wreaked havoc on farmlands, and destroyed irrigation sources. Overgrazing, trampling of the soil by livestock, and fires at the canyon heads were found, in an analysis published in 1934 by the U. S. Department of Agriculture, to be the principal causes of the flood menace. Following the study, livestock was excluded from the region, a 600-mile system of terraces was constructed on denuded areas by CCC workers, and oblique rock diversion walls were built along the highway to keep flood waters from farm houses. The terraces, planted with Douglas fir, have thus far controlled the run-off, and elimination of grazing has permitted revegetation of the slopes.

CENTERVILLE, 7.5 *m.* (4,246 alt., 670 pop.), hardly recognizable as a town, has business houses widely separated by farmlands. Orchards, interspersed with cottages and vegetable patches, cling to the foothills of the Wasatch. Bordering the highway are grain fields, truck gardens and retail fruit stands. Cherry season, in June, is hitch-hiking season on the highway between Centerville and Salt Lake City. The roadside is lined by youthful fruit-pickers eight to fourteen years old, who sit hopefully for hours, jerking vigorous thumbs at every passing car. Pickers' wages fluctuate from 25¢ to $2 (for an expert) per day, according to crops, prices, and the amount picked—

or eaten. Stomachache generally depletes the ranks of local pickers, and farmers supplement their crew with migratory workers.

BOUNTIFUL, 9.3 *m.* (4,408 alt., 3,341 pop.), second Mormon-settled city in the State, sprawls outward from Chapel Square onto broken foothills (L) and lakeshore flats (R). The business district is compacted alongside the highway. Primarily an agricultural center, Bountiful has several large greenhouses in which tulips, daffodils, and other bulb flowers are grown. Many workers commute from here to Salt Lake City, lending a semi-suburban character to the town. A municipally-owned plant provides light and power.

Peregrine Sessions, Mormon pioneer, camped on the site with a cattle herd in 1847. The following spring he built a cabin and began farming on land so badly cracked that his horses, while plowing, were in danger of breaking their legs. After the coming of other families the place was named Session's Settlement; later, for a country in the Book of Mormon, it was renamed Bountiful, "because of its much fruit." A horde of grasshoppers descended on the town in 1855, covering buildings, gardens, and fields with a "dark moving mass." The visit lasted overnight, but most of the crops were destroyed. The next morning the hoppers flew over Great Salt Lake.

The porticoed, five-spired MORMON FIRST WARD CHAPEL (*open on application to custodian*), on the square (L), is one of the oldest chapels in the State. The wood and adobe building was erected between 1857 and 1863. Iron nails, glass, and paint used in its construction were hauled across the plains by ox-team. In the assembly room is a portrait of Joseph Smith by Dan Weggeland.

At 10.5 *m.* is the junction with a dirt road; L. on this road to MUELLER PARK, 3.4 *m.* (*camp and picnic facilities, fishing*), a 1,000-acre mountain tract administered by the U. S. Forest Service as a bird and wild life sanctuary. There are several hiking trails, one of which leads to City Creek Canyon, north of Salt Lake City, a distance of about four miles.

At 11.2 *m.* is the south junction of US 91-Alt., with US 91.

US 91, south of the north junction with Alt. 91, by-passes the towns of Farmington, Centerville and Bountiful in a nearly straight stretch through meadow and pasture lands. Present-day travelers find this area easier to traverse than William Chandless, who complained, in *A Visit to Salt Lake* (1857), that "though the Mormons are certainly a hospitable people, they have a prodigious number of savage inhospitable dogs about their houses, and worse still, almost impassable ditches, so that the benighted traveller has pretty well as much work to find his way into a house to inquire, as to find the one he is inquiring for without information; even when ditch and dog are safely passed, you may find the householder a Dutchman or a Dane, which is perplexing to a bad linguist like myself, or possibly your Saxon ears are refreshed with 'Dim Sassenach' from a saint of a Welshman."

At 20.7 *m.* on US 91, is the junction with an asphalt road.

Left on this road to LAGOON, 0.5 *m.* (*open Memorial Day to Labor Day: adm. weekdays 25¢ per car to 6 p.m., 50¢ after; free Sun. and Mon. except on holidays; swimming, boating, dancing, picnic facilities*), a fifty-acre resort that advertises swimming "in water fit to drink." It also has a children's playground and carnival concessions.

At 21.1 *m.,* 25.9 *m.,* and 28 *m.,* on US 91 are junctions (L) with roads that lead to Farmington, Centerville, and Bountiful respectively.

At 29.2 *m.* is the south junction of US 91 with US 91-Alt. (*see above*).

At 30.1 *m.* is the junction with an oiled road.

Right on this road to WOODS CROSS, 1.3 *m.* (4,293 alt., 1,083 pop.), a canning and oil refining center.

At 31.2 *m.* is the junction with an oiled road.

Right on this road to the CUDAHY PACKING PLANT, 0.3 *m.* (*open workdays*), on a railroad siding and hemmed by stock yards. The plant, employing about 150 men, handles twenty-five million pounds of meat annually.

BECKS HOT SPRINGS (R), 33 *m.* (*open 9 A.M.-11:30 P.M.; adm. 25¢*), is an oblong building housing a pool filled daily with hot mineral water of asserted medicinal properties. Issuing at a temperature of 142 degrees, and at the rate of 900,000 gallons a day from a natural spring, the water is piped to a cooling tank before it is used in the pool.

The sludge-grimed batteries of stills, huge fractionating towers, pipes, and tanks of the UTAH OIL REFINERY (R), 35.1 *m.* (*open on application to main office, Salt Lake City*), sprawl over 120 oil-soaked acres. The plant, a subsidiary of the Standard Oil Company of Indiana, manufactures 125 petroleum products. A 438-mile pipeline from the Laramie, Wyoming, oil fields was completed in less than three months in 1939, at a cost of five million dollars, despite labor, legal, and political complications. The first crude oil was turned into the eight-inch line before the Utah end was completed, the molasses-like fluid requiring thirty-three days to reach Salt Lake City. The line flow is approximately 336,000 gallons in twenty-four hours.

At 36.3 *m.* is the north junction with US 40 (*see Tour 6c*) which unites with US 91 for 3.9 miles.

SALT LAKE CITY, 37 *m.* (4,366 alt., 150,021 pop.) (*see Salt Lake City*).

Section d. SALT LAKE CITY to SPANISH FORK; 56.9 m.,
US 91

Between SALT LAKE CITY, 0 *m.,* and Spanish Fork, US 91 threads its way through one of the most highly industrialized and intensively cultivated sections of Utah. Smelters, sugar mills, and grain elevators tower over the squared terrain of orchards and fields, and cities and towns are numerous. The level Salt Lake and Utah valleys, connected by the Jordan Narrows river passage, are exceptionally fertile. Trees grow where there are houses, and the odors of farms are mingled with pungent fumes from factory smokestacks.

At 3.2 *m.* is the southern junction (L) with US 40 (*see Tour 6b*), which is united with US 91 for 3.9 miles.

SOUTH SALT LAKE, 3.5 *m.* (5,617 pop.), is a closely populated suburb that incorporated in 1940 to bond itself for sewers and streets.

At 5 *m.* is the northern junction (R) with US 50 (*see Tour 7b, 7c*), which follows the course of US 91 southward for 52.4 miles.

Industry

UTAH COPPER CO.

27

MARION

COPPER PIT, BINGHAM CANYON

ORE CONCENTRATION MILL, PARK CITY

ORE TRAIN, BINGHAM CANYON

Lee A. Olsen

SMELTER SMOKE, GARFIELD

Courtesy Columbia Steel Co.

COAL MINERS, COLUMBIA

COAL LOADER IN A CARBON COUNTY MINE

Courtesy Aberdeen Coal Co.

STEEL INGREDIENTS—IRON AND LIMESTONE

TRUCKING SUGAR BEETS

Courtesy Utah-Idaho Sugar Co

Courtesy Utah-Idaho Sugar Co.

SUGAR IN STORAGE

CANNING—A LEADING UTAH INDUSTRY

IN A SALT LAKE CITY BREWERY

Courtesy Fisher Brewing Co.

SALT PILER, NEAR SALT LAKE CITY

PLOWING SALT

MURRAY, 7.3 *m.* (4,350 alt., 5,640 pop.), complete with false fronts and a clock-towered fire station, is a mixture of smelting town and rural trade center.

At Murray is the junction (L) with State 173 (*see Tour 1B*).

The AMERICAN SMELTING AND REFINING PLANT (R), 7.9 *m.*, was established in 1903 as a custom smelter for reduction of lead ores. The buildings in 1940 were almost hidden by a mesa of black slag, reaching around them on three sides, but the two smokestacks are visible from almost any point in Salt Lake Valley. The mills and furnaces, employing 350 men, have a monthly capacity of 45,000 tons of lead bullion.

Between Murray and southern Salt Lake Valley are prosperous farms, comfortable houses, and the orderly and colorful geometry of fenced fields. The principal products, attested by long rows of coops, dairy barns, and cement silos, are eggs, fryers, butter, and cheese, much of which is shipped by fast truck to the Pacific Coast.

At 9.7 *m.* is the junction (L) with an oiled road to Big Cottonwood Canyon (*see Tour 1B*).

At 11.3 *m.* is the junction (R) with State 48, to Bingham Canyon (*see Tour 1C*).

SANDY, 12.5 *m.* (4,450 alt., 1,436 pop.), consists in the main of comfortable houses set in large yards. In the boom days of the 1870's, when Sandy was a shipping point for ores, smelters lined the city limits. Collapse of Big Cottonwood mines and establishment of more direct shipping routes about 1900 left Sandy only its thin soil and slag dumps as sources of income. The town, however, survived admirably. The smelters have been replaced by ore-sampling works and by plants that manufacture rock wool from slag.

The UNITED STATES ROCK WOOL PLANT (L), 12.9 *m.* (*open workdays*), manufactures insulating material from abandoned slag dumps. The process was copied from the volcano of Hilo in Hawaii, where a small amount of rock wool—called by the natives "Pele's whiskers"—forms during each eruption. The rock wool plant imitates volcanic action by reheating slag to temperatures above 3,000 degrees, and by blowing the molten stuff out with steam. The product resembles uncarded wool, and is about thirty times as efficient an insulator as concrete.

At 13.4 *m.* is the junction (L) with a graveled road.

Left on this road to the mouth of LITTLE COTTONWOOD CANYON, 6.3 *m.*, the southernmost canyon recreation ground in the Salt Lake City area. Above the canyon floor immense granite ledges shoot skyward. Toward the head of the canyon, bare rock gives way to mountain soil and thick growths of trees and shrubs. Granite for the Mormon Temple (*see Salt Lake City*) was quarried in the mouth of Little Cottonwood Canyon.

ALTA, 17.8 *m.* (8,583 alt.), once a rip-roarin', rootin', shootin', mining camp, is now a winter sports resort. The old frame boarding house is the sole reminder of a once bustling city of 5,000.

The men who entered the valley from Colonel Patrick E. Connor's army camp, came for one purpose—to locate minerals. They were sharp-eyed, hard, and boisterous. The name of the first discoverer is lost, but J. B. Woodman is credited with early development of the great Emma silver mine in 1865, a discovery that almost caused international complications. The Prince of Wales and the South Hecla were other early mines. Among them, they brought thousands of people streaming up the canyon between 1865 and 1873. Woodman and his partners, who are now unknown, nearly starved those first few years. They offered a fourth interest for $3,000 but found no takers. They finally "rawhided" the ore in green cowhides down the canyon to ox-drawn wagons, which took the ore to the railroad at Ogden, whence it was shipped to San Francisco. There the ore was transshipped to sailing vessels, and sent around Cape Horn to Wales. After all transportation and smelting charges were deducted, the partners received $180 a ton, testimony to the richness of the ore. Once the mine started to produce, Walker Brothers, at that time Salt Lake City grocers, purchased a one-sixth interest for $25,000, and, in 1868, a Mr. Hussey bought a one-fourth interest for the same amount. Captain John Codman, in his book *The Mormon Country* (1874), writes that "These partners thereupon sold the whole to Parks and Baxter for three quarters of one million dollars," but George H. Watson, "Mayor of Alta," who moved to the camp in 1903, differs in some details with Codman. Whatever the true story, the Emma was now entering the international picture. Watson said in an interview,

Upon receipt of option, Parks went to Washington, D. C., and interested President U. S. Grant, and Grant introduced Parks to this minister to England, Schenck. . . . Schenck bought $50,000 in stock and became a director of the company. Schenck and Parks journeyed to London and sold the Emma for $5,000,000. The stock was listed in London stock exchange and shares rose [to] . . . a high of 31 pounds sterling, or about $150 per share. About this time the mine suddenly stopped producing, and a howl went up in England of fraud. . . . Congress felt that men as prominent as President Grant and his minister, Schenck, were entitled to a chance to vindicate themselves of threats—even threats of war. . . . Congress voted that a congressional investigation be called. Englishmen sent a boat of geologists from Heidelberg, and lawyers from London, and investigations started which covered 875 pages of testimony. Net result was that everyone connected with the transaction was fully exonerated of any wrong doing or wrong intentions. Facts brought out by geologists were that the ore body was cut off by a fault shortly after it was bought by the English.

The mystery of the lost vein did not dampen the spirits of the inhabitants. The Gold Miner's Daughter and the Bucket of Blood, most notorious of the twenty-six saloons, were not only busy serving drinks and raking in money over the tables, but were well occupied mopping up after the 110 killings as they occurred within the hospitable swinging doors. The men were buried in the little cemetery at the base of Rustler Mountain. Perhaps someone in Alta regretted the murders, for in the spring of 1873 a mysterious stranger appeared in camp, and offered to go to the cemetery and resurrect the dead. At first the people were disposed to accept the stranger's offer, but after giving the proposal some thought they decided that a general resurrection might be attended by numerous inconveniences. Widows and widowers who had remarried feared that the return of dead husbands and wives might disturb their domestic arrangements. Moreover, those who had inherited property soon recognized that the dead have no business out of the cemetery. Before many days the people of Alta took up a collection of $2,500 and presented it to the stranger, hoping the money would induce him to leave town. It did.

By 1872 Alta had reached its peak. More than a hundred buildings, some three stories high, were scattered over the flat; six of them were breweries. The population was 5,000.

Then came the "Crime of '73," as George Watson calls it. Congress demonetized silver. One by one the mines closed down, and the miners drifted out of the canyon. Those who hung on found that even nature was against them. Landslides and snowslides took more than 140 lives during the seventies. Between 1885 and 1940 the camp has produced fitfully. Alta came to life as a ski resort in 1937, when Salt Lake County provided year-round road equipment for the canyon. A three-story rustic lodge, built by the U. S. Forest Service in 1940, has a shelter lounge, ski repair shop, coffee shop, locker rooms, first-aid rooms, and an observation lounge. Rock for the walls was taken from old mine buildings. The first important ski meet was held in 1939, with participants from all over the United States. Events included downhill, slalom, and combined races for men and women. The course for men's events begins at an altitude of 10,996 feet in Peruvian Gulch and drops to 8,100 feet. The women start at about 9,900 feet and end at the same place.

"Mayor" Watson in 1940 was the owner of the old Emma mine, consolidated with thirty-three other locations. Watson had the old Emma geologized and diamond-drilled, and claims to have found the faulted segment of the ore body. The highway, open all year, allows for continuous development of the property, and miners occupying the old boarding house have relatively steady work.

At 17.2 *m.*, on US 91, is the intersection with State 111.

1. Right on State 111, graveled, to RIVERTON, 2.8 *m.* (4,435 alt., 1,326 pop.), a farming center with hay, grain, and sugar beets as the leading crops.

2. Left on State 111 oiled, to DRAPER, 1.3 *m.* (4,525 alt., 1,020 pop.), a community of scattered residences, large yards, and long rows of coops, set into a cove of the Wasatch Mountains. Draper exports poultry, eggs, and dairy products, but is chiefly known for two of its former residents, Dr. John R. Park, first president of the University of Utah, and Henry A. Pearson, first native Utahn appointed to the United States Naval Academy. Pearson, as an aide to Admiral Dewey at Manila Bay in 1898, cut Dewey's communications with the "strategy board" in Washington, D. C., a circumstance which was at least partly responsible for the American victory.

At 20 *m.*, on US 91, is the junction with State 161.

Right on State 161, graveled, to BLUFFDALE, 2.5 *m.* (4,435 alt.), so named for the near-by bluffs; L. from Bluffdale on State 68 to CAMP WILLIAMS, 4.6 *m.*, summer training quarters for the Utah National Guard, apparently selected with an eye to defense of communication lines through Jordan Narrows.

A ten-foot monument (R), 10.4 *m.*, commemorates the SITE OF A PONY EXPRESS STATION. Here for a time lived O. Porter Rockwell, who was Joseph Smith's bodyguard during the troublous days at Nauvoo, and was, according to legend, granted immunity to bullets for his loyalty. He accompanied Brigham Young westward in 1847, and served the community until his death in 1878 as a sort of Territorial marshal. Though he was in good standing in the Church, Rockwell clung tenaciously to monogamy and sometimes to a generous quota of whisky. What the gentiles thought of him is perhaps best summed up in a popular song to the tune of "Solomon Levi":

Have you heard of Porter Rockwell?
He's the Mormon triggerite.
They say he hunts for horse thieves
When the moon is shining bright.
So if you rustle cattle,
I'll tell you what to do,
Get the drop on Porter Rockwell,
Or he'll get the drop on you.

They say that Porter Rockwell
Is a scout for Brigham Young—
He's hunting up the unsuspects
That haven't yet been hung.
So if you steal one Mormon girl
I'll tell you what to do,
Get the drop on Porter Rockwell
Or he'll get the drop on you.

JORDAN NARROWS (R), 22.6 m., is a steep defile cut by the Jordan River. Here the highway swings sharply around POINT OF THE MOUNTAIN, affording a vista over Utah Valley, the meandering JORDAN RIVER, and the natural defenses of Camp Williams. The obvious parallel between the Utah river, which flows from fresh-water Utah Lake to salt-water Great Salt Lake, and the Jordan River of the Holy Land, which flows from fresh Galilee to the Dead Sea, impressed itself on Mormon explorers, who called the Utah river the "Western Jordan."

At 25 m. is the junction with State 80.

Left on State 80, improved dirt, through irrigated farmlands and arid bench country, to the junction, 5.9 m., with State 74 (see below). State 80 terminates at the junction and the route proceeds for 1.8 m. as State 146 (see below) to the junction with Forest Road 3 (see Timpanogos Cave National Monument).

LEHI, 28.4 m. (4,550 alt., 2,826 pop.), a farming community with intensively cultivated fields along Utah Lake, was settled in 1850 and named for a Book of Mormon character. Here, in 1890, the first successful sugar beet factory in the intermountain region was put in operation, and here also Isaac Goodwin planted the first alfalfa seed in Utah. Beets and alfalfa have become major crops in Utah. Lehi was hit hard by polygamy prosecutions of the 1870's and 1880's, and many residents were forced into hiding. A small boy of Lehi, ordered by Federal officers to point out a polygamist, led them solemnly and with much cautious circumspection to a chicken run and pointed out a rooster.

The JOHN HUTCHINGS ARCHEOLOGICAL COLLECTION, 2nd West and 6th North Sts., contains 5,000 classified arrowheads and artifacts excavated west of Utah Lake.

At 29.7 m. is the junction with State 68.

Right on State 68 to the junction, 1.2 m., with a dirt road; L. on this road to SARATOGA SPRINGS, 3.2 m. (open 9 A.M.-midnight, spring through fall; swimming, dancing, picnicking), a resort on Utah Lake. At 4.4 m. on State 68 is the junction with State 73; L. (straight ahead) on State 73 to the junction,

0.7 *m.*, with an unnumbered graded dirt road; L. on this road 3 *m.* to UTAH LAKE (*see Provo*), with catfish and bass fishing.

CEDAR VALLEY, 12.5 *m.* (5,125 alt., 233 pop.), on State 73, is a farming settlement mainly dependent on dry-farm wheat.

FAIRFIELD, 17.2 *m.* (4,876 alt., 129 pop.), settled in 1855, enjoyed a temporary boom during the years 1858-59 when Johnston's Army (*see History*) was encamped here at old Camp Floyd. The population in 1860 was about 7,000, mainly soldiers, teamsters, bawds, gamblers, and camp followers, and the metropolis swaggered under the unfelicitous pseudonym of "Frogtown." Johnston's cook at Camp Floyd was William Quantrill, leader of Quantrill's guerilla raiders in the Civil War, who massacred 140 people at Lawrence, Kansas, in 1863 (*see Kansas Guide*). The army concentrated 2,500 troops here until the outbreak of the Civil War, and the business of supplying them with foodstuffs was the first steady source of cash income for the Mormon colonists. The old army camp is completely effaced except for a monument and the military cemetery.

At 17.6 *m.* is the junction with a dirt road that leads to Mercur (*see Tour 6A*).

At 9.1 *m.* on State 68 is Camp Williams (*see above*).

AMERICAN FORK, 31.5 *m.* (4,566 alt., 3,330 pop.), a community of small farms and modest homes, is chiefly known as a poultry and egg producing center—an industry that is emphasized by an annual Poultry Day celebration in August.

Left from American Fork on State 74, oiled-gravel, to the junction, 4.1 *m.*, with State 80 (*see above*), and with State 146 (*see below*), alternate approaches to Timpanogos Cave National Monument.

ALPINE, 6 *m.* (4,957 alt., 548 pop.), on State 74, is a farming community set in a cove against the base of the Wasatch Mountains. Old adobe and log houses dominate the architecture, and the town retains a pioneer flavor.

At 34.4 *m.* is the junction with an oiled road.

Left (straight ahead) on this road to PLEASANT GROVE, 1.1 *m.* (4,621 alt., 1,754 pop.), named for the thick stands of cottonwood trees, which almost obscure the buildings. The bench lands about Pleasant Grove produce fruits and berries of excellent flavor, which are canned locally or shipped fresh, mainly to Pacific Coast markets, by refrigerator truck.

Left from Pleasant Grove on State 146, oiled, to the junction, 5.2 *m.*, with an oiled-gravel road; R. on this road to the west boundary, 0.7 *m.*, of the Wasatch National Forest on Forest Road 3 (*see Timpanogos Cave National Monument*).

At 7 *m.* on State 146 is the junction with State 74 (*see above*), which runs between Alpine and American Fork, and the east terminus of State 80 (*see above*).

Between the north junction with the Pleasant Grove road and Provo, US 91 follows a wide and fertile benchland divided into small farms. To the north, the full bulk of Mount Timpanogos (*see Timpanogos Cave National Monument*) sets solidly across the vision, and the east-lying mountains show high, pine-crenellated cliffs. Westward, Utah Lake glitters in the sun.

At 35.3 *m.* is the south junction with the Pleasant Grove road (*see above*), and the junction (R) with State 114, alternate route to Vineyard and Provo (*see below*) along the shores of Utah Lake.

LINDON, 36.5 *m*. (4,640 alt., 589 pop.), is chiefly devoted to the raising of berries and garden truck.

OREM, 39.1 *m*. (4,756 alt., 1,915 pop.), incorporated in 1925, produces garden stuff, much of which is canned at the Pleasant Grove Canning Plant in Orem, one of the largest tomato canneries in the Intermountain West.

Left from Orem on State 52 to the mouth, 3 *m.*, of PROVO CANYON (*see Tour 5*)

PROVO, 45.5 *m*. (4,549 alt., 17,956 pop.) (*see Provo*).

Provo is at the junction with US 189 (*see Tour 5*).

At 49.2 *m*. is the COLUMBIA STEEL PLANT (R) (*open by permission*), and the remnants of IRONTON (L) (*see below*). The immense hematite deposits near Cedar City (*see Tour 1f*) and a plentiful supply of coking coal in Carbon County (*see Tour 7b*), together with establishment of several steel fabricating plants on the Pacific Coast during and after the World War, led the Columbia Steel Company to establish reduction works at Ironton in 1924. The Ironton plant maintains a battery of fifty-six coke ovens, one blast furnace, and several by-product plants manufacturing ammonium sulphate, fuel gas, and benzene distillates. The blast furnace reduces about 500 tons of pig iron a day, most of which is shipped to the Pacific Coast. The Pacific States Cast Iron Pipe Company, however, immediately adjacent to the steel plant, utilizes up to 100 tons of the daily output. A village grew up on the mountainside east of the steel plant during its first years of operation, but near-by Provo and Springville, with already established conveniences, attracted most of the iron workers, and Ironton was allowed to decay.

The FEDERAL FISH HATCHERY (R), 50.5 *m*. (*open workdays*), was completed by the U. S. Bureau of Fisheries in 1916. It contains eighty hatching troughs and raises some four million game fish annually for distribution in Utah streams.

The UTAH STATE TROUT HATCHERY AND GAME FARM (L), 50.6 *m*. (*open workdays*), was begun in 1910 as a fish hatchery, and enlarged to include the game farm in 1924. Rainbow and Loch Leven trout are the principal stocks spawned here. The game farm serves as a breeding place for ring-necked pheasant, about 5,000 of which are released annually throughout the State. There is also a zoo, where animals and birds indigenous to Utah are shown.

SPRINGVILLE, 51.8 *m*. (4,516 alt., 4,777 pop.), because of its central situation in Utah, is the headquarters for many contractors, but it is most widely known as an art center.

A noted character in the town until late in the century was George "Beefsteak" Harrison, who acquired his nickname because of palatable steaks served at the Harrison Hotel. "George Harrison," says Kate B. Carter's *Military Life in the West,* "was one of the handcart boys who because of hunger left the Handcart Company and joined a tribe of Indians. Later he went to Fort Laramie, where he hired out as a cook for Johnston's army. . . . During the spring of 1858 he came to Utah . . . settling in Springville."

The SPRINGVILLE ART GALLERY (*open 9-5 daily*) was built in 1937 by the Works Progress Administration At that time the permanent student collection of Springville High School was valued at $150,000, and included works by such artists as John Costigan and John Hafen. The collection was assembled by gifts from artists and by purchases at a spring salon.

The PIONEER MOTHER MONUMENT and MEMORIAL FOUNTAIN in City Park are the work of Cyrus E. Dallin, known for his Indian studies; he was born in Springville.

SPANISH FORK, 56.9 *m.* (4,549 alt., 4,270 pop.), with a canning factory, a beet sugar factory, a foundry, and lumber yards, has an industrial aspect. Trees and spacious yards are in evidence, but the streets are crowded and there are factories on three sides of the town. Veterans of the Ute Black Hawk War hold their annual encampment each fall at Spanish Fork.

George Washington Brimhall, many-talented Mormon pioneer, lived here for a time; the house, if still standing, is not well known. His role in the commonwealth of Deseret is revealed in his rare volume, *The Workers of Utah:* "I continued about twenty years, seeking for water and timber in the valleys, mountain gorges and table lands, the best sites for cities, villages and farms, water power, roads and facilities to be employed by the incoming civilization." He was elected to the Territorial legislature in 1852 and soon acquired the title of "the Buckskin Orator." This venture as a lawmaker may have persuaded him "to study law at the feet of the Hon. Zerubbable Snow. . . . After engaging in this business for about three years I discovered that the intricacies of law were more difficult to follow than the trail of an Indian over the glaciers of ice or the flat smooth rocks of the mountains, and did not agree with my parent's blessings when I left home." Brimhall also served "the incoming civilization" as an Indian interpreter and treaty-maker (*see Tour 2A*).

Section e. *SPANISH FORK to BEAVER; 156.3 m., US 91*

South of SPANISH FORK, 0 *m.,* US 91 crosses an increasingly desert country. Small, intensely cultivated farms give way to large hay and grain fields and wide unfenced ranges. Intervals between towns are longer. The west-lying mountains are smaller, more arid, more distant, while those to the east, though pine-forested, are frequently obscured by low dry hills. It is a region of denim "britches," big hats, pole corrals, hay derricks, "roll-your-own" cigarettes, western self-sufficiency, tobacco-juice marksmanship, and big families. Its economy is based on the unexpressed theory that to make a profit the land must yield a product that can be walked to market, hence its devotion to cattle and sheep.

At 0.5 *m.* is the southern junction (L) with US 89 (*see Tour 2a*), which unites with US 91 for 75.6 miles, and US 50 (*see Tour 7b*), which unites with US 91 for 52.4 miles.

At 2.6 *m.* is a view (L) of the DREAM MINE, at the end of a zigzag road high on the face of the mountain to the east. About 1900, Bishop Koyle of Spanish Fork dreamed of rich bodies of ore in the mountain, and drove tunnels to recover them. During the succeeding forty years, Koyle, in spite of prosecutions for fraud and repeated disappointments, continued to drive tunnels. The mine has yielded small quantities of gold, silver, platinum, and lead, none of them in quantities to warrant processing. Among the many legends that have accrued to this enterprise is that of a Nephite or ancient Indian mine in the same region. Indeed, a short distance from the Dream Mine, there is an ancient tunnel, now caved in, its walls apparently chipped out with crude tools. Near this shaft on the cliff face is a petroglyph that represents beasts of burden, short-legged and thick-bodied like the South American llama, accompanied by drivers. From the mouth of the shaft, and reaching southwesterly across the valley, is what has been termed an ancient causeway, a ridge about fifteen feet wide that leads to what have been termed the ruins of a smelter and slag dumps.

SALEM, 4.4 *m.* (4,600 alt., 610 pop.), settled in 1851, was first named Pond Town for the small spring-fed lake about which the town grew up. The pond can be considered a lake only by desert standards, but it contains bass, perch, catfish, and rainbow trout, and is open to fishermen with licenses.

PAYSON, 7.6 *m.* (4,700 alt., 3,642 pop.), a community of old trees and solid homes, was settled in 1850. It is celebrated for its onions, and has an annual onion festival.

At 8.7 *m.* is the junction with an unnumbered dirt road.

Left on this road, known locally as the "Nebo Loop," through PAYSON CANYON, with its clear trout waters, around a shoulder of Mount Nebo, and through forested sheep and cattle range to the junction with State 189, 36.4 *m.* (*see below*).

SANTAQUIN, 13.8 *m.* (4,887 alt., 1,115 pop.), is a community of farmers and stockmen, its trees and meadows usually sprinkled with dust from the desert. The town was settled in 1851 and named for a Sanpitch Indian chief.

At 14.1 *m.* is the junction (R), in Santaquin, with US 6 (*see Tour 8*).

MONA (Manx, by the mountains), 26.1 *m.* (4,917 alt., 357 pop.), is chiefly remarkable for its late mornings—MOUNT NEBO, directly east (11,987 alt.), rises almost from Mona back yards, and withholds the sun for almost an hour after towns elsewhere in Utah have had their sunrise. SUNRISE PEAK (7,693 alt.), to the northwest, catches the morning sun long before Mona emerges from its matutinal eclipse.

NEPHI, 33.6 *m.* (5,096 alt., 2,844 pop.), Juab County seat, is on the sloping southwest buttresses of Mount Nebo in a region of farms and dry-land wheat ranches. The highway is the town's main thoroughfare, and residence districts on both sides are roomy and well-gardened. The city was settled in 1851, fortified with a moated wall, and named for the patriarch who in the Book of Mormon came with his family from Judea to the Americas in the time of the Babylonian captivity. Nephi's most important early event was the making of peace between Brigham Young and Chief Walker (Ute, Wah-kar-ar, yellow), somewhere near the city in 1854. According to S. N. Carvalho, who was present, Young, accompanied by 50 mounted men and 100 wagon loads ot curious settlers, came to Walker's camp. After a day of preliminary oratory and gifts, Walker began plaintively: "Sometimes Wakara take his young men and go far away to sell horses. When he is gone, Americats come kill his wife and children. Why no come fight when Wakara home?" But he concluded: "Wakara no want fight Mormonee. If Indian kill white man again, Wakara make Indian howl." There was consistent peace until 1865. After 1900, with development of dry-farm techniques, immense tracts in the hill country west of Nephi were put under cultivation, and the town grew as a shipping point for livestock and grain.

Nephi is at the junction with State 189 (*see Tour 2b*) and State 132.

Right on State 132, which runs through wheatlands west of Nephi and skirts the southern end of the arid East Tintic Mountains, to a junction, 23.6 *m.,* with US 6 at Jericho (*see Tour 8*).

At 38.5 *m.* is the junction with a dirt road.

Left on this road to the NEPHI-LEVAN RIDGE EXPERIMENTAL STATION (*open summer*), 0.5 *m.,* established by the Federal government to study techniques for raising grain without irrigation.

LEVAN, 44.6 *m.* (5,163 alt., 611 pop.), is the commercial center for the Levan Ridge country, Utah's most prolific dry-farm land. It is a desert town, its trees, lawns, gardens, and houses grayed with dust and sun.

Left from Levan on State 28, asphalt, through a valley of dry-farms, checkered by the green of growing fields and the red of the fallow, to LEVAN RIDGE, 8.8 *m.,* the proving ground for dry-farming in Utah. Where the land is uncultivated it supports stunted sage, and in the cultivated areas the merciless sun has seared even the fence posts—yet these red, orange, yellow, and blue-gray clays yield rich crops of grain.

At 31.2 *m.* is the junction with US 89 (*see Tour 2b*).

US 91 crosses the dam of SEVIER BRIDGE RESERVOIR, 62.4 *m.,* which holds back 236,000 acre-feet of water.

SCIPIO, 72.1 *m.* (5,300 alt., 544 pop.), lies in the sage-grayed hills of Sevier Valley, which support large herds of sheep and cattle, and irrigated lands about the town produce abundant crops of hay and grain.

At 72.3 *m.* is the junction with State 63.

Left on this improved dirt road through scattered farmlands, irrigated near Scipio, but cultivated dry a short distance south, and into a broad valley where sheep and cattle graze. The only signs of human habitation are drift fences and an occasional ranch house.

At 28.3 *m.* is the junction with US 89 (*see Tour 2b*).

HOLDEN, 85.5 *m.* (5,115 alt., 485 pop.), seems to have been settled on the pioneer maxim that where sage grows well, crops will thrive. Sagebrush stands about Holden, especially to the north and west, are jungle-thick and sometimes grow higher than a man's head, but the water supply has strictly limited the extent of cultivation.

FILLMORE, 96.3 *m.* (4,997 alt., 1,374 pop.), seat of Millard County, is a dry-farming and cattle town where "Levi's," five-gallon hats, and peg-heeled cow-punchers' boots are common habiliments. The spacious main street is lined by low-roofed stores, often with saddled cayuses hitched outside. Dusty stripped-down flivvers are common, with oversize tires signifying their use on the range. The city is one of the few in the nation that has no municipal taxes; all its expenses are paid out of municipal light plant profits.

The Territorial legislature in 1851 located the seat of government in Fillmore. Brigham Young selected the place for the capitol. Construction was begun, but lack of funds and too great distance from principal centers of population prevented completion of more than one wing of the State House. In the settlement's first criminal case, John Wigons, found guilty of "profane swearing" in 1852, was fined five dollars.

Fillmore is the birthplace of William H. King. Launched in politics before statehood, he was a member of the Territorial legislature, an associate justice of the Territorial supreme court, and a member of the U. S. Senate from 1917 to 1941.

The two-story red sandstone south wing of the FILLMORE STATE HOUSE, in City Park, was partially completed in 1855 and housed only the Territorial legislature of 1855-56, the seat of government being returned to Great Salt Lake City in 1856. Designed as a domed, three-winged structure by Truman O. Angell, the existing wing is now a museum for Indian artifacts and pioneer relics.

Left from Fillmore on a narrow dirt road to the mouth of CHALK CREEK CANYON, 1.7 *m.,* a steep-walled ravine densely clad with cottonwood, maple, box elder, and oak brush. The road crosses the west boundary, 3.2 *m.,* of FISHLAKE NATIONAL FOREST, and there are U. S. Forest Service campgrounds at 6.3 *m.* and at 7.3 *m.*

MEADOW, 104.2 *m.* (5,000 alt., 395 pop.), a livestock town, is surrounded by grain and alfalfa fields and pasture lands. West of the town rises the crystal-white cone of White Mountain, a volcanic dike between lime hills.

At 109.1 *m.* is the junction with a dirt road.

Left on this road to the KANOSH INDIAN RESERVATION, 2 *m.,* a village of about thirty Pahvant Indians under jurisdiction of the Uintah and

Ouray Agency at Fort Duchesne (*see Tour 6a*). They have an irrigation right, and most of them, living in log houses, have adopted the white man's way of life.

KANOSH, 110.3 *m.* (5,125 alt., 570 pop.), is a spread-out community of grain and alfalfa farmers, settled in 1859 and named for the Indian chief.

BLACK ROCK VOLCANO (R), 113.5 *m.,* is an extinct, coneless crater overgrown with sage.

Between Black Rock Volcano and Cove Fort US 91 crosses a grass and sage-covered flat and threads through Baker Canyon, incised in rolling mountains clothed with gray-green sage and electric-green juniper, which contrast sharply with the red soil and red rock.

COVE FORT, 131.4 *m.* (6,000 alt., 10 pop.), embraced by canyon walls, consists of a barn, farmhouse, and service station facing the well-preserved Mormon fort (R), walled with volcanic rock. Built in 1867, the fort is now a tourist camp. Its original rooms, backed against the enclosing wall, 100 feet square and 20 feet high, are screened and equipped with modern comforts. The well used by the pioneers is in the center of the square, and the bell, once a tocsin for Indian attacks, hangs in the front arch.

Left from Cove Fort on State 13, graveled, through CLEAR CREEK CANYON, (*camping, fishing*), with organ-like rock walls.
At 17.1 *m.* are eroded brown and white rock formations (L) resembling gigantic mushrooms.
At 19.9 *m.* is the junction with US 89 (*see Tour 2c*).

Between Cove Fort and Beaver the route is over rolling wastes of sage and juniper, punctuated by scattered wind- and sun-beaten ranch-houses between the towering forested crags of the Tushar Mountains (L) and castellated ridges of the Mineral Mountains (R). This is the region of the "Utah mile," which, in the way of distance, may be anything from a half-hour to an all-day hike. Speech becomes more languid, the western drawl begins to appear, and the main topics of conversation are the lack of rain, crops, and politics. Families are larger; there are few diversions except in distant larger towns.

At 134.3 *m.* is the junction with a dirt road.

Left on this road to SULPHURDALE, 1.3 *m.* (5,625 alt., 25 pop.), having Utah's only producing sulphur mine; the employees and the postmaster make up the town. The mine, an open-pit digging, is worked with draglines. Discovered in the 1880's, the mine was operated by Mormon pioneers to supply an element needed in gunpowder and in sugar refining.

At 156.1 *m.* is the junction in Beaver with oiled State 21.

Left on State 21 through BEAVER CANYON to the west boundary of FISHLAKE NATIONAL FOREST, 4.5 *m.* (*campgrounds, fishing, deer*).
At 11.7 *m.* the road begins a series of switchbacks that lift it high above the canyon floor.
PUFFER LAKE RESORT, 19.3 *m.* (*accommodations, boats, guides, horses*), is on the shore of a small lake. Deer are numerous in this vicinity.

19.7 *m.* is the junction with a dirt road; L. here to PUFFER LAKE, 0.1 *m.* (*trout*), a crystal mountain lake in view of Mounts Baldy (12,000 alt.), Belnap (12,131 alt.; *horseback trails to summit*), and Delano (12,162 alt.), highest peaks in southwestern Utah.

At 29.2 *m.* State 21 abruptly rounds the eastern slope of the Tushar Mountains, affording a sweeping view of the Sevier Valley far below, with its towns of Junction and Circleville (*see Tour 2c*). The road, descending by switchbacks to the valley floor, looks like a twisted tape flung out from the mountainside. A hairpin turn, 29.4 *m.*, brings the glistening hay-hook of Piute Reservoir into view below. This very steep grade should not be attempted by timorous drivers.

JUNCTION, 38.5 *m.* (6,250 alt., 252 pop.) (*see Tour 2c*), is at the junction with US 89.

BEAVER, 156.3 *m.* (5,970 alt., 1,673 pop.), a verdant city in the dusty red desert, is the center of a farming and stock-raising district and the seat of Beaver County. Settled in 1856, the town had a woolen mill, a $30,000 co-operative venture, by the sixties. Mormon settlers ignored the arid hills to the west, but gentile prospectors dug into them and found riches. A mining boom brought prosperity to Beaver, and with it came a horde of non-Mormon promoters, miners, card-sharps, and other "boomers." A rough-and-tumble crew, they derided the Saints. Antagonisms were encouraged by factional newspapers, and finally both sides asked for Federal troops to protect them from the Indians and each other. The mining boom subsided, leaving comparative peace in Beaver. In 1876, John D. Lee, a leader of the Mountain Meadows Massacre (*see Tour 1f*), was convicted here after a two-year series of trials.

A Deer Hunters' Dance is held annually in Beaver, on the eve of the season's opening. Allowed by a special city ordinance, it is planned as an all-night affair for the huntsmen and their ladies. With "enough liquid refreshments to go 'round," festivities achieve hilarious heights. On the first day of hunting the woods are apt to bristle with headaches, more abundantly than with deer.

Utah's Junior Senator, Abe Murdock, elected from the House of Representatives in 1940, is from a pioneer Beaver family, and makes his home here.

Beaver is at the junction (R) with State 21 (*see Tour 1D*).

Section f. BEAVER to ARIZONA LINE; 137.3 m., US 91

South of BEAVER, 0 *m.*, US 91 twists across sagebrush flats, across sage- and juniper-clad foothills, and, through wide windswept valleys, descends into Parowan Valley between the timbered Black Mountains and the dry bed of Little Salt Lake. South of Cedar City, the highway climbs red hills to the rim of the Great Basin and thence through canyons of flaming red winds down into "Utah's Dixie"—the green and red Mormon oasis in the southwestern corner of the State.

PARAGONAH (Paiute, many springs), 30.3 *m.* (5,897 alt., 384 pop.), is an agricultural settlement surrounded by green alfalfa and grain fields. Houses are of red adobe and native red brick, and, like the pink and red earth, contrast strikingly with the green vegetation. Paragonah has been a fruitful field for archeological research into remnants left by an adobe-building Puebloan culture.

Between Paragonah and Parowan the LITTLE SALT LAKE—called by the Paiutes Parowan, evil water—is visible (R) several miles distant. Virtually a dry lake bed, it gleams under the sun as convincingly as though fed by mighty rivers.

PAROWAN, 34.8 m. (5,990 alt., 1,474 pop.), Iron County seat and center of a sheep and cattle area, stands green and fresh in a hot, windy valley. Houses range from primitive pink adobe structures to modern firebrick houses, their colors cooled by the blue shadows of trees.

The Iron County Mission to Parowan and Cedar City was the first great Mormon colonizing expedition in Utah. Led by George A. Smith, it left Fort Provo in December, 1850, and consisted of 119 men, 310 women over fourteen years of age, and 18 children under fourteen. "I hope our ears will not be saluted," he admonished his followers, "with any profanity, swearing of blasphemous words, or taking the name of the Lord in vain. . . . We are going to build up the Kingdom of God." The 129 wagons contained, besides the colonists, pioneer armament, saddles, "lights of Glass," carpenter and blacksmith tools, various kinds of seeds, "pitt saws," plows, "syths and cradles," mill irons, cats, dogs, and chickens. Milk cows, beef cattle, oxen, mules and horses served as draft animals. The Parowan site, Smith found, had "red sandy soil covered with bunch grass, sage and rabbit brush and grease wood. . . . My wicky-up is a very important establishment, composed of brush, a few slabs and 3 wagons." The colony was reinforced by later settlers, including Dr. Priddy Meeks, who came "to help strengthen the place against Indians"—"verry doubtful neighbors," who were "verry saucy and turbulent especially among the women. One Indian struck John D. Lee's wife over the head and cut a gash some three or four inches long and we like to had war over it."

It was the business of the Parowan colonists to put in crops, so that following immigrants could open up the coal and iron deposits. Cedar City was the second settlement made. Two colonies so close together, at such a distance from Great Salt Lake City, stifled each other's growth after the iron manufacturing enterprise failed. Jules Remy, who passed through Parowan in 1855, found it "nothing more than a poor straggling village, built of wood and adobes of red earth."

Left from Parowan on State 143, graded dirt, through heavily timbered PAROWAN CANYON to the junction, 3.8 m., with a graveled road; L. on the graveled road to the VERMILION CASTLES, 1.3 m., brightly colored pinnacles and battlements above gray conglomerate walls. State 143 climbs steadily through Dixie National Forest, and at 16 m. arrives at the junction (L) with an improved road to BRIAN HEAD PARK, 2 m., a recreation area maintained by the U. S. Forest Service on the crown of Brian Head Peak (11,315 alt.), highest point in the area. There is a view from here into five States, above the cataclysmic scenic disorder of southern Utah.

At 17.4 *m.* on State 143 is the junction with State 55 (*see Cedar Breaks National Monument*), and the Panguitch Lake road (*see Tour 2c*).

At 53.7 *m.,* on US 91, is the junction with State 56 in Cedar City.

Right on State 56, oiled, concrete, and gravel, to the junction, 2.7 *m.,* with State 19; R. on State 19, oiled, to LUND, 31.4 *m.* (5,084 alt., 191 pop.), a treeless farming and railroad town on the forbidding Escalante Desert. Escalante crossed the eastern part of the desert, but was too preoccupied with dissensions in his party to record much about the desert since named for him.

Left (straight ahead) from Lund on a dirt road to the INDIAN PEAK INDIAN RESERVATION, 39.3 *m.* (*see Tour 1D*).

At 7.7 *m.* on State 56 is the junction with a dirt road; R. to IRON SPRINGS, 3.3*m.,* where *Union Pacific* was filmed among rolling sage plains and desert buttes. Many another picture, in whole or in part, has been filmed in the vicinity, including *Ramona, The Good Earth,* and *The Bad Man of Brimstone.*

NEWCASTLE, 29.1 *m.* (5,000 alt., 141 pop.), on State 56, defended from the desert by castellated rock formations, was settled in 1910. In possession of the Knell family here, until 1940 when it was placed in the L. D. S. Museum in Salt Lake City, was a faded water-color sketch, which recalls a moving incident of 1854. S. N. Carvalho, an artist with Frémont's fourth expedition, came to Cedar City, where he met a bereaved family who had lost their only daughter, aged six. Carvalho tells the story in his *Incidents of Travel and Adventure in the Far West:*

> Laid out upon a straw mattress, scrupulously clean, was one of the most angelic children I ever saw. On its face was a placid smile, and it looked more like the gentle repose of healthful sleep than the everlasting slumber of death. . . . I entered very softly, and did not disturb the afflicted mother. . . .
> Without a second's reflection I commenced making a sketch of the inanimate being before me, and in the course of half-an-hour I had produced an excellent likeness.
> A slight movement in the room caused the mother to look around her. . . . I tore the leaf out of my book and presented it to her. . . . She said I was an angel sent from heaven to comfort her.
> She had no likeness of the child. . . .
> When I was about starting the next day, I discovered in the wagon a basket filled with eggs, butter, and several loaves of bread, and a note to my address containing these words—'From a grateful heart.'

At 38.7 *m.* on State 56 is the junction (L) with State 18 (*see below*).

MODENA, 53.1 *m.* (5,462 alt., 102 pop.), on State 56, exists as a Union Pacific flag-stop on the southwestern edge of the Escalante Desert. State 56 here turns sharply southwest toward the Nevada Line, recalling its early importance as an arterial support of Pioche and Panaca, Nevada mining camps. Among the freighters who hauled supplies to Pioche in the seventies there grew up a legend that a rocky gorge near the Nevada Line was haunted by the Gadianton robbers, a terroristic brotherhood which the Book of Mormon explains as having sprung up among the Nephites and Lamanites in the century before Christ. Wide-eyed freighters told tales of rocks closing the way, and of the canyon folding up to entrap them.

UVADA, 62.1 *m.* (5,654 alt.), a Union Pacific station, clings to the western verge of the State.

At 62.6 *m.* State 56 crosses the Nevada Line (*see Nevada Guide*).

CEDAR CITY, 53.8 *m.* (5,805 alt., 4,695 pop.), was settled in 1851 by English, Scotch, and Welsh "miners and manufacturers" to open up the coal and iron deposits. In 1852 a hundred families of skilled Mormon converts were named to strengthen the "iron mission."

A multiplicity of difficulties finally doomed the iron manufacturing venture: There was trouble fluxing the ore; trouble finding sufficiently skilled workmen; trouble with floods, hard winters, and crop devastation; and, finally, iron brought in by Johnston's army and the transcontinental railroad made native production unprofitable. Cedar City grew, however, in consequence of extensive stock-raising in the area. Since the 1920's interest in scenic wonders has drawn outside people to the city, which is in easy reach of Cedar Breaks, Bryce Canyon, and Zion Canyon. The Dixie National Forest, to the east and west, annually attracts hundreds of deer hunters, fishermen, and vacationists. Cedar City is the most publicized mountain lion hunting center in the State (*see Richfield, Tour 2b*). Completion of a branch line of the Union Pacific Railroad in 1923 reawakened the old iron deposits, and thousands of tons of ore are shipped annually.

Cedar City is a cultural center of the area, having the Branch Agricultural College, a unit of the Utah State Agricultural College (*see Logan*); the faculty publishes the *Rocky Mountain Review,* a "little" magazine.

The CEDAR CITY MORMON CHAPEL (*open on application*) is built of vari-colored rocks from Utah and Arizona; the interior is of native cedar. Walter Granger, elected to Congress from Utah in 1940, makes his home in Cedar City.

At 53.9 *m.,* in Cedar City, is the junction with State 14.

Left on this gravel road (*impassable in winter*), to DEER HAVEN FOREST CAMP, 15.1 *m.* (*camping*), on a tableland and surrounded by aspen and pine.

At 20.5 *m.* is the junction (L) with State 55 (*see Cedar Breaks National Monument*).

At 29.1 *m.* is the junction with an improved road; R. on this road to NAVAHO LAKE, 4 *m.* (*fishing, trapshooting, camping*), which is surrounded by pink cliffs, black lava flows, and forests of pine, spruce, and aspen.

DUCK CREEK CAMP (L), 31.8 *m.* (*dancing, tennis, camping*), is on the banks of capricious Duck Creek, which springs up as a full-sized creek in a twenty-square-foot space at the side of the highway, and disappears in a space of similar size within two miles of its source. Left from Duck Creek Camp on a foot trail to ICE CAVE, 1.5 *m.,* a natural refrigerator large enough to admit a rotund person; one of its two rooms is filled with ice the year round.

LONG VALLEY JUNCTION, 45.9 *m.,* is at the junction with US 89 (*see Tour 2d*).

A HISTORICAL MARKER (L), 63.8 *m.,* set in a sage-covered valley, indicates the South Rim of the Great Basin. Mormon colonization south of this point in early times was characterized as "going over the Rim," and in colloquial usage the same phrase came to connote violent death.

KANARRAVILLE, 66.8 *m.* (5,750 alt., 279 pop.), is a ranching community, founded in 1861 and named for Chief Kanarra, leader of a Paiute band.

At 71.1 *m.* is the junction with State 144.

Right on gravel-surfaced State 144 to NEW HARMONY, 5.2 m. (5,250 alt., 178 pop.), at the base of the Pine Valley Mountains. John D. Lee established Fort Harmony, first settlement "over the Rim," in 1852. The settlement, four miles southeast, was abandoned because of the Walker War (*see History*), but Lee returned two years later and built a new fort. As "Indian farmer," Lee was living here at the time of the Mountain Meadows Massacre (*see below*) in 1857, at a point twenty miles west. Lee organized Washington County and for a while he was probate judge, clerk, assessor, and collector. In 1856, sitting in a carpenter shop, he heard the case of "The People of the Territory of Utah in Washington Co. V. S. Against Enos an Indian Native . . . for larceny—committed about the 25th. of Dec. 1855 & 1st. inst." The Indian demanded a jury trial, after which "a verdict was rendered that the Prisoner be punished by wearing a heavy chain on his leg and hard labor 3 months."

"Harmony No. 2," as Lee called it, was demolished in 1862 by a rainstorm that continued unceasingly for twenty-eight days. Lee did not remove his wet clothing for eight days and nights. Two of his children were killed when the walls of his home gave way. The Harmony colonists buried their dead and moved to the head of Ash Creek, where New Harmony was built to endure to the present.

ANDERSONS RANCH, 86.8 m. (3,700 alt., 8 pop.), is at the northern extremity of semitropical "Dixie." The Andersons Ranch area in 1880 was given by a miner to Peter Anderson, of Pintura. To modern times it is said "there was never a traveler turned away from Peter Anderson's ranch hungry."

Andersons Ranch is at the junction with State 15 (*see Tour 1E and Zion National Park*).

Between Andersons Ranch and Leeds, peaks in Zion National Park loom on the horizon (L), and the eroded slopes of Kolob Plateau are streaked by many-colored bands. The soil is pink sand, supporting white sage, "dagger weed," rabbit brush, and cacti.

At 90.7 m. is the junction with a gravel-surfaced road.

Right on this road to the junction, 1.2 m., with a dirt road; L. at the base of a red reef to SILVER REEF, 0.3 m., where, brooding and vacant-eyed, an old bank building watches over the grave of a once-famous silver mining camp. The nature-paved streets—huge boulders indifferently leveled—still wind along the ridge, but rattlesnakes, Gila monsters, tarantulas, and centipedes slither along where once hard men tramped. The ruined foundations of churches, saloons, dance halls, gambling dens, schools, and homes are weed-covered and tumbled-in, and brush-choked cellars gape lazily in the hot sun.

Various men have been credited with the discovery of silver at Silver Reef, some old-timers maintaining that the Spaniards once mined ore here, pointing to the old Spanish map brought in by Llewellyn Harris in the 1850's. The more generally accepted tale is that of "Metalliferous" Murphy, an optimistic assayer of Pioche, Nevada, whose reports on samples were so exuberantly high that miners distrusted him. When certain miners were debating one day where they could get an honest assay, two men rode in from Leeds with a load of wood and a grindstone. The miners dickered for the grindstone, pulverized it, and sent the "sample" to "Metalliferous" Murphy. The intent was to "sting" Murphy, for everybody knew, and the geologists said definitely, that silver could not occur in sandstone. When Murphy's assay on the grindstone "sample" showed 200 ounces of silver to the ton, the miners hit the ceiling. One account is that they hanged Murphy on the spot, another says that Murphy, infuriated by their doubts, traced the grindstone to the quarry and thus made the astonishing discovery that metals could be found in sandstone, upsetting all previous theories on the subject. Another tale gives credit to an unknown traveler who stopped at a house in Leeds one bitter cold night. A roaring fire was burning in the fireplace, and the traveler noticed something oozing out of the stone lining. He gathered some of the drops, which turned out to be silver. He had no trouble locating the quarry, and discovered horn silver in sandstone. Whether "Metalliferous" Murphy or the unknown traveler made the discovery, the disclosure was far-reaching. Geologists wrote long and learned articles on the matter, contradicting one another in measured scholarly terms.

The first recorded mine location in the district was that of John Kemple, who explored the area in 1866 and returned in 1870 or 1871 to file his first claim. He established the district, naming it the Harrisburg Mining District, and appointed a recorder. A few miners and prospectors came during the next two years, but it was not until 1874, when Elijah Thomas sent a sample of horn silver to Walker Brothers, Salt Lake City bankers, that any real interest was aroused. Walker Brothers dispatched William T. Barbee, Thomas McNally, and Ed Maynard, assayer, to the spot. Barbee became so enthused when he found horn silver even in petrified wood, that he located twenty-two claims on Tecumseh Ridge and hurried to Salt Lake City for supplies. Returning with a blacksmith, tools, and other mining supplies, he established "Bonanza City."

Although many Mormons resented the intrusion of miners in the territory, Apostle Erastus Snow thanked God for sending Brother Barbee to alleviate the hard times under which the settlers were struggling. Barbee's letters, published in the *Salt Lake Tribune,* brought thousands of miners into the district, and the boom was on. Pioche, Nevada, was almost deserted by miners rushing to Silver Reef in buckboards, wagons, carts, on horses, mules and burros. Among the new arrivals was Hyrum Jacobs, merchant, who set up his camp in the center of a ridge and named it Silver Reef. Between 1877 and 1903 more than 9,000,000 ounces of silver were removed from the reefs and sold for an average price of $1.15 an ounce.

The most beloved figure in Silver Reef was Father Scanlan, who came to Silver Reef on horseback in 1877. Funds were raised for the church, a hospital, and a school. In "Silver Reef, Personalities, Legends," Mark Pendleton throws new light on Mormon-gentile relations of the time: ". . . in 1879 . . . An invitation was extended Father, afterwards Bishop, Scanlan, by the Mormon authorities of St. George to hold services in their tabernacle. . . . A choir was needed, but as the tabernacle choir of the place did not know Latin, it was thought that the singing of the Kyrie Eleison and Gloria and Credo could not be carried out. The leader of the choir asked for Catholic music and being given Peter's Mass, in two weeks his choir knew the Mass and could sing it in Latin. . . . High Mass was sung in the tabernacle, the Mormon choir executing it with great credit to themselves, rendering the Gloria and Hosanna in clear, sweet tones."

In the late 1870's, when Silver Reef was at its peak, Federal officers began coming into town on their way to St. George to arrest polygamists. Silver Reef was a non-Mormon settlement, and the officers usually stopped there, but the telegraph operator was a Mormon. The St. George telegraph office was in a furniture store, and the Silver Reef operator would warn the town by wiring for "two chairs" when the officers appeared. St. George "polyg hunts" were never very successful, and the officers usually left town to the tune of derisive songs.

By 1880, the big ore producers were consolidated under various companies, each with its own amalgam stamp mill. Watson N. Nesbitt pioneered a hypo-sodium leaching plant in the Leeds mill, but the method was too expensive. The Buckeye mine in 1877 was turning out a thousand-ounce brick every day with an average purity of 990 (out of 1000). The Christy mill in 1878 reported milling 10,249 tons valued at $302,597, or $29.17 a ton. The price of silver fell, the ore became less rich, and water in the mines added to production costs. Wages were cut in 1881, and there was a strike. The strike leaders were jailed, but the loss to credit-burdened stores forced many shops to close. Silver prices continued downward, the old-timers left, newer men did not understand the mines or the men, and the companies ceased operations in 1891.

The following year there was a revival of mining that lasted until silver dropped to 65 cents in 1903. The camp was deserted until 1916, when Alex Colbath raised $160,000 and organized the Silver Reef Consolidated Mines Company. The rise in silver prices during the World War induced a New York company to lease the property in 1920, but a sharp decline in price prevented the construction of a large mill. Samuel M. Silverman of New York purchased the properties in 1928, and in the spring of that year the American Smelting and Refining Company purchased 51 per cent of the stock and sank a 541-foot shaft. When the price of silver dropped to 25 cents, all development stopped, and in 1940 the Reef was just a ghost town, with more past than future.

LEEDS, 91.3 m. (2,750 alt., 220 pop.), settled in 1867, was the center of much Silver Reef turmoil. Early a fruit region, Leeds was the birthplace of "fire-eating" Dixie wine, famous during the Silver Reef boom. Many old houses still stand. Dr. Priddy Meeks lived ten hard years near Leeds in the sixties, but had to sell out: "I had no money to pay my taxes & the boys [his sons] in debt and a kind of shut down in mining. . . . Right in the pinch here came a miner to buy my water in the Leeds field. I put him off. . . . It was against the principles I believed in to see [sell] to the gentiles but if I don't take this chance I shall be broke up. Now what shall I do, it now force-ably occurred to my mind to take the money from the gentile, for the same reason that David eat the shew bread . . . to keep himself from starving and this was the sole reason that caused me to sell out to the gentiles. Two neighbors posted right off to St. George to tell President Young what I had done. President Young said to them these words, I dont blame Bro Meeks one particle. So that settled the question."

HARRISBURG JUNCTION, 97.9 m., is a service station stand-ing sentinel over a fenced yard filled with oddly-shaped rocks.

Left from Harrisburg Junction on State 17 to an EXTINCT VOLCANO (R) 5.1 m. Several more craters (L), 6.9 m., lift their cold black rims to the sun.
HURRICANE, 8.5 m. (3,250 alt., 1,197 pop.), a fruit-raising town, took its name from Hurricane Fault, the long black ridge extending south of the town.
LA VERKIN, 10.1 m. (3,313 alt., 236 pop.), is the center of a small fruit-growing area.
At 11.2 m. is the junction with State 15 (see Tour 1E).

WASHINGTON, 103.1 m. (2,800 alt., 435 pop.), a leisurely group of red adobe and red brick houses, was settled in 1855, at the time of first experimentation with cotton in "Utah's Dixie." Enough was raised the first year, as Zodak Knapp Judd records in his manu-script autobiography, to give the planters "a sad experience picking the seed out. It was a slow business and made our fingers sore." A cot-ton factory was established at Washington in 1866, continuing inter-mittent production until 1900. A few cotton plants still grow in Washington gardens, as curiosities.

Pioneering was grim here, as it was generally in Utah—sugar was a medicine for babies, costing a dollar a pound; tea cost five dollars a pound; and flour, when obtainable, ten dollars a hundredweight. The imagination of pranksters, however, was not to be stultified. A mischievous youth carved a pair of huge wooden shoes with which he made immense tracks at night. Children were forbidden to play outdoors for fear of the "giant"; houses were kept securely bolted; men went armed to the fields. Meeting in anxious conference, the settlers determined to send to Brigham Young for advice. As the courier was mounting his horse, the prankster burst into helpless guffaws and Washington's "giant" vanished into the realm of splendid dreams.

At 106.1 m. is the junction with State 18.

Right on State 18, a rough graveled road, to two extinct BLACK VOLCANIC CRATERS (L), 12.9 m. and 13.5 m., their cold lava flows lying as they hardened in prehistoric times.

A sign (L), 33.8 m., indicates the situation of a monument (*on private property; permission must be obtained from near-by ranch*) marking the SITE OF THE MOUNTAIN MEADOWS MASSACRE. In September, 1857, a California-bound company of approximately 140 emigrants from Arkansas camped here to recruit their stock before pushing out into the deserts. They had passed down through Utah at a peculiarly tense time; complete uncertainty existed among the Mormons as to the intentions of Johnston's Army, then enroute to put down "rebellion" in Utah. Later the Mormons said that the Arkansans had poisoned springs, and beef given to the Indians, and had boasted that they meant to fall on the Mormons.

Although the dates are not accredited by all authorities, it has been believed that at daybreak on Monday or Tuesday, September 7 or 8, the unsuspecting emigrants were attacked by several hundred Paiute Indians. Seven were killed and sixteen or seventeen wounded at the first volley, but the emigrants killed a number of their attackers and entrenched behind wagons to resist a siege. White men were involved almost from the beginning. John D. Lee says, "The original plan was for the Indians to do all the work, and the whites to do nothing, only to stay back and plan for them. . . . Now we knew the Indians could not do the work, and we were in a sad fix." On the Thursday evening after the first attack, it was decided in council that the emigrants should be decoyed from their camp and slain.

On Friday morning William Bateman was sent with a flag of truce to the emigrant camp; he was met by an emigrant named Hamilton, who finally agreed that the arms and ammunition of the Arkansans should be placed in a wagon, all the young children in another wagon, and all the wounded in still another, the Mormons then to conduct the emigrants in safety to Cedar City, where they should be protected until there was an opportunity for them to travel on to California. Shortly after noon, Lee proceeded to the emigrant camp to lead the emigrants to their death. "As I entered the fortifications," he says, "men, women and children gathered around me in wild consternation. Some felt that the time of their happy deliverance had come, while others though in deep distress, and all in tears, looked upon me with doubt, distrust and terror. . . . I knew that I was acting a cruel part and doing a damnable deed."

Lee told the people they must put their arms in the wagon, to allay the animosity of the Indians. A short distance outside the camp, the emigrants were drawn up between a double file of settlers from Cedar City and the Santa Clara Valley, and between these files the wagons, the women and children, and the men passed in procession. The settlers then changed to single file, an armed settler marching on the right of each disarmed emigrant man. The march was now taken up toward Cedar City, the women and children about a mile ahead of the men. Meanwhile, the Indians had hidden in ambush. At a signal, whites and Indians fell on the unarmed emigrants. So sudden and ferocious was the onslaught that within five minutes the entire emigrant party, except for a number of children believed too young to talk, was massacred.

Lee, who had joined in the attack on the sick and wounded, says that, following the massacre, "the brethren were called up, and [John M.] Higbee and [Philip] Klingensmith, as well as myself, made speeches, and *ordered* the people to keep the matter a secret from the *entire* world. Not to tell their wives, or their most intimate friends, and we pledged ourselves to keep everything relating to the affair a secret during life. We also took the most binding Oaths to stand by each other, and to always insist that the massacre was committed by Indians alone." But the horror of this deed rested too heavily on the minds of the participants. Inevitably the story spread. John L. Ginn, an emigrant from Georgia, passed through the Meadows soon after the massacre and saw the unburied bodies; a scrap of paper disclosed their identity. After the arrival of Johnston's Army in Utah in 1858, the investigations of Judge Cradlebaugh disclosed the guilt of Lee, Isaac C. Haight, John M. Higbee, and other participants. They kept free of the law for many years, Lee settling at a remote spot on the Colorado River, subsequently known as Lees Ferry. Not until 1874, when Lee was caught at Panguitch, was anything done to punish those who had joined in the crime. He was tried at Beaver in 1875, the jury disagreeing. Tried again in 1876, he was convicted, and on March 23, 1877, he was brought to Mountain Meadows, and shot for his crime.

HAMBLIN, 35.5 *m.* (5,750 alt.), at the north end of Mountain Meadows, was located as a ranch by Jacob Hamblin in 1856. Here the seventeen children who survived the Mountain Meadows Massacre were distributed among those who had participated in the attack. They were cared for until Jacob Forney, U. S. Indian agent, sent them in 1858 to their relatives in Arkansas.

ENTERPRISE, 43 *m.* (5,500 alt., 464 pop.), began under another name, in another place. The need of a stock-raising area for Dixie led, in 1862, to the occupation of Shoal Creek and the building of Hebron, a short distance above the site of Enterprise. Hebron grew; the opening of Silver Reef and the mines near Pioche, Nevada, for a time was invigorating. As the mining towns declined, Hebron, as Orson W. Huntsman records, "began to go down, down, down. Some people moved away and drouth and discouragement took the place of moisture and ambition." Orson Huntsman planned a reservoir on Shoal Creek and removal of the town to its present place. "I preached reservoir," he says, "for about three years in all the surrounding towns." The indomitable dreamer at last found a sympathetic hearing among Church leaders in St. George, and in 1893 a company was organized. For sixteen years, impoverished settlers labored on their reservoir. "It was said that some lived on jackrabbits those sixteen years. They had no machinery of any kind; everything was done by hand." Some "tried to resurrect Hebron." A few settlers, however, moved to Enterprise townsite in 1895. "All [the next] ten years both Hebron and Enterprise stood still."

Like a sign from God, the earthquake that shook southwestern Utah in 1902, hit Hebron hardest. The people of Hebron sold their water to Enterprise, tore down their houses, and rebuilt them at Enterprise. The job took several years—"as the one town went down, the other was built up." When, in 1906, the West shook to the San Francisco earthquake, most of the remaining houses at Hebron were broken upon the ground; at Enterprise, every house stood firm.

At 51.5 *m.* is the junction with State 56 (*see above*).

ST. GEORGE, 107.9 *m.* (2,760 alt., 3,589 pop.), is marked by the white Mormon Temple, which rises dazzlingly above red soil, green trees and lawns, and trim red houses of adobe and brick. The seat of Washington County, St. George stands at the heart of Utah's Dixie, and is known for its long hot summers and mild winters.

The story of St. George's founding has an epic character. The success of cotton-raising experiments induced Church authorities in 1861 to undertake large-scale colonization of extreme southern Utah. Even then the area had a reputation as a hard place to live, and those "called" to the Dixie mission "to sustain Israel in the mountains," in many instances were not happy about it. One father, coming home from a hard day in the fields to be told that he had been "called" to Dixie, sank into a chair. "Damned if I'll go," he said. After sitting a few minutes, head in hands, he stood up. "Well, if we are going to Dixie, we had better be getting ready." Robert Gardner, notified that he was selected and expected to go right away, "looked and spat, took off my hat, scratched my head, thought, and said, 'All right!'"

By December, 1867, more than two hundred wagons were on the site of St. George, and the "town" was two long rows of wagons facing each other, with a ditch between. Before there was a single house in it, St. George was an incorporated town. Crops failed year after year, while heat, sand, and wind rasped at the nerves of the colonists. Visiting St. George in 1870, Orson Huntsman observed, "I believe we were close to hell, for Dixie is the hottest place I ever was in." A Dixie poet sang:

> The wind like fury here does blow that when we plant or sow, sir,
> We place one foot upon the seed and hold it till it grows, sir.

The colonists, however, stuck to their task, growing cotton and fruit and, in the seventies, experimenting with silk. Erastus Snow was the apostle designated to build up Dixie, and if life was hard for him and the other men, it was heartbreaking for some of the women. David Cannon's young wife, living in a willow lean-to in place of the luxury she had known, told her husband that if he could find just one flower fit to pin on a lady's dress, she would try to be satisfied. In the spring he presented her with a bouquet of orchid-colored sego-lilies, and she thought them as beautiful as any flower she had ever seen.

Polygamists were hunted by U. S. deputy marshals in the eighties, and while warnings passed on from Silver Reef (*see above*) were helpful, the polygamists led a grim life. Charles Walker wrote in his journal during May, 1888, "This month and part of April I have been obliged to hide up from the U. S. Deputies who are seeking me night and day to arrest me and drag me to prison for obeying the commands of God my Eternal Father. . . . They summoned my wife and daughters to Beaver 120 miles distant to testify against me. And this in a Christian country where everyone has the right to worship God according to the dictates of his own conscience."

The difficulties over polygamy passed in the nineties, and St. George settled down to agricultural development. The lack of railroad facilities made high freight rates a serious handicap, but the improvement of US 91 as an arterial highway opened truck routes to Salt Lake

City and the Pacific Coast. With the rise of tourism, St. George's position half-way between Salt Lake City and Los Angeles, and as a point of departure for near-by scenic wonders, revitalized the town. In 1940 it is a brisk town, flavored by its romantic past, sitting warm under the sun. The large white "D" on a black ridge flanking the town is emblematic of Dixie Junior College, founded in 1911 as the L.D.S. Dixie Normal College, and given to the State as a junior college in 1933.

Among the distinguished personalities associated with St. George is Henry W. Bigler, West Virginia-born Mormon whose diary fixed for history the date of gold discoveries in California. Bigler came to St. George in 1875 and lived here for twenty-five years, dying in 1900 at the age of eighty-five. He was a school teacher and penman and never entered into plural marriage. As a young man he went to California with the Mormon Battalion, and in January, 1848, while working at Sutters Fort, recorded in his journal, "Monday 24th this day some kind of mettle was found in the tail race that looks like goald first discovered by James Martial [Marshall], the Boss of the Mill. Sunday 30 clear & has been all the last week our metal has been tride and prooves to be goald it is thought to be rich We have pict up more than a hundred dollars woth last week." In the late years of his life, he gave this significant diary page to the California Historical Society, by whom it is preserved in Sacramento.

DIXIE SUGAR LOAF (R), in view north of the town, is a capstone of solid rock surmounting vermilion bluffs—"as bald as the head of the prophet Elisha," George Washington Brimhall said of it in 1864.

The MORMON TEMPLE (*not open to non-Mormons*), resting on a slight elevation, is visible for miles. The squarely built white stucco temple (L) has three tiers of tall round-arched windows, surmounted by a row of oval windows. It has a well-proportioned cupola with a weather vane, and covers nearly an acre within a ten-acre tract. Spacious green lawns, bordered with a profusion of colorful plants, accent the snowy exterior of the structure and tend to magnify its size. Completed in 1877, this was the first Mormon Temple erected in Utah. At night, floodlights on the building produce a cameo-like effect. Built on swampy ground, the foundations consist of hundreds of tons of black volcanic rock, beaten down by an old cannon used as a horse-power pile driver.

The MORMON TABERNACLE (*open on application*), completed in 1871, is a red sandstone structure in the simple proportions of a New England meeting house. It has a four-faced clock on a square tower, surmounted with a slender white wooden steeple. The small-paned windows form a pattern characteristic of the days when glass had to be shipped long distances in less breakable sizes.

The WASHINGTON COUNTY COURTHOUSE (*open 9-12, 2-5 week-days*), is a square two-story red brick building of Colonial design with a classical portico enclosing an iron-railed balcony at the second-floor level. The cupolaed building was erected about 1869; cattle rustlers have been tried here, occupying dungeon-like cells in the basement.

The BRIGHAM YOUNG WINTER HOME (*private*), SE. corner 1st West and 2nd North Sts., is a rectangular two-story buff adobe building with a porch, standing behind a wooden pale fence and shaded by tall trees. A white-plastered one-story building at the east end of the house was used by Brigham Young as an office when he wintered in "Dixie." The house, which was built in 1869, was a center for social and religious gatherings during the winter.

The ANGUS CANNON HOUSE (*private*), 75 S. Main Street, is a two-story adobe brick residence on a stone base, built by a St. George bricklayer in 1863. The second-story treatment distinguishes the building: A central door and flanking windows reach above the eave-level and are capped by dormer-like extensions from the sloping roof. The wood-shingled roof is surmounted by end-chimneys.

The ERASTUS SNOW HOUSE (*private*), built in 1875, is one of several erected in St. George by "the Father of Utah's Dixie." It is a one-story adobe cottage stuccoed and marked in squares to simulate cut stone. The house has a diminutive classical portico with sumac bushes growing on each side, an end-chimney, and an ell extending back from the main structure. Emma Lucy Gates, Utah's best-known vocal artist, was born in this house.

The JED GATES HOUSE (*private*), is a one-story adobe structure erected in 1863-65. A simple little dwelling of pleasing lines, it is representative of the smaller polygamous houses, having a door and a window in the same relationship for each half of the house.

SANTA CLARA, 112.6 *m.* (2,625 alt., 249 pop.), is a clustering group of light brown adobe, red sandstone, and modern brick houses shaded by green trees. Long orchards stretch away over the red earth at the edge of town. Jacob Hamblin and others settled here in 1854. Seven years later the colony was strengthened by Swiss settlers sent to the Dixie Mission. The Swiss were industrious, and despite the catastrophic flood of 1862, which all but destroyed the town, Santa Clara prospered. There was, however, some sense of differentiation between the Anglo-Saxon settlers of St. George and the Swiss of Santa Clara; only in recent decades has this antagonism modified.

The MARTIN BAUMAN HOUSE (*private*), centrally placed on the main street of Santa Clara, is a diminutive one-story white-plastered adobe house with a weathered shingle roof and a stubby chimney. It seems almost too small to accommodate the full-sized door and two windows that open under the little front porch. At one end a shed-type roof, supplemented by a vine-grown pole arbor, provides a cool spot in summer. The house was built in 1874.

The red stone JACOB HAMBLIN HOUSE (*private*), 113.1 *m.*, is a two-story structure (R) of random stone masonry, with a shingle roof and brick chimney. Built in 1862, the house was sturdy enough to withstand Indian attack, and a large upstairs room was used for social occasions.

Jacob Hamblin, an active force in the settlement of southern Utah, dedicated himself to the promotion and maintenance of peace between white settlers and Indians. Born at Salem, Ohio, in 1819, he emigrated to Utah in 1850. Four years later he was sent on a mission to the Indians of southern Utah, where he spent most of his remaining busy years, befriending the Indians of southern Utah and northern Arizona. Major J. W. Powell, explorer of the Colorado River, leaves a description of Hamblin in a familiar situation—around an Indian campfire: "He is a silent, reserved man, and when he speaks, it is in a slow, quiet way, that inspires great awe. His talk is so low that they must listen attentively to hear, and they sit around him in death-like silence. When he finishes a measured sentence, the chief repeats it, and they all give a solemn grunt. . . ."

Hoffman Birney, in his *Zealots of Zion,* prints Hamblin's "Rules and Ways of Managing Indians"—a diplomatic code worthy of general emulation:

1—I never talk anything but the truth to them.

2—I think it useless to speak of things they cannot comprehend.

3—I strive by all means never to let them see me in passion.

4—Under no circumstances do I show fear, thereby showing to them that I have a sound heart and a straight tongue.

5—I never approach them in an austere manner, nor use more words than are necessary to convey my ideas, nor in a higher tone of voice than to be distinctly heard.

6—I always listen to them when they wish to tell their grievances, and redress their wrongs, however trifling, if possible. If I cannot, I let them know I have a desire to do so.

7—I never allow them to hear me use any obscene language, or take any unbecoming course with them.

8—I never submit to any unjust demands, or submit to coercion under any circumstances; thereby showing that I govern and am governed by the rule of right and not might.

9—I have tried to observe the above rules for the past twenty years, and it has given me a salutary influence wherever I have met with them. I believe if the rules I have mentioned were generally observed there would be but little difficulty on our frontiers with the Red Man.

Hamblin is buried in Alpine, Arizona, where he died August 21, 1886, while in hiding from "polyg hunters."

The SHIVWITS-SHEBIT INDIAN RESERVATION, 120.2 *m.,* covers an area of about 27,000 acres. Its eighty-odd Indian inhabitants are the sole remnant of numerous tribes of southern Utah, northern Arizona, and eastern Nevada. The Indians rely for a livelihood upon Government work and the sale of baskets, gloves, purses, belts, and moccasins. Food supplies are purchased in St. George, and the Indian children attend white schools. Willow-covered summer sheds and one-room winter houses of frame or rock have replaced the old brush tepees. There are four graduates of Carlisle College on the reservation, Thomas Mayo, Tony Tillohash, Brig. George, and Foster Charles Toab, all members of Glenn S. (Pop) Warner's famous football teams of the nineties. Tillohash worked with Dr. Edward Sapir in assembling a Government bulletin on American Indians.

Southwest of the reservation, US 91 winds through the Beaver Dam Mountains at an altitude of 4,600 feet at the summit, 128.1 *m.* Between the Beaver Dam Mountains and the Arizona Line, the highway penetrates an undulating, semi-desert country, a land of militant Spanish bayonet, of spiny cactus, of weirdly-shaped Joshua trees, and of dense thickets known to the Southwest as chaparral. In spring and summer the air resounds with the bleat of thousands of sheep, and canvas-covered sheep-wagons dot the landscape.

At 137.3 *m.* US 91 crosses the Arizona Line.

Section 9. ARIZONA LINE to NEVADA LINE; 17.1 m., US 91

Between Utah and Nevada, US 91 clips the northwestern corner of Arizona, a section of desert which belongs politically to Arizona, geographically to Utah, and economically to a handful of cattlemen and farmers whose cars may wear licenses of either State or of Nevada.

South of the UTAH LINE, 0 *m.,* the highway parallels Beaver Dam Wash and the Virgin River, along which occasional farms break the succession of desert rock, sand, and spined vegetation.

BEAVER DAM, 7.2 *m.,* on the banks of Beaver Dam Wash (so named in 1861 for beaver colonies found along the watercourse) consists of a lodge and service station. The lodge caters to tourists and cowboys, and has rooms, meals, a water-cooled lounge, and a swimming place in Beaver Dam Wash.

At 17.1 *m.,* US 91 crosses the Nevada Line (*see Nevada Guide*).

Tour 1 A

Ogden—Huntsville—Woodruff; 65.4 *m.,* State 39.

Asphalt-paved road between Ogden and Huntsville; stretches of oiled, graveled and improved dirt road between Huntsville and Woodruff; closed between Huntsville and Woodruff in winter.
Stores and service stations in towns only; tourist camps at intervals in western section, none in eastern section.

State 39, through Ogden Canyon, shortens the distance between Ogden and Woodruff by 40 miles as compared with the all-year route, US 30S (*see Tour 4a*). State 39 in winter opens the way to an increasingly popular winter sports area, and in summer provides access to cool canyons and mountains. The road, which attains an elevation of more than 9,000 feet, is flanked by well-equipped camping and picnicking areas. This road, completed in the middle 1930's, provides the only outlet for several small farming communities having a short growing season due to the high altitude.

In 1860 the fast-growing town of Ogden needed building materials that were available in Ogden Canyon. A toll road, with a gate at the mouth of the canyon, was used by freighters and farmers. Since the toll was removed in 1882 the canyon has developed as a recreational area and summer home site.

State 39 branches east from US 91 (*see Tour 1b*) in OGDEN, 0 *m.* (4,299 alt., 43,719 pop.) (*See Ogden*), and follows 25th Street to Harrison Boulevard, 1.2 *m.,* where it turns north (L) to a six-foot granite marker (R), 3.2 *m.,* commemorating the old TOLL ROAD. Charges ranged from 25 cents for a saddle horse to $1.50 for a heavy vehicle. Ogden Valley settlers were often without money for years at a time; they hauled oats, potatoes, livestock, and firewood to Ogden and traded it for merchandise. The same commodities were accepted as toll.

The MOUTH OF OGDEN CANYON, 3.3 *m.* (*Caution: patches of poison ivy, poison sumac, and stinging nettle throughout the canyon*), is just wide enough for the highway and the Ogden River. The towering cliffs in the canyon, several thousand feet high, seem to block the way, but a passageway continually opens through vertical masses of pink quartzite. In the more eroded deposits of blue-gray limestone and sandstone, the canyon broadens into fertile glades. From the steep green-patched slopes, jagged monoliths lean far out over the road. Before construction of the toll road Ogden Canyon was impassable, except for an Indian trail high on the south wall.

State 39, in the canyon, runs through the MOUNT OGDEN GAME PRESERVE (*no hunting allowed; no firearms permitted outside of car*), an area of 130 square miles. The east drainage of this preserve was set aside in 1937 for deer hunting by archers only. Deer are numerous, beaver build their dams along the streams, and bobcats, coyotes, and smaller animals inhabit the area. Ruffed grouse, blue (pine) grouse and an occasional pheasant are to be seen on the preserve. Many species of birds find refuge here, including chickadees, thrushes, bluebirds, magpies, finches, falcons, and others indigenous to mountainous country. The stream beds are forested mainly with alder, willow, and cottonwood; in the lower levels grow chokecherry, scrub oak, maple, and pine, while in the upper areas are aspen, juniper, and spruce. The delicate beauty of geraniums, violets, columbines, blue bells, daisies, and wild pansies is contrasted with the hardy and more colorful Indian paintbrush, yarrow, grape, "niggerhead," and wild mustard.

At high-water season, the large ARTIFICIAL WATERFALL (L), 3.5 *m.,* made by releasing excess water from a hole in the OGDEN WATERWORKS CONDUIT, high on the mountainside, cascades seventy-five feet down the face of the cliffs. Five men, working on the original line in 1896, were killed by premature explosions while tunneling through the cliffs.

BLACK POINT (L), 7.9 m., has a large black seam of phosphate, closely resembling soft coal, in a Z-shaped fold.

At 8.5 m. are the junctions with a dirt road and State 162.

1. Right on the dirt road through WHEELER CANYON, a wild, heavily timbered gorge, to SNOW BASIN (formerly Wheeler Basin), 4 m., a 7,000-acre scenic area under development for winter sports in 1940.

2. Left on State 162, asphalt-paved, across PINE VIEW DAM, which fronts PINE VIEW RESERVOIR (boating, bathing, fishing). The dam and reservoir, a $4,000,000 Federal Reclamation Project, stores supplementary water for irrigation of more than 60,000 acres between Brigham City and South Ogden. A giant suspension syphon, a novel engineering feat, at the mouth of Ogden Canyon lifts the water to the HIGHLINE CANAL, which distributes water to five towns. Construction of the dam, an earth and rock structure, was begun in 1936. Beneath the artificial lake formed by the dam are fifty-one artesian wells, the principal source of Ogden's domestic water supply; the water flows through pipes under the reservoir bed. The deepest well extends 204 feet below the bottom of the lake. Sail and speedboat races are held on the reservoir in July, drawing as many as 10,000 spectators. The lake has a shoreline of more than 20 miles, upon which is parking space for 1,000 cars, on a peninsula west of Huntsville in a 60-acre pier and dock. Below the dam is a ten-acre picnic site.

EDEN, 4.1 m. (4,950 alt., 510 pop.), settled in 1859, is a quiet rural village. Entering this fertile valley through rough mountain passes, Mormon settlers thought they had found a garden of Eden, and so named it.

At 4.8 m. is the junction with a dirt road; R. here to PATIO SPRINGS, 2.6 m. (swimming; open July 1-Oct. 15), with a pool of clear cold water in a mountainous setting.

EL PATIO DEL RANCHO, 3.5 m. (open July-Oct.), on the dirt road, is the only dude ranch in the immediate vicinity of Ogden.

LIBERTY, 7.8 m. (5,110 alt., 280 pop.), on State 162, a farming hamlet, was settled in 1892.

At 8 m. is the junction (L) with a county road to North Ogden (see Tour 1b).

At 10.1 m. is the northern terminus of State 162 and the southern terminus of a county road to Avon (see Tour 1b).

HUNTSVILLE, 13.4 m. (4,920 alt., 496 pop.), is typical of the older Mormon villages, the people having their homes in the town and their farms beyond the city limits. Captain Jefferson Hunt, member of the Mormon Battalion (see History and Salt Lake City), founded the town in 1860 under the direction of Brigham Young. A temporary water supply was obtained by digging a ditch to the South Fork of Ogden River. When a band of Indians told the settlers to leave the valley or they would pollute the water, Captain Hunt told the Indians that at their first suspicious act he would burn all the water in the canyons. When they looked incredulous he seized a dipperful of colorless liquid—probably alcohol—and burned it before their eyes. The Indians resumed friendly relations.

An account by William Halls in the Deseret News for August 16, 1866, tells of the arrival of a numerous band of Shoshoni, led by their noted chief, Washakie: ". . . about 1,000 Indians, men, squaws, and papooses, came into this valley last Thursday, and camped a mile west of this settlement. . . .

"President [of the local stake] F. A. Hammond called for a donation to be brought in next day, and invited the chiefs and all the Indians to come on to the public square and receive presents. Yesterday morning early they formed in procession and marched slowly, dancing at intervals, to the public square . . . and the Indians sung and played on the square . . . and concluded by a sham fight. . . .

"After the performances they came to the bowery and received four beeves, nine sheep, several sacks of flour and from 50 to 75 bushels of potatoes, carrots, beets, turnips, etc. . . .

"They have gone away feeling well, and we feel well, for though their company is very agreeable, our philanthropy is so large that we are willing their presence should benefit other settlements as well as ours."

The MARY DILWORTH HAMMOND MONUMENT, on the Huntsville school grounds, honors the first school teacher (*see Education*) in Utah. She married and moved to Huntsville, where she resided until her death in 1877.

The MARY HEATHMAN SMITH MONUMENT, NW. corner of the Huntsville public square, a ten-foot white concrete shaft with a bronze plaque, honors the pioneer woman who was "lovingly known as Granny Smith. . . . She came to Utah in 1862 . . . serving as Doctor, Surgeon, Midwife, and Nurse for thirty years. . . . She brought into the world more than 1,500 babies."

The MAGPIE PICNIC GROUND (R), 19.2 *m.,* the SOUTH FORK PICNIC GROUND (R), 20.3 *m.,* and the MEADOW PICNIC GROUND (R), 21.1 *m.,* are maintained by the U. S. Forest Service.

LIMESTONE SPRING (R), 29.3 *m.,* heads Beaver Creek in the low-water season. Colonies of beaver have dams and brush houses just below the spring.

At 31 *m.* is a junction with a rough, unimproved dirt road.

Left on this road through ANT VALLEY, so called because of the great swarms of these insects that rise from the anthills in June, when they grow wings and take off on their mating flight. The males die after mating, and the fertile queens establish new colonies.

At 1.9 *m.* is the junction with a dirt road. Left on this road, the SITE OF THE SUNSET MINE is passed, just before reaching the ghost town of LA PLATA (Sp: silver), 25 *m.* (6,932 alt.). Rich galena ore was taken out of the Sunset Mine and a heavy rush started in the early 1890's. The town at one time had a bank, a newspaper, stores, saloons and gambling halls, and was widely publicized by "Coin" Harvey (*see Ogden*). The vein "played out," the inhabitants departed, and only a few broken-down shacks remain. The area is visited only by trappers, campers, and hunters, who report large bucks and an occasional bear.

At 16 *m.* is the junction (L) with a dirt road through BLACKSMITH FORK CANYON (*see Tour 1b*).

At 17 *m.,* on the main side tour, is the junction with State 145, which runs to LAKETOWN (5,989 alt., 408 pop.) (*see Tour 2a*).

State 39 winds through groves of fluttering aspen and sharp-pointed fir as it passes MONTE CRISTO PEAK (R), 39.9 *m.* (9,138 alt.), and crosses the highest summit (9,008 alt.), 42.5 *m.,* with magnificent views of distant mountains; the Uintas can be seen 100 miles south-east, with the highest peaks in the State.

MONTE CRISTO RECREATION GROUNDS (R), 43.6 *m.* (*tables, stoves, water, campground*), occupy land improved and maintained by the Forest Service in a glade surrounded by spruce, fir, balsam, and aspen. There is a pine-enclosed outdoor amphitheater, a playground, and a mile-square arboretum.

Through WALTON CANYON, 50.4 *m.*, the road winds along a willow-bordered stream, passing beaver dams at 51.2 *m.*, 52.6 *m.*, and 53.4 *m.* The country (*open range—watch for cattle*) to the east is a series of rolling sagebrush hills.

At 65.4 *m.* is the junction with State 3 in WOODRUFF (6,344 alt., 510 pop.) (*see Tour 2a*).

Tour 1B

Murray—Brighton; 22.2 *m.*, State 173, State 152, and Big Cotton-wood Road.

Asphalt-paved between Murray and west boundary of Wasatch National Forest, elsewhere graveled; sometimes closed in winter after heavy snows. Accommodations at Murray and Brighton only; campgrounds in canyon at short intervals.

The route passes through irrigated truck farms and orchards to wind over a benchland dotted with summer lodges of wealthy Salt Lake City people, and enters Big Cottonwood Canyon. In places the hard rugged walls of the glacier-cut canyon loom forbiddingly, but elsewhere they widen into tree-grown and flower-strewn glades. The turbulent stream rushes over rocks or winds between groves of birch, maple, aspen, and cottonwood, below the upward sweep of gnarled pines and craggy peaks. The canyon's streams, and mountain lakes high between the peaks, are stocked with fish; ski-lifts operate on the mountains in winter; camp and picnic grounds are numerous; bridle paths and hiking trails lead to craggy heights and hidden lakes.

State 173 branches east from US 91, 0 *m.*, at a point 0.2 miles south of Murray (*see Tour 1d*).

At 3.9 *m.* is the eastern terminus of State 173 and the junction with State 152. The main route turns R., following State 152.

The OLD MILL CLUB (L), 7.3 *m.* (*open weekdays on application to caretaker next door*), reconstructed in 1927 from ruins of a stone and adobe paper mill built by the Mormons in 1881, is a dance hall surrounded by trees and canyon shrubbery. Shortage of paper was keenly felt by the pioneers, who imported their supply from the East or from the Pacific Coast by wagon freight. To remedy this situation, Brigham Young imported $8,500 worth of machinery in 1850, and the first paper was made in Temple Square. Rags for paper-making were scarce, and the *Deseret News* issued pleas for rags, such as the following, in 1850: "Save your rags everybody in Deseret; old wagon covers, tents, quilts, shirts, etc., are wanted for paper. The most efficient measures are in progress to put a paper mill in operation the coming season in this valley and all your rags will be wanted." Several times the *News* was forced to issue "half sheets" and on August 10, 1854, the paper stated: "Doubtless the readers of the News [have noticed] that the paper has at last got a rather dark shade, and we do not fancy its color any better than you do. . . . But dark gray is better than no paper, which will soon be the case unless every person in our settlements throughout Utah gathers up and brings . . . all their paper rags." This objectionable shade of paper was used until October, 1854, when the *Deseret News* issued this statement: "We are happy in being enabled, by the arrival of our year's supply in the Church Train, to again issue the News on white paper, for we think our industrious subscribers will now be able to read their paper by candle light."

The original machinery was transferred from the mill at Sugarhouse to the New Granite Paper Mill (now the Old Mill Club), where paper was made from old paper, wood pulp, and straw. Following completion of the railroad, with the reduction in freight rates, the local mill was abandoned. In 1893 the building was partially destroyed by fire.

At 7.6 *m.* is the junction with Wasatch Boulevard at the mouth of Big Cottonwood Canyon. State 152 terminates here, and the route continues on Big Cottonwood Road.

At 8 3 *m.* the route crosses the west boundary of WASATCH NATIONAL FOREST. East of here the entire canyon is a game preserve (*no firearms permitted*).

STORM MOUNTAIN PICNIC AREA (L), 10.5 *m.* (*camping, picnicking*), is named for the massive, rocky peak (R).

The STAIRS POWER PLANT RESERVOIR (L), 10.7 *m.* (*rainbow and native trout*), was built about 1897 for a power plant. It has a storage capacity of twenty-seven acre-feet, and supplements Salt Lake City's culinary water.

East of MAXFIELD LODGE (R), 10.8 *m.,* the road winds around a series of S-curves, known locally as the CAT STAIRS, making a 2,000-foot change of altitude in three miles.

HIDDEN FALLS PICNIC AREA (L), 12 *m.,* is a picnic ground maintained by the U. S. Forest Service.

At 12.4 *m.* is the junction with a hiking trail.

Right on this trail, through Mill "B" South Fork Canyon, so named for sawmill "B" which once stood there, to LAKE BLANCHE, LAKE FLORENCE,

Town and City

Town and City

ROTUNDA, STATE CAPITOL

Highton: F. W. A.

STATE CAPITOL, SALT LAKE CITY

AIRVIEW OF TEMPLE SQUARE, SALT LAKE CITY

STATE CAPITOL

Courtesy Smith Printing Co.

UTAH STATE AGRICULTURAL COLLEGE, LOGAN

HIGH SCHOOL
GYMNASIUM, SPRINGVI

Lee A. Olsen

COMMENCEMENT PARADE, UNIVERSITY OF UTAH

MAESER MEMORIAL
BUILDING, BRIGHAM
YOUNG UNIVERSITY,
PROVO

DOWNTOWN OGDEN

WENDOVER, A DESERT TOWN ON THE NEVADA LINE

MAIN STREET, BRIGHAM CITY

SEAGULL MONUMENT, SALT LAKE CITY

and LAKE LILLIAN, 3 *m.*, limpid bodies of water at the foot of guardian peaks.

MOSS LEDGE FALLS PICNIC AREA (L), 12.8 *m.* (*picnicking, camping*), is a Forest Service camp among mountain trees and shrubbery.

North of the Moss Ledge Falls Picnic area, a hiking trail leads to Moss LEDGE FALLS, 0.7 *m.*, a tiny cascade of cold water feeding a crystal pool in a little mountain meadow.

The SPRUCES CAMP (R), 17.5 *m.* (*cabins, tents, stores and other camping facilities*), sheltered by evergreens at the base of lofty mountains, is a non-profit project operated by the Salt Lake City Chamber of Commerce and the U. S. Forest Service. It has a public shelter, with a fireplace, large enough to accommodate 250 persons; a public lunch room with space for 32 persons to eat their own lunches; six sleeping cabins for rent at 50¢ per person per night; and is equipped with electric lights and a telephone.

SILVER FORK CANYON (R), 19.3 *m.,* was the scene of a fatal snowslide in the 1880's. Eighteen men with horses, "rawhiding" ore (*see Transportation*) from a neighboring mine, were buried under tons of snow. Only two men escaped. Five bodies remained buried until spring. Big Cottonwood mines, formerly large producers, now yield sparingly, on account of underground water.

MOUNTAIN PARK CAMP (R), 20.2 *m.* (*camping, picnicking*), is maintained by the Forest Service; the canyon widens here, and the peaks surrounding Brighton are visible.

BRIGHTON, 22.2 *m.* (*hiking, swimming, fishing in summer; skiing in winter*), is a mountain resort (8,730 alt.) nestled in a bowl-like valley almost surrounded by craggy mountain peaks. The buildings are log cabins, log hotels and inns, log stores, and a log post office. The inns remain open all year and skiiers crowd the slopes and ski-lifts on weekends. A favorite overland ski trip is by a trail running northeast to PARK CITY (*see Tour 6b*). Surrounding Brighton are Sunset Peak, Mount Majestic, Mount Wolverine, Mount Millicent, and other lesser peaks. Water melting from the snows of these peaks and running into the Brighton basin provide a major portion of Salt Lake City's culinary supply. Hiking trails radiate in all directions to numerous lakes, set in flower-sprinkled mountain meadows. The lakes include Silver Lake, Lake Solitude, Twin Lakes, Lake Mary, Lake Martha, and Lake Catherine.

On cold winter nights at this altitude it is sometimes possible to see the aurora borealis. Wave upon wave of shimmering vari-colored lights pulsate across the midnight heavens. At times the whole celestial arch is tinted blood red, crags and peaks stand out as though cut from cardboard, and the snow glows ruddily. At other times, lambent fires weave back and forth across the heavens, or beat like summer lightnings, low on the horizon. Again, the glowing natural wonder appears a fan outspread, from which tongues, now rose-red, now dull green, pale gold, or silver, flick fitfully zenithward.

The MORMON TENTH ANNIVERSARY CELEBRATION MONUMENT, in Brighton, a natural granite shaft, bears an inscription describing the affair, in 1857, which was interrupted by news that a Federal army was on the way to Utah (*see History*).

Sir Richard F. Burton, who visited Brighton in 1860, noted that "All persons are forbidden to smoke segars or pipes, or kindle fires at any place in the kanyon, except on the camp-ground." He described the Brighton area as "a kind of punch-bowl, formed by an amphitheatre of frowning broken mountains, highest and most snowy on the southeast and west. . . . The level ground, perhaps one mile in diameter, was a green sward, dotted with blocks and boulders." The fish of the area, he said, were "principally mountain trout and the gymnotus eel."

Tour 1C

Junction with US 91—Midvale—Copperton—Upper Bingham—Utah Copper Mine; 19.6 *m.,* State 48.

Oil-surfaced road.
All types of accommodations in larger towns.

State 48 stretches toward the Oquirrh Range (Paiute, shining mountains; pronounced O-ker) over an irrigated and dry-farming country broken by occasional fields of yellow sunflowers and patches of lavender skunkweed. The mountains loom blue-gray, with the smoke of the smelters hanging motionless in the ravines. The highway gradually climbs to a bench of old Lake Bonneville, and, rounding a hill, enters Bingham Canyon.

State 48 branches west from US 91, at MIDVALE JUNCTION (*see Tour 1d*), 0 *m.,* and extends through a farming area.

MIDVALE, 1.1 *m.* (4,354 alt., 2,900 pop.), a smelting town on the east side of Jordan River, was settled in 1852. Originally a farming community, Midvale forsook the plow for the furnace when smelters and concentration plants were built on its outskirts.

The UNITED STATES SMELTING AND REFINING PLANT (R), 1.7 *m.* (*open workdays 9-5*), one of the first plants to operate as a smokeless smelter, occupies a steel and concrete building that has been enlarged several times since it was built in 1924; the plant handles 1,600 tons of ore a day and has a crushing and flotation plant as well as a smelter.

"Preferential flotation," says the *Mining Industry in Utah,* issued by the Salt Lake City Chamber of Commerce in 1939, "is one of the important metallurgical advances made in the past several decades and it is noteworthy that Utah has two companies that were well in the lead in the adoption of this process. . . .

"The company's mill is so designed that ores of four different characteristics, requiring different reagents in each case, can be treated concurrently to produce lead, zinc and iron concentrates, each separate from the other.

"The lead concentrates are hauled to the smelter proper where they are mixed with fluxes, roasted and finally sent to the blast furnaces to be reduced to metallic lead. Beginning with the preferential flotation process and continuing through the various stages of reduction in the smelter, large quantities of various chemicals, coke, scrap-iron, silica and limerock are required and must be used in accurate proportions with the ores, concentrates and roast products.

"The associated metallic minerals, zinc, silver and gold may be considered among the by-products of a lead smelter. Zinc, which some years ago was detrimental to the smooth operation of a lead smelter . . . is today commercially recovered from the sulphide ores by the flotation process. Gold and silver are recovered only through further processing and refining.

"The Midvale Smelter was also the first to successfully accomplish baghousing [filtering] of both roaster and blast furnace gases for the removal of the suspended solids. Retreatment of these baghouse products results in the recovery of an additional by-product—cadmium, one of the zinc series of metals now replacing nickel for plating because it tarnishes less rapidly."

West of Midvale State 48 climbs grass-grown benchland to the mouth of Bingham Canyon.

COPPERTON, 11.7 m. (5,617 alt., 800 pop.), a model mining town with copper-shingled, copper-screened brick houses, was built by operators of the Bingham mine. Its gardens and tree-shaded lawns contrast with barren hills roundabout.

The town of BINGHAM CANYON, 16.2 m. (6,100 alt., 2,957 pop.), slouches up a narrow V-shaped gulch, sprawls over the steep sidehills, and finally collapses near the enormous open-pit mine of the Utah Copper Company. The single street meanders up the canyon, framed by wooden houses and business buildings. Dwellings rise abruptly from the street, and second-story balconies lean precariously over the sidewalks. Unpainted lumber shacks are strewn carelessly over the canyonside, and here and there is a handkerchief-sized plot of grass. There is little or no class distinction in Bingham, where portly matrons chat amiably with girls from the "houses." Twice a day an ear-splitting whistle blows, warning of a coming blast at the pit. Housewives grab anything that might be jarred loose, including their children, for when the blast comes, the whole town bucks like a bronco. The night blasting can be heard in Salt Lake City—a deep rumble coming weirdly at three in the morning.

Forests of red pine, maple, and scrub oak grew on the hills around

Bingham when the pioneers came. Sanford and Thomas Bingham, sent out to settle by Brigham Young in 1848, farmed the canyon, and their herds grazed among the trees. Sawmills sprang up in the canyon, and soon the generously timbered slopes were completely cut off. The Bingham boys turned to prospecting, but Brigham Young put a stop to that: "Instead of hunting gold, let every man go to work at raising wheat, oats, barley, corn and vegetables and fruit in abundance that there may be plenty in the land." So the Bingham boys covered their ore-finds and returned to farming.

George Ogilvie, hearing of Colonel Patrick E. Connor's interest in mining, sent a galena ore sample to the soldier in 1863. The lead ore was rich in gold and silver, and Connor issued a letter on War Department stationery informing the public of Utah's wealth, and insuring all comers protection of the army. In the ensuing rush for claims, women staked out "the Women's Lode," subject to the same conditions as those of the men.

Lack of transportation and expense of materials almost caused abandonment of the raw new town. Discovery of placer mines saved the community. The richest placer was Clay Bar, which produced $100,000 by 1868. The Clay brothers gave up the bar at water level, and reworked the tailings dumps, which netted them $7 to $15 a day each. In the tailings Dan Clay found what is said to be Utah's largest gold nugget, valued at $128. Reports from the Clay Bar attracted other placer miners, and by 1868 more than $2,000,000 in gold had been removed. Placer mining died out after 1870, when completion of the Bingham and Camp Floyd Railroad revived interest in lode mining.

During the seventies the population jumped from 276 to more than 1,000, and substantial frame buildings replaced ramshackle shanties. Since the population was predominantly male, recreation was robust. At nightly track meets men hurdled powder boxes, broad jumped on the dumps, and pole vaulted with lead pipes. Boxing matches were weekly events, and the men fought to a standstill to the music of mouth organ, zither, and jewsharp. Gambling gradually replaced more virile forms of activity, and many miners deserted the mines for the softer life of a professional gambler. Faro, poker, craps, and roulette were popular, and gambling houses ran on shifts, staying open twenty-four hours a day. Thirty saloons were in operation by 1900, favorites being the "16 to 1" and the "Old Crow." In later years, free movies were introduced in the saloons, and patrons stood in darkened rooms to view the miracle. Vaudeville troupes performed in some of the saloons, forerunners of floor shows, and a piano was always in evidence.

The Buel and Bateman mill, first in the district, built in the early 1870's, was a highly successful enterprise. Bristol and Bateman of Nevada erected the Winnamuck smelter in 1872-73, and lode mining came into its own. The first concentrating plant, built in 1874 by A. H. Bemis for treatment of sulphide lead ore, gave the camp another boost. There were rich strikes at Yosemite No. 1, Brooklyn, No-You-Dont, Highland Boy, and Boston Consolidated.

Lead and silver mining flourished during the period 1880-96, and anyone who fooled around with copper, an inferior metal, was considered "tetched." The depression of 1893, which resulted in lowered silver, gold and lead prices, almost closed the camp. Samuel Newhouse and Thomas Weir of the Highland Boy built a cyanide plant in Carr Fork Gulch to extract gold, but large amounts of copper sulphide in the ore called for too much cyanide, and the plant shut down with terrific losses. Newhouse went East for money while Weir dug deeper, uncovering a vein of 18 per cent copper. The first shipment of copper ore was made in 1896. The Highland Boy was merged in 1899 with the Utah Consolidated, controlling interest being held by Standard Oil of New York; $12,000,000 changed hands, and John D. Rockefeller became one of the chief holders of the Utah mine. A smelter was built at Murray, but dissension with farmers forced the company to erect an aerial tramway from the mine to the smelter at Pine Canyon, near Tooele. Meantime, Colonel Enos A. Wall was quietly buying copper holdings and relocating old claims around Bingham. Secret tests revealed that the ore ran from 3 to 40 per cent copper. By 1896 Wall had acquired 200 acres, spent $20,000 in exploration, and was ready to develop. Bingham wiseacres ridiculed Wall for his interest in copper, and referred to his holdings as "Wall's rocks." Wall, keeping his mouth shut, was experimenting for a process to extract low-grade copper at a profit. He met defeat at nearly every turn, but Captain Joseph De Lemar, an old friend, finally bought an interest and took a six months' lease for $375,000. Lemar brought two young engineers, Daniel C. Jackling, now (1940) president of the Utah Copper Company, and Robert C. Gemmell from Mercur to investigate the property. Their joint report, published in 1899 (*see Mining*), changed the history of copper mining. Lemar took another option for $250,000, then lost interest. Jackling, convinced that large-scale surface mining was the only solution, interested Charles MacNeill and Spencer Penrose of the United States Reduction and Refining Company in his theory. A complicated deal was made, which gave Wall $385,000 for 55 per cent of his stock, MacNeill and Penrose buying Lemar's fourth interest. The Utah Copper Company was organized in 1903, and the following year erected a pilot plant. Underground mining methods were used at first, but Jackling's insistence on surface mining bore fruit in 1907, when plans were made for steam shovel operation. A merger with Boston Consolidated and Nevada Consolidated, in 1910, created a $100,000,000 copper company. For bringing about this merger Samuel Untermyer, a New York lawyer, was paid a fee of $775,000, the largest fee ever paid an attorney to date.

The smelter of the United States mine at Murray also ran into farmer trouble, according to an article published in the *Bingham Bulletin* in 1907: "The farmers of Salt Lake Valley now seem as anxious to have the smelters remain as they were a little while ago to give the 23 sign ['skidoo']. Just so soon as they found their bluff was taken in earnest, there was much hurrying to and from across the valley, and the prospects of seeing the easy money they had been getting from the smelters fade away, did not appeal to the gentleman with a bunch of whiskers on his chin. For the last four years the smelters have paid in damage suits, in and out of court, a half million dollars annually."

With the beginning of the century, the Denver & Rio Grande Western Railroad laid a standard gauge road to a point three-quarters of a mile from the camp. This did away with long hauls into the valley, and passenger trains ran daily to Salt Lake City, until they were replaced by auto stages. From 1912 to 1928 the camp underwent a period of electrification, including a lighting system, electric shovels, and locomotives.

A State law was passed in 1896 requiring an eight-hour day for underground and smelter employees. Safety measures were introduced —"hard boiled" hats, "hard toed" shoes, and body protectors. Except for minor violations of the eight-hour law, Bingham had no labor troubles until September, 1912, when the Western Federation of Miners organized the camp, and the miners struck for a fifty-cent raise. The National Guard dispatched fifty sharpshooters to Bingham, and 400 local men were deputized and armed. Strikebreakers coming in from other communities were sometimes manhandled. Railroad crossings and mines were floodlighted, saloons and gambling halls were closed. By the end of October half of the men had returned to work, and late in November, D. C. Jackling announced the mines were running "full blast." Grievances had been adjusted, but the union was not then recognized.

Rafael Lopez, a Mexican strikebreaker, came to Bingham during the strike. He stayed on afterward, leasing the Apex mine. One November night he beat up a Greek for molesting some girls, and was put in jail. After that, he had little use for officers of the law. When he was let out, Lopez got into an argument with Juan Valdez over, some say politics, some say a girl. Valdez drew his knife, and Lopez shot him. Lopez went home, got his rifle and ammunition, and left town. Four officers trailed him across forty miles of snow fields to a ranch on the edge of Utah Lake. Lopez shot and killed three of them. A posse, sent to the ranch, found only empty cartridges. Lopez backtracked to Bingham, and forced a friend, Stefano, to give him a rifle, ammunition, food, clothing, and bedding, which he made Stefano carry to the entrance of the Apex mine. Stefano hurried to the police, and guards were sent to the mine. The officers decided to smoke him out. The mine was closed down, forcing 200 men out of work. Outlets were sealed, bales of hay were placed at the only opening left, and set on fire. While officers were pushing bales into place, three shots rang out. One man fell dead, another wounded. More shots were fired as the posse tried to recover the bodies. "Finally on December 1," Miss Beatrice Spendlove writes in her thesis, *The History of Bingham Canyon,* "the burning of lump sulphur, damp gun powder, and cayenne pepper was begun. The fires were kept burning five days." The mine was ransacked, but all that was ever found of Lopez was his bedding and clothing. He was never apprehended.

Fires, cloudbursts, landslides, and snowslides have always menaced Bingham. The frame buildings make a fine fire hazard, and although they have been replaced somewhat in later years, a $400,000 conflagration almost wiped out the town in 1932. Starting in an old theater, supposedly by two children burning discarded film, the fire roared down the canyon, consuming everything in sight. Furniture carried into the streets was burned before it could be moved again. Stills blew up, flooding the streets with a questionable grade of liquor. When the fire was brought under control, Bingham was little more than charred ruins. Snowslides almost wiped out the little suburb of Highland Boy in 1926. The *Salt Lake Tribune* reported that "Seventeen dwellings and a three-story boarding house were swept from their foundations, and buried beneath the rushing thousands of tons of rock, snow, ice and other debris." Thirty-nine people lost their lives. A cloudburst hit Markham Gulch, part of Bingham, in 1930, burying houses, cars, and business buildings. Traffic was halted on highways and railroads. Land, loosened by water, slid down the steep-sided canyon; the damage amounted to $400,000. New fire regulations, retaining walls, and other safety measures have lessened the dangers somewhat.

In 1940 Bingham took pride in its Dr. Russell G. Frazier, surgeon-physician with Rear Admiral Richard E. Byrd's Government-sponsored Antarctic expedition. Movie houses and beer parlors had replaced saloons and gambling houses, and the old unruly spirit has been transformed into easy-going tolerance. Miss Spendlove suggests that "the towering mountains confining the people within such narrow limits have an effect in producing a closer bond of good fellowship."

West of the Bingham business district, the road passes through the north portal, 16.3 *m.*, of the BINGHAM TUNNEL, an arched 6,988-foot bore costing $1,400,000. The electrically lighted, cement-lined tunnel has a railed sidewalk for pedestrians and accommodates one lane of auto traffic. It carries county sewage lines and is ventilated by fresh-air ducts. The tunnel connects the town of Bingham with Upper Bingham.

UPPER BINGHAM, 17.7 *m.* (6,700 alt.), formerly known as Copperfield, was given its present name to avoid confusion with Copperton (*see above*).

The UTAH COPPER MINE, 19.6 *m.* (*open 9-5 workdays; guides*), presents a colorful view of the gray, green and red mountain, which is literally being eaten away by electric shovels that bite away seven tons of ore at a time. The mountain, or what is left of it, rises like a huge stadium, its levels like bleacher seats for giants. Ant-like electric shovels scurry back and forth on tracks along these levels, and snake-like ore trains crawl between the shovels and waiting railroad cars. With one long and three short blasts of the whistle, all work ceases, and charges of explosives are fired. There is a tremendous roar, and tons of earth avalanche downward over all levels. The mining and stripping area, in 1940, measured 650 acres, and the depth from the top level was 1,500 feet. Pit dimensions are constantly changing as earth is removed.

Although the copper content of the Bingham ores averages only about 1 per cent, or twenty pounds to the ton, the mining, transportation, and smelting of these ores is one of Utah's most important industries. Utah Copper produces more than 90 per cent of the copper mined in Utah, and one-twelfth of the total production of the world. Since its discovery, more than 200,000,000 tons of ore have been mined.

The mines of the West Mountain District have paid more than $200,000,000 in dividends and pay more than $60,000,000 annually in taxes. Production figures in the *Mineral Yearbook* for 1939 show that these mines in 1938 produced 129,388 ounces of gold, 3,671 ounces of silver, 212,098,500 pounds of copper, 82,668,239 pounds of lead, 46,192,937 pounds of zinc, valued at $33,707,918. The mines are said to have enough ore bodies to operate until 1990.

At the mine is the western terminus of State 48.

Tour 1D

Beaver—Milford—(Ely, Nevada); State 21.
Beaver to Nevada Line, 115.3 m.

Route intersected by Union Pacific R.R. at Milford; roughly paralleled by Union Pacific R.R. between Milford and Newhouse.
Oiled and graded dirt road. Open all year; winter traveling sometimes difficult in western section. Gas, water and traveling supplies should be checked before traversing road between Milford and Baker, Nevada.
Accommodations at Milford.

State 21, between Beaver and Milford, passes through the south end of the wooded Mineral Mountains, and through partly cultivated valleys. The Beaver Ridge, used primarily for irrigation, parallels the route in this area. West of Milford the highway crosses broad desert valleys, and skirts the southern foothills of the San Francisco Mountains. The towns are small and populated chiefly by miners and farmers. Some of the country appears desolate and barren, but there are a number of fertile irrigated valleys and some good range land.

State 21 branches west from US 91 in BEAVER, 0 m. (5,970 alt., 1,673 pop.) (*see Tour 1e*), between rows of tall black willow trees.

ROCKY FORD RESERVOIR (R), 12.2 m., four miles long and half a mile wide, impounds water from the Beaver River for irrigation of adjacent farming areas.

At 18.9 *m.* is the junction with a dirt road.

Right on this road to the junction, 4.5 *m.,* with a dirt road; L. on this road to the LINCOLN MINE, 0.1 *m.,* formerly called the Rollins Mine for James A. Rollins, who discovered it in 1858. Said to have been an old Spanish mine, Rollins worked it for the almost pure lead ore. Rollins erected a small Mexican style "furnace" in 1858 and extracted small quantities of pure lead, which was molded into bullets.

At 19 *m.* is the junction with an asphalt road.

Left on this road to MINERSVILLE, 0.3 *m.* (5,625 alt., 537 pop.), center of a small but rich agricultural district, where four crops of alfalfa are harvested annually; other parts of the State usually get only three cuttings. Corn, fruits, and early garden vegetables are supplementary products. Pioneer adobe and log houses stand among more recent frame and brick structures.

MILFORD, 32.6 *m.* (4,966 alt., 1,517 pop.), is a division point for the Union Pacific Railroad, a farming center, and an outfitting place for cattlemen and miners. The main street is two blocks long, with business houses and cafes on one side, and the Union Pacific depot on the other. Culinary water is obtained from municipally-owned artesian wells, and irrigation water is diverted from the Beaver River.

For several years after its settlement in 1870, Milford was a straggling frontier town, its business section consisting mostly of mine supply stores, dependent entirely upon the mines at Frisco and Newhouse. Ore seekers traveling to and from the "diggin's" in 1880 forded the Beaver River below a stamp mill. The crossing, known as the "mill ford," suggested a name for the town. When ore production fell off in the eighties, Milford lost heavily. Agriculture and railroading gradually took up the slack.

The UNION PACIFIC DEPOT (R), a yellow stucco structure, flanked by landscaped lawns, is a prominent landmark of the town. Sheltered by a pergola on the north lawn is an old stagecoach, one of the first used in this vicinity.

The twelve-bed MILFORD DISTRICT HOSPITAL (L), a converted dwelling near the western outskirts, serves a ninety-mile radius.

FRISCO (R), 47.8 *m.* (7,318 alt.), married to the Horn Silver Mine, died when the mine closed down after a cave-in. The mine was reopened in 1928, but the town was not rebuilt. With the exception of three dilapidated houses, a deserted school, the ruins of the company store, and a "match box" railroad station, Frisco is little more than a cross that marks the spot. "Desert amethysts"—bits of broken glass—are scattered through the old town, remnants of miners' whoopee and headaches long past.

Discovered accidentally in 1875 by two prospectors, James Ryan and Samuel Hawkes of Pioche, Nevada, the Horn Silver Mine, on the hill a mile west of Frisco, was the richest silver producer in Utah.

From a hole 900 feet long, 400 feet wide, and 900 feet deep, more than $54,000,000 was taken in ten years.

In a copyrighted article published (1936) in the *Salt Lake Mining Review* (partially reproduced by special permission), Murray Schick wrote:

> How many, for instance, know that the Horn Silver put a celebrated financier on his feet after he had lost his fortune trying to finance the building of the Northern Pacific railroad. That the first promoter of the Horn Silver died on a train as he was taking the financier to look at the mine. That Jay Gould, personally, had a hand in extending the first railroad to the mine. . . . Jay Cooke was the J. Pierpont Morgan of his day. His fame rested chiefly on his success in selling United States government bonds to finance the Civil War. . . . 'Solid as Cooke's bank' was a popular metaphor. . . . Cooke . . . committed himself, in 1870, to raise millions to build a railroad from Duluth to Seattle. . . . The . . . depression of 1873 put a strain on Cooke's banking business no bank could withstand, and it closed its doors, the railroad was stopped. . . . No one, Cooke least of all, could picture him in connection with a pair of sun-browned prospectors he had never seen piloting a burro train through sage-clad mountains twenty-five hundred miles away. . . . Water rather than minerals induced them to spread their blankets at a water hole in the San Francisco mountains called 'Squaw Springs.' Loath to leave the water, they scrutinized the neighborhood carefully.
>
> 'This ledge looks kind of good,' said one as he drove his pick into a limestone outcrop. It was good. Beneath the weathered surface galena ore glistened in the sun. . . . They agreed it was a 'bonanza' and scratched that name on a location notice.

They sank a twenty-five-foot shaft in solid ore, then sold out to Matt Cullen, Dennis Ryan, and A. G. Campbell, for $25,000. These three men sank the shaft to 280 feet and took out 25,000 tons averaging $100 a ton, and changed the name to Horn Silver, for its resemblance in texture and coloring to the horn of an animal; old-timers say it was so rich it could be whittled, and the slivers curved like the horn of a mountain sheep.

> Lycurgus Edgerton . . . associated with Jay Cooke in the Northern Pacific promotion . . . had . . . heard of the marvelous mine development in Utah [Schick continues]. On a visit to the East he told Cooke about the mine. . . . Cooke . . . started for Utah with Edgerton. Cooke arrived, but Edgerton died enroute from a heart attack.

Jay Cooke bought the property for $5,000,000 in 1879.

By this time, Frisco was booming. From Alta and Ophir, Utah, and from Colorado, Nevada, and Arizona came "boomers"—miners, gamblers, gunmen, and dance hall girls. A sheriff—Pearson, first name forgotten—who came from Pioche, was elected to clean up the town. With the simple philosophy that dead men give no trouble, he put on a law enforcement campaign; there were no fines to be paid, no jail sentences to serve, and burial expenses were not excessive. Pearson gave a man his choice—shoot it out, or leave town. Many tried to shoot it out, but Pearson had strong nerves and a quick trigger-finger. He was known to have killed as many as six men in one night, and it finally became necessary to hire a "body mover" to clean up after him. The "wagon" made the rounds every morning and hauled away one or two corpses; they were buried without questions or funeral announcements. Frisco acquired a reputation as the wildest camp in Utah. Each of the twenty-one saloons had its stories of killings. In one place two men were killed over fifty cents in a faro game.

Jay Cooke was not concerned with the morals of the town. He wanted a railroad to the place.

> At Salt Lake City [Schick writes], Cooke interested the heads of the Mormon Church in extending the railroad they already owned to the new mining district and they took a quarter interest in the railroad. Then Cooke was in a position to ask the Union Pacific company for the rest. Sidney Dillon was president of the railroad. Though Cooke had forgotten it, he had once loaned Dillon $20,000 to tide him over. When Dillon heard what Cooke wanted he stepped out of the room, and brought back a short man with a black beard. It was Jay Gould. Gould looked at his maps. . . . Before the end of the conference Gould and Dillon consented to supply the money for the construction and the building of the Horn Silver railroad was assured. [The railroad was completed to 'Frisco in 1880.]

From 1880 to 1885 the mine produced heavily. Men dropped in heat sometimes at 108 degrees, and dust from the ore sent as many as forty men a month to hospitals with "miner's con." The owners, feverish for more wealth, disregarded all mining tenets, and the "glory hole" caved in to the seventh level, taking the shaft with it. The night shift came off work, and the day men were lined up at the hoist house waiting their turn to go down. Mine officials stopped them, saying that there had been a trembling in the shaft. While the miners were standing around, the whole mine caved in with a crash that broke windows in Milford, fifteen miles away. A new shaft, 910 feet deep, was sunk through rhyolite at a cost of $26 a foot. Meantime, most of the miners moved out, taking their houses with them, and leaving residential Grasshopper Street a pile of ruins.

A company was organized in 1928 to take over the old interests, and since then the mine has been producing 10,000 tons a year. Frisco never had running water. Its water was hauled seven miles and sold for four cents a gallon. For that reason, old-timers say, Frisco will never live again.

At 53.2 m. is the junction with a dirt road (*very rough and in places cut by four-foot washes*).

> Right on this road to NEWHOUSE, 2.2 m. (5,250 alt.), an abandoned mining community with only a few rock formations to prove it ever existed. In its boom days, 1905 to 1910, Newhouse was a model mining camp. Miners' houses were comfortable, clubs and cafes were well furnished, and gun-play was not too frequent. The mine is about a mile east of the old townsite. Discovered in 1870, it was filed on as the Cactus. From its discovery until 1900 many unprofitable attempts were made to operate it. At that time it was acquired by Samuel Newhouse, who operated it from 1905 to 1910, when the ore body ran out. In that period the mine produced $3,500,000. The Newhouse Building, the Newhouse Hotel, and other buildings in Salt Lake City were built with profits from this mine.

Between Newhouse Junction and the Wah Wah Range, the high-way winds through Wah Wah Valley, spotted with white alkali flats, tumbleweeds, and stunted sage.

The summit, 66.1 *m.,* of the WAH WAH RANGE is bordered by a thick growth of tall juniper trees interspersed with piñon pines. The mountains, with a north-south trend, are barren and dry.

At 70.1 *m.* the highway crosses the east border of PINE VALLEY, a wide desert area overgrown with sagebrush and cactus.

At 75.4 *m.* is the junction with a dirt road.

Left on this road to INDIAN PEAK RESERVATION, 5 *m.,* a 10,240-acre tract, created a reservation by President Wilson in 1915 for two bands of Paiute Indians. Patches of potatoes, corn, and alfalfa are grown, but farming is hampered by lack of water. The gathering of pine nuts is the chief source of income. The reservation is heavily wooded with piñon pine, and several thousand pounds of nuts are picked in a good season. The roasted nuts are marketed wholesale at 20 to 30 cents a pound. "Old Jack," said to be more than a hundred years old (1940), lives in solitude on the reservation. His fine bows and arrows are purchased by white archers throughout the State. He handles a rifle with great accuracy, and bags a deer each year.

At 82.4 *m.* is the junction with a dirt road.

Right on this road to the DESERT RANGE EXPERIMENT STATION, 3.4 *m.,* a U. S. Department of Agriculture project for experimentation with desert plants. The station, a cluster of green-roofed white buildings in the center of Pine Valley, is surrounded by twenty-four paddocks used for grazing experiments. The paddocks are observed before and after grazing for the effect on various types of desert forage.

GARRISON, 113.9 *m.* (5,000 alt., 127 pop.), a ranching com-munity with windmills and tar-papered shacks, was settled in the 1850's by cattle rustlers, who corralled their stolen stock at a ranch hereabouts. They harvested hay along a near-by stream, and when pursued slipped from one State to another. The outlaws departed in the eighties, after a mining boom drew prospectors into the region. Garrison Ranch was established after the mine boom waned.

The motion picture, *Covered Wagon,* was filmed on the rolling hills and plains of this area in 1922. The picture was directed by James Cruze, and the female lead role was played by Betty Compson; both are natives of Utah.

State 21 crosses the NEVADA LINE, 115.3 *m.,* and continues as Nevada 14 (*see Nevada Guide*).

Tour 1E

Andersons Ranch—Zion National Park—Junction with US 89; 52.4 *m.*, State 15.

Oiled road; open all year.
Lodge and camps in Park; cabin camps in Rockville and Springdale; service stations at close intervals.

Between Andersons Ranch and Toquerville State 15 passes through groves of semitropical fruits. From Toquerville to Zion National Park (*see Zion National Park*), the highway runs through several villages where the houses of early pioneers still stand. They are all farming communities, raising figs, pomegranates, lemons, peaches, and other fruits. Areas between towns serve as an introduction to the Park, vivid red sandstone cliffs contrasting with black rocks near the roadside. Between Zion Park and Mt. Carmel Junction, on US 89, the route progresses by a series of switch-backs through the shoulder of the mountain, where a mile-long tunnel, blasted out of solid rock, carries the highway far above the river. Windows chiseled out of the rock along the tunnel-road provide magnificent canyon views.

State 15 branches east from US 91 at ANDERSONS RANCH, 0 *m.* (*see Tour 1f*) and crosses a narrow valley, with vineyards and pastures at the foot of towering cliffs, and fruit stands scattered along the road.

TOQUERVILLE, 2.7 *m.* (3,200 alt., 288 pop.), is one of the earliest settlements of southwestern Utah. The old Mormon meeting house, an old vinery, and a few of the original log cabins are still standing.

Brigham Young first visited Toquerville in 1861, and seemed impressed by the warm pleasant valleys hereabouts. Some of the first settlers had polygamous families, and "polygamy hunts" of the 1870's had humorous and tragic sides. Lorine Isabel Lamb Higbee recalls in an interview the time when U. S. marshals raided her house in the dead of night:

> They . . . started around the house. One going one way and one the other. I had some wooden tubs filled with clear water . . . at the back. They stumbled over these and fell into my yellow rose bush. You could hear them swear a mile. Isaac, my brother-in-law, heard them and decided who they were and got up and dressed and warned everyone who was living in polygamy so that the officers did not get anyone. John T. Beatty told his interviewer, Louise Slack, that The house I live in has three good hiding places. . . . One leads to the cellar, one under the floor but the best one is a set of hinged steps that were covered with rag carpet and opened

under the floor. One man, Dalton was his name, was shot by Federal officers and killed. He left two families of little children. . . . He was a big active young man and a fighter. . . . They shot him in the back as he was crossing the field.

At 6 m. is the junction with State 17 (see Tour 1f).

VIRGIN, 12.3 m. (3,400 alt., 198 pop.), was first known as Pocketville, the translation of an Indian word for the valley. This farming community is in a small pocket or canyon, sheltered by red sandstone cliffs. The town is strewn along the river banks; the green trees of the orchards contrast vividly with the cliffs.

Settlers came into the valley in the middle 1850's, when the Mormon Church sent colonies into "Dixie" to establish cotton plantations, sugar-cane fields, vineyards, orchards, and silk culture. Malaria swept the camps, crops were discouraging, and it was years before the orchards would bear profitably. Alice P. Isom, in her manuscript "Memories," excerpts from which are in possession of the Utah Writers' Project, tells how pioneer women made dyes:

> Blue took ten days more. The yarn had to be wrung out of the indigo every day and aired and put back until the desired shade. To make green, a yellow dye was made of peach leaves and the blue yarn scalded up in it. Red was colored with madder and sour bran-water set with lye made of ashes. For brown, the madder was set with copperas, for black we used logwood and copperas vitriol to set the color.

A prolonged rainstorm deluged the settlements in 1862. Crops were washed out, homes were flooded, and young trees swept from the ground. Neighbors held a bed above water while a woman gave birth to a child, subsequently named Marvelous Flood.

Sylvester Earl, in an interview with Louise Slack, tells of the Virgin oil boom in 1907, following the original discovery of oil in 1903:

> They drilled the well and struck oil on the fourteenth day of July in 1907. This was the first oil producing well in the State of Utah. It caused great excitement and a boom in Virgin City. We couldn't even feed the people who came in there, there were so many. In a few months there were seventeen oil rigs. . . . There were tent towns with two big tent hotels and saloons, but the money panic of 1907 came and knocked the bottom out of the whole proposition. . . . Since then the oil industry has been kept alive by promoters coming in and drilling a little and the refinery being set up but there has been very little excitement since the first boom.

ROCKVILLE, 21.8 m. (3,746 alt., 214 pop.), was settled by Mormon colonists in 1864, to produce cotton and fruit for the northern settlements. The fruit did well, and today neatly pruned orchards line the highway.

A double row of mulberry trees, planted for silkworm culture in pioneer days along Rockville's main street, was cut down in the spring of 1940 in the course of a road improvement program from Rockville to the mouth of Zion Canyon. Though the trees had a certain antique value, they dropped their juicy purple berries indiscriminately, and the Salt Lake Tribune reports that "Rockville's voting population of 120 almost unanimously voted for the end of the mulberries." Mrs. Warren Hirschi, however, was of another mind. She stood off workmen for a time with a rifle to prevent them from cutting down the eight trees fronting her property.

SPRINGDALE, 25.3 *m.* (3,913 alt., 246 pop.), is an agricultural community near the entrance to Zion National Park, from which the dazzling red cliffs and peaks of the park can be seen. Times were hard in the early days, following settlement. "Many men and women, nearly naked, had to subsist to a great extent on greens, broom corn and cane seed."

"Mrs. Eunice Mouk of Manti," says A. M. Woodbury in his manuscript on southwestern Utah, "recalled the Behunins telling her that the chickens in Zion Canyon went to roost soon after sundown, but the twilight was so long they got tired of waiting for darkness and came out again. The Behunins were real mountaineers," who carved a wash basin in the stump of a cottonwood tree, drained it through an auger hole, and plugged it from the outside.

State 15 crosses the south boundary, 26.7 *m.,* of ZION NATIONAL PARK at the South Entrance Checking Station. East of the station it runs through Zion scenery.

At PARK HEADQUARTERS, 28 *m.,* is the junction with the Zion National Park road (*see Zion National Park*).

State 15 winds (R) over one of the most spectacular pieces of highway engineering in the West—the ZION-MOUNT CARMEL HIGHWAY, 31.5 *m.,* where the road tunnels for a mile through the solid rock mountainside. At intervals, six great windows (L) are chiseled through the rock, providing breath-taking views (*parking space by windows*) of one of the canyons. Sloping all the way, the tunnel twists through the mountain, and the view from each window is different.

At 32.6 *m.* is the east entrance of the tunnel. The road passes through another short tunnel at 34 *m.,* and continues as a dugway blasted out of the rock; at 38.7 *m.,* it crosses the east boundary of the park.

At 52.4 *m.* is the junction with US 89 (*see Tour 2d*).

Tour 2

(Montpelier, Idaho)—Garden City—Logan—Brigham City—Ogden—Salt Lake City—Provo—Spanish Fork—Richfield—Panguitch—Kanab—(Fredonia, Ariz.); US 89.
Idaho Line to Arizona Line, 469.1 *m.*

Union Pacific R.R. parallels route between Logan and Spanish Fork; Utah-Idaho Central R.R. between Logan and Ogden; Denver & Rio Grande Western R.R. between Ogden and Marysvale; Bamberger Electric R.R. between Ogden and Salt Lake City; Salt Lake and Utah R.R. between Salt Lake City and Provo.

Improved gravel road between Idaho Line and Logan Canyon; elsewhere asphalt or concrete paved.

All types of accommodations in larger cities, at 5 to 50 mile intervals throughout route; service stations at short intervals.

US 89 is one of the two important north-south arteries of Utah. Like US 91, it has numerous branch roads entering from east and west.

Between the Idaho Line and Logan, the route skirts Bear Lake, and twists through broken and rugged terrain gashed by deep canyons. West and south of Logan, the road passes through a country rich in sugar beets, grain and alfalfa, along the brush-covered foothills of the Wasatch Mountains (L). Merged with US 91, the road in the north central section skirts the east shores of Great Salt Lake and Utah Lake.

Between Thistle and the Arizona Line, the road drives over plateaus, cleaves through a series of canyons, and traverses deserts of rock and sand, where there is a constantly sighing wind, and the soft, scaly rustling of sand. It is a region of grotesque formations, exotic coloring, strange fossils, brilliantly colored petrified trees, and areas, larger than some eastern States, of gashed barren rock.

Section a. IDAHO LINE to SPANISH FORK; 195.5 m., US 89

Along the west shore of Bear Lake, US 89, shaded much of the way by tall cottonwoods, is bordered (L) by green fields in which cattle and sheep graze. In the western background rounded hills rise through groves of pine and aspen. Through Logan Canyon the highway passes between sheer rocky walls. Between Logan and Brigham City the route loops around brushy limestone foothills of the Wellsville Mountains, a part of the Wasatch Range, and along the eastern margin of cultivated and irrigated Bear River Valley. South of Brigham City the route passes through farming towns and commercial cities.

US 89 crosses the IDAHO LINE, 0 *m.*, 25.4 miles south of Montpelier, Idaho, and follows the west shoreline of Bear Lake.

GARDEN CITY, 4.2 *m.* (5,950 alt., 261 pop.), an agricultural community on the west shore of Bear Lake, was settled by pioneers under the leadership of Charles Coulson Rich, Mormon apostle. Starting with two small cabins in 1864, the town acquired a flour mill, a sawmill, a blacksmith shop, a picker, carding machines, and looms. Later an irrigation canal was built, and the townsite was surveyed in 1877.

BEAR LAKE (5,924 alt.) (*fishing, boating, swimming*) dominates the scenery east of Garden City. This fresh water lake, thirty miles long and seven miles wide, lies half in Utah and half in Idaho. It has

white sand beaches, and because of its great depth has a wide range
of marine colors.

Utah, a desert State, has a "sea monster" story, with Bear Lake
as its locale. Shoshoni said that there was a great beast in the lake,
but that it went away after extinction of the buffalo by snowstorms in
1830. The *Deseret News* for July 27, 1868, reported "reliable" white
testimony to the existence of a monster in the lake. S. M. Johnson, of
South Eden, stated that he saw the head of the animal rising from the
lake, with "ears or bunches on the side of its head nearly as large as
a pint cup." The next day four people saw a large animal that "swam
much faster than a horse could run on land." Thomas Slight, Allen
Davis, and others soon after "saw" the monster. "Mr. Slight says he
distinctly saw the sides of a very large animal that he would suppose
to be not less than ninety feet in length. . . . It was going South, and
all agreed that it swam with a speed almost incredible. . . . Mr. Davis
says he never saw a locomotive travel faster, and thinks it made a mile
a minute, easy." The *News* asks, "Is it fish, flesh, or serpent, am-
phibious and fabulous or a great big fish, or what is it?" The newspaper suggested, "Here is an excellent opportunity for some company to
bust Barnum on a dicker for the monster . . . some of our settlers talk
of forming a joint stock arrangement and what they can do to the
business."

Left from Garden City on graveled State 3, which skirts the southwestern
shores of Bear Lake, to LAKETOWN, 10.8 *m.* (5,989 alt., 366 pop.), an agricultural settlement on the south shore of Bear Lake.
SAGE CREEK JUNCTION, 24.5 *m.* (6,260 alt., 122 pop.), is at the junction
with State 51; L. on this graveled road, through winding canyons and rocky
foothills to the Wyoming State Line, 4.7 *m.*, 29 miles west of Kemmerer, Wyoming (*see Wyoming Guide*).
RANDOLPH, 32.4 *m.* (6,287 alt., 656 pop.), on State 3, is a stockmen's
trading center and seat of Rich County. Randolph H. Stewart led the first group
of settlers from St. Charles (now in Idaho) to the present site in 1870. The
town was surveyed with a rope in the absence of a surveyor's chain, and
Brigham Young personally organized the town in 1871, when he made a treaty
with the Bannock Indians.
Rich County is regarded as the coldest in Utah; unofficial records show
that on January 14, 1888, a spirit thermometer registered 65 degrees below
zero at Randolph.
At 42.7 *m.* is the junction (R) with State 39 (*see Tour 1A*).
WOODRUFF, 43 *m.* (6,344 alt., 404 pop.), a farming center, is said to be
officially one of the two coldest spots in Utah, with a recorded temperature of
50 degrees below zero. It was settled in 1870-71 and named for Wilford
Woodruff, Mormon Church President.
At 53.3 *m.* State 3 crosses the Wyoming line 12.5 miles northeast of Evanston, Wyoming (*see Wyoming Guide*).

VIEW POINT, 10.6 *m.,* a favorite halting spot on US 89, unfolds
a view of Bear Lake, part of Wyoming, and a section of Idaho.

Between the summit, 11.5 *m.* (7,900 alt.), and Logan, US 89 passes
through LOGAN CANYON (*campsites with stoves, tables, firepits,
and drinking fonts*), which has almost perpendicular walls nearly a
mile high. Tiny lakes in the canyon are remnants of eleven prehistoric

glaciers. Logan River (*trout*), a favorite fishing stream, in 1924 yielded the largest German brown trout ever legally hooked; the fisherman was W. W. Smart, of Logan, and the fish weighed twenty-five pounds, five and a quarter ounces.

At 30.2 *m.* is the junction with a dirt road.

Right on this road to OLD JUNIPER CAMP, 0.3 *m.*, one of many shady campsites in the canyon; R. from Juniper Camp on a steep foot trail, ascending a small branch canyon through shady aspen and pine groves, to JUNIPER JARDINE, 1 *m.*, considered the oldest tree in Utah, and believed to be the oldest juniper in the world. The gnarled tree, forty-four feet high and more than fifteen feet in diameter, is more than three thousand years old.

At 30.4 *m.* is the junction with a foot trail.

Right on this foot trail to LOGAN CAVE (*flashlight necessary*), 0.1 *m.*, a double-mouthed cavern 1,500 feet long, inhabited by myriads of bats.

West of the Logan Cave trail junction, on the slopes of a series of crags (R), are two exposures of fossil seaweed, discovered during construction of the highway. One specimen is exposed for nearly forty feet; another extends over an area of about thirty square feet.

The highway passes through the mouth of Logan Canyon, 42.5 *m.* Shore lines of prehistoric Lake Bonneville (*see Geology*), which once covered the valley to a depth of 700 feet, are visible along the mountain slopes to the east.

LOGAN, 45 *m.* (4,535 alt., 11,875 pop.) (*see Logan*).

Logan is at the junction with US 91 (*see Tour 1a*) which unites with US 89 for 0.3 miles.

US 89 between Logan and Brigham City is sometimes used in winter as an alternate route for US 91, when the latter, through Sardine Canyon (*see Tour 1b*), is closed by heavy snows.

The STATE FISH HATCHERY (R), 47.1 *m.* (*open weekdays*), raises from 350,000 to 600,000 rainbow, Loch Leven, and cutthroat trout annually.

At 53 *m.* is the junction with State 142 (*see Tour 1a*) and graveled State 164.

Left on State 164 to MENDON, 3 *m.* (4,435 alt., 434 pop.), an agricultural town settled in 1859 by citizens of Wellsville. In early years, the crops were often destroyed by frost and grasshoppers, and the winter of 1873-74 was so severe that old straw from shed roofs was fed to cattle.

WELLSVILLE, 8.8 *m.* (4,495 alt., 1,401 pop.), is at the junction with US 91 (*see Tour 1b*).

At 60.4 *m.* is the junction with State 154, between US 89 and Riverside (*see Tour 3*).

COLLINSTON, 61.3 *m.* (4,460 alt., 114 pop.), is the shipping center of a dry-farming and cattle-raising area. Much of Collinston's history revolves about transportation. It was first named Hampton, for a Bear River ferryman of the sixties, and served as a station on the stage line between Utah, Idaho, and Montana. In 1880 it was renamed or Collins Fulmer, a conductor on the Utah Northern Railroad. During construction of the Hammond Canal, Collinston was a boom own—a city of saloons, gambling establishments, and frequent deaths. n 1907, upon completion of the canal, Collinston settled down.

DEWEYVILLE, 65.4 m. (4,323 alt., 256 pop.), is a farming nd livestock-raising community.

Deweyville is at the junction with State 102, between US 89 and JS 30S (see Tour 4b).

CRYSTAL HOT SPRINGS, 69.4 m. (picnicking, dancing, swimming), s a tree-shaded resort (R). The swimming pool is fed by two springs, ne hot and one cold.

HONEYVILLE, 71.1 m. (4,269 alt., 593 pop.), a farming town, s believed to have been named either by Abraham Hunsaker, a bee-eeper, or by early settlers to whom it suggested Canaan, a land "flow-ng with milk and honey."

At 79.7 m. is the north junction, in Brigham City (see Tour 1b), vith US 30S (see Tour 4b) with which US 89 unites for 31 miles.

BRIGHAM CITY, 81 m. (4,805 alt., 5,643 pop.), is at the north unction with US 91 (see Tour 1b), with which US 89 unites for 3.1 miles; at 104.1 m. is the south junction with US 91 (see Tour 1c).

At 110.7 m. is the southern junction with US 30S at the mouth of Veber Canyon (see Tour 4a).

Proceeding south, US 89 runs along the western foothills of the Wasatch Range between occasional farms and rocky, brushy slopes. Great Salt Lake (R) affords occasional magnificent views.

At 119.9 m. is a northern junction with US 91 (see Tour 1c) vith which US 89 unites for 75.6 miles (see Tour 1c, 1d); at 195.5 m. s the southern junction (see Tour 1e), in Spanish Fork (see Tour 1d), vith US 91 and the western junction with US 50 (see Tour 7b).

Section b. *SPANISH FORK to RICHFIELD; 121.5 m., US 89*

Between Spanish Fork and Richfield US 89 extends through fertile valleys, winding canyons, and across stretches of semi-desert.

East of its junction with US 91 (see Tour 1e), 0 m., US 89 unites with US 50 (see Tour 7b).

At 13.6 m. is the eastern junction of US 89 with US 50 (see Tour 7b).

THISTLE, 13.8 m. (5,033 alt., 288 pop.), is a railroad and high-way junction, settled in 1898 and named for thistles growing in the valley.

At 41.8 m. is the junction (L) with State 31 (see Tour 7a).

FAIRVIEW, 42.3 m. (6,033 alt., 1,120 pop.), a dairying and dry-farming town, was settled in 1859 by pioneers from Mt. Pleasant, attracted by meadows of wild hay. The water and light systems are municipally owned and the public library is maintained by the city.

MT. PLEASANT, 48.2 m. (5,857 alt., 2,284 pop.), is a leading Rambouillet sheep center, shipping 300,000 head annually, many of

334 UTAH

them to foreign countries; Rambouillets are sold chiefly for breeding
purposes, to improve herds elsewhere. Before the turn of the century
Mt. Pleasant people ranged their sheep municipally. The animals
were leased to herders, who guaranteed a specific increase; payments to
the herder were made *pro rata,* and he was given a bonus of all lambs
over the specified quota.

John Henry Seely, Mormon pioneer, a foremost advocate of blooded
stock, imported Rambouillet sheep and shorthorn cattle. Before
Seely's importations western sheep sheared two- or three-pound fleeces,
but by crossing with pure breds he developed individual sheep that
sheared thirty-five-pound fleeces. One ram was sold to the Russian
government for $6,000. Seely was born in the Mormon colony at
San Bernardino, California, and grew up as a herd boy, never owning
a pair of shoes until he was sixteen years old. In winter he attended
school barefooted, running along log fences to keep out of the snow—
he won his first pair of shoes in a foot race—and wore them only when
fishing.

SPRING CITY, 54 *m.* (5,685 alt., 992 pop.), a farming and
livestock community, was founded in 1852 by fifteen families from
Great Salt Lake City under the leadership of James Allred, bodyguard
of Joseph Smith.

PIGEON HOLLOW JUNCTION, 60 *m.,* was named for the
large number of mourning doves that nested in the valley when the
pioneers came.

Left from Pigeon Hollow Junction on State 189 to CHESTER, 3.9 *m.* (5,500
alt., 171 pop.), nearest town to the geographical center of the State.

MORONI, 7.7 *m.* (5,519 alt., 1,218 pop.), settled as a farming community
in 1859, has been a turkey-raising center since 1928. Turkey Day, in early
August, is an annual event. The town, among the foothills of the Sanpitch
Mountains, was named for Moroni, a Nephite prophet, who is said to have
revealed to Joseph Smith the golden plates, bearing the characters from which
Smith translated the Book of Mormon (*see Mormon Church*).

FOUNTAIN GREEN, 15.7 *m.* (5,994 alt., 982 pop.), a farming and sheep-
raising community, is known for its long-fiber wool. Previous to America's
entry into the World War, the quantity produced here, with the high price of
wool, made Fountain Green one of the wealthiest towns per capita in the
United States.

At 24.3 *m.* is the junction (R) with the Nebo Loop road (*see Tour 1e*).

The UNITED STATES GYPSUM PLANT (L), 28.4 *m.,* a one-story stucco building
capped by three tall smokestacks, was erected in 1909. An aerial tramway
carries gypsum from the mine, across the valley (R), to the plant, where it is
manufactured into plaster. Because of its color-retaining properties, plaster
from this plant was selected for use in the first colored, artificial travertine,
presented in exteriors and statues at the San Diego Fair in 1915; for palaces,
statues, and buildings at the Panama-Pacific Exposition in 1915; and for a
majority of plaster works at the San Francisco Golden Gate Exposition in 1939.

NEPHI, 30.1 *m.* (5,096 alt., 2,573 pop.), is at the junction with US 91
(*see Tour 1e*).

EPHRAIM, 64.8 *m.* (5,543 alt., 2,095 pop.), center of a turkey
and sheep raising area, was settled in 1853.

SNOW COLLEGE (*open schooldays*), in Ephraim, founded by the Mormon Church in 1883, since 1932 has been operated by the State Department of Public Instruction.

CENTRAL UTAH MUSEUM (*open 2-4 weekdays, Sept. to June*) has 11,000 specimens of Indian pottery, arrowheads, sandals, moccasins, one knives, and other artifacts.

At 65.2 *m.* is the junction with State 29 (*see Tour 7a*).

MANTI, 71.9 *m.* (5,530 alt., 2,200 pop.), Sanpete County seat, a livestock and poultry raising community. It was founded in 1849. The name is of Book of Mormon origin.

The MANTI MORMON TEMPLE (*not open to non-Mormons*) is built of white limestone on an eminence (L) overlooking the town, and visible for many miles. Started in 1877, the edifice was completed, at a cost of $1,000,000 in 1888.

At 79.9 *m.* is the junction with State 137.

At 86.4 *m.* is the junction (R) with State 28 (*see Tour 1e*).

GUNNISON, 86.8 *m.* (5,215 alt., 1,111 pop.), a sugar beet and poultry raising community, was founded in 1860 and named for Captain John W. Gunnison, United States topographical engineer. A small-pox epidemic here, in the winter of 1864-65, is thought to have been a factor contributing to the outbreak of the Black Hawk War (*see below*); several Indians contracted the disease, and some of them died. They blamed the epidemic on the white people, and a series of raids followed.

In 1911, a co-operative Jewish colony was started near Gunnison, in a little valley west of the highway. About one hundred families moved into the valley, each acquiring forty irrigated acres around a central commissary. Advice of natives to insulate the plank cottages with adobe or plaster was ignored, and the houses were freezing cold in winter and sweltering hot in summer. Many of the colonists were cultured people who found it impossible to adapt themselves to the handling of farm animals, and to the problems of cultivation and irrigation. They gradually drifted back to the cities, and by 1920 nothing remained of the experiment. Benjamin Brown, one of the settlers, organized the Utah Poultry Co-operative Association, which established a method for putting uniformly sized fresh eggs on the market.

At 87.6 *m.* is the south junction with State 137.

Left on State 137, graveled, to MAYFIELD, 8.2 *m.* (5,500 alt., 467 pop.), a quiet village on Twelve Mile Creek, surrounded by tall trees and high peaks. Wool, fruit, wheat, and hay are the principal products.

At 12.2 *m.* on State 137 is the north junction with US 89 (*see above*).

CENTERFIELD, 88.9 *m.* (5,125 alt., 554 pop.), refines some 5,000 tons of sugar beets harvested annually in the Sevier Valley.

REDMOND, 98 *m.* (5,135 alt., 641 pop.), is a trading center for rock salt mines in the vicinity, some of them working deposits 1,200 feet thick.

SALINA, 101.3 *m.* (5,160 alt., 1,614 pop.), is a shipping cent
for livestock, coal, salt, and farm produce. The name is derived fro
the salt deposits in the adjacent hills.

Salina, which was first settled in 1866, vacated during India
troubles of the sixties, and resettled in 1871, for many years had a
ordinance requiring business establishments to close on the Sabbat
The *Park Record* for March 1, 1902, reports that:

> The Sunday closing law is so strictly enforced in Salina, Utah, that t
> busy editor of the Salina *Sun* had to go to church to get the town counc
> together and secure a permit to accept one dollar on a subscription that o
> of his readers had traveled two days to give him. It was only after explai
> ing that it would cost one dollar and fifty cents to keep the subscriber ove
> thereby putting himself fifty cents in the hole, that the august body, t
> council, consented to allow the subscriber to deposit the dollar in a hole
> a fence post so that Howard could secure it when the midnight hour stru
> that night. Howard stood guard over that fencepost like a good 'Inju
> However, he caught a cold that it cost him three dollars and eleven cents
> buy mineral water and lime juice to cure.

Salina is at the junction with State 10 (*see Tour 7a*).

At 102.9 *m.* is the junction (R) with State 63 (*see Tour 1e*).

SIGURD, 112.5 *m.* (5,270 alt., 364 pop.), is a farming villa
in the Sevier Valley. Several small gypsum mines operate in t
vicinity.

Sigurd is at the junction with State 24 (*see Tour 2A*).

RICHFIELD, 121.5 *m.* (5,308 alt., 3,556 pop.), seat of Sevi
County and center of a dairying, farming and livestock area, has fi
cheese factories, three flour mills, one clay and metal mill, and co
and gypsum mines near by.

Richfield is one of several centers in Utah where packs of dogs a
maintained for hunting mountain lions, which are taken only in winte
when snow is on the ground. Good lion dogs were formerly mongre
of half a dozen breeds, but since about 1930 the choice has been
straight cross between a fox or coon hound and a bloodhound; th
have an exceptional trailing nose, show wisdom in their dealings wi
a deadly adversary, yet have no fear. Larger breeds of dogs have bee
tried and found wanting. At least four dogs ordinarily make up
pack, and the hunters ride trained horses, usually cow ponies. Whe
the dogs hit a hot trail and set up the deep-toned baying that is sym
phony to the hunter, the horsemen follow at full speed. The trail ru
hot and cold, fast and slow. Sometimes the riders are strung out fa
behind, and at others they have time to ease sideways in the saddle an
roll a smoke while the dogs are picking up the trail.

Mountain lions (they are known as panthers and cougars elsewher
but not in Utah) will "tree" when too closely pressed. Sometim
they "tree" in a high broken ledge of rock, at other times in a larg
cedar or pine. At bay on a ledge, with rock behind them, and guarde
by a long reach and deadly claws, they are dangerous customers. Foo

hardy dogs are often ripped into shreds, but the veteran hound knows enough to stay back, worrying the lion and holding him till the hunters come up. Sometimes the cat, by an incredible leap, will clear the cordon of dogs and get away, only to be trailed and cornered again.

A lion up a tree crawls out on a large limb, well above the ground, and faces the bole of the tree. Ordinarily, when no trophy is desired, the lion is shot with a pistol or small-caliber rifle, and the dogs tear the carcass as it strikes the ground. If the hide is wanted, the guide usually attempts to rope the animal. A lion cornered on a ledge, however, can strike a loop away, and branches interfere with the cowboy's art when the panther is up a tree. The technique is to climb the tree, to a point above the lion, with a lariat and forked stick about six feet long. The loop is worked over the lion's head, and the hunter may shoot his cat and let it hang till the dogs lose interest.

Mountain lions follow the deer, the U. S. Forest Service census estimating 550 in the State in 1939. Lions require from 50 to 100 kills to maintain themselves for a year, and sometimes five to ten deer are killed for the joy of killing. They do not, according to popular belief, leap upon their prey from above, but rush from a cover of brush, leap on the animal's back, and ride it to death. The U. S. Forest Service, the Utah Fish and Game Commission, and the U. S. Biological Survey, in the Federal Building, Salt Lake City, all encourage lion hunting. The Biological Survey has a list of packs and guides. Guides charge about $20 a day for horses, dogs, and their own services, and outdoorsmen say that with a good pack of dogs and a skilled guide the kill ought to be made in about three days. Cedar City is probably the most publicized lion-hunting center in the State, but there are also packs at Kanab, Kanosh, Salina, Henrieville, Panguitch, Nephi, Goshen, and Fruitland.

The BLACK HAWK TREATY TREE, a cedar in front of the Sevier Stake Mormon Tabernacle in Richfield, commemorates the treaty concluding Utah's Black Hawk War with the Ute Indians, in 1868. An annual Black Hawk celebration is held at Richfield.

The Black Hawk War began in April, 1865, the smallpox epidemic at Manti (*see above*) having apparently been a factor. Hostilities began here, when John Lowry pulled "Indian Jake" from his horse by the hair, and went home for a pistol. The Indians were gone before he came back, but the Ute Black Hawk War, most disastrous of all Utah's Indian wars for the white people, was launched. It consisted primarily of a series of guerilla raids on the part of the Indians, pursuit by the whites, and ambush by the Utes. Many Utah settlements were abandoned during the late sixties, including Richfield, and were not resettled until the early seventies. No detailed history of the conflict has been written. Raids, livestock thefts, and occasional killings on both sides continued for more than three years. In August, 1868, Colonel F. H. Head, Superintendent of Indian Affairs, held a council with the principal Ute chiefs, including Black Hawk, in the Strawberry Valley. A treaty was eventually drawn up and signed, and this is regarded as

the end of the war, though some raiding continued and other treatie
were necessary (*see Tour 2A*).

A telegram to the *Deseret News* dated September 27, 1870, from
Spring Lake Villa, between Payson and Santaquin, advised of Black
Hawk's death: "I hasten to tell you that Black Hawk, the India
desperado, is dead. . . . This is the place of his birth . . . and here h
came back to die."

RICHFIELD PARK (*open; playgrounds, picnicking*), is on the sit
of an old Indian village. In 1935, while attempting to level a san
dune, the sixteen-inch adobe wall of a five-room house was uncovered
containing crude agricultural implements, four skeletons, and tw
earthen pots filled with corn and a grain resembling wheat. Man
similar structures have been found in the vicinity.

Section c. RICHFIELD to JUNCTION WITH STATE 12; 86.9 m.; US 89

Between RICHFIELD, 0 *m.*, and Panguitch, US 89 follows th
Sevier River through a deep-walled canyon, winds among the tower
ing mountain peaks scarred by mine dumps and abandoned minin
claims, and passes hermit-like villages in narrow valleys. Sheep an
cattle range the forested slopes, and fertile bottomlands are checkere
with small farms. Between Sevier and Marysvale, the highway cut
through Marysvale Canyon, with spires and monoliths of many-hue
rocks rising from the broken and eroded mountainsides. The river i
dammed in seven places to furnish water for settlements and for irriga
tion. Between Marysvale and the junction with State 12 the highwa
leads over rugged plateaus or winds between blazing canyon wall
Side roads lead to scenic areas, and trails, known only by the native
reach into the Aquarius Plateau, Circle Cliffs, petrified forests, an
Smoking Mountain—areas larger than many eastern States, where ther
is not a single permanent inhabitant, white or Indian.

CENTRAL, 4.9 *m.* (5,345 alt., 277 pop.), is a farming and live
stock village guarded by the foothills of the Tushar Mountains.

At 6.7 *m.* on US 89 is the north junction with State 118.

Left on State 118 to MONROE, 3.5 *m.* (5,375 alt., 1,288 pop.), a lamb
raising and fruit-growing center, with broad tree-lined streets and houses c
the pioneer era. Modern dancers are inconvenienced by a local ordinanc
requiring the passage of visible light between partners.

MONROE HOT SPRINGS (open) is the only non-sulphurous body of hot wate
in the State. Medicinal qualities are claimed for the water.

At 9.4 *m.* on State 118, is the south junction with US 89 (*see below*).

ELSINORE, 8.3 *m.* (5,335 alt., 681 pop.), settled in 1864 an
named by Danish colonists for the site of "Hamlet's castle" in Den
mark, is a busy town surrounded by sugar beet fields and rolling foot
hills. It has a flour mill and sugar factory and is a shipping poin
for a portion of the Sevier Valley.

JOSEPH, 14.4 *m.* (5,435 alt., 297 pop.), strung along the highway among shade trees, is an agricultural community. "Old Joe Mountain" (R) is said to produce a good crop of deer in season.

Joseph is at the south junction with State 118 (*see above*).

At 17.9 *m.* is the junction (R) with State 13 (*see Tour 1e*).

Between the junction with State 13 and Marysvale, US 89 runs through MARYSVALE CANYON. Sunlight filters into the canyon for a few hours at midday, and wind-carved rocks march up the steep canyonsides.

BIG ROCK CANDY MOUNTAIN (R), 24.8 *m.,* is a rounded, lemon-colored hill sparsely covered with evergreens. No grass grows in the yellow soil, which is said to contain a low grade of alum.

WINKLEMAN RESORT (L), 24.9 *m.* (*cabins, meals, dancing*), is all that remains of a once prosperous mining camp (5,500 alt.). About the turn of the century alunite mines boomed in this district, but removal of the protective tariff on potash forced them to close down. Experiments with alunite, an aluminum and potash ore, and the discovery of valuable minerals in the ore, have reawakened interest in this district. A few small gold mines operate near here.

Left from Winkleman Resort, a dirt road extends into DEER CREEK CANYON. Cliff dwellings can be seen high on the smooth, red cliffs, from which relics and a few mummies have been removed.

The ALUNITE QUARRY, 3 *m.,* shows on the surface seven million tons of ore, which is surface-mined with steam shovels. Geologists estimate that nearly twenty million tons of ore are in this mountain.

MARYSVALE, 30.1 *m.* (5,866 alt., 471 pop.), in a little valley completely surrounded by mountains, is a center for the gold, silver, and potash mines of this district.

The PIUTE RESERVOIR (L), 40.7 *m.* (*fishing, hunting*), impounds water of the Sevier River for irrigation purposes. In autumn, the artificial lake is a gathering place for duck hunters.

JUNCTION, 45.4 *m.* (6,250 alt., 352 pop.), seat of Piute County, at the confluence of the East and South Forks of the Sevier River, is the trading center of a farming and livestock area. Mining activities are handicapped by the few miles of railroad in the county.

Junction is at the junction with State 21 (*see Tour 1e*).

At 47.5 *m.* is the junction with State 22.

Left on State 22 to ANTIMONY, 17.4 *m.* (6,500 alt., 239 pop.), a series of ranch houses stretching along the road for several miles. It was named for a near-by deposit of antimony ore.

WIDTSOE, 41.6 *m.* (7,623 alt.), was settled in 1876 and named for John A. Widtsoe, Mormon official and former president of the University of Utah. Scene of a Federal land utilization project, the town is abandoned, a few ruined frame houses providing a melancholy contrast with white and green Forest Service buildings. In the summer of 1935, Widtsoe had seventeen families, who could no longer make a living on their farms. The Government bought the property and resettled the clients, mostly in Utah County. The land is being reclaimed for grazing purposes.

Left from Widtsoe on State 23, an improved dirt road, through brilliantly colored canyons, to ESCALANTE, 27.9 m. (5,303 alt., 1,105 pop.), named in honor of Francisco Silvestre Vélez de Escalante, Spanish Catholic priest, who explored portions of Utah in 1776, but came no nearer this spot than 150 miles. It was settled in 1875 by Mormon pioneers and called Potato Valley, for a species of wild potato that grew here. Escalante is a "horse town"; people ride on horseback from one part of town to another, and newsboys deliver papers on horseback. An old-fashioned, isolated Mormon community, Escalante is one of the few remaining Utah places where ecclesiastical officials arbitrate civil problems. This settlement is on the Kaiparowits Plateau, which extends east to the Colorado River and south to the Arizona Line.

The Kaiparowits area has always been sparsely settled. The Cliff Dwellers and Indians found it unfriendly, isolated, and unproductive. Cliff houses are found in the region, but they suggest scattered outposts or temporary dwellings. "Without artificial irrigation," says Dr. Herbert E. Gregory in *The Kaiparowits Region,* "the food crops of the Kaiparowits region would be those of the cliff dweller and Piute—piñon nuts, cactus fruits, the seeds of the 'ak,' 'waiva' (wild millet), sunflower, goldenrod, some squash, and rarely corn, and when Pongonits, the wind god, dried up the springs and withered the grasses, reliance would be placed on deer, rabbits, badgers, porcupines, rats, mice, and lizards. . . . In practice it has been found unprofitable to supply water to as much as half of the otherwise available acreage." The total population of this vast area is only slightly over two thousand and thousands of acres contain not a single inhabitant. Cattle and sheep must range far to sustain themselves on the scant forage, and the herds are small. "The Kaiparowits region is essentially a grazing district," says Gregory, "perhaps the largest 'free range' in the United States. The villages and adjoining farms serve as headquarters for sheepmen and cattlemen, without whose interests the population of Escalante, Cannonvill, Tropic and Henrieville probably would be numbered by a few tens and Boulder might not exist at all."

The plateau is of interest to geologists, having upwarps, downwarps, anticlines, synclines, monoclines, faults, and thousands of vividly colored erosional forms. Pack trips into this region can be arranged at Escalante. Rates vary with the number in the party, but are as low as $3 per day for a guide and $1 per day for a horse.

Left from Escalante, the terminus of State 23, on a dirt road, through rock-tinted canyons, to the junction (L), 14.3 m., with a dirt road to Bicknell (*see Tour 2A*).

Southeast of the Bicknell road junction, almost at the summit of Roger Peak (10,133 alt.), are panoramic views of the Kaiparowits Plateau, Navaho Mountain to the south, and the Henry Mountains to the east. The scorched Escalante Desert, the colorful Circle Cliffs, the eroded Water Pocket Folds, and forbidding Fifty Mile Mountain form a barrier to the west, with the towering Aquarius Plateau (*see Tour 2A*) to the north.

HELLS BACKBONE, 25.4 m. is a knife-edged ridge with a bridge on top, spanning a streamless crevice no wider than the bridge itself. On both sides are precipitous walls that drop hundreds of feet, with Death Hollow on one side and Sand Creek Canyon on the other. For years the residents of Boulder carried mail and packed provisions along this ridge.

BOULDER, 44.1 m. (6,023 alt., 216 pop.), settled in 1894 and named for massive, vari-colored boulders surrounding the town, has green alfalfa fields, grazing cattle, and scattered ranch houses, in amazing contrast to the desert wastes and rocky vastnesses surrounding the community. For years after settlement the tiny town was isolated from the world by towering walls of solid rock, 35 miles by pack train from Escalante. A man packed in a pick-up truck, in pieces, reassembled it, and ran it eight years without a license; gasoline, also "imported" on pack horses cost seventy-five cents a gallon. In 1923, President Harding set aside 130 acres of public domain for a townsite, but a survey was neglected, and for nearly ten years the residents were legally squatters," immune from taxation. Mrs. Maggie Baker in 1932 asked for permission to buy the lot on which her house stood, and the Federal Land

Office made a survey so lands could be purchased. At about the same time the town filed on 3,000 acre-feet of water and built a reservoir to impound it. Work was begun on the Hells Backbone bridge, but it was not until about 1935 that Boulder ceased to be a "packhorse town"—said to be the last in the country—with a highway that could be used by wagons and automobiles. Between Boulder and the junction with State 117 the dirt road runs along the base of the Aquarius Plateau.

At 75.2 *m.* is the junction with State 117.

State 22 runs south through forests and canyons to the junction, 55.2 *m.*, with State 12 (*see Tour 2c*).

CIRCLEVILLE, 52.1 *m.* (6,061 alt., 436 pop.), is chiefly a stock raising community, as it was during the boyhood of George LeRoy Parker, alias "Butch Cassidy," Utah's most notorious bandit, who was born here (*see Tour 7b*).

PANGUITCH, 79.9 *m.* (6,624 alt., 1,968 pop.), a small metropolis between forested mountains, is the Garfield County seat. Inhabitants of the county derive their livelihood chiefly from livestock raising, but many obtain seasonal employment at local mines, sawmills, and the cheese factory. Panguitch hunters, like those at Richfield, keep packs of trained dogs for hunting mountain lions (*see above*).

Panguitch was first settled by Jens Nielsen, who led a group of settlers into the valley in 1864. They were snowbound the first winter, and kept alive on frosted wheat and beef fat until supplies were brought in. Good crops were harvested the next year and a gristmill was erected. Because of the Black Hawk War the town was abandoned in 1867 and resettled four years later.

The STATE FISH HATCHERY (*open workdays*), in Panguitch, annually rears six million fingerlings for planting in streams and lakes of this region. Fishing and deer hunting are good in the adjacent mountains.

Right from Panguitch on the Panguitch Lake road (dirt) to the east boundary, 7.5 *m.*, of the DIXIE NATIONAL FOREST. Between the east boundary and Panguitch Lake, the road passes through a desolate canyon and emerges among lofty pine-clad mountains. Great beds of lava, poured out in some ancient time, overlay the granite and red sandstone rocks. The lava flow winds in and out among canyons, varying from fifty feet to a mile wide. Horses cannot keep their footing on the glass-like rock, and the edges cut shoe-leather to ribbons.

At 18.3 *m.* is the junction with a dirt road; R. here to PANGUITCH LAKE, 0.2 *m.* (*fishing, hunting, camping*), which fills a volcanic basin a mile long and three-quarters of a mile wide. Along the lake shore are playgrounds, an outdoor theater, picnic grounds, and a ball park.

At 32.8 *m.* is the junction with State 55 (*see Cedar Breaks National Monument*), and State 143 (*see Tour 1f*).

At 86.9 *m.*, on US 89, is the junction with State 12.

Left on State 12, asphalt-paved, to the mouth, 2.5 *m.*, of RED CANYON, a brilliantly-colored gorge which is often mistaken for Bryce Canyon. Although full of color this little canyon does not compare with Bryce.

At 14.1 *m.*, where State 12 turns R. (*see Bryce Canyon National Park*), is the junction with State 22 to Widtsoe (*see above*) and State 54; L. (straight ahead), State 54, graveled, passes through the northeastern section of Bryce Canyon National Park (*see Bryce Canyon National Park*).

TROPIC, 7.7 *m.* (6,298 alt., 515 pop.), on State 54, is a farming community surrounded by orchards and vineyards.

CANNONVILLE, 12.8 *m.* (6,000 alt., 250 pop.), on State 54, was locally known as "Gun Shot," the settlers maintaining that it was not large enough to be called a cannon. Water is brought a long distance to irrigate this quiet little valley.

HENRIEVILLE, 16.8 *m.* (6,000 alt., 241 pop.), on State 54, is a farming community in a small valley, strung along the highway like a necklace. Since 1930, scientists have made this town a base for expeditions into the Kaiparowits Plateau (*Caution: This is a several weeks' pack-trip and should not be attempted without competent guides and adequate equipment*). Among its wilderness of stark rocks, within reach from Henrieville, are cliff dwellings, flaming monoliths, strange fossils, dinosaur tracks, slashed canyons, inaccessible tablelands, sand dunes, small lakes, cave dwellings, burial mounds, and petroglyphs. In one of these ancient pictures women kneel with out-stretched arms in prayerful supplication; in another fourteen hands, red, yellow and green, point toward a mural of golden butterflies.

The Chinle formation, so common in this area, is described by Byron Davies, of Provo, an archeology student who explored the area in 1938-39, and is (1940) preparing a paper on his discoveries:

> No matter how many colors we could conjecture, and all the resultant blends, there were still shades and tones . . . which we had not imagined existed before we studied this Chinle. All the possible tones that may be achieved from such colorful mineralizing agents as manganese, nickel, antimony, copper and iron are represented here. Scarlet, purple, green, yellow and lavender merge and blend into each other, with a grace and delicacy like the richness of faint spices in something good to eat.

SMOKY MOUNTAIN, south of Henrieville, is accessible through a canyon containing more than three hundred caves, once inhabited by prehistoric peoples. Millions of tons of material have issued forth from the side of this mountain, "not like slag, but rather it has created a patchwork of colors . . . spotted with sharp lines between hues. . . . From cracks in the mountain running down to an abysmal depth, smoke billows up in Satanic and diabolical fury. As the smoke comes to the surface, it brings with it a yellow, waxy material which adheres to the sides of the rocks. The yellow contrasting with other blackened surfaces resembles . . . the gaping maw of some hellish pagan monster." The fumes come to the surface at a number of places in an area twenty miles square. In places, subterranean bubbling is plainly audible. Also in the Kaiparowits country, Mr. Davies discovered and named Turtle Mountain, where he found complete and fragmentary fossil turtle shells. About equidistant from Henrieville and Escalante, near the Canaan Mountains, is a forest of petrified trees, with many of the trees still standing. One giant measures thirteen feet in diameter.

Section d.   JUNCTION WITH STATE 12 to ARIZONA LINE;
65.2 m., US 89

Between the junction with State 12, 0 *m.*, and the Arizona Line, US 89 stretches across sagebrush-covered mesas and undulating foothills, with the gray-blue Paunsagunt Plateau looming to the east. Between Long Valley and Kanab, red sandstone outcroppings stand out vividly among serrated gray granite rocks, and the Pink, White, and Vermilion Cliffs dominate the eastern landscape. Cedars replace

the sage, and the green of trees is emphasized by the brilliant sandstone.
LONG VALLEY JUNCTION, 21.1 *m.*, is at the junction with
State 14 (*see Tour 1f, and Cedar Breaks National Monument*).
At 22.6 *m.* is the junction with State 11.

Left on this graded dirt road to ALTON, 3.9 *m.* (6,875 alt., 193 pop.), on
a mountain top cleared of trees, with houses clustered at the foot of pink and
white cliffs. Laid out in 1907, the town devotes itself mainly to dairying and
poultry farming. Quietly and scenically situated, away from the main highway,
Alton has aspirations as a summer resort and winter sports area.
Alton is at the junction with State 136 (*see below*).

GLENDALE, 35.6 *m.* (5,824 alt., 239 pop.), on US 89, is a
sheep and cattle center. A coal mine near by furnishes some employment, and orchards flourish in the small valley.
ORDERVILLE, 39.8 *m.* (5,250 alt., 439 pop.), was one of the
principal sites of the United Order (*see History*). Settled in 1864,
the town was vacated in 1866 because of Indian uprisings, but was
resettled in 1871. Four years later it became the center of one of the
major economic experiments of the Mormon Church. The people
pooled all their wealth, and so lived as to insure unity in moral, material, and spiritual life. They ate at a common table, met morning
and evening for worship, and carried on all activities under supervision
of a Board of Directors. Everyone turned the fruits of his labor into
a common storehouse and all shared equally in the proceeds. In most
communities where it was tried the Order lasted rarely more than three
years, but in Orderville the application of a community of effort was
practiced for eleven years.
Failure came as a result of cumulative difficulties. Security was
complete, but, especially after 1882, when southern Utah mines were
booming, young men complained. The boom brought their neighbors
brilliant economic opportunities; they had money, dressed fashionably in
"store clothes," and poked fun at the home-spuns of Orderville people.
Skilled workers were then paid more than common laborers, but this
arrangement, in a community where all effort was theoretically of equal
value, led to bitter feelings. The difficulties of trying to live under
one social and economic system, surrounded by an entirely different
one, slowly stifled Orderville. Because of high taxes and illegality of
its charter, the experiment was discontinued upon advice of Church
authorities.
In the *Utah Historical Quarterly* for October, 1939, Mark Pendleton tells the story of a romantically inclined young man who thought
he needed a new pair of trousers, though there were no holes or patches
in the pair he was wearing. His application was denied. When the
lambs were docked that spring the young man gathered the amputated
tails and sheared them, trading the wool at Nephi for a pair of store
pants.
"On his return he wore his new pants to the next dance. . . . The
story is that one young lady rushed to him, embraced and kissed him.
The president of the Order demanded an explanation, and when it was

truthfully given, he said: 'According to your own story these pants belong to the Order. You are requested to appear before the Board of Management tomorrow evening at half past eight and to bring the store pants with you.' The young brother was commended for his enterprise. He was told that all pants must be made of cloth of the same quality; that the store pants would be unseamed and used as a pattern for all pants made in the future, and that he should have the first pair."

MT. CARMEL, 42.5 m. (5,197 alt., 133 pop.), is a farm and livestock community, with a specialty of raising pinto ponies. These strikingly-colored "calico" horses, with the endurance and sure-footedness of their mustang ancestors, make excellent saddle horses and sagacious cow-ponies.

Between Mt. Carmel and Kanab, US 89 passes through Three Lakes Canyon, with its cave lakes and vari-colored, wind-blown sandstone formations, called locally "fossilized sand dunes."

MT. CARMEL JUNCTION, 44.3 m., is at the junction with State 15 (see Tour 1E and Zion National Park).

KANAB CREEK, 57.5 m., spanned by a concrete bridge, flows through KANAB CANYON (L), important for its archeological sites.

The JACOB HAMBLIN MONUMENT (R), 61.3 m., made of petrified wood, honors the most noted Mormon missionary to the Indians (see Tour 1f).

KANAB (Ute, willow), 61.7 m. (4,973 alt., 1,364 pop.), Kane County seat, is the commercial center of a vast farming, cattle-raising, and sheep-raising area. Zane Grey lived at Kanab in 1912 while writing the *Riders of the Purple Sage,* and the desert country eastward to the Kaiparowits Plateau is thought to be the locale of the story. Old-timers and guides of Kanab can still show the way to desert watering places of wild horses, and can occasionally capture an animal considered of value. Kanab hunters keep packs of trained mountain lion dogs and conduct hunts into likely lion country (see Tour 2c).

Kanab is a tourist center, catering to sightseers visiting scenic areas of southern Utah and northern Arizona. The Kanab Lions Club presents an annual "Forty-niners' Ball," in late autumn, with prizes for costumes and whiskers.

The O. C. BOWMAN ARCHEOLOGICAL COLLECTION (open 9-6 weekdays), in a grocery store at Center and Main Sts., contains prehistoric Indian mummies, skulls, implements, textiles, and pottery.

At 62.2 m. is the junction with State 136.

Left on State 136, an improved dirt road, to the junction, 8.3 m., with a dirt road; R. on the dirt road to the PETRIFIED FOREST, about 10 m., a small but colorful remnant of a prehistoric woodland. Fragments of these trees, when cut and polished, make exquisite jewelry.

JOHNSON, 12.6 m. (5,000 alt.), on State 136, more a string of ranch houses than a town, has frequently been used by movie colonies on location, and several films have been made in JOHNSON CANYON near by. Near the northern end of the canyon are several extinct volcanic craters. Volcanic dikes and lava flows can be seen along the road.

North of Johnson, State 136 passes PICTOGRAPH ROCK, covered by ancient drawings on the west and south faces of the cliff. Mummies have been taken from the little cave in the base of the cliff, now used by a rancher as a grain bin. There are several cliff dwellings just east of the cave (*guides at ranch*).

At 25 *m.* is the junction with a dirt road; R. on this road to SKUTUMPAH (Navaho, bad water) or ROBINSON RANCH, one of the oldest ranches in Kane County. John D. Lee, who was executed for his part in the Mountain Meadows Massacre (*see Tour 1f*), used this secluded ranch as a hideout, and his old house still stands. Before the turn of the century hundreds of cattle grazed at the foot of the cliffs and enormous roundups were held here; in 1940 the ranch made a specialty of its purebred cattle and sheep.

ALTON, 45.5 *m.* (6,875 alt., 193 pop.), is at the junction with State 11 (*see above*).

At 65.2 *m.* US 89 crosses the ARIZONA LINE (*see Arizona Guide*).

South of the Arizona Line, US 89 and Arizona 67 represent the only practicable hard-road approach to the North Rim of the Grand Canyon, used by many tourists combining a visit to southern Utah parks and monuments with a view of the Grand Canyon.

South from ARIZONA LINE, 0. *m.* on US 89 to JACOB LAKE, 33.3 *m.* (6,950 alt., 19 pop.), a ranger station and campground, is at the junction with Arizona 67. South on this is GRAND CANYON LODGE, 77.7 *m.* (8,153 alt.) (*cabins, lounge, restaurant, cocktail room*), from which a path leads L. to the tip of Bright Angel Point (*see Arizona Guide*).

Tour 2A

Sigurd—Loa—Torrey—Greenriver; 176.4 *m.*, State 24.

Graveled road between Sigurd and Torrey; dirt between Torrey and Greenriver. Accommodations at Loa and Torrey; cabin camps at Fruita (*Caution: Carry extra supplies and water between Fruita and Greenriver*).

State 24 winds around the flanks of red-topped, forested mountains and through narrow canyons. Narrow alluvial valleys are hemmed in by cliffs so brilliantly colored that in places the rocks seem luminous. The highway runs through Capitol Reef National Monument, and traverses the desert wasteland of the San Rafael Swell—some of it so barren that only stunted sage and cacti can survive. Arroyos and gulches incise this country, which is only partially explored, inadequately mapped, and so barren that few have penetrated it.

State 24 branches southeast from US 89 at SIGURD, 0 *m.* (5,270 alt., 364 pop.) (*see Tour 2b*), and winds through canyon country. Small farms cling to benchlands, and villages are cramped into thin strips of valley.

At 21 *m.* is the junction with State 62.

Right on State 62 to BURRVILLE, 2.5 *m.* (7,000 alt.), a farming town at the foot of COVE MOUNTAIN (10,750 alt.), a volcanic formation covered with dense stands of white pine and cedar. Cove Mountain is one of southern Utah's most popular deer-hunting areas.

KOOSHAREM, 7.1 *m.* (6,850 alt., 319 pop.), an agricultural and stockraising community, was named with a Paiute word for "wild red clover," a plant similar in shape and flavor to carrots. In Grass Valley, near Koosharem, is a portion of the KOOSHAREM INDIAN RESERVATION, where a small band of Paiute Indians live in tepees, sometimes visible from the road. A few own land and farm machinery, and several of the younger women have sewing machines. Most of these Indians make beaded buckskin gloves and moccasins, and gather pine nuts, which they sell or trade at neighboring towns.

At 29.5 *m.* is the junction with State 25.

Left on this graveled road (*Warning: on last three miles of road look out for deer crossing highway*) to FISH LAKE, 7.3 *m.* (*hotels, cabins, meals, dancing, boats, guides, fishing table, camps*), Utah's most popular fishing area.

In a region of past volcanic and glacial activity, Fish Lake is five and a quarter miles long, three-fourths of a mile wide, and is fed by six streams. It has an average depth of ninety feet and a surface temperature in midsummer of 64 to 69 degrees. The area abounds with wild life. Deer, elk, snowshoe rabbits, and other small animals and birds can be seen by day, and mountain lions are plentiful, preying on the 50,000 deer in Fishlake National Forest; at night, the indescribable wail of the coyote can be heard. There are grass-grown meadows, spire-shaped pines, white-boled aspens, and stately spruces, white sego-lilies and yarrow, red baneberry, yellow columbine, blue lupine, and purple and pink asters. In autumn the trees and underbrush are aflame with color, mingled with the blue-black of evergreens.

Game fish taken from the heavily stocked lake include rainbow, brook, and mackinaw trout. Trolling is most popular, but fly fishermen get creel limits from shore waters and from creeks, particularly Sevenmile. Many notables visit the lake, including Wallace Beery, motion picture actor, and Captain G. E. T. Eyston, former holder of the world's auto speed record.

The FISH LAKE TREATY MARKER (L), 7.6 m., marks the scene of a treaty with the Fishlake (Ute) Indians in June, 1873, preliminary to another treaty in July of that year, "ending" the Ute Black Hawk War (*see Tour 2b*). The record is by no means clear, but this is apparently the treaty described by G. W. Brimhall in his rare volume, *Workers of Utah* (Provo, 1889), only two copies of which are known to exist. Officially the Black Hawk War closed with signing of a treaty in Strawberry Valley in August, 1868, but unrest persisted thereafter. Brimhall attended the council, "taking my two ponies, and little boy, Omer, about ten years old, but large of statue and a good shot." At the treaty grounds, "everything looked gloomy, no Indians, no white men, no news, game scarce." Finally the representatives of both races arrived and "War Chief Ungustroup, great civil commissary, or high bishop," presented his indictment against the white men:

"The Mormons are bad to let the Mericats (Americans) or McCarthy's bring a big herd from Arizona here to eat all the grass and order his men to go and kill the squaw's tame deer . . . and never give squaw any money and in the fight the Mormons kill old man Indian, and shoot good old bishop in the mouth, and was not careful enough to let the bullet go out of their gun and kill Ipeds (little children), that is all." Another chief asked why A. K. Thurber, mayor of Spanish Fork, was not there, and answered his own question: "Maybe Squaw sick, maybe children sick, maybe mule lost, iron of one wheel, hind foot kick much up mountain, maybe so, wagon lost moccasin of fore foot, maybe so. . . ."

Judge John Cox, whom the Indians called "Corkees," then defended the accidental shooting of "Poikneapsy, the bishop":

"My best brother, Poikneap, his mouth very big now, but I love him, and the Great Spirit loves him too, or the bullet would make moccasin track down his ear canyon, and he would not have been here. . . . But Black Hawk, like snake on little rocks, creep to Gibbons wickiup, and kill father and mother and three little girls and two small babies. . . ." Brimhall spoke, realizing that "not to agree, means the bow strung tight, the arrow point sharp, like the rattle snake's tooth," and the council adjourned to the next day.

Following the pipe, and long silences, Ungutsup "arose, and, looking off horizontally, straightened himself up, stepping forward with the right foot, extended his right arm, and said: 'I, Ungutsup, have slept with treaty all night. . . . I have put Norman's shoe on my right foot, and keep Indian's moccasin on my left foot. Now if Mormons will put Indian's moccasin on his right foot, and keep Mormon's shoe on his left foot, then we will go down in the same trail to the creek and run into the river and fill up the great lake, and there be still, and our mud settle to the bottom and always be good water. . . .'" Poikneap was the next speaker: "'I am Poikneap. . . . The treaty has laid with me all night in my couch, and we did not sleep. . . . I put on both Mormon shoes. Mormons wear Indian moccasins, and carry treaty in their hearts all the time and keep good peace forever. . . . Now the Great Spirit . . . with his own finger write in with big marks on the hearts of the fathers, so when the little Indians come, and the little Mormons come into the wickiups and houses, and then all of us can see it forever. I am Poikneap all the time.'

Brimhall then gives his own speech:

'I am George . . . I speak with Brigham's heart. . . . I am with Great Chiefs . . . that make the pipe to smoke all around to make the treaty of peace, into one great biscuit, and eat it up. . . . I make Poikneap's treaty of peace . . . and we and our squaws and ipeds have plenty, and our hearts be glad, and laugh much for this, and many new moons, on the trail where the sun, moon and stars make tracks, and time for snows in winter, and rain in summer, to make leaves on the trees and grass in the valleys, and little hills for Indian squaw's tame deer and Mormon's cow to eat together and be fat. . . . I am George that strike the hot iron and make iron moccasin to put on pony's foot. . . .'

At 50.9 m. on State 25 is the junction with State 10 (see Tour 7a).

At 42.5 m. is the junction with State 72.

Left on this graveled road to the junction, 11 m., with a dirt road; R. on this road to ELK HORN RANGER STATION, 5.2 m. (camping facilities), at the summit of Thousand Lake Mountain (11,295 alt.). Here, to the east, is a view of Utah's PAINTED DESERT, best in early morning, when the sunlight, casting shadows from cliff to cliff, combines with the haze of dawn to produce a constantly-changing color screen over the landscape. On a clear day the Henry Mountains can be seen to the southeast, the Aquarius Plateau to the south, and the dim purple outline of the Colorado's gorge, to the east. Thousand Lake Mountain has by no means so many lakes; local residents say map makers confused this area with Aquarius Plateau (see below).

At 35.9 m., on State 72, is the junction with State 10 (see Tour 7a.)

LOA, 43 *m.* (7,000 alt., 408 pop.), on State 24, Wayne County seat, was named by Franklin B. Young, Mormon missionary, for the Hawaiian volcano, Mauna Loa. Every house in Loa, and in several other Wayne County towns, is a corner house; the remainder of each block is reserved for garden space. Wayne County people, like those of several other southern Utah areas, have their own "beef trust," taking turns at killing a beef to satisfy the local demand. Visitors cannot buy beef in the county; there are no butcher shops.

BICKNELL, 52 *m.* (7,125 alt., 228 pop.), was named in 1914 for Thomas W. Bicknell, an Easterner, who offered a library to any town in Utah that would take his name. This town, then called Thurber, and Grayson, in San Juan County, accepted. Thurber got half of the library, and the name; Grayson got the other half and became Blanding (*see Tour 10*), taking the maiden name of Mrs. Bicknell.

At 54.4 *m.* is the junction with a dirt road.

Right on this road to BICKNELL BOTTOMS, 0.3 *m.*, a stretch of low marshy land along the Frémont River, and an important feeding ground for migratory waterfowl. Duck hunters usually bag the limit here during the open season. The Frémont River is a muddy, slow-moving stream, partially used for irrigation, which winds its lazy way across Wayne County to the Colorado. Major J. W. Powell, Colorado River explorer, originally named it the Dirty Devil, by which it is still locally known, but himself later changed the name.

At 56.6 *m.* is the junction with State 117.

Right on State 117 to TEASDALE, 1.3 *m.* (7,000 alt., 224 pop.), and GROVER, 10.7 *m.* (6,750 alt.); R. from Grover, pack trails lead to the uninhabited AQUARIUS PLATEAU (*guides and horses absolutely necessary*), rising directly west of Grover to altitudes of 10,000 to 12,500 feet. The top of this little explored tableland, with an area of 49 square miles, is crowned with dense stands of conifers and aspens. The Aquarius is a remnant of a vast plateau that once extended east and south of the present channels of the Green and Colorado rivers, attaining, in prehistoric times, heights nearly a mile above those of today. Here are numerous lakes, many of them seldom fished. Here are wide, sage-silvered deserts, colossal mesas, pinnacles and spires that spring from the sand, floor-like areas heaped with vividly colored rocks. Untracked canyons and vertical walls force long detours, and the water supply is uncertain.
At 11.3 *m.* is the terminus of State 117 and the junction with a county road to Boulder and Escalante (*see Tour 2c*).

TORREY, 60 *m.* (7,000 alt., 217 pop.), a farming and livestock community, lies beside Cooks Mesa, a reef of magnificent red sandstone, which extends from Bicknell to Fruita (*see Capitol Reef National Monument*). Citadels, temples, and walls of red, white and yellow rock striped with purple, distinguish the local landscape. Bishop E. P. Pectol's private museum displays relics from cliff dwellings of the region. Charles W. Lee's underground museum is said to be one of the most curious collections of prehistoric Indian paraphernalia in the country. A mile north of Torrey is an Indian cemetery called the "Battleground," from which skeletons, some in a mummified state, have been disinterred.

At 62.5 *m.* the road skirts the border of Capital Reef National Monument, winds through Granite Wash, and dips into deep draws where wind and water have carved intricate designs on the sandstone walls.

At 71.7 *m.* the road crosses the west boundary, and at 85.2 *m.* the east boundary, of Capitol Reef National Monument (*see Capitol Reef National Monument*).

NOTOM, 86.7 *m.* (5,250 alt.), a discontinued post office, is a group of ranch houses strung along the road, where the canyons fade away and the land opens to wide desert vistas.

Between Notom and Hanksville the highway crosses a region of utter desolation. Irresistible sand dominates the region—shifting, blowing, covering everything; some ranches have been abandoned because of it. Soft sandstone spires and monuments have fallen; broken and buried, they make softly-clothed mounds in a wasteland of sand dunes. The late afternoon sun paints the dunes, mesas, and mountain walls in delicate mirage-like pastels.

CAINESVILLE, 96.4 *m.* (4,608 alt.), a string of ranch houses in a narrow valley, is spread out along five miles of highway. To the southeast (R) is a rock castle in a desert of dunes.

GILES, 107.8 *m.* (4,432 alt.), is a small farming community on the Frémont River. Irrigation dams have washed out so often that most of the settlers have gone away. The recreational hall, the school house, and scattered dwelling ruins remain to tell the story of dirty work by the Dirty Devil (Frémont River).

State 24 crosses Blue Valley, where the road is so slick in wet weather that the traveler is obliged to wait till it dries.

HANKSVILLE, 117.6 *m.* (4,125 alt., 185 pop.), isolated and secluded, was used, in the eighties and nineties, as a rendezvous for the Robber's Roost gang (*see Tour 7b*). The gang held sway over all the territory south and east of Hanksville; some people welcomed them in the small settlements, perhaps because the outlaws were good spenders. The large cattle companies were their chief victims.

Right from Hanksville on a dirt road to HITE, 60 *m.* (3,480 alt.), a "town" on the Colorado River with two stone buildings and a population of one! Cass Hite, supposed renegade and former member of Quantrill's Civil War guerillas, built a rock hovel here in the early 1870's. For years he existed by washing out "flour" gold from the sandbars of the Colorado. In 1893, when in one of the larger settlements for supplies, he was diligently questioned about gold on the Colorado. Whether to keep prospectors away from his hideout, or in sincerity, he said that the coarse gold had washed down to the riffles and sandbars at the foot of Navaho Mountain (*see Rainbow Bridge National Monument*). A gold rush was started, ferries were built, and great dredges were hauled to the Colorado, where they still lie, twisted and rusting. Finding no gold, disappointed prospectors "went after" Hite, intending to kill him. The resourceful isolationist went into hiding for two years until the incident blew over. Hite's crossing, which he called "Dandy Crossing," was consistently used by the Indians. It is one of four, and perhaps the best natural crossing of the Colorado. Captain Gunnison's crossing, at present Greenriver (*see Tour 7a*), the so-called Crossing of the Fathers, and a crossing on the Virgin River, now inundated by Lake Mead, are the others. Meager information led the pioneers to use Halls Crossing, Hole in the Rock (*see Tour 10*), and Lees Ferry. The cliffs of the Colorado open out at Hite, and the river slows down. Dr. A. L. Inglesby has launched several river expeditions from White Creek Canyon, a wide, shallow tributary entering from the east. The solitary dweller (1940), and the population of one, is Arthur Chaffin, who also has boats, and goes to Hanksville for supplies.

Between Hanksville and Greenriver the highway fords a series of streams and washes—dangerous to cross during heavy rains, when great walls of water may sweep down at any moment. For crossing sandy washes on this stretch, the traveler should carry several gunnysacks, which can be partly filled with sand or brush to aid traction in spots of soft sand. Semi-deflation of tires is helpful, if stuck.

At 172.6 *m.* on State 24 is the junction with an unnumbered dirt road.

Right (south) on this road through eroded uplands, across the mesa-lined valley of the San Rafael River, and onto a high mesa of shifting dunes, to BARRIER CANYON, 65 *m.*, where several groups of archeologically important aboriginal cliff paintings have been discovered. A guide (obtainable at Greenriver) is advisable. Barrier Canyon, locally known as Horseshoe Canyon, is a meandering gorge that works northward to the Green River from highlands west of the Orange Cliffs and Horse Thief Pasture Mesa. Its head is in Robbers Roost (*see Tour 7a*) and the canyon once served as an avenue by which fleeing outlaws reached their badlands refuge. Entry into the canyon is possible only at widely spaced intervals—in the area of the paintings there is but one horse trail into the gorge for ten miles in either direction. The walls rise sheer from three to five hundred feet above the canyon floor—massive bulwarks that scale off flecks of buff and magenta sandstone as large as houses. Near the bases, where water has worn the cliffs smooth or where cleavages have left flat facets, a prehistoric race carved and painted naive representations of its people and the things they did. The carved designs (petroglyphs) are small, from six inches to two feet high, and were apparently made by pecking into the soft sandstone with a piece of flint. They represent men, sheep, deer, antelope, and, apparently, dogs, accompanied by undecipherable symbols with lines as uncertain as twentieth-century doodles. The paintings are more restrained in subject matter—they depict men, animals, and hands. They are predominantly red, and are made of iron ore dyes with animal fat for a binding medium. The most imposing of these murals is about three miles up-canyon from the point of entry. Here, the figures are as much as nine feet high, and are occasionally bedecked with ceremonial regalia. In the summer and fall of 1940, the Utah Art Project reproduced these murals on canvas for an exhibition in the Museum of American Art, New York City, in the late winter and early spring of 1940-41.

GREENRIVER, 176.4 *m.* (4,079 alt., 474 pop.), is at the junction with US 50 (*see Tour 7a*).

Tour 3

(Malad, Idaho) — Plymouth — Garland — Junction with US 30S; US 191.
Idaho Line to Junction with US 30S, 21.6 *m.*

Oiled road; open all seasons.
Oregon Short Line (U.P.) R.R. roughly parallels route throughout.
Accommodations at Plymouth and Garland; service stations at convenient intervals.

US 191 traverses the productive Malad and Bear River valleys, transformed by water from a sagebrush-covered desert into one of the finest farming valleys in the State. The highway rolls between irrigated farms, and the outlying benchlands and foothills produce dry-farm wheat. The land drained by these rivers, equal in area to the State of Rhode Island, lies between the Wasatch Range on the east and the rolling Blue Hills (6,430 alt.) to the west.

This region was no doubt crossed many times by trappers, but the Stansbury Expedition was the first party of record over the route by wagon, in 1849, while exploring a route between Salt Lake City and Fort Hall, Idaho. "The valley of the Malade," Stansbury wrote, "is extremely level, free from underbrush, with very little artemisia [sagebrush], and affords ground for an excellent wagon-road. . . . Several fine springs were passed, in which the water was cold and clear."

At the turn of the century, with good prices for wheat and vast acres of dry land that could be farmed profitably by clearing it of sagebrush, middle western farmers were attracted to the district. In 1940 there were 182,000 acres in dry farms and 52,000 acres under irrigation; the principal crops are grain, alfalfa, sugar bets, potatoes, and vegetables.

US 191 crosses the IDAHO LINE, 0 *m.,* thirteen miles south of Malad, Idaho (*see Idaho Guide*).

At 4.3 *m.* is the junction with a dirt road.

Right on this road to WASHAKIE, 2.2 *m.* (4,773 alt., 166 pop.), a self-supporting Indian community, named for the Shoshone Indian leader, who was friendly to the whites and sought to educate his people in the ways of the white men. Not a reservation, the only Government institution at Washakie is a school supervised by the Indian agent at Fort Hall, Idaho; the settlement is under his jurisdiction, but the people are so law-abiding and self-sustaining that very little supervision is required.

The Washakie people appealed to Brigham Young for land in 1875, and he granted it. The Indians "proved" their land and received title, but were hampered by lack of water. On a trip to Cache Valley, Brigham Young studied the country from a hilltop. Pointing toward present Washakie, he said: "There is where I want the Indian colony to locate, this is the wrong place." The move was made, and the Indians have remained. Some of the land at Washakie is owned by the L.D.S. Church and cultivated by the Indians, but many of them own original homesteads. Nearly all of them are actively affiliated with the Church. For many years a white bishopric presided over the ward but Moroni Timbimboo, a full-blood Indian, was the bishop in 1940. Misunderstandings are normally adjusted by the bishopric and it is unusual for a county peace officer to visit the community. The principal source of Washakie income is from the farms, supplemented by day labor. The Washakies make beaded buckskin moccasins, gloves, and jackets of fine craftsmanship, which are traded at the stores as other farmers trade eggs and butter.

The last chief, Yeagah Timbimboo, who died in 1936, told in 1855 of seeing his people plowing, dressed in full war regalia. These Indians were among the first farmers in the State to raise dryland grain with modern machinery. They tell that in 1850, when their village stretched three and a half miles along the Malad River, 500 Indians died of smallpox, brought to them by a white trader. Only a few, those who stood in sagebrush smoke, survived. The bodies of the dead were devoured by dogs, for none was left to bury them.

PORTAGE, 5.4 m. (4,370 alt., 382 pop.), an irrigated farming community, was first settled about 1854. A strange treaty, which endured for many years, was consummated following the birth of a baby girl to the Waldron family in 1856. The Shoshone chief promised to bury the hatchet if he could name the baby. This concession was made, and the girl was named Eliza. The story is, however, that the mother had the name suggested to him by one of his squaws.

'PLYMOUTH, 9.7 m. (4,400 alt., 315 pop.), a dry-farming and stock-raising community, was settled in the spring of 1869, when cattlemen pitched their tents and grazed their stock over the surrounding area. During the first year the settlers made an effort to dry-farm, but a plague of crickets swept the fields clean. Discouraged, they turned to their livestock, which was the chief industry by 1877. Dry farming later met with more success, and this industry gradually outgrew stock raising.

At 14.1 m. is a junction with an improved dirt and oiled road.

Left on this road to FIELDING, 1.4 m. (4,389 alt., 333 pop.), a farming community first settled in 1893 and named by Joseph Fielding Smith, then President of the Mormon Church. There is some irrigated land, large areas of dry farms, and fat cattle graze on the neighboring hill. When the country was first reconnoitered in 1877, it was covered with sage, to the height of a mounted man's head.

UDY HOT SPRINGS (R), 2.6 m., is a resort with dancing and bathing facilities.

RIVERSIDE, 15.9 m. (4,400 alt., 216 pop.), on the north bank of the Bear River, is a farming community, which was laid out in 1893 under the supervision of the Bear River Canal Company and the Corinne Mill, Canal and Livestock Company. The prosperous Bear River Valley was occupied by struggling dry farmers and homesteaders before the waters of Bear River came winding down the canal in the early 1890's. Hundreds of people then filed on homesteads. Utah pioneers had learned how to put water on their land, but those who came into the valley, especially a German colony from Illinois, damaged their farms by too much water and too little drainage; alkali salts rose to the surface, and some lands were abandoned. The U. S. Department of Agriculture in 1934 sent Charles F. Brown, a drainage expert (a graduate of Utah State Agricultural College) to study the problem; he showed that over-irrigation can be overcome by proper drainage at a cost of 5 to 10 per cent of the land's value.

At 19.1 m. is the junction with an asphalt-paved road.

Right on this road to GARLAND, 0.7 m. (4,344 alt., 914 pop.), essentially a twin city with Tremonton (*see Tour 4b*). Together they constitute the trading center for a large agricultural area raising grain, sugar beets, and apples. Garland has one of Utah's largest sugar factories, and its annual Wheat and Beet Day, usually held in August, publicizes agricultural possibilities and accomplishments. Programs include band concerts, games, rodeos (at which Washakie Indians are enthusiastic performers), shooting exhibitions, and a flower show.

Farming activities of the surrounding region are dependent on the fortunes of the sugar industry, for its staple crop is the sugar beet. The harvest is determined by laboratory tests, showing when the beets have the highest sugar content. After harvest, the beets are trucked to the factory, where they are washed and passed into the slicer, which cuts them into pieces resembling shoestring potatoes. Sliced beets are dumped into diffusion tanks or "batteries," where hot water is added. The pulp is then separated and saved for cattle feed. The liquid is drained into carbonators and purified by limestone and lime gas (carbon dioxide). Drawn into a huge press, the juice is then filtered, siphoned into large "vaps" or evaporators, and reduced to a thick syrup. While still liquid it is forced into vacuum pans, the pressure reduced and the temperature increased, until the syrup becomes impregnated with sugar crystals. Separation of sugar from "molasses" is done in a centrifugal machine a "spinner," which revolves at great speed, forces out the syrup, and leaves sugar crystals. The molasses is mixed with various types of cattle feed. The crystals, still hot and moist, are elevated to a heated, rotating drum and dried as they pass through a flume. An enormous hopper is placed at the end of the flume and mechanically adjusted to regulate the flow of sugar as it is drawn off by sackers. Beet farmers are often carried over into the factory, as they are released from the fields. The factory "run" varies from 90 to 100 days, usually closing around the first of the year.

At 21.6 m., on US 191, is the junction with US 30S (*see Tour 4b*).

≪≪≫≫

Tour 4

(Evanston, Wyo.)—Ogden—Brigham City—Tremonton—(Burley, Idaho); US 30S.
Wyoming Line to Idaho Line, 83.1 m.

Union Pacific R.R. parallels route between Wyoming Line and Corinne; roughly parallels it between Corinne and Tremonton. Utah-Idaho Central R.R. parallels route between Ogden and Brigham City.

Asphalt and concrete between Ogden and Brigham City; concrete between Brigham City and Tremonton; elsewhere asphalt; open all seasons; heavy snows and drifts in winter.

Accommodations at short intervals in central section, and in larger towns elsewhere.

US 30S passes through canyons of eroded sandstone, with rock formations of nearly every geologic age, along juniper-dotted foothills of the Wasatch Mountains, over a mountain range covered with tawny June grass and scattered dark juniper trees, and through gold and green wheat and sugar-beet regions, dry, sage-clad uplands, and wide, rolling valleys. The flavor of the years lingers especially on the eastern section of the route. The canyons have reëchoed to the passage of Indians, trappers and explorers, Pacific emigrants, Mormon pioneers, wagon freighters, California gold-seekers, Pony Express riders, Overland Stage drivers, and travelers of every description. The first transcontinental railroad followed the beaten path through Echo and Weber canyons. Like dragon's teeth, railroad spikes sprouted railroad towns, which stagnated as the rails moved westward. Farmers settled in the canyon valleys, to till the soil and build sturdy villages; farming remains the chief source of income, heartened by trains that roar to markets east and west.

Northwest of Brigham City, the highway strikes into a region charted less early, but the wheels of pioneer wagons gradually wore a crude road, which in 1926 achieved the status of a Federal highway. In summer, the dry-farm wheatfields between Brigham City and the Idaho Line are a flowing golden sea.

Section a. **WYOMING LINE to BRIGHAM CITY; 93.8 m.,**
US 30S

This section runs through Echo Canyon, a cavernous ravine in which sounds reverberate weirdly from towering walls; thence down the gorge of Weber Canyon, carrying the turbulent Weber River, through the massive Wasatch Mountains; and across a thickly settled alluvial strip between the Wasatch Mountains (R) and Great Salt Lake (L).

US 30S crosses the WYOMING LINE, 0 *m.,* 5 miles west of Evanston, Wyoming (*see Wyoming Guide*) along gently rolling hills matted with wild grass and scrubby brush, where livestock graze and browse. The desert here has a moving beauty at dusk when the hills roll out under the sky in magical velvet tones of silver-blue and violet. Between the Wyoming Line and Echo Junction, US 30S is combined with US 189.

WASATCH, 4.8 *m.* (6,816 alt., 75 pop.), at the crest of the divide between the Bear and Weber rivers, is a sun-beaten, treeless railroad town built in two sections—yellow and white railroad houses and depot several hundred yards from the highway (R), and the corrugated iron road maintenance sheds and one- and two-room houses bordering the road (R). A black wooden water tank, rising high above these structures, dominates the town. Nearly every house is flanked by a stack of old railroad ties, to be sawed into stove-lengths and neatly piled for fuel.

At the head of ECHO CANYON, 6 *m.*, US 30S runs along the south slope of a shallow gully, in which Echo Canyon Creek, rising from springs (R), begins its winding course.

Low growths of silver-green sagebrush unroll on both sides of the road, representative of a plant, sometimes six or seven feet high, that covers much of the arid land in Utah, Wyoming, Idaho, and Nevada. Stubborn and tough, the sagebrush (*Artemisia tridentata*) thrives on land where grass perishes for lack of water. Under the sun's heat it has a strange, bitter and pleasurable aroma, the very hallmark of the American desert. Its gnarled gray wood has fed thousands of cheerful campfires, and to the westerner no smell so elementally recaptures the wide earth, star-strewn skies, and sweeping night winds as the deep fragrance of burning sagebrush. However, as Mark Twain observed, "as a vegetable it is a distinguished failure. Nothing can abide the taste of it but the jackass and his illegitimate child the mule. But their testimony to its nutritiousness is worth nothing, for they will eat pine knots, or anthracite coal, or brass filings, or lead pipe, or old bottles, or anything that comes handy, and then go off looking as grateful as if they had had oysters for dinner." In the late 1930's, University of Utah chemists experimented exhaustively on the uses of sagebrush, but when their retorts and Bunsen burners were put away the chief value of sagebrush was still its bright pungent blaze in campfires.

At 9.3 *m.* is the junction with a dirt road.

Left on this road (*open on application at ranch house 0.4 m. L.*) to CACHE CAVE, 1 *m.*, in which early-day trappers *cached* (hid) supplies. The advance company of westward-bound Mormon pioneers visited the cavern in July, 1847. Orson Pratt wrote in his journal: "The opening resembles very much the doors attached to an out-door cellar, being about 8 feet high and 12 or 14 feet wide. . . . We went into this cave about 30 feet, where the entrance becoming quite small, we did not feel disposed to penetrate it any further. On the under side of the roof were several swallows' nests." The cave was a prominent landmark on the old Mormon Trail, and was known as a "register of the desert," because many early emigrants and Mormon soldiers carved their names on its walls. Cache Cave also played a part in the career of Isaac Potter and Charley Wilson, western outlaws who, with a band of Ute Indians, terrorized northern Utah settlements in the sixties. Potter appropriated a consignment of grain for Fort Bridger, and hid it in the cave; later, with Wilson, he tried his hand at cattle rustling. Both were killed in Coalville during an attempted jailbreak.

The OLD MORMON TRAIL MARKER (L), 10.5 *m.*, a seven-foot granite monument, commemorates a route that was long-used before the Mormons traversed it in 1847. Sioux, Cheyenne, and Crow war parties came west by this route to raid Shoshoni and Utes. Trappers usually approached Great Salt Lake Valley via Cache or Malad valleys, but Étienne Provot apparently came west this way in 1824. James Clyman, a former Ashley trapper, recorded his impressions of Echo

Canyon in 1846; "the Bluffs of this ravin are formed of red rock made of smoothe water washed pebbles and the North side in particular are verry high and perpendicular and in many places hanging over the narrow vally is completely Strewn over with the boulder which have fallen from time to time from the cliffs above." The Harlan-Young party made the first wagon tracks down Echo Canyon in 1846, and were followed a week or ten days later by the tragically famous Donner-Reed party. These emigrant trains broke a road that saved the Mormons of 1847 enormous labor.

Orson Pratt took an advance company of "23 wagons and 42 men" into Echo Canyon in July, 1847, while Brigham Young, ill with "mountain fever," laid by to rest. ("Under the generic popular name 'mountain fever,' " says Sir Richard F. Burton in his *City of the Saints,* "are included various species of febrile affections, intermittent, remittent, and typhoid; they are successfully treated with quinine." Some present-day physicians think "mountain fever" was typhoid). "Our journey down Red Fork [Echo Canyon]," Pratt wrote, "has truly been . . . exceedingly picturesque. We have been shut up in a narrow valley from 800 to 1200 feet, and the most of the distance we have been walled in by vertical and overhanging precipices of red pudding-stone, and also red sand-stone. . . . These rocks were worked into many curious shapes, probably by the rains. . . . There is some willow and aspen in the valley and upon the side hills, and some scrubby cedar upon the hills. . . ."

In the vicinity of CASTLE ROCK, 14 m. (6,233 alt., 43 pop.), a railroad town named for a salmon-colored, castellated rock formation, erosion takes violent fancies. The red sandstone canyon walls (R), rising at some points a thousand feet from the valley floor, are carved into fantastic shapes—Steamboat Rock, Giant Teapot, Sphinx, Gibraltar, Sentinel, The Cathedral, and Pulpit Rock.

On the canyon wall (R), 20.3 m., strata of light-colored conglomerate sandstone, slanting under the weight of layers of red sandstone, contain fossils of Cretaceous plants, 55 to 95 million years old. The precipitous cliffs are pock-marked with holes, housing countless swallows.

In SAWMILL CANYON (R), 26.2 m., are Indian petroglyphs, scratched or chipped on the rocks in prehistoric times.

Ruins (R) of the OLD MORMON BREASTWORKS at THE NARROWS, 26.4 m., with cramped red walls and boulder-strewn canyon floor, recall the Mormon determination in 1857-58 to halt the U. S. Army during the "Utah War" (*see History*).

ECHO, 31 m. (5,460 alt., 175 pop.), a straggling railroad town, has a more colorful past than present. The town lies a half mile northwest of the site of the original Weber River stagecoach station, erected in 1853. The station was eagerly hailed by travelers, who often met with a riotous reception. A group of Shoshoni who lived near by made it a habit to descend hair-raisingly on the station as the stage-coaches drew up.

At one time the station was beset by a hard-shelled group of thieves known as the "Racket gang," who levied on horses and ponies, returning them promptly when rewards were posted. Down came Jack Slade, division superintendent for the Overland Stage line, of whom it was said, "Although a walking arsenal, he was not a killer at heart and only shot in self-defense or for the company's protection." Slade planted a few of the horse thieves in sterile canyon graves, and conditions improved. He met a gunman's death in Montana in 1864, being thoroughly hanged by vigilantes.

During railroad construction in 1868, tent saloons, gambling houses, and brothels sprang up to fleece the Irish "Paddies." Men often disappeared overnight. Seven unidentified bodies were removed from one hole, under a saloon and gambling hall; it was thought that the tent covered a trap door, through which dead men and refuse were dumped. The town quieted as the rails moved west, and the old Weber Station survived long enough to become a filling station. When it was razed in 1931, its thick old walls gave up a love letter from an eastern girl to a Pony Express rider, some small change, a five dollar gold piece, a Pony Expressman's gun case, and a pair of gold-rimmed spectacles.

West of Echo, US 30S enters the broad Weber Valley (*fishing, camping*), with its snug farms and small towns. Alfalfa and grain fields alternate in green disorder behind barbed strands of wire fence; brown-faced cows stand contentedly in creek beds, switching their tails. Under the green brush and grass on the rolling canyon sides, the earth stands forth in tones of dun and red. The course of the Weber River (L), is marked by a tall dark column of cottonwoods meandering down the canyon. In winter the cottonwoods are an unimpressive ashy tangle of branches except when transformed by snowfalls, but in spring their budding limbs are transformed to an incredibly delicate filigree of tender green. After midsummer the massed green of their foliage ripens into gold and runs like an amber fire through canyons already aflame with the scarlet brilliance of scrub oak and yellow-blazing aspen.

In the lower canyon of the Weber, streams, rain, and wind over long ages have carved fantastic forms on the hillsides. Conspicuously exposed are THE WITCHES (R), 32.4 *m.,* a group of natural rock monuments bearing top-heavy "witches' caps."

WEBER RIVER, 34.8 *m.,* even at flood, would be by eastern standards only a moderate-sized creek, but it is one of Utah's major streams and of inestimable importance to irrigators. From beginning to end it is, except for the Provo, the most heavily fished stream in Utah. Storms roil it heavily, and when the river is at its chocolated best anglers report that the fish get stuck in the mud and can't be pulled out. Besides rainbows and native cut-throats, German brown trout of large size inhabit the stream, much too canny to get caught except by accident or during high water, when no wisdom avails a Brown against an angleworm. The Weber (pronounced (WEE-ber) is presumed to have been named for Captain John G. Weber, who claimed to have joined General Ashley as a trapper in 1823. The Weber was also called Weaber and Weaver, and may have been named for Pauline Weaver, Arizona frontiersman.

HENEFER, 35.5 *m.* (5,337 alt., 413 pop.), a farming and live-stock community, uses US 30S for its main street, along which are several stores and gas stations, and a frame post office. A few gray log cabins still stand among more recent structures of stone and brick.

The old Mormon Trail parts company at Henefer with US 30S. The Clyman party of 1846 came from Great Salt Lake Valley this way. Because the Harlan-Young party, guided by Hastings, experienced such terrible difficulties in getting through lower Weber Canyon, the Donner-Reed train turned south at Henefer and broke the trail used by the Mormons through Emigration Canyon in 1847. Most immigration during the next dozen years followed the trail of 1847. Johnston's army came this way to Salt Lake Valley in 1858 and the route was used by the Overland Stage and the Pony Express. The superior merits of the more circuitous Parley's Canyon road, however, eventually prevailed, and the last section of the old Mormon Trail (State 65), is now rarely traversed.

West of Henefer, the canyon narrows, the red walls rise sometimes to a height of 4,000 feet, and the river fills the bottom of the canyon. Hasting's company found the way all but impassable, moving its wagons along the canyon wall where the railroads tracks now run. The gorges below Henefer prevented effective travel in lower Weber Canyon until construction of the railroad in 1868-69. The Union Pacific awarded Brigham Young the contract for grading down Echo and Weber canyons; Young let sub-contracts, and this difficult section of road was built by Mormon settlers, given grateful employment following the grasshopper plagues of 1866 and 1867.

At 39.3 *m.* is the junction with State 58, a dirt road leading to Lost Creek (*fishing*).

Right on this road to the Union Portland Cement Plant (L), 0.4 *m.*, and quarry. Constructed in 1906, this lime-dusted plant has a capacity of about 2,600 barrels of cement a day. The plant is dwarfed by its raw materials, since the whole mountainside supplies limestone and shale. Portland cement is manufactured by taking exact amounts of raw materials, such as limestone, marl, shale, clay, and blast furnace slag, grinding them to extreme fineness, roasting them at a temperature that would melt steel, and then regrinding the resultant clinker to a powder so much finer than flour that it can penetrate waterproof mesh. More than eighty operations are necessary before the cement is ready for market.

At 9.5 *m.* is the junction with a dirt road; R. on this road to the junction, 2 *m.*, with a foot-trail (*traversable only in dry weather*) leading to CHINATOWN, a natural amphitheater with vividly colored walls fifty feet high. Exquisitely carved natural rock formations occur here, shaped like Chinese pagodas, a huge ball in balance atop a supporting pillar, and Totem Pole Park—a group of eroded pillars resembling Indian totems.

DEVILS SLIDE (L), 39.7 *m.*, a geologic formation resembling a playground chute, consists of two parallel, vertical limestone reefs twenty feet apart, standing out forty feet above the canyonside. The Weber

River, here about twenty feet wide, flows slowly westward between the highway and the slide.

MORGAN, 47 *m.* (5,063 alt., 1,077 pop.), is the center and county seat of a rich agricultural district, with canning its chief industry. Morgan is especially noted for its fine peas. The compact business district, on the west side of the road, gives way to long rows of dwellings fronted by green lawns. Settled in 1860, the community, originally called Monday Town, was relocated and renamed in honor of Jedediah Morgan Grant, who died in 1856 shortly after the birth of a son, Heber Jeddy Grant, who in 1940 was president of the Mormon Church.

COMO SPRINGS (*cabins, swimming, dancing, boating*), in Morgan, is a popular resort, its mineral waters reputedly of medicinal value.

Left from Morgan on State 66, a narrow dirt road, impassable in wet weather, to EAST CANYON RESERVOIR, 11.5 *m.* East Canyon is a favorite haunt for fishermen on the opening days of the season when, it is said, so many hooks are dangled into the stream that the water rises a foot. Trout that survive the initiation are so hardened that for the rest of the season East Canyon anglers do their most effective fishing at the meat market. East Canyon reservoir is an important source of irrigation water for farms below the mouth of Weber Canyon.

PETERSON, 55.5 *m.* (4,889 alt., 400 pop.), a farming settlement, is at the point where the Bryant-Russell mounted party of 1846 crossed into Weber Canyon. The Harlan-Young wagon party, as shown by one of the few surviving narratives, printed in *The California Gold Book,* had great difficulties here:

The [Weber] canyon is scarcely wide enough to accommodate the narrow river which traverses it, and there was no room for roads between its waters and the abrupt banks. . . . Three times spurs of the mountains had to be crossed by rigging the windlass on top, and lifting the wagons almost bodily. The banks were very steep . . . so that a mountain sheep would have been troubled to keep its feet, much more an ox team drawing a heavily loaded wagon. On the 11th of August, while hoisting a yoke of oxen and a wagon up Weber mountain, the rope broke near the windlass. . . . The faithful beasts . . . held their ground for a few seconds, and were then hurled over a precipice at least 75 feet high, and crushed in a tangled mass with the wagon on the rocks at the bottom of the canyon.

West of Peterson US 30S passes through a narrow, V-shaped gorge, and the plunging stream is harnessed at several points to generate power. Below a series of hydroelectric plants, the water is released for irrigation.

DEVILS GATE, 61.9 *m.,* a narrow gorge flanked by vertical cliffs, provided another formidable barrier for the emigrants of 1846. The wagons and livestock were finally passed through with windlasses and ropes.

At the mouth of WEBER CANYON, 64.1 *m.,* is the eastern junction with US 89 (*see Tour 2a*), which is combined with US 30S for 6.6 miles. Great Salt Lake Valley opens to the west, the rolling, sage-clad foothills of the Weber Valley merging in the distance with the lake plain. Great Salt Lake is a long, slate-blue streak against low-lying Frémont Island to the southwest, and the taller heights of the Promontory Mountains to the northwest.

UINTAH, 65.3 m. (4,497 alt., 304 pop.), lies in a cove at the mouth of Weber Canyon, its neat, rectangular farms of gold and green like the sign and symbol of rural well-being. The first settlers came in 1850-51, and the town expanded swiftly; it is said for a short time to have exceeded Ogden in size, but most of the settlers moved on. Charcoal burning was an important early industry, but it disappeared with the juniper trees. Manufacture of sorghum molasses, when sugar sold for $1 a pound, was important for a time. For a short period after the Union Pacific laid its rails through the town in 1869, Uintah boomed as a point of transshipment to Salt Lake City. Old-timers remember when there were nearly a hundred business concerns, including hotels, restaurants, saloons, barber shops, tobacco shops, dry goods stores, grocery stores, and a hard-worked brewery. Completion of the Utah Central between Salt Lake City and Ogden in 1870, however, nipped Uintah's boom. In "The Life of Jonathan Dyer," published in his book, *Forays and Rebuttals* (1936), Bernard DeVoto has written understandingly of his Mormon grandfather, who settled at Uintah to raise fruit trees. DeVoto owes the small-boy memories of trains passing terrifyingly in the night, written into the opening passages of his first novel, *The Crooked Mile* (1924), to his early associations with Uintah.

Left from Uintah on a dirt road to SOUTH WEBER, 3 m., THE SITE OF THE MORRISITE WAR. An obscure English immigrant, Joseph Morris, in the late fifties announced that God had revealed to him his destiny "to be a mighty man, yea, to be a prophet in Israel." Morris wrote the Church heads many letters, advancing his claims and identifying himself as the "Seventh Angel" foretold by Daniel, but his letters were ignored and he made no converts until 1860. In that year he settled at South Weber, and thereafter he issued revelations in abundance—a doctrinal book, "*The Spirit Prevails*," contains 304. He and sixteen adherents were excommunicated in 1861, but organized their own church, predicting that the judgments of God should come as a whirlwind to wreak havoc among His enemies. Proselytes "consecrated" their property to his church, but dissension arose, and the Morrisites came into conflict with the courts. Believing the Millennial Day at hand, the Morrisites ignored court writs, and a military posse was sent to enforce them and arrest Morris and his lieutenants. After a three-day battle, the Morrisites surrendered. In a scuffle that followed, Morris was slain, a disciple writing, "Such was the earthly end of Joseph Morris, but he still lives in the hearts of his followers." Six Morrisites, including two women, and two posse members were slain in the "Morrisite War." Survivors were taken to Great Salt Lake City, where some were fined and sentenced, but the governor pardoned them. General Patrick E. Connor settled some of the Morrisites at Soda Springs in what is now Idaho, while others scattered into Oregon and California; they rapidly disintegrated as a religious organization, although a few faithful members in the West still preach the cause.

Northwest of Uintah, US 30S climbs the foothills along the old Bonneville benches and circles the abrupt face of the Wasatch Moun-

tains to Ogden. Great Salt Lake Valley opens out to the north and
south. In the distant southwest is a shoulder of the Oquirrh Mountains, hazed by the smoke of the Garfield smelters. The highway runs
past farm houses and cultivated fields.

At 70.7 *m.* is the southern junction with US 91, with which US
30S is combined, through Ogden (*see Ogden*), for 23.1 miles (*see Tour
1b and 1c*).

Section b. *BRIGHAM CITY to IDAHO LINE; 83.1 m., US 30S*

US 30S passes through a rich agricultural district, over mountain
ranges blanketed with June grass and scattered juniper trees, past
wheat and sugar beet fields, sage-covered dry-lands, alkali flats, and
wide, open valleys.

West of BRIGHAM CITY, 0 *m.* (4,439 alt., 5,643 pop.) (*see
Tour 1b*), US 30S skirts the edge of Box Elder lake, and strikes out
across marshlands, drab foothills, sage-dotted flats, past farms and
ranches.

BEAR RIVER, bridged at 5.9 *m.,* here a slow, brackish stream,
heads in the Uinta Mountains, meanders over a 350-mile course through
Wyoming and Idaho, and returns to Utah to empty into Great Salt
Lake at a point only ninety airline miles from its source. Dams, at
various intervals along its course, impound and divert the waters for
industrial and agricultural purposes. More than 52,000 acres of fertile
valley lands are irrigated by this sluggish stream.

CORINNE, 6.7 *m.* (4,229 alt., 411 pop.), dreams in the sun, like
an old man remembering his youth. The once roaring, fighting, hilarious rakehell town has little to show for its riotous past. A handful
of houses, a few weather-stained business buildings, a church, and a
school, are all that remain of a city of more than 2,000 people. A
discerning eye can trace the boundaries of the old city, but the men
who dreamed and slaved to make it a great railroad and steamboat
center have long since gone. It is hard to imagine that this little
farming village was once the gentile stronghold, once aspired to become
the capital of Utah, once had hopes of becoming a great agricultural
center, and was once so wild it had to hire an "outlaw-tamer" to rid
itself of undesirables.

In 1868 Mark A. Gilmore, with five gentile companions, stood on
the west bank of the Bear River and visioned a throbbing gentile
metropolis, a great railway junction, and steamboats plying back and
forth across Great Salt Lake from the mines to the south. They made
haste to acquire the land. A contract was made with the Union Pacific
Railroad to survey and lay out the town, with alternate lots for compensation. The men felt secure with such a powerful ally behind them.
Utah was the Mormon stronghold, and, with a vivid tradition of
eastern persecution, the Saints would not look with favor upon any
gentile settlement. The Mormons were staunch in their beliefs, insisted
upon conformity to their standards, and had as a fixed purpose the

creation of a State of their own. On the other side were men, brought in by the railroads, who were more absorbed with railroad and mining economy than with religion. Within two weeks more than 300 frame buildings, shanties, and tents were erected, and the population rose to 1,500, excluding the 5,000 Chinese left behind by the railroad. To handle this influx, a temporary city government was set up. Two years later, in 1870, the Territorial legislature incorporated the town under the name of Corinne City and granted a charter.

Corinne at once became a thorn in the side of Mormon authorities in their determined effort to control the Territory. With completion of the transcontinental railroad in 1869, thousands of freighters swarmed into the "Burg on the Bear," making it their headquarters. Most of them were rough, hard-boiled adventurers, fresh from the Civil War, with fairly stable desires and demands, all of them elemental. They spent weeks away from civilization, and when they reached Corinne they wanted a good time. Corinne gave it to them.

One enterprise did a thriving business in Corinne. Divorces were granted for $2.50 without the presence of applicants. This practice was stopped after some 2,000 persons had received "divorces" which were later threshed out in courts all over the country. Undesirables flooded the town. Daniel Ryan, a former Civil War officer, who had a reputation as a "law and order" gun-fighter, was appointed Corinne's "outlaw-tamer" in 1869. He either drove the outlaw out of town, or shot it out with him. He cleaned up Corinne, and died a natural death in his old age.

Fateful for Corinne was the decision settling the point of junction for the Union Pacific and Central Pacific railroads. Promontory, where the rails met in 1869, was unsuitable; Brigham Young was determined to make Ogden the junction; and Corinne fought desperately for it. The junction point was finally settled at Ogden. "The Gentile City" became the butt of sarcastic editorials, jokes, and ridicule as business institutions migrated to Ogden.

But the founders of Corinne were fighters. They formulated a plan for diverting the waters of the Bear River for irrigation. This enterprise would take more money than the little settlement could raise, so a memorial was addressed to Congress urging a grant of public land in Bear River Valley: "It is the only place where a truly American community can be brought into permanent and successful contact with the Mormon population, whose feet have trodden and who hold in their relentless grasp, every other valley in Utah. . . . It is a notorious fact that everywhere in this territory the Mormon prophet and his coadjutors have acquired control of the water courses issuing from the mountain sides, that can be used for irrigation and of all the canyons that afford any valuable timber within reach of cultivated lands. This monopoly . . . has enabled them to confine immigration to those of their own creed." A bill giving effect to this petition was introduced in the House and Senate, but nothing ever came of it. An item in the *New York World* in 1870 shows that Corinne had not given up the hope of being a great city: "Congress proposes removing the capital of Utah from Salt Lake City to Corinne, which, containing but a few Mormons, is deemed a fitter place to put the military corps in."

The defeat of the memorial was a shock to Corinne, but the founders turned from the railroad and the land to Great Salt Lake. In 1871 a stern-wheel steamboat was built to navigate the lake, and Corinne became a "port of entry." The *City of Corinne,* 70 feet long, had three cargo decks. The first trip was made to Lake Point in 1872, with machinery for the smelter at Stockton, and the boat returned with ore from the Tintic district and Nevada. The second boat, the *Kate Connor,* was launched shortly after, but the "curse of Corinne" still held. The *City of Corinne* did not pay, and the *Kate Connor* found her destiny on a mud bar in Bear River. The *City of Corinne,* renamed the *General Garfield,* became an excursion boat and finally ended as a pavilion at Garfield Beach, south of Great Salt Lake.

From 1870 to 1874 Corinne was the stronghold of the Liberal Political Party, headed by the anti-Mormon General Patrick Connor. A convention was held at Corinne in 1870, and General George E. Maxwell was nominated for Congress. Like all of Corinne's ambitions, this one also blew up. By condemning polygamy, they alienated the "Godbeites," who, although they had left the Mormon Church, still practiced polygamy. Maxwell was defeated. The *New York Herald* remarked that "The Gentile town of Corinne polled more votes than it had inhabitants," which was no doubt true, since transient railroad workers were registered. Maxwell ran again two years later and was again defeated.

In 1872 a diphtheria epidemic swept the community. Hundreds died, and people began to desert the city. More families left in 1876, when Indians surrounded the town, helping themselves to anything they wanted until troops from Fort Douglas drove them out. Still more families departed when alkali worked to the surface of the ground, laying waste to fields and orchards. The final straw to break Corinne's back was the Lucin Cutoff, constructed in 1903, which left Corinne far inland from the new roadway. In 1940 the town was striving to overcome the threatening alkali, in a comeback as an agricultural community. Even Corinne's old enemies admit that the town did much to establish the commercial status of Utah. Failure dogged all of its ambitions, but it was the first gentile town in Utah, had the first gentile school, was the home of the first political party to oppose the Mormon People's Party, and was the first to put steamboats on Great Salt Lake.

At 6.9 *m.* is the junction with State 83.

Left on this improved dirt road (*difficult in winter*) to SULPHUR SPRINGS, 6.7 *m.* (*duck hunting*), flowing from the base of Little Mountain, and forming a series of pools. In late autumn, mallards fly north over the scalding springs in great flocks.

At 20.6 *m.* is the junction with a poor dirt road; L. on this road through sage-covered hills to PROMONTORY POINT, 30 *m.* (4,217 alt.), from which Great Salt Lake spreads out in panorama. The Southern Pacific's Lucin Cutoff across Great Salt Lake skirts the shore for four and a half miles. West of the point are extensive salt beds. State 83 crosses a valley dotted by half a dozen ranches. Dry-land wheatfields roll back from both sides of the highway, like warm restless sunlight. Wild horses run in the mountains beyond.

At 24.6 *m.* is the junction with a dirt road; L. on this road to PROMONTORY, 1.2 *m.* (4,902 alt.), where the fulfillment of one epic American dream is marked by the GOLDEN SPIKE MONUMENT. Here the Central Pacific's *Jupiter* steamed across the last-laid rails on May 10, 1869, to bang its iron snout against the Union Pacific's *No. 119,* completing the railroad linkage of a continent (*see Transportation*).

At 30.9 *m.* on State 83, is the junction with a dirt road; L. on this road to ROZEL, 4 *m.* (4,593 alt.), which sprang up with the railroad. Steamboats on Great Salt Lake at one time carried wood to Rozel for locomotive fuel. In the 1920's the town became a center for intermittent oil-drilling activities, and, a decade later nearby asphaltum deposits attracted attention (*see Mining*).

Near LAKE, 35.6 *m.* (4,213 alt.), a railroad station, is the point, marked by a wooden sign, where on April 28, 1869, a Central Pacific track-laying crew established a record that still stands by laying ten miles of track in one day. Grenville Dodge, Union Pacific engineer, was not, however, greatly impressed: "They took a week preparing for it, and embedded all their ties beforehand. . . ."

KOSMO, 40.9 *m.* (4,222 alt.), is visible from afar as a silver shaft upthrust from the drab surrounding land; the shaft is a sixty-foot grain elevator rising above scattered houses.

LOCOMOTIVE SPRINGS (L), 48.1 *m.,* pour out their waters from the center of a large flat, creating thousands of acres of marshland, wild hay fields, and sloughs. Thousands of brant, snipe, and ducks frequent the marshes, which are included in a migratory bird refuge.

KELTON, 60.3 *m.* (4,222 alt.), which for several years after completion of the railroad served as a junction for stage and freight lines from Oregon, was the center, in 1934, of the severest earthquake since white occupation of Utah, though there were no casualties and no serious damage. From the rent earth at Kelton gushed muddy water and black slime; the cracks—in some places three feet across—were plainly visible along the highway for several years. Houses in Kelton were swung awry, and for a time school was held in a house, propped up by railroad ties and beams, which leaned at an angle of almost 30 degrees. Subsequently the school was transferred to a passenger car donated by the Southern Pacific Railroad. Salt Lake City experienced mild tremors from this earthquake (*see Salt Lake City*). Kelton is a shipping center for Idaho grain, and has a small store, a few buildings constructed of ties, and a large red warehouse.

At 71.5 *m.* is the junction with State 70 (*see below*).

BEAR RIVER CITY, 11.6 *m.* (4,253 alt., 436 pop.), on US 30S, is an agricultural community, sugar beets its chief crop. Dry farming in Utah (*see Agriculture*) had its beginning here in 1863 when Scandinavian settlers experimentally planted wheat on non-irrigable sagebrush land and were rewarded with a fair crop.

The JIM BRIDGER MONUMENT (R), 13.1 *m.,* a cobblestone structure bearing a bronze plaque, honors the frontiersman who came this way to his discovery of Great Salt Lake (*see Great Salt Lake*).

ELWOOD, 17 *m.* (4,290 alt., 520 pop.), is flanked on all sides by apple orchards. Originally settled for grazing, the district became a dry-farming and horticultural center.

At 18.6 *m.* is the junction with US 191 (*see Tour 3*).

TREMONTON, 19.9 *m.* (4,322 alt., 1,444 pop.), an agricultural and railroad shipping center, producing chiefly sugar beets and alfalfa, was settled in 1888. A business boom followed laying out of the townsite in 1903, and Tremonton now boasts a public library, a three-story hospital, and a Mormon chapel. The town dresses and ships 100,000 turkeys annually.

Between Tremonton and Blue Creek, US 30S winds over smooth, rolling hills and through open valleys in which grain fields ripple with the wind. Rows of Lombardy poplars anchor the farms, in pleasing contrast with the desolate, uncultivated upland.

At 22.8 *m.* is the junction with an oiled road.

Left on this road to PENROSE, 8 *m.* (4,300 alt., 155 pop.), a branch station of the Malad Railroad, which runs from Tremonton to Penrose for the benefit of beet growers and dry farmers. The town was named for Charles W. Penrose, editor, poet, and Mormon Church official, who wrote some of the Mormons' sweetest hymns. "O Ye Mountains High," still a Mormon favorite, he wrote as an English convert, before he ever laid eyes on Zion's mountains.

At 13 *m.* is the junction with State 83 (*see above*).

BLUE CREEK, 41 *m.* (4,660 alt.), is a farming town with a few scattered houses and a ·post office.

Left from Blue Creek on an unimproved road to BLUE CREEK RESERVOIR, 4 *m.*, one of the few resorts for Utah bass fishermen.

SNOWVILLE, 57.3 *m.* (4,544 alt., 168 pop.), the center of Curlew Valley farming and dairying activities, was not named for the climate, though temperatures range from 100 degrees in summer months to 40 below zero in winter. Snowville was settled in 1871 by Idahoans, and named for Lorenzo Snow, who later became fifth President of the Mormon Church. Curlew Valley is bisected by meandering Deep Creek. This stream, Snow predicted, would be "an everlasting stream whose water should never diminish, and one from which many should come to drink." The prediction has thus far been valid; even in parched years Deep Creek has not lowered.

Between Snowville and the Idaho State Line, the highway crosses gray sage-covered flats and desert.

At 75.8 *m.* is the junction with State 70.

Left on graveled State 70 where, in summer, the heat waves obscure the land like rippling water as the sun beats down on the baked, white clay flats, to BLACK BUTTE (R), 11.7 *m.*, a black volcanic knoll surrounded by lava ridges, rising in sharp contrast from the white clay plain.

At 18.5 *m.* is the junction with State 83 (*see above*).

PARK VALLEY, 20.5 *m.* (5,600 alt., 167 pop.), was settled by ranchers in 1869, the rich grass in the valleys supporting large herds of cattle, though scarcity of water always counterbalanced fertility of the soil. More lively days came with mining excitement in the late years of the century. A vein of gold was struck, and, as recalled by C. W. Goodliffe, early settler, for some time "everything was hustle and bustle. A small five-stamp mill was erected and money was turned out at the rate of $500 per day."

In 1914 a group of Russians moved in to colonize the valley, but successive years of drouth forced abandonment of their project in 1920. Sheep- and cattle-raising has become the chief source of income for settlers of the region. In

1937 a range rider, hunting coyotes, fell with his horse down a thirty-foot well abandoned by the Russians. Horse and rider landed right side up. The horseman managed to throw his lariat out of the well and was drawn up by a companion; it took forty-eight hours to extricate the horse.

ROSETTE, 25.6 *m.* (77 pop.), serves a few scattered farms. Many of the original settlers were Swiss. Between Rosette and Lucin, State 70 skirts the edge of the Salt Desert (*see Tour 6c*).

LUCIN, 76.8 *m.* (4,471 alt., 259 pop.), is a sun-baked, weather-beaten hamlet clinging for life to the railroad (*see Great Salt Lake*).

At 84.3 *m.* State 70 crosses the Nevada Line (*see Nevada Guide*).

At 83.1 *m.* US 30S crosses the IDAHO LINE (*see Idaho Guide*).

Tour 5

Junction with US 30S—Coalville—Kamas—Provo; 76.7 *m.*, US 189.

Route paralleled by Union Pacific R.R. between Echo Junction and Wanship; by Denver and Rio Grande Western R.R. between Kimballs and Park City, and between Heber and Provo.
Concrete-paved between Coalville and Wanship; elsewhere asphalt-paved and improved dirt. Heavy snows and drifts in winter between Heber and Provo. Hotels and tourist camps in larger towns; other accommodations at short intervals.

US 189 skirts the east shore of Echo Reservoir along rolling foot-hills; passes through mountainous regions and fertile valleys; skirts the eastern end of the Uinta Range, highest in Utah; and in the southern third of the route extends through timbered, scenic Provo Canyon. Before, and for several years after, the advent of the trans-continental railroad, the highway between Echo Junction and Wanship was used by freighters operating between Salt Lake City and Fort Bridger, Wyoming. Fleet coaches of the Overland Stage operated for a while over the same route. Side trips into the mountains, including the High Uintas Primitive Area, pass through woodlands at the foot of snow-lined peaks. Fishing is excellent in streams and lakes, and hunting is good in season.

US 189 branches south from US 30S at ECHO JUNCTION, 0 *m.* (5,460 alt.) (*see Tour 4a*), and parallels the Weber River (R).

ECHO DAM and RESERVOIR (R), 0.9 *m.*, a $2,500,000 Federal Reclamation Project built in 1930, impounds water for nearly 80,000 acres of farm and orchard land in the lower Ogden and Weber valleys. The earthwork and concrete dam, 155 feet high and 1,887 feet long, forms a reservoir with a capacity of 74,000 acre-feet of water.

COALVILLE, 5.6 *m.* (5,571 alt., 948 pop.), Summit County seat, situated on a bench of land sloping from the narrow mouth of Chalk Creek Canyon to the Weber River, is a supply center for farmers and ranchers. Dial telephones, the first in Utah, were installed here in April, 1939.

Summit County has been an accurate political indicator since the turn of the century. The *Saturday Evening Post* for January 21, 1939, suggests that the straw-vote takers poll this county: "It wouldn't cost much; Summit County numbers only 2500 families. . . . since 1900 it has been an accurate vest-pocket barometer of every presidential election except one: In 1912 it went for Taft. In the last three presidential elections, it represented the national vote . . . within 1 per cent."

William H. Smith, while freighting through this area in 1858, noticed that wheat spilled from the wagons grew to maturity. Where wheat would "volunteer," he decided, was a good place for a settlement. The following spring, Smith settled here with several other families. Thomas Rhodes in 1858 found an outcropping of coal in Chalk Creek Canyon. The first mine was opened in 1859, and more mines were developed in succeeding years. In 1940, however, only a few small mines were producing.

J. Will Robinson, Utah Representative in Congress since 1932, was born in Coalville.

Left from Coalville on State 133, a dirt road, to the mouth of CHALK CREEK CANYON, 1.1 *m.* Chalk Creek is a favorite trout stream for weekend visitors from Salt Lake City.

HOYTSVILLE, 8.8 *m.* (5,663 alt., 353 pop.), is a farming town, settled in 1859. The settlement was first known as Unionville, because its fort, built in the 1860's, was a common gathering place during Indian alarms.

WANSHIP, 13.6 *m.* (5,862 alt., 205 pop.), settled in 1859 and named for a Ute chief, retains many of its original frame buildings, set close together along the highway. The houses were built of native lumber, sawed at pioneer mills in the mountains. In 1872, when the population was three times the present number, Wanship was an important stage station on the Overland route. Visiting Indians treated the white men in a friendly manner and made no attempt to damage the station or delay the stages, but they had a reputation for carrying away anything that was not nailed down.

Right from Wanship, on State 530, through Silver Creek Canyon to KIMBALLS STATION MONUMENT (R), 9.4 *m.*, two stone columns supporting a wooden sign. The old stagecoach road can be seen 100 yards behind the monument. This monument commemorated the KIMBALLS STAGE STATION (R), 9.6 *m.* (*private*), a two-story, red-tinted stone building with a shingle roof, used in 1940 as a dwelling on the Bittner ranch. Herds of sheep and white-faced cattle graze through the valley, and the creeks are open to fishermen. One of the few original Overland Stage stations still standing, it was built in 1862 by William H. Kimball, Mormon pioneer, after the original Mormon Trail had been abandoned in favor of a more desirable route from the east down Weber Canyon to Echo, thence up Silver Creek to this point, and down Parley's Canyon (*see Tour 6b*) to Salt Lake City.

KIMBALL JUNCTION, 11.2 *m.,* is at the junction with US 40 (*see Tour 6b*).

ROCKPORT, 17.5 *m.* (6,009 alt.), a village on the Weber River, was settled in 1860 by Henry Reynolds, who built a log house here. The winter of 1861-62 was severe, hay was scarce, and the livestock suffered. Too poor to pay cash, the settlers jointly mortgaged a portion of their next year's grain to buy a piece of fresh beef for Christmas dinner. Because of threatened Indian trouble the settlers were advised to move to Wanship in 1865. Begging to remain, they were allowed to do so if they would build a fort. The old "Rockfort" still stands, its stone walls two feet thick and eight feet high.

PEOA, 21.7 *m.* (6,191 alt., 211 pop.), was settled in 1857 and named Pe-OH-a, a Ute word meaning to marry. The chief products are grain, hay, and poultry.

OAKLEY, 24.6 *m.* (6,517 alt., 371 pop.), is built around a flour mill, a post office, a sawmill, and a creamery. It was first settled by William Stephens in the 1860's, and his son built a burr-type flour mill. Equipped with roller machinery, the Oakley mill remains an important local industry.

KAMAS, 30.2 *m.* (6,473 alt., 668 pop.), is an incorporated city on Beaver Creek. Thomas Rhodes, a hunter, obtained permission from Brigham Young to settle here with twenty-five others in 1857. During the hard winter of 1861-62 they ground wheat in a coffee mill, their only available machine.

Kamas is at the junction with State 34 and State 150.

1. Right on State 34, a poor dirt road, to a junction with US 40, 4.3 *m.* (*see Tour 6b*).
2. Left on State 150, a graded dirt road, the route zigzags along pine-clad slopes, past high mountain peaks, through park-like meadows and narrow canyons, to BALD MOUNTAIN PASS (11,000 alt.), 29.8 *m.,* the highest auto road in Utah with a grade of not more than 8.5 per cent.
At 31.4 *m.* is the junction with a dirt road to MIRROR LAKE, 0.6 *m.* (*see High Uintas Primitive Area*), on the shore of which is MIRROR LAKE LODGE (*cabins, meals, supplies, boats*). The lake is at the foot of Bald Mountain (11,947 alt.). Seventy-five other lakes, well stocked with fish, are within a radius of six miles.

FRANCIS, 32.4 *m.* (6,525 alt., 345 pop.), is a farming community in Rhodes Valley.

Left from Francis on State 35 (*sometimes impassable in winter*) to CAMP KILLKARE (R), 7.2 *m.* (*cabins, fishing*), a summer resort catering to Provo River fishermen; the South Fork dashes down the steep floor of the canyon.
At 11.4 *m.* State 35 crosses the east boundary of the Wasatch National Forest and the west boundary of the Uintah National Forest. A GRANITE MARKER (L), 16.9 *m.* honors Masashi Coto, a Japanese aviator on an attempted globe-girdling flight, who crashed near by in 1929.
At 19.8 *m.* is an exceptional view (R) of the Wasatch Mountains. The

road traverses a series of switchbacks; in places it is so narrow that two cars cannot pass except at turnouts blasted from the cliffs.

WOLF CREEK PASS CAMPGROUND (R), 20.4 *m.* (9,480 alt.), a Forest Service facility, is on the summit of a mountain, where surrounding peaks seem leveled off, and the road appears to take off into space (*caution: test brakes before descending*). The road penetrates heavily forested areas above which tall barren peaks raise their heads.

State 35 bridges the North Fork of the Duchesne River at the junction, 32.7 *m.*, with a dirt road; L. here to SAVAGES RANCH, 6 *m.* (7,700 alt.), a dude ranch with a large plank-and-log ranch house accommodating fifteen persons, and a campground near by. Pack and fishing trips can be made from this point into the Uinta Mountains (*see High Uintas Primitive Area*).

STOCKMORE RANGER STATION (L), 33.1 *m.* (6,960 alt.), on State 35, is surrounded by a grove of cottonwoods and aspens.

HANNA, 34.8 *m.* (6,250 alt., 306 pop.), is a farming community, with houses strung along the highway for more than five miles.

DEFAS PARK, 38.6 *m.* (*cabins $1 to $1.50 a day; fishing*), on the Duchesne River, has a few houses, a filling station, and a dance hall. Cabins along the river are usually rented by fishermen. Horses and guides can be obtained here for trips to the high mountains to the north (*see High Uintas Primitive Area*).

TABIONA, 43.8 *m.* (6,750 alt., 170 pop.), is a cluster of frame houses edging the highway, and its one street is crowded with ranchers and "cow-pokes" on Saturday. Tabiona, on the Duchesne River, was settled in 1906 on land belonging to a Ute chief named Tabby. At first it was called Tabbyville, but the name was later refined to Tabiona.

At 63.6 *m.* is the junction with State 134, an improved dirt road; L. here to the junction, 8 *m.*, with a logging road; L. on the logging road to TALMAGE, 0.7 *m.* (6,830 alt., 243 pop.), a farming community. The logging road continues up Rock Creek to UPPER STILLWATER, a widening of Rock Creek, and leads to a Forest Service Camp, which is the end of the road and the beginning of a popular trail into the High Uintas (*see High Uintas Primitive Area*). Guides and horses are obtainable at the camp. North of the Talmage road junction State 134 winds through timbered country to MOUNTAIN HOME, 14 *m.* (6,994 alt., 273 pop.), a farm village. L. from Mountain Home on a dirt road to BROWN DUCK LAKE, the eastern entrance to many mountain lakes. North of Brown Duck Lake a trail extends to the High Uintas Highline Trail (*see High Uintas Primitive Area*).

State 35, south of its junction with State 134, parallels the Duchesne River.

DUCHESNE, 70.2 *m.* (5,517 alt., 907 pop.), is at the junction with US 40 (*see Tour 6a*).

West of Francis, US 189 runs (R) through a narrow canyon, carrying the waters of Provo River. ELKHORN CAMPGROUND (L), 36.1 *m.*, is an area set aside by the Forest Service for the public convenience.

HAILSTONE, 39.9 *m.* (5,959 alt.), is at the western junction with US 40, which unites briefly with US 189; at 48.7 *m.* is the eastern junction with US 40 (*see Tour 6b*).

CHARLESTON, 52.6 *m.* (5,433 alt., 343 pop.), on the east bank of the Provo River, is noted for its fine Hereford cattle and Percheron horses. Whiting Brothers, Winterton Brothers, and J. M. Ritchie, three of the leading breeders of Herefords in the West, have won livestock prizes at shows from Chicago to San Francisco. Fish in the streams of this area are reputed to have read a copy of Walton's *Compleat Angler,* and know all the tricks. Deer hunting in the neighboring hills is said to be good. Swimming in the Hot Pots at near-by Midway (*see Tour 6b*), is a favorite recreation.

Between Charleston and Wildwood, work was in progress (1940) to change the highway route; when the road is opened, mileages will be at variance with those given here.

DEER CREEK DAM AND RESERVOIR (L), 58.7 *m.,* under construction in 1940, when completed will be an earth-fill dam 155 feet high and about 1,400 feet wide. When full, the reservoir, impounding waters of the Provo River and its tributaries, will be seven miles long and three-quarters of a mile wide, with a capacity of 150,000 acre-feet. Work was begun in 1938. The project will augment the supply of irrigation water for lands in Utah and Salt Lake valleys, supplement the culinary water supply of Salt Lake City, Provo, and other towns, and provide water for industrial purposes. Further plans include a diversion tunnel near Hanna (*see above*) to bring Uinta drainage waters into the Provo River, and a diversion canal leading south from Oakley (*see above*) to carry surplus waters from the Weber River into the Provo River basin.

The idea for such a project was advanced in 1856 by Brigram Young, who said in an address at Great Salt Lake City: ". . . we shall continue our exertions, until Provo River runs to this city. We intend to bring it around the point of the mountain to Little Cottonwood, from that to Big Cottonwood, and lead its waters upon all the land from Provo canyon to this city." Building of the dam resulted from the endeavors of a group of citizens led by Leland H. Kimball, engineer for the project. They worked for years with the complex problems of prior water rights, and those of construction.

WILDWOOD, 63.2 *m.* (5,250 alt.), is a summer resort and private colony (*camping, 25¢ a day; fishing, riding, children's playground; open May 1-Oct. 1*), part of which is open to the public. In summer, swimming and fishing in Provo River are popular sports; in winter, skiing and skating are favorite diversions. Wildwood is at the junction with State 166 (*see Timpanogos Cave National Monument*).

At 64.3 *m.* is the junction with a graded road.

Left on this road to VIVIAN PARK, 0.1 *m.,* a 200-acre canyon resort, with a baseball park, children's playground, and restaurant. The park is the scene of many outings and conventions in summer.

BRIDAL VEIL FALLS, 66.2 *m.,* is a misty cataract descending in two graceful cascades. A broad zigzag trail, taking fifteen minutes to climb, leads to the top of the falls, a point used as a lookout while Mormon pioneers were awaiting Johnston's army in 1858 (*see History*). In the spring the canyon walls and pathway are a riot of wild flowers, blooming shrubs, and trailing vines.

Between Bridal Veil Falls and the mouth of the Provo Canyon, the highway follows the course of the river through rock walls clad with pine, birch, box elder, and scrub oak. In autumn the view is spectacular.

The narrow mouth of PROVO CANYON, 70.1 *m.,* is marked by a natural gateway of high cliffs. To the west towers massive and free-standing Mount Timpanogos (*see Timpanogos Cave National Monument*).

At 70.3 *m.* is the junction with State 52, an oiled road between US 189 and Orem (*see Tour 1d*) on US 91.

PROVO, 76.7 *m.* (4,549 alt., 17,956 pop.) (*see Provo*).

Provo is at the junction with US 91 (*see Tour 1d*).

Tour 6

(Craig, Colo.)—Vernal—Duchesne—Heber—Salt Lake City—Grantsville—Wendover—(Elko, Nev.) ; US 40.

Colorado Line to Nevada Line, 336.5 *m.*

Asphalt-surfaced road, except short concrete section in vicinity of Salt Lake City.

Route paralleled by branch line of Denver and Rio Grande Western R.R. between Park City and Salt Lake City, by Western Pacific R.R. between Salt Lake City and the Nevada Line.

Accommodations of all kinds in cities and towns; distances between towns often more than 20 miles.

US 40 traverses two thinly populated areas—the Uintah Basin and the Great Salt Lake Desert, eastward and westward of Utah's largest city. The basin is a semiarid depression between the Uinta Mountains and the Colorado Plateau. Scattered through the basin are a score of small towns, none of which has a population of more than 2,000; stock raising is the principal industry. The desert is the barren bed of ancient Lake Bonneville. Dreaded by slow-moving early travelers, it contains today the world's fastest automobile speedway and a bombing range for Army aviators. In the eastern half of the desert is Great Salt Lake, remnant of the older lake. Separating the basin and the desert are the forested Wasatch Mountains, with Salt Lake City at the western base.

Section a. COLORADO LINE to DUCHESNE; 92 m., US 40

Between the Colorado Line and Fruitland, a distance of approximately 125 miles, US 40 runs through the Uintah Basin, a wide depression approximately 6,000 square miles in area, bounded on the north by the lofty Uinta Mountains and on the south by the rugged

Colorado Plateau. Here, in the time when little eohippus, four-toed ancestor of the horse, roamed North America, an inland sea since called Lake Uinta extended for the full reach of the basin and beyond into Colorado.

An exploration party sent into the Uintah Basin by the Mormon Church in 1861, reported the area "measureably valuless . . . except to hold the world together . . . consequently all arrangements for establishing a settlement there have ceased." The following month the basin was designated an Indian reservation, and in 1868 Captain Pardon Dodds, Indian agent, established his headquarters at Whiterocks. In the seventies, livestock men moved into the area. By 1930 the "valuless" area supported a score of farming and livestock communities, with a population of more than 10,000.

US 40 crosses the COLORADO LINE, 0 m., at a point 96 miles west of Craig, Colorado. The highway for several miles traverses an uninhabited and sparsely vegetated desert. Scattered mats of prickly pear hug the ground, brightening the landscape with yellow, pink, and crimson flowers. A few miles north (R), the pink-tinted escarpment of CLIFF RIDGE forms a sheer wall hundreds of feet high.

A HISTORICAL MARKER (R), 15.9 m., one of a series erected by the Utah State Road Commission in 1939, honors "the first white men in Utah"—Father Dominguez and Father Escalante, who penetrated the Uintah Basin in 1776 (see History). SPLIT MOUNTAIN GORGE, six or seven miles north (R), is a jagged gash through which the Green River escapes into the Uintah Basin. The massive peaks of the Uinta Mountains, snowcapped most of the year, are dimly visible to the north.

A steel bridge spans the muddy GREEN RIVER, 17.1 m., largest tributary of the Colorado River (see Tour 7a).

JENSEN, 17.8 m. (4,739 alt., 415 pop.), is a farming community surrounded by alfalfa and grain fields. Weathered log houses with dirt roofs are shaded by huge cottonwood trees.

At Jensen is the junction with State 149 (see Dinosaur National Monument).

Between Jensen and Vernal, US 40 runs through rolling brush-covered country, with a few ranches along the road.

VERNAL, 31 m. (5,322 alt., 2,111 pop.), in a large green valley is a trade center for sheepherders and cowhands; broad-brimmed Stetsons, high-heeled boots, and jangling spurs are commonplace. Approximately 200,000 sheep and 25,000 cattle are grazed in the surrounding country, and clover blossoms provide the basis for another industry—bee culture.

Settled in the late 1870's, Vernal was plenty tough. The first saloon, a heavy plank laid across two water barrels, opened for business with five gallons of whisky. According to custom, the first round was "on the house." Thereafter, everybody took a turn at bartending, with drinks dispensed by the same philanthropic arrangement. When the proprietor came to the next morning his gross returns amounted to 1 hang-over. The second saloon fared no better; the bartender demanded cash for every drink, but his unsold stock, apparently too well "rectified," froze in the bottles.

In the 1890's Vernal was enlivened by "Butch" Cassidy's "Wild Bunch," operating from Browns Hole, a valley occupying a corner of Utah, Wyoming and Colorado (see Tour 7b).

The BANK OF VERNAL, 3 W. Main St., is constructed of brick sent from Salt Lake City by parcel post. It was erected in 1919, when freight was $2.50 a hundred pounds and parcel post only $1.05. Postal regulations prohibited mailing more than 50 pounds in one package or more than 500 pounds in a shipment to one address. Bricks were mailed in packages of seven, addressed to a dozen different Vernal residents. The Salt Lake City, Price, and Vernal post offices were flooded with bricks. Vernal farmers, becoming parcel-post conscious, ordered tools, wagon parts, and canned goods by mail. Farm products were mailed to market; one shipment of corn required ten four-ton trucks. Mail trucks were often loaded to capacity without carrying a single letter. Federal parcel post regulations were changed shortly thereafter, preventing shipment of more than 200 pounds a day to any addressee. The Vernal star route, from Salt Lake City, is the longest in the United States, 188 miles, serving fifty post offices.

NEWTON BROTHERS LEATHER PLANT, 44 N. Vernal Ave., one of the largest leatherwork shops in the West, manufactures boots, saddles, harness, belts, and other leather goods. The business was founded in 1905 by William B. Newton, blinded by a childhood accident, and his brother, Isaac, who lost his sight in 1920.

THORNE'S PHOTOGRAPH SHOP, 122 S. Vernal Ave., has a small MUSEUM (adm. with 25¢ purchase) containing a collection of firearms, Indian artifacts, and a mummy.

Right from Vernal on State 44, an improved dirt highway through the Uinta Mountains. Hundreds of deer range in the forests of cedar, aspen and pine. State 44 crosses BRUSH CREEK (trout), 11.2 m. The highway climbs through miles of densely grown cedar and crosses the south boundary, 15.4 m., of ASHLEY NATIONAL FOREST, in which approximately 10,000 cattle and 100,000 sheep are grazed during the summer. In the distance (L) is RED MOUNTAIN (7,776 alt.), a conspicuous ruddy uplift.

At 22.1 m. is the junction with a dirt road; L. to IRON SPRINGS CAMPGROUND, 3 m. (8,750 alt.), from which a foot trail leads (L) 0.5 m. to BIG BRUSH CREEK CAVE, an ice-filled cavern penetrating several hundred feet into the mountainside. The campground side road continues to BULLIONVILLE, 4 m., a ghost mining camp, and TROUT CREEK RANGER STATION, 15 m.

At 26.9 m. on State 44 is the junction with a dirt road; R. to DIAMOND GULCH, 5 m., named for one of the greatest mining swindles in American history. In 1871 two prospectors, Philip Arnold and John Slack, deposited several sacks of rough diamonds in the Bank of California, San Francisco. They told William Ralston, the bank's president, that they had discovered a diamond field a thousand miles east of San Francisco. D. C. Colton, Southern Pacific Railroad official, examined the field and reported acres of precious gems. Henry Janin, mining engineer, estimated that twenty laborers could wash out a million dollars worth of diamonds a month. A ten-million-dollar company was organized, and even the Rothschilds of London purchased stock. Then Clarence King, head of the fortieth parallel Survey, made a visit to the

field. He found diamonds in tree forks and rock crevices, but none in the
underlying rock. Finally he uncovered a large diamond bearing stonecutter's
marks, showing that the field had been "salted." The gems were South
African "niggerheads," purchased in Amsterdam and London. The "prospec
tors" got away with $660,000, and Ralston shouldered the loss, hanging the
framed receipts on his office wall.

State 44 crosses the 8,100-foot highway summit at 30 m.

RED SPRING CAMP (L), 32.9 m., is one of a score of Forest Service camp
grounds in this area.

At 41.5 m. is the junction with a dirt road; R. on this road to GREEN
LAKE, 0.9 m. (season, June to October; cabins $1.50 up; privately-stocked
lake, no license required; boats 25¢ per hour). Green Lake, twenty
three acres in area, lies almost on the rim of Red Canyon. The side road con
tinues along the canyon (R), with short driveouts to the rim at 1.8 m. and
2.9 m. RED CANYON is one of the major gorges of the Green River, and
there is a breath-taking view from the rim, with the winding stream 1,57
feet below.

CARTER CREEK CANYON (R), 49.3 m., carved by a small tributary of
the Green, is a steep-walled ravine, 800 feet deep. State 44 parallels the
canyon rim for three miles, descends a dugway to the bottom, crosses CARTER
CREEK, 54.1 m., and ascends the opposite slope.

PALISADE PARK FOREST CAMP, 61.5 m., at the junction of Hope Creek and
Sheep Creek, occupies a forested site surrounded by 1,500-foot sandstone wall
of many colors.

At 67 m. is the junction with a dirt road; R. along Sheep Creek to the
junction, 4 m., with a second dirt road; R. 2 m. into HIDEOUT CANYON
where the Green River runs between rugged walls 1,500 feet high. At 6 m
the first dirt road enters HORSESHOE CANYON, where the Green makes
sharp bend in a canyon more than 1,000 feet deep. "Where the river turns to
the left," writes Major John Wesley Powell, who explored the river in 1869
"it takes a course directly into the mountain, penetrating to its very heart
then wheels back upon itself, and runs out into the valley from which it
started only half a mile below the point at which it entered, so the canyon i
in the form of an elongated letter U, with the apex in the center of the moun
tain. We name it Horseshoe Canyon."

MANILA, 73.7 m. (6,376 alt., 256 pop.), on State 44, is a clean-swep
town in Lucerne Valley, at the base of a flat-topped pink ridge running eas
and west along the Utah-Wyoming Line. The site was being surveyed i
1898 when Admiral Dewey captured the Philippine capital, and the town wa
named for that event. When Daggett County was created in 1918, Manila
became the smallest county seat in the State. Daggett County, without a
felony until 1938, got its first glimpse of a district jurist when Judge P. C
Evans came to Manila to hear an assault case.

LINWOOD, 77.9 m. (6,024 alt., 72 pop.), is a group of weathered log
buildings on HENRYS FORK, five miles east of its confluence with the Green
River. At this junction—or a few miles up Henrys Fork, on the Wyoming
side, some historians say—the first rendezvous of American fur traders wa
held in the summer of 1825 (see History and Ogden).

In the spring before the rendezvous, Ashley's men had persuaded a party of
Hudson's Bay trappers to desert their British employer and bring their beave
to the American rendezvous. This was a serious breach of contract, but ther
was an argument-settling difference between the $5 per pelt paid by General
Ashley and the $2 per pelt paid by the British company. No international com
plications resulted, but it was a lively subject for a while, and it did not serv
to improve relations between American and British traders.

At 78.2 m. State 44 crosses the Wyoming Line, 54 miles south of Green
River, Wyoming.

US 40, between Vernal and Duchesne, traverses a sparsely vegetate
area punctuated by flat-topped hills and ridges. Northward, 25 to 5

niles, is the 125-mile length of the UINTA MOUNTAINS, dom-
nated by KINGS PEAK (13,498 alt.), highest point in Utah. Rela-
ive to this area, Sir Richard F. Burton, in his *City of the Saints*, speaks
f mountain men as "transcendental liars." An old mountaineer, asked
vhat difference he had noticed in the country since he first settled in it,
aid "Wal, stranger, not much, only when I first came here, them there
nountains," pointing to the massive Uintas, "was a hole in the
round!"

A few miles south of Vernal, not visible from the highway, is
ASPHALT RIDGE, containing plentiful deposits of asphalt. Much
f this asphalt, mixed with sand, has been used in the construction of
JS 40 in eastern Utah.

At 55.5 *m.* is the junction with State 88.

Left on State 88, an oiled road, to FORT DUCHESNE, 1.1 *m.* (4,991 alt.,
ɔ2 pop.), headquarters of the UINTAH AND OURAY INDIAN RESERVA-
ʾION (1,346 pop.), occupied by the Whiteriver, Uintah, and Uncompahgre
ands of Ute Indians, originally inhabitants of Colorado. The reservation
ɔvers approximately 384,000 acres, including 36,000 acres of irrigated land.
ʾhe reservation was created by executive order of President Lincoln in 1861,
nd originally occupied nearly all of the Uintah Basin. The Indians derive
ɪeir livelihood from farming, stock raising, and labor. In 1939 the annual
er capita income was $187. Most of the Indians live in frame cottages, but
few still insist on tepees. Before 1930 few Indians would submit to medical
eatment, but in 1939 the reservation hospital had 561 patients. Indian handi-
:raft and farm products are displayed at the annual Indian Fair held at
ort Duchesne in September. At the same time, whites and Indians join in
ɪe three-day Uintah Basin Industrial Convention. The Bear Dance and the
un Dance (*adm. 25¢*) are annual events on the reservation. The four-day
ear Dance, which celebrates the advent of spring, is held at Whiterocks,
•uray, and Myton, late in March or early in April, and is performed in a
rush enclosure, the women choosing partners. The partners face each other,
ɪke a few steps forward, then a few steps backward, repeating indefinitely.
ʾhe musical accompaniment is supplied by placing a notched stick on a res-
nator—usually a piece of tin or an old tub—and rubbing it with a smooth
ick. Marriages are often consummated at the Bear Dance, by rolling the
ɔuple in a blanket overnight.

The Sun Dance, a religious ceremony designed to cure or avert physical
ifirmities, is held at Whiterocks, late in July or early in August. Only men
articipate—the old to cure their ailments, the young to test their endurance.
ʾhe dance is performed in a circular brush enclosure, about sixty feet in
iameter, erected around a central pole. The dance begins in the evening
nd ends at the third sunrise. The dancers rest about half of the time, but
bstain entirely from food and water. At the third sunrise, all of the dancers
ice the sun, and the medicine man gives each an emetic drink.

OURAY, 20.2 *m.* (4,655 alt., 40 pop.), at the confluence of the Duchesne
nd Green Rivers, is one of three places the Indians of the Uintah and Ouray
eservation hold their spring Bear Dance.

FORT ROBIDOUX MONUMENT (L), 57.3 *m.,* on US 40, com-
ɪemorates the Indian trading post established, 8 miles east of the high-
vay, by Antoine Robidoux about 1832. The fort was destroyed by
ndians in 1844.

At 57.3 *m.,* opposite the monument, is the junction with a gravel-
ɪrfaced road.

Right on this road is WHITEROCKS, 13.1 *m.* (6,050 alt), an Indian settlement on the Uintah and Ouray Reservation, centered about the WHITEROCKS INDIAN SCHOOL, accommodating 150 pupils. The school provides academic training for first to ninth grade pupils and vocational training in manual arts, home economics, dairying, and gardening.

Whiterocks is one of three places at which the Bear Dance is held and is the only place at which the Sun Dance is held.

ROOSEVELT, 62.7 *m.* (5,084 alt., 1,264 pop.), a trading center for farmers and ranchers, lies in an open valley surrounded by flat topped red ridges.

US 40 crosses the DUCHESNE RIVER, 72 *m.*, a major tributary of the Green River. The Duchesne and its tributaries drain nearly the entire southern slope of the Uinta Mountains.

MYTON, 72.4 *m.* (5,085 alt., 395 pop.), a stock-raising community, lies on an alkali flat, thinly vegetated with greasewood and salt grass. In a strip of land, 20 miles wide, extending sixty miles southeast from Myton to Watson, are the only commercially important veins of gilsonite in the United States. Gilsonite, sometimes called uintaite, is a black, lustrous, brittle asphalt. It resembles glossy coal and melts at 325 degrees, but will not burn. Gilsonite is resistant to acids and alkalies and is used in the manufacture of varnishes, paints, rotogravure ink, waterproofing compounds, electrical insulation, telephone mouthpieces, roofing materials, and floor coverings. The Uintah Basin deposit was discovered in 1885 by Samuel H. Gilson, prospector, Indian scout, and Pony Express rider. In an interview with a *Salt Lake Tribune* reporter in 1938, Mrs. Gilson told the story of her husband's discovery: "An Indian Chief at Fort Duchesne told Mr. Gilson the tribesmen had found a substance which wouldn't burn. The Indians took Samuel to a ledge that contained the black mineral. I'll never forget the day he brought the substance home. Then began a series of experiments . . . every place I turned there was some of the sticky stuff. He made chewing gum, paint, insulation for wires. . . ." Mr. Gilson was a persistent experimenter with "whittle-out" model airplanes years before aviation became a practical reality. It is estimated that the Uintah Basin contains thirty-two million tons of gilsonite, which occurs in vertical veins 1,000 feet deep.

At 74.2 *m.* is the junction (L) with State 53 (*see Tour 7a*).

DUCHESNE, 92 *m.* (5,517 alt., 907 pop.), is a ranch-outfitting center at the mouth of Indian Canyon, through which the Uinta Basin population has its most immediate access to a railroad. A 46-mile trip leads through this canyon and over a 9,100-foot summit to Castlegate, on the Denver and Rio Grande Western Railroad (*see Tour 7b*).

At Duchesne is the junction with State 33 (*see Tour 7b*) and State 35 (*see Tour 5*).

The Setting II

ee A. Olsen

TAKING OFF AT 9,000 FEET, ALTA SKI RUN

Shipp: U. S. Forest Service

FOREST RANGER ON MT. TIMPANOGOS TRAIL

PACK TRIP IN
THE HIGH UIN

*Robert Davis:
Utah Recreation
Project, WPA*

VIEW ACROSS THE WASH IN CAPITOL REEF NATIONAL MONUMENT

BRIDAL VEIL
IN PROVO CA

Courtesy Provo
Chamber of Com

IN THE AMERICAN FORK CANYON, WASATCH NATIONAL FOREST

WHITE WATER
FISHING, LOGAN CANYON

Koziol: U. S. Forest Service

DEER HUNTERS' CAMP IN BEAVER CANYON

ASPENS ON BOULDER PLATEAU

Swan: U. S. Forest Service

Shipp and Parkinson: U. S. Forest Service

BUCK AND FAWN

SEAGULLS, GREAT SALT LAKE

BOAT BASIN, GREAT SALT LAKE

Darel McConkey

Section b. DUCHESNE *to* SALT LAKE CITY, *119.4 m.* US 40

Between Duchesne and Salt Lake City, US 40 traverses the west end of the Uintah Basin and passes through a series of verdant canyons and green valleys.

West of DUCHESNE, 0 *m.,* US 40 runs through miles of sagebrush country.

FRUITLAND, 25.4 *m.* (6,609 alt., 121 pop.), is a ranching community, settled in 1907 and named by land promoters who hoped to attract settlers.

Between Fruitland and Strawberry Reservoir, US 40 passes through DEEP CREEK CANYON, its rolling, mountainous slopes vegetated with sagebrush, aspens, and evergreens.

At 40.8 *m.* is the junction (L) with an improved dirt road which makes a 15-mile loop around STRAWBERRY RESERVOIR (7,600 alt.) (*trout fishing, boats, campgrounds*), returning to US 40 at 47.8 *m.* The reservoir is visible for several miles from the main highway. Completed in 1915, it was the State's first important Federal Reclamation Project, diverting irrigation water into Utah Valley through a 19,000-foot tunnel. The reservoir lies within the boundaries of the STRAWBERRY VALLEY BIRD REFUGE.

Between Strawberry Reservoir and Heber, US 40 winds through DANIELS CANYON, its curved slopes supporting a dense growth of trees, shrubs, and wild flowers. DANIELS CREEK (L), a trout-stocked stream, is bordered by willows and cottonwoods. There are Forest Service campgrounds at intervals along the highway.

At 70.5 *m.* is the south junction with US 189 (see Tour 5). Between this junction and Hailstone, US 40 is united with US 189.

HEBER, 71.6 *m.* (5,595 alt., 2,750 pop.), trading center of a large ranching area, lies in the center of a green valley, encircled by pastures, hayfields, and forested mountains. Pioneer dwellings, built of red sandstone or gray limestone, mingle with buildings of more recent vintage.

Left from Heber on State 113 to the junction, 2.8 *m.,* with a dirt road; R. here to the junction, 0.7 *m.,* with a second dirt road; L. here to the junction, 0.9 *m.,* with a third dirt road; R. here to LUKE'S HOT POTS, 1.1 *m.* (cabins, chicken dinners, swimming in the hot water of extinct geysers).

MIDWAY, 3.3 *m.* (5,567 alt., 568 pop.), on State 113, is a rural village settled in 1859. In the vicinity are numerous limestone craters like the Hot Pots, averaging about 20 feet in diameter, formed by deposition from springs or geysers. Inhabitants of Midway use limestone, which cuts easily but weathers out hard, for building houses and fences. Right (straight ahead) from Midway on an improved dirt road, to the junction with a dirt road which leads to SCHNEITTER'S HOT POTS, 1.7 *m.,* a twin resort to Luke's Hot Pots.

CHARLESTON, 6.7 *m.,* is at the junction of State 113 with US 189 (*see Tour 5*).

A concrete bridge spans PROVO RIVER, 78 *m.,* a noble fishing stream, which furnishes electric power and irrigation water for Utah Valley.

HAILSTONE, 79.4 *m.* (5,959 alt.), is a lumber camp where 300,000 feet of lumber, 15,000 railroad ties, and 400,000 feet of mine props are cut annually. Nobody seems to remember why the place was named Hailstone.

At Hailstone is the north junction with US 189, with which US 40 is united to Heber.

At 82.8 *m.* is the junction (R) with State 34 to Kamas (*see Tour 5*).

At 89.3 *m.* is the junction with State 6.

Left on State 6, an oiled road, to PARK CITY, 0.8 *m.* (6,980 alt., 3,735 pop.), the gamin silver mining camp of Utah. Adhering faithfully to the past, Park City has gray, battered frame buildings interspersed with brick stores. Dingy houses cling tenaciously to the canyonsides, one row on each side of the narrow street. The business section begins where three canyons meet and widen; here several streets run parallel. First floor entrances face on the lower streets, and second floors open on upper streets. The town was settled by hard men, and, although it is no longer necessary for the editor of the *Park Record* to complain, as he did in 1884, that "There is too much promiscuous shooting on streets at night," Park City is still a mining town.

In 1853 cattle were grazing in the high, cool meadows during the short summers, and the winters were locked in long, snowy silences. Then, in the winter of 1869, ore was discovered. The solitude was shattered by the tramp of prospectors' feet, by the ring of picks on hard rock, by the rumble of blasted earth, and by the laughter of hard-fighting, fast-living men.

According to General William Henry Kimball, keeper of the stage station (*see below*) a few miles from Park City, three soldiers from Colonel Patrick E. Connor's company ran across a bold outcrop of quartz about two miles south of Park City. They broke off a chunk, marked the spot with a red handkerchief, and hurried down the canyon. The assay disclosed 96 ounces of silver, 54 per cent lead, and one-tenth ounce of gold. It was not until 1870, however, that they began operation, naming the claim the Flagstaff.

The opening of the Flagstaff started a stampede. Tents and brush shanties sprang up along the canyon, followed by a boarding house, a general store, a blacksmith shop, a livery stable, a meat market, and saloons.

The Walker and Webster Gulch finds were made in the early 1870's, followed by the McHenry Gulch strike (now part of the Park Utah Consolidated), and a short time after the Jones bonanza was discovered (later known as the Daly-Judge mine). Rector Steen located ore running 400 ounces of silver in the ton in 1872, and named the claim the Ontario. Steen and his partners sold out for $27,000 that same year to a Mr. Stanley and George Hearst, father of William Randolph Hearst, chain newspaper publisher. Thomas J. Kearns, later U. S. Senator (*see Salt Lake City*), and David Keith, a large stockholder in the Silver King Coalition, got their start in Park City. During the 1870's the surface of the mountains was dotted with claims, but the ore ran deep, and not many of the small claim-owners had the capital to go down for it; the few who did struck water and were flooded out. Claim-owners finally combined their resources and sank long drain tunnels. Mergers later brought most of the property under the heads of two companies, the Park Utah Consolidated and the Silver King Coalition. The Consolidated produced 72,245 ounces of gold, 244,901 ounces of silver, 7,097,906 pounds of lead, 8,911,940 pounds of zinc and 25,759 pounds of copper in 1939. The Silver King mines shipped ore having a metallic content of 1,307 ounces of gold, 924,873 ounces of silver, 14,746,345 pounds of lead, 10,180,823 pounds of zinc, and 447,098 pounds of copper in the same year. Total valuation of all ores mined in Park City district in 1939 was $3,825,233, according to the tentative estimate of the U. S. Bureau of Mines.

By 1880 Park City was a good-sized town. The *Park Mining Record,* later called the *Park Record,* was established by the Raddon family, and has continued under their management. The first telegraph line was completed from Park City to Echo; a Catholic church was erected; and a water system, consisting of a small reservoir and a pipe down one street, was installed. Amusements were simple, and, as befitted the men of the district, generally muscular—boxing matches, wrestling matches, and foot or snowshoe races.

Until the 1880's, stages were the only means of transportation, but in 1881 the Salt Lake and Park City Railroad (a narrow gauge) filed articles of incorporation to build a railroad from Park City to Salt Lake City and a branch line to Coalville. That same year, Utah Central and Union Pacific trains ran out of Park City by way of Coalville, and the Sevier Valley, Salt Lake and Park City, and the Rio Grande Western merged under the name of the Denver & Rio Grande Western Railroad. Railroads crowded the stages out of business, but years later the act was reversed when automobile stages cut railroad business to one train daily.

Chinese laborers working on the railroads stayed in Park City and developed their own district. One moon-eyed celestial had the habit of lying under a table behind a curtain to enjoy his pipe of opium. This was all right, but he always took a lighted candle with him, and the result was nearly always the same; the curtain would catch fire, and the fire department would get a hurry call. In reporting the death of one of the older Chinese residents the *Park Record* said: "He had been ailing for a long time and for some time past looked as though he was simply living to save funeral expenses. He was buried by his fellow 'chinks' . . . with his hat on so he would not catch cold on the way to his Happy Hunting Grounds." Feeling between Mormons and gentiles flared in 1886, when the Loyal Legion called a meeting. The *Record* reported that "It is an open secret that the Mormon Church is about to publicly renounce polygamy and try for admission as a state. Fear that Anti-Mormons would be asked to leave the State was expressed forcefully. . . . Fear was expressed the Mormons would cripple the mining industry, and [the Legion wanted] more particularly to protect silver and lead." The *Park Record* acquired a rival in 1887 when *The Call* hit the streets, but it lasted only eighteen months. Other editors tried to "buck" the *Record* but soon gave up: The *Miner* ran from 1890 to 1892, the *Utah Patriot* from 1895 to 1897, and *The Park Miner* from 1902 to 1903. Strangers coming into the district were amazed to find the old "sourdoughs" toting tins of morphine into the hills. It was always necessary to explain that a man alone in the mountains, miles from assistance in case of a bad accident, needed the stuff. An overdose of morphine was preferable to starvation, freezing, or being eaten alive. What happened to one old-timer is shown in a story from the *Park Record* in 1905: "Twelve years ago two old time prospectors, while exploring a small drift at the bottom of an abandoned shaft, stumbled on to the skeleton of a man. . . . The heavy shoes . . . encased gruesomely the shiny bones of the feet . . . a sheet of paper was found . . . upon which was written in a faltering and uncertain hand, a short but pitiful story . . . 'Dear God. I am dying. I have found wealth at the cost of my life. The samples in the bucket are from a ledge on —my hand trembles, my eyes grow dim—I am—.' Here the message becomes a senseless jumble."

The acting abilities of John L. Sullivan failed to impress a Park City audience. The occasion was reported tersely by the *Park Record:* "John L. Sullivan made an appearance at the local playhouse. . . . Comment was that he made a better fighter than actor." Later issues noted that a bank—with the largest plate glass window in Utah Territory—was being erected, a library started, and a flock of Angora goats brought in to range the hills around town. Park City experienced its first gambling raid in 1888 and reformers took over the town for a short period. Respectable citizens had been complaining about the "Shirt Tail Factory" in the residential section. A new marshal was appointed, and orders were given to the "madam" of the "Shirt Tail Factory" to move in thirty days, or else. The "madam" bought a lot near the "Green House," another establishment, and built small brown houses. Fines were levied in lieu of a license; in 1888 and 1889 the operators were rounded up every three or four months and fined $35 or $40 for the "madam" and $20 for each girl. The girls were not permitted on the main streets, but a big white light on a pole lighted the way for visitors. This arrangement appeased respectable citizens. The next move was to raise the license fees of all saloons. "Tin horn" gamblers were rounded up and fined. Many of them left town, along with the owners of cheap saloons.

Bad luck stalked the camp in the 1890's. The panic of 1893 dealt Park City a hard blow, and a series of fires nearly wiped it off the map. The first fire broke out in a furniture store. Next to go was the sampling works, followed by the most disastrous conflagration of all, the hotel fire of 1898. It started in the kitchen, and, fanned by a canyon breeze, spread so rapidly that firemen were unable to control it. When the smoke cleared away, Park City counted a million-dollar loss. The town dug in, and within ninety days a new business district arose. There were rumors of a "fire bug." The *Park Record,* always a barometer of public opinion, wrote: ". . . should anyone be caught in the act of setting fire to a building his life would not be worth a straw. . . . Murder may be committed and the law allowed to take its course, but the line is drawn on the fire bug and God help the man. . . . A long rope and a short-shift will be his portion as sure as fate."

When the miners got a fifty-cent cut in July, 1897, they took it philosophically. One said, "Four years ago the Cleveland panic took 50¢ off each day's wages; now the McKinley boom strikes us and away goes another 50¢." The Miners Union did succeed in getting fourteen cents a day reduction at the company boarding house, but the next month the Ontario and Daly mines shut down for the first time in twenty-five years. Miners left the camp in droves. An advertisement in the *Park Record* for November 20, 1897, shows the extremes to which some men were driven: "A competent sawmill man wishes a situation. Can run a sawmill and keep it in repair from engine to slab pile. P.S. If I cannot get a situation in a mill, would be perfectly willing to accept a situation with some widow (no matter how grassy) until the roses bloom again."

The reforms of the eighties and nineties were soon forgotten, and by 1901 the evangelists and reformers were sadly moving away. The *Park Record* of that year notes the departure of "Rev. French Oliver . . . who considered Salt Lake City the wickedest city in the United States, Park City only forty rods from hell, and the *Park Record* editor as the ring leader of the whole business." The rise of silver prices in 1901, reopening of the big mines, and the return of easy money no doubt hastened the collapse of the reform.

The Miners Union, discouraged by long trips to Salt Lake City before injured miners could be treated, began a drive for a miners' hospital in Park City. Subscriptions amounting to $5,000 were raised, and the building was opened in 1903. When the Daly-West mine tried to introduce oil lamps in 1906, the miners walked out, claiming that the lamps were "unhealthy, dirty and inconvenient." The strike was settled nine days later, the men returning to work with their old candlesticks. Most of the Park City strikes in 1906 and 1907 were settled by arbitration. When W. D. "Big Bill" Haywood, secretary of the Western Federation of Miners, was acquitted of the murder of Governor Steunenberg of Idaho in 1907, the mines were closed for the day, and a big parade was staged, 650 union men marching under a long banner labeled "Undesirable Citizens." The city went through another period of reform in 1907, when Mayor Welsh ordered all the gambling places closed. "For the first time in years all gambling was stopped," reported the *Record.* "Slot machines were turned to the wall, the little ivory ball was silent, the high card was no longer high, the rattle of 'craps' had ceased. Faro banks, wheels, games of chance for merchandise or otherwise went out of business. . . . Many of the 'green cloth men' left town feeling that the condition would last for some time." The condition did last for a couple of years. A great percentage of the city's revenues were derived from the various forms of gambling, and from fines levied on the "soiled doves" of the restricted districts, so the shut-down put the city's finances in a precarious position for months. In 1909 gambling returned to Park City and the city fathers closed their eyes to it. The city collected $1,010 in fines before the reform element took over in 1910, and this time the sheriff closed the town up tight. The saloons, however, continued to do a land-office business. A temperance worker told the *Park Record* that he "watched one of the leading saloons in Park City and counted the men that went in and out, from 7:30 p.m. till 8 p.m. The result one hundred and fifty-three went in and one hundred and sixty-four came out." With the advent of prohibition in 1917, twenty saloons went out of business, reducing the city's revenues $22,000 a year. On the last day of July the miners tried their best to drink up all the supply on hand: "The stocks of all the saloons were completely sold out two hours before the deadline. Bartenders could not serve the patrons fast enough so the patrons served themselves, some paid, and some stole until at midnight the 'grave digger' bell, tolled by the gravedigger [sexton] himself, warned all that prohibition had come."

The coming of prohibition, the World War, the slump in silver prices, the depression, labor troubles, and the death of many of the old-timers, combined to partially tame this once wide-open town. Although stills blowing up could be heard in the mountains, and the residents were able to find a species of alcoholics when they wanted to, the town never really recovered from the shock of prohibition. Beer parlors and State liquor stores replaced the palaces of drink; fighting on the streets became more scientific and less spectacular; and automobiles took the miners into other towns on pay day. Gambling was carried on furtively behind closed doors, and characters like "First Class" Sickler, who thought all ore looked first class, grew scarce. Park City's light has dimmed, but there clings an aura of the past. Park City is still the slightly uncouth mining camp of yore.

KIMBALLS, 94.8 *m.* (6,366 alt.) a ranching community, was named for George Kimball, who operated the Overland Stage station here in the 1860's.

At Kimballs is the junction (R) with State 530 to Wanship, which follows the route of the old Overland Stage (*see Tour 5*).

Between Kimballs and Salt Lake City, US 40 follows the course of the old "Golden Pass" toll road, opened for travel by Parley P. Pratt in 1850.

ECKER SKI HILL (L), 96.6 *m.,* is the site of many record ski jumps. In 1937, Alf Engen, Salt Lake City skier, leaped 245 feet to set a world's record for amateurs.

GORGOZA, 97.2 *m.* (6,328 alt., 20 pop.), a railroad siding, was named for Rodriguez Velasquez de la Gorgozada, a Spaniard, said to have invested almost a million dollars in a narrow-gauge railroad from Park City to Salt Lake City. John W. Young, son of Brigham Young, failing to raise money in the United States, went to France to solicit the financial support of Gorgozada. The Spaniard was persuaded to sponsor the project after Young drew the picture of a large city and offered to name it for the financier. A narrow-gauge railroad was built, operated for five years, and became bankrupt. Later it was made a branch line of the Denver & Rio Grande Western Railroad. Gorgoza is at the junction with State 6 (*see Tour 4a*) to East Canyon.

MOUNTAIN DELL RESERVOIR (R), 105.8 *m.,* largest storage unit in Salt Lake City's waterworks system, has a capacity of one and one-half billion gallons. The water is impounded by a concrete dam, 100 feet high and 560 feet wide, completed in 1924.

Between the reservoir and Salt Lake City, US 40 winds through PARLEYS CANYON, a rugged and tortuous gorge named for Parley P. Pratt. In the spring, deer often browse near the road.

A driveout at the mouth of Parleys Canyon, 111.2 *m.*, affords a spectacular view of Salt Lake Valley.

At 116.2 *m.* is the south junction, in Salt Lake City, with US 91, with which US 40 is united for 3.9 miles (*see Tour 1c, 1d*).

SALT LAKE CITY, 119.4 *m.* (4,266 alt., 150,021 pop.) (*see Salt Lake City*).

Section c. SALT LAKE CITY to NEVADA LINE, 125.1 m. US 40

Between Salt Lake City and Wendover, on the Nevada Line, US 40 traverses a desolate yet fascinating country, with but one incorporated town and a total population of less than 1,500 along the entire route. West of Salt Lake City the highway for a few miles parallels the south shore of Great Salt Lake. East of Grantsville is Utah's "dust bowl," and westward the road winds through rolling hills. Between these hills and the Nevada Line the highway is a black ribbon across the barren gray Great Salt Lake Desert.

The conquest of this desert forms a dramatic chapter in western history. It was first crossed by white men in 1827, but the present highway was not completed until almost a century later. Today, where early trail breakers dared death from thirst and suffocation, dark-goggled tourists and travelers on two railroads travel in speed and relative comfort. Mirages that once tortured thirst-crazed minds are now merely curious optical illusions, and the once-dreaded salt flats, where ox-teams once dragged reluctant wagons, now provide the fastest automobile speedway in the world and a bombing range for Army aviators.

West of SALT LAKE CITY, 0 *m.*, US 40 extends across on unsettled and uncultivated alkali flat.

At 0.7 *m.* is the north junction with US 91, with which US 40 is united for 3.9 miles (*see Tour 1c, 1d*).

The 50,000-watt KSL RADIO TRANSMITTER, 11.1 *m.* (*open by arrangement at KSL studios, Union Pacific Building, Salt Lake City*), with its twin 230-foot aerial towers (R), was established in 1922. The transmitter, constructed in 1932, uses Great Salt Lake as a grounding field.

The ROYAL CRYSTAL SALT COMPANY PLANT (*open on application*), 11.1 *m.*, is flanked by long windrows of gray salt (L) paralleling the highway. The plant screens and grades some 80,000 tons of salt annually. Water is pumped from Great Salt Lake into large concentration ponds, where the salt, averaging 99.5 per cent pure, is precipitated by solar evaporation. The salt is loosened by tractor-drawn plows, piled in long mounds for curing, and later hauled to the mill for refining and packing. Several brands of salt are processed here. Salt workers, oddly, consume more salt in their food than average persons.

At 14.3 *m.* is the junction with an oiled road.

Right on this road to SALTAIR, 1 *m.* (*open Memorial Day to Labor Day, adm. 25¢; bathing, dancing, and amusement concessions*), largest and most noted resort on Great Salt Lake (*see Great Salt Lake*). The principal building is a large two-story structure of Moorish architecture, with an immense ballroom on the upper floor. The Saltair resort, constructed in 1898, was built on ten-inch pilings driven into the lake bottom through salt dissolved by steam. Upon this platform were erected the bathhouses, amusement concessions, and other buildings. The resort was destroyed by fire in 1925, but the old pilings were not burned, and the resort was rebuilt on a nine-acre concrete platform.

The SALT LAKE SODIUM PRODUCTS PLANT (*open on application*), 14.4 *m.*, in a three-story frame and sheet-iron building (R), manufactures sodium sulphate from Glauber salt, a colorless crystalline deposit underlying a shallow layer of sand near Great Salt Lake. The sand is scraped off, and the Glauber salt is put in solution to rid it of impurities. The solution is then clarified, and the water is evaporated, leaving pure sodium sulphate. The principal use of this compound is in the processing of wood pulp for kraft paper. The Salt Lake plant has a daily capacity of 100 tons and is one of the few plants in the United States manufacturing sodium sulphate as the principal product.

The SALT LAKE YACHT CLUB HARBOR (R), 17.8 *m.*, has a rock-fill boat pier 860 feet long and 15 feet wide, where members keep launches, motorboats, and sailboats for navigating Great Salt Lake. "Some of the fellows," says the *Improvement Era* for January, 1932, "make anchors of [compressed] salt. . . . Instead of being eaten by the salt water, they may even grow a little." There is an excellent view of the lake and its islands from the pier.

At 17.8 *m.* the GARFIELD COPPER SMELTER (*see Tour 7c*) is visible (L), at the base of the denuded Oquirrh Mountains; their plant life was stifled by sulphurous smoke.

At 18.1 *m.* is the junction with a dirt road.

Right on this road to SUNSET BEACH and BLACK ROCK BEACH, 0.5 *m.* (*adm. 10¢; bathing, dancing*), two privately-owned lake resorts. Black Rock was named for a dark core of rock rising from the lake bed south of the resort. Seagulls fly about the beaches.

BLACK ROCK CAVE, in the Oquirrh Mountains (L), was the site of an important archeological discovery in 1931, when Dr. Julian H. Steward, then an archeologist at the University of Utah, unearthed a child's skeleton believed to be more than 7,000 years old, antedating by several thousand years the Basket Makers, oldest known inhabitants of the intermountain region.

Between LAKE POINT JUNCTION, 19 *m.* (4,240 alt.), and the Nevada Line, US 40 and US 50 (*see Tour 7c*) are united.

MILLS JUNCTION, 24.7 *m.* (4,330 alt.), so named because Brigham Young owned several mills in the vicinity, is at the junction with State 36 (*see Tour 6A*).

The UTAH WOOL PULLERY (*open on application*), 25.3 *m.*, occupies a group of buildings (R) in which nearly a million pounds of wool are pulled from pelts annually. Near the pullery is BRIGHAM YOUNG'S GRISTMILL (*open on application*), an old frame building still used as a flour mill.

Between Mills Junction and Grantsville, road signs warn that this is a dangerous dust area. Flat gray country extends for miles in every direction, pocked with gaping holes. Overgrazing made this area the cradle of Utah's worst dust storms until efforts of the U. S. Soil Conservation Service brought the wind erosion under control.

GRANTSVILLE, 35.1 *m.* (4,304 alt., 1,201 pop.), a "one-street" town that stretches along the highway for nearly five miles, is a typical rural Mormon community, deriving its livelihood from alfalfa, grain, sheep, and turkeys. Squat adobe houses built by the first settlers rub shoulders with later brick dwellings. Water is obtained from artesian wells.

Grantsville was the birthplace of J. Reuben Clark, Jr., Mormon Church official and United States Ambassador to Mexico, 1930-32. It was the boyhood home of Elijah Nicholas Wilson, author and hero of *White Indian Boy—The Story of Uncle Nick Among the Shoshones.* "Uncle Nick" was born in Illinois in 1842, crossed the plains by ox-team, and settled at Grantsville in 1850. When only 12 years old he ran away with a band of Shoshoni and lived with them for two years.

In the GRANTSVILLE HIGH SCHOOL (*open 9-5 schooldays*) is a small collection of pioneer relics and Indian artifacts. Parts of a wagon, a child's shoe, and other articles found on the Salt Desert tell of the hardships encountered by the Donner-Reed party (*see below*).

West of Grantsville US 40 runs along the foothills of the brush-covered STANSBURY MOUNTAINS (L). Near these mountains have been discovered almost 200 single-room, semi-subterranean prehistoric Indian pit-houses.

At TIMPIE JUNCTION 48.7 *m.* (4,266 alt.), an improved dirt road extends southward from US 40.

Left on this road to IOSEPA (Hawaiian, Joseph), 15.4 *m.* (4,500 alt.), a ghost town settled in 1889 by Hawaiian converts to Mormonism. Natural springs supplied irrigation water for a 960-acre tract, and salt grass provided forage for livestock. The first party consisted of fifty-three islanders, who drew lots for their land. Houses, a chapel, and a school were provided by the Church. In one year more than $20,000 was derived from sale of grain, hay, and livestock.

In 1893 an outbreak of leprosy caused many to lose faith. A hospital was built, the afflicted were quarantined and not many cases developed. Although the people were unable to adapt themselves entirely to the climate, the project continued until 1916, when a Mormon Temple was built in Hawaii, and many returned home. By 1917 Iosepa was almost completely abandoned.

The SKULL VALLEY INDIAN RESERVATION, 25.6 *m.* (37 pop.), consists of 18,640 acres of desert land set aside for the Gosiute Indians, who herd a few sheep, gather pine nuts, till small poverty-stricken farms, and rent part of their grazing land to ranchers.

Between Timpie Junction and Low Pass, US 40 cuts across the north end of SKULL VALLEY, said to have been named for the numerous Indian skeletons found here by pioneers. Skull Valley is arid and unproductive, the low mountains intercept very little moisture, and the sparse rain evaporates almost immediately, leaving the ground as thirsty as ever. Nevertheless, early travelers found small bands of Gosiute Indians living here. Thomas J. Farnham described them in 1843: "They wear no clothing of any description—build no shelter. They eat roots, lizards, and snails. . . . And when the lizard and snail and wild roots are buried in the snows in winter, they . . . dig holes . . . and sleep and fast till the weather permits them to go abroad again for food. . . . These poor creatures are hunted in the spring of the year, when weak and helpless . . . and when taken, are fattened, carried to Santa Fe and sold as slaves." To avoid capture, the Gosiutes carried water in *ollas* and remained away from springs.

Between Skull Valley and the Great Salt Lake Desert, US 40 runs through Low Pass, between the thinly vegetated LAKESIDE MOUNTAINS (R) and CEDAR MOUNTAINS (L).

Between Low Pass and Wendover, US 40 spans the mud flats and salt beds of the GREAT SALT LAKE DESERT. On the edge of the desert brush and grass supply winter forage for thousands of sheep; in the heart of the desert nothing grows. With hardly a curve in more than 50 miles, the highway forms a black ribbon across the salt and alkali. Mirages are numerous. Small mountains seem like floating islands, with ends turned up like the toes of wooden shoes. In places the mountains appear to be upside down, with gigantic tunnels through them. Realistic water mirages are everywhere, and distances are tremendously deceptive.

The DONNER-REED TRAIL MONUMENT (R), 72.7 *m.*, commemorates a party of California-bound emigrants (*see below*) who, in 1846, struggled across this treacherous desert and were trapped by early snows in the Sierra Nevadas.

KNOLLS, 85.9 *m.* (4,239 alt.), is a cluster of buildings on the eastern edge of the desert. There are no settlements along the 40 miles of highway between Knolls and Wendover. Horace Greeley, who was in Utah in 1859, said of the desert: "If Uncle Sam should ever sell that tract for one cent per acre, he will swindle the purchaser outrageously."

The first recorded crossing of the Salt Desert was made from west to east by Jedediah Strong Smith and two other fur trappers on their return from California in 1827. Their course was over the southern edge of the desert, but Smith's uncomplaining 137-word description of the trip indicates some of the difficulties: "After travelling twenty days from the east side of Mount Joseph, I struck the southwest corner of Great Salt Lake, travelling over a country completely barren and destitute of game. We frequently travelled without water, sometimes for two days over sandy deserts where there was no sign of vegetation, and when we found water in some of the rocky hills, we most generally found some Indians who appeared the most miserable of the human race, having nothing to subsist on (nor any clothing) except grass-seed, grasshoppers, etc. When we arrived at the Salt Lake, we had but one horse and one mule remaining, which were so feeble and poor that they could scarce carry the little camp equipage which I had along; the balance of my horses I was compelled to eat as they gave out."

In 1833 Joseph Walker's detachment of Captain Benjamin L. E. Bonneville's party circled the northern edge of the desert en route from Wyoming to California. No other crossing was attempted until 1841, when the California-bound Bartleson wagon train skirted the north end of Great Salt Lake and cut over the northern part of the desert. Many of their oxen dropped from exhaustion and the owners, taking with them only such possessions as they could carry, left their wagons and completed the journey on foot. The party arrived at Sutter's Fort with nothing but their rifles and the rags on their backs.

Captain John Charles Frémont, exploring the West for the United States Government in 1845, with Kit Carson as guide, charted a route over the desert from Skull Valley to Pilot Peak, 20 miles north of Wendover. Mounted on horseback, Frémont's party completed the trip with comparatively little difficulty. Failing to consider the slowness of heavy wagons, Frémont reported that the route was feasible.

Lansford Warren Hastings, empire dreamer, occupies an important if infamous place in the history of the Salt Desert. Having led emigrant trains to Oregon and California in 1842 and 1843, Hastings apparently had an idea of conquering Pacific Coast territory and setting himself up as president. He returned East in 1844 and prepared his *Emigrant's Guide to Oregon and California,* then organized a party to return with him to California. They followed the Oregon Trail to Fort Hall, Idaho, and then branched southwest to California. Seeking a shorter route, Hastings and a small party started eastward in 1846 with James Clyman, trapper, as a guide. Mounted on good horses, they took the route surveyed by Frémont and Carson, and completed the trip with no serious trouble, though Clyman wrote in his diary, "This is the most desolate country on the whole globe, there being not one spear of vegetation, and of course no kind of animal can subsist." Continuing to Fort Bridger, Wyoming, Hastings recommended the route to everyone he met.

At Fort Bridger, Hastings found four parties, totalling eighty wagons and including the parties of Samuel C. Young and George Harlan, who accepted his offer to guide them over the shorter desert trail. Hastings, however, had a penchant for trying new and uncharted routes. Deviating from the trail with which he was familiar, he attempted a new course between Fort Bridger and Great Salt Lake, and his party had great difficulties in crossing the Wasatch Mountains. Eventually, however, they emerged through Weber Canyon (*see Tour 4a*), bringing the first wagon to enter Salt Lake Valley by any route. Skirting the south end of Great Salt Lake and traversing Skull Valley, the company began the first crossing ever attempted by wagon over the center of the desert. The distance was greater than they had anticipated, and they found no water. Oxen dropped from exhaustion and wagons were left strewn along the trail. When the emigrants finally reached the springs at Pilot Peak, they hauled water and grass over the back trail to save stock and to bring in abandoned wagons. Many days were required to collect their possessions before they could continue to California.

A week or ten days behind the Hastings party came the Donner-Reed wagon train. The caravan spent two weeks trying to get through a canyon, then found the route impassable. Eventually they worked their way down Emigration Canyon into Salt Lake Valley. It was early September when the Donner-Reed party began its tragic trek over the Salt Desert. After two and a half days of travel without water, Reed volunteered to ride in search of a spring. He found no trace of water until he reached Pilot Peak, 30 miles ahead. Returning, he met the first of his party still 20 miles out. The oxen were falling one by one and being left on the desert. Wearied by five days and nights without sleep, Reed found his wagon mired down. Carrying their small children, he and his wife began the long walk across the wasteland. Meantime Jacob Donner reached Pilot Peak, watered his oxen, and started back for the Reed family. He found them exhausted, resigned to death on the desert. Several wagons were abandoned and many cattle died, but the entire company survived. The delay, however, was costly. They reached the Sierra Nevadas too late to cross before winter, and became snowbound a hundred miles from Sutter's Fort. Many perished of starvation and exposure. Others survived by cooking and eating their boots, harness, and the flesh of dead members of the party. Of the eighty-seven emigrants who began the journey, only forty-four reached California.

Evidence of the Donner-Reed crossing is still preserved in the surface of the desert. Tracks made nearly a hundred years ago by wagons too heavy for the thin salt crust are still visible. The route of the Hastings Cutoff has been retraced and many articles left along the trail have been gathered. A few of these relics are on display at the Grantsville High School (*see above*); others are in the Archeological Museum of the University of Utah; a larger collection is on exhibit at the Fort Sutter Historical Museum in Sacramento, California. Charles Kelly made the desert crossing in 1927 and 1928, while gathering information for his book, *Salt Desert Trails*. In 1936 Dr. W. W. Stookey followed the trail in a caterpillar tractor towing a rubber-tired trailer. He called it the "Salt Desert Limited," because "its speed was limited to three miles an hour and its capacity to four passengers, two of whom had to walk."

The experience of the Donner-Reed party discouraged further attempts to cross the desert until 1849, when Captain Howard Stansbury was sent by the Government to survey Great Salt Lake and the surrounding country. Circling the north end of the lake, he followed the Bartleson route across the desert to Pilot Peak. Here he rested a few days, and began a second desert crossing—eastward over the Hastings Cutoff to the southern end of the lake. He saw evidences of the Donner-Reed journey—several wagons, a cart, skeletons of oxen, and discarded personal property. Stansbury's arrival at Salt Lake City completed the first circuit trip around Great Salt Lake. During the California gold rush of 1849-50, the desert route was again used by over-eager westbound travelers, and again wagons and oxen were abandoned along the trail.

In 1854 Lieutenant E. G. Beckwith was sent to Utah by the Government to make a survey for a railroad to the Pacific. Laying his course a little south of the old Cutoff, he found water at convenient intervals and made the trip without mishap. Building of the railroad was postponed, but the route was used for many years by wagon freighters. The Beckwith road had a steep grade over the Cedar Mountains, and Captain J. H. Simpson, another Government surveyor, came to Utah in 1859 to find a better route. His course led south through Tooele Valley and then west, crossing the desert farther south than previous roads. The Pony Express and the Overland Stage followed this route, and ruins of the old stone relay stations still exist at Fish Springs and Callao.

Travelers were frequently attacked by Indians and outlaws. In 1852 Major Jacob Holeman, Indian Agent, wrote from Salt Lake City to Luke Lee, Commissioner of Indian Affairs in Washington: "We are in great confusion here. We want a few troops on this route very badly. The *white* Indians, I apprehend, are much more dangerous than the red. The renegades, deserters and thieves, who have had to fly from justice to California, have taken refuge in the mountains, and having associated themselves with the Indians are more savage than the Indians themselves. . . . Their object is to plunder, and all who travel that road leading from the states to California." The next month Major Holeman wrote from Carson Valley (now Nevada) : "It is my painful duty to report to you, that from all the information I can get from Whites and Indians, the great, almost the sole cause of all the difficulties, the destruction of life and property on this route is owing to the bad conduct of the whites who were the first to commence it. . . . Whites are in the habit of shooting the Indians whenever and wherever they can find them, whether the Indians are molesting them or not. . . . The Indian knows no difference between the white men, if injured by one he takes revenge upon another."

Garland Hurt, Territorial Indian Agent, in a letter to Brigham Young in 1855, presented the Indian's grievances: "The Indians claim that we have eaten up their grass and thereby deprived them of its rich crop of seed which is their principal subsistence during winter. They say too that the long guns of the white people have scared away the game and now there is nothing left for them to eat but ground squirrels and pis-ants."

The next attempt to plan a route over the desert came in 1896, when William Randolph Hearst, chain newspaper publisher, decided, as a publicity stunt, to send a message by bicycle from his *San Francisco Examiner* to his *New York Journal*. William D. Rishel of Salt Lake City was delegated to map out a portion of the course. Rishel and C. A. Emise took a train to Lucin, Utah, where they unloaded their bicycles and started back to Salt Lake City, laying their trail over the desert around the south end of the lake. The first few miles over the salt beds provided an excellent course, but when the bicycles struck the mud flats the cyclists were frequently compelled to carry their bicycles and walk. After twenty-two hours they arrived at Grantsville—the first and only persons ever to cross the desert on bicycles. Having discovered that the desert crossing was impractical, Rishel surveyed a course around the north end of the lake. Six hundred cyclists, riding in relays, completed the transcontinental trip in thirteen days.

In 1903 the Southern Pacific Railroad built the Lucin Cutoff (*see Great Salt Lake*) across Great Salt Lake and the Salt Desert. In 1907 the Western Pacific Railroad laid its rails across the desert, closely following the Hastings Cutoff. Early attempts to build a highway over the desert were unsuccessful. In most places the salt is many feet deep and when it was dissolved by winter moisture the road was "absorbed" into the desert. The present highway, completed in 1925, an oil-surfaced gravel grade, utilizes a new principle in road engineering—it is protected against the undermining action of water by a mud-filled trench under the roadbed.

In June, 1940, the War Department instructed the Army Air Corps to develop a bombing range, 2,000 square miles in area, on the Great Salt Lake Desert. The area is so remote from settlements that there will be no menace to persons or property. The salt flats are hard and smooth, making runways unnecessary, but hangars for airplanes and "igloos" for storage of bombs must be constructed. Bombing planes will operate from the air base near Ogden.

The BONNEVILLE SPEEDWAY (R), 113.6 *m.*, fastest automobile course in the world, is formed by 100 square miles of level salt, as hard as concrete, looking very much like an immense lake of snow-covered ice. Here—and nowhere else in the world—automobiles have attained speeds in excess of 300 miles per hour. The remarkable qualities of this natural course was first shown in 1914, when Teddy Tetzleff, nationally-known race driver, set an unofficial world record of 141 miles an hour for a measured mile. In 1926 Utah's Ab Jenkins drove for 24 hours without relief, and broke almost every world speed record by traveling 2,710 miles at an average speed of 112 miles an hour. During the following years his records were broken several times, but in 1937, Jenkins, with the assistance of two relief drivers, drove his *Mormon Meteor* in a continuous forty-eight-hour run, during which he regained almost every world record, and established marks of 157 miles an hour for twenty-four hours, and 148 miles an hour for forty-eight hours.

World-wide attention was attracted to the speedway in 1935, when

Sir Malcolm Campbell, London sportsman, drove his specially-built *Bluebird* over the salt flats at an official speed of 301 miles an hour for a measured mile, breaking his own former world's record of 276 miles an hour established at Daytona Beach, Florida, where the fastest records had been made up to that time. Campbell, who was the first person in the world to drive an automobile in excess of 300 miles an hour, later wrote: "These vast salt flats are the future testing grounds of those inevitable developments in racing engines on whose results we shall base the practical everyday lessons which will govern the motor car and, to a certain extent, the aeroplane." His record stood until 1937, when another British driver, Captain George E. T. Eyston forced his seven-ton *Thunderbolt* over the course at 311 miles an hour. On September 16, 1938, a third British driver, John Cobb, raised the mark to 350 miles an hour, but the following day Eyston regained the record by driving 357.5 miles an hour. Cobb returned to the salt flats in 1939 and boosted the world's record to 368.9 miles an hour—traveling a mile in less than ten seconds.

At 118.9 *m.* motorists can leave the highway and drive as fast as they like across the level surface of the salt beds (R)—the only place in Utah where there is no speed limit.

WENDOVER, 124.6 *m.* (4,246 alt., 205 pop.), is a railroad town on the western edge of the Great Salt Lake Desert. The railroad roundhouse and the large yellow frame depot are conspicuous among the unpainted frame houses.

Left from Wendover, on a graded road that skirts the west edge of the Great Salt Lake Desert and wanders across the Nevada line and back into Utah. Between Wendover and Gold Hill, the road parallels the Deep Creek Railroad, an abandoned single-track line operated from 1917 to 1939 by Percy T. Hewitt, engineer, and Mason Moore, manager, superintendent, roadmaster, conductor, clerk, stenographer, and track laborer. In cold weather the combination passenger-mail coach was heated by old-fashioned stoves. Passengers were picked up or let off at any convenient point, and freight was delivered as close as possible to its destination. The accommodating engineer frequently stopped the train to allow passengers to shoot jack rabbits or coyotes, and once, when the stork was delivering twins to a family along the line, the engineer obliged the attending nurse by drawing water from the locomotive boiler.

GOLD HILL, 51 *m.* (5,321 alt., 72 pop.), named for gold deposits near by, is almost a ghost town. The district has produced gold, silver, lead, copper, arsenic, tungsten, and other minerals, but shipments from its mines are said to be "more remarkable for their variety and diffusion than for their tonnage." Valuable ore was first discovered about 1858 by California-bound gold seekers traveling along the Deep Creek Mountains, but the hostility of Indians discouraged development. In 1869 a mining district was organized, and in 1871 a crude smelter—"a stack furnace operated with three blacksmith bellows"—was built. Profits were small until 1892, when Colonel J. F. Woodman, who had taken a fortune from mines in the Tintic district, located two mines near Gold Hill and erected an amalgamation plant. Woodman, over a period of four years, extracted bullion valued at $300,000 but work was suspended after his death. The town had a brief revival in 1905, when a considerable amount of copper ore was extracted, and again in 1923, when scorodite, a form of arsenic fatal to the cotton boll weevil, was discovered. Scorodite solution is sometimes sprayed from airplanes on cotton fields in the South. The "one-man" Rube Mine was discovered by Loeffler Palmer about 1920, after a near-lifetime of fruitless prospecting. Palmer, working alone, spent months loading a single car, but received $6,000 or more for each shipment. When he sold the mine in 1932 he had extracted $112,000 in gold.

IBAPAH (Gosiute, deep down water), 65 *m.* (5,288 alt., 219 pop.), a farm and livestock center, was settled in 1859 by a Mormon missionary who established a farm here to teach agriculture to the Indians. The project was abandoned the following year because of Indian hostilities but later reestablished.

Left from Ibapah on a dirt road to the GOSHUTE INDIAN RESERVATION, 12 *m.* (153 pop.), a fifty-five-acre tract set aside in 1914. The younger Indians can read and write, and to a considerable extent they have abandoned their native dress in favor of white men's clothes. Log huts have been built for all of them, but some of the older Gosiutes still prefer tepees in summer. They cultivate small fields, graze small herds of sheep, gather pine nuts, and make grass baskets, beaded gloves, and moccasins. The miserable condition of the Gosiutes before Government became effective is noted by Mark Twain in *Roughing It:* "We came across the wretchedest type of mankind I have ever seen. . . . I refer to the Goshute Indians . . . small lean scrawny creatures . . . having no higher ambition than to kill and eat Jackass rabbits, crickets and grasshoppers, and embezzle carrion from the buzzards and coyotes."

The main side road crosses the Nevada Line, 69 *m.*, east of Tippett.

US 40 crosses the NEVADA LINE, 125.1 *m.*, at a point 110 miles east of Elko (*see Nevada Guide*).

Tour 6A

Mills Junction—Tooele—Stockton—Junction with US 6; 64.8 *m.* State 36.

Road asphalt-surfaced for north 20 miles; elsewhere gravel-surfaced and improved dirt.
Union Pacific R.R. parallels route throughout.
Accommodations at Tooele; filling station at Stockton.

State 36 parallels the mineral-producing Oquirrh Mountains, in a series of sagebrush valleys. Along the highway are mining and smelting centers and rural hamlets.

State 36 branches south from US 40 at MILLS JUNCTION, 0 *m.* (*see Tour 6c*).

Between Mills Junction and Stockton the highway traverses TOOELE VALLEY, a semi-arid area, 10 to 15 miles wide, bordered on the east by the Oquirrh Mountains and on the west by the Stansbury Mountains.

At 8.4 *m.* is the junction with State 178.

Left on State 178, asphalt-surfaced, to the junction, 2.6 *m.*, with a dirt road; L. here to the million-dollar ELTON TUNNEL, 1 *m.*, construction of which began in 1937. When completed the tunnel will be twelve by twelve feet in cross-section and 23,000 feet long, running eastward into the Oquirrh Mountains to connect with the Rood mine shaft in Bingham, 2,500 feet below the surface. A conduit will drain water from mines in Bingham (*see Tour 1c*), making possible the irrigation of 2,000 acres of land in Tooele Valley, where 1,000 new houses will be built for miners now living in narrow Bingham Canyon. These miners will be transported to and from work through the tunnel, on an electric railway which will also haul ore to the Tooele smelter. At present (1940) this ore is raised to the surface in Bingham and conveyed by aerial tramway over the summit of the mountains to the smelter. Drainage of the Bingham mines will also open additional ore deposits.

The INTERNATIONAL SMELTING AND REFINING PLANT, 4.2 *m.*, was constructed in 1910 at a cost of three million dollars. The plant smelts a million tons of copper ore annually, by a process identical with that used at Garfield (*see Tour 7c*).

TOOELE, 9 *m.* (4,923 alt., 4,984 pop.), seat of Tooele County, is a mining and smelting center. The name, pronounced too-IL-luh, may have derived from the Spanish *tule,* for bulrushes; from the Indian *tuilla,* for a species of flag; or from the name of a Gosiute chief, Tuilla. Mining and smelting brought many foreign-born workers into the community, and the city has two residential sections separated by a strip of unimproved land about a quarter of a mile wide. The eastern section is inhabited by Italians, Greeks, and Austrians, and the western by native-born and English inhabitants. The population mingles freely in work, play, business, and school, but each individual returns at night to his side of town.

Tooele was settled in 1849, and a number of the early stone buildings still stand. During the Civil War many Easterners, to avoid being drafted into the army, went to California "for their health." From these travelers early residents of Tooele obtained horses, sheep, and goats. It is said that the fine-wooled white Merino sheep was introduced into Utah through one of these trades.

At 12.9 *m.* is the junction with State 179.

Right on State 179, a gravel-surfaced road, to BAUER, 1.7 *m.* (5,050 alt.), with its COMBINED METAL REDUCTION PLANT, where ores are concentrated by the flotation process. The plant, established in 1923, has a capacity of 700 tons a day. A large apple orchard on the edge of Bauer is irrigated with water pumped from a mine.

STOCKTON, 15.5 *m.* (5,068 alt., 351 pop.), is a tumble-down town named for Stockton, California, by Colonel Patrick Edward Connor, who constructed Utah's first large smelter here in 1864, following the discovery of valuable ore deposits by Fort Douglas soldiers in the mountains near by. Mines in the vicinity have produced millions of dollars in gold, silver, and lead.

Between Stockton and Vernon, State 36 passes through RUSH VALLEY, a wide brushy flat bordered on the east by the Oquirrh Mountains and on the west by the Onaqui Mountains. Through this region ran the Overland Stage.

At 20.5 *m.* is the junction with State 180.

Left on State 180, a gravel-surfaced road, to the junction, 5.1 *m.*, with a gravel-surfaced road; L. here to the mining town of OPHIR, 3 *m.* (6,498 alt., 170 pop.), which, contrary to the claim of one old codger, did not derive its name from the expression, "Oh, fer Gods sake." The town was named by Colonel Patrick E. Connor's soldiers for the fabulous mines of King Solomon. Ophir has risen from the sick bed so often, the very buildings seem bored with constant resurrection. The lop-sided, caved-in ruins lean on their elbows and complacently view the goings-on of each new strike. Frame structures of every period mark the dates of Ophir's revivals.

Indians mined silver and gold for trinkets, and lead for bullets, in this little canyon. Connor's men, hearing of the Indian mine, staked the St. Louis Lode in the late 1860's. The strike touched off a boom. Miners and prospectors dashed into camp from Nevada and California, and soon the Pocatello, Velocipede, Wild Delirium, and Miner's Delight were located. Mack Gisborn, who made his stake at Mercur, built a toll road from Ophir to Stockton. Wagons hauled ore over this road and north to Lake Point, on Great Salt Lake, where it was boated to Corinne and the railroad. The usual "boomers" hurried into camp and threw up shacks. Saloons lined the street, interspersed with brothels and gambling dens.

One poker game is still remembered. An eye witness tells in the *Park City Record* of the game between "Digger" Mike and Frank Payton:

I walked over to the corner table and took a position where I could see the players. "Digger" had . . . about $6,000 in front of him while Payton had about $7,000. Both men played cautiously for a while, or until there was a jack pot which "Digger" opened with a bag of gold dust. Payton staid and raised him two hundred fifty dollars, which the "Digger" saw and went him five hundred dollars (gold dust) better. Payton just called this, then skinned his hand and asked for one card. "Digger" dealt it to him and then threw five hundred of his dust into the pot remarking, "I don't need any." Payton skinned his hand again and after going through the usual motions of looking at his antagonist for a few minutes he saw the five hundred and went it five hundred better. "Digger" was more prompt in raising this four bags of dust, and Payton even more promptly saw the raise and went it two thousand better. . . . They continued to raise each other as they made bet after bet until the "Digger" shouted for a showdown, saying he couldn't call another cent. Both hands went down on the board at the same moment and then Payton reached over and began to scoop in the gold dust and chips. He had a pair of fours, while "Digger" had been bluffing on a "kelter" [absolutely nothing]. "I didn't think you had enough nerve to follow me, Frank," was all he said as he got up from the table to leave the place to go back to the diggings to toil for more gold dust.

Payton left the saloon, and that was the last time he was seen until his body was picked up a week or two later in a ravine. His skull was crushed and his money was gone. His murderer was never found.

The mines at Ophir furnished Marcus Daly, Montana copper king, with his start to riches. Fired from the Emma Mine at Alta, Daly was hired by the Walker Brothers, Salt Lake City bankers, to work their property at Ophir. He staked the Zella claim for himself, and profits from that mine helped develop Anaconda Copper in Montana. George H. Dern, later Secretary of War, got his start as a bookkeeper at Mercur (*see Salt Lake City*). The Kearsarge Mine, at Ophir, is said to have produced a million dollars from one stope. One of the largest silver nuggets ever mined was sent from this property to the St. Louis World's Fair in 1904. The ore beds at Ophir were shallow and soon exhausted, but since 1930 deeper shafts have been sunk, and, with more efficient methods of smelting, the mines are coming back. In 1938 Ophir District produced 140 ounces of gold, 144,919 ounces of silver, 874,102 pounds of copper, 4,025,543 pounds of lead, and 3,786,812 pounds of zinc, all valued at $551,189. The camp may be convalescent, but it is a long way from dead.

Beyond the Ophir junction State 180 winds along the foothills of the Oquirrh Mountains (L). At 9.6 m. the road enters a narrow canyon and winds eastward to MERCUR, 12.6 m. (6,700 alt.) a mining town that refuses to be a "good Indian"—it will not stay dead. The ruins—an old jail cage, two whisky cellars, a bakery oven, and a jewelry store vault—cock a humorous eye at the newly-built, unpainted shacks and the flapping tent-houses. A few old walls still stand, but the only impressive marks of yesterday are the huge slag dumps, which, paradoxically, are the foundation of Mercur's newest boom. Streets were never a problem; the town straggled wherever it pleased.

Mercur came to life in the late 1860's when Colonel Patrick E. Connor's soldiers discovered silver ore in the canyon, but early yields were disappointing. The Floyd Silver Mining Company optimistically put $700,000 into development of property that returned only $175,000. Mack Gisborn started the stampede, however, when he lifted $80,000 from his hole in the ground, the Carrie Steel. Silver seekers fought their way into the new camp in every kind of conveyance, and the stage companies ran six trips a day. News of the strike brought business men, gamblers, saloon keepers, and the usual camp parasites. Buildings sprang up along the gulch, and the new town was named Lewiston. Hotels and "hook shops" did a land office business, and if they missed extracting all of a miner's money, the saloons and gambling houses finished the job. A million dollars was taken out, but in 1880 the boom folded up and everybody left.

Arie Pinedo, a Bavarian prospector, drifted into the district in 1882, and located the Mercur lode, a cinnabar or quicksilver deposit, which gave the town its present name. Assayers found gold in all samples, but the prospectors were unable to pan any of it. Pronouncing a curse on all assayers, the prospectors, including Pinedo, departed. In 1889 Joseph Smith rediscovered gold on the Pinedo claim. Smith "rawhided" (see Transportation) ore to the amalgamating mill at the bottom of the canyon, but no gold would come out. Smith was determined to get at the gold, and while experimentation continued, he and his partner, L. S. Manning, set out to find Pinedo. After a chase through North America, South America, and Europe, Pinedo was finally overhauled. He wanted $100,000 for his interests, but Smith arranged a deal for $30,000. The gold remained elusive, and Smith's promoters dropped out—at the wrong time, for Colorado engineers discovered the cyanide process in 1893 and Mercur hit the headlines again.

Mercur was a lively town in the late 1890's, but the fights were mostly fistic. One notable battle stands out, between Soda Water Fred and the Horse Jaw Kid over Katie, the lovely waitress. Jack Schaefer, proprietor of the Mercur Hotel, suggested they fight it out in public, the winner to take the girl and the gate receipts. They hired a dance hall, Schaefer acted as referee, his partner, H. O. Milner, tended the gate. The fighters started slugging, and Schaefer was afraid the match would not last long enough to satisfy the customers. He asked Horse Jaw to lay down, but Soda Water, not hearing him, kept boring in until Horse Jaw claimed a foul. Schaefer let the foul go, and Horse Jaw up and quit. Staggering to the center of the ring he yelled, "Milner took the money at the gate, Schaefer refereed the fight, and Soda Water owes Schaefer twenty dollars, so how in the hell can I win this fight?" Schaefer said of the bout, in an interview, "Katie was in cahoots with me on the deal. The fight ended with the gate $20.15 and Soda Water Fed and Horse Jaw losing out on the deal, girl and all." Katie married an Easterner, and is known in society from coast to coast.

Old-timers blame the exuberance of the populace on the quality of Mercur's sidehill whisky, but insist that the citizens had to drink whisky—water was too expensive. John Nicholsen owned the only spring in the district; the water was hauled a mile and dispensed in cups and buckets. In 1895 water was struck in Ophir, and a pipe line was laid to Mercur, ruining Nicholsen's monopoly.

About this time the railroad came, and by 1896 the population had jumped from 400 to 6,000. A move was made to incorporate the town on Statehood

Day, January 6, 1896, but a fire swept the town, leaving little to incorporate. The "Hook Department" went into action. Water was scarce and the volunteer fire department used a long pole with a hook on the end, with which they dragged flaming shacks into the street and let them burn. In spite of the fire, however, the town was incorporated.

Mercur was going along nicely again in June, 1902, when somebody saw a curl of smoke coming out of the Preble Hotel. This time dynamite, hooks, and bucket brigades were useless. By evening all that remained of Mercur was smoking ruins. The camp was never rebuilt. In 1913 the Golden Gate shut down, and the few remaining residents tore down their buildings and left. Cloudbursts finished the job of wiping out the camp. The $20,000,000 ore body was worked out, it was said, but Horse Thief Gulch took on new activity in 1934, when the Snyder Brothers located a rich claim. The company is also reworking the tailing dumps to recover gold and silver lost by old smelting methods. Old-timers go back to Mercur once a year, during the first week in September, for the Mercur Pioneer Reunion. The usual events and contests are held, but the old-timers like best to tell of the days when the raw, rejuvenated mining camp was a boasting, swaggering city.

At 24.5 m. on State 180 is the junction with State 73 (see Tour 1d).

VERNON, 41.6 m. (5,511 alt., 341 pop.), is a farming and ranching community centered around a dusty blue frame chapel and a yellow brick schoolhouse.

South of Vernon, State 36 winds and dips through a narrow sagebrush valley, bordered on the east by the West Tintic Mountains and on the west by the Sheeprock Mountains. The blue summit of Mount Timpanogos, highest peak in the Wasatch Range, is visible fifty miles eastward.

KNIGHT, 61.2 m. (6,572 alt.), a shipping point on the Union Pacific Railroad, with a 50,000-bushel grain elevator and an emergency landing field, was named for Jesse Knight, who was responsible for development of much of the mining property in the Tintic District (see Mining and Tour 8).

At 64.8 m. is the junction with US 6 (see Tour 8).

Tour 7

(Grand Junction, Colo.)—Greenriver—Price—Helper—Spanish Fork —Magna—(Elko, Nev.); US 50.
Colorado Line to Nevada Line, 385 m.

Asphalt paved throughout.
Denver and Rio Grande Western R.R. parallels nearly entire route.
All types of accommodations in larger towns.

US 50 feels its way over a plateau region, past billowing foothills sparsely covered with sagebrush and cacti, through winding canyons, and across clay flats. The colorful Book and Brown Cliffs hem the highway on the north while the canyons of the Colorado River are glimpsed across the barren wasteland to the south. A few scattered farms push their way toward the red sandstone cliffs. The semiarid desert is perpetually harassed by winds, which cover everything with a fine, red dust. The flats—baked hard by the hot summer sun—are cracked and broken by the winter's frost. Between Greenriver and Woodside, the San Rafael Swell is blackly silhouetted against the southern sky. West of Woodside, the highway penetrates Utah's fuel center, and the settlements draw closer together; thousands of tons of coal are shipped daily from these mines. Mining towns straggle over the mountainsides between Price and Soldier Summit. West of Soldier Summit, the road gradually loses the accompanying red sandstone formations, and picks up the gray-white limestone of canyons flanking the highway to Spanish Fork. Between Spanish Fork and Salt Lake City, US 50, united with US 91, skirts the western slopes of the Wasatch Mountains, and west of Salt Lake City, united much of the way with US 40, the route penetrates smelting towns and crosses the Great Salt Lake Desert.

Section a.   COLORADO LINE to PRICE; 137.4 m., US 50

Desolate wastes stretch on both sides of US 50 as it crosses the rolling mesas of the Grand River Valley. Rabbit grass and stunted sage dot the red semi-desert, and the distant Book Cliffs catch and hold the glaring sunlight. West of Greenriver the country is more rugged, and cliffs move in to hedge the highway.

US 50 crosses the COLORADO LINE, 0 *m.,* 35 miles west of Grand Junction, Colorado (*see Colorado Guide*), and ascends a gently rolling plateau.

HARLEY DOME, 5.9 *m.,* with one house and a service station, was named for the man who drilled the first gas well in this section. Analysis of the gas revealed that Well No. 1, drilled in 1925, contained 2.25 per cent helium. Well No. 2, drilled the following year, had 7 per cent helium. The wells were capped and set aside in a government reserve.

CISCO, 23.8 *m.* (4,352 alt., 193 pop.), a few houses and shipping corrals, was built in the center of a red mesa by the Denver & Rio Grande Western Railroad to serve sheep and cattle ranchers. The barrenness of the region is deceptive, for a variety of hardy plants make it important for grazing. Rich deposits of vanadium, uranium, and copper have been found in the hills, but they remain undeveloped.

The Colorado Museum of Natural History sent an expedition into the Book Cliffs near Cisco in 1939 to excavate cliff dwellings. The expedition has found a series of curved, unconnected walls, and significance of which has not been determined, and, according to *Southern*

Utah News and Views, "A new type of fire pit, circular in form and of material baked to bricklike consistency."

At 25.7 *m.* is the junction with State 128 (*see Tour 9*).

Between Cisco and Thompsons the landscape is one of straight lines and sharp angles. Rugged plateaus and mesas south of the highway are separated by vertically walled canyons.

THOMPSONS, 46.3 *m.* (5,134 alt., 102 pop.), is a watering point on the Denver & Rio Grande Railroad.

Thompsons is at the junction with a dirt road and State 94.

1. Right on State 94 to a narrow defile, 3.4 *m.,* of the Book Cliffs, where petroglyphs and pictographs, badly marred by vandals, are on the walls (R and L).

SEGO, 4.8 *m.* (6,000 alt., 223 pop.), a mining camp producing anthracite coal, never knows when a paleontologist will pop up. In 1931 officials of the Chesterfield mine sent a dinosaur track, four feet five and a half inches long, and thirty-two inches across the side toes, to Pennsylvania State College. The dinosaur is thought to have slipped in soft peaty mud, causing the extreme length of the track. The same year, R. M. Magraw, general manager of the mine, sent another track, forty-four by thirty-two inches, to the American Museum of Natural History, New York City. The museum sent an expedition to the region in 1937, and Barnum Brown, curator of fossil reptiles, reported in the March, 1938, *Natural History* that "Footprints of a giant with a 15-foot stride, and estimated to tower 35 feet, are among the valuable specimens brought back."

2. Left from Thompsons on a dirt road to the junction, 9 *m.,* with US 160 (*see Tour 9*).

CRESCENT JUNCTION, 52.2 *m.* (4,778 alt.), is at the junction with US 160 (*see Tour 9*).

ELGIN, 71.7 *m.,* a name on a railroad signpost, is at the junction with a poor dirt road.

Left on this road to Utah's OLD FAITHFUL "GEYSER," 8.5 *m.* (*adm. 50¢ a car*), which came into existence when Glen M. Ruby, geologist, began drilling for oil in 1936. Gas flows and a tremendous volume of water forced Ruby to abandon the well at 2,000 feet. The "geyser," local people say, spouts water ninety feet high every fifteen minutes.

At 72 *m.* US 50 crosses the GREEN RIVER, one of Utah's largest streams, which heads in the Wind River Mountains of Wyoming, and, sixty miles below the crossing, flows into the Colorado River. Here the Green River, beckoning with one hand and thumbing its nose with the other, lures the riverman. It is a wolf in sheep's clothing, hiding behind a bland and limpid surface its turbulent upstream past, and giving no hint of its crashing, thrusting, downstream future.

Trappers used sections of the river in the 1820's, but if they reached the junction of the two rivers, it has not been recorded. The first man to attempt the Green appears to be General William H. Ashley, who went downstream almost to Greenriver, Utah, in 1825. The name, "D. Julien," with the date 1836, appears several times on the walls of the canyons of the Green River, but little else is known of his trip.

The one-armed Major John Wesley Powell may not have been a good manager, but there can be no question of his daring. He made two assaults upon the rivers, one in 1869, the other in 1871. Without maps or charts Powell made his way along the Green and Colorado to the Grand Canyon. Leaving Green River, Wyoming, May 24, 1869, Powell set out with four boats and a crew of nine. The boats passed uneventfully through U-shaped Horseshoe Canyon, and Kingfisher Canyon. While camped along this stretch, Powell made a discovery, which he outlined in his present-tense journal, *Exploration of the Colorado River of the West:* "On looking at the mountain directly in front, the steepness of the slope is greatly exaggerated, while the distance to its summit and its true altitude are correspondingly diminished. I have heretofore found that to properly judge the slope . . . you must see it in profile. . . . Now lying on my side and looking at it, the true proportions appear. This seems a wonder and I rise up . . . and view it standing. . . . Musing on this I . . . find . . . the reason is simple. . . . The distance between the eyes forms a base-line for optical triangulation."

In Lodore Canyon, Powell had his first accident, resulting in the loss of a boat. The men were saved, but it was thought that all the barometers, which were on this boat, had been lost. Powell sent two men through the rapids to the still intact cabin the next day, and they returned triumphantly with the barometers and a three-gallon keg of whisky. Powell, because he had only one arm, almost lost his life in Split Rock Canyon (*see Dinosaur National Monument*).

At the junction of the Uinta, Powell went to visit the Indian reservation—located in 1868 at Whiterocks—and Frank Goodman left the party. He had been on the boat that was lost, and Powell intimates that he had lost his nerve, but the Major was not always fair to the men who left him. Above Stillwater Powell gazed upon "a strange, weird, grand region. The landscape everywhere, away from the river, is of rock—cliffs of rock; tables of rock; plateaus of rock; terraces of rock; crags of rock—ten thousand strangely carved forms. Rocks everywhere, and no vegetation, no soil, no sand . . . a whole land of naked rock, with giant forms carved on it; cathedral shaped buttes, towering hundreds or thousands of feet; cliffs that cannot be scaled, and cañon walls that shrink the river into insignificance, with vast, hollow domes, and tall pinnacles, and shafts set on the verge overhead, and all highly colored—buff, gray, red, brown, and chocolate; never lichened; never moss-covered; but bare, and often polished."

Between Lees Ferry and the Grand Canyon, three of his men, thoroughly fed up with the management of the party, with the roar of water, with high enclosing walls, and fearing great rapids below, left the expedition. Shivwits Indians, refusing to believe their story that they came from the river, killed them.

Powell seems to have taken his second expedition lightly. According to the journal of William Clement Powell, his nephew, dissension began early. The party left Green River, Wyoming, May 22, 1871, and by June 11, Frank Richardson was ready to leave the party, "at the Maj. request." F. S. Dellenbaugh, expedition artist, was only 17 at the time, but from young Powell's account he was quite a man. Dellenbaugh's two books, *The Romance of the Grand Canyon* and *A Canyon Voyage,* have been used as guides for river trips ever since. Powell neglected to meet the party at designated places, failed to send supplies, and kept the men waiting in confining canyons for days while he went "scouting" with Jacob Hamblin, Mormon missionary to the Indians.

Nate Galloway, a trapper, was probably the first man to run the rivers alone. In 1895, he made the trip from Green River, Wyoming, to Jensen, Utah, where he meant to disembark a load of beaver pelts. However, he preferred river hazards to officers looking for beaver poachers, and continued on to Lees Ferry, Arizona, by himself. He made repeated trips through Cataract Canyon and Grand Canyon before leading the Julius F. Stone expedition. Charles S. Russell, E. R. Monnette, and Bert Loper started from Greenriver, Utah, in 1907 in steel boats. Loper laid up at Hite to repair his boat, and the others reached Needles, California, in February, 1908.

The Julius F. Stone expedition of 1909 left Green River, Wyoming, in September, with four boats designed by Nate Galloway, and reached Needles in November, bringing two boats through without a spill. Stone gives the story in *Canyon Country.* He returned to the river in 1939 at the age of 83, and with boats furnished by Dr. A. L. Inglesby made another trip with Charles Kelly, Dr. Inglesby, Dr. R. G. Frazier, now (1940) with Admiral Byrd in the Antarctic, William A. Chryst, who helped Kettering develop the automobile self-starter, and George Stone, son of Julius. The party found a carved date, "1642," not yet identified, and an "1837" with some unintelligible lettering.

Emery C. Kolb, James Fagin, and Ellsworth Kolb, with two flat-boats designed by Nate Galloway, left Green River, Wyoming, in September, 1911, and arrived at the Bright Angel Trail in November. The brothers resumed their trip, and arrived at Needles in January, 1912. Ellsworth went on alone to the Gulf of California, in May, 1913, making the run in eight days. A record of their trip, *Through the Grand Canyon from Wyoming to Mexico,* was written by Ellsworth.

Boyhood dreams were realized by Clyde Eddy when in 1927 he made the trip from Greenriver, Utah, to Needles. Eddy made another trip in 1934, accompanied by Dr. R. G. Frazier, Bill Fahrni of Bingham, and three men from Vernal. They made a complete photographic record of the river from Lees Ferry to Boulder Dam.

The next trip to attract public attention was the "lone wolf" voyage of Buzz Holmstrom, who left Green River, Wyoming, in October, 1937. Buzz studied each rapid before attempting it, and more than once had to portage or line his boat over the rocks. He emerged at Boulder Dam, fifty-two days later.

GREENRIVER, 73.2 *m.* (4,079 alt., 472 pop.), is nationally known for its watermelons and cantaloupes. Settled in 1878, the town was a mail relay station between Salina, Utah, and Ouray, Colorado, until the Rio Grande Western Railroad entered in 1882. With the coming of the railroad, a short-lived land boom hit the little settlement. In an interview Chris Halverson stated that he and his brother caught 180 beaver the first winter, selling the hides for 50¢ to $1.50. Prospectors found gold in the region, but it was "flour" gold, too fine to sift out. Eastern farmers tried to irrigate with water from the Green River. The river was hard to handle—it still is—and crop after crop flooded out. The few who succeeded took land along small streams that could be controlled. Melon-growing began in 1917, but it was not until 1926 that local melons reached New York City, where they have since commanded premium prices.

Greenriver is at the junction with State 24 (*see Tour 2A*).

Between Greenriver and Woodside a portion of the San Rafael Swell (L) stands black against the skyline. Resembling the ruins of an ancient city, the immense pinnacles, as sharply defined as broken glass, glow softly at sunset.

WOODSIDE, 96.8 *m.* (4,633 alt., 83 pop.), is a farming community. Midway between the town's two service stations is the WOODSIDE "GEYSER." The railroad drilled for water at this spot in 1910, and got it, but it was so vile nothing could be done with it. The well spouted seventy-five feet in the air and refused to be capped. Humans avoided the poisonous water, but cattle died from drinking it. In 1940 it barely rose above ground.

An undulating plateau of clay and shale, resembling the gray, wrinkled backs of gigantic elephants, borders the highway between Woodside and Wellington.

At 121.7 *m.* is the junction with State 123.

Right on this paved road, to the junction, 8.2 *m.*, with State 124; R. on State 124 to COLUMBIA, 3.3 *m.* (7,800 alt., 646 pop.), a model steel company town that supplies coking coal to the blast furnaces at Ironton (*see Tour 1d*). Trim lawns and gardens circle neat houses, and the miners have a tennis court and swimming pool.

SUNNYSIDE, 11.7 *m.* (413 pop.), on State 123, is a declining coal and coke town operated by a "ghost crew." When Sunnyside was a town, there existed a strong feeling between southern Europeans and "whites," as the American-born were locally known. Prejudice was not so pronounced where Negroes were concerned. The "whites" heartily sanctioned Negro action against a school teacher who had beaten colored children: The Negroes ran him out of town. Andrew W. Dowd, community doctor, did much to further the assimilation of foreigners by enforcing rules of sanitation; he discouraged scalding slaughtered hogs in the bathtub, giving chickens the right-of-way in the house, and raising rabbits under the bed.

Children, however, were fascinated by foreign customs. Mrs. Lucile Richens, formerly of Sunnyside, is quoted in the manuscript *History of Carbon County,* by the Utah Historical Records Survey, to illustrate this point: "We children used to go down to Jap town after school to watch the Japanese fly kites. . . . They used to make wooden men, painted in bright colors . . . joined at the elbows, shoulders, waist and knees and worked by a windmill in such a way that, when the wind blew, it looked like the wooden men were turning the windmills." Jefferson Tidwell found a seam of coal in 1898 and sold it to he Utah Fuel company for $250. A year later more than 1,200 men were employed in the mines at Sunnyside. Coke made here was shipped to Castlegate (*see below*) for use in smelting. In 1902-03 more than 400 coke ovens were burning at Sunnyside. It boomed as a coke town until 1929, when other products were introduced for smelting. Of the 816 coke ovens once in use, only six were operating in 1940.

ROCK ASPHALT DEPOSIT, 16.7 *m.*, has enough oil-impregnated sandstone to pave everything in sight. The deposit was first utilized in 1892, but serious development waited until 1928. The stone is quarried here, trucked to a mill, and crushed to the consistency of coarse sand. It can be laid cold.

US 50 continues through a region of plateaus and mesas, with the Book Cliffs (R) standing guard over the wasteland.

At 127.4 *m.* is the junction with State 53.

Right on this graveled road (*carry extra water and supplies*) to MINNIE MAUDE CREEK, 37 *m.*, flowing into Nine Mile Canyon (R). Alfred Lund settled here in 1885, naming the place Minnie Maude, for two girls.

Right here from State 53 over a poorly defined trail into downstream NINE MILE CANYON, where Donald Scott of the Peabody Museum, Harvard University, made exhaustive studies of cliff dwellings and petroglyphs in 1936. He found Basket Maker remains, evidenced by "square-shouldered figures of typical basket-maker pattern on the walls and rock shelters." Four types of Pueblo houses were found. "The site called . . . the 'sky house' is the most important," the *Salt Lake Tribune* reports. "In its details, it represents a type of house which has not hitherto been excavated in any part of the world. . . . The house is located atop an isolated pinnacle, the top of which is roughly round and about 25 feet in diameter. . . . The roof and superstructure were supported on a heavy framework of logs held by four pillars of wood about nine inches in diameter. . . . In the center of the hard-packed floor, an elaborate fireplace was found . . . paved with thin slabs of limestone and surrounded by a double rim of adobe bricks." Archeologists estimated the date of occupation at 890 to 1000 A. D.

At 69.1 *m.* is the junction with US 40, 1.9 miles west of Myton (*see Tour 6a*).

At 130.4 *m.* is the junction with a dirt road.

Left on this road to the CARBON DIOXIDE WELL, 0.3 *m.*, where "dry ice" and carbonic gas are manufactured for refrigeration and beverages. As it comes from the well, the gas is changed to a solid by running it through a heater; it is then treated chemically to remove other gases. The carbon dioxide, now a liquid, passes through a nozzle and emerges as a fine spray, which crystallizes into "snow." The snow is transferred to moulds, where it is compressed by hydraulic pressure into cakes about a foot square. "Dry ice," having a temperature of 114 below zero, does not melt, but evaporates, leaving no moisture residue. Before mechanical coal stokers came into common use, when lump coal was in demand, liquid carbon dioxide was popularly used for blasting coal. Put up in cartridges, it was electrically detonated.

PRICE, 137.4 *m.* (5,566 alt., 5,212 pop.), Carbon County seat, is a moneyed town, with modern buildings, numerous cafes, saloons, and behind-the-scenes gambling houses. If there is a touch of coal dust in the air, it is a dust that means cash, and local people do not give it too much time to settle.

Caleb Rhodes saw possibilities in the valley when he passed through with a herd of cattle in 1877. Farming was begun along the Price River two years later, but active settlement was delayed until the coming of the railroad in the early 1880's. Discovery of coal opened a new source of income. The wealth of the town made it a stopping place for the outlaws of Browns Hole (*see Tour 6a*) and Robbers Roost (*see below*). Butch Cassidy, leader of the Robbers Roost gang, came here to view his body. Word was spread that the outlaw had been killed by a posse in the San Rafael Swell, south of town. Cassidy, concealed in a covered wagon, drove past the place where his "body" was lying "in state." Several days later, officers discovered that the slain man was Jim Herron, a minor outlaw.

Price was the home of Matt Warner, one-time member of the Robbers Roost gang, who died in 1938. For years he terrorized the country as far west as Oregon, and east to Colorado. Warner served time in the State penitentiary, and later took up ranching near Price. He served two terms as Price city marshal and one term as justice of peace at Carbonville (*see below*).

The first week in September is set aside for the Robbers Roost Roundup, a rodeo reviving the wild and woolly West. The Intermountain Band Contest, for high school bands, held each spring, draws more than 2,500 contestants and 20,000 visitors from surrounding States.

The PRICE ART GALLERY (*open 8-8 weekdays, adm. free*), on the second floor of the modern Municipal Building in Price, was opened by the Utah Art Project in April 1940, when it showed the paintings of Lynn and Dean Fausett, Price artists. Gallery exhibitions are principally those circulated among seventy-two Federal art centers throughout the country by the WPA Art Program.

Left from Price on State 10, a paved road to the junction, 7.6 *m.*, with State 122; R. on this road to three coal mining camps, HIAWATHA, MOHRLAND, and WATTIS.

At 20.2 *m.* on State 10 is the junction with State 155; L. on this graveled road to CLEVELAND, 6.1 *m.* (6,000 alt., 294 pop.). East of the town on Red Plateau, Lee Stokes, a local resident and Princeton student, in the fall of 1939 uncovered a deposit of fossil dinosaur bones, covered with a layer of volcanic ash.

At 21.7 *m.* on State 10 is the junction (R) with State 31, an alternate route (*closed in winter*) running through the Manti National Forest and connecting with US 89 at FAIRVIEW, 45.3 *m.* (6,033 alt., 1,120 pop.) (*see Tour 2b*).

HUNTINGTON, 22.4 *m.* (5,900 alt., 995 pop.), is an agricultural community.

At 27.7 *m.* is the junction with State 29; L. on this road to the junction, 3.9 *m.*, with a paved road; L. here to ORANGEVILLE, 0.3 *m.* (5,772 alt., 532 pop.), supported principally by farming. It was settled in 1877 and named for Orange Seely, a man who weighed more than 320 pounds. "His feet were only number five in length but were almost as wide as they were long." A Utah Historical Records Survey manuscript says: "People came from thirty to fifty miles for him to set broken bones and pull teeth, or if they could not come to him he set out cheerfully on horseback to go to them." Mrs. Seely is quoted as saying, "The first time I ever swore was when we arrived in Emery County and I said 'Damn a man who would bring a woman to such a God Forsaken country!'"

At 12 *m.* on State 29 is a view (L) of NORTH HORN MOUNTAIN (9,050 alt.) looming skyward through a tangle of pines and aspens. In the summer of 1937, remains of a fossil titanosaur, never before found in North America, were uncovered on this mountain by George B. Barnes of an exploring party from the Smithsonian Institution. The animal was about fifteen feet tall, and and had a fifty-foot tail.

EPHRAIM, 42.7 m. (5,543 alt., 1,966 pop.), is at the junction with US 89 (see Tour 2b).

CASTLE DALE, 31.4 m. (5,771 alt., 839 pop.), on State 10, a solid town with prosperous farms and fat livestock, is named for castlelike rock formations in the vicinity. Orange Seely first entered this section in 1875, bringing herds for grazing. Outlaws, hiding out at Robbers Roost to the south, plagued the settlers with cattle-rustling raids in the eighties and nineties.

Left from Castle Dale on an oiled road to SAN RAFAEL BRIDGE, 2 m. Completion of the bridge in 1937, and improvement of the highway to the south, opened an untamed area—the SAN RAFAEL SWELL. Among the vari-colored spires, pinnacles, monoliths and domes, in the highest and most inaccessible section of this great area, is ROBBER'S ROOST, outlaw hideout in the eighties and nineties. Undeveloped oil fields, supposed to contain large quantities of oil and gas, are near the road. The Swell has undeveloped deposits of radio-active carnotite and uranium ores. Outstanding scenic attractions in the area are the DEVIL'S STEWPOTS, thousands of hollowed-out mounds resembling giant bowls; BUCKHORN FLAT, a 50,000-acre plain as level as a dance floor; LON CHANEY PEAK, the "mountain with a thousand faces"; SENTINEL PEAK, standing guard and pointing a slender red finger as though in exhortation; SINBAD, an area of arabesque monoliths in every imaginable color and shape; and BUCKHORN WASH, a narrow defile with low rock walls. During the rainy season, the wash is a trough for raging torrents, but in summer it is a dry stream bed. A frieze of petroglyphs, two feet high and a thousand feet long, has eluded erosion on the canyon walls.

MOORE, 52 m. (6,250 alt., 114 pop.), until 1940 named Rochester, had its name changed to honor L. C. Moore, manager of the local farm project since 1907. Philatelic enthusiasts sent letter covers here to be postmarked "Rochester" on one day and "Moore" the next, when the name was officially changed.

"County banks," or small coal mines, provide the citizens of EMERY, 58.3 m. (6,247 alt., 620 pop.), with a good income. The mines are operated by residents, and the coal is trucked to near-by towns. Emery is entirely surrounded by high, rugged mountains. Casper Christensen settled Emery in 1881, and pioneers bored a 1,240-foot tunnel to tap Muddy Creek for irrigation water.

FREMONT JUNCTION, 74.4 m., is at the junction with State 72 (see Tour 2A).

Between 76.4 m. and 107 m., eastern and western boundaries of FISHLAKE NATIONAL FOREST, State 10 traverses some of the best elk and deer country in Utah.

SALINA, 110.8 m. (5,160 alt., 1,383 pop.), is at the junction with US 89 (see Tour 2b).

Section b. PRICE to SALT LAKE CITY; 121.5 m., US 50

Between PRICE, 0 m., and Helper, US 50 closely parallels the Price River, where rich bottomlands are green with irrigation. Roads branch off from the main highway to coal fields in various canyons. West of Helper, steep-walled Price River Canyon makes a shadowy corridor through which the highway twists toward Soldier Summit. Wriggling through a small draw, US 50 runs through Spanish Fork Canyon, past small railroad sidings and scattered mining camps, and into the open Utah Valley. North of Spanish Fork, US 50, united with US 91, runs along the western base of the Wasatch Mountains.

At 4.9 m. is the junction with State 139.

CONSUMERS, 10.7 *m.* (7,500 alt., 475 pop.), a model mining camp, has the largest coal mine in the district. A. E. Gibson, with his partner, located a nine-foot coal seam in 1920, and, though hampered by snowdrifts, crude machinery, and lack of food, shipped thirty-four carloads the first winter. Outside interests later purchased the mine, and built up the town.

At 5.9 *m.* is the junction with State 137.

Right on this road to KENILWORTH, 3.9 *m.* (6,604 alt., 877 pop.), a modern coal camp with an almost entirely American population, which is rare in this district. Heber J. Stowell discovered the first vein of coal here in 1904, and the mine was a big producer during and after the World War. Three tipples operate during the winter season.

HELPER, 7.2 *m.* (5,829 alt., 2,843 pop.), overflows on both sides of Price Canyon. Houses cling precariously to the steep walls, barely keeping their feet out of the street and Price River. The narrow street is crowded with American, Italian, Greek, Austrian, Japanese, and Chinese miners, who depend upon the twenty-eight mines in the area for a livelihood. Railroad men mingle with the crowd, and there is a sort of an armed neutrality between them and the miners.

Teancum Pratt brought his two wives here in 1870 while he prospected for coal. For many years the family lived in a dugout, but eventually Pratt acquired nearly the whole district. Helper is platted according to his original survey. He sold his property to the Denver & Rio Grande Western in 1883, and a narrow-gauge railroad was brought in. Standard gauge replaced the narrow gauge in 1890, and two years later a depot, roundhouse, oilhouse, coal chute, and hotel for trainmen were erected. The town became known as Helper in 1892 because extra engines or "helpers" were kept here to push trains up the heavy grade to Soldier Summit.

Helper went through a period of outlawry, gambling and killings when gunfights were too common to attract any attention, and the Robbers Roost gang (*see below*) often visited the town.

Mines in the district are either shaft or drift mines. A shaft mine is reached through a vertical shaft like an elevator; a drift mine is entered horizontally, through the side of a hill along the plane of the coal seam. Cutting machines make a slot along the bottom of the seam, explosives are inserted, and the blast blows the coal down. It is shoveled by hand into squat mine cars. Rock-dust, a fine, damp powder, is sprayed on the mine walls, where it absorbs the explosive coal dust. Mine ventilation systems keep up a constant circulation of air, and draw out inflammable gases. Miners wear "hard hats," similar to soldiers' helmets, and battery-fueled electrical head-lamps. Electrically-operated trains carry the coal out to the tipple, a specimen of side-hill architecture that straddles a railroad track, where it is cleaned, sized, and in some cases waxed. Shaker screens with different size meshes separate the coal into slack, pea, nut, stove lump, and furnace lump, and clanging metallic belts carry it into railroad cars lined up beneath the tipple.

The CIVIC AUDITORIUM (R), on Main Street, is the only building of its kind in Utah (1940). It is a modern brick structure with meeting-rooms, card-rooms, and a library, dedicated in 1937. The HELPER ART GALLERY (*open 1-9 P.M.; adm, free*), on the first floor, is staffed by the Utah Art Project and shows current exhibitions circulated by the WPA Art Program to eighty-odd centers of the United States. From the time of its opening in late December, 1939, to the end of May, 1940, the gallery, in a town of 2,800 people, entertained 5,100 visitors.

At 8.3 *m.* is the junction with an oiled road.

Right on this road to the mining camps of PEERLESS, 3.1 *m.*; SPRING CANYON, 4 *m.*; STANDARDVILLE, 5.2 *m.*; LATUDA, 6 *m.*; RAINS, 7 *m.*; and MUTUAL, 8 *m.*; all were settled and developed between 1912 and 1918. These camps reached the peak of their productivity during the World War, when each turned out approximately 2,000 tons daily. Increased use of natural gas and oil-burners had, by 1940, halved their output.

CASTLEGATE, 10.7 *m.* (6,147 alt., 840 pop.), named for the castellated formations guarding the entrance to the valley, has fought its way through floods, explosions, and outlaw raids to become one of the outstanding coal mining camps in Utah. The red-roofed frame houses seem to remember the turbulent days of the 1890's. They stand a little pathetically against the rising red cliffs, and keep watch down the winding street.

Castlegate mine-owners kept an alert eye open for the Robbers Roost gang, knowing the large pay roll would attract attention. It did, in 1897. Butch Cassidy (born George LeRoy Parker, of Mormon parents at Circleville, Utah), had the advantage of being unknown in Castlegate. He came into town dressed as an ordinary cowpuncher, hung around the railroad station, apparently getting his horse used to the roar of the engine, and applied to different ranchers for a job. Charles Kelly writes in *Outlaw Trails:*

> To the depot loafers he was just another crazy cowboy. On . . . April 21, 1897 . . . the Rio Grande train from Salt Lake City pulled in and Cassidy rode to meet the train as usual. Dismounting, he left the gray horse standing quietly, tied to the ground [reins dangling]. . . . The mail and express was loaded onto trucks and hauled into the baggage room. E. L. Carpenter, paymaster, then entered the express office accompanied by two men, Phelps and Lewis. When they came out each was carrying a heavy bag of money . . . Phelps . . . with $700 in gold, Carpenter . . . with $8,000 and Lewis . . . with $100 in silver. The company office was over a store, 75 yards from the station, entered by an outside stairway. At the foot of the stairs two men were loafing. Just as Phelps started to go up, Butch Cassidy stuck a gun in his ribs. . . . [Phelps] started to push past, but was knocked out with a blow on the head from Elza Lay's six-shooter. . . . Carpenter handed over his $8,000 without argument. Lewis . . . dropped his $100 in silver and dived into the open door of the store. Frank Caffey . . . was leaning against the counter . . . when Lewis dived in. . . . Caffey stepped to the door. . . . Lay whirled, drew a bead on his rather broad belt line and yelled: "Get back in there . . . or I'll fill your belly full of lead!" Caffey got. Two or three riders then fell in behind and all left town in a cloud of dust. . . . Word was telephoned to Castle Dale, Huntington and Cleveland, and posses were sent out.

This was Castlegate's only contact with the gang that terrorized the country from Canada to Mexico and from Nebraska to the Pacific Coast, between 1870 and 1904. In later years the gang turned their attention mainly to cattle rustling.

There was a touch of Robin Hood in Cassidy's blood. Anyone in hard luck could go to him for help. If he didn't have the necessary cash, he'd go out and get it. While operating in the West, he is never known to have killed a man. After the break-up of the gang in the early 1900's, Cassidy is supposed to have gone to South America and started a cattle ranch. The most authentic story seems to be that he was killed there. Many claim, however, that he has been seen since then in the United States, and even in Utah.

The worst flood in the history of the county hit Castlegate in 1917. Water poured through the narrow canyon, washing houses and bridges before it, twisting steel rails like pretzels. Debris covered the territory for miles, and for ten days no trains passed through the city. Strangely, only one life was lost.

Early in the morning of March 8, 1924, three terrific explosions shook the town. Accumulated gas and coal dust ignited at the No. 2 mine and took the lives of 173 men. The force of the explosions tossed water pipes like jackstraws, steel rods as large as a man's forearm were blown to bits, and the heavy timbers in the main haulageway were hurled to the opposite side of the canyon, a mile away. Debris, water, fire, and gas hindered the rescue work, and it was nearly ten days before all of the bodies were removed. Every canary bird in Carbon County was brought into service in the rescue work, since the birds die from slight traces of gas, long before man is aware of its presence. In a number of homes every male member of the family was lost. In seven instances, both father and son were killed. Wholesale funerals were held in all churches, and many of the victims are buried in the small cemetery atop the workings in which they met their death.

Right from Castlegate on graveled State 33, a commonly used short route, through Willow Creek Canyon and Indian Canyon across a 9,100-foot summit, to DUCHESNE, 44.4 *m.* (5,517 alt., 907 pop.), at the junction with US 40 (*see Tour 6a*).

ROYAL, 12.6 *m.* (6,344 alt., 315 pop.), rests at the foot of Castle Rock, at the confluence of the Bear and Price River canyons. The pink rock fortress rises on both sides of the highway, almost shutting out the light.

US 50 winds through PRICE RIVER CANYON, 13.5 *m.* (*Caution: Watch for rock slides, and heavily loaded trucks*), walled with buff sandstone. As the road climbs the dugway, Price River is a silver thread glittering on the canyon floor.

COLTON, 24.7 *m.* (7,188 alt., 55 pop.), a railroad junction, is set amid broad, tilted hills of oil shale, a vast potential source of petroleum.

At 25.1 *m.* is the junction with State 96.

Left on this gravel road to SCOFIELD RESERVOIR (R), 10.4 *m.* (*fishing*), which covers an area of 18 square miles. The dam, 60 feet high and 600 feet long, impounds 43,000 acre-feet of water. Farm produce raised in this district is sold at the coal camps.

SCOFIELD, 17.4 *m.* (7,702 alt., 234 pop.), is a coal mining town shut in by towering hills. Work in the mines has decreased since 1930, and Scofield is almost a ghost town. John Henry Evans writes in *The Story of Utah* that "At one of the mines belonging to this company [Pleasant Valley Coal Company] a gang of Chinese was employed [1880]. They used no powder, but only picks and shovels. And the work on the sides and over-head is described as 'The most beautiful one could wish to see.'"

The Daily Tribune of Salt Lake City reports Utah's worst mine disaster:

At Winterquarters mine near Scofield at 10:25 on the morning of May first 1900. From outside the mine a low thud was heard, and experienced miners knew that there had been an explosion. They didn't know . . . that of the 310 men working in the . . . mines . . . only 104 would escape alive. The others were entrapped in a lethal chamber which did an efficient job, leaving 199 dead, no injured. . . . It is reasonably certain that a dynamite explosion . . . ignited the coal dust in the air, and that like oiled lightning the explosion spread to every part of the mine. . . . The Pleasant Valley Coal Co. had orders for 2,000 tons of coal a day, so the mines were worked day and night. . . . In some places the miners worked in dust ankle deep. . . . The bodies as they were brought out were placed in company buildings, boarding houses, the Mormon Church, the school house, and all available buildings. . . . 105 widows . . . visited the places . . . and there were 270 children whose fathers were laid out. . . . Coffins came to Scofield by the car loads, and as the supply in Utah ran short, some were sent from Denver. At nearly every home caskets could be seen, either on the porch, or through the open door, sometimes one, sometimes several. . . . President McKinley expressed his condolence, and President Loubet of France sent a message of sympathy.

The OZOKERITE MINES (R), 31 *m.,* yield a mineral wax found only in Utah and Galicia, Austria. The Utah field extends from Colton westward for twelve miles, in a belt two miles wide. The ore is crushed, put into tanks of water, and boiled. The wax rises to the surface as it melts, and is skimmed off and cooled. *The Salt Lake Tribune* in 1912 described ozokerite as "a wax with a melting point from 160 to 190 degrees Fahrenheit, as against 130 degrees for paraffin wax . . . odorless and tasteless; occurs dark bottle green to dark brown and turning nearly black on exposure to air; plastic without being soft; acid and alkali proof; can be bleached to pure white and then made any color. . . . It is used in place of beeswax, for high priced altar candles, wax figures and dolls, waterproofing indurated paper, keg and barrel linings, lining of tanks used in the manufacture of the most powerful acids, sealing wax, matches, shoe blacking, floor polish, waterproofing cartridges and textile fabrics, sole leather dressing, lumber pencils, and insulation. As an insulator it is the most perfect known, Edison giving it a resistance of 450,000,000 megohms, as against 110,-000,000 for paraffin. It is also used in making phonographic records, and one of its largest uses is in the manufacture of linen fabrics." The mines were not active between 1920 and 1940, but because of world conditions they are resuming operations.

SOLDIER SUMMIT, 31.7 *m.* (7,440 alt., 319 pop.), a railroad shipping point and the highest point on US 50 in Utah, received its name from the fact that several soldiers are buried here; who the soldiers were, however, is a matter of spirited local disagreement. Soldier Summit is on the dividing line between the Great Basin and the Colorado River drainage system. Rain falling on the west side flows into Great Salt Lake; rain falling on the east side flows down the Price, Green, and Colorado rivers to the Pacific Ocean.

Between Soldier Summit and Thistle, US 50 runs through UPPER SPANISH FORK CANYON.

TUCKER, 38.4 *m.,* is a railroad siding serving the coal camps.

Left from Tucker on Skyline Drive, a dirt road (*closed in winter*) along the crest of the Wasatch Mountains at an elevation of 9,000 to 11,000 feet. Below the highway, range after range of purple-blue peaks lie in shadowy layers. To the east and south, gem-like lakes dot the landscape, and Fish Lake gleams near the end of the road.

At 56.5 *m.* is the east junction, in Thistle, with US 89 (*see Tour 2b*) which unites with US 50 for 65.7 miles.

The GOLD MEDAL EXPLOSIVE PLANT, 65 *m.,* a division of the Illinois Powder Manufacturing Company, supplies acids and explosives to smelters and mines.

US 50 traverses the checkered fields of Utah Valley, where orchards meet the foothills. In the distance, Utah Lake sparkles in the sunlight.

At 69.4 *m.* is the south junction, in Spanish Fork (*see Tour 1d*), with US 91 (*see Tour 1e*) with which US 50 unites for 52.4 miles.

At 121.5 *m.* is the north junction with US 91 (*see Tour 1d*) in Salt Lake City.

Section c.   *JUNCTION WITH US 91 to NEVADA STATE LINE; 126.1 m., US 50*

US 50, west of its junction, 0 *m.,* with US 91, is almost a straight line through fields of alfalfa, corn, garden truck, and sugar beets. Near the Oquirrh Mountains, the highway runs through an important smelting district where blue-gray smoke hangs heavily upon the air. Great Salt Lake, with its barren islands, shimmers steel-blue in the distance.

KDYL RADIO STATION (L), 1.6 *m.,* is an intermountain outlet for the National Broadcasting Company, with studios in Salt Lake City.

At 10.7 *m.* is the junction with State 159.

Left on this gravel road to BACCHUS, 2.1 *m.* (4,910 alt., 225 pop.), a town concentric in form, with homes separated by wide lawns and trees. It was created in 1913 by the Hercules Powder Company and its plant, with an annual capacity of 18,000,000 pounds of powder, employs approximately 90 men.

At 11.2 *m.* is the junction with State 48 (*see Tour 1c*).

MAGNA, 12.7 *m.* (4,278 alt., 1,604 pop.), is on the dividing line between cultured fields and structures of the mining industry. The town began its career in 1906 when ore concentrating plants were built. Mill laborers first lived at the foot of the mountain in tents and shanties, but when the company erected 300 cottages, "Ragtown" disappeared.

Sprawled on the slopes of the mountains which shadow the town, is the MAGNA CONCENTRATION MILL (L) erected in 1906. Gold, silver, lead, copper and other minerals are treated here preliminary to smelting.

The immense ARTHUR CONCENTRATION MILL (L), 14.8 *m.*, is also used to prepare ore for smelting. A barren, yellow-gray flat has been formed by the tailings (waste) of the mill.

DEAD MAN'S CAVE (L), 16 *m.*, a large opening in the face of a rock jutting against the highway, received its name when, at some forgotten date, the body of a suicide was found hanging inside. The cave was once the home of prehistoric Pueblo peoples. The bubbling spring behind the cave is bitter with minerals, but the water can be used. Artifacts discovered by Elmer Smith, archeologist of the University of Utah, in 1939, indicate that the cavern was inhabited around 1100 A.D. Arrow points, handstones, bone awls, and pottery remains from this site are displayed at the university archeological museum. "Dead Man points"—chipped flint arrowheads with ears—differing from anything ever discovered in the West, have been found here.

GARFIELD, 16.4 *m.* (4,240 alt., 2,047 pop.), is a company-built town of smoke-shrouded buildings lying at the base of a denuded peak.

The GARFIELD SMELTER (L), 16.8 *m.*, a huge steel and sheet-iron building, is one of the largest smelting plants in Utah. Here blister copper is produced from concentrates of the Magna and Arthur mills, and is sent to refineries at Baltimore, Maryland, and Tacoma, Washington. The black column of smoke arising from the tall smokestacks can be seen for miles.

The ore is sampled, a small quantity being treated by essentially the same process as in large-scale smelting. The samples are then assayed, and the metallic content is used as a basis for settlement between shipper and smelter.

The main body of ore is thoroughly crushed and moved into charge bins holding 2,000 to 5,000 tons. Different ores are mixed together to condition them for smelting, placed in roaster ovens, and subjected to temperatures ranging from 500 to 1,200 degrees. Roasters are vertical steel cylinders about twenty feet in diameter and thirty feet high. A revolving axis stirs the seething ore and drives out the sulphur-dioxide. After roasting, the ore is placed in a reverberatory furnace, built of silica and magnesite brick, about 130 feet long and 25 feet deep. In heating, the metals—called matte—sink, and the waste, or slag, rises to the top and is drained off. The matte is next placed in converters—cylindrical steel devices about thirty feet long and thirteen feet wide, mounted on rollers—which force off iron and sulphur, and the remaining metal is blister copper. This metal is reheated in a casting furnace and poured into water-cooled molds, producing slabs of 98 per cent pure copper, weighing about 400 pounds. The slabs are shipped to refineries where gold, silver, and impurities are removed.

At 18 *m.* the highway dives through an underpass, beneath the track over which molten slag is carried from smelter to dump. On both sides of the road is a huge black mound of this waste. At night, the glow of the molten rock can be seen for miles as it runs down the side of the dump.

At LAKE POINT JUNCTION, 20 *m.* (4,278 alt.) US 50 joins US 40 (*see Tour 6c*), and runs concurrently with it to the NEVADA STATE LINE, 126.1 *m.* (*see Nevada Guide*).

Tour 8

Santaquin—Eureka—Delta—(Ely, Nevada); US 6.
Santaquin to Nevada Line, 168.5 *m.*

Route paralleled by Union Pacific R.R. between Elberta and Delta.
Asphalt road between Santaquin and Eureka; oiled road between Eureka and Lynndyl; elsewhere improved gravel and dirt road.
All types of accommodations in larger towns (*Caution: Carry extra supplies between Hinckley and Nevada line*).

US 6 swings west from US 91 through a semi-mountainous area and semi-arid lands and strikes out across desert wastes to the Nevada Line. Several ranges of rolling, juniper-covered hills flank the road; there are scattered farms in the valleys, irrigated lands around Lynndyl and Delta being quite productive. A few dull-looking but productive mining towns break the monotony of the yellow-gray landscape. The stretch westward from Hinckley appears barren, but among its rolling hills and shifting sand dunes grow 1,050 different flowering plants and 90 species of grasses. The rolling plains supported herds of antelope, and deer browsed on the timbered hills before the white man came with his long-range rifles and brought the seeds of tumbleweed, white top, and wild mustard. Jack rabbits, cottontails, and other small life of the desert are still plentiful, and the spine-chilling wail of the coyote can be heard every night.

US 6 branches west from the southern junction of US 91 at SANTAQUIN, 0 *m.* (4,887 alt., 1,115 pop.) (*see Tour 1e*), and winds through irrigated farmlands.

GOSHEN, 6.7 *m.* (4,530 alt., 669 pop.), is a tree-shaded livestock and farming community, settled in 1856, with a typical small-town business district, a residential section where old houses rub elbows with new, and outlying farms that crowd the city limits. Pioneers in the valley moved from place to place to find suitable homesites. According to Solomon Hale, Brigham Young, who made a special trip from Great Salt Lake City to select this site, chided the people for their constant moving: "Your chickens have been moved so many times that every time they see a wagon they just turn over and stick their feet in the air to be tied for another moving." Utah Lake extended to Goshen in pioneer days, but is has receded four miles since 1910 because so much of it is pumped out for irrigation (*see Provo*).

ELBERTA, 9.9 *m.* (4,657 alt., 21 pop.), is an agricultural settlement named for the Elberta peach, which thrives here.

Right from Elberta on a dirt road to the ghost town of MOSIDA, 11.5 *m.* (4,500 alt.), one of the few agricultural ghost towns in the State. Mosida was established in 1910, and electric pumps were installed to take water from Utah Lake to irrigate an 8,000-acre tract. A $15,000 hotel and a $3,000 schoolhouse were built, and 50,000 bushels of wheat were harvested and 50,000 fruit trees were planted in 1912. The community seemed to thrive, but by 1915 the company was hopelessly in debt. Landowners clamored for larger canals, more water, and better pumping equipment. The company went into receivership in 1918. Nothing remains of the briefly prosperous community.

Between Elberta and Eureka, US 6 traverses rock-strewn and sagebrush-covered flats and hills, where tumbleweeds dance across the road at the whim of the wind.

At 15.3 *m.* is the junction with a dirt road.

Left on this road to DIVIDEND, 0.8 *m.* (5,952 alt., 204 pop.), a model mining town, built by the Tintic Standard Mining Company. It has modern stores, an ice plant, community recreational facilities.

US 6 passes through a winding canyon on the east slopes of the East Tintic Range. There are no permanent streams in these mountains, but mine and spring water provides for the mining camps. Scattered over the hillsides are old shafts, trenches, abandoned dumps, weatherbeaten camps, and prospecting holes.

In EUREKA, 20.7 *m.* (6,396 alt., 2,290 pop.), wooden houses painted long ago, and squat brick buildings hug the narrow streets. In some sections of the town brick bungalows stand beside tumbledown, weather-beaten buildings. The dump of the Gemini mine— symbol of twofold prosperity in the past—almost pushes into the lobby of the leading hotel, and newer stores stand scornfully beside false-front structures of another day. There is an occasional tree, vividly green. Constant blasting, deep underground, shakes the "jerry-built" houses. Beneath the streets, in tunnels and drifts that honeycomb the earth, miners stolidly tear the ground to pieces, taking out millions of dollars worth of gold, silver, copper and lead. Huge trucks roar through the streets, some carrying armed guards to protect the fabulously rich ore. Eureka, surrounded by ghosts of former mining camps, is the focal point in the Tintic district.

The Tintic Valley was a favorite Indian campground long before the Mormons came. The grass grew high then, the springs and streams ran full, and game was plentiful. A minor Ute chieftain, Tintic, claiming all the land in Tintic Valley, bitterly resented invasion by white men and carried on guerilla warfare. His band was repeatedly pursued by the Territorial militia, but always managed to escape. Peteetneet, friendly with the whites, said "Tintic has ears that are no good and no use to him, as he had good council given him, but he would not hear it." Dimmick B. Huntington reported to the Mormon Church historian in 1856 that he "had an interview with Arrapeen. . . . He does not countenance Tintic in the course he has taken and says that he need not go to any of the Nation for favors, for they all have thrown him away, and he need not go to the Snakes, for they will kill him." Tintic went to the Uintas, but they refused to aid him. He then made his way to Manti, where he died in 1859. The *Deseret News,* reporting his death, said, "Tintic, the notorious Ute Chief, died on the morning of the 15th. . . . The citizens of this territory who have been acquainted with his history will not much deplore his death." Tintic could have been a Croesus of his time: Beneath his old camp-site were found some of the richest mineral veins in Utah.

The riders of the "Jack-ass Mail," as Major George Chorpenning's mail-carrying enterprise of 1851 was known, did not hesitate long enough in the valley to spot the outcrops. Stage drivers, dashing between Salt Lake City and the Pacific Coast, were intent upon getting through without Indian attacks. The Pony Express rider was also plenty busy, as I. E. Diehl shows in his manuscript account of "Broncho Charlie" Miller, the last surviving Pony Express rider (1939): "In 1860 the wildest 'blood n' thunder' stretch of the Pony Express was east of Carson City, Nev. Several riders had been killed by the Indians and Charlie, who lived at Carson with his parents, was pressed into service. He was an experienced rider and a dead shot although only 11 years old. . . . After traveling a few miles over the desert trails war whoops resounded and Indians appeared ahead and in the rear. Drawing his two guns the lad started to shoot at the advancing redmen with one hand and with the other shot over his shoulders at the pursuers . . . he succeeded in escaping." Stockmen, entering the valley in the early 1850's, saw only the lush grass and the bubbling springs. Before long, charcoal manufacturing was begun, forests were slaughtered, the watershed was ruined, the high grass disappeared, and sagebrush crept in from the desert. Soon only sheep could survive on the range.

With the discovery of a "funny looking" piece of rock by George Rust, cowboy, in 1869, the valley arrived at its destiny. For several years, however, the shouts of rich strikes at Park City, Alta, and in the Cottonwood Canyons drowned out the news of more quiet prospecting in the Tintic Mountains. Five men fought their way through a blizzard to locate the "Sun Beam" in December, 1870, the first registered claim in the valley. In January, 1871, another group of men located the "Black Dragon," and in the same month the "Corresser

Lode," now known as the "Carisa," was discovered. By April Sunbeam ore was worth $500 a ton, Montana and Eureka ore $1,500 a ton, Mammoth ore $1,000 a ton, and the remaining thirteen mines ran down the scale to the Bull's Eye, which mined ore worth $86 a ton. An old mine, discovered the same year, ten miles south of Eureka, brought in ore valued at $6,000 a ton. Another old mine was discovered in the 1920's, and when boulders were rolled away from the entrance, two human skeletons were revealed. "No mineralized vein was discovered," writes Diehl in his Tintic manuscript. "The methods employed by those primitive miners is a marvel. They had no powder, nor even matches or tools except what they made for themselves, and yet they penetrated the solid rock for many feet. Some of the old Spanish workings show that fires had been built to heat the rocks which were then cracked by throwing water on them." Some old-timers believe these mines were operated by Indians.

By 1872 it was not uncommon for mines to ship ten-ton lots of ore assaying from $5,000 to $10,000. Specimens assaying 15,000 ounces of silver to the ton were sent to the Vienna Exposition in 1873. One fifty-ton lot from the Centennial Eureka netted the company $200,000, and the Grand Central, which was reopened in 1937, got $198,000 for a fifty-ton lot. In 1914, ore valued at $10,000 a carload was still being shipped from the district, and the year before the Colorado mine was shipping from a two-foot vein assaying 2,000 ounces of silver to the ton. Mining camps sprang up all over the mountains in the early 1870's, and Silver City, the first real camp, is described in Diehl's manuscript as having "a billiard saloon, blacksmith shop, grog hole, some tents, several drunks, a free fight, water some miles off, a hole down 90 feet hunting a spring without success, and any number of rich or imaginary rich lodes in the neighborhood. The owners are all poor, and the poor men work for them. By next spring the poor will be poorer."

Following the settlement of Silver City (1870), came Diamond (1870), Mammoth (1870) Ironton (1871), Homansville (1872), and Knightsville (1897). Silver City's population fell from 800 to almost zero when the mines reached water-level and the cost of pumping proved prohibitive. A new boom was started in 1908, when a smelter was built in Knightsville, but the plant ran only a few years. In 1940 the town had only a handful of people to keep its memory alive. The last house in Diamond, named for crystals found near by, was moved away in 1923, and all that remains of this once bustling camp of 900 persons is the cemetery, a few old mine dumps, and yawning holes that were once cellars. Homansville, once an important well-site with a population of 300, is now a pumping station for the Chief Consolidated mine, with a lime quarry and lime hydrating plant, and a couple of watchmen. Ironton once aspired to be a railroad terminus for the mines, and during the 1870's more than forty wagons hauled iron ore to its station. Interest has revived in the iron mines, but no effort has been made to rebuild the town. Jesse Knight, whose Godiva,

Uncle Sam, May Day, Humbug, and Yankee mines were coining money, purchased a tract of land two miles south of Eureka in 1897, and laid out Knightsville. When rich silver-lead ore was struck in the Beck tunnel in 1907, Knightsville experienced a boom that boosted the population from 300 to more than 1,000. In 1940, only the concrete foundation of the school building remained, but Knightsville was still remembered as the only camp without a saloon.

Tintic Mills, once known as Shoebridge, has completely disappeared. The story of Tintic is the story of the Shoebridge mine. In 1870, William McIntosh, after nearly starving his family and himself, located a rich vein of ore on the surface near Diamond. He established claims and called his mine the Shoebridge. A mill was built the following year, and twenty-five log cabins were erected. The Crismon-Mammoth mill was erected in 1877, and Samuel McIntyre, czar of the Mammoth mine, built a palatial brick residence. By 1884, twenty-two furnaces were in operation at the smelter. The plants closed down, and Samuel McIntyre abandoned his fine home to move to Salt Lake City. It was used for years by cowboys and ranchers, but was torn down in 1933.

During the 1870's, such mines as the Joe Bowers, Showers, Tesora, Butcher Boy, Ajax, Tintic, Crismon-Mammoth, and Bullion-Beck were in operation. Scarcity of water hindered development to some extent, but wells were sunk at Homansville and water was pumped to various mines. Water hauled into Eureka for domestic use sold for ten cents a gallon. A wooden pipe line was constructed from Jenny Lind Spring in the 1880's, and householders carried water in pails. This was the only water supply until 1893, when the Cherry Creek line was installed.

Ore picked up on top of the ground in 1870 by Paul Schettler, George Beck and Gotlieb Beck, resulted in sale of their original claims for $1,000 to Joab Lawrence, who organized the Eureka Mining Company. Horn silver, valued at $1 a pound, was taken from gopher holes, and $50,000 worth of silver was found in large boulders, which were rolled down the canyonside and loaded into wagons. Lawrence and John L. Whitney sold their interest to Captain E. B. Ward in 1872 for $350,000; they went to New York City, and Ward had them arrested on a charge of stock swindling when the vein petered out. Finally convinced that the transaction was not fraudulent, Ward returned to dig deeper and reap a rich reward. Several times claim-jumpers tried to appropriate the property, and on one occasion an armed gang was repulsed by Ward's men in a rock fort. John Q. Packard purchased an interest in the mine for $300,000. There are no figures showing the actual earnings of this mine, which is now part of the Chief Consolidated chain, but estimates run as high as $50,000,-000 worth of ore, and more than $3,500,000 in dividends have been paid. The mine in 1940 was being worked by lessees.

At this period of its history, Eureka knew such men as John Beck, who literally rolled down hill onto his Bullion-Beck mine; Samuel and William McIntyre, who built a tight little empire around the Mammoth mine, and anyone caught trespassing was shot first and questioned afterwards; Jack McChrystal, who sent his new "under-slung" car hurtling off the Gemini dump, because it got hung up once too often on high-centered roads; John Q. Packard, who would walk the twenty-one miles from Santaquin to Eureka to save carfare, but who donated a $20,000 lot and a $100,000 building to Salt Lake City for a library and died leaving a $20,000,000 estate; and E. J. Raddatz, who nearly starved to death before he could interest capital in his Tintic Standard mine, one of the biggest present-day Utah producers. Scattered over the hill were lesser characters, all filled with their hopes, and nearly all doomed to disappointment. Matteo Messa was one. Born in Sonora, Mexico, he came to Utah with Johnston's army, and stayed to make a fortune at Ophir. He gave most of his money away and died broke in a little cabin in Eureka where hundreds of Bull Durham sacks hung from the rafters. He claimed they kept the evil spirits away, and the flies. "Buffalo Dave," last name unknown, had his hopes, but he drowned them in liquor, and finally sold his body to a medical society to raise money for whisky; he died in the insane asylum at Provo. Mrs. Anna Marks, an illiterate Russian-Jewess, came to Eureka in the 1880's. The first thing Mrs. Marks did was have her landlord, a Chinese, arrested for assault. The Chinaman left, and Mrs. Marks confiscated the building. She gradually acquired more real estate, and any trespass upon her land was a declaration of war. John Cronin started to build a fence to separate his property from that of Mrs. Marks. When he ignored her order to cease digging post holes, she grabbed the shovel and filled them in as fast as he dug them, finally jumping into one of the holes. Cronin then proceeded calmly to bury her. As she scrambled out of the dirt, Cronin threw her down and sat on her. The indignant woman took the matter to court, but lost. When Harvey Tompkins started to build a fence between her property and the Tompkins Hotel, she grabbed her gun and started shooting. A bullet pierced a plug of tobacco in the workman's pocket, saving his life, another shot struck Tompkins' daughter, and the fight ended with Tompkins the winner. The Rio Grande Railroad found her too much for them when they attempted to build a spur across her property; they finally settled for $500. The town drew a sigh of relief when Mrs. Marks died in 1912, leaving an estate valued at $70,000.

Wealth pouring out of the hills started an epidemic of "high-grading," which forced some of the mines to shut down. Miners sneaked rich ore out of the mines in their lunch buckets, up their noses, in special pockets in their overalls, and once a whole carload of exceedingly rich ore disappeared from the railroad station. Tracers were sent out, and the car—empty—was finally found in Mexico. The mystery was never solved. The Mammoth roughly estimated that it had lost $150,-000 to "high-graders."

Mine "salting" was another little game played in the district. Sometimes the "salted" mine turned out to be a rich producer: The men who purchased the Wyoming mine from a Mr. Pease, were so pleased with the rich ore in the shaft that they gave him $20,000 in cash, the remaining $2,000 to be paid within a week. Pease accepted the $20,000 and disappeared. The strangers built a mill, but found that Pease had dumped two carloads of rich ore from the Eureka Hill down the shaft. They were forced to use custom ores at the mill, but later uncovered a rich vein that brought them $1,000,000. Salting of mines sometimes worked the opposite way: A superintendent would open a rich vein, "salt" the vein with low grade ore, and report to the company that it was not worth developing. Later he would lease the mine and make his fortune.

The Utah Southern Railroad reached the Tintic district in the 1870's, and by 1878 had extended its rails to Ironton. Between then and 1890, several railroads were built into the district, most of which were later absorbed by mergers. The Union Pacific has maintained bus service to the camps since 1932. The branch line of the Rio Grande Western, now the Denver & Rio Grande Western, built from Springville to Silver City in 1891, is an outstanding feat of railroad engineering. The road winds around the mountains, first on one side of the canyon, then on the other. Tunnels were driven through the mountains, and long, high trestles across the canyons. In one place a loop bridge was built to gain altitude: The tracks run along the canyon floor, wind around the mountain, and return to the same spot, on a high bridge over the lower track. Large "S" turns were utilized to gain altitude in Homansville Canyon.

The *Eureka Reporter,* established in 1885, tells of two races held in Eureka in the 1890's, both with unexpected results. A bewhiskered tramp came into town driving a measly-looking pinto pony in a rattle-trap buggy, and declared his horse could beat any nag in town. The miners raised a $100 pot. Jake Sullivan was chosen to ride a locally unbeatable horse. Sullivan rode his best, but the tramp beat him by rods, riding all the way backward. The tramp then challenged anyone to race him on foot. Dan Fields, local sprinter, took the challenge. The tramp won easily, running the last ten yards backward, thumbing his nose at the puffing local boy. A few weeks later it was discovered that the "tramp" was Harry Bethune, fastest sprinter of his time.

Little Billie King, a roving printer who loved his liquor, wandered into town in 1899. He soon became known as the "Belfast Spider" because of his tales of championship prize fights he had won. For years he lived in a plank cottage at the head of Church Street, and built fires only when he cooked. In summer, it was Billie's custom to hie himself to a nice sunny hillside and sleep off his latest jag, thus combining a steam bath and a good long rest. Awakening one day from his nap, still groggy, he spotted a man running around the hill with a fish net, apparently trying to pull a fish out of the air. Billie walked over to him, placed his hand on his shoulder, and said, "You'd better come to town with me, friend." The stranger explained that he was searching for bugs. Billie smiled indulgently and said, "Sure, I know. I've had 'em myself, but you better come to town with me."

The stranger, convinced by this time that Billie was crazy, decided he had better humor him, and allowed himself to be led to town. Later Billie discovered that his "crazy man" was Tom Spalding, the man who put Utah on the entomological map. Spalding, a natural-born collector, sold one collection for $1,400, and another is included in the $3,000,000 Barnes collection at Decatur, Illinois. Spalding first came to the notice of entomologists in 1910, when he captured a little blue butterfly, the first of its kind ever found; it was named *Philotes spaldingi*. Twelve other unusual specimens were named for Spalding. He died in Salt Lake City in 1929.

The early 1900's ushered in a mild epidemic of killings. In 1902 William Dryburn and Barney Dunne were getting quietly drunk in their tent, and they disputed as to who was the best shot. Dryburn dared Dunne to shoot his hat off. Dunne raised his rifle and shot. Both men lost—Dryburn, his head, and Dunne, his wager, because he missed the hat and hit Dryburn square in the forehead. In 1904 E. H. Weeds of Fish Springs drove into Eureka looking for the sheriff. He had the blanket-wrapped body of his partner, A. F. White, on the floor of his buckboard. He explained that White insisted upon singing while he was trying to read. He served ten months in the county jail, reading his books in peace and quiet.

By 1910 most of the mines in the Tintic district were under the ownership of the Chief Consolidated Mining Company and the Tintic Standard, which controlled various mines, and in 1937 became one of the mines in Eureka Lily Consolidated. All options called for payment in gold coin, and when a company made a purchase they would have the gold shipped from Salt Lake City. In 1910, the Chief secured an option on some claims belonging to Dick Tyner for $25,000 in gold. Tyner refused to bank the money, having lost one fortune in a bank crash in the 1890's. He put his gold in sacks, had a drayman haul it to his cabin, and forced the Eureka police to guard him and his wealth. He was finally prevailed upon to place the money in a New York State bank, and went there to spend the rest of his days.

For three years, 1919-21, Eureka was haunted by the "Woman in Black." Night after night, in different parts of town, she would step from the shadows in the path of some woman, and stare. She never spoke, never touched anyone. One man claimed she stopped him, and he knocked her down, but she sprang up and ran away. Another man said she pointed a gun at him and asked if he was "So and So." When he replied that he was not, she turned and walked away. Where she came from, who she was, or where she finally disappeared to, has never been found out.

By the 1920's, the mines of the Tintic district were all tapping deeper ores by means of perpendicular shafts, 2,000 feet deep or more. The levels (floors) are usually one hundred feet apart, and from these stations, long drifts (halls) run from the shafts. Through the drifts ore and waste are transported to the shaft for hoisting to the surface. Between the main drifts are intermediate or sub-levels, which are connected with the main drifts by raises or winzes. Trammers, on the sub-levels, load from a chute transferring the material to the main level. The trammer handles one car at a time. On the main level, mine cars are handled in trains of from three to twelve cars. Some mines use mules to haul the cars, others use electric locomotives. The average capacity of a mine car is one ton. Main drifts often are a mile or more in length, and considerable man-power is required to handle 100 or more cars in an eight-hour shift. Most main drifts slope downward to the shaft, and the upward pull is with empty cars.

Mine mules, before being lowered through the small opening in the shaft, are fed short rations for several days before entering the mine. When the time arrives for the lowering operation, the cage is hoisted clear of the collar of the shaft, and a bulkhead is placed over the opening. The mule is led to the shaft and placed in an especially constructed harness, with his legs tied close to his body so they will not become entangled in the shaft timbers. The harness is then fastened to the bottom of the cage, and the mule is lowered to the level where he is to be worked. The mule is released on a bulkhead over the shaft, and is taken to a barn within the mine. He is fed extra rations for several days, and becomes accustomed to the darkness. Put to work on a regular shift, the mule remains underground until he is no longer of service.

Figures in the *United States Bureau of Mines Yearbook* show that between 1869 and 1938 the Tintic District produced 2,394,527 ounces of gold, 244,532,264 ounces of silver, 229,422,014 pounds of copper, 1,748,854,741 pounds of lead, and 36,999,120 pounds of zinc all valued at $363,133,791.

The day of the small operator has passed, and the mines are under the control of large companies who can afford to sink deeper shafts, install pumping equipment, construct long tunnels, run underground railroads, and provide the other necessities of modern mining. Pines and the firs grow no longer on the hills, springs have ceased to tumble down the mountainside, and even the indomitable sagebrush is stunted and scant. Irish and Cornish work side by side, and a few miners straggle in and out of the beer parlors, or gather in groups along the one main street. Occasionally someone works up enough energy to start a fight. Churches, schools, and movies have replaced gambling dens and dance halls. Eureka has at last bowed its head to the times.

The late Amelia Earhart, noted aviatrix, made a forced landing in a plowed field near Eureka in 1928, which hastened construction of an emergency field six miles northwest of town.

A pack of wild dogs roams the North Tintic hills. They are relentlessly hunted, with a bounty on their scalps, but few have been killed. Occasionally they can be heard as they run down and kill a deer, colt, or calf; their baying brings chills of fear to anyone on foot after dark. In 1934 a stray female dog of uncertain ancestry made her den in a mine tunnel northwest of Eureka, where she gave birth to a litter of mongrel pups. The dogs subsequently crossbred with coyotes and other mongrel dogs, and attaining formidable numbers they reverted to the pack-hunting instincts of the wolf, combined with the sagacity of the dog. Heber Fields, of Eureka, found and killed a female with four whelps; for seven months he made every effort to domesticate one of the pups. The animal was so vicious it had to be killed.

At 22.2 *m.* is the junction (R) with State 36 which runs between US 6 and US 40 (*see Tour 6A*).

At 23.7 *m.* is the junction with an asphalt road.

Left on this road to MAMMOTH, 0.6 (6,026 alt., 492 pop.), its main street consisting of a few bleached, false-fronted buildings. Residents live in decrepit plank shacks, some of them painted a dirty yellow, and dry barren hills close in upon the town. The Mammoth Mine, where most of the male population works, is one of the richest in the district (*see above*).

At 24.7 *m.* is the junction with an asphalt road.

Left on this road to SILVER CITY, 0.5 *m.* (6,100 alt., 111 pop.), a trading center for numerous small silver, gold, and lead mines in the district. The Swansea mine was developed by William Hatfield, the first man in this region to extract ore below the water level; it produced nearly $700,000. Silver City was the boyhood home of George Sutherland, one-time Associate Justice of the United States Supreme Court.

JERICHO (R), 39.4 *m.* (5,311 alt.), has large sheep corrals in which thousands of sheep are sheared each spring. Although this is one of the leading wool shipping points in the West (*see Agriculture*), Jericho has no population except in shipping season.

At shearing time the corrals are jammed, engines puff back and forth shunting cars on the sidings, gas engines snort as they generate power for buzzing machines. The sheep are wrangled through a series of corrals to the shearing platforms. Men with electric shearing machines strip the sheep of wool almost to the skin. Fleeces fall at the rate of one every three to four minutes. The clip is tied twice around, clean side out, with a paper string, and thrown into a huge long wool sack. When the sack is filled it is sewed and rolled aside for shipment. The unsung hero of the shearing corrals is the "wool tromper." The wool sacks, about eight feet long, are suspended from a rack and a few fleeces thrown into the bottom. The "tromper" jumps into the sack, tramping the fleeces tightly. Fleeces are thrown in on him, sometimes with a choking smother of dirt, dust, and effluvium. As the "tromper" works his way to the top, and raises his head and shoulders into comparatively pure air, he is, often as not, struck in the face with another dirty fleece.

After shearing, the sheep are turned into a receiving pen where they are dipped to eliminate ticks and stamped with the brand of their outfit. They are then turned into a large corral, where ewes and lambs scramble to find each other. Ewes call and lambs answer, each with its distinctive and recognizable voice timbre.

Right from Jericho on a dirt road to the SITE OF THE WEST TINTIC AGRICULTURAL COOPERATIVE COLONY, 7.5 m., established in 1920 by a group of Mormons. The colony consisted of ten families, who pooled their resources and worked under a co-operative plan. Buildings were erected, land cleared, machinery purchased, and a food store established. Their attempts at farming were unsuccessful. When the colony was about a year old the leader had some "revelations," one of them urging the practice of "wife sacrifice," which appeared to be nothing newer than an exchange of wives. Mormon authorities investigated and excommunicated most of the members.

The leader of the cult was Moses S. Gudmundson, a former professor of music at Brigham Young University, about 35 years old at the time of the Church trial at Eureka. Evidence showed that the exchange was "confined solely to married couples," and was intended to "overcome selfishness." The leader had some difficulty in explaining why he had neglected his own wife to lavish attentions upon his neighbor's. Two members, tried in district court, were sentenced to three years in the penitentiary, but the leader was acquitted.

At 39.9 m. is the junction with State 132, which runs between US 6 and Nephi (see Tour 1e).

US 6 penetrates the Great Pahvant Valley, an area of 5,000 square miles, several hundred of which are under irrigation.

At 49.9 m. are shifting sand dunes (R). This is the northern edge of the Sevier Desert, and hundreds of sandhills and hummocks can be seen from the highway. About the turn of the century a miner from Mammoth (see above), exploring these shifting sands, found a low ledge of mineral-bearing rock. His samples assayed high-grade lead ore, but work in Mammoth kept him away for several weeks. Returning to place location notices, he could find no trace of the ledge; moving sand had covered it, and changed the terrain entirely. The outcropping has never been found.

LYNNDYL, 57.1 m. (4,785 alt., 372 pop.), a division point on the Union Pacific Railroad, is a trading center for Pahvant Valley farmers. The yellow frame railroad station is a landmark, and the main street is fronted by unpainted frame buildings.

At 68.5 m. US 6 crosses the Sevier River, a source of irrigation water.

At 73.6 m. is the junction with State 135.

Left on this gravel road to OAK CITY, 13.5 m. (4,700 alt., 340 pop.), with frame and adobe dwellings, and brick business buildings. The quiet main street is lined with trees and flower gardens, and water flows along each side of the road.

At 74.3 m. is the junction with State 26, a much-traveled road between US 6 and US 91.

DELTA, 74.5 m. (4,649 alt., 1,183 pop.), a farming town and shipping center for small mines, has clean wide streets, modern homes, and a prosperous business section. The Great Pahvant Valley was condemned as wasteland in 1900, but five years later a group of Fillmore men purchased a half interest in the Sevier River Reservoir, and 10,000 acres of land, to found a settlement on the Sevier River delta. Reasonably priced farms were parceled out, with one share of water for each acre. Town lots sold at $15 each. Plentiful water contributed to cultivation of many crops, especially alfalfa. Cleaning, grading, and marketing of alfalfa seed developed into an enormous business, and in 1940 nearly one-fourth of the alfalfa seed in the United States was produced in the Delta district. The contiguous valley provides farm families of the area an average annual income of $2,500.

HINCKLEY, 80.9 *m.* (4,600 alt., 678 pop.), is a residence for farmers and livestock men. The town has a small commercial center, and its frame or brick dwellings peep from behind tall poplar trees.

At 81 *m.* is the junction with State 140.

Left on State 140 to DESERET, 3.7 *m.* (4,512 alt., 411 pop.), a quiet, well-ordered farm hamlet where life centers around a white frame grocery store.

Right from Deseret on a dirt road to DESERET FORT, 1.6 *m.,* erected by order of Brigham Young in 1866 as a protection against Indians during the Ute Black Hawk War. Competing teams built one end and a bastion. Mud and straw was trampled by oxen to make the walls, which are still partially standing.

At 85.4 *m.* is the junction with a poor dirt road.

Left on this rough, unimproved road to the junction, 1.2 *m.,* with a dirt road; the main side route continues L. At 2.7 *m.* is the junction with a dirt road; L. on this road to GUNNISON MONUMENT, 0.3 *m.,* a cobblestone marker commemorating the spot where Captain John W. Gunnison and seven of his men were killed by Pahvants in 1853 (*see History*).

US 6 traverses a flat country covered with stunted sage and interspersed with patches of dark volcanic rock.

At 110.7 *m.* is the junction with a dirt road.

Right, through juniper dotted hills, to the junction, 5.1 *m.,* with an improved dirt road; R. on this road to the SWAZEY PEAK (9,678 alt.) area. A surveying party found well-preserved fossil trilobites around the peak in 1870. Remains of the extinct beetlelike marine creatures of the middle Cambrian period, more than 430 million years old, were thickly strewn in tiny reefs of rocks. Perfect specimens ranged in size from one-sixteenth of an inch to two inches long. Scientists tried for more than fifty years to relocate the deposit, which was rediscovered by Frank Beckwith, Sr., of Delta, in 1927. Another deposit was subsequently found at Blue Knoll near Antelope Springs (*see below*). More than 3,300 specimens, of different species, some of them extremely rare, were sent to the Smithsonian Institution.

ANTELOPE SPRINGS issues from the hillside above a CCC camp, at 23 *m.,* on the main side road. Near here Arm Nay, early-day bad man, occupied a cave known as Robber's Roost. Part of the old corral, in which stolen livestock was kept, is still standing.

MARJUM PASS, 123 *m.* (6,250 alt.), is an opening between narrow cliffs, towering 500 feet above the highway.

OLD SPRING (L), 123.7 *m.,* flowing into a concrete trough by the side of the road, is marked by a wooden sign; it was a watering place for early emigrants.

Through COWBOY PASS (5,714 alt.), 144.8 *m.,* US 6 crosses the rolling hills of the CONFUSION MOUNTAINS, so named for a bewildering maze of gullies that crisscrosses the range.

At 148.2 *m.* is a view (straight ahead) of the green and brown SNAKE VALLEY, in the center of which is a large alkali flat. The pine-covered summits of the Snake Mountains (R) loom dark blue.

At 155.3 *m.* is a series of grassy knolls (R and L) with small artesian springs slowly exuding from their rounded summits.

ROBISONS RANCH, 163 *m.*, a hamlet in Snake Valley, consists of a few log houses surrounded by orchards and poplar trees. The adjacent country is good grazing land. West of Robisons Ranch US 6 is a series of roller-coaster dips for approximately a mile.

At 168.5 *m.* US 6 crosses the NEVADA LINE 60 miles east of Ely, Nevada (*see Nevada Guide*).

Tour 9

Crescent Junction—Moab—Monticello—(Cortez, Colo.); US 160.
Crescent Junction to Colorado Line, 105.5 *m.*

Oil-surfaced road between Crescent Junction and a point 12 miles north of Monticello; elsewhere gravel-surfaced. Open all seasons; occasional snowdrifts in winter.
Accommodations and service stations at Moab and Monticello only.

US 160 runs through a country in which shades of red permeate almost everything—plains, deserts, hills, cliffs, canyons. Only the greenness surrounding the La Sal and Abajo Mountains challenges the dominance of this color, and near these mountains are the only settlements. The country is crossed by the Colorado River, but water is scarce in most areas, and the land is devoted almost exclusively to the grazing of cattle and sheep.

US 160 branches south from US 6-50 at CRESCENT JUNCTION, 0 *m.* (4,778 alt.) (*see Tour 7a*).

For fifteen miles the highway follows an almost straight course over a broad, brush-covered plain. Low table-topped ridges of red, yellow, and gray are scattered over the area, but the distant Henry Mountains (R), 80 miles southwest, and the nearer La Sal Mountains (L), 35 miles southeast, loom high above the intervening landscape.

At 1.5 *m.* is an OIL WELL (R), one of several being drilled (1940) at widely separated points in southeastern Utah. The State has not yet produced fluid oil in commercial quantities.

At 10.5 *m.* is a view (L) across six miles of thinly-vegetated plain to a long red and yellow ridge fronting the DEVILS GARDEN (*see Arches National Monument*).

At 14.5 *m.* is the junction with an improved dirt road.

Right on this road (*Carry water*), to the BIG FLAT, 25 *m.*, a 90,000-acre livestock range developed by the U. S. Grazing Service through the drilling of two wells; powered by windmills, they provide water for 2,000 cattle and 6,000 sheep.

At 27.3 *m.* is the junction with a dirt road; R. on this road to THE NECK, 7.9 *m.*, where a tributary gorge of the Colorado River (L) and a tributary gorge of the Green River (R) are separated by a narrow ridge less than 40 feet wide, which constitutes the only passageway to a 40,000-acre mesa—a "peninsula" surrounded by air and depth. Steep cliffs form the sides of the mesa, which could be fenced with a forty-foot fence.

The main side road ends, 35.1 *m.*, in a grove of green cedars growing out of red sandstone, and a short trail leads to DEAD HORSE POINT. The point is shaped like a blunt arrowhead, 30 yards wide at the neck and 400 yards at its greatest width. It is, by western standards, "sorta level," which means that there are no deep gullies. The trail crosses the neck, a narrow strip of land separating two yawning gorges each more than a thousand feet deep. These gorges dwindle into insignificance when the trail comes to a dizzy, teetering halt at the rim of the UPPER GRAND CANYON OF THE COLORADO. Here the face of the earth breaks away into a 3,000-foot chasm, offering perhaps the most sensational canyon panorama in Utah.

The point overlooks 5,000 square miles of the red and rugged Colorado Plateau. The view sweeps east to the La Sal Mountains, south to the Abajo Mountains, southwest to the Henry Mountains, west to the Aquarius Plateau, and down into a tremendous gorge, at the bottom of which, in a canyon within a canyon, the silt-laden Colorado River flows through a maze of buttes and mesas. The river is visible in a dozen places as it winds sinuously from the east, makes a great loop toward the point, doubles back on itself, and finally meanders off to the south.

Ages ago the Colorado River was a wide shallow stream flowing aimlessly across the flat and unscarred Colorado Plateau. At first its channel was very wide, but as the land uplifted and the stream cut deeper into the sandstone, its channel became narrower. The process of deepening and narrowing continued, and the river now runs between step-like walls, 3,000 feet below the surface of the plateau.

The origin of the name of Dead Horse Point is probably a better index to its character than any description yet written. A band of wild desert ponies was herded onto the point, the best of the "broomtails" were culled for "cow service," and the rest were left to return to the range. Confused by the peculiar topography of the point, the horses wandered around in circles, and eventually died of thirst in full view of the Colorado River, half a mile away —straight down.

At dawn, when the La Sals are silhouetted against the rising sun, the canyon is a bottomless black bowl, still and foreboding, but as the sun arches into the sky its rays penetrate into the canyon, resurrecting the cliffs and mesas. The contrast of sun-tinted formations against purple shadows gives the canyon great width and depth. With field glasses many remarkable formations are visible in the canyon and across the plateau. A heart-stopping feat, most safely performed with help, is to stand near the rim and look across the canyon through field glasses, slowly lowering the glasses until one's feet come into the line of vision. Long before this visual traverse is completed, there is a sensation of tumbling into the canyon void—and that is where a helper with a good grip comes in, to keep the sensation from becoming a reality.

For several miles US 160 winds through a series of eroded red hills. Everything is red. Even the scattered growths of cedar are powdered with red dust.

At 19.9 *m.* is the junction with State 93 (*see Arches National Monument*).

On US 160, at 20.2 *m.,* is a view (L), across six miles of red desert, of two natural arches called The Windows (*see Arches National Monument*).

At the JUMPING-OFF PLACE, 23.9 *m.,* early settlers of Moab experienced great difficulty in lowering their wagons into Moab Canyon. A dugway eases the descent for present-day motorists. Oliver B. Huntington, who kept the official journal of the Mormon Elk Mountain Mission (*see below*), wrote in 1855: "Most of the *teams* were near giving out when they came to the canyon descent leading to the Grand River. . . . The 'jumping-off place' is a perpendicular ledge . . . down which Wm. Huntington and Jackson Stewart, the year previous, let five wagons with their loads by ropes, taking their wagons to pieces. The knowledge of this induced President Billings to take a company of twelve horsemen in the morning and move rapidly to the canyon . . . and at the 'jump-off' they worked a road over a point of the mountain covered with very large rocks; in half a day they completed a very passable road. . . . By doubling teams up and all the men that could be spared to steady the wagons down we got all our wagons down safely about nine o'clock at night."

MOAB CANYON is a beautiful and rugged gorge, four miles long, between towering cliffs and jagged mountain walls, gorgeously colored with orange and black, white and gray, red and purple, and numerous other tints and shades. Oliver Huntington described the canyon as "narrow, crooked, and rough with rocks."

US 160 crosses the COLORADO RIVER, 29.4 *m.,* over a long steel bridge, completed in 1912, which replaced ferryboats operated here since 1881. The Elk Mountain Mission party spent four days crossing the river in 1855, and Huntington wrote in the official journal: "President Billings, with five others, crossed the river with horses. . . . The remainder of the company was left under the charge of Jos. Rawlins, getting cattle over the river. Some Indians were about but appeared friendly, although the day before an arrow was found sticking in Brother Ivie's ox about an inch. This arrow was shot by a small boy, whose father apologized and made the excuse that his son could not shoot straight."

Norman Taylor operated the first ferry, a 28-foot boat not large enough to transport wagons without taking them apart. This was replaced two or three years later by a larger boat on which loaded wagons could be carried. The fare for each wagon was $2.50 until 1897, when Grand County purchased the ferry and reduced the charge to fifty cents. Faun McConkie Tanner says, in her *History of Moab* (1934), "It used to be said of this town, 'Moab is the only town in Utah to which admission is charged. In fact, it costs quite as much for an exit fee as for entrance.'"

At 29.5 *m.* is the junction with State 128.

Left on State 128, an improved dirt road, is a scenic canyon drive not recommended for squeamish drivers or timid passengers (*road impassable in winter and during spring floods; inquire at Moab or Cisco*). Between the junction with US 160 and that with the Castleton Road, State 128 parallels the turbulent and treacherous COLORADO RIVER, 150 to 200 yards wide, as it flows through a canyon of red sandstone. Much of the way the road climbs and dips along a narrow winding dugway overlooking the river; in other places the canyon walls pinch together and massive cliffs, towering to a height of 1,500 feet, crowd the road to the river's edge. The Colorado River originates near the Continental Divide in Rocky Mountain National Park, Colorado. Its largest tributary—larger than the Colorado itself—is the Wyoming-born Green River (*see Tour 7a*), which joins the Colorado 65 miles southwest of Moab.

Almost without exception, explorations of the Colorado River by boat have started at some point on the Green. In 1889, however, Frank M. Brown led a party down the upper Colorado River to make a preliminary survey for a "water-level" railroad route from Colorado to California. The party set out from Grand Junction, Colorado, and reached the confluence of the Colorado and the Green without mishaps. Below the junction, Brown was swept to his death in the Soap Creek Rapids. The reorganized party continued to Needles, California, reporting the route impractical because of periodic floods.

NIGGER BILL CANYON (R), 3.2 *m.*, was named for William Granstaff, a mulatto who came to Moab Valley in 1877. He departed hurriedly through this canyon in 1881, when some of the white settlers charged him with contributing to Indian troubles by selling whisky. "The men are gathering up guns to hunt Indians," he said, as he saddled his horse, "but I think maybe I'm the Indian they're after."

At 16.2 *m.* is the junction with the Castleton Road; R. on this dirt road, through a maze of red hills, into CASTLE VALLEY, 2 *m.* At 5 *m.* (L) is the red sandstone PRIEST AND NUNS, which, at 5.4 *m.* becomes CASTLE ROCK, a tall slender shaft on a conical base.

CASTLETON, 9.4 *m.* (6,750 alt.) is a cluster of weathered log houses occupied in summer by bachelor sheepherders who graze their flocks in the La Sal Mountains. At Castleton is the northern terminus of the La Sal Mountain Road (*see below*).

At 20.5 *m.* is the junction with the Onion Creek Road; R. here on a poor dirt road (*not recommended for motor travel*). At 1 *m.* the road reaches ONION CREEK (*poisonous water; contains arsenic*), a small, deceitfully clear stream of water. Sheepherders, driving their flocks through this region, lose many sheep from drinking this water. For nine miles the route is along the gravel bed of this stream, winding between red sandstone bluffs; the clear water, splashing on fenders or windshields, leaves albuminous splotches. The TOTEM POLE, 5 *m.*, is a tall pinnacle on the edge of a cliff. At THE NARROWS, 6 *m.*, the gorge is squeezed to a width of 10 feet by sandstone walls 400 feet high. For a mile the passageway twists between these walls, permitting a view of only a few feet forward or backward. GAUDY GARDEN, 8 *m.*, is a conglomeration of fantastic formations and bizarre colors. The road winds through a succession of shale hills—yellow, brown, gray, green, and purple, against a background of red towers. FISHER VALLEY, 14 *m.*, locally known as "Forbidden Valley" because of its inaccessibility, is a green farmland at the base of the La Sal Mountains. Three miles wide and eight miles long, it is surrounded by pink sandstone cliffs.

At 21.5 *m.* State 128 crosses a shallow wash, 20 feet wide, in which flows Onion Creek (*poisonous*).

At 24.3 *m.* the canyon widens, permitting a view (R) to the reddish-purple FISHER TOWERS, a remarkable group of pinnacles and spires, 800 to 1,700 feet in height. Merel S. Sager, of the National Park Service, describes them in the *American Planning and Civic Annual* for June, 1937: "From a distance, these red sandstone formations suggest the skyline of Manhattan. . . . Some have dominant, unbroken vertical lines of the modern skyscraper, while others resemble Gothic cathedrals with delicate carvings. They are different and distinct in a region where red sandstone pinnacles are common." North of this point State 128 parallels the Colorado River (L) through a steep-walled canyon so deep that the stream and the road are in almost perpetual shadow.

DEWEY, 31.3 *m.,* is a tiny settlement of five or six log houses at the confluence of the Colorado and Dolores rivers. At Dewey, State 128 crosses a cable suspension bridge over the eddying Colorado River, here approximately 150 yards wide.

At 43.4 *m.* is the junction with US 50 (*see Tour 7a*).

MOAB, 31.9 *m.* (4,042 alt., 883 pop.), seat of Grand County, is the commercial center of an extensive sheep and cattle country, and since 1930 has achieved importance as a point of departure for scenic attractions in southeastern Utah. Though isolated it has a small business district, selling everything from hay and gasoline to malted milk and liquor—the only "legal" liquor in the county. Squat red adobe houses stand neighbor to more pretentious firebrick houses. In the evening neon lights illuminate the business district, but after midnight, except on Saturdays, the town does a complete "blackout."

Moab has green trees, green lawns, green fields, but even this greenness comes from red soil. The town is on the Colorado River, which has an average annual flow of more than six million acre-feet, but gets its water from Mill Creek and Pack Creek, small streams flowing out of the La Sal Mountains. The Colorado's water-level fluctuates so greatly that any attempt by Moab farmers to divert its water would be an invitation for the river to flood the town. As a matter of historical record, in 1884 the river rose so high that, without benefit of diversion canals, it flooded the lower end of the valley.

The first attempt to settle Moab Valley came in 1855, with establishment of a mission in the Elk Mountains (now the La Sals). Advance preparations were made in 1854, when five wagon-loads of provisions were cached in the valley. The following spring, the Church called forty-one men to establish the mission. The group left Great Salt Lake City in May, taking with them fifteen wagons, thirteen horses, sixty-five oxen, sixteen cows, two bulls, one calf, two pigs, twelve chickens, four dogs, flour, wheat, oats, corn, potatoes, peas, five plows, twenty-two axes, and other tools.

The company reached the Colorado River in mid-June, and found the valley "abounding with the largest sage-wood any of us had ever seen, which we took as an indication of good farming land. . . . About the center of the valley we came to the lands cultivated by the Indians. . . . Loose soil and rubbish was piled in ridges, forming dams, by which the land was flooded in small quantities." Soon "all hands were busily engaged in grubbing brush, plowing land, building a dam . . . but the dam being in sandy land, it broke away . . . and ruined the site, which obliged us to go a mile farther up the creek and take water from a beaver dam."

By mid-July the men had planted crops and built a stone fort. They held friendly meetings with the Indians, converted and baptized some of them.

During late September, in a sudden series of attacks, Indians killed three of the Mormons and set fire to haystacks and log fences. The missionaries abandoned the fort the next morning "without eating breakfast." They departed so hurriedly that water was left running in the irrigation canal from Mill Creek. Water continued to run through this ditch, year after year, until eventually it carved an arroyo twenty-five feet deep.

The next settlers were probably two brothers, George and Silas Green, who brought 400 cattle into the valley about 1875. They were apparently killed by Indians. In the summer of 1877 two prospectors, William "Nigger Bill" Granstaff, a mulatto, and a French-Canadian known only as "Frenchie" took possession of the fort, and laid claim to the valley. In 1878 A. G. Wilson made a trade with "Frenchie" for his land, but when he returned with his family the following spring the Frenchman had traded the same land to Walter Moore, and had left the valley. The mulatto, however, remained until 1881. In that year the settlers had their last trouble with the Indians. A band of Paiutes and Navahos from Colorado came into the La Sal Mountains, killing and plundering settlers who grazed their cattle there. After a running fight in which ten whites and twenty-seven Indians were killed, the Indians were driven back to their reservation. During this trouble "Nigger Bill," accused of selling whisky to the Indians, fled into Colorado by way of Nigger Bill Canyon (*see above*).

A post office was established in 1879, and a committee chose the Biblical name Moab for the town. Grand County was created in 1890, and Moab was named the county seat. The population of the county in 1940 was approximately 2,000, most of whom derived their livelihood from sheep and cattle. The Grand County Fair, a three-day festival held in October, includes a rodeo and livestock show. Supervisory offices of the La Sal National Forest are at Moab.

The OLD IRRIGATION CANAL ARROYO, 50 to 300 yards west of US 160 through Moab, is the channel carved by the irrigation stream left running when Indians drove Mormon missionaries from the valley in 1855.

The BIG COTTONWOOD TREE, northwestern Moab, is the largest known tree in Utah. Its trunk is 8.2 feet in diameter. Planted about 1880 by L. B. Bartlett, it now stands in the middle of a road; sheer size saves it from removal.

Boats and guides are available at Moab for trips down the Colorado River. The 75-mile trip from Moab to the head of Cataract Canyon, 10 miles below the junction of the Colorado and the Green, can be made with comparative safety. Below this point navigation is difficult and dangerous. A 90-mile trip can be made up the Green from its junction with the Colorado to the town of Greenriver.

Beginning with the launching of the *Major Powell* in 1891, unsuccessful attempts were made to establish navigation service between Moab and Green-river (*see Tour 7a*). Improved overland highways ended these experiments, and today (1940) navigation is mostly confined to sight-seeing trips. In 1923

Ross Thomson and Mike O'Neil made the 65-mile trip from Moab to the junction in a 16-foot canoe, covering the distance in 10 hours and 21 minutes. The following year William Tibbetts and Tom Perkins also made haste down the river. Escaping from the Moab county jail, where they were being held for cattle theft, they started in a rowboat. They were pursued by officers in a motorboat. Almost overtaken, they landed and escaped into the adjacent canyon country. They were never recaptured.

West of Moab, the Colorado pierces towering cliffs that surround the valley, and begins its long imprisoned journey through canyons thousands of feet deep. Along the route are natural bridges, arches, windows, buttes, pinnacles, monuments—a continuous, constantly-changing display of strange and remarkable formations carved in naked red rock.

At HYS BOTTOM, 3.5 m., a foot trail (L) leads up the side of the cliff, through a cleft in the sandstone walls, then follows the canyon rim for a short distance, and descends to the PETROGLYPH OF THE MASTODON, the "riddle of the Colorado." The "mastodon" is an ancient drawing chipped in red sandstone. It measures 42 inches from snout to rump, and is 14 inches high at the shoulders. The upturned trunk is shorter than that of an elephant. The petroglyph was discovered in 1924 by John Bristol, Moab newspaperman, but little information regarding the strange carving was circulated until 1933, when Dr. Lawrence M. Gould, geologist-geographer on Byrd's first Antarctic Expedition, visited and photographed it. Weathering of the sandstone in which the drawing is cut proves that it is very old. It is 300 feet above the present river bed—far above other petroglyphs along the stream. Scientists are generally agreed that early man carved only images of what he actually saw, but the mastodon is said to have been extinct for 30,000 years—15,000 years before the supposed advent of man. This gives rise to speculation as to whether man was here 30,000 years ago, or whether the mastodon survived until 15,000 years ago. The Mastodon petroglyph remains the "riddle of the Colorado."

The junction of the Colorado and the Green, 65 m., is between walls 1,300 feet high. Major John W. Powell, who sailed down these rivers in 1869, climbed, with a companion, "as men would out of a well," to see the confluence from above: "From the northwest comes the Green, a narrow winding gorge. From the northeast comes the Grand [Colorado] through a canyon that seems bottomless from where we stand. Away to the west are lines of cliffs and ledges of rock—not such ledges as you may have seen where the quarryman splits his blocks, but ledges from which the gods might quarry mountains . . . and not such cliffs as you may have seen where the swallow builds its nest, but cliffs where the soaring eagle is lost to view ere he reaches the summit. . . . Wherever we look there is but a wilderness of rocks; deep gorges, where the rivers are lost below the cliffs and towers and pinnacles; and ten thousand strangely carved forms in every direction; and beyond them mountains blending with the clouds."

South of Moab, US 160 traverses a rolling semiarid strip of land, thinly vegetated with greasewood and prickly pear. A few miles east of the highway are the LA SAL MOUNTAINS (L), second highest range in the State. The La Sals (Sp., the salt) were formed by doming, caused by the intrusion of igneous rock between the lower sedimentary beds. The range is roughly 15 miles long and 6 miles wide, but high mesas radiating from the main mass cover a much larger area. Mount Peale, the highest peak, has an elevation of 13,089 feet. Forests of pine, fir, and aspen cover the higher slopes; cedar, scrub oak, and sagebrush grow on the lower slopes. Thousands of sheep and cattle are grazed here each summer.

US 160 crosses MILL CREEK, 33.4 m., and PACK CREEK, 34.3 m., the streams from which Moab gets its water.

At 41.7 *m.* is the junction with a gravel-surfaced road.

Left on this road to the junction, 1.1 *m.,* with the La Sal Mountain Road (*closed in winter*) ; R. on this improved dirt road.

At 4.2 *m.* is the junction with an improved dirt road; R. here to PACK CREEK CAMPGROUND, 3 *m.,* in La Sal National Forest. East of this junction the main road follows a steep, winding dugway ascending the western slope of the LA SAL MOUNTAINS. There are spectacular views from here (L) across the broken red country of the Colorado Plateau to the hazy blue Henry Mountains, nearly 100 miles southwest.

At 6.6 *m.* the road crosses the west boundary of LA SAL NATIONAL FOREST (North Division), and the sharp crest of MOUNT TUKUHNI-KIVATZ (Ute, place where the sun shines longest; 12,004 alt.) pierces the sky (R), hiding MOUNT PEALE (13,089 alt.), highest of the La Sal peaks.

At 11.1 *m.* is the junction with an improved dirt road; R. here to GEYSER PASS (10,750 alt.) 7 *m.,* named for Al Geyser, who grazed cattle in this region in the 1880's. The road runs between HAYSTACK MOUNTAIN (11,500 alt.), on the left, and MOUNT MELLENTHIN (12,750 alt.), on the right. The view from the summit stretches eastward into Colorado, to the Continental Divide, and westward across the Colorado Plateau. North of this junction the main road descends into HORSE CREEK CANYON, 12 *m.,* where there is a Forest Service campground in a grove of aspens.

At 14.2 *m.* is the junction with an improved dirt road; R. here, across Bald Mesa, to WARNER CAMPGROUND and WARNER RANGER STATION, 4 *m.,* near the summit of the La Sal Mountains.

North of this junction the main road again runs along the mountainside, with a succession of green peaks (R) sweeping upward from the road.

At 19.2 *m.* there is a view downward through Porcupine Draw (L) to the red sandstone statues of Castle Valley. In the background are towering red cliffs flanking the Colorado River.

At CASTLETON, 25.6 *m.* (6,750 alt.) (*see above*), is the northern terminus of the La Sal Mountain Road. From this point the Castleton Road continues 9.4 *m.* to the junction with State 128 (*see above*).

CANE SPRINGS (R), 48.2 *m.,* was for many years a watering place for early-day travelers. In the cliff on the opposite side of the highway is a cave, converted into a ranch house by construction of a wall across its opening.

The BIG MULE SHOE, 51.3 *m.,* is a sharp curve by which the highway crosses a wide, deep wash. The topography of southeastern Utah makes curves of this type necessary in many places.

At LA SAL JUNCTION, 55.9 *m.,* is the junction with State 46.

Left on this gravel-surfaced road to LA SAL, 8.9 *m.* (7,125 alt., 280 pop.), a ranching community settled in the early 1930's, when Old La Sal, twelve miles east, was abandoned. Ranchers graze their sheep and cattle in the mountains in summer and on the sagebrush plains in winter.

OLD LA SAL, 19.5 *m.* (7,500 alt.), was settled by cattlemen in 1877 and abandoned in the early 1930's because of frequent floods. In 1940 only a few ramshackle buildings remained.

At 22.8 *m.* State 46 crosses the Colorado Line, 90 miles west of Montrose, Colorado.

LOOKING GLASS ROCK (L), 59 *m.,* on US 160, is a salmon-colored sandstone wall pierced by an opening 25 feet high and 50 feet wide. It is so named because the view through the opening seems to be a reflection of the opposite wall.

In dry weather US 160 crosses HATCH WASH, 60.6 *m.;* in wet weather Hatch Wash crosses US 160. There is no bridge. The wash comes out of a deep rocky gorge (L), crosses the highway, and drops a sheer 150 feet into another gorge (R). Near the road (R) the torrential flood waters have gouged a "well," 75 feet deep.

SUGAR LOAF (R), 73.3 *m.,* is a red mound resembling a gigantic loaf of bread. Its top is hollowed out by erosion, and in pioneer days teamsters stretched tarpaulins inside the depression to catch rain water for their horses.

In this vicinity in the early 1900's lived "Rimrock" Annie, noted for her ability to work like a man. She broke her own broncos, roped her own mavericks, and branded her own livestock. Then one day romance "got her," and she gathered to her bosom a widower with seven children and left the valley. Her last act was the breaking of four wild horses for work. "Rimrock Annie was quite a character," remarked one oldtimer. "She was a good woman in her way, but she was as wild as the horses she broke."

At 74 *m.* is the junction with a dirt road.

Right on this road to the HOME OF TRUTH COLONY, 0.6 *m.,* a religious community founded in 1933 by Mrs. Marie M. Ogden, formerly a prominent welfare worker in New Jersey. At first membership in the colony totaled almost one hundred, but it has since dwindled to less than ten. Members are required to transfer ownership of all property to the leader for use of the entire group, and are thereafter entitled to food, clothing, and shelter. Should a member leave the colony, none of his property is restored, and he can take nothing with him except the clothes he wears. Mrs. Ogden claims that she founded the colony under divine guidance and that she receives revelations regarding its management. The doctrine of the sect allows members no meat, except fish and chicken, and forbids the use of tobacco and alcoholics. Mrs. Ogden owns the county's only newspaper, the *San Juan Record,* printed at Monticello.

The Home of Truth Colony is divided into three sections—the Outermost Point, the Middle Section, and the Outer Portal. The OUTERMOST POINT, 0.6 *m.,* consists of a group of unpainted frame buildings for the use of non-members and visitors. The colony has no electrical nor sanitary conveniences; light is provided by candles and oil-lamps, and water is obtained from outdoor hand-pumps.

The MIDDLE SECTION, 1.7 *m.,* is another group of unpainted frame buildings, used by members. In one corner of an unfinished cobblestone church is a small chapel for Sunday worship.

The OUTER PORTAL, 3 *m.,* is a third group of unpainted frame buildings in PHOTOGRAPH GAP, so called because of the vista between its walls. This unit has community buildings, and five or six houses, one of them occupied by Mrs. Ogden. The cult leader has prophesied that the grazing land beyond the gap will eventually be populated by thousands of Home of Truth colonists, and that the faithful will live in peace and prosperity while the rest of the world is caught in the destruction and misery of war.

SHAY MOUNTAIN (9,987 alt.), 15 miles southwest of the colony, is the sacred peak of the Home of Truth. During the summer the colonists make frequent trips to this mountain, remaining at its base while their leader ascends to the summit to receive revelations.

North of Monticello, US 160 skirts the west edge of the SAGE PLAIN, 1,200 square miles of monotonously level country sweeping eastward to the Dolores River in Colorado. Visible across this im=

mense plain are the San Miguel, La Plata, and Ute Mountains in Colorado.

The ABAJO MOUNTAINS (R), known locally as the Blue Mountains, are a prominent feature of the landscape for many miles. The "formal" name, when used, is pronounced "uh-BAH-hoe." These mountains, like the La Sals (*see above*), are of laccolithic origin. Herbert E. Gregory of the U. S. Geological Survey describes them in *The San Juan Country:* "The Abajo Mountains rise from Sage Plain . . . to eight independent summits. Below 8,000 feet the mountains constitute a single mass about 16 miles long and 10 miles wide, scalloped by radial valleys except on the west, where the flat-topped Elk Ridge abuts against its flanks. Above 9,000 feet . . . are four groups of peaks . . . much alike in form and structure. Their tops are rounded, some of them nearly flat; their sides slope steeply and evenly and not far from the summit develop long spurs, which likewise have broad tops and smooth sides.

"The Abajo Mountains give rise to many permanent streams. . . . In general, dense forests cover the northern and northwestern slopes; grasses cover the southern and eastern slopes."

MONTICELLO, 88.4 *m.* (7,066 alt., 665 pop.), seat of San Juan County, is a cool green town on the east slope of the Abajo Mountains. It was named for Thomas Jefferson's home in Virginia, but the name is pronounced "mon-ti-SELL-o" instead of "mon-ti-CHELL-o" as in the East. Temperatures here rarely reach 90 degrees —the highest ever recorded was 98; the lowest, 21 below zero. Hot days are followed by cold nights, and the temperature may drop as much as 50 degrees after sunset. The growing season is short—one year it was only 78 days. The community derives its livelihood principally from sheep and cattle.

Topographers with the Hayden Survey found no white men here in 1874, and it is probable that a cattleman named Patrick O'Donnell, who built a cabin here in 1879, was Monticello's first resident. Monticello was founded in 1887, when the Mormon Church "called" five families to settle the site.

Among the first settlers was Parley Butt, still alive in 1939, when Ernie Pyle, Scripps-Howard's traveling columnist, visited Monticello: "He's a character if I've ever seen one. He was in the Mormon scouting party that first penetrated southeastern Utah. He was a member of the fated group that made Mormon history by their experiences at 'The Hole in the Rock'. . . . Parley Butt was in Bluff in '78. He must be close to 80 now . . . a lovable rascal. Ugly as a mud fence (aw, don't get nervous; he won't mind), with huge, queer gold teeth in his lower jaw. He doddles around with a fly swatter. . . . When I said good-by to him he said, 'Well, give my regards to all the good-looking people in the world.' I kinda doubt if a guy like that will ever die."

In 1892 Monticello was caught in the San Juan River "gold rush" (*see Tour 10*). Prospectors, disappointed with their luck, came north to the Abajo Mountains. Most of them found nothing. The following year two prospectors found placer gold in Johnson Creek, and soon gold ore was found at the head of the stream. News of the discoveries precipitated a rush. Three hundred claims were staked, but the deposit was soon exhausted and the "boom" collapsed.

In 1894, a group of Coloradoans, under the leadership of David F. Day, Indian agent, influenced the U. S. House of Representatives to pass a bill awarding land in San Juan County to the southern Ute Indians in exchange for land in southern Colorado. A House committee was told that San Juan County was desolate desert, inhabited only by a small colony of Mormons and roving outlaws, and that it was unfit for anyone but Indians. After the House approved the bill, and without awaiting action by the Senate and President Cleveland, Day instructed the Indians to move into the county. Eight hundred came, bringing goats and ponies, taking over springs and water holes, and driving settlers' cattle from water and forage. Residents of the county sent a protest to the Territorial governor, Caleb W. West, who referred the problem to Washington. No immediate action was taken, and the settlers circulated a letter notifying all men in the county to prepare to drive the Indians out. A copy of the letter fell into the hands of Day, who wired Governor West: "Hold back your long-haired Armenians until I can get my squaws and papooses out of your God-forsaken country." Day, with Governor West and officers of the Utah State Militia, met with the settlers and Indians at Monticello. The Indians refused to go. "Our grandfathers owned and hunted 'buckskin' here for many hundred years; Washington 'Big Chief' say all right for Indians to set down in San Juan. We stay." Word was sent for soldiers to make ready to entrain from Salt Lake City. C. L. Christensen, interpreter, pleaded with the Indians through the night. By morning most of the Indians had agreed to return. A few remained, and they and their descendants still live (1940) on the reservation south of the San Juan River (*see Tour 10*), in Allen Canyon (*see Natural Bridges National Monument*), and on Montezuma Creek.

At Monticello is the junction with State 47 (*see Tour 10*).

Right from Monticello on a dirt road to the ABAJO MOUNTAINS (*see above*), 2 *m.* W. H. Jackson, who was with the Hayden Survey in 1874, wrote feelingly of this section: "Clear and cold mountain streams ripple down through ravines overhung by groves of willow, maple, and quaking aspen, with splendid little oaks and stately pines scattered over the uplands, and an abundance of rich, nutritious grass everywhere, that our poor, half-starved animals knew well how to appreciate. The blacktail deer and grouse were in goodly numbers, starting up from under our very noses."

The road (*inquire at Monticello regarding passability*) runs up North Canyon to COOLEY PASS, 10 *m.*, near the summit (L) of ABAJO PEAK (11,357 alt.), highest point in the Abajo Mountains. "The view from the top of Abajo Peak is of unusual interest," writes Herbert E. Gregory in *The San Juan Country.* "The prominent features of the marvelously carved and marvelously colored Colorado Plateaus within a radius of 100 miles are plainly visible. On clear days the sweep of vision is limited eastward only by the San Miguel and

La Plata Mountains, southward by Black Mesa, westward by Kaiparowits and Aquarius Plateaus, and northward by the Book Cliffs. In the distant views the La Sal Mountains, Henry Mountains, Ute Mountain, and Navajo Mountain . . . appear on the horizon as solitary peaks dwarfed in size by the enormous expanse of surrounding flat surface. . . . It is not difficult to foresee the time will come when they [the Abajo Mountains] will become a center of scenic interest. Of all the high isolated mountains affording extensive views of the plateau country this group is the most easily accessible."

Between Monticello and the Colorado Line, US 160 makes the only east-west crossing of SAGE PLAIN, 1,200 square miles of level brush-covered country deeply gashed by a network of canyons.

At 105.5 m. US 160 crosses the Colorado Line, 51 miles west of Cortez, Colorado (see Colorado Guide).

Tour 10

Monticello—Blanding—Bluff—(Kayenta, Ariz.) ; State 47.
Monticello to Arizona Line, 102.4 m.

Gravel road between Monticello and Blanding; improved dirt road between Blanding and Arizona Line.
Rooms and meals at Blanding, Bluff, Mexican Hat, W-Bar-L Ranch, and Goulding's Trading Post.
Caution: Unbridged washes south of Bluff, dangerous when in flood. When driving in sand, carry shovel and reduce air pressure in tires.

State 47 runs at the base of green-forested mountains, over deserts of sand, and spans a stream that often carries more silt than water. It passes through a town whose settlers spent four months constructing a road that was never used again. It traverses a land of cliff-dwellings whose inhabitants, once twice as numerous as the present population of the same country, disappeared for no known reason. It crosses a Navaho Indian reservation and runs through a wonderland of huge natural bridges, strange erosional formations, and nameless canyons. It penetrates a sparsely settled corner and offers access to the largest unsurveyed and unexplored region in the United States. It is one of the country's few remaining "adventure" highways. Less than one thousand people live along the entire route.

State 47 branches south from US 160 at MONTICELLO, 0 m. (7,066 alt., 496 pop.) (see Tour 9).

For several miles the highway traverses an area of rolling green brush-covered land paralleling (R) the lofty Abajo Mountains (see

Tour 9), known locally as the Blue Mountains. Sweeping eastward into Colorado is the vast deceptive terrain of Sage Plain (*see Tour 9*), mainly useful as winter range for sheep and cattle.

VERDURE, 6.7 *m.* (6,925 alt., 25 pop.), is a cluster of houses huddled in a green pocket enclosed by mountainous slopes. The San Juan pioneers, who first came north from Bluff (*see below*) in search of new and less grudging farmland, settled at Verdure in 1887.

State 47 descends several hundred feet into DEVIL CANYON, 11.9 *m.* For much of the year the stream-bed is dry, but after a rainstorm it is swept by a swift, roaring torrent. Before the creek was bridged, heavily-laden freight wagons were occasionally trapped by unexpected flood-waters and dashed to pieces against the canyon walls. Even today the bridge is sometimes submerged.

The highway crosses RECAPTURE CANYON, 17.8 *m.,* named by Peter Shirts, a hermit who settled in the San Juan country in 1877. Shirts believed that Montezuma escaped from his Spanish captors and was recaptured in this canyon.

BLANDING, 22.1 *m.* (6,105 alt., 555 pop.), is a farming community on White Mesa, surrounded by fields of hay and grain; its residents derive their livelihood mainly from sheep and cattle. Northwest of the town are the pyramidal bluegreen Abajo Mountains. Westward, buttressing their south slope, is Elk Ridge. Blanding was settled in 1905, and within ten years became the largest town between Moab and Arizona, a distance of more than 150 miles. In 1940 with less than 600 inhabitants, it was the most populous town in San Juan County, which has an area of 7,761 square miles, equivalent to the combined areas of Connecticut, Delaware, and Rhode Island, but the total white population is less than 5,000. "San Juan County," writes the geologist Herbert E. Gregory, "is essentially a grazing district—a great expanse of free range. The villages serve primarily as homes and supply points for cattlemen and sheepmen. . . . Soil is deficient in amount and in fertility. Over large areas it is merely . . . sand temporarily holding its position on windswept rocks. . . . Large areas have no soil at all." Only the San Juan and Colorado rivers flow the year around. "Many of the streams . . . flow only in direct response to rainfall. During most of the year the stream channels . . . are dry beds of sand, boulders, or bare rock; yet . . . the driftwood perched on the valley sides testify to the strength of occasional floods."

"Blanding," says Gregory, "owes its existence to . . . Walter C. Lyman, the father of the irrigation project that brought the waters of the Abajo Mountains to some 3,000 acres of favorably lying land. . . . In 1905 the first settlers arrived—chiefly those whose farms had been ruined by the San Juan River at Bluff and those driven from Mexico by political and religious persecution." Blanding stands on land once occupied by prehistoric Indians, and ruins of adobe and rock were used in constructing some of the older buildings. The town was first named Grayson, but was renamed in 1915 when Thomas W. Bicknell, an Easterner, offered a library to any Utah town that would take his name. Two towns, Grayson and Thurber, accepted. A compromise was arranged whereby Thurber became Bicknell and Grayson became Blanding, taking the maiden name of Mrs. Bicknell; the library was divided between them.

Only a north-south highway connects Blanding with the outside world; it is served by no railway or airline. A road east to railroad points in Colorado is talked about, but it would have to cross ten Sage Plain canyons in the first fifteen miles.

Blanding is at the junction with State 95 (*see Natural Bridges National Monument*).

Along more than 80 miles of highway southward from Blanding into Arizona the total white population is less than 100. Excepting three or four families, all of these people live at Bluff. Between Blanding and Bluff, State 47 runs along the flat divide between COTTONWOOD CANYON (R) and RECAPTURE CANYON (L). The canyons are not always visible from the road, but at one place they are less than thirty feet apart. The road traverses the southwest corner of Sage Plain, running through miles of gently rolling sagebrush, greasewood, and rabbitbrush, with distant mountains in view eastward in Colorado and southward in Arizona.

At 37.7 *m.* is the junction with a primitive dirt road (*see Hovenweep National Monument*).

At 43 *m.* there is a view (R) across ten miles of rolling and rugged country to the jagged gray edge of COMB RIDGE, extending southward 100 miles from the Abajo Mountains into northern Arizona; it can be crossed only at two places.

State 47 descends from Sage Plain to the valley of San Juan River through COW CANYON, 47.6 *m.* The NAVAHO TWINS (R), 48.7 *m.,* are massive formations of red sandstone.

BLUFF, 49.1 *m.,* (4,320 alt., 70 pop.), consists of a score of dusty red brick houses, built of the soil on which they stand. Five artesian wells provide water for an oasis-like growth of shade trees and fruit orchards. Bluff has an Indian trading post where Navahos are frequent visitors, bringing wool, silver work, goat meat, and hand-woven rugs to trade for groceries and clothing. Bluff is the southward terminus for telephone lines, and the traveler will go deep into Arizona before finding another 'phone connection.

Attention of the Mormon Church was first attracted to this region by Jacob Hamblin, missionary to the Hopis, who investigated the area in 1879. John Taylor, Church President, sent an exploration party led by Silas S. Smith to make a more detailed survey. The expedition traveled south from Cedar City, crossed the Colorado River at Lees Ferry, continued southeast to Tuba City, and entered the San Juan Valley from the south. A fort was constructed on Montezuma Creek, and two families were left there. The explorers returned to Cedar City via present Moab, Greenriver, and Salina. In five months they completed a 1,000-mile loop through a little known region.

The Church "called" 200 members to settle the San Juan country, to "cultivate the good will of the Indians and to preserve law and order." Both of Smith's routes were considered too circuitous, and a traverse directly east from Panguitch was decided upon. With little more investigation than a glance from the rim of Glen Canyon across the Colorado River, the journey to the San Juan was begun in December, 1879. Kumen Jones, who made the trip with Smith and with the main company, tells in the *Utah Historical Quarterly* for January, 1929, that after the company had arrived at the last camping place before crossing the Colorado River, "exploring parties were sent out to see just what was ahead of us. The discovery was soon made that we had been led into a trap, as deep snows had fallen on the mountains back of us, and the next to impossible loomed up before us."

The journey is vividly described in Hoffman Birney's *Zealots of Zion*. Of the crossing of Glen Canyon, he writes:

The trail they built cannot be called a road by any present standards of highway construction. Leaving the plateau, it pitched directly toward the river through the famous Hole. Below that [four-foot] cleft, blasted to a width sufficient to permit the passage of a wagon, was a turn into a long diagonal where the lavish use of powder had made a path across the face of the cliffs. At other points the workers constructed "dugways"—a term coined by the Mormon road-builders. . . . It is merely a rut dug so deep that a wagon wheel, once in the slot, cannot possibly get out. Gravity takes care of the rest. The wagon goes down, although the dugway builders offer no guarantee that all of the vehicle will reach the bottom at the same point. . . . "Those Mormon roads," said one old-timer who had used many of them, "are somethin' like th' cowboy's beefsteak—just done enough to eat raw!"

After two weeks of hard work on the trail, an effort was made to move some of the horses down from the plateau to a bench above the Colorado. . . . The majority of the animals made the treacherous descent without mishap, but nine horses were unable to keep their footing on the glassy rocks. They slipped, slid over the smooth slope to the rim of the cliffs, and crashed down to death. After considerable more work the first wagon began the descent through the Hole-in-the-Rock. The wheels were locked and men, hanging back on long rope, checked its speed until it had been guided around the turn below the cleft and headed for the dugways. . . . The wagon struck the built trail, bounced over the rocky barrier, gained momentum on the steep grade, and reached the bottom riding on the crest of a miniature landslide of its own making. By the time the last of the eighty-odd vehicles had made the descent, the roadway was as bare of loose rock as it had been before the work began.

Four men, sent ahead to find the best route, returned in twenty-five days, a month before the crossing of the Colorado was completed. On the second day they came to the Slick Rocks, an area of steeply sloped sandstone, impossible to avoid and apparently impossible to descend; a scout followed a herd of mountain sheep across it.

They were forced many miles to the north by the rough terrain . . . and the necessity for discovering a pass through the Clay Hills [Birney continues]. They found that pass, the only one in the range, by following another dim trail made by the ancient inhabitants of the land. . . . East of the Clay Hills . . . lay a many-branched gorge so vast that they christened it the Grand Gulch. . . . On Christmas Day . . . they cooked the last of their food. That Christmas dinner was "a slapjack of flour and water baked in a frying-pan.".

Late in the eleventh day, after four days without food, the men staggered into a cabin on the present site of Bluff. The following morning they continued to the settlement at Montezuma, and after a single day's rest began the return trip, with a forty-eight-pound sack of flour for food. When they got to the Colorado River they were tired and discouraged. The company, however, had no choice but to move forward: Heavy snows made it impossible to return; lack of forage made it impossible to remain. They hauled lumber 60 miles from Escalante to build a ferryboat, and blasted a road in the east wall of the canyon.

To tell of the journey of that caravan [writes Hoffman Birney], would be virtually to repeat the tale of the sufferings of the four pathfinders and to multiply five-fold the labor that had been necessary to descend through the dreaded Hole to the river. . . . The Hobbs party made the trip in eleven days; to cover the same ground with heavily-laden wagons took just five times as long—a daily average of less than three miles. . . . Conditions at the Slick Rocks prohibited the building of anything even resembling a road. . . . After seven days of toil, the colonists achieved what they called a "shoot the chute." All of the wagons reached the bottom, but extensive repair work was necessary before many of them resumed the journey. There are limits to what even an emigrant wagon will stand. . . . At the foot of the pass, as the party faced the long drag about the head of Grand Gulch, a blizzard buried the campsite in deep drifts and set the hungry oxen and horses to pawing through the snow for their forage. . . . Five days were required to build a road in and out of the canyon of upper Grand Gulch . . . and progress from there on across the [densely wooded] southern spur of Elk Ridge was possible only through the labor of a corps of axemen who preceded the train and cut a passage for the wagons.

It was a severe winter [recalls Kumen Jones] but the pilgrims enjoyed good health. Each Sabbath day was duly observed by all resting from their labors and holding services. Each night before retiring the bugle sounded as a signal for all to observe evening prayers. Dancing parties were frequently held on the flat bed rock, also singing, games, readings and other amusements. Three babies were born on the way, and with the assistance of two old-time nurses, and the blessing of the Good Father, all went well with mothers and children.

East of Elk Ridge the company descended into the canyon of Comb Wash and turned south to the San Juan River, reaching the mouth of Cottonwood Creek in April, 1880. Still 15 miles from the Montezuma settlement, this was "the first place they had found to stop and also the first place from which they had no strength to go on." Exhaustion had halted the company at the most suitable site on the San Juan River.

The geologist Gregory retraced the route of the Bluff colonists: "My traverse of the Escalante-San Juan road on foot, on horseback, and by swimming makes it easy to understand why it was used but once. . . . It seems clear that missonary zeal rather than a knowledge of topography guided this heroic but futile undertaking." Hoffman Birney evaluates the journey thus: "It was labor beside which the toil of the emigrant trains that crossed the entire continent to California and Oregon was child's play. . . . Nowhere in the history of America is there a more impressive example of the power of a creed, of the faith that moveth mountains, than in the conquest of the Hole-in-the-Rock and the story of the Saints of the San Juan."

An act of the Territorial legislature created San Juan County in February, 1880, when it had no permanent inhabitants, and leaders of the Mormon company were appointed its officials while still struggling eastward from the Colorado River crossing. Bluff became the county seat and remained so until 1895, when it was removed to Monticello (see Tour 9). The population of Bluff in April, 1880, was approximately 225; it has never since reached that figure. During the first year "about half the population moved away." Yet as the manuscript "San Juan Stake History" records, "somehow, in this wonderful colony which had come through from Escalante whether it could or not, there remained a splendid element of invincibility. When the dissatisfied and disheartened ones moved on to the east, and back to the west, that invincible spirit clenched its jaws the tighter, and attacked the Bluff ditch with angry force. It brought out a stream of water, it broke the virgin soil and planted long cherished seeds. It built a bullfence, fitting the crooked stakes and riders of the crooked cottonwood limbs into a hocus-pocus barrier, which is responsible for the generation of breachy cows which have pestered Bluff ever since.

"More still, it undertook from that same rams-horn breed of trees, to select logs and build houses, whose walls bowed in and out with wonderful irregularity. . . . It roofed them with quick coats of sand, which feathered out into a crop of runty sunflowers and stinkweeds, if the weed-seed had time to sprout before the wind carried the sand away. But whether it raised weeds or blew away, it never turned the rain, which dripped dismally from it long after the sky was clear. These houses had doorways without doors, windows without glass, and floors which required sprinkling at intervals to lay the native dust and tempt the soil to harden."

With the nearest white settlement more than seventy miles away, the colonists had difficulty with the Paiutes and Navahos. A fort was built to protect women and children, but when Indians stole cattle and horses, the settlers dared do little about it. The most they usually accomplished was to retake the stock. The settlement was not entirely free from Indian trouble until 1923, when Old Posey, chief of the dispossessed Paiutes, died. For twenty years he had done almost everything to make himself unpopular. His career came to an end when he and his band assisted in the escape of two Paiutes who had been arrested for robbing a sheep camp. A posse pursued the Indians for several days, killed one of them, wounded Old Posey, and captured the rest. Old Posey escaped to an abandoned cave in Comb Wash, where he died, his wounds stuffed with weeds, his lifeless face toward the approaching enemy.

More serious were the vagaries of the San Juan River. Time after time the settlers attempted to divert water from the river, but each

Yesterdays

Yesterdays.

OLD SALT PALACE, SALT LAKE CITY

EARLY STREET SCENE, SALT LAKE CITY

OLD COVE FORT

Note remnants of rifleman's platform over gate.

OLD RANCH HOUSE, NEAR IBAPAH

Lee A. Olsen

EMPEY HOUSE (c. 1855), SALT LAKE CITY

This house was designed by Truman O. Angell, architect of the Mormon Temple.

ERASTUS SNOW HOUSE
(1875), ST. GEORGE

BAUMAN ADOBE HOUSE
(1874), SANTA CLARA

OGDEN CANYON (c. 1870)

The photographs on these two pages were made by William H. Jackson, official photographer for the Hayden Survey of the Territories in the 1870's.

GREEN RIVER

QUARRYING GRANITE FOR THE MORMON TEMPLE (c. 1871)

FRISCO, UTAH'S RICHEST SILVER TOWN, IN THE 1870'S

"BUTCH" CASSIDY (*Right*) AND HIS GANG IN 1900
N. H. Rose Collection, San Antonio, Texas

A C. R. Savage Photograph

MEETING OF THE TRAINS AT PROMONTORY (1869)
This celebration marked the completion of the first transcontinental railroad.

PACK-MULE POST TO BOULDER
This means of mail delivery was in use until 1935.

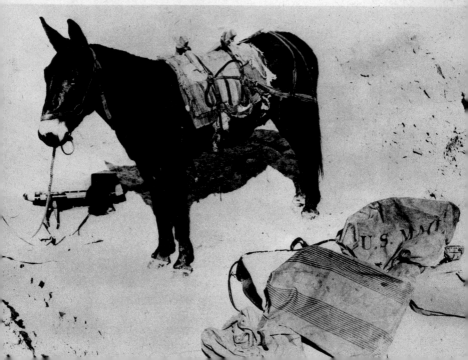

PRINCESS ALICE (b. 1875)

This animal, a popular attraction at the Hogle Garden Zoo, Salt Lake City, was the first elephant to calve in America.

time the stream rose unexpectedly and flooded the fields. The Church sent Francis A. Hammond to act as president of the San Juan Stake. He moved most of the people to Monticello (*see Tour 9*), and stock-raising replaced farming as the primary industry. By 1935 the twenty miles of farmland that existed along the San Juan River in 1880 had been reduced by floods to 200 acres at Bluff. By that time, however, the townspeople had begun to irrigate with water from artesian wells.

For two decades Bluff was "the end of the line." The road from Bluff to Mexican Hat was constructed during the "oil boom" at the turn of the century (*see below*). Between Bluff and the Arizona line there are no towns—only a ranch, a tourist lodge, and an Indian post, all of which provide tourist accommodations, guide service, pack and saddle horses, and "desert" automobiles with over-size low-pressure tires for travel over the sand. "The region is distinctly," as Gregory says, "a 'foot and horseback country'; most of it is accessible only by pack train. . . . Except under the direction of men acquainted with the topography of the plateau province and experienced in finding water holes, tourists are advised to limit their travels to areas reached by auto-mobiles or by frequently used trails."

Between Bluff and Mexican Hat, in a distance of 27 miles, State 47 crosses a dozen unbridged washes. In case of a characteristic torren-ial rain, care should be exercised in crossing them.

The road climbs steep-sided COMB RIDGE, 56.2 *m.*, by a series of switchbacks, and winds over the summit through a rocky pass. At the base of NAVAHO HILL, 57.9 *m.*, on the east slope of Comb Ridge, a trail leads (L) 100 yards to NAVAHO SPRINGS, where good water is available.

For a mile the road weaves through SNAKE CANYON, 59.5 *m.*, where some of the curves are so sharp that a motorist almost collides with his own tail light. The canyon winds through red eroded hills, and is said to have received its name when an unfortunate snake broke his back trying to crawl through it.

West of Snake Canyon the road crosses LIME RIDGE, a brush-covered dome. The red pinnacles and buttes of Monument Valley, along the Arizona line, are hazily visible from here.

At 73.9 *m.* is the junction with a dirt road.

Right on this road to the junction, 0.8 *m.* with another dirt road; R. here to the mesa-shaped stone lodge of W-BAR-L RANCH, 7 *m.* (*meals, cabins, guides, horses*), at the base of high-cliffed CEDAR MESA.
Buck Lee, whose name is reputedly William, widely known for a genial hospitality that is unpredictably laconic and garrulous by turns, and generally conceded to be the "best damn artist" in the San Juan, is part-owner of the W-Bar-L. Mr. Lee works in oil and leather—he has exhibited paintings and carved saddlery in the State Capitol—but he is most proud of his faultless tall tales and of his "desert broiled" steaks. The latter are carved into slabs two or three inches thick, smeared with a mixture of lard, salt, and pepper, laid on grills about four inches above a bed of coals, and allowed to sizzle until the surface is cooked into a hard crust. The meat, with the hot juices caught and ember-seasoned, like ripe scotch with peat smoke, is a desert delicacy.

As to his stories, Lee likes light, for solemn-faced telling is half the yarn. The coals are built up to a blaze to eat by, and he begins without asking:

I caught a bear onct.

This here bear got so tame I used to ride him after cattle. Only just two things was wrong with him. He et too much and he had one ear off. I called him Herkimer.

One day me and Herkimer was out for some yearlings, and we run smack into another bear. My outfit growls, the other bear growls, and first thing I know me and Herkimer light right on top of that other bear. I yell, I throw rocks, and I can't get that outfit split—and what's more, Herkimer ain't doing so well. I get me a club and by banging both of them get the outfit squared off long enough to climb on Herkimer and make tracks with that wild bear about six feet behind. The wild one ain't got no rider to carry and he gains on us, growling like all hell. I sock in my spurs and grab Herkimer's ear—and then [pensively] by gad I notice I'm hanging onto that outfit with both hands—and I got me an ear in each hand.

Lee's method at this point is to pay no attention to the results of his story. The idea is to drain a cup of coffee with sage-ash in it, and begin another while his listeners are still protesting the first.

One morning when I was a boy [it is a western convention that really heroic events happen to the teller] my mother sent me out to hoe the garden. I begun chipping at the string-beans, and bingo, an ole desert rattler slapped his fangs into the hoe handle. The handle began to swell, and swelled fast. It mashed three rows of string-beans, a couple of rows of strawberries, and got "clean to the goose-berries before the snake poison give out." The Lee family assembled to consider the damage and to "reckon" what was to be done. They sawed up the sequoia-size hoe handle, and made a bunk house out of it. That was all right, and it made an "OK" bunk house for several years. The Lees prospered. Their cattle increased, they built fences, and improved all the water holes. And one day they got so prosperous that they painted all the buildings. It worked all right on the barn, the hog pen, and the ranch house, but when the paint "hit" the bunk house it began to shrink. It got littler and littler, and in two days there wasn't nothin' left of it but a pile of toothpicks on the heatin' stove. The turpentine in the paint had counteracted the snake poison.

Trips can be arranged from the ranch to many parts of this vast unsurveyed country, to countless points of scenic interest, to scores of nameless canyons and hundreds of ancient cliff-dwellings, and to the incredible route of the Hole-in-the-Rock Mormon colonists (see above). A specially-equipped car with a driver-guide is available for automobile trips to various points of interest such as the GARDEN OF THE GODS, a remarkable group of red sandstone formations 100 to 400 feet in height. There are no roads in this area. The driver "takes off" across the desert and removes brush and boulders as circumstances require.

A pack-trip requiring six or more days can be taken to GRAND GULCH, the tremendous box canyon that forced Bluff colonists far off their course. Here are several hundred cliff-dwellings, few of them fully explored and many of them entirely untouched since they were abandoned centuries ago. Existence of the Basket Maker culture was first substantiated by T. M. Prudden as the result of collections made in Grand Gulch in the 1890's (see Archeology).

The main side road continues to the GOOSENECKS OF THE SAN JUAN RIVER, 5.1 m., one of the world's most magnificent examples of an "entrenched meander." Here, in a mud-gray canyon more than 1,200 feet deep, the San Juan makes a series of symmetrical bends, around which it flows six miles to travel an airline distance of one. The river is viewed from the north rim at it flows north, then south, then north again, and finally south again, in a series of close-set curves. The center bend is three miles around, but the dividing ridge, at its narrowest point, is less than 100 yards wide. According to geologists the San Juan once meandered over the surface of a level plain; a slow regional uplift forced the stream to cut deeper and deeper into the plain. Eventually, eons hence, the meanders may cut through, leaving a series of gigantic natural bridges (*see Natural Bridges National Monument*).

MEXICAN HAT BUTTE (L), 75.4 *m.*, on State 47, a cone-shaped mound of red shale nearly 400 feet high, derives its name from an eroded rock formation on the summit, resembling a gigantic Mexican sombrero balanced on its crown. The brim of the "hat" is 62 feet across. In the background are cliffs containing the RAPLEE ANTICLINE, "on upfold or arch of stratified rock," so remarkable because of its symmetry that photographs of it are used in geology texts. The anticline is 15 miles long and 1,500 feet high at its crest.

MEXICAN HAT LODGE, 77.4 *m.* (*meals 75¢; rooms $2 and $3; guide $5; "desert" car and driver-guide $15; guided boat trips $5 and up*), in a desert valley north of San Juan River, provides a base for trips to scenic areas of southeastern Utah and to numerous cliff-dwellings, including PONCHO HOUSE, in Chinle Wash. This ancient ruin, one of the largest in the Southwest, is four stories high, 600 feet long, and contains 125 rooms. Mexican Hat Lodge (4,244 alt.) is operated by Norman D. Nevills, "white water" boatman. His "adventure" trips range from a four-mile boat ride on the San Juan, costing $5, to a 200-mile, eight-day trip on the San Juan and Colorado, from Mexican Hat to Lees Ferry, Arizona, with a side trip to Rainbow Bridge National Monument, which costs $300 for a party of four. The 33-mile San Juan River trip from Bluff to Mexican Hat requires one day and costs $50 for a party of four.

In midsummer, 1940, Nevills announced discovery of GREGORY NATURAL BRIDGE, a huge span in a side canyon of the Escalante River, which enters the Colorado River from the west, at a point about 15 miles north of Rainbow Bridge. Nevills reported that the bridge has a height of 305 feet, only three feet less than that of Rainbow Bridge, and a span of 293 feet, nearly twenty feet longer than that of Rainbow. Nevills was at the time on a canyon expedition from Green River, Wyoming, to Boulder Dam. The newly discovered bridge was named for Herbert E. Gregory, Government geologist and authority on the Navaho country.

The muddy SAN JUAN RIVER, 78.1 *m.*, is spanned by a suspension bridge. The river rises in the San Juan Mountains of southern Colorado, flows into New Mexico, back into Colorado, enters Utah near the Four Corners, and flows westward to its junction with the Colorado River near the Arizona Line. Discovery of gold along the upper tributaries of the San Juan led E. L. Goodridge to make the first known boat trip down the river in 1879. He found only minor quantities of flake gold, but "little streams of oil coming from loose boulders" induced him to seek funds for development of an oil claim near the present San Juan bridge. The venture was eventually financed in 1907, and the following spring Goodridge brought in "a gusher, throwing oil to a height of 70 feet." By 1911 there were twenty-seven drilling rigs in the field, a small town had sprung into existence at Goodridge (now Mexican Hat), and a bridge was constructed over the San Juan River. Most of the wells produced only a little oil and gas, and many were "dry holes." None produced oil in commercial quantities.

In 1891 rumors began to circulate that San Juan sands were rich in gold. The "gold rush" of 1892-93 followed, bringing almost 2,000 men into the region. A few prospectors recovered enough gold to make day wages. Many prospectors drifted north to the Abajo Mountains (*see Tour 9*), but found only added disappointment.

From the Colorado Line to a point midway between Bluff and Mexican Hat the river occupies a flood plain half a mile to a mile wide, bordered by low walls. West of Bluff the river follows a meandering canyon to the Colorado River. The airline distance from the head of the canyon to the Colorado is only 63 miles, but the distance by stream is 133 miles. The most closely spaced bends are the Goosenecks (*see above*), but at the GREAT BEND the river makes a nine-mile loop and returns to within half a mile of its starting point. At the west end of this loop the Colorado is only 5 miles away, but the San Juan travels 34 miles before the two streams meet. The depth of the canyon varies from a few hundred feet to half a mile.

The 1921 expedition of the U. S. Geological Survey, led by K. W. Trimble, was the first to make a survey of San Juan Canyon. The party descended the river in two sixteen-foot rowboats and spent more than two months making a study of the river, the canyon, and the adjacent country. Hugh D. Miser, geologist with the party, reports kaleidoscopic colors in the canyon—gray, buff, brown, red, pink, lavender, green, yellow—and describes "sand waves" of this silt-laden stream at flood: "The advancing front of each surge was marked by a ragged splashing wave as much as 6 feet high."

R. C. Pierce, who made a study of the San Juan River, reports in a U. S. Geological Survey water-supply paper, that "A sample taken by the writer just after the peak of a sudden heavy flood . . . and examined after settling for 24 hours, showed that 75 per cent of the original volume of sample was silt and red sand, chiefly the latter. . . . At the peak of the flood and for almost an hour afterward the river ran with a smooth, oily movement and presented the peculiar appearance of a stream of molten red metal." From 1927 to 1933, maximum flow of the river was 70,000 second-feet in September, 1927, and the minimum was 26 second-feet in December, 1932. Normally one of the largest streams in the State, the San Juan ceased to flow in 1896, and in 1934.

Nineteen hundred and nine was a low-water year and James Douglas, prospecting the river, discovered a bonanza sand bar. Then the river rose and the bar disappeared. Douglas waited patiently for the river to go down, waited year after year, but his bar remained flooded. In 1929, after twenty years of vigil, his patience exhausted and his hair white, the old man jumped off Mexican Hat Bridge, leaving this note behind him:

> When this you see
> My old body in the river will be
> There is no one in the world
> To blame for this
> Only me.

San Juan folk were touched. They named Douglas Mesa, west of the Goosenecks, for him. Five years later the river went dry.

Between the San Juan River and the Arizona Line, State 47 crosses the NAVAHO INDIAN RESERVATION, which occupies the entire strip of land from the Colorado River on the west to the Colorado line on the east. Only one automobile crossed this strip before 1921, but the scenic beauty of the region has since attracted many visitors. In 1939 it was used as the location for filming *Stagecoach*. Those acquainted with the valley were amused, in the cinema production, to see the stagecoach traveling first in one direction, then in another. For several miles the road runs through Monument Valley. Only a small part of the Navaho population lives in Utah, as compared with Arizona and New Mexico, but their dress, customs, and activities are uniform over the area. White men have had little influence on them, few speak or understand English, and nearly all cling to their primitive customs and beliefs. Their summer *hogan* or house, is a thatched roof supported by posts; the winter *hogan* resembles an Eskimo igloo, but is built of posts, brush, and mud. The principal industries of the Navahos are sheep-raising and rug-weaving. They move from place to place with their herds as the supply of forage and water requires, but confine their movements to a somewhat limited area.

Ethnologists believe that the Navahos came into the Southwest about 500 years ago. They speak an Athapascan language, similar to that used by tribes in northwest Canada. Early Spanish records indicate that they were a warlike people. They eventually became so troublesome that in 1863 Colonel Kit Carson led an expedition into their country, rounded up all the tribe (except a band in Monument Valley, who refused to surrender), numbering at that time about 4,000, and took them to Fort Sumner, New Mexico. After four years of "Babylonian" captivity they were given a few sheep, released, and permitted to return to their own country. Navahos today are principally known for their hand-woven rugs. Apparently they began weaving about 1780, imitating the loom of the Pueblos and acquiring wool from the Spaniards, to make striped blankets for their own use. Later they began trading blankets to the Spaniards, but weaving was not an important industry until after their release from captivity, when traders induced them to make rugs instead of blankets. Zizzag and diamond designs were introduced in the early 1800's, but did not gain popularity until after the release from captivity. Use of a border began at the turn of the century. No design, however, is completely enclosed, a thread leading out for the evil spirits to escape, lest the weaver lose her sight or mind.

All weaving is done by women. The Navaho woman uses wool from her own sheep, processed entirely by her own hands. She keeps the design in mind and develops it as she weaves, starting from the bottom and working up. When she has woven half way, she turns the rug over, begins at the bottom, and weaves toward the middle until the two halves are joined. The value of a rug is determined by its weight, the closeness of the weave, and the complexity and symmetry of the design. A well-woven rug, traders say, will shed water.

Navaho Indians and their customs are described in the Arizona State Teachers College bulletin, *The Navaho,* written by the Federal Writer's Project. The principal places of prestige, this book shows, are occupied by medicine men, who heal by chanting. There are perhaps twenty-five chants, but a medicine man usually knows only one. Sand paintings, four to twelve feet across, are an essential part of all chants, and, though elaborately made with colored sand, they must be destroyed before sunset.

According to Dr. John P. Harrington, Smithsonian Institution ethnologist, the Navahos are responsible for Utah's name. "Ute" is derived from a Navaho word meaning "upper," and was a name applied to these Indians because they lived in mountainous country.

ALHAMBRA PEAK (R), 79.5 *m.,* is a jagged black volcanic mass, contrasting with the red of the surrounding country.

HULKITO WASH, 88.5 *m.,* is one of the major intermittent streams of this region.

MONUMENT PASS, 95.7 *m.,* is the north entrance to MONUMENT VALLEY, where maroon buttes and pinnacles rise, like skyscrapers, out of the red desert, and tower nearly a thousand feet above the valley floor. Between the monuments, distant ranges in Colorado, New Mexico, and Arizona can be seen. Agathla Peak, a metallic blue volcanic spire, stands out in the red Arizona desert. The road parallels a row of descriptively named monuments (L)—Emperor, Stagecoach, Bear and Rabbit, and Castle Rock, 96.5 *m.,* Big Indian Butte, 97.1 *m.,* and Brighams Tomb, 98.1 *m.* Far west, across the desert (R) are the Clay Hills, Train Rock, and the Henry Mountains.

At 101.9 *m.* is the junction with a dirt road.

Right on this road to GOULDING'S TRADING POST, 2 *m.* (*rooms, with meals, $4 and $5; guides $5; horses $2; special "desert" car, with driver-guide, $15 and up*), operated (1940) by Harry Goulding, whom the Navahos call T'payeh-nez, or Long Sheep, either because he is tall, and owned sheep when he came into the valley, or because he had many sheep. Goulding's Post (5,275 alt.) is a solidly-built two-story structure—a house, a lodge, and a trading post. Here the "Navvies" bring their wool, rugs, and silverwork to trade for food and clothing. Occasionally, when things are especially bad, a Navaho will pawn his personal jewelry. From Goulding's Post pack-trips can be arranged to Navaho Mountain and Rainbow Bridge (*see Rainbow Bridge National Monument*), to twenty natural bridges, dozens of unnamed canyons, hundreds of cliff-dwellings, and countless remarkable remnants of erosion.

Between the Goulding's Post road and the Arizona Line, State 47 follows the floor of Monument Valley, paralleling an area of monuments (L), including one of the MITTENS, 102.2 *m.,* and MERRICK BUTTE, 102.3 *m.,* named for a prospector killed by the Navahos in the 1880's.

At 102.4 *m.* State 47 crosses the Arizona Line. Forty desert miles eastward along the line is FOUR CORNERS, only point common to four States. Navahos say the desert is exactly the same on all four sides of the cairn at Four Corners. Ernie Pyle, Scripps-Howard columnist who trekked to the cairn in 1939, sat on a pile of rocks, put his feet in two different States, and reached down to touch two more with his hands. He ran around the cairn, traveling through four States in something under ten seconds—and ended up feeling a little ridiculous. Zeke Johnson, custodian of Natural Bridges National Monument, wrote in 1940 that an old friend asked him how come he had lived in San Juan for so many years; Zeke replied that he "was so close to 4 Corners that no sheriff could catch him."

State 47 at the Arizona line is 93 miles north of Tuba City, Arizona (*see Arizona Guide*).

PART IV

Parks and Primitive Areas

Arches National Monument

Highway Approaches: Windows section, 9 miles on State 93, which branches E. from US 160, 12.2 *m.* north of Moab, thence by foot trail, 3 *m.* round trip, 4 hours from Moab to Moab; Courthouse Towers section, from US 160, 4.5 *m.* north of Moab, thence by foot trail, 5 *m.* round trip, 2½ hours from Moab and return; Klondike Bluffs section from Salt Valley Road (right at 10.1 *m.*), which branches E. from US 160, 26 *m.* north of Moab, thence by foot trail, 3 *m.* round trip, 6 hours from Moab to Moab; Devils Garden section, via Salt Valley Road, which branches E. from US 160, 26 *m.* N. of Moab, turning left on Salt Valley Road at 13 *m.*, thence by foot trail 3.5 *m.*, or 10 *m.* round trip, 4 to 10 hours from Moab to Moab, depending on length of tour; Delicate Arch section, from terminus of Salt Valley Road (at 22 *m.*), thence by foot trail, 3 *m.* round trip, 6 hours from Moab to Moab. Roads are unimproved, but patrolled six days each week, and offer no difficulties if speed is kept below 35 m.p.h.

Administrative Offices: Custodian's home at Moab; Park Cabin on State 93, 5 *m.* E. of US 160.

Information: Moab Garage, *Moab Times-Independent,* Moab Lions Club.

Accommodations: Hotel, tourist camps, guest homes at Moab. Hotel at Thompsons. No improved campsites in Monument.

Transportation: Private car. Horses for pack trips available at Moab; prices variable.

Communication: Telephone and post office at Moab and Thompsons. Express office at Thompsons. No telephone at Monument (1940).

Climate, Clothing, Equipment: Elevation of Arches National Monument is 4,000 to 5,000 feet; winter snowfalls seldom exceed 4 inches or last more than a day. The diurnal temperature range, however, is large. Warm clothing the year round is advisable for evening wear. For daytime, except in winter, light rugged clothing. Cowboys wear denim jeans and long-sleeved shirts. Straw hats, unless chin-strapped, are fairly useless in a region where the wind blows hard enough to carve through solid rock. Rubber soles are helpful for climbing "slickrock," but oxfords are an abomination in deep sand. Carry own water and camping equipment for overnight stays. Film in special sizes sometimes difficult to obtain in near-by towns.

Recreational Facilities: Photography, hiking, climbing, horseback riding (western style, an English saddle is useless in the up-down terrain of the Monument). One of the finest areas in Utah for photographing erosional curiosa.

Warnings and Regulations: Usual regulations applying to areas administered by the Park Service. Do not destroy property, carve initials, or remove artifacts, plants, or other natural objects. Guide essential in Devil's Garden, Klondike Bluffs, and advisable in other sections. Monument trails not posted (1940).

Admission: Free. Guide service to any or all of the sections furnished without charge by custodian.

ARCHES NATIONAL MONUMENT lies in the redrock country north of Moab, between the Colorado River and US 160. It is a region of desert sandstone, of deep and tortuous canyons, and its thin, multicolored topsoil supports piñon and sage. From the highway, except for the castellated pile of the Windows section, the whole area appears to be a flat and desiccated plain, intersected by occasional reefs that glow redly against the gray-green desert. Southward the pyramided La Sal Mountains rear, alien blue, from the valley floor, and the high peak Tukuhnikivatz, a Ute name meaning "place-where-the-sun-shines-longest," shows snow the year around. Northward are the Book Cliffs of Tavaputs Plateau, but eastward and westward the desert rolls out interminably, with a deceptive levelness. Squat hillocks of sand conceal gorges two, three, and four hundred feet deep, their sheer or overhanging crests revealed only from the rim. Many of the canyons have sweetwater springs in them, and patches of meadow in sandy alluvium, but are accessible only at the canyon mouths or at rare points where side-canyons intersect.

In the Monument proper, the wind has carved these canyon walls into forms that, even in a region noted for spectacular erosion, are remarkable. Here are arches and windows through solid stone, from a size that can scarcely be crawled through to immense spans that would accommodate a troop of cavalry; monoliths measured in hundreds of tons balanced on decaying bases; chimneys, deep caves, and high, thin, sculptured walls of salmon-hued rock. There are arches in all stages, from caves not yet cut through, to towering spans that have fallen, their buttresses pointing skyward. Although the terms "arch" and "bridge" are, in keeping with western informality, used somewhat loosely by Grand County people, there is a difference between them. A bridge usually occurs in a canyon as the effect of stream erosion (*see Natural Bridges National Monument*), and it spans something. An arch occurs in reefs, often where there is no stream course, and is in the main the product of wind weathering.

The rock in Arches National Monument was laid down as sediment in a Jurassic sea, which in the time of dinosaurs and northern tropical forests extended almost through the Colorado Plateau. The lowest exposed strata is a close-grained, gray and buff Navaho sandstone, 300 feet thick. Above it is a 50-foot layer of dark red sandstone known as the Carmel formation. The third layer is Entrada sandstone, which has a fine, even-grained texture and ranges from buff to light red in hue, and atop it there are remnants of a red, sandy mudstone known as the Summerville formation. In the Monument the Navaho sandstone usually serves as a platform upon which the various erosional forms stand, and the Carmel appears at the base of cliffs where talus debris has washed away. The cliffs themselves and the great walls into which the arches and monoliths have been carved are of Entrada sandstone. The Entrada, because its cementing material is readily dissolved and because the quartz grains which make up its main bulk are small and uniform in size, weathers easily into massive round-edged ledges, low configured domes, spool-shaped monuments, and hourglass forms that, wearing through at the waist, topple the upper half or leave it in precarious balance. In the Arches region the full thickness of the Entrada has been fractured by a criss-cross of cracks from ten to twenty feet apart. Rain water, seeping through, has carried with it the cementing material and small grains of sand, enlarged the cracks to crevasses and gorges, and left immense upright slabs or "fins" of pink and orange sandstone standing between. The wind, driving crumbled sand, has found weak spots and pecked windows through, chiseled out pinnacles, and chipped the contours of a stubborn piece of stone into life forms and ragged battlements. The wind is tireless— cowboys say it is useless to build a pine board fence in the desert. If the knots loosen, the wind blows through the holes and wears the boards out, "which," they add, "is how come an arch."

The whole area is rich in desert flora, especially in the canyon bottoms. Piñon pine, desert ash, and juniper are the only trees found in abundance, but sage, cacti, and grasses are everywhere. Uinta wildcat, coyote (found wherever cattle and sheep range in the West), western red fox, Great Basin skunk, Colorado cottontail, jack rabbit, chipmunk, gopher, pack rat, porcupine, and mule deer fatten the whole year on grass, shrubs, and seeds. Birds are numerous, with the smaller species predominating, though golden eagles, American ravens, and red-tailed hawks are frequently seen.

Enterprising cattlemen moved into the valley about Moab in the 1870's, and were ranging the whole countryside by 1885. Many of the canyons now in the Monument afforded good range, and since it was legend among cowboys that the frugal Mormons never lost a cow if she could be followed, it is not unreasonable to assume that the intricacies of the canyons were well known to them. Some of the arches carried, besides their sanctioned names, range designations that bespeak long and perhaps affectionate familiarity. Double Arch, for example, was known as the "jughandles," and Delicate Arch as "the schoolmarm's pants." And the Turnbow or Wolf Ranch cabin at the terminus of the road into the Delicate Arch section, though still serving line riders in 1940, possesses a venerable decay that could scarcely have accumulated to it in less than 50 years. Credit for "discovery" of the Arches has been tentatively given to Alexander Ringhoffer, a miner who worked his way into the section in 1922. Dr. J. W. Williams and L. L. "Bish" Taylor, in 1940 Editor of the *Moab Times-Inde-*

pendent, packed in shortly thereafter and began a long siege to arouse the interest of the National Park Service, which was persuaded to recommend establishment of the Monument in 1929.

Harry Reed, an eastern photographer, came to Moab in 1935 to test descriptions of the Arches scenery. He found few people who knew where the Arches were, and a smaller number who had visited them. Inquiries among cowboys disclosed that "they wa'nt nothin' out there. Jest a lot of holes in rocks"—this notwithstanding that one of the "holes" was just nine feet short of a Utah city block—or a football field—in length. The following year, Reed was appointed part-time custodian of the Monument, and in the fall, Harry "Long-Sheep" Goulding, trader to the Navahos of Monument Valley, drove to the Windows section in a specially equipped car. In 1937 Grand County ran a bulldozer and grader over Goulding's course, and the first tourists visited the Monument. In 1938, President Franklin D. Roosevelt, by proclamation, enlarged the boundaries of the Monument to the present 33,680 acres. The Monument, in spite of its right-angled boundaries, is roughly crescent-shaped, with the horns pointing west. It has five sections, each different in geologic interest and scenery: The Windows, centrally located; Courthouse Towers, in the southern extremity; Klondike Bluffs, at the point of the northern horn; Devils Garden and Delicate Arch, comprising the remainder of the northern horn. The U. S. Park Service, which administers the area, distinguishes sharply between a park and a monument—the former is scenic and inspirational, the latter is primarily educational. Arches National Monument was set aside to preserve and make accessible its splendid examples of wind erosion. Various sections should be visited in the company of a guide (furnished through the custodian) who will explain the invisible geology behind the visible forms.

THE WINDOWS

The Windows section is an eroded reef of ruddy Entrada sandstone, 9 miles east of US 160 on State 93. From the highway its battlemented contour, half mosque, half feudal castle, dominates the skyline, and patches of blue show clearly through two of its arches. State 93, after the manner of desert roads, threads somewhat uncertainly through hillocks, washes, and around outcroppings of sandstone bedrock. The road, however, offers no difficulties, aside from slow driving over rough spots and staying on the road in sandy stretches, and affords besides a chance to observe that the desert is much maligned, that it is full of green things and has even an occasional patch of grass. Five miles from the highway is Willow Springs cabin, a water tank, and a corral used by cattlemen whose herds range the public domain adjacent to the Monument. At 8 *m.* from the junction with US 160 is a 200-foot pinnacle of hard stone (200 yds. L) that has survived erosion, and atop it is BALANCED ROCK, a 50-foot block of even harder stone, its edges extending precariously past its base. A walk of 200-odd yards (L) from this point (best conducted by guide) leads to a vantage point from which Delicate Arch and Devil's Garden can be seen to the north. At 8.5 *m.* are ADAM and EVE (L), cleanly sculptured and complete even to the apple, with Adam holding the malignant fruit to take the first bite. Near by, on a 250-foot pinnacle, EAGLE ROCK surveys the business with aquiline unconcern.

The road ends at 9 *m.,* and a ten-minute hike through the COVE OF CAVES, an amphitheater whose wind-pocked walls return echoes that double back on themselves, leads to DOUBLE ARCH, sometimes known as the "jughandles." Here, two massive arcs of streaked salmon-pink stone swing outward and downward from the common abutment of Windows Reef. The larger extends 165 feet from reef to base, and towers 156 feet above the debris below. The smaller, though not by any means dwarfed by its companion, has as yet been considered too insignificant (by a people who take the spectacular calmly) to merit measurement. It probably is no more than high enough to shelter a three or four story building (much of the estimating of dimensions in this region is done by simple triangulation, using the thumb or forefinger for transit and a guess for a base line). From Double Arch, the foot trail leads by a sculptured butte, where SATAN uncovers ominous tushes in Mephistophelean approval of the doings of Adam and Eve, and a PARADE OF ELEPHANTS marches in echelon, trunk to rump. The butte is 300 feet high, and the Entrada formation and its Carmel base are plainly discernible. A short distance beyond is SOUTH WINDOW, 65 feet high and 130 feet long, and hard by, its companion, NORTH WINDOW, of like size. Both are less smoothly sculptured than Double Arch, but both are imposing in size and regularity, and frame imposing desert vistas.

TURRET ARCH, last major formation in the Windows area, is so named because the reef in which it is found terminates in a great spearheaded tower. The arch itself is shaped something like a keyhole (of Brobdingnagian proportions) and is accompanied by a smaller window which had not in 1940 been deemed sufficiently remarkable to merit a name. A favorite trick of photographers is to walk through the South Window and snap Turret Arch in its frame. It is well to remember, when photographing arches and other eroded formations in the Monument, that the whole country is of tremendous proportions and that without some index to actual size pictures are apt to be disappointing. The most common method, of course, is to include human figures in the picture.

COURTHOUSE TOWERS

The Windows section is in a reef that stands out 300 to 400 feet above the desert; the Courthouse Towers section lies in a system of canyons cut as deep below the desert. It is best reached by foot trail from US 160, 4.5 *m.* north of Moab, which transcends the north wall of Moab Valley and descends into PARK AVENUE, the main scenic route through the section. The trail offers no difficult climbs, though it is impossible to enter the canyon of Park Avenue except at its head. The main scenic route leads along a continuous slab of Entrada sandstone from 150 to 300 feet high, perfectly vertical and intricately eroded. Only the more spectacular forms had been named in 1940. SAUSAGE ROCK, the first of the named forms, is a balanced and symmetrical pinnacle some 40 feet high. Northward from it the trail works through wind-carved piles to UNJOINED ROCK, an undercut block of stone 20 feet thick, which overlooks the canyon from its wall 300 feet above, and to the THREE GOSSIPS, who take form at the top of a fin 400 feet high and no more than 50 feet thick at the base. Here also is THE ORGAN, a V-shaped fin, knife-thin at the top, and 700 feet high. The continuous fin that walls in Park Avenue terminates at SHEEP ROCK, and permits a view of the La Sal Mountains southeastward and the Windows section to the north. The trail continues about half a mile into COURTHOUSE WASH, passing two unnamed arches, and bringing up against the sheer north wall of the wash. Here are visible the battlemented and towered piles from which the section takes its name.

KLONDIKE BLUFFS

The Klondike Bluffs section was in 1940 the least known portion of the Monument. Cowboys report that it is impossible to get a horse more than fifty feet into the area anywhere, but a good foot trail leads to two points of interest. The Bluffs are a jungle of salmon-hued sandstone, not very large in area, but endless in variation. One sculptured butte discloses JOSEPH SMITH, the Mormon Prophet, at the moment of his discovery of the Golden Plates, from which he translated the Book of Mormon. Into another butte the wind has carved beautifully symmetrical TOWER ARCH. Trails have been proposed for the Bluffs which will make them more accessible.

DEVILS GARDEN

Devils Garden, which contains sixty-four of the Monument's eighty-one known arches, is the largest and most complex section of the Monument. It extends along a continuous sandstone ridge, eroded into jungles of upright fins, huge amphitheaters with sinuous interconnecting passageways, and wind-gnarled monoliths. Small parks with sweetwater springs are secreted here and there, surrounded by vertical slabs of sandstone, and sometimes joined to natural "slickrock" corrals that are used by cattlemen at branding time. It is distinctly a foot and horseback region. Those who know the Garden say it is impossible to get lost in it, because "you have to come out the way you go in." The lower portion, known as the FIERY FURNACE, is so rough and broken up, with abrupt walls and ledges, that it has been but cursorily explored. However, according to the Park Service, it contains many arches and windows and "other formations that are among the finest examples of wind erosion in the world," and trails are planned that will open it to visitors not equipped with the impedimenta of mountain climbing.

The most frequently-taken hike into Devil's Garden leaves the Salt Valley road 13 *m.* east of its junction with US 160, traverses the eastern slope of Salt Valley to the base of the Garden, and ascends to a point beneath ARCH-IN-THE-MAKING, high in the cliff face. Here an immense block has been wedged from the wall of sandstone by the expanding action of ice, and wind-driven sand has already begun its work of chipping through the cavity. Northward, the trail follows the cliff for six miles, passing forty-five arches on the way, only a few of which are named. PINE TREE ARCH, half a mile beyond Arch-in-the-Making, is 30 feet wide and 60 feet high, and takes its name from a hardy pine that grows immediately beneath it. HOLE-IN-THE-WALL, another half mile northward, is high in the cliff face and commands a wide sweep of desert, a kind of Gargantuan peephole.

LANDSCAPE ARCH, near mid-point of the hike, is perhaps the most spectacular formation in the region. Its slender ribbon of banded black and salmon stone, only a few feet in thickness, has a length of 291 feet, and is 118 feet above the canyon floor. Its span is believed to be the longest in the Americas. There are those, seeing it and the warm-hued desert vista it frames, who are content to turn back without further exploration. Most others push on through scored corridors to DOUBLE-O ARCH, a pair of windows arranged in double-deck—as if to keep alive an appetite jaded by mere single windows. The last eroded form in the Garden that bears a name is DARK ANGEL, a towering and ominous creation that might have been done by Gothic gargoyle-carvers. The monolith looks out southward, brooding over a kind of solidified Pandemonium, whereof Harry Reed says, "You can almost smell the brimstone."

DELICATE ARCH

In Delicate Arch section there is but one arch of any consequence, yet it is probably the most popular section with return visitors. Salt Valley road terminates at Turnbow's cabin, a specimen of frontier log-and-mud-chink architecture almost completely identified with the ground on which it stands. From the cabin, the west buttress of Delicate Arch is visible against the skyline. The trail begins in the canyon bottom, ascends from it after a quarter of a mile, and climbs across slickrock to the top of the canyon wall. Below, in a shallow depression, its sides rising like those of an irregular saucer, is a platform that rises almost as high as the walls, and atop it, alone and sharp against the sky, is Delicate Arch. Descent into the bowl and the climb up the platform is slow but not dangerous. The slickrock is truly "slick," and when it catches the slanted rays of the sun in its wind-made whorls, it spatters the light almost as flint does. The arch can be made to serve splendidly as a frame for the La Sal Mountains, for Tukuhnikivatz, and for the Colorado River country between.

Bryce Canyon National Park

Highway Approach: Via State 12, turning east from US 89 seven miles south of Panguitch.

Season: Open all year. Road south of Inspiration Point usually closed by snow, November-April. Bryce Canyon Lodge open May 30-September 30. Cabin camp and cafeteria open about May 15-Oct. 20. Free public camp ground open about May 15-Oct. 30; longer if weather permits. Camps and lodges adjacent to park are open all year.

Administrative Offices: Administered jointly with Zion National Park. Address: Superintendent, Zion National Park, Utah. Information obtainable from rangers or museum.

Admission: Combined admission price for Bryce Canyon and Zion national parks, $1 per car and $1 per trailer. Garage service at Bryce Canyon Lodge.

Railroad and Bus Service: By rail, to Cedar City on the Union Pacific or to Marysvale on the Denver and Rio Grande Western, thence by motor bus to the Park. Rim Road trip in Bryce, $3. Union Pacific motor bus transportation to Bryce, Zion, Cedar Breaks and North Rim of Grand Canyon available from Cedar City. For rates, inquire of railroad passenger agent, Utah Parks Company, Cedar City, or at information office in Park.

Saddle Horses and Guides: Horses in park, $1.50 for two hours or less; $5 for eight hours. Escorted trips daily to Bryce Natural Bridge, $5. Half-day trips into canyon, $3. Special guides, if available, $3 for half-day, $5 for day. Riding clothes rented at lodge.

Airplane Service: Small airport for private planes at junction of State 54 and State 12. Charter trips available from Las Vegas, Nevada, with landing on North Rim of Grand Canyon. Trips booked by United Air Lines and Thompson Flying Service, Salt Lake City.

Accommodations: Free camping area open about April 15-Nov. 15. Cabins from $2.50 to $8.25 per day, according to number. Meals and groceries available in park. Cabins and lodge also at entrance of park.

Climate, Clothing and Equipment: Cool to chilly evenings, days may be quite warm; dress accordingly. In winter, low temperatures and high winds, too cold for winter camping. Lodge carries camera supplies, groceries, curios, and Indian handicrafts. Bring own camera, comfortable clothes, and hiking shoes.

Medical Service: Registered nurse in attendance at Lodge. Dentist at Panguitch.

Warnings and Regulations: Carry chains in winter. In early spring, trails may be slightly washed out before repairs are made. Drive carefully, especially at intersections and viewpoints. Parking permitted in designated areas, and for short periods on roadside. Picnicking and lunching permitted only in public auto camp. Picking of flowers or defacing trees and rocks strictly prohibited.

Recreational Facilities: Conducted hikes over several trails daily. Inquire time and starting points from rangers or information office at Museum. Automobile caravans led free from Bryce Canyon Museum by ranger-naturalist each day, summer, 10 A.M. and 2 P.M. Illustrated lectures at lodge and entertainment by student personnel nightly. Frequent special programs, campfire lectures, etc. Bryce is magnificent for color photography.

Communication: Post office and express service, telegraph and long distance telephone at Bryce Canyon Lodge. Address, when lodge is open, Bryce Canyon National Park, Utah.

BRYCE CANYON NATIONAL PARK, covering 55 square miles, is really not a canyon, but a series of "breaks" in fourteen enormous amphitheaters extending down a thousand feet through the pink and white limestones of the Paunsaugunt Plateau. Neither the English, nor perhaps any other language is sensitive and various enough in distinctions of form and color to give more than an obtuse characterization of this amazing area. The best Paiute Indians could do was to call the area *Unka timpe-wa-wince-pock-ich,* which means "red-rocks-standing-like-men-in-a-bowl-shaped-canyon." In regard to colors, it is said that sixty tints have been recognized; and in regard to form, it can be said that almost every conceivable shape can be found in the myriad of fantastic figures. Bryce Canyon is popular with tourists, accommodating well over 100,000 each year.

The entire park area, plus some thirty miles of the Pink Cliffs, can be seen from Rainbow Mountain at the southern end of the Park. In addition, there are magnificent views across the "land of the purple sage" to Navaho Mountain, 80 miles to the east, and to the Kaibab Plateau and Trumbull Mountain to the south, the latter 99 miles distant. The Kaiparowits Plateau, the largest unknown and unexplored area left in the United States, is to the east and southeast.

Although chiefly known for its scenic and geological interest, Bryce has fairly abundant wildlife, of which the most common large animal is the Rocky Mountain mule deer. Coyotes are often heard. Bobcat tracks and signs of mountain lion are frequently observed after rain or snow. Small animals such as porcupine, marmot, chipmunk and gray squirrel are seen in abundance. Bird life includes crossbills, Clark nutcrackers, and gray jays, commonly known as "camp robbers."

Zion is entered from the floor, with trails leading to the rims; Bryce is entered at the rim with trails leading to the floor. The Rim Road, called the most colorful twenty miles in the world, is a misnomer because only in a very few places does it approach the rim, but parking places are provided and numerous short hikes can be taken to the rim at the north and south ends of the park. All the trails are relatively short and of easy grade. At appointed hours, there are short lectures on geology, and a guide-naturalist leads the most popular trail tour. Near the public campground is a museum with exhibits of flora and fauna of the park.

Predominant forms in Bryce are domes, spires, and temples; predominant colors are red, pink and cream. The first adjectives that come to mind are possibly grotesque, bizarre, and weird. Like Cedar Breaks, the Bryce and other amphitheaters can be regarded as the workshops of ancient sculptors of gigantic size and ambition, who were defeated by the splendor of their craftsmanship and left it unfinished; or as great tubes of paint that have exuded from the canyon floors and solidified; as the ruins of an ancient city; or as the graphic representation of a magnificently insane mind.

Zion is chiefly Grecian in its architecture; Bryce at first glance seems to be rampantly Gothic. It is Gothic in its unrestrained profusion of decoration, its apparent allegory and symbolism, its world of monsters and grotesque beasts which fill the capitals, grin from gargoyles and corbels, and look across the parapets. Less obviously, it also is Gothic in its roofless interiors, which are forests of slender stone piers, engaged like pilasters or detached like columns. That Zion is classic and Bryce wildly romantic is clear at a glance. But close study demands more than a similitude with the Gothic. In the overwhelming picture of gorgeous ruins, the larger structures often bear striking resemblances to cathedrals, to castles and temples; and among the smaller ones are lions couchant, gargoyles, dragons, idols and heathen gods, limboes and purgatories and torture chambers, nave and architrave, pagoda and pantheon and mosque. Much of the statuary seems to be imperfect only because it has been unprotected for ages against wind and weather, and many of the architectural forms seem to have fallen only from disuse. Many cliffs and bluffs, walls and palisades, do not suggest the workmanship of human hands, but there are shafts and bulkheads, capitals and entablatures that look like the craftsmanship of ancient workmen. A turret or newel or facade resembles the work of a forgotten genius, but side by side with them are forms that seem to be the crude efforts of the most primitive art. Much of the handiwork has crumbled, but some of it has been surprisingly fine and durable. Here is a wainscot, there a stuccoed wall, yonder a lacquered capital, a mansard roof, or a plastered arcade, that have withstood the ravages of time. The columns and pillars and colonnades, the steeples and spires, the windows and arches and doorways, have suffered more. Many have crumbled and fallen. Others are so gouged and eroded that they look more like enormous segmented reptiles of stone stood on end than examples of chaste and perfect art.

Close and prolonged study disabuses the mind of Gothic likeness, except in the general and panoramic aspect, and finds more definite similarities with the architecture of other peoples and times. The Egyptian is more apt, for here are the monstrous figures in the Great Temple of Ipsambul or Amen-Ra, and there are ancient subterranean grotto temples with the earth-roof cleared away. The Wall of Windows more than faintly resembles the Basilica of Constantine. The final appraisal comes to this, that in these amphitheaters are types of all periods and kinds of architecture from the most savage to the most civilized. A Roman entablature or a Doric column may be neighbor to the ruins of a Coptic church or a pagan altar. A Romanesque column stands in the foreground of a cliff dwelling or a rococo wall. Perhaps the adjective that most fully sums up the area is megalithic; for here indeed are thousands of monuments made up of great stones; and here is cromlech and menhir, trilithon and cyclolith, of remarkable perfection.

In coloring, not least astonishing are the changes that come with the changes in light. This is especially so on a cloudy day, when the sun alternately appears and disappears. A group of monuments may in one moment be a dull orange and in the next a brilliant yellow. A sullen red statue of a heathen god becomes almost vermilion; golden dunes flash as if a carload of diamonds had been scattered upon them; and a shrouded wall stands forth in blinding glory. The colors not only shift in tints with morning, noon or evening sun, or after dusk; the shapes grow and diminish in size, become invested with new meanings and symbolisms. By moonlight, deep shadows set brilliant white spires aglow with a light that is almost phosphorescent. When the morning sun lights up the canyon, it resembles a huge bowl of glowing embers.

Fifty-odd million years of geological history is covered in the book of the rocks at Bryce, tracing the earth's history since the Cretaceous Period, or Reptile Age. Not least astonishing is the fact that the story goes on today; older forms are crumbling, new ones appear. The rim of the canyon is receding at a rate that undermines trees, some of which cling precariously with roots exposed. At times, Bryce was covered by the sea; at times, broad rivers flowed across it, at still other times it was swept by hot desert winds. A great block of the Pink Cliffs was raised from near sea level to a high altitude, steepening the pitch of the streams, causing them to flow and erode more rapidly. Running water, frost and rain, ground water and chemical agencies active through eons carried billions of tons of ground-up rock to the Colorado.

The Paiutes say in a legend that Bryce was built as a city for the people of Coyote—the birds, animals, lizards, and those that looked like humankind. The Coyote people displeased Coyote because they worked too long beautifying their city. Coyote was angry, and he turned over the paints they were using, and he turned the people all to stone. They are still standing there, stone rows of them. And their faces are painted with the war paint they were using when Coyote was angry and threw it in their faces.

The Kanarra Cattle Company and several sheepmen used the plateau adjacent to Bryce for grazing in the early seventies, but the first permanent settler was Ebenezer Bryce, pioneer cattleman, who took up a homestead in the fall of 1875. When asked about the canyon to which Bryce had given his name, he made the classic remark, "Well, it's a hell of a place to lose a cow."

The first person to cross the park in a wagon was Orley Bliss, who traveled over the mountain near the present highway leading to Tropic in 1875. "The hill was rough and steep, both rear wheels were locked, that was not enough. John Davis, then working for the Kanarra Cattle Company, tied a rope to the rear axle and to the horn of his saddle. The mule he was riding was a good cow mule. The old mule hung back serving as a brake, and in that way the wagon was lowered to the bottom."

The earliest written description of Bryce was by T. C. Bailey, U. S.

Deputy Surveyor, in 1876: "There are thousands of red, white, purple and vermilion rocks, of all sizes, resembling sentinels on the Walls of Castles; monks and priests with their robes, attendants, cathedrals and congregations. There are deep caverns and rooms resembling ruins of prisons, Castles, Churches, with their guarded walls, battlements, spires and steeples, niches and recesses, presenting the wildest and most wonderful scene that the eye of man ever beheld, in fact it is one of the wonders of the world." Bailey "lost" two days at Bryce Canyon, looking for his large meerschaum pipe, which was usually chained to him. The hunt was unsuccessful, but the pipe turned up several years later.

Ruben C. Syrett purchased 160 acres of land adjacent to Bryce in 1916, and made homestead entry on another 160 acres within the present park. In the spring of 1920, after he received patent for his homestead, he built a small lodge and cabins near Sunset Point and began entertaining tourists. The same year he was made the first postmaster of Bryce Canyon. Water was hauled for three miles to the camp. In the fall of 1923 the Utah Parks Company purchased his improvements, and the following year he opened Rubys Inn. Today he operates a large dude ranch just outside the Park, and regales the tourists with tall tales.

Bryce Canyon National Park was established in 1928. By authority of President Hoover, the park was greatly enlarged in 1931 to its present 35,240 acres. The Rim Road was completed in 1934. Not until it was extensively advertised in the early 1930's by the Union Pacific Railroad, who built lodges and provided transportation, did Bryce become known, even within the State.

BRYCE CANYON ROADS, TRAILS AND VIEWS

State 12 branches eastward from US 89 at a point 7 miles south of Panguitch (*see Tour 2c*). Fourteen miles east of this point State 12 makes a junction with State 22 and State 54. Turning south on State 12 the highway enters Bryce Canyon National Park. At 3 *m.* is the official checking station, where a $1 fee is paid for entrance to Bryce and Zion National Parks.

A road leads L. 1.1 *m.* to FAIRYLAND, a huge amphitheater, most beautiful in early morning light. Fancy can run riot here and still be at a loss, but the character of the area can be suggested by saying that it is a three-dimensional Arabian Nights. In the foreground are walls and columns, rose-colored below and with cream colored capitals; in the center is a huge crumbling monument that looks like a thousand tons of disintegrating copper; and beyond to the right and left are acres of ruins. They stand in barbarously eroded abutments and terraces, their gaunt and wind-beaten skeletons softened by the play of sunlight upon the deep rose and red, and yellow and gold, of the stone.

Many formations that stand alone look for all the world, especially at a distance, like the images of heathen deities; for time and erosion have carved many a likeness of the human face in this amphitheater. A hundred yards down the trail there is the monumental figure of a parent and child, and totems so fierce that they would frighten almost anything except another totem. The eastern rim gives way to soft ravines and ridges in alternating strata of tinted chalk and powdered gold. Far beyond, in the east, and not within the Park, is a mountain that should be viewed under the evening sun, when its main bulk is layer upon layer of softly luminous colors, above which is superimposed a crest of evergreens, like a purple reef down the sky.

This part of Bryce is called Fairyland. All in all, it seems to be a most appropriate home for Snow White and the Seven Dwarfs. A description, by Maurice Howe, carries out the fairy tale motif:

> Bryce, where the quick dawn caught the goblins and ghosts while rois-tering on the pinnacles and froze them into stone ere they could hide away in the shadows.
> Bryce, where friendly little gnomes invited one to enter a gigantic toy-land, where merry "children," carved in crimson stone, beckoned to wander in a world of dreams, weird and enchanting.
> Bryce, where Mother Nature's subtle fingers wrought flames in stone and topped them with angels, snowy white; then sensing incompleteness, made all the beast and birds in wondrous art and spilled the paint pots of the gods upon her handiwork, scattered seeds of pine and cedar, and left the scene for man to contemplate.
> Bryce, ten thousand eons in the making, where frost and wind and rain labored for ten million lifetimes to chisel out each grotesque statue. Amaz-ing Bryce—a poem—an artist—a treasure of form and color.
> Bryce—a sunset—petrified!

PARK HEADQUARTERS, 4.4 *m.,* has in its vicinity a public camp-ground, a cafeteria, cabins, store, museum, Bryce Canyon Lodge, and a garage. The Rim Road leads south, but there are well-marked turn-offs to the principal views, parking spaces, and short trails to the rim.

From SUNRISE POINT, on the trail east of the lodge, the eastern view reveals a gently rolling landscape that looks like fields of spun gold. Its structures are more massive than those of Fairyland; the great walls, saturated with red, are in sharp contrast with monuments that seem to be of white chalk. The sculpturing here is more gigantic, is less barbarous, though there are many lean shafts, emaciated bulk-heads, and weirdly lacquered crags. In the foreground the erosion is more spectacularly purposeless than on the far side, where huge castles need only windows and doors to be complete. Glasses show that portions of the roofs have fallen in, staircases and mezzanine floors are crumbling, vestibules are too rugged for human occupancy, and corridors have lost most of their vaulted ceiling, but the excellent stucco of the walls is intact. Some of the roof fragments seem to be elaborately adorned with cupolas and steeples, but the walls below have a chaste restraint. The white formations, when brought close, are seen to be not a part of the castles, but silent figures who stand or kneel upon the battlements. In the south, there is a striking figure called Thor's Hammer, but it looks more like an Egyptian priest, sitting on a throne and facing the rising sun, with an enormous stone crown on his head.

SUNSET POINT, half a mile south of Sunrise Point, offers a broader panorama. The immediate foreground of Sunrise Point is a series of massive welded structures, with great segmented columns of yellow and orange rising to a garden of ragged spires on the left, and to orchid and pale-rose pediments on the right. The columns support capitals that look like solidified cream. Directly below 'Sunset Point is the Hammer. On the right, the chasm is full of ruins. Down below is WALL STREET, a long, narrow corridor, and on the right of it are acres of brilliant upthrusts like a field of stalagmites. Just to the left, the well-preserved ruins of a castle embody a half-dozen savage architectural motifs and cap them all with three colossal columns. The walls here are honeycombed as if bees as large as dragons had worked in them for ages. The colors are rose and orange and yellow in a number of tints.

Beyond, to left and right, the forms approach the Grecian, with more severe lines, leaner columns, and more austere buttresses. The far view is deceptive; when brought close with glasses, this area is a menagerie of statuary, idols of men and beasts standing on picturesquely extravagant pyramids and escarpments. In the far left center is FAIRY CASTLE. For some, the forms much more closely resemble a cemetery, with a magnificent mausoleum in the center, flanked on either side by rows of white headstones. There is probably no lovelier view in the Park than these monuments upon a hill.

INSPIRATION POINT, a mile south, offers the most comprehensive and overwhelming view. On the right is the Wall of Windows; below it is an area of old-rose battlements, adorned with rows of pale mauve spires, and far beyond is the cavernous southern wall reaching from the floor to the rim. Most spectacular is the view toward Sunrise Point— for here is Bryce in all its barbarous glory. The first impression may be of a mountainside of thousands of segmented columns; the second of countless jointed monuments standing row on row from the floor of the canyon to the rim; but the third and most satisfying summary is of all the finest cycloliths of ancient times, brought to this amphitheater to be preserved unto posterity.

The Rim Road proceeds southward to other views including BRYCE POINT, RAINBOW POINT, PARIA VIEW, and BRYCE NATURAL BRIDGE, a ragged arch in yellow and orange and gold; but after the view from Inspiration Point, everything southward is anticlimax.

Trails: All of the trails to the floor are easy and safe. Though saddle horses are available, and horseback trips are made daily during the summer to Peek-a-boo Canyon, Campbell Canyon, and Fairyland, by far the most popular trip is by foot. It begins at Sunset Point and follows the Comanche and Navaho trails; a naturalist-guide conducts this hike daily. Of interest at closer range on this trip are Wall

Street, the Temple of Osiris, Queen Victoria, The Pope, and the Elephant followed by the Wise Man. The climb out of Wall Street, over what the guide calls thirty-five zags and thirty-four zigs, is alone worth the trip.

Capitol Reef National Monument

Highway Approach: 71.3 m. SE. of Sigurd on State 24.
Season: Open all year, but best in the late spring or fall.
Administrative Offices: Superintendent, Zion National Park. Acting custodian at Fruita.
Admission: Free.

Accommodations: Tourist rooms at Loa; rooms and cabins at Torrey; limited ranch accommodations at Fruita and Notom; unimproved campsites in Monument. Note: The Monument is undeveloped for tourists and it is advisable to make reservations in advance.

Transportation: Automobile or horseback. No direct bus service to Monument. Nearest railroad connection via Denver and Rio Grande Western to Sigurd. Mail stage Mon., Wed., Fri., Sigurd to Fruita.
Climate, Clothing, Equipment: Monument undeveloped (1940), carry own camping equipment, including food and supplies; none on sale in Monument. Meals and gasoline in Fruita. Wear rough clothing, cord rubber soles, and gloves for climbing. Unimproved and unmarked trails—use guide if venturing far off road through Capitol Reef. Take camera with extra film. Field glasses desirable and fishing tackle for use in Powell or Fishlake National Forests near by.
Post Office: Fruita via Torrey.
Medical and Dental Service: Loa or Richfield.
Communication and Express: Long distance telephone at Loa. Express Office at Sigurd.
Speed Limits: Road east of Torrey rough in spots; safe when not driven at excessive speed. Road through Capitol Wash is bottom of the gorge, with large rocks.

Naturalist Service and Information: Acting custodian at Fruita. Information from Bishop E. P. Pectol and Charles W. Lee, Torrey; Dr. A. L. Inglesby and W. C. Chestnut, Fruita.

Recreational Facilities: Hiking, climbing, horseback riding. Excellent fishing, hunting, and camping in adjacent national forests. Color photography. Pack trips into least known and least explored area in United States for those accustomed to hardships of desert travel with dry camp every other night.
Warnings and Regulations: In case of rare desert cloudburst, *GET OUT OF DRY WASHES IMMEDIATELY*—there may be ten feet of flood water in half an hour. Guide necessary for trips far off main trails or road. Do not remove artifacts, petrified wood, or plant life, including wild flowers. Be careful in climbing—the walls are sheer, rocks are slippery, footholds none too sure. Check mechanical condition of car and tires before trip. *Guides and Horses* available at ranches adjacent to Monument at Torrey, and in Fruita. Varying rates. Inquire at Fruita for available guides.

CAPITOL REEF NATIONAL MONUMENT preserves erosive formations—steep scarps, goblin rocks, carved pinnacles and gorges—that give it the impression of having combined the fantasy of Bryce and the grandeur of Zion National Parks, with more color than either. It also contains numerous archeological remains, and petrified forests. The great temples and walls resemble those in Zion, the Monument has huge arches, and the contrasting colors run in streamers, bands, and layers, both vertically and horizontally. There are gorgeous blues and greens here, in broad stripes; purple and orchid and lavender give remarkable softness to the walls; and every primary color is visible in any one of a dozen different formations.

The reef, which gives its name to the Monument, fits a definition, popularly used in the West, for an upthrust area with a cliff face. The great ridge of rock, 20 miles long, stands high above its surroundings, buttressed with talus slopes. White Navaho sandstone domes, topping reddish brown Wingate sandstone, supposedly resemble the National Capitol at Washington.

Since the cataclysm that heaved the crust of the earth sixteen thousand feet high, above the present 11,000-foot Aquarius Plateau, erosion has gnawed perpetually at the high peaks. The strata of Capitol Reef lie in relatively the same position they occupied before the disturbance, but they are deeply gashed by Frémont Gorge and its branches, Grand Gorge, Capitol Gorge, Sheets Gulch, and Pleasant Creek. The reef itself is a part of what geologists call the Water Pocket Fold or Flexure, so named because of numerous natural "tanks," which hold thousands of gallons of ground water in the spring. Natives attribute construction of the tanks to the Indians, but they are geological formations, possibly great potholes pounded out by waterfalls after the upthrust. A man could die of thirst within sight of rocks containing a "tank" without knowing it was there or being able to reach water without a guide. Triassic and Jurassic strata—of the "Age of Reptiles"—are exceptionally well displayed, and numerous marine fossils, agatized wood, and jasper have been found.

Petrified forests that flourished millions of years ago abound in the Monument. The area north of the road from Cathedral Cliffs to Chimney Rock, about 26 square miles, is rich in petrified and fossilized remains. Petrified wood fragments run from small twigs to seventy-five-foot lengths, five and one-half feet in diameter. One tree, in the Circle Cliffs about 30 airline miles south of Fruita, discovered by Charlie Lee, is claimed to be 185 feet long and 12.5 feet in diameter. Standing petrified trees have been found, but most have fallen. Several have been broken up by ranchers getting rid of "rocks," or looking for uranium.

The following Paiute legend, gathered by William R. Palmer, and published in the *Utah Historical Quarterly* for April, 1933, gives the Indian's theory of the origin of petrified forests:

> Tobats is the great god. . . . Tobats made the world. He made the Indians and put fish in the water. . . . He made all the animals.
> Shinob is the second great god. He is brother to Tobats. . . . Tobats is old, he was always old, but Shinob is young. . . .

Tobats made tu-weap, the ground, and timp-i-ah, the rocks, and kaib-a, the mountains, and pau, the water. . . .

Shinob looked over the world that Tobats had made and said, "It is good. It is strong. It is pretty. It is useless." Tobats answered, "It is not done. . . . I will make, mav, the trees. I will make flowers. I will make grass. I will make willows and brush. I will make everything." Tobats did as he said. He made them all of stone so they would endure forever. Then Tobats made Nung-wa, the Indians, and all the animals. . . .

Shinob came and looked. . . . Shinob went to Tobats and said, "Tu-weap is very beautiful but all the animals must die. They can drink only water. There is no food for them to eat. They are very poor. The Indians are very unhappy. The wind blows and the rain and snow falls and the living things are very cold. There is no fire. They cannot make houses to shelter them. The willows break when they would make baskets. Your stone trees bear no fruit. The living things can only eat each other. It is not good."

Then Tobats said to Shinob, "Go to tu-weap, the earth, and give the Indians fire. Put fire in everything. . . . Put water also in the trees and in the brush and the willows and the grass so they will bend and not break. . . ."

Shinob did as he was told. He came and called from far off to all the tribes of Indians to send men to him for fire—ten strong men from every tribe.

It was done . . . and as the Indians came the god handed to each group a stick with fire on one end to carry back to their tribe. . . .

When the Indians started homeward, Un-nu-pit, the devil found them. His evil spirits fell upon them and tried to steal the fire or to kill it. . . .

During this great struggle ashes and sparks were flying everywhere. Whatever was touched by them partook of Shinob's fire. . . . The trees and willows and grass and brush caught most of the sparks. They now burn best. Tu-weap got the ashes and not much fire. Tim-i-ah, the rocks, locked the fire up. Hit them together quick and they let a little out and then shut it up tight again. . . .

In the big fight . . . a few trees here and there escaped the touch of flying sparks. You may find them yet in the old forests. Some are standing and some are fallen and broken but they still are stone. . . .

Petrified trees in the Capitol Reef area recall Jim Bridger's celebrated "tall" tale about Yellowstone Park, which applies equally well here: "They was peetrified trees a-growing, with peetrified birds on 'em a-singin' peetrified songs." Bridger also told about riding his horse on the level right across a canyon and concluded afterward that the force of gravity was "peetrified" in that place.

Archeologically, Capitol Reef and its adjacent territory are exceptionally rich. The small museums in Torrey owned by Bishop Ephraim P. Pectol, and by Charles D. Lee, grandson of John D. Lee, contain artifacts found in this area (*see Tour 2A*). Prehistoric Basketmaker and Pueblo peoples have carved petroglyphs and painted pictographs on the cliff walls. Some of them were the prehistoric ancestors of the Hopi, who built crude, small adobe and stick granaries; because they are too small to admit an average-sized person, the mistaken notion has arisen that pygmies lived here. Many of the more accessible sites were looted by "pot hunters" before passage of the Antiquities Act of 1910. On the perpendicular cliff walls, backing up the green of peach orchards at Fruita, are petroglyphs representing sheep, serpents, and human figures. Many less accessible ethnological sites remain undisturbed. Perhaps a lone cowboy has tied a lariat to a cedar and swung himself down for a look into a dwelling, but usually he has left things as he found them.

In 1875 Mormon pioneers established a small settlement on the river which Major J. W. Powell first called the Dirty Devil and later renamed the Frémont. Fruita was settled in 1878 by Franklin D. Young. Other settlers followed, homesteading the river bottoms.

Bishop Ephraim P. Pectol, of Torrey, becoming interested in the "Wayne Wonderland" as a potential park area in 1910, induced Robert Adams, a photographer, to make the first pictures. With the election of Joseph S. Hickman, a teacher at Wayne High School, to the legislature, a 160-acre site at Fruita was set aside as a State park by the legislature of 1925-26. Dr. J. E. Broaddus, writer and lecturer of Salt Lake City, did much to publicize the region. In 1933, Bishop Pectol was elected to the legislature and memorialized Wayne Wonderland to Congress as a national park, a move strongly endorsed by Secretary of War George H. Dern. The Monument was set apart in 1937, largely through the efforts of Bishop Pectol, Dr. Broaddus, and Dr. A. L. Inglesby of Fruita, an authority on the lesser known portions of Utah.

Capitol Reef and the Wayne Wonderland have had many colorful characters, including Charlie Gibbons, of Greenriver, the cowboy who captured the stallion "Wildfire" in Zane Grey's novel of the same name. Many old-timers recall the "Wild Bunch" who hid out in Robbers Roost during the last of the nineteenth century, and who used Capitol Gorge as one of the main outlets for the "Outlaw Empire" of San Rafael Swell. Exploration continued in the Monument early in 1940, when a hitherto undiscovered natural bridge was found three and a half miles southeast of Fruita, by Owen Hibbert, W. C. Chesnut, and Fred Fagagreen.

Desert and semi-desert plants grow plentifully in Capitol Reef National Monument. In late April, May, and June, several dozen varieties of hardy desert wildflowers are in bloom. Several varieties of cacti continue in flower through most of the summer. Among numerous other forms of plant life reported from the Monument and vicinity are cedar or juniper, desert primrose, red, yellow, and green cactus roses, Indian paintbrush, Spanish bayonet, desert geraniums, sagebrush, and prickly pear. Areas that seem barren often have sagebrush, rabbit brush, saltbush, blackbush and greasewood, clumps of gramma grass, and an occasional yucca.

While there are few rattlesnakes, bullsnakes and gartersnakes are plentiful in the Monument. Small animal life includes field mice, cliff mice, "trade" rats—which usually leave something for everything they take, according to old-timers—ground squirrels, chipmunks, coyotes, and a number of species of lizards. Herds of wild horses formerly ranged the area, but of late years are seldom seen. Piñon jays, sage sparrows, rock wrens, and sage thrashers are the principal birds found in the area.

CAPITOL REEF ROADS, TRAILS AND VIEWS

The best and most practicable approach to the Monument is on State 24 (*see Tour 2A*), turning east from US 89 at Sigurd. The west boundary is 71.3 *m.* southeast of Sigurd. The road is paved nearly all the way to Loa and graveled to Torrey, but east of that point it is graded dirt highway, and through Capitol Wash it is just the bottom of the gorge. Capitol Reef, first viewed from the road two miles north of Teasdale and frequently from that point into the Monument, loses its resemblance to the Capitol dome on closer approach.

An opening at the left, just as the western monument boundary is crossed, is called the HARBOR OF SANTIAGO, a genie-like transition from the SLEEPING UTE, seen just before entering the Monument. At 0.4 *m.* after crossing into the Monument, a massive red rock formation projects toward the highway, its cliff face rising precipitously for hundreds of feet above a steep talus slope of warm-hued rocks, with lavender, gray, and brown stirred in. To the right a rich red strata curves down toward the road and tips out of sight, to accent the green of orchards and fields beyond. Opposite the first house of Fruita is SERPENT'S LAST BITE (R), a writhing formation and large boulder.

FRUITA (5,418 alt.), 1.4 *m.,* an eleven-house village of many orchards, is set in a pocket surrounded by towering cliffs. Horses and guides are available for trips to Broad Arch and other points of interest in the Monument. The INGLESBY HOUSE, in Fruita, is built of logs, petrified wood, and ripple-marked sandstone. It is surrounded by a fence made entirely of great slabs of ripple-marked stone, bolted together to enclose the rich green of the garden, seeming greener than it is against the colored cliffs. Some 500 feet left of Fremont River Bridge is the mouth of COHABITATION CANYON, shortened to "Cohab" Canyon, so named because it was the hideout of polygamists and their wives after the passage of anti-polygamy laws in 1886 (*see History*). The canyon, narrow and fractured, and with a maze of side canyons, was well chosen to avoid the pursuit which failed to materialize.

Down RIVER GORGE OF FREMONT RIVER is a trail that leads to BROAD ARCH, 3 *m.* It is only a few hundred yards from Fruita in an airline but the country is so broken that the trail has to wander far around. Horses are desirable for transportation, for the river is crossed several times, and the trail is rocky. The massive arch of pink and white sandstone, 15 feet thick at the narrowest point, is 133 feet from rim to rim, and 72 feet above a line connecting its abutment bases, but is dwarfed by cliffs rising jaggedly for 2,000 feet. On the way to the bridge the trail passes a well-preserved cliff dwelling, obscure among the rocks, and a tiny natural bridge.

At 2.1 *m.* the road enters GRAND WASH, bordered by rolling red hills on the right and by castellated red and ivory-tinted cliffs to the left. The cliff bases range through green, lavender, and several shades of reddish brown.

A poor road joins State 24 (L) at 3.8 *m.,* and a car can be driven with care down the bottom of the wash into GRAND GORGE, the most beautiful canyon in the Monument. In green clay mounds (L), 0.3 *m.*, are the standing stumps of petrified trees, some of them four feet in diameter. A mile down the wash, a red cliff rises (L) perpendicularly hundreds of feet from the road, like the wall of a giant's house. Left of this cliff, and about 400 feet above the floor of the wash, is the second largest natural bridge in the Monument, usually missed without a guide. SINGING ROCK, 1.2 *m.*, is a gigantic arched grotto in the wall of the wash (R), 600 feet high and 400 feet across. The grotto, which has unusual acoustical properties, was used for dedication ceremonies at the opening of Capitol Reef National Monument in 1937.

The GREAT CURTAIN, 1.3 *m.*, on both sides of the road, is 200 feet high, its walls are smooth and glistening from top to bottom, with bands of color ranging from dark brown through red, rust, rose, orchid, lavender, pink, gold, and lemon yellow, and vertical streaks of black. One can gaze intently at the Curtain for an hour and still be astonished by the richness of its color-banding.

At 1.4 *m.* there is a view of a high white monolith on a red, cliff-banked base, bearing a remarkable likeness to the Great White Throne in Zion National Park. A court, 2.5 *m.*, completely surrounded by towering cliffs, pinnacles, and monoliths, is the extreme point that can be reached safely by car. A hike of a little more than a mile leads to the gorge of the Frémont River. The canyon is narrow beyond this court; at a distance of 400 yards, the water has cut under the cliff at the left, forming a cave about 100 feet long, 30 feet deep, and 20 feet high. Between a distance of 600 and 700 yards from the court, there is a narrow section, 15 to 20 feet wide, completely surrounded by insurmountable steep-walled cliffs, 600 feet high, and no outlet is visible—an uncomfortable spot for claustrophobiacs. At a distance of 800 yards, the walls of the gorge draw close together, leaving a passage only 15 feet wide. Beyond this point the gorge widens somewhat, and at 2,100 yards opens into the Frémont River Canyon.

Back at the junction with the main road, continuing through Grand Wash, the castellated wall continues on the left for several miles, stained with softer tints of red, purple, orchid, old rose, pink, pale green, and delicate blue. On the right are rolling red hills.

At 8.4 *m.* is the junction with a poor dirt road (R), which leads to FLORAL RANCH, 2.6 *m.* In this arid land, with water from Pleasant Creek, the proprietor has grown squashes weighing as much as ninety-two pounds. On and around the ranch are Indian petroglyphs, pictographs, and ancient dwellings. Petrified wood specimens in the area include a log, two feet thick, with an exposed length of forty-five feet; and another log, six feet in diameter and eighteen feet long.

CAPITOL GORGE is entered at 8.5 *m.* between widely separated NORTH PORTAL (L) and SOUTH PORTAL (R), castellated formations set high on sloping purple bases, their summits 1,200 feet above the canyon floor. Small pieces of petrified wood are often found here. The gorge is walled by red and cream-colored cliffs, hundreds of feet high, and throughout this portion of the drive there is a tremendous variety of cliffs, monoliths, and pinnacles, all magnificently colored.

The THREE WISE OWLS (R), 11 *m.*, are pinnacles of red and gray stone. Half a mile farther, the canyon pinches in to a width of only eighteen feet, its walls rising an abrupt thousand feet. Late July and August cloudbursts, rushing off the non-porous landscape, sometimes millrace through the NARROWS, tumbling boulders weighing tons. They would do the same to an automobile. *GET OUT* OF THE

NARROWS AT THE FIRST SIGN OF RAIN. Ahead, through the Narrows, can be seen a scarlet-topped mountain rising three thousand feet above its base, highest point in the Monument. This, with its massive golden cliffs, is the GOLDEN THRONE.

At the east end of the Narrows, 11.9 *m.,* natural tanks (L) in the rock were used as a watering place by Indians. Here also is a small natural bridge, with a span of ten or twelve feet. The tanks and bridge are reached by steps carved out by the Indians so long ago that they have since been worn by erosion. Eastward from this point, the cliff walls are lower, still many-colored, but more like massive quarried stone blocks than natural temples. As the road emerges from the gorge at 13.5 *m.* it reaches the desert, where hills roll away, pink, gray, and yellow far into the east and southeast.

State 24 continues northeasterly (*see Tour 2A*) toward Greenriver.

Cedar Breaks National Monument

Highway Approaches: 20.4 m. E. of Cedar City, via State 14 to the junction with State 55; 26.8 m. W. of Long Valley Junction (on US 89), via State 14 to the junction with State 55.

Speed Limits: Not advisable to drive over 15 m.p.h.

Season: June 1-Nov. 1; highway closed by snow in winter and until late spring.

Administrative Offices: Administered jointly with Zion National Park and Bryce Canyon National Park. Address of Suprintendent: Zion National Park, Utah. Information at Lodge or from ranger-naturalists.

Admission: Free.

Medical and Dental Service: Doctor and dentist at Cedar City.

Accommodations: Cedar Breaks Lodge, operated by Utah Parks Company, June 1-Sept. 20. Cabins and meals, also housekeeping cabins. Groceries, campers supplies, gasoline, and oil available in Monument. Curio store sells magazines, films, cigarettes, etc. Public campground with water, fireplaces and fuel in Monument and at Forest Service camps near by.

Express (Baggage): Arrangements must be made with Utah Parks Company at Cedar City; trunks are not carried on motor busses. No storage charge on hand baggage or trunks checked with Union Pacific Railroad on route of ticket while the owner makes park tour. Express to Cedar City.

Transportation: Monument included in loop bus tours of Utah Parks Company. Union Pacific R.R. to Lund or Cedar City.

Climate, Clothing, Equipment: Nights cool, days may be warm; sudden temperature changes due to altitude (10,700). Stout hiking shoes and outdoor clothing, riding breeches, and puttees desirable. Serviceable gloves add to comfort in climbing or riding. Bring camera with extra film, especially color film. Field glasses useful.

Mail Service: Care of Cedar Breaks Lodge, Cedar City, Utah.

Communications: Long distance telephone and telegraph service at Cedar Breaks Lodge.

Recreational facilities: Hiking, riding, fishing near by. Hunting in season adjacent to Monument. Color photography, ranger-naturalist lectures, campfires, entertainments at Lodge.

Warnings and Regulations: Usual regulations applying to National Parks and Monuments. Narrow road from Cedar City to Cedar Breaks, climbs more than 4,000 feet in 20 miles.

CEDAR BREAKS NATIONAL MONUMENT, set aside by presidential proclamation in 1933, covers 5,837 acres in the high Markagunt Plateau. It is a vast amphitheater, almost a half-mile deep and two miles from rim to rim, enclosing several semicircular basins. Its walls are furrowed, eroded and broken into massive colored ridges radiating from the center (fitting the western definition of breaks—an abrupt, broken, and deeply eroded canyon or amphitheater), and painted like the wheel of a gigantic circus wagon. Myrtle Decker Janson writes, "Cedar Breaks displays a wilder, loftier beauty on a much wider scale than Bryce. Both are masterpieces of the marvelous sculptor and architect, erosion. Both are abysmal basins with serrated floors and millions of architectural or sculptural forms. But, Cedar Breaks is carved on larger proportions; it lacks the lacy fretwork, the intricate mazes, the labyrinths and grottoes of Bryce but surpasses Bryce in its more massive Gothic walls, and Sphynx-sized statues. It exhibits more terraces, each with precipitous alluvial fans at the base."

Although Cedar Breaks is cut from the same geological formation as Bryce, it is 2,000 feet higher. The cliffs are white or orange at the top, breaking into deep rose and coral. The Pink Cliffs here have a thickness of nearly 2,000 feet and innumerable warm shades of red predominate. Color, which caused the Indians to name Cedar Breaks, "circle-of-painted-cliffs," is the chief feature of the Monument. It blazes with reds, is sultry with yellows, blinds with sun-reflecting whites, is drenched with molten golds and orange, and in the shadows, as they lengthen toward evening, it is deep purple and cool blue.

In the alpine country surrounding the Breaks is an expansive forest free from underbrush, lush with mountain meadows and grassy parks, streams and lakes where big trout wait. A good road leads to the summit of Brian Head, 11,299 feet, highest in southwestern Utah. From its observation station, a sweeping view encompasses the country surrounding Zion and Bryce, country draining to the Colorado and reaching out to the seared Nevada desert. Large Engelmann spruce predominate in the typical timberline forest cover on the rim, which includes fir, balsam, and bristlecone (foxtail) pine, and farther down the mountain is the white-boled quaking aspen. One large bristlecone on the rim is estimated to be more than 2,000 years old. From mid-July to mid-August alpine flowers garland the mountain around the Breaks—pentstemon, lupine, bluebells, enormous white starlike columbines, and the vivid blues of fringed gentian, larkspur, and bluebonnet. Bird life is more common than in other Utah parks and mule deer are often seen. The coolness of the high forested region in the vicinity of Cedar Breaks is a welcome retreat from the summer heat of the desert regions.

CEDAR BREAKS ROADS AND VIEWS

The usual entry to Cedar Breaks is by way of Cedar City, turning eastward from US 91 on State 14 and traveling 20.4 miles to the junction with State 55. It may also be approached on improved road by turning west from US 89 at Long Valley Junction and traveling 26.8 miles west on State 14 (*see Tour 1e*). Northward on State 55 from State 14 the road passes through mountain meadows dotted with fir trees and enters Cedar Breaks National Monument. At 3.2 *m.* is the Monument checking station, and the public auto camp (R) is four-fifths of a mile farther. At 3.9 *m.* is a junction with a road. Left on this road 0.2 *m.* is the information office and museum, and

POINT SUPREME; a car can be driven to the very edge of this amazing break.

At Point Supreme, Cedar Breaks is suddenly and magnificently present. It is hard to tell whether the brilliant coloring of the Breaks or its grotesque sculpturing is the more remarkable. In the former, forty-seven tints have been counted by an artist; and in the latter, though the variety is less astonishing than in Bryce, the formations nevertheless run the gamut from cathedrals to tombstones. For those who gaze into this enormous basin, the physical aspects suggest a multitude of similes. It is surprising to find a natural amphitheater so huge and at the same time so perfect. As one gazes down upon the hundreds of columns and towers, balconies and pinnacles, arches, gateways and standing walls, it is not difficult to pretend that an ancient civilization, with an architectural taste for the Gothic, was once crowded into this huge bowl. High against the orange rim is a cream-colored shelf fashioned in a broad arc. When brought close with powerful glasses it is seen to be of remarkable perfection, as though a mason had laid it carefully stone by stone. Just beyond it, and below the rim, are soft golden flanks that lie like painted hills. The ancient builders were prodigal with their paint, and must have spilled it by the barrels. It is equally obvious that for brilliant hues they had the passion of a Titian.

Upon the next level below, and on the far side, is an area resembling a large cemetery wherein all the dead were given a monument of the same formidable size. Below these are the ruins of two gigantic structures that some might fancy as cathedrals and others as medieval castles, with their walls laid in big blocks of old rose and coral and burnt orange, their windows and doorways tumbled in. Still farther down, the structures are more crumbling still, and have the clean windswept beauty that only the ruins of once beautiful architecture can have. There are high thin walls, thin as blades, standing alone, as though the other walls had fallen and long ago disappeared. Of what was once a noble edifice, there may be left only a solitary tower or an arch or a colony of thin golden spires. So many mansions have disintegrated and fallen that the floor of the amphitheater is piled deep with ruins.

One can fancy that some prehistoric sculptor of gigantic size had his workshop in the Breaks and set out to carve from forty-seven tints in stone. Of insatiable ambition and undirected purpose, he left nothing finished, nor perhaps even fully realized what he was trying to do. In the center close to the floor is the fine Gothic arch of a medieval castle, or the entrance to a court. The Great Sculptor built the gateway, then left it standing in an isolation of its own. If glasses are used to bring the craftmanship closer, a huge bronze statue of a woman holding a babe to her left breast, with the babe's face to her left cheek, is seen to the right. The Sculptor must have liked this creation, for it is the most nearly finished piece of his stupendous graveyard of forgotten things. Centrally placed in regard to breadth and depth is a person with head bowed in prayer before an altar; and a hundred yards to the left on the same plane, is, ironically enough, an almost flawless dress-shop dummy. In the same plane, too, but far to the left, is a kneeling group. For the most part, however, the sculptor's genius seems to have been devoted to rough designs in cathedrals and castles, to promenades and minarets, to weird totems that stand row on row, to mountainside cemeteries in which everyone rests under a tombstone unsurpassed in size or splendor by his neighbor's, or to great solitary obelisks to time and the wind.

Two other points of vantage are worth while, SUNSET VIEW at 4.2 *m.* (25-yard walk L. to edge of break), and DESERT VIEW at 5.3 *m.* (two-fifths of a mile L. to the rim), but none is so impressive as Point Supreme.

For the fullest appreciation—not of his care, for he was a most careless sculptor—but of the richness of the world of Balzac done in stone, the amphitheater should be viewed at sunset, when the thousands of formations stand gloriously desolate in their ruins.

Dinosaur National Monument

Highway Approach: State 149, 7 *m.* N. of Jensen (on US 40).
Season: Open all year; best time for visit is spring or fall.
Admission: Free.
Administrative Office: Custodian's office in Monument.

Accommodations: No accommodations in Monument; hotels, camps, and cabins at Vernal, 13 *m.* W. of Jensen on US 40.

Transportation: By private car only from Jensen; bus service to Jensen.
Clothing and Equipment: Sports or outdoor clothes for spring, summer, and fall. Cord or rubber soled shoes for rock climbing. Bring camera; local film supplies doubtful. Nearest place for purchasing all equipment is Vernal; clothing, food and staples are of ranch type; prices not excessive. Unusual, seldom called for, and "dude" items are not stocked.
Post Office: At Jensen.
Medical and Dental Service: At Vernal.
Speed Limit: State 194 is an improved dirt road, good in dry weather. Drivers unfamiliar with country should not exceed 30 m.p.h., and should proceed with great care in wet weather.
Recreational Facilities: Camping, fishing, photography, hiking.
Guides and Horses: Ranchers can be hired to act as guides; fees vary from $2 to $5 per day; ranch horses $1.50 to $3 per day.
Warnings and Regulations: Do not remove or chip fossils, nor mark or deface rocks. Usual regulations governing Federal parks and monuments.

Set aside by presidential proclamation in 1915, DINOSAUR NATIONAL MONUMENT, America's most important natural display of fossilized reptile bones, includes about 78 square miles in the badlands of northeastern Utah and 247 square miles in Colorado. President Franklin D. Roosevelt increased the area to its present size in 1938. The center of activities (1940) is in Utah, seven miles north of the point where highway US 40 passes through the little town of Jensen. Here the National Park Service has a camp and a small temporary museum, and scientists expect soon to begin work in a quarry on Dinosaur Peak, to cut away the enshrouding rock and exhibit, in Borglumesque bas-relief, the bones of strange reptiles that roamed this country millions of years ago.

The quarry is approximately 40 feet high, 400 feet long, and 40 feet wide. No bones have been removed for several years, but fractures in the rock have been cemented to protect the fossils from weathering. An adequate structure will be built along the cliff face to house the exhibit of dinosaur remains. Although the quarry is the dominant feature of Dinosaur National Monument, the museum, a quarter of a mile west, contains a collection of geological specimens. Among them are dinosaur bones scarred by the teeth of ancient carnivores, smooth rocks which the huge reptiles are believed to have swallowed to help them grind their food, imprints of leaves, fossilized shells, volcanic rock, soft coal, and dinosaur teeth so perfect that even the nerve sheaths are preserved.

The region surrounding the quarry is the epitome of barrenness and desolation—a vast waste scarred by innumerable washes and strewn with dingy yellow-gray mounds of disintegrating stone. Isolated buttes rise abruptly out of the valleys, and naked hills hunch against the skyline like silhouettes of prehistoric monsters. South of the quarry the Green River creeps sluggishly across the desert floor toward Desolation Canyon, and to the east a series of broken upturned ledges in pastel shades of red, gray, and brown merge into the shattered pile of rocks that forms Split Mountain.

Northeastern Utah was not always a desert highland. More than 100 million years ago, probably in the Jurassic period of Mesozoic time, the site of Dinosaur Monument was an area of low relief, where a river with its tributary streams flowed northward through a broad valley. In some places ox-bow lakes and pools green with scum marked abandoned stream channels, and occasional shallow lagoons flooded the valley floor. The waters teemed with crocodiles, fishes, and amphibians, while in the swampy marginal lands reeds, ferns, grasses and trees grew in luxuriant profusion. Myriads of insects swarmed above the marshes; strange creatures, half bird, half reptile, spread their leathery wings and flapped across the sky. Huge beasts wallowed clumsily through the muddy swamplands, and small primitive mammals roamed the higher ground. The Mesozoic era, however, was an age of reptiles. In every favorable habitat throughout the world, the dinosaurs were supreme. They developed in amazing variety, until there were no less than 5,000 distinct species. Some of these reptilian creatures were no larger than a hen, but others, huge hulks of flesh and bone 100 feet in length, weighed thirty or forty tons. The largest dinosaurs inhabited the marshes and fed upon succulent water plants, but many carnivorous varieties lived on dry land and preyed upon their larger but more defenseless neighbors. Some of the dinosaurs, with huge underslung bodies governed by two-and-a-half ounce brains, were too ponderous and slow to put a decisive end to an argument; for protection they developed spiked faces and tails and a protective covering of bony armor. Some varieties had sharp dagger-like teeth; others were toothless. Some hopped or ran on their hind legs; others moved awkwardly on all fours. During the Jurassic period the great reptiles reached their ascendancy, and by the end of the Mesozoic era the advent of a different climate, or some other cause, resulted in their extinction.

The dinosaurs lived millions of years without a name, and left their bones to be found by a new race of animals—man—millions of years later. John M. Mills of Ogden, one of Utah's leading educators, points out that this new race grew slowly into many branches, developed languages that grew and changed, and, with their people, died. Later peoples, with other systems of speech, appealed to the dead languages for word-combinations to name the ancient monsters. The Greek provided *dinos* (terrible) and *saurus* (lizard) to make a general name, dinosaur, for a large class of extinct animals, and the same language provided scores of other names—such as brontosaurus, tyrannosaurus, ichthyosaurus, stegosaurus, diplodocus—for different kinds of "terrible lizards."

A number of explanations have been advanced to account for the dinosaur-bearing deposits. It is probable that when these animals died, they left their bodies strewn over a wide area in the river valley. Sometimes the flesh decayed, and the scattered bones were washed away to lower ground; sometimes the flood waters carried the carcasses into the rivers and deposited them on sand bars or on the margins of lakes. Many complete bodies and thousands of individual bones converged in a relatively small space and at length were covered with sand and gravel. Silica in the water percolating through the sediments replaced organic material of the bones and resulted in fossilization. Toward the end of the Mesozoic era, the sea encroached upon Utah land, and the sediments containing the dinosaur bones were covered with hundreds of feet of marine sediments. Early in the following era, the Cenozoic, the land was folded and raised above the water, and a new erosion cycle began. Through millions of years the marine deposits weathered away until finally the bones were exposed.

No doubt the Indians who roamed through northeastern Utah long ages before the coming of the white man were the first to see the dinosaur bones. Perhaps they wondered about them. Father Escalante, who crossed the Green River in the vicinity of Jensen in 1776, gives no indication in his journal that he noticed the great bones. Ashley's trappers, who came down the Green River in 1825, were more concerned with beaver than with fossils.

Major John Wesley Powell led an expedition down the Green River through the present Monument in 1869. Powell named the Canyon of Lodore, in the Colorado portion of the Monument, for Robert Southey's poem, "The Cataract of Lodore"; later maps misspell it Ladore. The major narrowly escaped death while climbing the cliffs of the Green River Canyon downstream from the Yampa River mouth. The incident Powell describes is all the more vivid because he had only one arm (he lost the right in the Battle of Shiloh): ". . . we proceed, stage by stage, until we are nearly to the summit. Here, by making a spring, I gain a foothold in a little crevice, and grasp an angle of the rock overhead. I find I can get up no farther, and cannot step back, for I dare not let go with my hand. . . . The moment is critical. Standing on my toes, my muscles began to tremble. . . . At this instant it occurs to Bradley to take off his drawers, which he does, and swings them down to me. I hug close to the rock, let go with my hand, seize the dangling legs, and, with his assistance, I am enabled to gain the top."

Ironically, when Powell, who twelve years later became director of the U. S. Geological Survey, went out to "spend the day among the rocks, studying an interesting geological fold and collecting fossils" in Split Mountain Canyon, within the Utah portion of Dinosaur National Monument, he found nothing more important than fossil corals and fossil shellfish. He did, however, leave a description of the view, essentially the same today, from the summit on the east side of Split Mountain Canyon:

> We are standing three thousand feet above its waters, which are troubled with billows, and white with foam. Its walls are set with crags and peaks, and buttressed towers, and overhanging domes. Turning to the right, the park is below us, with its island groves reflected by the deep, quiet water. Rich meadows stretch out on either hand, to the verge of a sloping plain, that comes down from the distant mountains. These plains are of almost naked rocks, in strange contrast to the meadows; blue and lilac colored rocks, buff and pink, vermilion and brown, and all these colors clear and bright. A dozen little creeks, dry the greater part of the year, run down through the half circle of exposed formations, radiating from the island-center to the rim of the basin. Each creek has its system of side streams, and each side stream has its system of laterals, and again, these are divided, so that this outstretched slope of rock is elaborately embossed. Beds of different colored formations runs in parallel bands on either side. The perspective, modified by the undulations, give the bands a waved appearance, and the high colors gleam in the midday sun with the luster of satin. We are tempted to call this Rainbow Park. Away beyond these beds are the Uinta and Wasatch Mountains, with their pine forests and snow fields and naked peaks. Now we turn to the right, and look up Whirlpool Cañon, a deep gorge, with a river in the bottom—a gloomy chasm, where mad waves roar; but, at this distance and altitude, the river is but a rippling brook, and the chasm a narrow cleft. The top of the mountain on which we stand is a broad grassy table, and a herd of deer is feeding in the distance. Walking over to the southeast, we look down into the valley of White River, and beyond that see the far distant Rocky Mountains, in mellow, perspective haze, through which snow fields shine.

When the Uintah Basin was opened for settlement, ranchers collected fossil remains, but it is unlikely that anyone appreciated their significance. For more than twenty years one man walked every day over a doorstep made from a slab of sandstone in which a dinosaur had left his footprints.

In 1908 the Carnegie Museum of Pittsburgh, Pennsylvania, sent Dr. Earl Douglass into the Uintah Basin to search for fossil mammals. During this expedition ranchers called his attention to dinosaur bones protruding from a bluff near the Green River, and the following year he returned to make a systematic search for reptilian fossils. According to a newspaper account, "a ledge of sandstone which contained scattering bones was followed down one side of a canyon or ravine and up the next hill. On arriving at the top of the hill the hunter was startled by seeing a series of articulated joints of a huge animal weathered out in relief on the face of the sandstone ledge." The exposed bones were part of the tail of a large dinosaur, and quarrying operations revealed the complete skeleton of a brontosaurus. From the time of this discovery until 1923 the Carnegie Museum removed from the quarry nearly a million tons of rock and bone. Various institutions, including the Smithsonian and the University of Utah, continued the work. Twenty-two complete skeletons and thousands of individual bones have been found in the Monument, representing five species of dinosaurs, primitive mammals, crocodiles, invertebrate forms, and plants. These fossils have been sent to almost every important museum in the country. In 1924 Dr. Frederick J. Pack, then professor of geology at the University of Utah, brought nineteen wagons loaded with dinosaur fossils to Salt Lake City. As the caravan paused in one of the smaller towns, an inquisitive old woman asked Dr. Pack the age of the bones. When she received an answer in terms of millions of years, she was visibly annoyed. "But that can't be right," she said. "You told me the same thing last year."

The American Museum of Natural History became actively interested in the fossil deposits about 1931, and in 1934 the museum's curator of fossil reptiles, Dr. Barnum Brown, became consulting paleontologist for the Monument. Since 1933, when Dr. A. C. Boyle assumed the duties of custodian and resident geologist, the program of development at the quarry has been under the direction of the National Park Service. In 1934 about 100 transients were employed in cleaning out the old quarry and making various improvements. Between 1936 and 1940 the Monument has been developed by WPA labor.

Almost 15,000 persons visit Dinosaur National Monument every year. Some of them are geologists and paleontologists who make painstaking examinations of the fossils, take copious notes, and speak in scientific language, but many more are simply inquisitive tourists who ask absurd questions and make facetious remarks. "How many undiscovered skeletons are there in the quarry?" asks one visitor. The guide is preparing a courteous answer when a high school lad, who has been gazing thoughtfully upon a huge bone, finds an opportune moment to remark that the dogs must have enjoyed life in those days. The laughter is cut short by the squeal of a feminine tourist, startled by a small dun-colored lizard perched upon a huge bone, panting in the sun. Nobody takes time to observe, nor does the lizard, that he is a member of an ancient order, the Sons of the Dinosaurs.

Great Salt Lake

Highway Approach: 14.3 *m.* W. of Salt Lake City, on US 40, a concrete highway. Views of lake from many other highway vantages.
Season: Highway open all year; lake resorts open May 30 to Labor Day.
Admission: At beaches, 10¢ and 25¢.

Accommodations: Meals at resorts; other accommodations at Salt Lake City.

Transportation: Salt Lake, Garfield and Western R.R. (electric) maintains regular service in season to Saltair; Southern Pacific R.R. runs across lake, between Ogden and Lucin, and Western Pacific R.R. skirts the southern shore. Sight-seeing busses from Salt Lake City.
Recreational Facilities: Bathing, boating, dancing, amusement resorts. No fishing.
Warnings and Regulations: Do not visit islands inhabited by birds during nesting season (April 15 to July 15). Do not molest sea gulls, pelicans and other island birds. Do not venture on lake when storms threaten; waves are heavy and dangerous. Do not dive into lake; solidity of water makes it dangerous. Do not get water in eyes or throat; causes painful smarting and strangulation.

GREAT SALT LAKE, Utah's unique inland sea, has been called exciting and disappointing, magnificent and desolate, sublime and fearful, grand and bleak. Its temper and appearance change with the season, the weather, the time of day. Its size varies from year to year and from season to season. Roughly, the lake is 75 miles long and 50 miles wide. The largest lake in the United States west of the Mississippi, it is more noted for its salt content than for its size. The average salinity of the lake is six to eight times that of the ocean. The water contains an estimated six and a half billion tons of salt, which gives the water great buoyancy. Horace Greeley wrote, in 1859, "You can no more sink in it than in a clay bank."

The most popular approach to Great Salt Lake is US 40 (*see Tour 6c*), which parallels the south shore for several miles, passing all the beach resorts. A description of the lake is difficult because of the constantly changing water level. In 1925 the water came within a few feet of the highway; five years later it dropped to its lowest recorded level, receding nearly a mile from the road and leaving the Saltair beach pavilion high and dry. When the water is low, the view from the highway reveals comparatively little of the lake. Barren salt flats occupy the foreground, and the lake is visible as a thin horizontal line of water in the distance. The surrounding land is little higher than the lake itself, and a good view can only be obtained from an elevation.

By day, the lake is impressive chiefly because of its size. Far across its surface, the dull gray-green of the water fades imperceptibly into the horizon. Here and there the bright rays of the sun are caught in the sails of occasional small boats. Gulls fly overhead. At sunset the lake awakens with brilliant reflections.

Few forms of life exist in Great Salt Lake. Dr. Angus M. Woodbury, associate professor of zoology at the University of Utah, names them in *Ecology* for January, 1936:

> The Great Salt Lake, with its saline content approaching saturation, presents a hostile environment to most living organisms. . . . The principal food-makers of the lake are blue-green algae. . . . These are undoubtedly the food base for very limited fauna . . . which can withstand immersion in the water of the lake. . . . Of the visible forms, the brine shrimp . . . and two brine flies . . . are common inhabitants of the lake . . . these arthropods have been enabled to multiply with little or no molestation to the limit of the food supply. . . .

Great Salt Lake, according to geologists, is the remnant of a much larger body of fresh water called Lake Bonneville, which 25,000 to 100,000 years ago filled the eastern half of the Great Basin (*see Geology*). Discovery of Great Salt Lake is ordinarily credited to Jim Bridger, early mountaineer. Sir Richard F. Burton, in his *City of the Saints,* writes that "the early Canadian *voyageurs* . . . recounted to wondering strangers its fearful submarine noises, its dark and sudden storms, and the terrible maelstrom in its centre, which, funnel-like, descended into the bowels of the earth." There was also a belief that Great Salt Lake was connected subterraneously with the Pacific Ocean.

While camped near Utah Lake in 1776, Father Escalante was informed by friendly Indians of a salt lake a short distance north: "The other lake that joins this one, occupies, as we are told, many leagues, and its waters are very harmful and very salty; the Timpanois assured us that anyone who moistened any part of the body with it would at once feel the part bathed greatly inflamed."

During the winter of 1824-25, Jim Bridger, while trapping on Bear River, discovered the lake as the result of a bet on the probable course of the river. Bridger went down the river in a "bull boat," and arrived at Bear River Bay, northeastern arm of Great Salt Lake. Taking a drink of the water, he spat it out with the ejaculation, "Hell, we are on the shore of the Pacific!" This misconception was dispelled a year later when James Clyman and three others, searching for beaver streams, "circumambulated" the lake in round "bull boats" made of buffalo skins; they reported that the great body of water had no outlet. Colonel Henry Inman, explorer and author, has preserved a story told him by Bridger, a noted teller of tall tales, to the effect that in the winter of 1830 it began to snow in Salt Lake Valley and continued for seventy days without cessation. The whole country was covered to a depth of seventy feet and all the buffalo in the region perished in the storm. Their carcasses, however, were preserved by the cold and "when spring came," Bridger said, "all I had to do was tumble 'em into Salt Lake an' I had pickled buffalo enough for myself and the whole Ute nation for years. On account of this terrible storm there are no more buffalo in the valley."

In September, 1843, Captain John C. Frémont visited Frémont Island in "a frail batteau of gum cloth distended with air." He found that, "Roughly evaporated over the fire, the five gallons of water yielded fourteen pints of very fine-grained and very white salt, of which the whole lake may be regarded as a saturated solution."

In 1848, nine months after arrival of the Mormons in Salt Lake Valley, a party of six men spent five days exploring Great Salt Lake. One of the men suggested, according to Albert Carrington's report, "what we considered a very appropriate and characteristic name for the lake, viz. 'the briny shallow' in contradistinction to the 'briny deep.' " He concludes: "We were highly fortunate in our expedition, with constant good feelings, which we attributed to our custom of attending to our prayers daily night and morning, having no disposition to shove prayers off the great checker board of duties in this probation."

In 1849, Captain Howard Stansbury, of the U. S. Army, came west to make a detailed survey of Great Salt Lake and the surrounding country. His view of the lake from Promontory Point was disappointing: "The stillness of the grave seemed to pervade the air and water; and, excepting here and there a solitary wild-duck floating motionless on the bosom of the lake, not a living thing was to be seen. . . . The bleak and naked shores [were] without a single tree to relieve the eye." Stansbury skirted the lake, "being the first party of white men that ever succeeded in making the entire circuit of the lake by land."

Stansbury established a base on Antelope Island, from which he conducted his survey during the spring of 1850. His commentary on Salt Lake bathing is still valid: "A man may float, stretched at full length, upon his back, having his head and neck, both his legs to the knee, and both arms to the elbow, entirely out of the water. If a sitting position be assumed, with the arms extended to preserve the equilibrium, the shoulders will remain above the surface. The water is nevertheless extremely difficult to swim in, on account of the constant tendency of the lower extremities to rise above it. The brine, too, is so strong, that the least particle of it getting into the eyes produces the most acute pain; and if accidentally swallowed, rapid strangulation must ensue. . . . After bathing, it is necessary to wash the skin with fresh water, to prevent the deposite of salt arising from evaporation of the brine. Yet a bath in this water is delightfully refreshing and invigorating." Stansbury also found the water useful for preserving meat: "A large piece of fresh beef was suspended by a cord and immersed in the lake for rather more than twelve hours, when it was found to be tolerably well corned."

Since 1851 a continuous record has been kept by various agencies of the annual rise and fall of Great Salt Lake. Between 1851 and 1940 the water level has varied more than 18 feet. This variation has affected the size of the lake tremendously, in some places altering the shoreline as much as 15 miles. Because of the gradual slope of the lake bottom, it is estimated that a ten-foot change in water level will cover or uncover 480 square miles of lake bed. The water was highest and the lake largest in 1873, when it covered an area of 2,250 square miles. The water was lowest and the lake smallest in 1935, when it covered only 1,420 square miles. Measurements of the water level are usually stated with reference to a gauge on which the zero level is 4,196.85 feet above sea level. The highest reading was 14.65, in 1873. The level dropped below zero for the first time in 1902, and fell to the lowest recorded level, 3.1 below zero, in 1935. In 1940 the lake shrank under drought conditions to a new low, 3.2 below zero, but at the end of the year began another rise.

Great Salt Lake, as compared with other lakes of similar size, has been sailed by few large boats. All boats ride high in its dense waters. Though calm in fair weather, a sudden storm can quickly transform the lake into a surging mass of heavy wild waves. The *Timely Gull,* launched by Brigham Young in 1854, was destroyed four years later in a gale. A three-decked stern-wheel steamboat, the *City of Corinne,* was launched in 1872 to haul Tintic ores from Lake Point to Corinne (*see Tour 4b*). The boat reached Corinne by sailing 20 miles up the Bear River, but in 1874 the level of the lake began to fall, and the river became unnavigable. For a few years thereafter the steamer was used as a passenger boat. Other large boats sailed for brief periods on the lake, but most were wrecked by storms. Smaller boats now sail the lake, some of them specially constructed for lake conditions, but all stay near the shore when stormy weather threatens.

SALT LAKE ISLANDS

Great Salt Lake contains approximately ten islands, the exact number varying with the level of the lake. When the water is low, many islands become peninsulas, connected with the mainland; when the water is high the lake contains two large islands—Antelope and Stansbury—and nine or more islets. Four islands—Gunnison, Bird, Egg, and White Rock—are inhabited by birds, and should not be visited during nesting season (about April 15 to July 15). The birds may be frightened from their nests and their eggs eaten by gulls, or spoiled by the sun's heat. Pelicans are especially timid. In 1936 a party became marooned, resulting in the loss of the entire pelican crop.

ANTELOPE ISLAND, in the southwestern part of the lake, the largest, is 15½ miles long, 5½ miles wide, and has an area of 23,175 acres. Osborne Russell, a trapper, who was on the shore of Great Salt Lake in 1841, was the first to report antelope and buffalo on the island, and the first to mention the fluctuating level of the lake. He talked with an old Indian chief, who "could recollect when buffalo passed from the mainland to the island without swimming. The depth of the water was increasing, and the buffalo had long since left the shore of the lake." The island was named by Captain John C. Frémont when he visited the lake for the second time, in 1845. In *Memoirs of My Life* he writes:

> There is at this southern end of the lake a large peninsular island which the Indians informed me could at this low stage of the water be reached on horseback. Accordingly . . . I took with me [Kit] Carson and a few men and rode . . . across the shallows. . . . On the island we found grass and water and several bands of antelope. Some of these were killed, and, in memory of the grateful supply of food they furnished, I gave their name to the island. . . .

It became known as Church Island about 1849, when the Mormon Church began to use it as a herding ground. Brigham Young frequently visited the island, and sometimes entertained guests with programs that ranged from bathing to broncho-busting. Wild horses were captured, broken, and taken to the mainland for use on farms.

When Captain Howard Stansbury made his survey of Great Salt Lake in 1850, he used Antelope Island as the base for much of his work. "Like all the other islands in the lake," he writes, "it consists of a long rocky eminence, ranging from north to south, rising abruptly from the water, and attaining an elevation of about three thousand feet above the lake."

Romance came to Antelope Island in 1857 when an eloping couple spent their honeymoon there, eluding the bride's father, who considered her too young to be married, and placed her under guard; they remained on the island until the father became reconciled to the marriage. Five years later the island was the scene of a more unpleasant episode. A grave digger called Jean Baptiste was caught robbing a grave in Salt Lake City. Feeling against him ran high, and Alfred Lambourne, in *Our Inland Sea,* tells the sequel: "Branded and shackled, the man, himself, was once kept, a solitary prisoner, on one of these neighboring islands. He attempted escape. By one of the river mouths, a skeleton was lately exhumed—a fetter and a link of chain were still on his ankle bone. It was the remains of Jean Baptiste. He had met his death by drowning."

On Antelope Island once lived, with his wife and six children, George Frary, who knew the lake perhaps better than anyone. Fifty years of his life were spent in building boats to sail and explore the inland sea. Frary's wife died and was buried on the island in 1897, but Frary remained for many years thereafter. He assisted in making the first soundings for the Lucin Cutoff (*see below*), and his daughter was a passenger, in 1903, on the first scheduled train that crossed the lake.

Antelope have disappeared from the island—the last were seen in 1870—but buffalo again graze the rugged slopes. They are not native, but descendants of a dozen head placed on the island in 1892 by William Glasmann, Ogden publisher. The herd once numbered more than four hundred, but in 1940 it had been reduced to twenty-eight head. Buffalo stampede scenes in *The Covered Wagon* were filmed on Antelope Island in 1922. The island is privately owned and is used principally for grazing sheep and cattle.

FRÉMONT ISLAND, in the east central part of the lake, is 5 miles long, 2 miles wide, and has an area of 2,945 acres. Stansbury named it for Captain John C. Frémont, who had called it Disappointment Island. Frémont describes it as "simply a rocky hill, on which there is neither water nor trees of any kind."

When Stansbury visited Frémont Island in 1850, "Search was made for the cover to the object-end of Frémont's telescope, which he had left on the summit of the island, but it could not be found." Alfred Lambourne, who lived on Gunnison Island in the late 1890's, mentions Frémont's telescope cover, and observes that "This object has been much sought after." It had not, so far as known, been found up to 1940.

GUNNISON ISLAND, in the northwestern part of the lake, is less than a mile long and has an area of only 163 acres. It was named for Lieutenant John W. Gunnison, chief assistant to Captain Howard Stansbury in his survey of the lake. The island is the largest of four having bird rookeries. It is estimated that 80,000 gulls, 10,000 pelicans, 100 herons, and 100 cormorants nest on the islands of Great Salt Lake in the summer. On Gunnison Island, gulls and pelicans are most numerous, but there are also a few herons.

In 1886-87 Alfred Lambourne, Utah artist and writer, preempted a homestead on Gunnison Island, where he lived for fourteen months. Out of this hermit existence came his illustrated book, *Our Inland Sea,* and many of his best paintings. "From my father," he writes, "I have inherited these—a love for an island and a love for a vine," and he planted a vineyard. With the eye of a poet Lambourne observed the seasonal aspects of the lake and its surroundings. In winter "the distant mountain heights smoke in the dawn like tired horses, or the sun rises like a disk of copper, ruddy through the spindrift brine." Of summer he exclaims, "O, the glare of the light upon the waters of the Inland Sea! Like polished steel gleams the briny surface; and across it, the sun's path is like that same steel at molten heat." In autumn, "A mighty drowsiness is on the land. The Harvest-Moon—the Indian's Moon of Falling Leaves—has supplanted the Moons of Fire. . . . Haze-enwrapped are the distant Wasatch; through deepening shades of saddened violet, the Onaqui lapse into melancholia. The western headlands, the jutting promontories, appear as if cut from dim, orange crepe, or maroon-colored velvet. Wistful and vague stand the peaked islands, and shell-like is the gleam of the far-stretched brine."

Guano-gatherers were on the island at the same time as Lambourne, but efforts to market bird guano, or manure, deposits on the island have never been commercially successful.

BIRD (or HAT) ISLAND, in the southwestern part of the lake, is less than a quarter mile in diameter and has an area of only 22 acres. "Merely a pile of granitic conglomerate," it is, nevertheless, inhabited by thousands of birds, principally seagulls and pelicans. The safety of isolation must have prompted so many birds to nest here, for there is no food on the island itself, nor in the surrounding salt water. The pelicans fly as much as a hundred miles to obtain fish from fresh-water streams and lakes. The gulls are scavengers, content to eat whatever they can find. In the spring, great flocks of gulls follow the plows, picking up insects. Since about 1920 the gulls have learned to eat cherries and other fruits. Neither of the birds has appreciable economic value, but both are protected by law—the pelican because it is in danger of extermination, and the gull because of its timely intervention during the cricket plague of 1848 (*see Salt Lake City*).

EGG ISLAND, north of Antelope, and WHITE ROCK, west of Antelope, are also occupied by waterfowl. Only gulls nest on White Rock, but Egg is also inhabited by a few herons and by the only cormorants on the lake.

CARRINGTON ISLAND, in the southwestern part of the lake, is a circular isle, slightly more than 2 miles in diameter, with an area of 1,767 acres. It was named by Captain Stansbury for Albert Carrington, a Mormon (later an apostle) who assisted with the 1850 survey. The summit, Stansbury reports, "consisted of ledges of excellent roofing slate."

MUD ISLAND, 8 miles northeast of Frémont Island, is an island only when the lake is low. At other times it is merely a sandbar, with an area of approximately 600 acres. Stansbury found "A belt of soft, black mud, more than knee-deep . . . between the water and the hard, rocky beach, [which] seemed to be impregnated with all the villainous smells which nature's laboratory was capable of producing."

STANSBURY ISLAND, in the southwestern part of the lake, has not actually been an island since the 1870's, when Great Salt Lake was at its highest recorded level. For decades it has been connected with the mainland, and is more accurately a peninsula. Nevertheless, the "island," capped by rugged mountains rising 3,000 feet, is described as being 11½ miles long, 5½ miles wide, and 22,314 acres in area. It was named for Captain Howard Stansbury by officers of his party, during the survey of the lake in 1850.

STRONGS KNOB, in the west central part of the lake, is connected with the mainland except when the lake is high. It is geologically a part of Strongknob Mountain, from which it takes its name, and has an area of 703 acres.

DOLPHIN ISLAND and CUB ISLAND are the two northernmost islands in the lake. Both are small and barren. When the water is low, Dolphin is connected with the mainland, and Cub is a part of Gunnison.

ACROSS THE LAKE BY RAIL

Special arrangements can be made with the Southern Pacific R.R., at Ogden or at Lucin, for a stop at Lucin, not a regular passenger stop. A daytime round-trip tour by train can be made across Great Salt Lake, but schedules and rates are subject to change—inquire at railroad station.

The LUCIN CUTOFF (pronounced Lu-SIN), completed by the Southern Pacific Railroad in 1903, extends 102 miles between Ogden and Lucin and includes 30 miles of trestlework and rock fill across Great Salt Lake. The Cutoff replaced the longer railroad route around the north end of the lake, shortening the distance by 44 miles and eliminating numerous curves and grades. Construction required one and a half years of work by three thousand men, cost more than eight million dollars, and used hundreds of trainloads of rock and the timber from 38,000 trees.

West of Ogden the route is through level green farmland. Near the lake, fields and pastures give way to marshland and barren salt flats. REESE, 8 *m.* (4,224 alt., less than 50 pop.), is on the border between irrigated farms and flat sandy marshes. West of the town are great salt-grass pastures, growing sparser, due to alkalinity, near the lake.

From LITTLE MOUNTAIN (R), 15 *m.,* Captain John C. Frémont obtained his first view of Great Salt Lake in 1843, and there is a monument to him here. Between Little Mountain and Promontory Point the tracks are laid on a rock fill separating the partially freshened water of Bear River Bay (R) from the salt water of the lake (L). In winter the bay may be entirely frozen over, but the lake remains open in coldest weather, because of its high content of salines.

PROMONTORY POINT STATION, 23 *m.* (4,217 alt., less than 50 pop.), named for Promontory Mountain, a north-and-south peninsula dividing Bear River Bay from Great Salt Lake, has a salt works (R) which produces 10,000 to 15,000 tons of salt each year. From Promontory Point there is a view (L) across the lake to Frémont Island and Antelope Island; sheep are ferried in flatboats from the Point to these islands for winter grazing. Thirty miles to the north is Promontory, where the last spike was driven, May 10, 1869, in the first transcontinental railroad (*see Transportation*).

Between Promontory Point and Lakeside the railroad crosses the center of the lake. Part of the way is over rock fill, but twelve miles is over wooden trestlework.

SALINE, 27 *m.* (4,219 alt., less than 50 pop.), is the quarters of the bridge safety patrol. On the fill (L) are landings for motorboats used by the patrol in making their rounds to check up on fills and trestlework of Lucin Cutoff.

BRIDGE, 30 *m.,* is a telegraph station and quarters for operators. A short distance west is the western end of the fill and the eastern end of the twelve-mile wooden trestle, built on pilings 100 feet long. Officials of the Southern Pacific Railroad say that from year to year this bridge becomes stronger as the salty waters preserve and harden its timbers. The lake, as seen on this rail trip, is a place of mirages, the waters serving as a background for islands seemingly suspended in midair.

MIDLAKE, 37 *m.* (4,217 alt.), is a station and passing track, with living quarters for bridge attendants, who live a lonesome life, stationed several miles from land.

LAKESIDE, 47 *m.* (4,216 alt., less than 100 pop.), is on the west edge of Great Salt Lake, sheltered by the gray cliffs of Lakeside Mountains, from which thousands of tons of rock were quarried to build the Cutoff. Cars loaded with boulders weighing many tons stand in readiness here, awaiting the report of the safety patrol, following a storm, of boulders washed out of the rock fill. The lake waters are so dense that they move boulders of unbelievable tonnage when lashed by a storm. Residents of the settlement include an agent, operators, power-house operators, track workers, and quarrymen. Some of the townspeople make miniature houses, windmills, and other objects, which they hang in the lake. In a few days they are covered with half an inch of sparkling salt crystals; eastern curio dealers provide an outlet for these strange products. The town proper is three-quarters of a mile west of the depot. In 1936, Preston Thomas, son of the local postmaster, assisted his father in transporting the mail by hitching his dog, Molly, to a small handcar running on a sidetrack from the main line. The beef-steak-powered "houndmotive" made two trips daily to the depot, returning sometimes with as much as 750 pounds of mail.

Great trackless salt flats extend westward from Lakeside, dazzling white, a field for mirages and optical illusions. Residents of this exposed locality are careful to keep all light household objects fastened down, else they might sail or roll for miles before the unhindered winds, without meeting any obstruction to stop them. North of Lakeside is Gunnison Island (*see above*).

HOGUP, 61 *m.* (4,220 alt.), is a siding and telegraph station, operated only occasionally during the summer months. Hogup Mountains, to the north, are a winter range for sheep, the annual snowfall in this region being very light. Prehistoric remains indicate that villages existed in this area hundreds of years ago. The only available water for many miles is at the station, piped there by the railroad company. The vegetation of this area is mostly sagebrush and desert grasses. In the spring there is a burst of bright-colored flowers—wild geranium, desert pea, larkspur, bluebell, and Indian paintbrush—appearing for a short time on the lower slopes of near-by hills.

ALLEN, 66 *m.* (4,224 alt., less than 50 pop.), is a siding and living quarters for track workers. Here are a few green trees, planted and watered by residents. This is one of the driest areas in Utah, with an annual precipitation of about one inch.

GROOME, 71 *m.* (4,221 alt.), is a loading siding for copper and lead ore, trucked from the Newfoundland Mountains, in sight to the south. The slopes of these mountains provide winter grazing for herds of sheep. Westward, gray salt flats continue for many miles.

LUCIN, 102 *m.* (4,471 alt., less than 100 pop.), is the junction of Lucin Cutoff with the old railroad line circling the north end of the lake. It is the southern outlet for Grouse Creek Valley, a ranching area about thirty miles to the north, lying between the Raft River Mountains on the west and the Independence Mountains on the east.

High Uintas Primitive Area

Highwy Approaches: Via Kamas to Mirror Lake (*see Tour 5*); via Lonetree, Wyoming, up the headwaters of Henrys Fork; via Mountain Home, up Rock Creek to Big Kidney Lake; via Hanna and. Savage's Ranch (*see Tour 5*), to the Grandaddy Lakes.
Season: June 15 to Nov. 1.
Administrative Office: Wasatch National Forest, 350 South Main, Salt Lake City.

Accommodations: Campgrounds and lodge to accommodate 15 guests at Savage's Ranch (only spot in area approximating a dude ranch); cabins at Moon Lake and Defas Park; filling station, cabins and hotel at Hanna, rates $1 to $1.50 per day; campground with commercial packing facilities (*guides and horses*) N. end of Rock Creek Road.

Transportation: Private cars afford the only means to these "road-end" points; the region is remote from railroads and bus lines. A Department of Commerce emergency landing field is maintained 1 *m.* NE. of Wanship.
Climate, Clothing and Equipment: Region of perpetual snow, with peaks above timberline. Semi-arctic conditions exist in the higher areas, with cool nights even in midsummer in lower portions. Wear cord soled walking shoes for hiking and select equipment for service and utility; except for horses and saddles nothing can be obtained within the area. Bring camera and photographic supplies and *always carry* pocket knife, compass, matches, mosquito dope, and a Forest Service map of the area.
Medical and Dental Care: Doctor and dentist at Duchesne and Park City; doctor at Kamas. Small hospital at Park City.
Speed Limit: Not safe to exceed 20 m.p.h. on roads to points of entry.
Warnings and Regulations: Forest Service rules must be abided by; these include registry at nearest ranger station, put fires *dead out,* burn or bury all refuse, break all matches with one finger on burnt end.

Naturalist Service and Information: Administrative Office, Wasatch National Forest, Salt Lake City, for general information on area; for more technical naturalist information see biologists and geologists at University of Utah, Salt Lake City.

Free Maps of Primitive Area, showing all trails, obtainable at headquarters of Wasatch National Forest, Salt Lake City.
Recreational Facilities: Fishing, hiking, photography, horseback riding, pack trips, camping, and mountain climbing. Little hunting, since game goes down from heights by opening of hunting season in fall.
Guides and Horses: Both at Savage's Ranch; horses at Moon Lake and Defas Park (*see Tour 5*). Ranch hands, excellent guides, are available at Hanna, and at Peterson's Ranch on the Lower Stillwater of Rock Creek (*see Tour 5*) when ranch work is not pressing. Commercial packer (*guides and pack horses*), at Upper Stillwater of Rock Creek July 1-Sept. 30.

THE HIGH UINTAS PRIMITIVE AREA, a 243,957-acre saddle across the backbone of the Uinta Mountains, occupying portions of the

Wasatch and Ashley National Forests, was set aside by the U. S. Forest Service in 1931. The area is almost pear-shaped, with the stem pointing westward and the bud end east by north. Kings Peak (13,498 alt.), the highest peak in Utah, could be termed the bud, with the stem south of Haydens Peak (12,485 alt.) and northwest of Grandaddy Lakes.

The purpose for which this primitive area is set aside, says the Forest Service, is to prevent the unnecessary elimination or impairment of unique natural values and, so far as economic conditions will permit, to afford the public opportunity to observe conditions which existed in the pioneer days of the Nation, and to engage in the forms of out-door recreation characteristic of that period, thus helping to preserve national traditions, ideals, and characteristics, and promoting a true understanding of historical phases of national progress. This area will be preserved in a "wild" state, in the sense that it will not be developed by road building, or by any form of permanent occupancy. Prospecting, mining, and grazing of livestock will be permitted and the orderly utilization of timber and water resources may be allowed. Travel in the area is only on foot or horseback. Dense forests, varied by glacial canyons and myriads of lakes, are walled in and divided by high mountains.

The Uinta Range, part of which is included in the Primitive Area, in general form is a broad, elongated, flat-topped arch. The culminating peaks and ridges lie for the most part along the north side of the arch. The plateau-like summit in many places is deeply dissected and eroded into jagged peaks and ridges; at their bases are immense amphitheaters, and below are deep canyons. The central part of the range, along the anticlinal crest, is formed of nearly horizontal rock strata, buried at many places beneath glacial material, which impounds numerous lakelets and ponds. A great portion of this region is occupied by grassy parks, open meadows, and heavily forested slopes, above which the barren peaks rise boldly. The northern flank of the range slopes off steeply to the undulating Green River Basin of Wyoming. The southern slopes drop more gently to an extensive plateau region and then into the Uintah Basin. These slopes are deeply incised by streams, many of them with canyon channels from 1,000 to 2,000 feet deep. In this most heavily timbered region in the State the rock coloring is delicate, ranging through the rich warm colors of the spectrum to mellow blends of green, blue, lilac, pearl, amethyst, and purple.

No one knows the actual number of lakes within the Primitive Area. Only a few of the larger ones have been named; it is thought that there are approximately 1,000, of which 100 have never been fished. Mirror Lake is a mile long, a half mile wide and in some places 100 feet deep; within a radius of six miles are 78 smaller lakes. Grandaddy Lake is one and a half miles long and three quarters of a mile wide; the Grandaddy Basin alone contains more than 350 lakes and lakelets. Moon Lake, Mirror Lake, and their adjacent meadows and streams—all accessible by car—have convenient campsites and accommodations. They offer almost an exact counterpart of the scenery, fishing, and rare atmosphere of the higher, more remote regions. Women, children, and those physically unable to hike or ride, find primitive country in these areas. The water in Uinta lakes and streams is cold, and the fish are full of fight. Gourmets claim the fish caught in these icy waters have a superior flavor. Lake shores are usually clear of line-snagging trees and brush.

Five plant zones are represented in the Primitive Area: the Arctic, on the grassy moss- and lichen-covered but treeless peaks above 11,000 feet; the Hudsonian, marked by Engelmann spruce and alpine fir, usually from 9,000 to 11,000 feet; the Canadian, with white balsam, blue spruce, and aspen as low as 7,000 feet; the Transition between 6,000 and 7,000 feet, represented by scrub oak and yellow pine; and the Upper Sonoran, with its juniper and sage below 6,000 feet. Indigenous flora includes twenty-five genera of grasses, thirty different shrubs, and more than one hundred types of herbs and weeds. The pine, spruce and fir are varied with quaking aspen, piñon pine, mountain ash, hickory, juniper, and scrub oak. Bird life comprises all species indigenous to the western Rockies, augmented by many migrants.

Animals are abundant. Bighorn sheep roam the crags, elk browse in the valleys, bear put on fat before their long winter sleep. The most plentiful big game animal is the mule deer. Badger, porcupine, Canadian lynx, mountain lion, and coyote are numerous, and there is a great variety of smaller animals.

The origin and age, as mountains, of the Uinta Range is part of what geologists call the "Laramide Problem." It is supposed that they were uplifted at about the same time as the rest of the Rocky Mountains, and that the cause was the so-called Laramide Revolution, but so many complex factors are involved that there is little agreement among geologists as to what caused the stresses which forced the rocks into a great arch, or in what period it occurred. Geologists also differ as to the ice ages of this region, some claiming that there were three, while others say five. They are agreed that it was completely covered with ice as recently as 25,000 years ago, and that some of its glaciers were twenty miles long. Glaciers carved out the great amphitheater-like cirques, their debris dammed up hundreds of lakes, and water melting from them wielded the principal erosional tools that cut scores of deep canyons.

Ute Indians hunted in the Primitive Area before the coming of the white man, following the game up the mountains in summer, drying the meat, tanning the hides, and gathering and drying berries.

The first white man known to have crossed the Uintas, in 1825, was General William H. Ashley, leader of the first trapping expedition to reach present Utah (see History). A shortage of food among Mormon settlers in the fall of 1847 led to the next known penetration of the High Uintas, by Mormon hunters. "I used to be a good hunter," writes Priddy Meeks in his journal, a copy of which is in possession of the Utah Historical Records Survey, "and I believe the Lord will bless me with good luck and I will trust in him like old Lehi and try it." He met "Brother Gustin" on the way and they went together:

So we traveled some 50 or 60 miles untill the second night and camped with a perpendicular wall of rock behind us and a little stream of water in front of us. A good place not to be discovered by Indians. . . . [The following morning] "The red clouds in the east was beginning to shine very bright," and Meeks, while "musing in my mind over our condition," saw an elk against the red clouds and shot it. Now we did rejoice exceedingly believing with all our hearts that the Lord sent that elk right straight to us to furnish our wives and children with food, who we had left behind with little or nothing to eat. . . . I looked on the top of the mountain I saw an elk looking down at me. It was so high it looked not much larger than a goat. I turned and climbed the mountains, I used my gun as a walking stick, also catching at roots, twigs and grass, sometimes making a foot hold in the ground to place my foot in. Finaly I got up and stopped and looked all around but saw no elk. It was a beautiful place up there with small valleys with small springs of good water and heavily set with the nicest kind of grass, with nice groves of quaking asp but no under brush.

While I was amusing myself in looking at the wonders of the world away up there I saw an elk. . . . It took up the mountain that appeared to be as much higher as the one I had come up and I think I went to the top of the third mountain which appeared to be one mountain on top of another mountain before I was in reality on top. . . . Here I took a survey of all the kingdoms of the world that were in my sight at any rate, but I was not tempted to accept any of them, but returned to camp. . . .

In later years wandering prospectors, cowboys, and sheepherders penetrated the forests and climbed the peaks, leaving only burnt sticks and tin cans to mark their passing. A Swedish prospector was working with his partner in the Rock Creek country. The Swede felt that he had found what he always wanted—gold near running water, lakes, trees, flowers, and a fishing stream right in camp, but his partner yearned for the fleshpots of the mining camps. After many heated quarrels the partnership was broken up in a fierce fight. The winner— the peace-loving Swede—sucked his bruised knuckles and yelled after his ex-partner: "Yah, now run qvick to Park City vit its hussies and saloons. Anyhow! you are yust a snoose-chewing, coffee-grinding, visky-drinking, ski-yumping, fisk-eating yackass, anyhow!" Homesteading pioneers preferred better land in lower valleys, irrigable with water from these mountains. Some logging was done, but the roads were too rough and the distance to the large centers too far to make it profitable. All things seemed to conspire to leave the High Uintas a primitive area, just as it was in the days of Ashley, Priddy Meeks, and the Swede.

The trend started early toward fish-stocking in the highland lakes of the Uintas. Sheepherders and prospectors found higher lakes empty of fish, natural barriers preventing the fish from spawning farther up. They would catch a few fingerlings in a bucket, carry them up, and empty them in good but unproductive lakes. This method of transplanting fish was the only one used in this area until 1910, when official stocking of rainbow and eastern brook trout was begun. Montana grayling were introduced in Hoover Lake in 1934, in the following year California golden trout were placed in the Mirror Lake Basin, and for several years native eggs have been planted in barren lakes with exceptional results. It was time then, in an age of air-conditioning, for people to seek an upland country that was naturally air-conditioned, with a frigidaire in every stream, and inquisitive little neighbors that might be the originals of Walt Disney's animal creations.

HIGH UINTAS HIGHLINE TRAIL

The Highline Trail runs in a general east-west direction along the crest of the Uinta Mountains; it is the only feasible path through the lofty passes. There is a network of trails across the area, with the Highline Trail the trunk or main artery. Well-marked connecting trails lead to highway points of entry (*see Tour 5*). A round trip, made as described in the following one-way log, requires eight days on horseback, stopping only for meals and sleep. Food, first aid supplies, fishing equipment, warm bedding or a medium-weight sleeping bag, and warm clothing must be carried for the entire trip.

From the west, the Uinta Mountains are first entered at Kamas, from which a winding dirt road leads 32 miles to Mirror Lake (*see Tour 5*). Here guides, pack horses, saddle horses, and supplies are available.

East from MIRROR LAKE, 0 *m.*, the Highline Trail skirts BONNY LAKE (L), 2.5 *m.*, with good fishing for rainbows. The trail climbs northeast, through tall forests, with Bald Mountain in the background and Mount Agassiz looming to the northeast, and winds through flowering meadows. SCUTTER LAKE (R), 6 *m.*, during the summer is covered with water lilies.

The trail crosses the NORTH FORK of the Duchesne River, 8 *m.*, well stocked with native and rainbow trout. At 9 *m.* is a junction with a trail (R), to FOUR LAKE BASIN, 4 *m.* Within a radius of a few miles from this basin are perhaps a dozen lakes. Four Lakes and those near by are heavily stocked with fish.

From the junction, the Highline Trail climbs towards ROCKY SEA PASS, to the northeast. The only water available between the west and east slopes of this steep pass is a spring, 11 *m.*, which boils unexpectedly out of dry rocks. Two miles of rough, rocky and steep trail traverse the pass. At 13 *m.* is a large meadow dotted with lakes; the trail passes between two of them.

A tributary, 14.5 *m.*, of Rock Creek, crossed by the trail, empties from RAINBOW LAKE (L), in which there is good fishing. There are campsites on the east side of the lake. Somewhere in Upper Rock Creek Valley is supposedly one of the "lost" Caleb Rhodes mines. While no one has ever been able to find a trace either of his placer or his lode mine, it is well established that he left a fortune when he died.

The trail descends from Rainbow Lake through a forest to the floor of the valley, crossing ROCK CREEK proper at 15.5 *m.*, east of which is a junction with a north-south trail paralleling Rock Creek.

Left on a branch trail to SQUAW BASIN, 2 *m.* Right on a branch trail to LOWER STILLWATER, 20 *m.* (*see Tour 5*).

The Highline Trail rounds a towering rock point (L), at 18 *m.*, and leads north to a small lake (L), crowded between two solid rock cliffs and fed by small springs issuing in a smother of spray from a cliff face. The trail zigzags up to the summit of DEADHORSE PASS, 20 *m.* Perpetual cool winds blow over this high pass, and the view from the summit can hardly be surpassed by climbing the higher surrounding peaks.

A small blue lake (L), 21 *m.*, is the head of the West Fork of Blacks Fork Creek; lake and stream are well stocked with rainbow trout. The Highline Trail continues east to the junction, 21.1 *m.*, with a branch trail, which leads L. to the BLACKS FORK RANGER STATION, 7 *m.*, and R. to a near-by stream.

The summit, 24 *m.*, of RED KNOB PASS presents a magnificent view. Denuded craggy peaks, including Mt. Lovenia (13,277 alt.), with clouds hiding their tops, are to the north and south; to the east and west are dense forests dotted with lakes, like a handful of newly minted coins thrown at random on a green lawn, connected by silvery stream-threads.

The trail reaches the junction, 27 *m.*, with several posted trails. Southeast (R) along the Lake Fork Creek trail to MOON LAKE, 14 *m.* (*see Tour 5*).

At 35 *m.* the trail crosses PORCUPINE PASS; the rugged mountain to the northeast is Wilson Peak (13,095 alt.). YELLOWSTONE CREEK VALLEY, with its trout lakes, is entered at 36 *m.*

The main trail continues L., past NORTH STAR LAKE, 37.5 *m.*, and ascends ANDERSON PASS, 42 *m.*, which is just north of KINGS PEAK (13,498 alt.), the highest mountain in Utah. From the summit of the pass a short hike (R), not too difficult, leads to the "highest point," where the "Record" is kept. In a stone cairn is the log which is usually signed by those who visit this lofty peak. Colorado, Wyoming, and Idaho mountains can be seen from here, and streams heading apparently at the foot of the peak diverge and flow into these three States.

At 44 *m.* is the junction with two trails; the north (L) trail leads to LAKE ATWOOD, 4 *m.*, and CHAIN LAKES, 10 *m.*, stocked by the Government in the middle 1930's and very infrequently fished. The southeast (R) trail follows the North Fork of the Uinta River for several miles, where it joins the Uinta River proper, which it follows for 40 miles to the Indian settlement of WHITEROCKS (*see Tour 6a*).

The Highline Trail continues to the top, 41.5 *m.*, of GUNSIGHT PASS, from which the vast meadows of Henrys Fork drop off to the north. An alternate trail (R), 42.5 *m.*, leads three-quarters of a mile northeast from this junction to DOLLAR LAKE, while the main trail (L) winds across the valley floor to HENRYS FORK LAKE, GLASS LAKE, and BEAR LAKE.

At 46 *m.* is the junction with a marked east-west trail. The east (R) trail leads to FISH LAKE, 21 *m.,* in the eastern end of the Uintas. The west (L) trail runs to the EAST FORK, 7 *m.,* of Smiths Fork Creek, a fine fishing stream, in a wild and beautiful valley, walled by high and gorgeously colored mountain peaks. At the head, 12 *m.,* of the East Fork of Smiths Fork Creek are several small lakes within a radius of about 5 miles.

The route continues through dense timber and lush meadows to HENRYS FORK PARK, 56 *m.,* eastern terminus of the Highline Trail, where campsites are maintained by the U. S. Forest Service. This is the only practical entry to the High Uintas Primitive Area from the north. From Henrys Fork Park a dirt road leads northeast 13 miles to Lonetree, Wyoming, and a gravel road north of Lonetree connects with US 30S, near Lyman, Wyoming (*see Wyoming Guide*).

Hovenweep National Monument

Highway Approach: From Utah by an unimproved unnumbered desert road that leads east to the Monument from State 47, 12.2 *m.* north of Bluff; from Colorado on an unnumbered dirt road W. from Cortez 25 *m.* to McElmo, thence 12 *m.* NW. on an unnumbered dirt road to the Ruin Canyon group, or 16 *m.* SW. to Cajon Canyon group. The Colorado approach is better, and gives the visitor an opportunity to obtain free guide service at Mesa Verde National Park. All roads are patrolled at regular intervals.
Season: All year. Best in spring or fall.
Administrative Office: Superintendent of Mesa Verde National Park, Mesa Verde, Colorado.
Admission: Free.

Accommodations: None at Monument. Rooms and meals at Cortez and McElmo, Colorado, and at Bluff and Blanding, Utah.

Transportation: Private automobile only.
Climate, Clothing, and Equipment: Altitude of Hovenweep is about 5,000 feet, nights are usually cool and days hot during the spring and fall. Light rugged clothing and shoes, with coat for evening wear. Certain canyons in Monument contain springs, but it is well to carry a small supply of drinking water. Carry own equipment for camping.
Warnings and Regulations: Usual, applying to national monuments. Do not remove artifacts or carve initials on dwellings. Monument is best visited with a guide (supplied without charge by superintendent at Mesa Verde). To see all dwellings in Hovenweep requires a full day and a hike of about 12 miles.

HOVENWEEP NATIONAL MONUMENT, in the remote canyon country north of the San Juan River by the Colorado-Utah line, was established by presidential proclamation in 1923 to extend Park Service protection to the ruins of a numerous prehistoric civilization. The reserve, though small—it is no larger than a middle-sized farm by desert standards—contains four separate groups of buildings, perhaps suburbs of a single city, among which are several towers that are of great interest to archeologists. The Monument includes four large and several tributary canyons in the mesa between Montezuma and McElmo creeks, the principal ruins being in Ruin and Cajon canyons in Utah, and Hackberry and Keeley canyons in Colorado. Sage Plain, the mesa into which the canyons of Hovenweep are cut, is horizon-wide in all directions, broken only by the blue Abajos and the distant La Sal Mountains northward. Over it, sage grows everywhere, sometimes in thick stands from three to five feet high, interspersed with piñon and scattered juniper. In the canyons, especially in those with springs, there are small parks, patches of meadow, and growths of cottonwood trees. It is a cattle and sheep range. Herbert E. Gregory, an eloquent and authoritative spokesman for San Juan winds, says of them in his

Geologic and Geographic Reconnaissance of Southeastern Utah, "They blow in and out of canyons, up canyons, down canyons, around buttes and mesas. They blow up over the box heads of canyons during the day, only to return down canyon at night. During the hot summer days they seem to head from all directions toward sand flats and stretches of naked rocks." The whorled cliffs and denuded patches of slickrock, in Hovenweep, bear Gregory witness. It is difficult for many to believe that Hovenweep once supported a large population, perhaps more people than there are today in the whole county of San Juan. Old-timers, however, point out that "Hovenweep" in the Ute Indian tongue (the "o" is long, as in "over") means "deserted valley," and often add "no wonder."

Padres Escalante and Domínguez passed by the region of the Hovenweep dwellings in 1776, discovered one ruin in what is now south-western Colorado, damned it with a passing reference, and left it for W. H. Holmes and W. H. Jackson of the Hayden expedition to rediscover, together with others on McElmo Creek, an even century later. In 1879, Peter Shirts, a roving trapper who by repute had more experiences than furs at season's end, was camped at the mouth of Montezuma Creek, and a family named Mitchell was living at the mouth of McElmo Creek. Settlement of San Juan Valley by the Mormons in 1880 threw no new light, as far as known, on the ruins of Hovenweep, but stockmen who succeeded the farmers toward the end of that decade ranged the country from one end to the other. By 1910 the dwellings in Ruin and Cajon canyons were well-known landmarks, a few of them had been looted, and archeologists were interesting themselves in the tower structure at canyon heads. J. Walter Fewkes, chief of the Bureau of American Ethnology, published a comprehensive study of the Hovenweep ruins in the annual report of the Smithsonian Institution for 1923.

Ruin Canyon and its south fork, sometimes called Square Tower Canyon, contains the most numerous and important group of buildings in the Monument. The canyon heads about twelve miles north of the San Juan River and drains to it by way of McElmo Creek. Gregory speaks of Sage Plain as "deeply dissected by streamways that begin as canyons and continue as canyons all the way to the San Juan." Ruin Canyon fits this description; it appears without warning, 300 to 500 feet deep, and as sheer-walled as a sewer trench. It has no gradual beginning, but presents an abrupt drop from the mesa at its head. Along this ledge, in caves within the canyon wall, and along its base, are the prehistoric ruins. HOVENWEEP HOUSE stands at the cliff rim in the head of Square Tower Canyon. It was, in the times of its Pueblo builders, a large semicircular structure that housed perhaps fifty families, and included circular underground rooms (now called *kivas*) for priestly rites and a large D-shaped tower that rose from the middle of the house. Under the cliff below Hovenweep House are the remains of another large dwelling, and atop a pinnacle that rises from the canyon is SQUARE TOWER, the remarkable ruin from which the canyon takes its name. HOVENWEEP CASTLE, on the north rim of Square Tower Canyon, is the best preserved building in the Monument. It was built in two wings, not unlike the L-shaped feudal manors of Europe, and contained, besides sleeping and living chambers, several towers and underground ceremonial *kivas*. The walls of this building are massive affairs of rock and mud mortar, some of them still rising more than twenty feet. At the apex of the peninsula that separates the north and south forks of Ruin Canyon is another tower, which commands a splendid vista eastward over the main canyon, and below it, on the canyon floor, are several dwellings.

On the north rim of Ruin Canyon, a short walk from Hovenweep Castle, is the UNIT TYPE HOUSE, a circular *kiva* surrounded by rectangular rooms. Down-canyon on the north rim are still other dwellings, among which is picturesque STRONGHOLD HOUSE. The best preserved structures in Ruin Canyon are, however, on the south rim. ERODED BOULDER HOUSE, perched atop a projecting rock much like Square Tower, is chiefly remarkable for its position, but the dwellings adjacent to it show clearly the method by which the Pueblos laid their mortar. TWIN TOWERS occupy a platform at the cliff rim and are separated from the main body of the mesa by a deep cleft. The foundation of the larger tower is oval, that of the smaller, horseshoe-shaped; the walls of both are in a fair state of preservation.

Cajon Canyon, a few miles southwest of Ruin Canyon, contains one major ruin called COOL SPRING HOUSE because the canyon below it flows with sweetwater. Hackberry and Keeley canyons, over the Colorado line a short hike eastward from Ruin Canyon, contain additional dwellings and towers, the most important of which are HACKBERRY CASTLE and HORSESHOE HOUSE.

Of the folk who built the dwellings in Hovenweep very little is known beyond what has been gleaned from deserted houses and burial grounds. Archeologists agree that the houses have not been occupied in 600 years, perhaps longer, and Fewkes concludes that the origin of these sedentary aborigines in canyons of the San Juan probably antedates written history. They seem to have migrated from the north, for their progress southward through the Colorado Plateau toward the Rio Grande is marked by increasingly complex dwellings. When they first settled along the tributaries of the Colorado River in what is now Utah, they had not yet learned to build above ground nor to bake pottery. They lived in pit dwellings, cultivated corn, and worked river reeds into baskets to carry their possessions. The Basketmakers (*see Archeology and Indians*) in the security of their hidden gorges and scarcely accessible mesas began to build more enduringly, higher and higher above ground, became more dependent on their corn patches, and ultimately developed fixed communities, which archeologists call pueblos. The similarity between this prehistoric Pueblo culture and that of contemporary rural America is in many respects remarkable. To the pueblo-builder the canyon or stream course was a highway as well as a water-source, and he built villages at important and easily defended points. Between these villages isolated small farmhouses dotted the course of travel. A village, as for example the important cluster of dwellings at the head of Ruin Canyon, then as now, probably served as a market and cultural center for the farming regions strung out about it. Fewkes found evidences of both cultures, or both stages of the same culture, in Hovenweep, the houses of the Pueblo peoples having been constructed over more primitive earth lodges.

That the people of Hovenweep were skilled farmers at the peak of their civilization is evidenced by remains of check dams and irrigation ditches near their cornfields. Their pottery is of a high order, and the masonry of their adobe-cemented stone buildings shows skillful workmanship. The readiness with which their houses have broken down at the corners indicates, however, that they did not master the business of "tying" the walls together. They built as high as three stories and raftered each floor with cedar logs. The towers of Hovenweep have been variously explained as forts, storage bins (not unlike a twentieth-century grain elevator), observatories, lookout towers, and as temples for the performance of religious rites. Probably they were put to all these uses: several are in canyon bottoms where they have no view at all, others are built directly over subterranean *kivas,* which are known definitely to have been consecrated to religious ceremonies, others occupy strategic cliff-edge positions that seem to have been selected with an eye to defense. Fewkes suggests that since the Hovenweep Pueblos were an agricultural people, their towers may have been observatories from which planting time was determined by priestly observations of the sun's rising and setting. He adds that "a building from which aboriginal priests determined calendric events by solar observations very naturally became a room for sun worship." As to the *kivas,* which frequently appear beneath the towers, they were retained for the celebration of rites to the mother earth.

The reason for complete disappearance of the Hovenweep people is even more problematical than the function of their towers. It has been suggested that the pueblo-building Zuñi and Hopi of Arizona and New Mexico are the only survivors of this once numerous cliff-dweller nation, though neither of the modern tribes claims the old folk for its ancestors. In Navaho *hogans* south of the San Juan River, the venerable and garrulous keep alive a story of Navaho invasion, so long ago that no man's father remembers it. The invaders, they say, found a weak and effeminate race living in the cliff houses, drove them into rivers, and saw them changed to fish. A primitive *blitzkrieg* may conceivably have descended upon the cliff-dwellers. Kitchen crockery, corn, stone knives, and other artifacts were not removed (the Navaho regards these conquered folk with a proper sense of racial superiority, not without an intermingling of superstitious regard for their abandoned dwellings). Archeologists, however, suggest again that as the northernmost pueblos grew in size, arable lands may have given out, and communities that depended on them were forced to migrate by slow stages southward. More pessimistic scientists advance the theory that the cliff-dwellers civilized themselves into extinction, or that, not having any adequate concept of sanitation, they bred plagues in their compact communities. Most likely, all of these possibilities contributed to the ultimate eradication of the prehistoric pueblo-builders. The fact that the Ute tongue bears close affinities to that of the Hopi has not been sufficiently investigated. The cliff-dwellers may have been assimilated by nomadic tribes that occupied the Southwest when white men came (most modern tribes of Utah have practiced slavery within the memory of their old men, and they seldom erected caste taboos between slave and master).

Indians

Indians

MAKING NAVAHO BREAD

"MASTODON" PETROGLYPH, NEAR MOAB

ROCK PICTURES, NATURAL BRIDGES NATIONAL MONUMENT

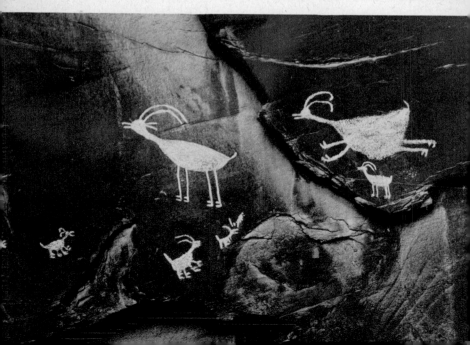

RUINS OF PREHISTORIC HOUSES,
HOVENWEEP NATIONAL MONUMENT

PONCHO HOUSE, SOUTHEASTERN UTAH

NAVAHOLAND—MONUMENT VALLEY

Roy and Brownie Adams

NAVAHO HOGAN

Charles Kelly

NAVAHOS ON THE MOVE

Charles Kelly

Roy and Brownie Adams

NAVAHO MEDICINE MAN IN COSTUME

R. M. Jones   *Smithsonian Institution*

PAINTING BY GORDON COPE
OF JOHN DUNCAN, UTE CHIEF

OURAY (*Center*) AND SUB-
CHIEFS OF THE SOUTHERN UTE

UTE INDIAN (c. 1860)   UTE FARMER

A C. R. Savage Photograph: *Courtesy U. S.*
Courtesy L. D. S. Church   *Indian Service*

Roy and Brownie Adams

NAVAHO MEDICINE MAN WITH SAND
PAINTING USED IN HEALING RITES

HOGAN ON THE SHIVWIT RESERVATION

Dr. D. E. Beck

Natural Bridges National Monument

Highway Approach: 51.1 *m.* W. of Blanding on State 95, improved dirt road.
Season: Open all year, but Bears Ears Pass closed by snow, December 1 to April 15.
Administrative Offices: At Monument in summer.

Accommodations: Small hotel, tourist cabins at Blanding. Administration building in Monument, with sleeping and eating accommodations May 1-Nov. 30. Excellent campsites in southern area of La Sal National Forest, on way into Monument. Garage at Blanding.

Admission: Free.
Transportation: Private automobiles can be hired at Blanding. Nearest railroad station at Thompsons, on Denver & Rio Grande Western R.R. Motor stage, Thompsons to Blanding.
Climate, Clothing and Equipment: Summer temperatures may vary 50 degrees in a single day from hot days to cool nights. Low humidity, heat not oppressive. Outdoor clothing, including riding clothes and stout shoes for hiking. Camera, extra films. Carry own water, food, gasoline, and oil—not available between Blanding and Monument.
Post Office: Blanding.
Medical Service and Dentist: Doctor and dentist at Blanding. Nearest hospital at Moab.
Communication: Long distance telephone at Blanding.
Speed Limits: Low gear driving in spots on State 95.
Naturalist Service: Custodian at Monument.
Recreational Facilities: Hiking, climbing, horseback and pack trips by advance arrangement. Fishing or hunting in season in adjacent La Sal National Forest.
Warnings and Regulations: Do not remove artifacts, wild flowers or other objects. Do not carve initials on rocks. Usual regulations applying to national monuments.
Guides and Horses: Arrange with custodian. Guides $5 per day, horses $3 per day.

NATURAL BRIDGES NATIONAL MONUMENT is an area of spectacular erosive formations, its chief attractions being three immense water-carved bridges and a number of prehistoric cliff-dweller villages. Eastward, the green-wooded diagonal rise of Elk Ridge leans against the sky; in all other directions the unending red and dun of the plateau face rolls with deceptive and innocent smoothness toward the horizon; forty miles westward the Colorado River gnaws sluggishly at the mesa walls of Glen Canyon. From high places the castellated buttes of Moki Canyon are dimly visible. In the canyons of the Monument the dominant red of the plateau country is broken into endless gradations, from a metallic yellow where the sun glints, to deep and misty violet in the shadows, with streamers and blotches of lichen green.

The entire region between Blanding and the Colorado River is, in a sense, a single plateau, overlain by smaller plateaus that ascend and descend stepwise, or rear up as isolated buttes, or reach from horizon to horizon as immense mesas. The whole system is composed of sedimentary rock laid down by Triassic and Permian oceans and raised above the waters about the time of the dinosaurs. The forces which raised the plateaus tilted them gently, forming the essential features of the Colorado drainage system, and rain water, working oceanward through it, carved a meshwork of intricate cracks and cleavages, and enlarged the cracks to box-walled gorges and canyons sometimes as much as 2,500 feet deep. Where soft and hard beds of stone alternate in the canyon, the soft beds have been eroded out, leaving massive overhangs, caves, alcoves, fluted columns, and bridges. The meandering course of San Juan waterways often takes the form of great loops. The streams, throwing their force against the loop necks, in time cut through and leave islanded buttes beside the new course. Where the capstone is hard and the underlying beds soft, the water carves deep, overhung alcoves in the soft stuff, and eventually may punch completely through it in a narrow neck, leaving an island that is joined to the "mainland" by a bridge of capstone. Subsequent erosion of the new channel cuts it deeper without affecting the overspanning capstone, and a bridge such as the Sipapu is tediously formed. According to Zeke Johnson, "one of the most noted geologists said in his opinion Owachomo, which is considered the oldest bridge, was at least ten million years old. That was on the 14th day of July, 1926, so if he was right, the bridge was 10,000,014 years old in July, 1940. I will continue to keep track of their age after this." On the plateau faces, water and "her handmaiden wind" have carved whorls, turrets, potholes, windows, and have contoured the rock with whimsical designs as complex as those of a Persian rug. Of soil there is very little, except in the canyon bottoms. The people of San Juan have a saying about this country: "A lot of rocks, a lot of sand, more rocks, more sand, and wind enough to blow it away."

Wild life and vegetation on the plateau are diverse. The igneous Abajo Mountains, 10 miles north of Blanding, have been driven up wedgewise through the plateau face to altitudes of 10,000 feet and they are heavily wooded, as is Elk Ridge, about half way between Blanding and the Monument. Desert shrubs, piñon, and juniper subsist somewhat thinly in the coarse dry patches of soil on the plateau face, but in the well-watered canyons it is not uncommon to see pine, white fir, black balsam, manzanita, and snowberry growing beside saltbush, chapparal, greasewood, and yucca. In Dark Canyon and Grand Gulch plateaus bighorn sheep, mule deer, mountain lion, bobcat, bear, and beaver have been sighted, though the habitat is more native for coyotes, lizards and pack rats. Several varieties of snakes are found in both alpine and desert regions of the plateaus, but poisonous species are rare in both places. Birds of the high mountains and those of the desert nest within a few miles of each other—magpies, mourning doves, piñon jays, sage sparrows, canyon towhees, bluebirds, rock wrens, swallows, and chickadees are the most plentiful, though eagles, ravens, meadowlarks, cranes, finches, grouse, and water ouzels are sometimes seen.

In prehistoric times the plateau was occupied by a primitive people sometimes called Cliff Dwellers. White and Allen canyons and Grand Gulch have large clusters of houses (built sometimes of fitted stone, sometimes of adobe) that yield fine examples of pottery, and stone and bone implements; smaller communities have been found elsewhere in the area. Herbert E. Gregory, of the U. S. Geological Survey, was so moved by the remarkable preservation of the dwellings that he felt "the families have merely gone on a long visit." The Cliff Dwellers of this region, however, were displaced at least 500 years ago by the Ute and Paiute Indians, whose descendents now occupy Allen Canyon. The first white visitors are anonymous. A few trappers may have traversed the country, but they left no record. In the 1880's, Cass Hite, a desert misanthrope whose name still graces a one-man town in the Colorado River (*see Tour 2A*), worked his way through this country, and according to historical gossip of San Juan oldtimers, brought back accounts of many wonders including three "whoppin'" natural bridges. About 1885, cattlemen began filtering into the Grand Gulch and Dark Canyon country, and some of them stayed. In 1895, cattleman Emery Knowles saw the bridges in White Canyon and later in the same year, James Scorup visited them. In 1903, Scorup guided Horace M. Long to his find, and in August 1904, W. W. Dyar published an account of their explorations in *Century Magazine*. By 1908 the bridges were sufficiently well known to be set aside as a national monument, and in 1928 a road was "extended" from Blanding to the Monument.

BLANDING TO NATURAL BRIDGES

West of Blanding, State 95 traverses the arid mesas of Sage Plain, Brush Basin, and Dark Canyon Plateau, transcends pine-wooded Elk Ridge, and descends abruptly to the sandstone floor of Grand Gulch Plateau. The road is, according to Zeke Johnson, custodian of the Monument in 1940, "not too good, not bad." Herbert E. Gregory, who made a geologic reconnaissance of the San Juan County between 1909 and 1929, says that off the road "A few trails are kept open by cattlemen, and in many places the topography marks out feasible routes for pack trains," but that "most travel consists of rough scrambles in and out of canyons at places that seem at the time most favorable." The region is devoted primarily to grazing—"Panhandle style" say local cattlemen, who assert that a paltry thousand acres will support one steer in bovine luxury, "if he's tough."

At 12.6 *m.*, the road zigzags down a steep dugway into COTTON-WOOD WASH. Disappearing into Cottonwood Wash (R) is a natural causeway, ten feet wide and straight as a boulevard for several miles, which local romantics solemnly claim is an ancient highway.

Boulders have been piled along it by flood waters; cuts and fills are claimed for it; and the grade is uniform from beginning to end.

An INDIAN TRADING POST, 14 *m.*, offers Paiute, Navaho, and Hopi craftworks for sale. Visitors may obtain blankets, baskets, turquoises, and Navaho silver work at reservation prices.

At 15.6 *m.*, a dirt road (R) leads 2.2 *m.* to ALLEN CANYON INDIAN AGENCY, a farm of 8,800 acres, of which perhaps 80 were under desultory cultivation in 1940. Allen Canyon, a characteristic plateau fantasia of mesas, columns, and whorled abutments in the inevitable red sandstone, in prehistoric times sheltered a large Cliff-Dweller suburb; in historic times a band of Paiutes, who steadfastly refused to be removed to other reservations, were allotted farming lands in the canyon. In 1934, Gregory said that, although a sympathetic agent was attempting to make them self-sufficient, "it has been found impractical to discontinue food rations."

At 17 *m.* a posted trail (L) leads (100 yds.) to the GOBLET OF VENUS, a piece of freak weather tooling in vermilion sandstone. The goblet bowl, six or seven feet in diameter and weighing about five tons, is delicately balanced atop a symmetrical stem six feet long and not much thicker than a man's leg.

At 18.3 *m.* the road enters the southern section of LA SAL NATIONAL FOREST. Desert vegetation yields, as the road ascends the outermost escarpment of Elk Ridge, to yellow pine, oak, scrub maple, willow, manzanita, sagebrush, and, on the high places of the ridge, to aspen. Elk Ridge is actually a domed plateau of the same character and composition as the desert regions about it but its altitude, which averages 8,000 feet, permits alpine vegetation. KIGALIA RANGER STATION (R), 30 *m.*, is occupied during the summer months and is the only place between Blanding and Natural Bridges National Monument where first aid can be obtained.

At 30.5 *m.*, the road skirts the rim of the Elk Ridge plateau, affording a tremendous sweep of desert vista such as Zane Grey called "the yellow-and-purple corrugated world of distance." Southward, the towering buttes of Monument Valley, 50 miles away, are visible over the face of Grand Gulch Plateau; eastward, Sage Plain, walled off from Grand Gulch Plateau by battlemented Comb Ridge, extends deep into Colorado; westward, the view ranges over Dark Canyon Plateau, White Canyon, Red House Cliffs, the buttes and ridges of Moki Canyon, to the dim outlines of Kaiparowits Plateau beyond the Colorado River. Beginning almost in the talus at the foot of the rim, the sheer gorge of Arch Canyon yaws across the face of Grand Gulch Plateau, the walls whitening as they descend to the inaccessible canyon floor.

At 34.8 *m.* the road passes between the twin peaks called BEARS EARS (9,059 and 8,508 alt.). The reason for the name is obvious for miles before they are reached.

MAVERICK SPRING (L about 150 yards), 36.8 *m.*, is the last readily available water between Elk Ridge and Natural Bridges National Monument, and is a favorite camping spot for Indians; their pine-bough windbreaks are usually found near the spring.

MAVERICK POINT, 39.7 *m.,* commands a second sweeping vista over the stepped mesas, south, east, and west. In *Rainbow Trail,* Zane Grey said ". . . his judgement of distance was confounded and his sense of proportion was dwarfed one moment and magnified the next. Then he withdrew his fascinated gaze to adopt the Indian's method of studying unlimited spaces in the desert—to look with slow, contracted eyes from near to far." There is no better advice. The tremendous masses of upflung, reddened stone, the carved buttes and monoliths in the gray distance, even the horizontal mass of the configured plateau beneath the Point, will by such scrutiny reveal their bulk and intricate form. The Point is the outermost rampart of Elk Ridge, and from it descent to Grand Gulch Plateau is abrupt. At 50 *m.* the road enters upon a series of contorted writhings locally designated as "Zeke Johnson's Last Half Mile," and breaks out suddenly at 51 *m.,* onto an improved parking and camping space, in full view of Owachomo Bridge on the southern boundary of the Monument. At this point is the headquarters of the caretaker. One hundred feet westward is the brink of Armstrong Canyon, 200 feet deep, carved from pale sandstone.

OWACHOMO BRIDGE, 100 yards by foot trail, named Little Bridge by Long and Scorup, and renamed Edwin for a time, is ten feet thick and spans 200-foot Armstrong Canyon at a height of 108 feet (Long, triangulating with his thumb, said 142 feet). The word Little is appropriate only in comparison with the other two bridges. Owachomo, a Hopi word meaning "flat-rock mound," was chosen for a near-by promontory. The stone of Owachomo Bridge is light, a pale salmon pink, shot through laterally with vermilion streaks, and accented here and there by green and orange lichens. The "slickrock" canyon walls beneath and beyond it are "most voluptuously" whorled and as delicately colored as the bridge itself. By evening light the hard stone seems velvet soft, and it glows until the coyotes begin to howl. Almost beneath the bridge is a "tank" or pothole in the slickrock such as desert men cherish as sources of drinking water—this one, however, is commonly known as "Zeke's bathtub."

Many visitors do not leave their cars and the camp tables at the end of the road, but Zeke Johnson, custodian since 1916, whose enthusiasm for the bridges was legend as early as 1930, says that "it is customary to walk" a nine-mile triangular trail that leads to the other two bridges.

From Owachomo, a well-marked foot trail works southward through Armstrong Canyon. At 3 *m.* is KACHINA BRIDGE. Scorup stipulated as part of his agreement to Long for guiding him that he should be permitted to name one of the bridges for his wife. He chose this one, and called it Caroline. Government officials, in the proclamation establishing the Monument, substituted the name Kachina (a Hopi word meaning "sacred dance") because there were dance symbols carved on the bridge. Kachina is the most massive of the three bridges, 107 feet thick at its narrowest place, and the stone of which it is composed is a deeper red. Its span is 186 feet, and it rises 205 feet above the canyon floor. At Kachina Bridge a fork (L) of the trail leads downstream about 200 yards to a scattered community of cliff dwellings and several excellent rock pictures. The main trail turns (R) up White Canyon, almost under the Bridge. The scalloped walls of White Canyon vary in color from a warm pearl gray to brick red; at several points they widen, forming small parks, and as often they contract until the overhanging lip of the plateau above almost shuts out the sky. The canyon throughout its length is well watered and supports lush vegetation.

SIPAPU BRIDGE, 3.5 m., is the most impressive of all. To Dyar, it seemed "a structure so magnificent, so symmetrical and beautiful in its proportions, as to suggest that nature, after completing the mighty structure of the Caroline, had trained herself for a finer and nobler form of architecture." Long, following Scorup's precedent, named the bridge for his wife, who was "very appropriately" christened Augusta. The name Sipapu was taken from Hopi legend and it refers to "the gateway through which the souls of men come from the underworld and finally return to it." The Hopi say that formerly the souls of men were shut up under the earth. The animals, when they learned this thing, set out to release them. Coyote dug for a while, and after him almost all of the animals worked to deepen the hole, but Badger, who is the real digger of the animals, finished the job. When Badger's claws poked through the crust, men were released from the underworld, but when earth is through with men, they must return to underworld the same way they came out—through the arched cave carved by Coyote and Badger and the other animals. Subtle ones among the whites say that the legend is an allegory of the pelvic arch and the return to prenatal simplicity. Be that as it may, most present-day Indians are reluctant to visit the vicinity of natural bridges, which strongly resemble the opening clawed out by Badger. The 261-foot span of Sipapu would give egress to an army, and the bridge arches 222 feet above the canyon floor—the Capitol at Washington, D. C., could sit under it very nicely, and have fifty feet to spare. Dyar estimated that the tallest Sequoia in Calaveras Grove, if planted under the bridge, would have thirty feet to grow before its tallest tip would brush the under side of the span.

Sipapu Bridge was marred by initial-carvers in 1926, and the incident furnishes Zeke Johnson, the custodian, with one of his most oft-told tales:

A group of boys was going out to the bridges from Blanding, and I told them not to scratch their names on rocks inside the Monument. One man who went along with the boys (I will just call him John Doe) told his boy that that man Zeke Johnson had no police authority over those rocks, and he and his son wrote their names on top of Sipapu Bridge and dug it deep. Well of course I explained the law and told him to get back out and rub it off, and he told me to go "places." The invitation to go some place was repeated several times, and I found it necessary to write to the director of national parks in Washington, D. C. The defendant got a letter telling him that unless he immediately complied with Custodian Johnson's instructions he would have a free ride at his own expense from Blanding to Washington, D. C., to be arraigned before the U. S. Government. He soon hunted me up and asked what he should do. I said just do as I told you, track back out there and take off those initials. He offered me twenty bucks if I would do it, but I told him nobody could do it but him, and it was a five-day horse-back trip in those days. Since then he has been a help to me. Several initial-cutters have been caught, and when they tried to lobby with me I just told them to step across the street and talk with Mr. John Doe. I can't give you chapter and verse, but the law is very plain, and I am obliged to enforce it.

At Sipapu, a trail (L) continues northeasterly up White Canyon 0.5 *m.*, to a Cliff Dweller community that extends along the left wall of the canyon a mile and a half. The houses occupy alcoves in the wall from ten to fifty feet above the canyon floor, and are in an excellent state of preservation. At 1.2 *m.*, is a large group of dwellings in a cave about forty feet above the stream bed. These are reached by the original ladders—now decrepit with age but reinforced somewhat with "Mormon buckskin," which is to say, baling wire. Zeke Johnson's customary advice to tourists wishing to climb into this dwelling is, "I'll tell you where they are, but I won't advise you." Included in the group are two-story structures, small storage rooms, and a *kiva* with its sooted ceremonial rock and incised wall-symbols still intact.

The main trail turns southward (R) from Sipapu Bridge, climbs steeply out of White Canyon, and returns 3 *m.* across the rolling mesa face to its starting place at Owachomo Bridge. The entire length of the Monument trails, including side paths to cliff dwellings, is about 12 miles; they can be traversed in a day's walk.

Rainbow Bridge National Monument

Highway Approach: 107.4 *m.* NE. of Tuba City, Arizona, to Rainbow Lodge, 14 *m.* SE. of Monument. Two-day pack trip from Rainbow Lodge.

Season: Weather permitting, the Monument may be reached at any time of year, but it is advisable to inquire locally before leaving main highways. Rainbow Lodge open only during summer months.

Administrative Office: Superintendent of Southwestern National Monuments, Coolidge, Arizona. No resident custodian.

Admission: Free.

Accommodations: Rainbow Lodge. Authorized trading post, furnished cottages, supplies.

Transportation: Nearest railroad station · (Santa Fe) at Flagstaff, Arizona. Arrangements for auto transportation to Rainbow Lodge can be made through Fred Harvey Tours, Grand Canyon, Arizona; Jack Wilson, Nava-Hopi Tours, Flagstaff, Arizona; or Little Colorado Trading Post, Cameron, Arizona.

Climate, Clothing and Equipment: Occasional severe winters, hot in summer. Advisable to wear western cowpuncher clothing. Cord-soled hiking shoes, riding boots, compass, first aid kit, smoked glasses, camera, and films. This is a strenuous trip, far from help or supplies; visitors should be good horsemen and in better than average health.

Medical and Dental Service: Hospitals, doctors, and dentists at Winslow and Flagstaff, Arizona.

Speed Limits: From Red Lake to Rainbow Lodge the road is merely two wheel tracks winding through sand-filled washes or crossing hazardous rock ledges. It is passable for modern cars if driven with care, but easier with models having higher wheel bases. Use extreme care not to high center and puncture oil pans.

Recreational Facilities: Pack trips, hiking, climbing, photography, exploring, and scientific study. Beyond the Lodge with guides only.

Warnings and Regulations: National Park rules must be obeyed; do not damage Government property or carve initials on rocks. Trust your guide, and obey him completely; it may mean your life. The entire region is criss-crossed by Indian trails, many of which look like main trails. The main trails have been much improved since first laid out, but still have hazardous stretches. To stray from the main trail or become lost may result in death by thirst.

Guides and Horses: At Mexican Hat or Goulding's Trading Post, Utah; Kayenta or Rainbow Lodge, Arizona. Write for reservations and rates. Average cost is approximately $15 per person per day, for saddle horses, pack horses, guide, meals, and bedding. Two-day trail trip, including meals and bedding, Rainbow Lodge to Rainbow Bridge and return, $30 per person. Carry all personal equipment, such as spare clothing and cameras, that may be needed for entire trip.

RAINBOW BRIDGE NATIONAL MONUMENT, in southern Utah, is about 6 miles north of the Arizona line, and 10 miles southwest of the Colorado River junction with the San Juan River. It includes 160 acres around the largest natural bridge yet discovered, and was set apart by President Taft as a monument in 1910. The bridge is not accessible by car, a two-day pack trip northeast from Rainbow Lodge, Arizona, being necessary to reach it. Longer pack trips can be taken from Mexican Hat or Goulding's Trading Post, both in Utah.

The Monument borders the least known uninhabited area in the United States. The Colorado River, a busy and efficient hydraulic excavator, has made it impractical for roads to reach the region. The thinly vegetated country surrounding Rainbow Bridge supports only a few goats and sheep belonging to scattered bands of Navahos and Paiutes. Navaho Mountain looms southeast of the bridge, more than 10,000 feet above the sea, but seeming much lower because of its rounded slopes. The Navahos avoid it, the dwelling place of their thunder god. The tops of plateaus, mesas, and mountains in the area around Rainbow Bridge are rounded; natives call them whalebacks and baldheads. To traverse such slanting surfaces is sometimes as hazardous as scaling the perpendicular, since the rocks are best described by their familiar name—"slickrocks." Native horses and mules, and even Indian ponies, sometimes slide disastrously when taken off established trails. There is no soil, only finely pulverized sand and accumulated humus in the bottom of gorges. The shoes of the white man's horses ring on the smooth rocks or swish through the soft heavy sand, which pervades everything.

This is a country, as Irvin S. Cobb puts it, "where Old Marster stacked it up and scooped it out and shuffled it together again so violently, so completely and with such incredibly beautiful tonings, such inconceivably awesome results." The bare naked rocks blaze with blended colors; curves and outlines display stark massive strength. There is, in the country, a vivid eternal peace, vastness, and power. Intermingled with the serenity of solitude, yet causing no apprehension to the seasoned desert dweller, is the ever-present thirst menace of the region. Yet Bridge Canyon, spanned by Rainbow Bridge, is an inconceivably green oasis, spattered with brilliant flowers.

Father Escalante skirted this country in 1776, crossing the Colorado River roughly 20 miles west of Rainbow Bridge. The peaceful *padre's* diary says that his party was suffering, short of food, tortured by infrequent water, yet borne up by an abiding faith. Cass Hite, who built a cabin at Hites Crossing, existed for many years by washing out flour gold. He was responsible for one of the pathetic episodes of this area. In 1890, when questioned by greedy prospectors about the gold near his home, he stated that all the heavier gold would positively be found north of Navaho Mountain, washed there by the river. A gold rush followed. Great dredges now lie twisted and rusting on sandbars in the Colorado, abandoned because the gold was too flour-fine to recover. All the efforts of man, even those stimulated by the lust for gold, were frustrated and thrown back by this inaccessible country. It remains today as it was before the coming of white men. There are relics of the ubiquitous cliff dwellers near Rainbow Bridge, and petroglyphs and pictographs can be seen all over the region.

Rainbow Bridge is in the Navaho country. In 1906, John Wetherill and his young bride drove rumbling freight wagons north from Kayenta, Arizona, to establish the first trading post in the region. This courageous woman grew to love the desert. To the Indians she was *Shema Yazi,* Little Mother. They told her their lore and tales of their wanderings in strange desert places. They brought her their troubles and their babies. Finally came Nashja, a Paiute, with a strange story. He had seen *Nageelid Nonnezoshi,* the-hole-in-the-rock-shaped-like-a-rainbow. And there was sweet water, and grass to feed many goats. But the trail was hard. Indian ponies, he said, could travel it, not white man's horses.

Mrs. Wetherill interested Professor Byron S. Cummings of the University of Utah in a trip to discover the great bridge. The expedition was made in 1909, with John Wetherill and Nashja-begay, son of Nashja, as guides, W. L. Douglass, surveyor of the U. S. General Land Office, and two student assistants. Douglass' story is that he had word of the bridge direct from the same Indian, and that the two expeditions, started separately, continued together. There was an acrimonious debate in after years as to whether Cummings or Douglass first saw the bridge. The question was quietly disposed of in 1927, when the Wetherills erected a bronze plaque at the bridge to Nashja-begay, "who first guided the white man to Nonnezoshi."

Professor Cummings published probably the first printed description of the bridge in a University of Utah pamphlet in 1910. He gave the dimensions of the gigantic red and yellow sandstone arch as 308 feet high and 275 feet between abutments. The bridge was formed through the same process of undercutting by stream meanders, Cummings said, as that which resulted in the concentration of three giant bridges in White Canyon (*see Natural Bridges National Monument*). The professor likened the natural structure to an "enormous flying buttress" rather than a bridge, because of the form taken by the gracefully curved "arm of the cliff." On a bench almost beneath the bridge, Professor Cummings found fire-blackened rocks, indicating that prehistoric peoples had probably used the site as a shrine for building sacred fires. His imagination kindled at the thought, and he could visualize a firelit congregation of cliff-dwellers assembled in this awesomely beautiful spot, paying reverence to their pagan gods. Present-day Indians still regard the bridge with feelings of religious awe. C. A. Colville, who visited the arch late in 1909, led by a Paiute guide, Whitehorse-biga, relates that the Indian would not pass under the bridge because he had forgotten a prayer required by Paiute custom before such a venture could be safely made.

The Navahos, too, have a long-lost prayer they must say before they will go under the bridge. Mrs. John Wetherill recovered it from an Indian child and translated it in *Traders to the Navahos,* which she wrote in collaboration with Frances Gillmor, published in 1934 by the Houghton Mifflin Company:

Mountain where the head of the War-God rests,
Mountain where the head of the War-God rests,
Dark Wind, beautiful chief, from the tips of your fingers a rainbow send out,
By which let me walk and have life.
Black clouds, black clouds, make for me shoes,
With which to walk and have life.
Black clouds are my leggings;
A black cloud is my robe;
A black cloud is my headband.
Black clouds, go before me; make it dark; let it rain peacefully before me.
Before me come much rain to make the white corn grow and ripen,
That it may be peaceful before me, that it may be peaceful before me.
All is peace, all is peace.

Iridescent Wind, beautiful chieftainess, from the palm of your hand a rainbow
     send out,
By which let me walk and have life.
Iridescent clouds, iridescent clouds, make for me shoes,
With which to walk and have life.
Iridescent clouds are my leggings;
An iridescent cloud is my robe;
An iridescent cloud is my headband.
Iridescent clouds, come behind me; make it dark; Earth Mother, give me much
     rain,
To make the iridescent corn grow and ripen,
That it may be peaceful behind me, that it may be peaceful behind me.
All is peace, all is peace, all is peace, all is peace.

Theodore Roosevelt, guided by John Wetherill, visited Rainbow Bridge in 1913, and described it for *The Outlook* of October 11 that year. The season was apparently a wet one, for "T. R." found deep pools of water in the canyon under the bridge. The former President, hailing an opportunity for a bath after a hard, dry, desert journey, floated luxuriantly on his back in the water, with the great arch towering above him. To Roosevelt the bridge was a triumphal arch, greater in its lonely majesty than any monument ever erected by a conqueror. When twilight came, the guides built a fire under one of the great buttresses, and the fire flared up now and then, illuminating the under side of the bridge. White men and Indian packers ate together, and afterward sat around the fire. The night was clear, and a full moon came up beneath the curve of the bridge. Roosevelt waked several times during the night and looked for a long time at the looming arch against the night sky.

Charles L. Bernheimer was so fascinated by the bridge that he made three trips to it in four years, each time accompanied by John Wetherill, and Zeke Johnson, custodian (1940) of the Natural Bridges National Monument. On each trip they sought a shorter and easier trail, and eventually found it. Bernheimer published his book, *Rainbow Bridge,* in 1926. To him the bridge was a unique and stupendous monument, with a lean and effective muscular strength. "Where the strain is greatest, its contour suggests the arm and shoulders of a trained athlete." Yet, as he pointed out, its size is such that the national Capitol at Washington, D. C., could be placed beneath it and have ample clearance above.

Timpanogos Cave National Monument

Highway Approaches: 8.1 *m.* N. and E. of American Fork on State 74, State 146, and Forest Road 3; 9.6 *m.* N. and E. of Pleasant Grove on State 146 and Forest Road 3; 9.8 *m.* E. of US 91, at a point 3.4 *m.* N. of Lehi, on State 80, State 146, and Forest Road 3; 17.6 *m.* NW. of Wildwood on State 168 and Forest Road 3.

Season: Cave open all year, with guide service, but April to November is most favorable time for visiting area.

Admission: Entry to Monument area free; to cave, including guide service, adults 50¢, children 25¢.

Administrative Office: Custodian at Monument headquarters, American Fork Canyon.

Accommodations: Campgrounds with water, tables, and fuel, and a store where lunches, meals, and foodstuffs are available, at U. S. Park Service camp, foot of trail to Timpanogos Cave. Hotels at Provo, tourist camps at American Fork.

Transportation: Timpanogos Loop tours (Gray Line) daily from Salt Lake City in summer $5; $1 lunch at Monument, cave admission extra.

Climate, Clothing and Equipment: Cold nights and cool days in summer; snow between November and April usually makes area too cold for winter camping. Hiking shoes for steep climb to cave, jacket to wear in cave, where temperature is 42 degrees; hiking or climbing togs for ascent of Mount Timpanogos and glacier. Camera film available at the Park Service camp store.

Post Offices: Pleasant Grove and American Fork.

Medical and Dental Service: Doctors and dentists at American Fork, Pleasant Grove, Lehi, and Provo. Hospitals at Lehi, American Fork, and Provo. Directions to first aid stations posted along road throughout canyon.

Speed Limit: Wide graveled and asphalt road, with gentle curves; safely driven at posted speed limit of 35 m.p.h.

Warnings and Regulations: Do not damage natural objects within Monument. Do not touch formations in cave; acids from human body are deleterious to them. In his proclamation for Timpanogos Cave in 1922, President Harding warned the public "not to appropriate, injure, deface, remove, or destroy any feature of this national monument." Forest Service regulations on fire and sanitation should be observed in remainder of Mount Timpanogos area.

Naturalist Service and Information: Custodian's office in Monument, Timpanogos Cave Committee at American Fork, Brigham Young University in Provo, National Park Service, Zion National Park; for adjacent area, Wasatch National Forest Headquarters, Salt Lake City.

Recreational Facilities: Well-equipped picnic and camp grounds, numerous small and a few established hiking trails, trout-stocked stream, and countless natural subjects for photography.

Guides: At cave entrance.

TIMPANOGOS CAVE NATIONAL MONUMENT, a 250-acre area containing Utah's outstanding scenic cavern, is on the precipitous northern slope of Mount Timpanogos in the Wasatch Range, and is reached by a trail up the south wall of American Fork Canyon. The Monument is in a small area, easily accessible from good roads and only a few miles from towns and accommodations. Crowded into a restricted section around it are scenic wonders and natural phenomena on a grandiose scale. The roads that swing in a rough circle around the larger area of Mount Timpanogos are known as the Timpanogos Loop. Within the "loop" are the limestone cave, a rugged canyon, a towering mountain, an outdoor summer school and theater, and a tiny "glacier."

The cave is approached, from the highway on the canyon floor, by a mile-long zigzag trail that climbs 1,200 feet up a sheer cliff-wall. Tickets are purchased (*daily 3-4*) at the Park Service camp store or at the ranger station across the road. The well-advised visitor to the cave wears low-heeled hiking shoes (low heels are even more of a help coming down than going up), and carries a jacket to put on when he enters the cavern. A good, steady stride, with occasional stops at benches to get the second, third, and fourth wind, will take the climber to the cave in the average time of one hour. The ramp-like trail follows a naturally flower-bordered course up the spasmodically wooded steep slope. There is a pungent aroma of sun-warmed pine as the trail climbs higher, and signs warn against picking flowers or taking short cuts. Most people are not tempted to disobey the second injunction, for the near-perpendicular mountainside is covered with loose flinty rocks that promise a quick, pants-warming descent, in addition to setting off a miniature landslide dangerous to those below.

The westward view, between the steep walls of American Fork Canyon, takes on a different character at every turn of the trail, as altitude and perspective change. Productive Utah Valley opens out beyond rugged canyon walls, its cultivated fields cut into geometric blocks of tilled and crop-greened land. An optical illusion convinces the climber at these altitudes that the valley slopes upward from the mouth of the canyon; in fact, it steps down in a series of benches before trending upward west of the Jordan River. The opposite canyon wall, clearly and closely visible, presents an intricate study of mountain architecture, with its cliffs, towers, washes, talus slopes, scrub growth, evergreens, and a wooden water main snaking around the mountain and tunneling under occasional spurs of rock.

The rocks along the way are inconceivably old. Quartzite near the bottom of the canyon is of Cambrian age, containing little or no remains of fossil life. It is surmounted by a shaly strata, and all above that, on this trail, is limestone, mainly of Carboniferous age. Minute marine plant and animal life, including coral, can be found by a trained eye in this great bed of limestone, which extends upward for five thousand feet; it is marked by a sign at the lower edge. The limestone has been intricately cracked by terrestrial disturbances, and the cracks filled with white calcareous matter, similar to that of the cave formations. Survival of this exposed limestone mass is clearly owing to the arid climate; in a humid region, with plentiful water dashing upon and over it, dissolving and carrying away its soluble lime, the deposit would quickly, in a geologic sense, have been undermined, and more resistant rocks from above would have tumbled down to cover the outcrop.

As the trail climbs higher, portions of it can be seen below, cutting sharp M's and W's in the mountainside. High above, perched like a swallow's nest, is a little stone rest station, and a black-shadowed arch west of it indicates the cave entrance. Once the rest station is reached, there is only one more long ramp, through an arch in the trail, to the cool, man-made grotto where visitors register, put on their jackets, and, with the guide, enter a wooden door into the cave.

TIMPANOGOS CAVE (6,776 alt.), half a mile long, is in reality three caves, connected by man-made tunnels. They are all part of the same geologic structure, a fissure along the lines of a fault that occurred probably in Eocene time, some fifty million years ago. It is thought that the fissure was washed out by waters of a stream corresponding to American Fork Creek, which in the succeeding epoch, the Miocene, began cutting American Fork Canyon. Deposits within the cavern—icicle-like stalactites, upthrust stalagmites, and the branched, oddly-angled helictites—are thought to have required the same time to grow as the cutting of American Fork Canyon. Once the stream bed was cut below the cavern-fissures, water was scarce, and dripped rather than flowed. As the calcium-saturated drops came slowly down, evaporating the while, they began to deposit limy material on the ceiling of the cave, the beginning of stalactites. Falling to the floor, they deposited other infinitesimal particles, and began to build stalagmites upward. In the course of time some of the stalactites and stalagmites joined, to form columns; others occur in the cave that have not yet joined. The "macaroni-like filigree" of helictites apparently formed where less moisture was present; they branched in every direction, even forming complete circles, having left deposits where water was drawn out by capillary action and evaporated completely.

HANSEN CAVE, through which entrance is made, was discovered in 1887 by Martin Hansen, who then owned the land. The cave was almost completely stripped of formations, some of which were sold to curio-hunters, some of which were taken by chance visitors. This, like the other caverns, is ingeniously lighted by a system of indirect electric lights. The guide, who knows where the light switches are concealed, turns off a circuit behind and turns on another ahead, sometimes leaving visitors in absolute darkness for a moment, to give them a notion of the profound Stygian gloom. At such times, when there is a tendency to listen, the only sound that can be heard is the dripping of water. The way trends downward and eastward, the caverns passing through the mountain behind the stone rest station. An 85-foot arched tunnel, built by hand, leads to Middle Cave.

MIDDLE CAVE, discovered in 1922, in the course of penetrating Timpanogos Cave proper, is a narrow, winding channel with a high vaulted ceiling, sometimes reaching a height of 125 feet. When first entered, from the top, explorers let themselves down with ropes. One man fell and was injured, resting on a ledge until rescued. The top entrance was closed in the course of development, to prevent terrific drafts from outside. A series of winding passages, stairs, and grilled footways leads from one area in the cave to another. Here the formations are for the most part unspoiled, in colors that range from pure white through lemon yellow, ivory, coral, brown, and mauve. In an inaccessible portion of this cave are formations indicating a slight movement in the mountain, thousands of years past: Formation of a stalagmite, by dripping from a stalactite above, was abandoned, and a new stalagmite was begun three-quarters of an inch away.

TIMPANOGOS CAVE proper, connected to Middle Cave by a 190-foot man-made tunnel, reaches an area abounding in coloration, odd forms, and curious resemblances. There is a hidden lake, and hundreds of formations, configuring to the imagination of each person a different set of resemblances—the Dove's Nest, the Reclining Camel, Father Time's Jewel Box, Mother Earth's Lace Curtains, the Chocolate Fountain (well named), a seal, a dressed chicken, and scores of others. The "Heart of Timpanogos," bearing a remarkable likeness to the human vital organ, is illuminated with a red light from behind; variations in opacity give it a lifelike appearance. A thermometer in this cave has a constant all-year reading of 42 degrees. By means of doors it is kept the same throughout the caverns, to maintain the proper humidity, which gives color to formations and encourages continued deposition. There is more to see after the heart, more marvels of lighting, form, color, more likenesses pointed out by the guide, more of that vague loss of direction within a cave, more dripping of water. Finally there appears ahead and below a faint shining of blue light, as if the electrician had prepared a new and different set of glows and indirects. It is the sunlight, shining in around the wooden exit door. The eyes, accustomed to half a mile of yellow or red artificial light, refuse temporarily to accept all the colors of sunlight, and translate only the blue.

Timpanogos Cave was probably discovered as early as 1915 by "a group of Lehi people," who kept its whereabouts a secret, and attempted to lease a "mining claim" from the Forest Service, in order to develop it commercially. Official discovery of the cave is credited to Vearl J. Manwill, who tells the story in the *American Fork Citizen* for April 28, 1939:

We had a group of "outdoor minded" people from Payson that went on a canyon or mountain-climbing trip about every two weeks during the summer months.

In the summer of 1921, this group joined the annual Mt. Timpanogos hike. . . . After the hike was over we discussed plans for our next outing, and I remembered that I had just recently seen an article in the American Fork newspaper. . . . I was led to believe that the cave was known and it was being kept secret. . . .

I made inquiry of Martin Hansen concerning the cave, and he told me its whereabouts was unknown, but if we wished to look for it, he would suggest looking near Hansen cave or on about the same level. . . .

After scouting the hillside for about an hour, I sat down to rest, and noted the rocks about ten feet from where I was sitting had a very artificial appearance, so I moved over to the spot and kicked one loose. This exposed a hole in the rocks, which proved to be the entrance to what is now known as Timpanogos cave. I called the rest of the party and we went in and explored it. . . .

That night in camp, around a fire, we discussed ways and means of protecting the cave against a vandalizing public. . . .

The Forest Service took the cavern under its protection, and a trail was built. Civic groups contributed to development of the cavern, and about 10,000 persons visited it the first year, 1922; on the average about an equal number have visited the cave annually in subsequent years. The cave, 600 feet long when opened, was declared a national monument the following year. A lighting system was installed in 1923-25, and replaced in 1939. A trail to Hansen Cave was completed in 1936; necessary tunneling was done, and beginning in 1938 the cavern trip was made, as now, through the three caves. No further extensions are known, but there is a persistent local rumor of another giant cavern in the vicinity.

TIMPANOGOS LOOP AND TRAILS

The west end of Forest Road, 3 *m.*, at the junction with State 146, is at the mouth of American Fork Canyon. The canyon is wild and rocky, among the most rugged in Utah.

TIMPANOGOS CAMP (L), 1.4 *m.*, in a widening of the canyon floor, is equipped with picnic and campground facilities; it is operated by the U. S. Park Service. The store (R) has various supplies for sale, and is at the junction with the foot trail to Timpanogos Cave (*see above*).

At 4.3 *m.* is a junction (L) from which a side road leads up American Fork Canyon; the SOUTH FORK RANGER STATION of the U. S. Forest Service stands at the junction. The main road leads up the south fork of American Fork Canyon, climbs a dugway, from which there is a good view of the canyon, and at 5.9 *m.* there is a view (L) of the rocky summit of MOUNT TIMPANOGOS (12,008 alt.), originally named Pa-ak-ar-et Kaib, "very high mountain," by the Paiutes. The Provo River was called Timpanogos, "water running over rocks." Escalante, in 1776, called it Sierra Blanca de los Timpanogos, "the White Mountain of the Timpanogos." His name for the peak has not been changed, but the river has been renamed for a trapper. A more recent interpretation is that Timpanogos is a Paiute word for "woman lying down," and it is true that, from a certain perspective on the southwest, the mountain assumes the shape of a reclining female figure.

This mountain, according to Professor Fred Buss, in the booklet *Timpanogos,* issued by Brigham Young University, "owes much of its grandeur to the fact that it rises so steeply from the bed of old Lake Bonneville with only inconsequential foothills on its flanks, while Provo River on the south and American Fork River on the north have carved their canyons to the very base of the range, thereby leaving Timpanogos standing apart from the other peaks in a state of splendid isolation. Geologists attribute the form and position of the mountain to its being a faulted block of the earth's crust which has been lifted by the great internal forces of the globe to its present heights above a correspondingly depressed block under Utah Valley. The western face of Timpanogos is believed to be the fault scarp." Five plant zones are represented on Mount Timpanogos, Upper Sonoran, Transition, Canadian, Hudsonian, and, above timberline, the Arctic or Alpine. The rise from agricultural Utah Valley, therefore, to the bald top of Timpanogos reveals the same climatic and vegetative changes that would be encountered on a journey from Provo to the Arctic Circle.

CAMP TIMPANOKE (L), 7.7 *m.,* is at the junction with a six-mile trail (R) up the north face of the mountain. At least six trails wind to the top of this Wasatch giant, three from Pleasant Grove on the west face of the mountain, and two scaling the north walls. This route from American Fork Canyon is the oldest and newest path to the summit. For many years sheep have been driven this way to the upland valleys for summer pasture. The Forest Service has improved the trail, which is used by hundreds of mountain climbers. It is of even grade all the way up, and passes rushing torrents, waterfalls, canyons, and farflung mountain views.

Forest Road 3 continues up the floor of the canyon, with a turn (L) at 7.9 *m.,* and reaches the summit of the canyon at 9.5 *m.;* from here there is another view (R) of Mount Timpanogos and a canyon vista across the way just traveled.

ASPEN GROVE (7,000 alt.), 18.8 *m.,* has a store and a playground. BRIGHAM YOUNG UNIVERSITY SUMMER SCHOOL (*open*), a high-altitude branch of Brigham Young University (*see Provo*), and TIMPANOGOS THEATER, an outdoor theater sponsored by the university and by the U. S. Forest Service, are at Aspen Grove. The school includes an art gallery where summer students exhibit their work, and a scientific display showing the rocks, birds, flowers, animals, and insects of the area. Concerts and plays are presented here in summer. Around the grove of fir, spruce, and aspen, rise lofty peaks; small waterfalls sparkle in the sun, and short trails lead to many scenic vantage points.

Leading from Aspen Grove is the most popular trail to the summit of Timpanogos, five miles long, with a lift of 5,000 feet, having been used as the route of the annual Timpanogos Hike since it was started by the physical education department of Brigham Young University in 1912. A thousand or more climbers take part annually. The date for the hike varies a few days each year, but it is always held near the middle of July. Hikers assemble at Aspen Grove the night before, and there are campfires, plays, skits, and songs. An early start is made, in order to reach the summit at sunrise. Timpanogos Hike buttons, placed at the top of the mountain before the hike, are distributed when the summit is reached.

After a mile of almost level grade, the trail starts zigzagging up the steep, glaciated canyon, passing UNNAMED CATARACTS, MOSS FALLS, BABY FALLS, LECTURE LEDGE, COLUMBINE FALLS, AMPHITHEATER FALLS, and numerous others unnamed. There is, in effect, an intermittent waterfall plunging down the side of Mount Timpanogos, dropping a mile and a half; about 50 cascades attain the proportions of waterfalls, and about 150 smaller ones bubble and trickle over moss-covered rocks or drop short distances over flower-grown cliffs. A natural rock garden in a wild setting a mile and a half above sea level has a profusion of mosses, ferns, Indian paintbrush, cliff roses, pentstemons, columbines, violets, marigolds, geraniums, hollyhocks, and bluebells. The cirques, or giant glaciated amphitheaters, are filled with snow at midsummer, and along the edges of snowbanks and lakes are flowers abloom in rich variety. From the amphitheater floor there is a hundred-yard trail to the left, leading to HIDDEN LAKE, but EMERALD LAKE, a placid mountain pond formed by melting from the "glacier," is on the main trail. At Emerald Lake the trail branches, and the hiker may gain the summit either by climbing directly up the face of the "glacier" or by taking a circuitous but easier route (northerly) to the American Fork or Timpanoke Trail.

TIMPANOGOS "GLACIER," near the summit, is about a mile long and 300 feet thick. Like similar bodies, large enough to be called glaciers without quotation marks, it is formed by packed snow, which never melts at this altitude; it exerts downward pressure, and drops tiny icebergs from the lower end, which tumble into the frigid waters of Emerald Lake. Slow melting, caused by the friction of movement and the summer sun, provides water for streams below. A hundred-yard slide on the "glacier" provides heart-stopping thrills. There is a sheer fifty-foot drop, and the slider is retarded by a series of "shoot the chutes" before coming to a full stop. During hot summers, when the "glacier" is shortened by heavy melting, the feat is of doubtful safety.

At the SUMMIT OF TIMPANOGOS (12,008 alt.) is a galvanized iron and glass shelter, eight feet square, called the "Glass House," containing indicator-bars, which show the direction of peaks and cities within the range of vision from the summit. In the words of Harrison R. Merrill, there is a view of "rich fields and plains, tiny roadways, thread-like ribbons of steel and, farther off, lakes and hills and peaks and distances . . . draped in mists of blue, and drab and lavender."

Between Aspen Grove and Wildwood, on State 168, there is a series of horseshoe bends.

WILDWOOD, 34.5 m. (5,250 alt.), is at the eastern terminus of State 168, and at the junction with US 189 (see Tour 5). Between Wildwood and Provo US 189 is part of what is known as Timpanogos Loop. Between Provo and Pleasant Grove, US 51-91 (see Tour 1d) forms part of the Loop, and State 146 (*see Tour 1d*) between Pleasant Grove and the mouth of American Fork Canyon closes the circle. Alternate routes between—State 52, State 74, and State 80 (*see Tour 1d*)—are also considered a portion of the Loop.

Zion National Park

Highway Approaches: Entrance 26.7 *m.* E. of Andersons Ranch on State 15, 25.7 *m.* W. of Mt. Carmel Junction on State 15.
Season: Roads to and within the Park are open the entire year.
Administrative Office: Superintendent, Zion National Park.

Accommodations: Zion Lodge, open May 30-Sept. 30. Cafeteria, store, and housekeeping cabins, and South Entrance Free Campground, are open throughout the year. Grotto Campground open May 1-Nov. 1.

Admission: Jointly with Bryce Canyon, $1 per automobile, and $1 for trailer.
Transportation: By rail on the Union Pacific to Cedar City, from which the Utah Parks Company provides bus service to Zion, and make daily trips within the Park; from Zion Lodge to Temple of Sinawava, $1; special trips can be arranged. Private car and horse travel are most popular, and foot trails are heavily used.
Climate, Clothing and Equipment: Sports clothing is appropriate, lightweight preferable in midsummer. For hiking trips serviceable shoes (not oxfords) should be worn. Water should be carried on some trips; inquire at Zion Lodge or Office. Jackets needed for evenings during spring and fall, heavier clothing for winter.
Post Office: Zion Lodge, Zion National Park, Utah (summer).
Medical and Dental Service: Cedar City and Kanab. Registered nurse at Zion Lodge, May 30-Sept. 30.
Communications and Express: Telegraph and long distance telephone at Zion Lodge.
Speed Limits: Roads are posted; 20. m.p.h. is safe.
Warnings and Regulations: U. S. National Park regulations, conspicuously posted within the park, must be obeyed. Keep to posted trails unless accompanied by guide.

Naturalist Service and Information: Office and Museum at Park Headquarters. Ranger-naturalists conduct nature study parties twice daily, on variable schedule posted at Museum. Evening lectures daily at public auto camp and Zion Lodge. Service is free.

Recreational Facilities: Horseback riding, hiking, motor trips, and swimming (in Lodge pool), nature and scientific study, and photography (including color).
Guides and Horses: Special guides $5 a day or $3 for a half day or less. Saddle horses $1.50 for 2 hours or less, $3 for 4 hours or less, and $5 for 8 hours. Escorted horseback trips to East or West Rim, $5; escorted half-day trips to The Narrows or Angels Landing, $3. Women's riding togs for rent at lodge. Horses are well broken and accustomed to country.

ZION NATIONAL PARK, an area of 94,888 acres in southwestern Utah, is the best-known example of a deep, narrow, vertically-walled canyon readily accessible for observation. Through much of its course it is about as deep as wide, though in the Narrows it is 2,000 feet deep and less than 50 feet wide. The park area is one of towering walls and steep slopes, which here and there recede into alcoves and amphitheaters, everywhere decorated by broad arches, pilasters, statues, balconies, and towers. Beneath the white and red of the higher walls are the purple, pink, lilac, yellow, blue, and mauve shades in the most brilliant-colored rocks, and the colors shift constantly with the light and seasons. In winter, when the upper reaches are blanketed with snow, the lower walls are by contrast all the more brilliant; in autumn they are a gorgeous backdrop for the yellow and golden foliage of deciduous trees and shrubs on the canyon floor; and in the spring innumerable cascades plunge down the vast escarpments, some of them dropping a sheer thousand feet, colored by their burden of sand, each waterfall sometimes of a different hue from its neighbor.

This is a realm of temples and cathedrals. Some of the names were bestowed by persons who were members of no church, but no other nomenclature would fit: Mountains of stone are called temples, patriarchs, Angels Landing, thrones, and cathedrals. Easter services, held annually in Zion since 1935, attract an ever-increasing number of visitors; the region impels to awe and prayer.

All visitors enter on the canyon floor, and most of them are content with the grandeur that towers above them. The few who climb to the east or west rim, to the summit of Lady Mountain, or even to Angels Landing, get a vista of a far different kind. From the floor, the beholder is walled in by blazing cliffs that rise half a mile in places; from the summits he looks out over a breath-taking landscape, an Aladdin's carpet of wondrous pattern and riotous colors spread far below. On all sides, extending for miles, is a tumultuous ocean of colors, as if a million rainbows had been melted in the bowl of the sky and poured out on the rocks. Light is a potent factor—there is a remarkable difference in looking into the sun or away from it, into canyons where the splendor of daylight is a dazzling glory, or where the shadows deepen and soften the bold tints and blend them into colorful mists. White summits are as bright as clouds under sunlight; red walls are half a mile of solid flame; pink ridges become long burning reefs; and evergreen terraces are luminous in golden haze.

The elevation at Zion Lodge is 4,275 feet; the main mountain tops are West Temple, 7,795 feet; East Temple, 7,110 feet; and the Great White Throne, 6,744 feet. These altitudes provide the Park with a cooler atmosphere in summer than the surrounding section of southern Utah. Compared with desert country roundabout, the streams and cascades, the trailing ferns and flowering plants, the pines and firs, make Zion a multi-colored oasis. Mule deer abound in the park. Bighorn sheep remain on the highest peaks unless driven down by heavy snows. Mountain lions, coyotes, and bobcats leave their tracks after rain or snow. Porcupines, marmots, chipmunks, and squirrels appear as frequently, almost, as the many types of harmless lizards. Bird life includes the forms typical to areas of heavier rainfall with those indigenous to arid and semiarid country.

The sedimentary rocks exposed in Zion are assigned by geologists to the Triassic, Jurassic, and Cretaceous periods of the Mesozoic era, and to the Eocene or "dawn" epoch of Tertiary time. According to Dr. Herbert E. Gregory, most of the rocks were laid down by water as gravel, sand, mud, and slimy ooze. They have been converted into solid rock by the weight of layers above them and by cementing lime, silica, and iron. Embedded in the rocks are fossil sea shells, fish, trees, snails, and the bones and tracks of land animals. The most conspicuous remains are those of dinosaurs—huge reptiles which so dominated the life of their time that the Mesozoic is known as the "Age of Dinosaurs."

Today, Zion is an area of gorges, cliffs and mesas. From the hard surfaces, softer layers have been stripped by water and wind. The principal canyon, North Fork, was cut by the Virgin River. Originally a shallow valley, it has become a narrow trench between towering walls, but the river follows the same meanders as it did millions of years ago when it was 5,000 feet above the present level. The stream, having nine times the fall of the Colorado River, is still impressively busy, carrying out of the park about 180 carloads of ground rock daily. Adding to the erosive process are rainfall, surface run-off spilling over the high rims, ground water emerging as springs, frost, and growing tree roots, which loosen great slabs, and chemical agencies that weaken the stone. Continuous sapping and undermining have developed alcoves, opened fissures, and spilled blocks from the cliffs upon the conical talus slopes below.

Long ago Zion was the home of a prehistoric people, cliff ruins having been discovered in the Park. The principal ruins are in Parunuweap Canyon, 8 miles from the nearest road, and not accessible to casual visitors. These ancient people "farmed" near the creeks and rivers, raising corn, squash, and melons. Their dwellings, perched high above, like the nests of swallows, gave them protection from marauding enemies.

Zion Canyon was discovered in 1858 by Nephi Johnson, a Mormon pioneer, who rode up the canyon as far as the present Zion Stadium. Three years later Joseph Black explored the region and led farmers and stock-growers into the canyon, where their descendants tilled and grazed the land until it was proclaimed a national park. In 1872 Major Wesley Powell visited the canyon and applied the Indian names, Mukuntuweap to the North Fork of the Virgin River, and Parunuweap to the East Fork. Indians refused to live in the canyon and were fearful of being overtaken by darkness there. This happily provided a sanctuary for the Mormons, who called their small settlement Little Zion. When Brigham Young told them it was not Zion at all, they called it, for a while, Not Zion.

A portion of the area was set aside as Mukuntuweap National Monument by President Taft in 1909. Nine years later the Monument was enlarged by President Wilson and the name changed to Zion. In 1929 the status was changed by act of Congress to that of a national park, and the following year the park was enlarged to its present area.

ZION ROADS, TRAILS, AND VIEWS

Entering Zion National Park from US 91 the SOUTH ENTRANCE CHECKING STATION (L) is 1.4 *m.* N. of Springdale (*see Tour 1E*), and 1 *m.* S. of the Park Headquarters and Superintendent's Office (L). From US 89 via the Mount Carmel Highway and Tunnel there is a short "Y," making two junctions with the main Park road; one (R) leads to the north and Zion Lodge, the other (L) leading to the South Entrance Checking Station where visitors register and pay their fee. Midway between the Park Heaquarters and the South Entrance are the Public Campgrounds, cafeteria, store, and housekeeping cabins (*see Tour 1E*).

There are 20 miles of improved roads in Zion Park, including the 11.5 miles of Zion-Mount Carmel Highway within the boundaries. The main road, with several short branches to points of interest, runs north from Park Headquarters to the Temple of Sinawava. Closed-car travelers find it advantageous to make frequent stops, since the top of the car obscures the lofty tops and sheer walls. Approximately 26 miles of well-kept trails lead to sections of the Park not reached by roads. They can be used at all seasons, except those to the canyon rims, which are closed by snow in winter. Two major horseback trails lead to the east and west rims.

Roads and trails covered in this log are from the Park Headquarters north to the Temple of Sinawava. The road from the South Entrance and Checking Station north to the Park Headquarters, and the Mount Carmel approach from US 89, are treated in *Tour 1F.*

PARK HEADQUARTERS, 0 *m.,* in a canyon of nearly perpendicular sides more than half a mile high, half a mile wide at the floor, and a mile wide from crest to crest, is surrounded on all sides by stupendous formations. Soaring skyward to the west is the highest point in the park, WEST TEMPLE (7,795 alt.), its great height belied by its mammoth proportions. The formation rises 3,805 feet above the canyon floor, and its eastern side is like a smooth wall of veined marble. Across the canyon from it, and of even more startling color and design, is THE WATCHMAN, with red dominating the orange and rust, green and rose; in design, it looks as if a dozen Gothic skyscrapers had been stood side by side, heated, and welded into one enormous cathedral. Under sunset, the colors glow as if a great furnace burned in the interior; at dusk, after the sun has set, The Watchman resembles nothing so much as a monolith saturated with heat and slowly cooling.

On the east side is BRIDGE MOUNTAIN, guarded on either side by structures that look like two sons of The Watchman. The Bridge is named for a "flying buttress" or natural bridge on the face of the mountain—a slender arch of stone 150 feet in length. Even through powerful glasses (*mounted and free to visitors*) the bridge looks like a thread of rock that a man could put on his shoulder and carry away; its insignificant size against the wall emphasizes the colossal proportions of these monuments. Beyond Bridge Mountain to the right is EAST TEMPLE, in form and color closely resembling its companion to the west.

ZION MUSEUM, at Park Headquarters, has an exhibit of plant and animal life of the region, and a large-scale relief map portraying the topography of the Park. Lectures on reptiles, using live specimens, are given at the museum several times daily during the summer months.

THE SENTINEL (L), 1.5 *m.,* is a truncated dome, tinted with cream and orchid and purple. The TWIN BROTHERS (R), 1.8 *m.* (6,850 alt.), two massive summits of vari-colored stone, are seen together after a turn in the road. The west rim of the canyon recedes from the river to form the cool green COURT OF THE PATRI-ARCHS, 1.6 *m.,* over which loom three lofty peaks (L), the THREE PATRIARCHS themselves. Opposite is the MOUNTAIN OF THE SUN, catching the first golden rays of sunrise and the last brilliant colors of sunset. At 1.6 *m.* is a short branch road (L) to the garage and service station.

After skirting the eastern base of the Three Patriarchs is the junction (R), 2.8 *m.,* of the loop road to ZION LODGE, 3 *m.* A horseback or foot trail (L) backtracks from here along the west of the road to a point above the garage and makes a loop at the feet of the Three Patriarchs. GROTTO TRAIL (R) to the north, ends at the Grotto, a cavernous arch in the side of the mountain.

LADY MOUNTAIN (6,940 alt.), overshadows SPEARHEAD POINT to the north. Gazing at the steep wall of Lady Mountain (L) it seems incredible that a trail could go up it. It starts at Zion Lodge, and hikers making the trip should wear good shoes, be in sound physical condition, and carry water or a few oranges. From the summit of Lady Mountain is perhaps the finest view from a foot trail in the Park. The Great White Throne, to the north, resembles the ruins of an old castle; on its eastern face is an arch of tremendous size. Directly north is a section of the trail leading to OBSERVATION POINT (6,508 alt.). To the left is Angels Landing, looking quite dwarfed from this eminence. To the west is a canyon with a sheer wall 2,000 feet high, and across it on the far rim is a collection of huge sculptured faces that might have been cut by a giant ancestor of Gutzon Borglum.

The EMERALD POOL TRAIL begins at Zion Lodge and joins the West Rim Trail (which should be attempted only on horseback). The EMERALD POOLS are small pockets of water formed by ribbon-like waterfalls that plunge hundreds of feet down the face of steep cliffs.

Leaving Zion Lodge the main road at 3.4 *m.* makes a loop (R) to the Public Campground, Grotto Ranger Station, and Temple of Sina-wava.

The ranger station is the center of an area for viewing vividly colored waterfalls that appear in the Park immediately following a shower. Sometimes of only a few minutes' duration, they are exquisite while they last. As many as thirty have been counted from a single point. The water carries richly tinted silt and sand from the plateaus above, coloring the falls yellow, red, chocolate, orange, and even black. Streamer after streamer of colored water swoops from the high rims, dyeing the Virgin River like a mottled Easter egg. These waterfalls are the joy and aggravation of color photographers, who are tempted to wait, and pray for rain, until they occur.

At 3.5 *m.* a sign with an arrow posts the way to West Rim Trail, Angels Landing, Emerald Pools, and Court of the Patriarchs.

WEST RIM TRAIL, oil-surface for the first mile, begins opposite the Public Campground, leaves the canyon floor at the foot of Angels Landing, and is benched along a precipitous ledge of the west wall for 600 feet into Refrigerator Canyon. Hewn into the face of the almost vertical cliff, it winds through cool narrow gorges, and comes out on top of bare rock ledges. The trail zigzags up, nearly to the level of Angels Landing, and turns north, continuing over the colorful sandstone formation for two miles before making the final ascent to the rim. Coming out on top, it extends along the rim to Potato Hollow on HORSE PASTURE PLATEAU. From the rim there is a view of Zion Canyon, with all its startling color and strange formations, and into the broken wilderness of West Canyon. With these colorful chasms as a foreground, the vista includes parts of Utah, Arizona, and Nevada.

A sign, 4.7 *m.,* pointing right, shows the trail to East Rim and Weeping Rock.

EAST RIM TRAIL leaves the canyon floor at the foot of CABLE MOUNTAIN (R) and ascends its north flank. There are wonderful views of Zion Canyon from various points on the trail, but the finest, that from OBSERVATION POINT, is reserved for the last. From this point Kaibab Forest can be seen on the North Rim of the Grand Canyon, far to the southeast; Cedar Mountain, in the Cedar Breaks country, looms on the northern horizon; and to the southwest is the Virgin River Valley and the settlements of Utah's Dixie, visible as far as St. George, 55 miles away.

There is a good view of THE ORGAN (L) at 4.9 *m.,* and at 5.2 *m.* is a roadside halting place with a view of the GREAT WHITE THRONE (L) through the saddle between the Organ and Angels Landing.

The road continues to the base of THE GREAT WHITE THRONE (6,744 alt.) best known monolith in the park. The summit of this gigantic truncated mass of white sandstone has been reached only a few times. A number of hikers have been injured in attempting to scale its precipitous walls; the climb should be attempted only by experienced alpine climbers with professional equipment. Directly opposite is ANGELS LANDING (5,785 alt.), its dull red color in contrast to the glittering white of the Throne. A trail from the Campground leads to the summit of this peak.

Leaving the Throne, the road and the river make a great bend around the colossal ORGAN, a red spur projecting outward from Angels Landing. Opposite is a circular parking area, from which a short trail leads to WEEPING ROCK. Water seeping from the rocky walls moistens the soil to which cling cool green mosses and drooping ferns, intermingled with gay yellow columbines, purple shoot-ingstars, and scarlet monkeyflowers.

The auto road terminates at the TEMPLE OF SINAWAVA, 6.4 *m.,* a natural amphitheater almost surrounded by clifflike walls. The floor is a flower-covered carpet shaded by deciduous trees.

The oil-surfaced NARROWS TRAIL begins here, over which ranger-naturalists conduct parties twice daily. A trailside exhibit at this point includes charts, diagrams, and labels explaining the geology of The Narrows. At one point on the trail the complete process of plant fossilization can be seen and studied. A hundred yards up the trail there is a good view, looking south, of the top of the Great White Throne. Half a mile up is ZION STADIUM, a walled-in amphitheater with wild flowers growing from crevices and clinging to the steep sides; on the canyon floor is a pool of cold lucid water. At THE NAR-ROWS, a mile up the canyon, the walls rise vertically for 2,000 feet, but are only 50 feet apart at the stream. At the end of the trail the walls of the canyon close in, and those who would venture farther must wade along the river edge.

ZION NATIONAL MONUMENT

Zion National Monument, northwest of Zion National Park, is entered by an unimproved dirt road leading northeast from the little town of Virgin (*see Tour 1E*). The road runs almost directly north to a point equal with the north boundary of the Monument, then branches northwest to connect with US 91 a short distance north of Kanarraville and about 2 miles south of Cedar City. This extremely rough and in places doubtful road is used only by cattle and sheep men and wood haulers. Although it passes through some extremely rugged and scenic country, visitors say that the area does not compare with Zion Park. It is practically unexplored, and accessible only for horse-back and pack trips.

The Monument contains a portion of the Hurricane Fault, visible to the east of US 91 (*see Tour 1f*) at a point 20 miles south of Cedar City. The fault forms a bold, jagged escarpment, with an edge as ragged and sharp as a ripsaw, having an elevation of nearly 7,000 feet. In this section are the Kolob Canyons, 2 miles east of US 91, midway between Cedar City and Andersons Ranch. The other-worldly beauty of the canyons undoubtedly prompted Mormon pioneers to name them for the central star of the universe in Mormon "Book of Abraham" cosmogony—Kolob, "the great one . . . nearest the throne of God," its revolution requiring a thousand years. Red cliffs rise abruptly from the canyon bottom, breaking into a series of eight rugged canyons with walls 1,500 to 2,500 feet high. The most easterly canyon carries the waters of La Verkin Creek, which flows south between Andersons Ranch and La Verkin (*see Tour 1E*). Sparkling streams from the Kolob Plateau flow through some of the eastern canyons, covering the floors with a profusion of wild flowers and dense vegetation. However warmly these verdant canyons may welcome the visitor, once away from streams and familiar roads they can become harsh and cruel—malevolent desert country, far from towns or accommodations.

PART V

Appendices

Chronology

1540   Captain García Lopez de Cardenas approaches Utah south of the Colorado River.

1776   Father Silvestre Vélez de Escalante and Father Francisco Atanasio Domínguez make first comprehensive exploration of Utah.

1813   "Old Spanish Trail" in use between Santa Fe and Utah Lake.

1820   Religious revivals on New York frontier lead to first Joseph Smith vision.

1824   General William Henry Ashley's trappers cross South Pass and enter Utah. Jim Bridger discovers Great Salt Lake.

1825   Ashley explores Green River. First trappers' rendezvous held on Henrys Fork of Green River.

1826   Trappers circumnavigate Great Salt Lake. Jedediah S. Smith traverses Utah en route to Southern California in first American overland journey to California, returns to Utah next year in first white eastward passage of Sierra Nevada mountains and central Nevada deserts.

1830   Buffalo rendered virtually extinct in Utah by tremendous winter snows. American Fur Company extends operations to intermountain region and institutes bitter ten years' rivalry with Hudson's Bay and Rocky Mountain Fur companies.
        Book of Mormon published. April 6. Mormon Church organized at Fayette, New York.

1832   Antoine Robidoux establishes first fixed white post in Uintah Basin.

1837   Denis Julien makes first known white explorations of lower Green and Colorado canyons.
        Fort Davy Crockett established in Browns Hole by Philip Thompson and William Craig. L.D.S. Church begins world-wide proselyting.

1839   Nauvoo, Illinois, named as gathering-place for harassed Mormons.

1840   Bottom falls out of market for beaver fur, dooming mountain fur trade.

1841   Bartleson-Bidwell party, en route to California, brings first emigrant wagons across Utah.

1843   Captain John Charles Frémont explores northern Great Salt Lake; goes on to Oregon and Southern California, and next year traverses Utah north to Utah Lake, thence east through Uintah Basin and Browns Hole. Joseph Smith issues revelation on plural marriage at Nauvoo.

1844   Joseph and Hyrum Smith shot to death by mob at Carthage, Illinois; Quorum of Twelve Apostles, headed by Brigham Young, accepted as presiding authorities of Mormon Church.

531

1844-45 Miles Goodyear builds on Ogden site first permanent white post in Utah west of Wasatch Mountains.

1845 Frémont, returning west, circles southern shore of Great Salt Lake and breaks new trail across Salt Desert to California.

1846 Harlan-Young and Donner-Reed emigrant parties break wagon trails across Utah.
Mormons begin migration from Nauvoo. Mormon Battalion enters U. S. Army for service against Mexico.

1847 Advance companies of Mormon pioneers arrive in Great Salt Lake Valley. Mormon irrigation begins. Brigham Young named president of Mormon Church.

1848 Mormon Battalion members participate in discovery of gold in California. Treaty of Guadaloupe Hidalgo ends war with Mexico; Utah area passes under United States sovereignty.
Ogden founded as Browns Fort. Gulls help destroy marauding crickets. First petition drawn up to Congress for Territorial government.

1849 Colonization begins, with settlements in Utah, Sanpete, and Tooele valleys. Gold rush brings thousands west, many through Great Salt Lake City. Captain Howard Stansbury commences survey of Great Salt Lake, finishing next year.
Constitution adopted for Provisional State of Deseret; Brigham Young named governor.
Perpetual Emigrating Company organized to aid poor Saints to Utah.

1850 General Assembly of Deseret charters University of the State of Deseret, first university west of Missouri River, and third west of Mississippi (renamed University of Utah, 1892).
Deseret News begins publication as first intermountain newspaper. Population of Utah, 11,380. Congress creates Territory of Utah to supersede State of Deseret.

1851 General Assembly of Deseret charters Great Salt Lake City, Ogden, Provo, Manti, and Parowan.
Brigham Young takes oath of office as governor of Utah Territory; first Territorial legislature meets. Fillmore named Territorial capital. Colonization continues in Sanpete, Sevier, Little Salt Lake, and northern valleys.

1852 Plural marriage proclaimed to world as Mormon doctrinal tenet. First Utah iron smelted in Cedar City.

1853 Ground broken for Mormon Temple in Great Salt Lake City.
Walker War with Utes begins in Utah Valley, continuing until following May. Captain John W. Gunnison and seven men killed by Pahvants on Sevier River.

1854 Grasshopper infestations begin. Deseret alphabet originated.

1855 Grasshoppers destroy almost all crops.

1856 Famine conditions prevail. Tintic War with Utes fought in Utah and Cedar valleys.

"Reformation," initiated by Jedediah M. Grant at Kaysville, results in two years of intense religious feeling.

Hand-cart migrations across the plains begin, continuing until 1860; many lost the first year when caught by early snows along Sweetwater River in Wyoming.

1857 Severe winter is followed by best harvest since Mormon arrival in Utah. Territorial seat returned to Great Salt Lake City.

Government orders west an army to quell "rebellion" in Utah; army is forced into winter quarters near Fort Bridger.

Upwards of 120 Arkansas emigrants slain in Mountain Meadows Massacre.

1858 Territorial seat moved from Great Salt Lake City to Parowan; next year returned in fact though not formally by law, to Great Salt Lake City. Colonel Thomas L. Kane negotiates end of "Utah War"; Mormons return to abandoned homes; Federal troops settle at Camp Floyd in Cedar Valley.

1860 Pony Express commences east and west operations through Utah. Population of Utah, 40,273.

1861 Territory of Nevada created out of western Utah; Colorado Territory created out of part of eastern Utah.

Overland Telegraph completed between Great Salt Lake City and "The States." Dixie Mission begins, marking effective colonization of southern Utah.

1862 Salt Lake Theater dedicated.

State of Deseret "ghost government" established; exists until 1870.

Congress passes Anti-Polygamy bill.

Colonel Patrick Edward Connor and his regiment of California-Nevada volunteers locate Camp Douglas.

1863 Connor crushes Shoshone band at Battle of Bear River.

George Ogilvie registers first mining claim in Oquirrh Mountains.

Dry farming begins in Utah.

1865 Congregationalists establish first non-Mormon church in Utah.

Ute Black Hawk war begins, continuing until 1868.

1866 Utah loses 20,850 square miles to newly created State of Nevada.

Deseret telegraph line opened between Great Salt Lake City and Ogden; subsequently extended up and down Territory.

1867 Grasshoppers begin new series of onslaughts on crops; famine is a specter for some years.

Tabernacle completed in Great Salt Lake City.

1868 Zion's Co-operative Mercantile Institution begins operations in re-named "Salt Lake City."

Creation of Wyoming Territory cuts Utah to present-day dimensions.

1869 United States land office opens in Salt Lake City, enabling settlers to obtain title to their lands.

Union Pacific and Central Pacific railroads meet in Golden Spike ceremony at Promontory.

Major John Wesley Powell commences explorations of Green and
Colorado rivers, continuing intermittently until 1872.

First Utah ore shipped to California.

1870   Utah Central Railroad completed between Salt Lake City and Ogden.
Anti-Mormons and Godbeite Mormons organize Liberal political
party.

Large-scale importation of sheep begins.

Population of Utah, 86,786.

1871   Utah Northern Railroad organized to link Ogden and Montana.

1872   First smelting and refining company commences operations in Salt
Lake Valley.

Salt Lake City Gas Works introduces gas as fuel.

First street car system opened in Salt Lake City.

1874   United Order established in Mormon towns and settlements.

Congress passes Poland Bill, to further prosecution of polygamists.

1875   Brigham Young Academy founded by Brigham Young; becomes
university in 1903.

1876   John D. Lee convicted for participation in Mountain Meadows
Massacre; he is shot next year at Mountain Meadows.

Organization of Pleasant Valley Coal Company marks first important exploitation of Carbon-Emery coals, and functional beginning
of Utah coal industry.

1877   St. George Temple, first completed in Utah, dedicated by Brigham
Young.

Brigham Young dies in Salt Lake City.

1879   First telephone line put in at Ogden.

1880   John Taylor succeeds Brigham Young in Mormon Church Presidency.

Electric lighting instituted in Utah.

Population of Utah, 143,963.

1882   Congress passes anti-polygamic Edmunds Law, disfranchising polygamists.

1883   Denver & Rio Grande Western Railroad completed between Denver
and Salt Lake City.

1884   Prosecutions commence under the Edmunds Law.

1885   Virtually all grazing lands in Utah are occupied by herds.

1886   First commercial canning begun at Ogden.

1887   Congress passes Edmunds-Tucker Act in its warfare on polygamy.
John Taylor dies in hiding and is succeeded in the presidency of the
Mormon Church in 1889, by Wilford Woodruff.

Utah Supreme Court appoints receiver to take over Mormon Church
property confiscated under Edmunds-Tucker Act.

1888   Utah State Agricultural College established.

1889   Liberal party wins first major victory in Ogden election.

1890   Liberals carry Salt Lake City for first time.

Wilford Woodruff issues manifesto advising Church membership
to refrain from contracting polygamous marriages.

Natural gas transported to Salt Lake City in wooden pipelines from Davis County.

Free school system established throughout Territory.

Population of Utah, 210,779.

1891 Republican and Democratic parties organize; Mormon People's Party dissolves. Lehi opens first successful sugar beet factory in Utah.

1892 First cattlemen's congress in the West is held at Ogden.

1893 President Benjamin Harrison issues manifesto of amnesty to polygamists; Mormon Temple dedicated.

Congress authorizes return of confiscated property to Mormon Church.

Liberal party disbands.

1894 Legislature passes eight-hour day law.

1895 May 8. Seventh constitutional convention signs Constitution of Utah.

1896 January 4. President Grover Cleveland signs proclamation admitting Utah as Forty-fifth State. January 6. First State legislature convenes.

1897 Uinta Forest Preserve, first "national forest" in Utah, is established.

1898 Park City largely destroyed in million-dollar fire, most disastrous in Utah history.

Wilford Woodruff dies and is succeeded in Church Presidency by Lorenzo Snow.

1899 Legislature creates Utah Art Institute, to sponsor fine arts.

1900 Approximately 200 die in explosion of Winter Quarters coal mine, worst Utah mine disaster.

Population of Utah, 276,749.

1901 Lorenzo Snow dies, and is succeeded by Joseph F. Smith as Church President.

1903 Reed Smoot is elected U. S. Senator by State legislature; begins four-year struggle for his seat.

Three huge natural bridges "discovered"; included in Natural Bridges National Monument in 1908.

Lucin Cutoff completed across Great Salt Lake.

1905 San Pedro, Los Angeles, & Salt Lake Railroad completed at Caliente, Nevada, brings Utah into direct rail communication with southern California.

American Party, new anti-Mormon political organization, carries Salt Lake City election.

1906 Uintah Indian reservation partially opened to homesteading; fully opened in 1914.

Exploitation of low grade copper deposits commences at Bingham.

1907 First oil wells in Utah sunk at Virgin.

1908 First junior high school in Utah instituted at Ogden by John M. Mills.

Western Pacific Railroad completed between Salt Lake City and San Francisco.

Important dinosaur remains found near Jensen; area set aside as national monument in 1915, enlarged in 1938.

Bamberger line, completed between Salt Lake City and Ogden, is first interurban railroad in the West; road is electrified in 1911.

1909 Rainbow Bridge discovery in expedition guided by Nashja-begay; made a national monument the following year.

Zion Canyon is set aside as Mukuntuweap National Monument; status changed to national park in 1929.

1910 Population of Utah is 373,351.

1911 U. S. Reclamation Service completes Strawberry reservoir, first large reclamation project in Utah to divert water from Colorado basin to Great Basin.

Three Brigham Young University professors resign in controversy over teaching of evolution.

1913 Legislature establishes first women's minimum wage laws.

1914 Cave-in at Centennial Eureka mine kills eleven, leads to enactment of mine safety laws.

1915 Good-roads agitation reflects increasing importance of automobile transportation.

Farm Bureau movement begins.

State Capitol completed in Salt Lake City.

Seventeen University of Utah faculty members resign in controversy over free speech.

1917 Utah musters men and capital for World War.

Prohibition laws are extended over the State.

1918 Joseph F. Smith dies; is succeeded in presidency of Mormon Church by Heber J. Grant.

1920 Population of Utah, 449,396.

First commercial airports instituted.

1921 Utah unsuccessfully attempts to prohibit cigarettes; law is repealed in 1923.

Timpanogos Cave "discovered"; is made a national monument the next year.

KSL radio station begins broadcasting.

1922 Arches area "discovered"; is set aside as national monument in 1929.

1923 Floods at Willard and Farmington take nine lives and cause half million dollars' damage, awaken State to need for watershed control and range conservation.

Hovenweep prehistoric Indian remains declared a national monument.

1926 Commercial airlines begin operations in Utah.

Columbia Steel Company opens plant at Ironton, bringing heavy industry to Utah.

1927 Utah has pari-mutuel horse racing; legislature subsequently passes prohibitory laws.

1928   Bryce Canyon National Park established; enlarged in 1931.
1929   Natural gas piped into Utah from Wyoming's Baxter Basin; marks beginning of effectual use of this fuel.
1930   Population, 507,847.
1931   Banks fail; restored in 1933 by Federal Deposit Insurance.
       High Uintas "saddleback" set aside as permanent primitive area.
1932   Mormon Church presents academies to State for junior college purposes.
       State joins in Democratic upheaval; George H. Dern made Secretary of War in Roosevelt cabinet.
1933   State repeals dry law and becomes thirty-sixth to ratify constitutional repeal amendment.
       Cedar Breaks National Monument established.
1934   Official automobile racing begins on Bonneville Salt Flats.
       Dust storms wreak havoc in Tooele County; are brought under control in following years by government efforts.
1935   Legislature passes unemployment insurance laws.
1937   Old age benefits provided by legislature, through co-operation with Federal Social Security Board.
       Act creating Utah Art Institute amended to allow co-operation with Federal cultural projects. Utah State Institute of Fine Arts established.
       Capitol Reef National Monument established.
       Commercial airline accidents in 1937-38 lead to safe-altitude rulings in intermountain area.
1940   Population of Utah is 550,310.
       Utah State Symphony Orchestra founded and first concert given.
       Gregory Natural Bridge discovered by Norman Nevills.

Selected Reading List

Needs more special than those satisfied by this list, will be aided by institutional collections. In Salt Lake City is the L.D.S. Church Historian's Office and Library, its collection the most important group of Mormon source materials in the world. Other book and manuscript collections are those of the Utah State Historical Society, the Daughters of the Utah Pioneers, the University of Utah Library, the Utah Historical Records Survey, WPA, the Utah Writers' Project, WPA, and the Salt Lake City Free Public Library, which has a major collection of books and early newspapers in addition to many volumes of miscellaneous *Mormon-Utah Pamphlets*. The Brigham Young University Library at Provo possesses many manuscripts and other works; the Utah State Agricultural College Library at Logan contains works of utility; the Carnegie Free Public Library at Ogden possesses in its "Golden Spike" collection an important group of printed western Americana; and significant manuscript material is owned by the public libraries at Cedar City and St. George. Valuable materials on Utah and the Mormons are also to be found in great libraries outside Utah, particularly the Library of Congress, Washington, D. C., the Bancroft Library, Berkeley, California, and the New York Public Library. Much untouched manuscript material is in The National Archives, Washington, D. C.

AGRICULTURE AND IRRIGATION

Johnson, Alvin, and Branson, E. C. *Economic Problems of Reclamation.* Washington, Govt. Print. Off., 1929.

Mead, Elwood. *Report of Irrigation Investigations in Utah.* Washington, Govt. Print. Off., 1903. 330 p. (U. S. Department of Agriculture, Office of Experiment Stations. Bulletin 124.)

Smythe, William E. *The Conquest of Arid America.* New York and London, Harper & Brothers, 1900. Rev. ed. New York, Macmillan, 1911.

Stewart, George. "History of Range Use." *Western Range.* Washington, Govt. Print. Off., 1936, pp. 119-133. (Senate Document 199.)

Stewart, George, and others. *Range Conditions in the Uinta Basin, Utah.* Logan, Utah State Agricultural College, 1938.

Thomas, George. *Development of Institutions Under Irrigation.* New York, The Macmillan Co., 1920. 293 p.

Utah State Planning Board. *Irrigation in Utah.* Salt Lake City, 1934. 19 p.

Widtsoe, J. A., and Merrill, L. A. *Arid Farming in Utah*. Logan, Utah State Agricultural College, n.d. Bulletin 91.

Zink, Norah E. *Dry Farming in Utah*. Chicago, University of Chicago Press, 1937. 69 p., mimeo., maps, illus.

ARCHEOLOGY AND INDIANS

Gottfredson, Peter. *History of Indian Depredations in Utah*. Salt Lake City, Skelton Publishing Co., 1919. 352 p.

Hodge, Frederick W., ed. *Handbook of American Indians*. Washington, Govt. Print. Off., Part 1, 1907. 972 p. Part 2, 1910. 122 p. (Bureau of American Ethnology. Bulletin 30.)

Judd, Neil M. *Archeological Observations North of the Rio Colorado*. Washington, Govt. Print. Off., 1926. 171 p. (Bureau of American Ethnology, Bulletin 82.)

Steward, Julian H. *Ancient Caves of the Great Salt Lake Region*. Washington, Govt. Print. Off., 1937. 131 p., illus. (Smithsonian Institution, Bureau of Ethnology. Bulletin 116.)

Steward, Julian H. *Basin-Plateau Aboriginal Sociopolitical Groups*. Washington, Govt. Print. Off., 1938. 346 p., maps. (Smithsonian Institution, Bureau of American Ethnology. Bulletin 120.)

Steward, Julian H. "Changes in Shoshonean Indian Culture." *Scientific Monthly*, Dec. 1939, p. 524-537.

Steward, Julian H. *Pueblo Material Culture in Western Utah*. Albuquerque, University of New Mexico Press, 1936.

Wilson, Elijah Nicholas. *Among the Shoshones*. Salt Lake City, Skelton Publishing Co., 1910. 222 p. (Rep. as *Uncle Nick Among the Shoshones*, and *The White Indian Boy*.)

BIOGRAPHY AND AUTOBIOGRAPHY

Beardsley, Harry M. *Joseph Smith and His Mormon Empire*. Boston, Houghton-Mifflin Co., 1931. 421 p., illus.

Brimhall, George Washington. *The Workers of Utah*. Provo, The Enquirer Co., 1889. 95 p.

Brown, James Stephens. *Life of a Pioneer*. Salt Lake City, George Q. Cannon & Sons Co., 1900. 520 p., port.

Clayton, William. *The Life of William Clayton*. (William Clayton's Journal.) Salt Lake City, The Deseret News, 1921. 376 p.

Egan, Howard. *Pioneering the West, 1846-1878*. Salt Lake City, Utah, The Skelton Publishing Co., 1917. 302 p.

Evans, John Henry. *Charles Coulson Rich, Pioneer Builder of the West*. New York, The Macmillan Co., 1936. 400 p., illus.

Evans, John Henry. *Joseph Smith, an American Prophet*. New York, The Macmillan Co., 1933. 447 p.

Hickman, W. A. *Brigham's Destroying Angel*. Edited and with notes by J. H. Beadle. New York, George A. Crofutt Co., 1872.

Jenson, Andrew. *Autobiography.* Salt Lake City, Deseret News Press, 1938. 705 p.

Lee, John D. *Mormonism Unveiled; The Life and Confessions of John Doyle Lee.* Ed. and comp. by W. W. Bishop. St. Louis, The Bryan-Brand Co., 1879. 406 p. (Abridged form printed as *The Mormon Menace,* ed. by Alfred Henry Lewis. New York, 1905.)

Little, James A. *Jacob Hamblin, a Narrative of His Personal Experiences.* Salt Lake City, Deseret News Press, 1909. 144 p.

Pratt, Parley P. *Autobiography.* Ed. by Parley P. Pratt, Jr. Chicago, Law, King & Law, 1888. 502 p.

Roberts, Brigham H. *Life of John Taylor, Third President of the Church of Jesus Christ of L.D.S.* Salt Lake City, George Q. Cannon & Sons, 1892. 468 p., illus.

Spencer, Clarissa Young, and Harmer, Mabel. *One Who Was Valiant* (Brigham Young). Caldwell, Ida., The Caxton Printers, 1939.

Stanley, Reva. *The Archer of Paradise.* (Parley P. Pratt.) Caldwell, Ida., The Caxton Printers, 1937. 349 p.

Toponce, Alexander. *Reminiscences of Alexander Toponce, Pioneer, 1839-1923.* Ogden, Century Printing Co., 1923. 248 p., illus.

Werner, M. R. *Brigham Young.* New York, Harcourt, Brace & Co., 1924. 478 p., illus.

EXPLORERS, FRONTIERSMEN AND EMIGRANTS

Alter, J. Cecil. *James Bridger.* Salt Lake City, Shepard Book Co., 1925. 546 p., illus.

Beckwith, Lieut. E. G. "Report of Exploration for the Pacific Railroad on the Line of the Forty-First Parallel of North Latitude." *Reports of Explorations and Surveys to Ascertain the most Practicable and Economical Route for a Railroad from the Mississippi River to the Pacific Ocean,* v. 2. Washington, Govt. Print. Off., 1854.

Bidwell, John. *Echoes of the Past.* Chico, Cal., Chico Advertiser, n.d. 92 p.

Birney, Hoffman. *Grim Journey.* New York, Minton, Balch & Co., 1934. 275 p. The story of the Donner Party.

Bonner, T. D. *The Life and Adventures of James P. Beckwourth.* Ed. by Bernard DeVoto. New York, Knopf, 1931. 405 p.

Bryant, Edwin. *What I Saw in California.* New York, D. Appleton & Co., 1848. 455 p. London, Richard Bentley, 1849. 412 p. (Rep. as *Rocky Mountain Adventures,* 1855.)

Camp, Charles L., ed. *James Clyman, American Frontiersman, 1792-1881.* Cleveland, The Arthur H. Clark Co., 1928. 247 p.

Carvalho, S. N. *Incidents of Travel and Adventure in the Far West.* New York, Derby & Jackson, 1857. 380 p., illus.

Dale, Harrison Clifford. *The Ashley-Smith Explorations and the Discovery of a Central Route to the Pacific, 1822-1829.* Cleveland, The Arthur H. Clark Co., 1918. 352 p., maps, illus.

Dellenbaugh, Frederick S. *A Canyon Voyage.* New York, G. C. Putnam's Sons, 1926. 277 p.

Escalante, Silvestre Vélez de. "Diary and Travels." In Harris, W. R. *The Catholic Church in Utah.* Salt Lake City, Intermountain Catholic Press, 1909., pp. 34, 124.

Frémont, John Charles. *Memoirs of My Life.* Chicago, Belford Clark & Co., 1887. 655 p.

Hafen, Leroy R. *The Overland Mail, 1849-1859.* Cleveland, The Arthur H. Clark Co., 1926. 361 p.

Hill, Joseph J. "Spanish and Mexican Exploration and Trade Northwest into the Great Basin." *Utah Historical Quarterly,* Jan. 1930.

Irving, Washington. *Adventures of Captain Bonneville in the Rocky Mountains and Far West.* New York, Putnam, 1849. 428 p. First ed. 1837.

Kelly, Charles, and Howe, Maurice L. *Miles Goodyear.* Salt Lake City, Western Printing Co., 1937. 152 p., bib., illus.

Kelly, Charles. *Salt Desert Trails.* Salt Lake City, Western Printing Co., 1930. 178 p.

Nevins, Allen. *Frémont, Pathmarker of the West.* New York, D. Appleton-Century Co., Inc., 1939. 639 p.

Powell, John Wesley. *Exploration of the Colorado River of the West.* Washington, Govt. Print. Off., 1875. 291 p., maps, illus.

Phillips, Paul G., ed. *Life in the Rocky Mountains.* Denver, The Old West Publishing Co., 1940. 350 p.

Reagan, Albert B. "Forts Robidoux and Kit Carson in Northeastern Utah," *New Mexico Historical Quarterly,* April, 1935, pp. 121-32.

Root, Frank A., and Connelley, William Elsey. *The Overland Stage to California.* Topeka, Kan., The Authors, 1901. 630 p. Best account of the Pony Express.

Russell, Osborne. *Journal of a Trapper, 1834-1843.* Boise, Ida., Syms-York Co., Inc., 1921. 149 p.

Sabin, Edwin. *Kit Carson Days.* New York, Press of the Pioneers Inc., 1935. 488 p.

Simpson, James Henry. *Report of Explorations Across the Great Basin of the Territory of Utah for a Direct Wagon Route from Camp Floyd, in Carson Valley, in 1859.* Washington, Govt. Print. Off., 1876. 518 p., plates, maps.

Stansbury, Howard. *Exploration and Survey of the Valley of the Great Salt Lake of Utah.* Philadelphia, Lippincott, Grambo & Co., 1852. 487 p., maps, illus.

Sullivan, Maurice S. *Jedediah Smith, Trader and Trailbreaker.* New York, Press of the Pioneers Inc., 1936. 233 p.

Wilson, Rufus Rockwell. *Out of the West.* New York, Wilson-Erickson Co., 1936. 480 p.

THE FICTIVE SCENE

Benoit, Pierre. *Salt Lake, A Novel.* New York, Alfred A. Knopf, 1922. 377 p. Tr. from the French. Deals with events during the "Utah War."

DeVoto, Bernard. *The Chariot of Fire*. New York, The Macmillan Co., 1926. Study of frontier religion.

———. *The Crooked Mile*. New York, Minton, Balch & Co., 1924. 432 p. Sequel to *The House of Sun-Goes-Down,* though written earlier.

———. *The House of Sun-Goes-Down*. New York, The Macmillan Co., 1928. 408 p.

Dougall, Lily. *The Mormon Prophet*. New York, Appleton & Co., 1899. 427 p. Based on Joseph Smith's life.

Ertz, Susan. *The Proselyte*. New York, D. Appleton-Century Co., 1933. 359 p. Concerned with the psychological problems of polygamy.

Fisher, Vardis. *Children of God*. New York, Harper & Brothers, 1939. 769 p.

———. *In Tragic Life, Passions Spin the Plot, We Are Betrayed, No Villain Need Be*. Caldwell, Ida., The Caxton Printers, 1932-36. An autobiographical tetralogy.

Gates, Susan Young. *John Stevens' Courtship*. Salt Lake City, The Deseret News, 1909. 377 p. Deals with the "Utah War."

Robertson, Frank Chester. (Frank Chester Field.) *The Rocky Road to Jericho*. New York, Hillman, 1935. 288 p.

Snell, George Dixon. *Root, Hog and Die*. Caldwell, Ida., The Caxton Printers, 1936. A study of Utah beginnings.

Stokes, Jeremiah. *The Soul's Fire*. Los Angeles, Sutton House, 1936. 291 p. Story of crossing the plains.

Whipple, Maurine. *The Giant Joshua*. Boston, Houghton-Mifflin Co., 1941. 367 p.

Woodman, Jean. *Glory Spent*. New York, Carrick & Evans, 1940. Serious novel of contemporary Mormonism.

HISTORY, GENERAL

Alter, J. Cecil. *Utah: The Storied Domain*. Chicago, American Historical Society, 1932. 3 vols.

Bancroft, Hubert H. *History of Utah*. San Francisco, The History Co., 1890. 808 p.

Creer, Leland Hargrave. *Utah and the Nation*. Seattle, University of Washington Press, 1929. 275 p.

Evans, John Henry. *The Story of Utah: The Beehive State*. New York, The Macmillan Co., 1933. 445 p.

Neff, Andrew Love. *History of Utah, 1847-1869* Ed. by Leland H. Greer. Salt Lake City, Deseret News Press, 1940. 955 p.

Utah State Historical Society. *Utah Historical Quarterly*. Salt Lake City, 1928-1933; 1939-   , Vols. 1- .

Warrum, Noble. *History of Utah Since Statehood*. Chicago and Salt Lake City, S. J. Clark Pub. Co., 1919. 3 Vols.

Whitney, Orson F. *History of Utah*. Salt Lake City, The Deseret News, 1916. 588 p., portraits, illus.

Work Projects Administration. Historical Records Survey. "The State of Deseret." *Utah Historical Quarterly,* April-Oct. 1940, pp. 65-251.

Young, Levi Edgar. *The Founding of Utah.* Boston and New York, Charles Scribner's Sons, 1923. 445 p.

HISTORY, LOCAL

Forsgren, Lydia Walker, comp. *History of Box Elder County.* Privately printed, n.d. 390 p.

Gardner, Hamilton. *History of Lehi.* Salt Lake City, The Lehi Pioneers Society, The Deseret News, 1913. 463 p.

Jensen, J. Marinus. *History of Provo, Utah.* Provo, New Century Printing Co., 1924. 410 p.

Lever, W. H. *History of Sanpete and Emery Counties.* Ogden, Utah, The Author, 1898. 681 p., illus.

Longsdorf, Hilda Madsen, compiler. *Mount Pleasant.* Mount Pleasant, Utah Pioneer Historical Association, 1940. 338 p.

Tanner, Faun McConkie. *History of Moab.* Moab, Ut., Press of the Times-Independent, 1937. 86 p.

Taylor, Frank J. "The Story of Utah's Dixie." *Sunset Magazine,* Mar. 1929, pp. 20-23.

Tolton, J. F. *History of Beaver.* Beaver, Utah, Carleton Publishing Co., n.d.

Tullidge, Edward W. "History of Provo." *Tullidge's Quarterly Magazine,* July 1884. Vol. 3, pp. 233-285.

――――. *History of Salt Lake City, and its Founders.* Salt Lake City, The Author, 1886. 1058 p.

――――. "History of Spanish Fork." *Tullidge's Quarterly Magazine.* April 1884. Vol. 3, pp. 137-170.

――――. *Histories of Utah.* Salt Lake City, The Author, 1889. Vol. 2. 540 p. Northern Utah and southern Idaho counties.

――――. "History of Utah County." *Tullidge's Quarterly Magazine,* Jan. 1885, pp. 337-453.

Work Projects Administration. Utah Historical Records Survey. *A History of Ogden,* 1940. 77 p.

――――. Utah Historical Records Survey. *Inventories of the County Archives of Utah.* Ogden and Salt Lake City, 1937-   , published and in preparation.

――――. Utah Writers' Project. *Origins of Utah Place Names.* Salt Lake City, State Department of Education, 1940. 3rd ed. 47 p.

MINING

Brighton, T. R. "Salt Making on the Great Salt Lake." *Journal of Chemical Education,* Mar. 1932.

Butler, B. S., and others. *The Ore Deposits of Utah.* Washington, Govt. Print. Off., 1920. 700 p., illus. (U. S. Geological Survey. Professional Paper 111.)

Clark, Frank R., and Wegeman, C. H. *Coal Fields in New Mexico and Utah.* Washington, Govt. Print. Off., 1914. 74 p. (U. S. Geological Survey. Bulletin 541.)

Kiessling, O. E. *Mineral Resources of the United States, 1930; Part I, Metals.* Washington, Govt. Print. Off., 1933. 1142 p., statistics. (U. S. Bureau of Mines, Mineral Resources.)

———. *Mineral Resources of the United States, 1930; Part II, Non-metals.* Washington, Govt. Print. Off.; 1932. 876 p., statistics. (U. S. Bureau of Mines, Mineral Resources.)

Lewis, R. S. *Mining, the Priceless Heritage.* Salt Lake City, University of Utah, 1939.

——— and Varley, Thomas. *The Mineral Industry of Utah.* Washington, Govt. Print. Off., 1919. 201 p., illus. (U. S. Bureau of Mines. Bulletin 12.)

Utah. State Planning Board. *Summary of Data on Minerals and the Minerals Industry of Utah.* Salt Lake City, The Author, 1935. 55 p., mimeo., charts.

Winchester, Dean E. *Oil Shale of the Rocky Mountain Region.* Washington, Govt. Print. Off., 1918. 54 p., illus. (U. S. Geological Survey.)

MORMONS AND ANTI-MORMONS.

Allen, Edward J. *The Second United Order Among the Mormons.* New York, Columbia University Press, 1936.

Allred, B. Harvey. *A Leaf in Review.* Caldwell, Ida., The Caxton Printers, 1933. 222 p. A brief for polygamy.

Arbaugh, George Bartholomew. *Revelation in Mormonism.* Chicago, University of Chicago Press, 1932. 252 p.

Baskin, R. N. *Reminiscences of Early Utah.* Salt Lake City, The Author, 1914. 252 p.

Beadle, John Hanson. *Polygamy: Or the Mysteries and Crimes of Mormonism.* Philadelphia, The National Publishing Co., 1886. 572 p. The author has written other colloquial, unreliable works.

Bennett, John C. *The History of the Saints; or an Expose of Joseph and Mormonism.* Boston, Leland and Whiting, 1842. 344 p.

Birney, Hoffman. *Zealots of Zion.* Philadelphia, Penn Publishing Co., 1931. 317 p.

Bonwick, James F. *The Mormons and the Silver Mines.* London, Hodder & Stoughton, 1872. 418 p.

Brooks, Juanita. "A Close-Up of Polygamy." *Harper's Magazine,* Feb. 1934, pp. 299-307.

Browne, Albert G. "The Utah Expedition." *Atlantic Monthly,* Mar.-May 1859.

Burton, Sir Richard F. *The City of the Saints.* New York, Harper & Brother, 1862. 574 p.

Chandless, William. *A Visit to Salt Lake.* London, Smith, Elder & Co., 1857. 346 p.

Cutten, George Barton. *Speaking with Tongues.* New Haven, Yale University Press, 1927. 193 p.

Daines, Franklin D. "Separatism in Utah, 1847-1870." (In American Historical Association, *Annual Reports, 1917-18.*) Washington, Govt. Print. Off., 1921, pp. 332-343.

DeVoto, Bernard. *Forays and Rebuttals.* Boston, Little, Brown & Co., 1936. 403 p. Contains important essays on the Mormons and the West.

———. "Utah." *The American Mercury,* Mar. 1926, pp. 317-323.

Ericksen, Ephraim Edward. *The Psychological and Ethical Aspects of Mormon Group Life.* Chicago, Chicago University Press, 1922. 101 p.

Ferris, Benjamin G. *Utah and the Mormons.* New York, Harper & Brother, 1854. 340 p.

Gardner, Hamilton. "Communism Among the Mormons." *Quarterly Journal of Economics,* Vol. 37, 1922-1923, pp. 134-174.

———. "Cooperation Among the Mormons." *Quarterly Journal of Economics,* Vol. 31, 1916-1917, pp. 461-499.

Geddes, Joseph A. *The United Order Among the Mormons.* Salt Lake City, The Deseret News, 1924.

Gibbs, Josiah F. *Lights and Shadows of Mormonism.* Salt Lake City, Tribune Publishing Co., 1909. 535 p.

Goodwin, Samuel H. *Mormonism and Masonry.* Salt Lake City, Grand Lodge F. & A. M., Utah, 1934. 78 p.

Gove, Jesse A. *The Utah Expedition, 1857-1858.* Concord, The New Hampshire Historical Society, 1928. 442 p.

Gunnison, Lieut. John Williams. *The Mormons.* Philadelphia, J. B. Lippincott, 1856. 168 p. First ed. 1852.

Howe, E. D. *History of Mormonism.* Painesville, O., The Author, 1840. 290 p. First ed. 1834 in *Mormonism Unveiled.*

Hyde, John Jr. *Mormonism; Its Leaders and Designs.* New York, W. Fetridge & Co., 1857. 335 p.

Jenson, Andrew. *Church Chronology.* Salt Lake City, The Author, 1899. 259 p.

Kelly, Charles, and Birney, Hoffman. *Holy Murder.* New York, Minton-Balch & Co., 1934.

Larson, Louis W. "Mormon Polygamy: The Last Phase." *The American Mercury,* July 1933, pp. 284-291.

Linn, W. A. *The Story of the Mormons From the Date of Their Origin to the Year 1901.* New York, The Macmillan Co., 1902. 637 p.

Morris, Joseph. *The "Spirit Prevails."* San Francisco, George H. Dove, 1886. Contains revelations and miscellaneous papers of Morris.

Musser, Neil B. "A Mormon Boyhood." *The American Mercury,* Jan. 1930, pp. 14-21.

Quaife, Milo M. *The Kingdom of St. James.* New Haven, Yale University Press, 1930. 284 p. The story of the Strang heresy.

Remy, Jules, and Brenchley, Julius. *A Journey to Great Salt Lake City,* London, W. Jeffs, 1861. 2 vols.

Roberts, Brigham H. *A Comprehensive History of the Church of Jesus Christ of Latter-day Saints.* Salt Lake City, Deseret News Press, 1930. 6 Vols.

Robinson, Phil. *Sinners and Saints.* London, Sampson Low, 1883.

Rogers, Fred B. *Soldiers of the Overland.* San Francisco, The Grabhorn Press, 1938. The story of Connor's men in Utah.

Smith, Joseph. *History of the Church.* Ed. by Brigham H. Roberts. Salt Lake City, Deseret News Press, 1902-1932. 7 vols. (Abridged from the "History of Joseph Smith." *Millennial Star,* 1852-63; Vols. 14-25.)

Smith, Joseph Fielding. *Essentials in Church History.* Salt Lake City, Deseret News Press, 1922. (New edition 1938.)

Stenhouse, Fanny (Mrs. T.B.H.) *Tell It All.* Hartford, Conn., A. D. Worthington & Co., 1875. 623 p.

Stenhouse, T. B. H. *Rocky Mountain Saints.* New York, D. Appleton & Co., 1873. 760 p.

Twain, Mark. *Roughing It.* Hartford, Conn., American Publishing Co., 1879. 591 p.

Tyler, Daniel. *Concise History of the Mormon Battalion in the Mexican War (1846-1847).* Washington, The Author, 1881. 376 p.

Waite, Catherine V. *The Mormon Prophet and His Harem.* Cambridge, Mass., Riverside Press, 1868. 318 p.

Works Progress Administration. Federal Writers' Project of Illinois. *Nauvoo.* Chicago, A. C. McClurg, 1939, 49 p.

Young, Ann Eliza. *Wife No. 19.* Hartford, Conn., Dustin, Gilman & Co., 1876. 605 p.

Young, Brigham, and others. *Journal of Discourses.* London, F. D. & S. W. Richards, 1854-1884. 26 vols. Contains important addresses of Church leaders during the critical years of the Church in Utah.

MORMON DOCTRINE

The Book of Mormon. First ed. pub. at Palmyra, N. Y., E. B. Grandin, 1830. 588 p. Many subsequent eds.

Doctrine and Covenants. Salt Lake City, George Q. Cannon & Sons, 1891. 503 p. Many eds.

The Pearl of Great Price. Liverpool, Albert Carrington, 1882. 90 p.

Roberts, Brigham H. *Defense of the Faith and the Saints.* Salt Lake City, The Deseret News, 1912. 2 vols.

Smith, Joseph Fielding. *The Way to Perfection: Short Discourses on Popular Themes.* Salt Lake City, Genealogical Society of Utah, 1931. 365 p.

Talmage, James E. *Articles of Faith.* Salt Lake City, Church of Jesus Christ of Latter-day Saints, 1924. 537 p.

————. *The Vitality of Mormonism.* Boston, Richard G. Badger, The Gorham Press, 1919. 361 p.

Widtsoe, John A. *Priesthood and Church Government.* Salt Lake City, Deseret Book Co., 1939. 410 p.

NATURAL SETTING

Atwood, W. W. "Lakes of the Uinta Mountains." (American Geological Society, *Bulletin,* 1908. p. 12-18.)

Bailey, Reed W.; Forsling, C. L.; and Becraft, R. J. *Floods and Accelerated Erosion in Northern Utah.* Washington, Govt. Print. Off., 1934. 21 p. (U. S. Department of Agriculture. Misc. Publication 196.)

Bernheimer, C. L. *Rainbow Bridge.* Garden City, N. Y., Doubleday, 1924. 180 p., maps, illus.

Borah, Leo A. "Utah, Carved by Winds and Water." *National Geographic Magazine,* May 1936. pp. 577-625, illus.

Boutwell, John M., ed. *The Salt Lake Region.* Washington, Govt. Print. Off., 1933. 149 p.

Bradley, Wilmot H. "The Biography of an Ancient American Lake." *Scientific Monthly,* May 1936 (Rep. in Proceedings of Smithsonian Institution, 1937).

Campbell, Marius R. *Guidebook of the Western United States.* "Part E., The Denver & Rio Grande Western Route." Washington, Govt. Print. Off., 1922. 266 p. (U. S. Geological Survey. Bulletin 707.)

Cummings, Byron. "Great Natural Bridges of Utah." *National Geographic Magazine,* Feb. 1910. pp. 157-167.

Dutton, Clarence Edward, and Gilbert, G. K. *Report on Geology of the Henry Mountains.* Washington, Govt. Print. Off., 1877. 160 p., plates, maps, illus. (U. S. Department of the Interior.)

————. *U. S. Geographical and Geological Survey of the Rocky Mountain Region.* Washington, Govt. Print. Off., 1879. 2nd ed., 195 p., maps, illus.

————. *Geology of the High Plateaus of Utah.* Washington, Govt. Print. Off., 1880. 307 p., atlas, illus. (U. S. Department of the Interior; Geographical and Geological Survey of the Rocky Mountain Region.)

Eyston, George, and Bradley, W. F. *Speed on Salt.* New York, Scribner, 1936. 84 p., illus.

Gilbert, Grove Karl. *Lake Bonneville.* Washington, Govt. Print. Off., 1890. 438 p. (U. S. Geological Survey, Monograph No. 1.)

Gregory, Herbert E. *Geology of the Navajo Country.* Washington, Govt. Print. Off., 1917. 161 p., plates, illus, index. (U. S. Geological Survey. Water Supply Paper 93.)

Gregory, Herbert E, and Moore, R. C. *The Kaiparowits Region.* Washington, Govt. Print. Off., 1931. 161 p. (U. S. Geological Survey. Professional Paper 164.)

————. *The Navajo Country.* Washington, Govt. Print. Off., 1916. 219 p., plates, index. (U. S. Geological Survey. Water Supply Paper 380.)

———— with contrib. by Thorpe, Malcolm R. *The San Juan Country.* Washington, Govt. Print. Off., 1938. 123 p., maps, illus. (U. S. Geological Survey. Professional Paper 188.)

Judd, Neil M. "Beyond the Clay Hills." *National Geographic Magazine,* Mar. 1924, pp. 275-302.

Lambourne, Alfred. *Our Inland Sea.* Salt Lake City, The Deseret News, 1909. 256 p., vignettes. Life of a homesteader on Gunnison Island.

Lee, Willis T., and others. *Guidebook of the Western United States.* "Part B., The Overland Route." Washington, Govt. Print. Off., 1916. 251 p. (U. S. Geological Survey. Bulletin 612.)

Pack, F. J. *Lake Bonneville.* Salt Lake City, University of Utah, 1939. 113 p., illus. (Bulletin 4, v. 30.)

Powell, J. W. *Report on the Lands of the Arid Region of the United States.* Washington, Govt. Print. Off., 1879. XV. 195 p., maps, indexed.

Schneider, Hyrum. "Geologic Processes and Their Relation to Human Activities in Utah." Provo, Utah Academy of Sciences, Arts and Letters, *Proceedings,* 1935. v. 12.

Scoyen, Eivind T., and Taylor, Frank J. *Rainbow Canyons.* Palo Alto, Cal., Stanford University Press, 1931. 105 p., index.

Stone, Julius F. *Canyon Country.* (The Romance of a Drop of Water and a Grain of Sand.) New York and London, G. F. Putnam's Sons, 1932. 442 p.

U. S. Department of Agriculture. *Climatic Summary of the United States;* "Section 20, Western Utah," 41 p., "Section 21, Eastern Utah," 23 p. Washington, Govt. Print. Off., 1936.

U. S. Forest Service. *What the National Forests Mean to the Intermountain Region.* Washington, Govt. Print. Off., 1930. 21 p.

Webb, Walter Prescott. *The Great Plains.* Boston, Ginn & Company, 1931. 525 p., illus.

White, Charles Langton. *The Agricultural Geography of the Salt Lake Oasis.* Worcester, Mass., a dissertation submitted to Clark University, 1925. 203 p., illus.

PLANTS AND ANIMALS

Barnes, Claude T. *Utah Mammals.* Salt Lake City, University of Utah, 1927. 183 p., illus., index.

Belle, William H. "Highlights of Ornithological Work in Utah." *Condor,* July 1938, pp. 165-173.

Carter, Kate B., comp. "Flowers of Utah," and "Trees of Utah." In *Heart Throbs of the West.* Salt Lake City, Daughters of Utah Pioneers, 1939.

Cottam, Walter P. *New and Extended Ranges of Utah Plants.* Salt Lake City, University of Utah, 1939. (Biological Series, v. 4, No. 4.)

Flowers, Seville. *Mosses of Utah.* Salt Lake City, University of Utah, 1934. Mimeo.

Garrett, A. O. *Spring Flora of the Wasatch Region.* Salt Lake City, Skelton Publishing Co., 1911. 106 p., index.

Paul, J. H., and Barnes, Claude T. *Farm Foes and Bird Helpers.* Salt Lake City, Deseret News, 1914. 192 p.

Paul, Joshua H., and Barnes, Claude T. *Forest Groves and Canyon Streams.* Salt Lake City, Deseret News Press, 1913. 228 p., illus.

————. *Out of Doors in the West: Plants, Birds, and Insects of the Rocky Mountain Plateau.* Salt Lake City, Skelton Publishing Co., 1911. 236 p.

Tanner, Vasco M. *Distributional List of the Amphibians and Reptiles of Utah.* Provo, 1928.

Tidestrom, Ivar. *Flora of Utah and Nevada.* Washington, Govt. Print. Off., 1925, maps, illus. (Smithsonian Institution, U. S. National Museum, Vol. 25.)

U. S. Department of Agriculture. *Forest and Range Resources of Utah; Their Protection and Use.* Washington, Govt. Print. Off., 1930. 101 p., index, illus. (Misc. Publication 90.)

Woodbury, A. M. *Key to the Birds of Utah.* Salt Lake City, University of Utah, 1933.

————. "Management of Aquatic Wild Life in the Great Basin." *Scientific Monthly,* April 1940.

————. "Planning the Conservation of Utah's Wild Life." *Utah Educational Review,* 1937, v. 30.

————. *The Reptiles of Utah.* Salt Lake City, University of Utah, 1931. 129 p., illus., index.

THE SOCIAL AMENITIES

Art Work of Utah. Chicago, The W. H. Parish Publishing Co., 1896. 2 vols.

Brandley, Elsie Talmage, and Merrill, Harrison R., eds. *Utah Sings.* Provo, Utah Academy of Sciences, Arts, and Letters, Brigham Young University Press, 1934. 320 p. An anthology of Utah verse.

DeVoto, Bernard. "A Sagebrush Bookshelf." *Harper's Magazine,* Oct. 1937.

Henderson, Myrtle E. *A History of the Theatre in Salt Lake City from 1850 to 1870.* Evanston, Ill., The Author, 1934. 161 p.

Lambourne, Alfred. *Play House.* Privately Printed, 1914. 64 p., illus.

Lindsay, John S. *The Mormons and the Theatre.* Salt Lake City, The Author, 1905. 178 p.

Lyon, John. *The Harp of Zion.* London, T. C. Armstrong, 1853. 225 p. Contains many early Mormon hymns.

Pyper, George D. *The Romance of an Old Playhouse.* Salt Lake City, Seagull Press, 1928. 342 p., photos.

Whitney, Horace G. *The Drama in Utah.* Salt Lake City, Deseret News Press, 1915. 48 p.

THE SOCIAL SCENE

Alter, J. Cecil. *Early Utah Journalism.* Salt Lake City, Utah State Historical Society, 1938. 405 p.

Beal, O. F. *Marriage and Divorce in Utah.* Ann Arbor, Mich., Edward Brothers, Inc., 1935.

Beeley, A. L. "Conserving the Cultural Resources of Utah." In Utah Academy of Sciences, Arts, and Letters, *Proceedings.* Provo, 1938. v. 15, p. 55 et seq.

————. *Social Planning for Crime Control.* Salt Lake City, University of Utah Press, 1937. 50 p.

————. "Utah Population: Some Significant Characteristics and Trends." (In Utah Academy of Sciences, Arts and Letters, *Proceedings.* Provo, 1932. v. 9, p. 65 et seq.)

Cowles, LeRoy E. *Organization and Administration of Education in Utah.* Ann Arbor, Mich., Edward Brothers, 1934.

Fries, Louis J. *One Hundred and Fifty Years of Catholicity in Utah.* Salt Lake City, Intermountain Catholic Press, 1926. 143 p.

Greenwood, Annie Pike. *We Sagebrush Folks.* New York, D. Appleton-Century Co., 1934. 438 p.

Hansen, George H. *A Regional Redistricting Plan for the State of Utah.* Provo, Brigham Young University Press, 1937. 57 p., maps, charts.

Harris, Chauncy Dennison. *Salt Lake City: A Regional Capital.* Chicago, Privately printed, 1940. 206 p., maps.

Harris, Franklin Stewart, and Newburn, Isaac Butt. *The Fruits of Mormonism.* New York, The Macmillan Co., 1925. 146 p.

Kelly, Charles. *Outlaw Trail.* Salt Lake City, Western Printing Co., 1938. 337 p. Story of the outlaw gangs in eastern and southern Utah.

Kenner, Scipio Africanus. *Utah As It Is.* Salt Lake City, The Deseret News, 1904. 639 p.

Merkel, Henry Martin. *History of Methodism in Utah.* Colorado Springs, The Denton Printing Co., 1938. 270 p.

Pendleton, Mark A. "The Orderville United Order of Zion." *Utah Historical Quarterly.* Salt Lake City, Vol. 7, Oct. 1939, pp. 141-159.

Seegmiller, Emma Carroll. "Personal Memories of the Orderville United Order," *Utah Historical Quarterly.* Oct. 1939, pp. 160-200.

Skidmore, Charles H., ed. *Utah Resources and Activities.* Salt Lake City, Department of Public Instruction, Paragon Press, 1933. 458 p.

Thomas, George. *Civil Government of Utah.* Chicago, D. C. Heath Co., 1912. 198 p.

Tittsworth, W. B. *Outskirt Episodes.* Des Moines, Ia., Success Printing Co., 1927. Reminiscences of Browns Hole.

U. S. Department of the Interior. *Survey of Education in Utah.* Washington, Govt. Print. Off., 1926. 510 p. (Bulletin 18.)

Utah. State Planning Board. *Review of Industrial Movements in Utah With Population Aspects.* Salt Lake City, The Author, 1935. 41 p., mimeo., charts.

Utah. State Planning Board. *A State Plan for Utah, Progress Report.* Salt Lake City, The Author, 1935. 159 p., mimeo.

Vandegrift, Rolland A., and Associates. *The Economic Dependence of the Population of Utah*. Salt Lake City, The Authors, 1931.

Work Projects Administration. Utah Historical Records Survey. *History and Bibliography of Religion in Utah*. Salt Lake City, 1940. 121 p.

Young, Kimball. "Story of the Rise of a Social Taboo." *Scientific Monthly*, May 1928. Concerning the seagulls.

List of Consultants

Adams, Thomas C., Associate Professor of Civil Engineering, University of Utah.

Alter, J. Cecil, Historian and Editor, Utah State Historical Society.

Beeley, Mrs. A. L., Salt Lake City.

Bennion, Glynn, L.D.S. Church Historian's Office.

Bird, Elzy, J., State Supervisor, Utah Art Project.

Boyle, A. C., Custodian, Dinosaur National Monument.

Bradley, Wilmot H., Geologist, U. S. Geological Survey, Washington, D. C.

Brown, Arnold, Librarian, *Salt Lake Tribune-Telegram*.

Canfield, David H., Superintendent, Rocky Mountain National Park, Estes Park, Colorado.

Cannon, Tracy Y., Director, McCune School of Music and Art.

Carter, Mrs. Kate B., Second Vice President, Daughters of Utah Pioneers.

Champ, Frederick P., Logan.

Christiansen, Francis W., Instructor in Geology, University of Utah.

Clark, Herald R., Dean of the College of Commerce, Brigham Young University.

Cook, Newell B., Commissioner, Utah State Fish and Game Commission.

Cowles, LeRoy E., Dean, Lower Division, School of Education, University of Utah.

Davis, John M., Assistant Superintendent, Zion and Bryce Canyon National Parks.

Durrant, Stephen D., Instructor in Zoology, University of Utah.

Fetzer, Henry, Architect, Salt Lake City.

Gerry, C. N., Statistician, U. S. Bureau of Mines.

Greenwell, Darrell J., Administrator, Utah WPA.

Gurr, James E., Supervisor, Wasatch National Forest.

Hanson, George, Professor of Geology and Geography, Brigham Young University.

Hart, Charles J., Assistant Professor of Physical Education, Brigham Young University.

Hibbert, Owen, Technical Engineer, Capitol Reef National Monument.

Jensen, J. Marinus, Associate Professor of English, Brigham Young University.

Johnson, Zeke, Custodian, Natural Bridges National Monument.

Kelly, Charles, Author and Historian, Salt Lake City.

Kimball, Ranch, Commercial Artist, Salt Lake City.

King, Dale S., Archeologist, Southwestern National Monuments, Coolidge, Arizona.

Knight, W. S., Utah Lake Investigator.

Lee, Hector, Instructor in English, University of Utah.

Lund, A. William, Assistant Historian, L.D.S. Church Historian's Office.

Margetts, Sumner G., Director, Utah State Planning Board.

Meeks, Heber, Area Manager, U. S. Bureau of the Census, Salt Lake City.

Miller, Hugh, Acting Superintendent, Southwestern National Monuments, Coolidge, Arizona.

Mills, John M., Ogden.

Miser, Hugh D., Geologist, U. S. Geological Survey, Washington, D. C.

Paulson, A. B., Architect, Salt Lake City.

Peterson, Elmer G., President, Utah State Agriculture College.

Pyper, George D., former manager, Salt Lake Theatre.

Richards, Heber G., Associate Professor of English, University of Utah.

Schmidt, Henry, Custodian, Arches National Monument.

Sinclair, Marguerite L., Librarian, Utah State Historical Society.

Smith, Alvin, Librarian, L.D.S. Church Historian's Office.

Smith, Elmer R., Instructor in Sociology and Anthropology, University of Utah.

Steward, Julian H., Bureau of American Ethnology, Washington, D. C.

Stewart, S. S., Associate Forester, U. S. Forest Service.

Tanner, Vasco M., Professor of Zoology and Entomology, Brigham Young University.

Walker, Thomas A., Custodian, Timpanogos Cave National Monument.

Woodbury, Angus M., Associate Professor of Zoology, University of Utah.

MAP OF
UTAH
IN SIX SECTIONS

LEGEND for STATE MAP

U. S. HIGHWAYS ▬▬【90】▬▬

STATE HIGHWAYS ▬▬[35]▬▬

CONNECTING ROADS ▬▬▬▬

POINTS OF INTEREST (SYMBOL) ■

NATIONAL FORESTS

INDIAN RESERVATION

NATIONAL PARKS
AND MONUMENTS

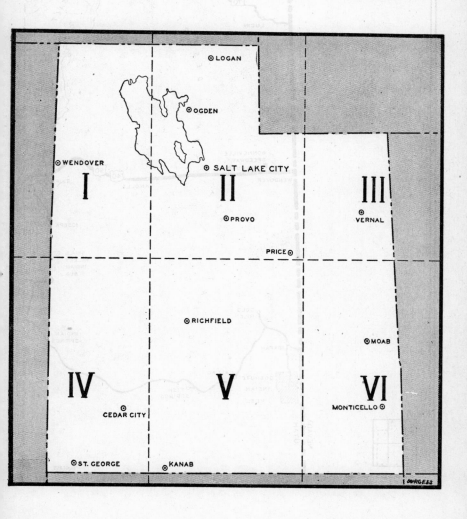

○ LOGAN

○ OGDEN

○ WENDOVER

I

○ SALT LAKE CITY

II

III

○ VERNAL

○ PROVO

PRICE ○

○ RICHFIELD

○ MOAB

IV

V

VI

○ CEDAR CITY

○ MONTICELLO

○ ST. GEORGE   ○ KANAB

BURGESS

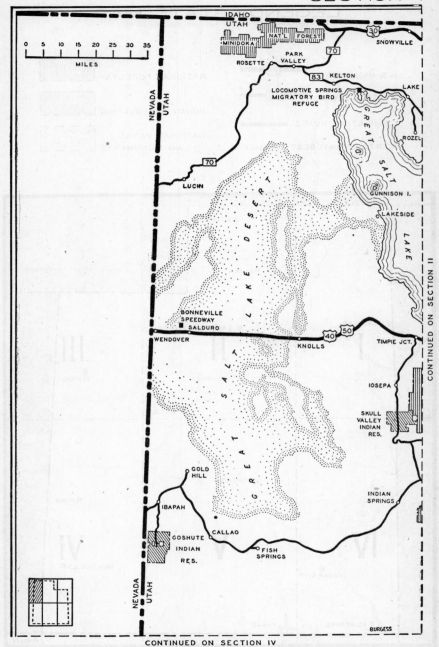

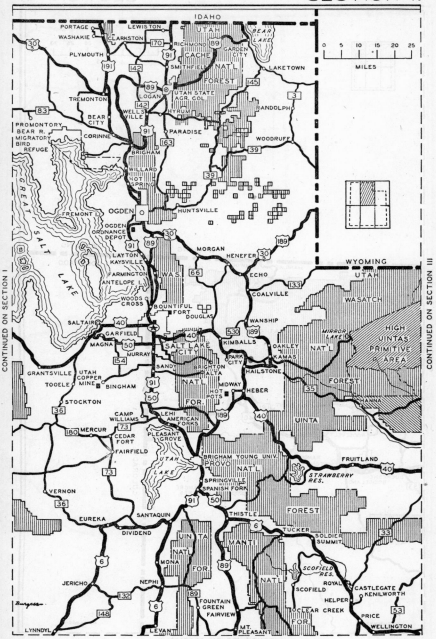

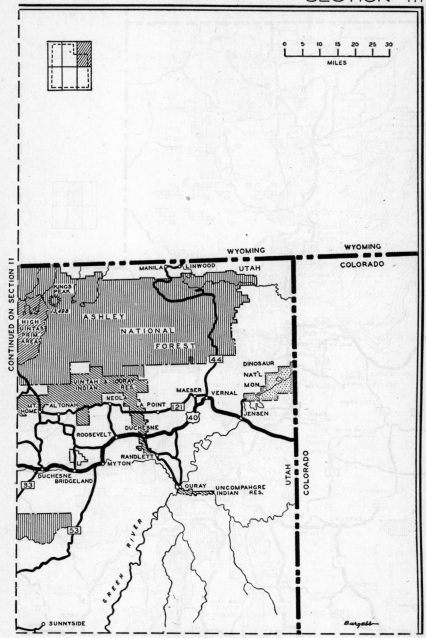

CONTINUED ON SECTION II

CONTINUED ON SECTION VI

MILES

WYOMING
UTAH

WYOMING
COLORADO

MANILA   LINWOOD

KINGS
PEAK
13,498

HIGH
UINTAS
PRIM
AREA

ASHLEY

NATIONAL

FOREST

44

DINOSAUR
NAT'L
MON.

UINTAH &
INDIAN   OURAY
RES.

NEOLA   A POINT   121

MAESER   VERNAL

ALTONAH

HOME

40

JENSEN

ROOSEVELT   DUCHESNE

RANDLETT

MYTON

DUCHESNE
BRIDGELAND

33

53

OURAY   UNCOMPAHGRE
INDIAN   RES.

GREEN RIVER

UTAH
COLORADO

SUNNYSIDE

Burgess

HINCKLEY
DESERET

ROBISONS RANCH

6

GARRISON

21

DESERT RANGE EXPERIMENTAL FARM

COVE FORT

NEVADA
UTAH

21 NEWHOUSE
FRISCO
MILFORD

91
BEAVER

PAIUTE INDIAN RES.

ADAMSVILLE
GREEN-VILLE
MINERSVILLE

19

LUND

27

LITTLE SALT LAKE

PARAGONAH
PARAWAN

MODENA

SUMMIT

DIXIE

NEWCASTLE

56

143

18
ENTERPRISE

16
PINTO

198

91
CEDAR CITY

14

CEDAR BREAKS NAT'L MON.

DIXIE
NAT'L

KANARRAVILLE

NAT'L

CENTRAL

NEW HARMONY

ZION NAT'L MON.

FOREST

VEYO

PINE VALLEY

FOREST

ANDERSONS RANCH
TOQUERVILLE
VIRGIN

ZION NAT'L PARK

GLENDALE
ORDERVILLE

LEEDS
LA VERKIN

15

MT. CARMEL

SHIVWITS INDIAN RES.

18

HURRICANE

SPRINGDALE
ROCKVILLE

89

NEVADA
UTAH

SANTA CLARA ST. GEORGE

59

91

164

UTAH
ARIZONA

0 5 10 15 20 25
MILES

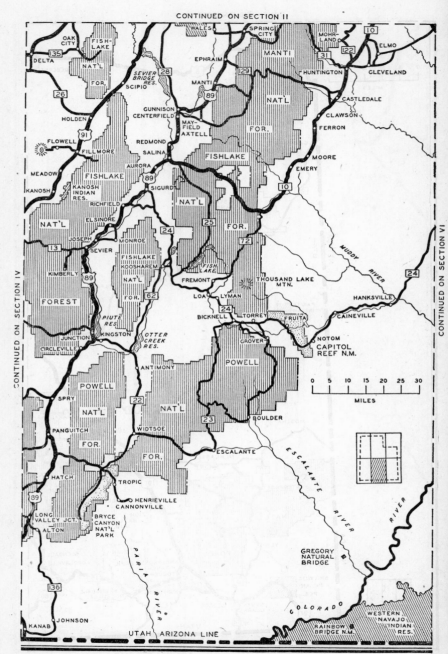

SECTION V

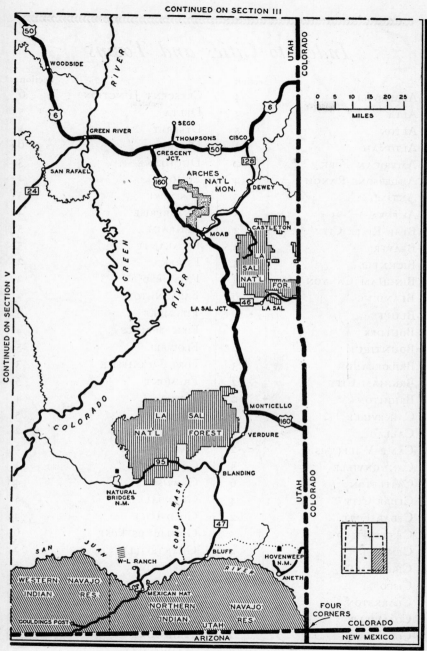

CONTINUED ON SECTION V

SECTION VI

Index to Cities and Towns

	Section		Section
ADAMSVILLE	4	CRESCENT JUNCTION	6
ALTA	2	DELTA	5
ALTON	5	DESERET	4
ALTONAH	3	DEWEY	6
AMERICAN FORK	2	DUCHESNE	3
ANDERSONS RANCH	4	ECHO	2
ANTIMONY	5	ELSINORE	5
AURORA	5	ENTERPRISE	4
BEAR RIVER CITY	2	EPHRAIM	5
BEAVER	4	ESCALANTE	5
BICKNELL	5	EUREKA	2
BINGHAM CANYON	2	FAIRFIELD	2
BLANDING	6	FARMINGTON	2
BLUFF	6	FILLMORE	5
BOULDER	5	FISH SPRINGS	4
BOUNTIFUL	2	FLOWELL	5
BRIDGELAND	3	FORT DUCHESNE	3
BRIGHAM CITY	2	FREMONT	5
BRIGHTON	2	FRISCO	4
CAINEVILLE	5	FRUITA	5
CALLAO	1	FRUITLAND	2
CAMP WILLIAMS	2	GARDEN CITY	2
CANNONVILLE	5	GARFIELD	2
CASTLETON	6	GARRISON	4
CEDAR CITY	4	GLENDALE	4
CEDAR FORT	2	GOLD HILL	4
CENTERFIELD	5	GOULDINGS POST	6
CENTRAL	4	GRANTSVILLE	2
CIRCLEVILLE	5	GREENRIVER	6
CISCO	6	GREENVILLE	4
CLARKSTON	2	GROVER	5
COALVILLE	2	GUNNISON	5
CORINNE	2	HAILSTONE	2
COVE FORT	4	HANKSVILLE	5

	Section
HANNA	2
HATCH	5
HEBER	2
HENEFER	2
HENRIEVILLE	5
HINCKLEY	4
HOLDEN	5
HOT SPRINGS	2
HUNTSVILLE	2
HURRICANE	4
HYRUM	2
IBAPAH	1
INDIAN SPRINGS	1
IOSEPA	1
JENSEN	3
JOHNSON	5
JOSEPH	5
JUNCTION	5
KAMAS	2
KANAB	4
KANARRAVILLE	4
KANOSH	5
KAYSVILLE	2
KELTON	1
KIMBALLS	2
KINGSTON	5
KNOLLS	1
KOOSHAREM	5
LAKE	1
LAKETOWN	2
LAPOINT	3
LA SAL	6
LA SAL JUNCTION	6
LA VERKIN	4
LAYTON	2
LEEDS	4
LEHI	2

	Section
LEWISTON	2
LINWOOD	3
LOA	5
LOGAN	2
LONG VALLEY	5
LUCIN	1
LUND	4
LYMAN	5
MAESER	3
MAGNA	2
MANILA	3
MANTI	5
MANTUA	2
MAYFIELD	5
MEADOW	5
MERCUR	2
MEXICAN HAT	6
MIDWAY	2
MILFORD	4
MINERSVILLE	4
MOAB	6
MODENA	4
MONROE	5
MONTICELLO	6
MORGAN	2
MOUNTAIN HOME	3
MT. CARMEL	4
MURRAY	2
MYTON	3
NEOLO	3
NEWCASTLE	4
NEW HARMONY	4
NEWHOUSE	4
NOTOM	5
OAK CITY	5
OAKLEY	2
OGDEN	2

	Section		Section
ORDERVILLE	4	SMITHFIELD	2
OURAY	3	SNOWVILLE	1
PANGUITCH	5	SPANISH FORK	2
PARADISE	2	SPRING CITY	5
PARAGONAH	4	SPRINGDALE	4
PARK CITY	2	SPRINGVILLE	2
PARK VALLEY	1	SPRY	5
PAROWAN	4	STOCKTON	2
PINE VALLEY	4	SUMMIT	4
PINTO	4	SUNNYSIDE	3
PLEASANT GROVE	2	SUNSET	2
PLYMOUTH	2	THISTLE	2
PORTAGE	2	THOMPSONS	6
PROMONTORY	2	TIMPIE JUNCTION	1
PROVO	2	TOOELE	2
RANDLETT	3	TOQUERVILLE	4
RANDOLPH	2	TORREY	5
REDMOND	5	TREMONTON	2
RICHFIELD	5	TROPIC	5
RICHMOND	2	VERDURE	6
ROBISONS RANCH	4	VERNAL	3
ROCKVILLE	4	VERNON	2
ROOSEVELT	3	VEYO	4
ROSETTE	1	VIRGIN	4
ROZEL	1	WALES	5
ST. GEORGE	4	WANSHIP	2
SALDURO	1	WASHAKIE	2
SALINA	5	WASHINGTON	4
SALTAIR	2	W-BAR-L RANCH	6
SALT LAKE CITY	2	WELLESVILLE	2
SANDY	2	WENDOVER	1
SAN RAFAEL	6	WIDTSOE	5
SANTA CLARA	4	WILLARD	2
SCIPIO	5	WOODRUFF	2
SEGO	6	WOODSCROSS	2
SEVIER	5	WOODSIDE	6
SIGURD	5		

Index

Abajo (Blue) Mountains, 10, 144, 422, 423, 431-435, 442, 496, 502
Acoma, 35
Adam, 91
Adams Canyon, 29
Adams: Elias, 29, 281; Frank, home and museum, 281; Robert, 467
Adult Education Project, WPA, 141
Aerial tramway, 319, 334
Agathla Peak, 444
Agriculture, 12, 30, 32, 35, 36, 39, 58, 61, 63, 73, 76, 82, 85, 88-90, 98-104, 112, 116-17, 120, 194, 203, 272, 332, 469, 522: Indian, 33, 34, 352, 391
Ahlander, Anders Frederik, 162
Air: base, 280; Forces, 254, 389; lines, 133, 267; planes, 133, 194; ports, 267, 395, 418, 536
Alfalfa, 9, 19, 30, 288, 294, 296, 323, 330, 340, 357, 365, 421
Alhambra Peak, 444
Alice Art Collection, 169, 249
Alkali, 10, 19, 30, 99-101, 278, 353, 363, 487
Allen, Capt. James, 57; Allen, 488; Canyon, 432, 503, 504; Canyon Indian Reservation, 504
Alpine, 289
"All-seeing eye," 77, 237
Alta, 15, 122, 132, 146, 285-87, 324, 393, 412
Alter, J. Cecil, 149-51, 272
Alton, 343, 345
Aluminum, 339
Amatrice, 125
American Fork, 136, 289: Canyon, 224, 513, 514, 516, 517, 519; Creek, 514; mining district, 122; River, 517
"American" political party, 87, 88
Americats (see Mericats)
Amphitheater Falls, 518
Amnesty, 72, 84
Anderson: Kirk, 149, 150; Mark, 224; Peter, 300
Anderson Pass, 494
Andersons Ranch, 300, 327, 526
Angel Moroni, 3, 237, 334
Angell, Truman O., 183, 184, 238, 243, 246, 256, 257, 294
Angels Landing, 521, 524, 525

Animal life, 24-8, 310, 451, 467, 491, 502, 521
Antelope, 24, 39, 41, 144, 410, 483, 484
Antelope Island, 16, 24, 226, 228, 482-484, 486, 487
Ant Valley, 312
Antelope Springs, 13, 421
Anthropological collection, 256
Antimony, 123, 339, 342
Anti-Mormonism, 5, 53-7, 67-9, 73, 78-80, 82, 84, 87, 88, 114, 120, 138, 150-2, 155, 156, 205, 362, 363, 379
Anti-polygamy legislation, 78-80, 82-84, 231
Apostasies, 77-9, 155-56, 369
"Apostolic interregnum," 82
Aquarius Plateau, 338, 340, 341, 347, 348, 423, 433, 465
Arch Canyon, 504
Archeology, 32-8, 235, 262, 297, 339, 340, 342, 344, 345, 348, 350, 383, 396, 397, 401, 409, 434, 440, 441, 465, 466, 475-79, 488, 496-501, 522
Archeological Museum of the University of Utah, 158, 262, 387
Arches National Monument, 11, 449-55
Architecture, 35, 40, 163, 180-87, 200, 208, 213, 216, 228, 237, 239, 241, 243, 244, 256, 282, 428, 443: Indian, 33-7, 40, 401, 498
Aricara Indians, 48
Arizona, 8, 10, 13, 33-5, 74, 95, 97, 131, 193, 346, 435, 443, 444, 499
"Arizona strip," 75
Armstrong Canyon, 505
Arrapeen, 412
Arroyos, 345
Arsenal, 232, 280
Arsenic, 123, 390
Art, 7, 36, 153-87, 235, 237, 247-49, 258, 262, 264, 290, 291, 298, 485: Barn, 169, 258; centers, 169, 402, 405; collections, 169, 249, 256, 258, 262, 264, 517; schools, 164-66, 169
Artesian wells, 132, 206, 311, 323, 384, 435
Artifacts, 32, 34, 37, 222, 235, 373, 384, 409, 499, 503
Ash Creek, 300

Ashley, Gen. William H., 48-51, 126, 202, 216, 229, 355, 358, 374, 397, 477, 491, 492
Ashley National Forest, 373, 490
Aspen Grove, 147, 220, 224, 517
Asphalt, 124, 125, 364, 375, 376
Asphalt Ridge, 375
Astoria, 48
Athapascan Language, 443
Auxiliaries, Mormon Church, 95, 96
Avon, 276, 311

Babbitt, Almon W., 62, 69
Baby Falls, 518
Badger, 25, 144, 340, 491, 506
Badlands, 147, 350
Bailey, T. C., 459, 460
Baker: Amenzo, 230; Jim, 203; Lydia Hamp, 193; Mrs. Maggie, 340
Baker Canyon, 295
Baldheads, 509
Bald: Mesa, 429; Mountain, 368, 493; Mountain Pass, 368
Ballads, 170, 171
Bancroft, Hubert H., 54, 113, 136, 156, 171
Banking, 114, 537
Bannock Indians, 202, 331
Baptism, Mormon, 92, 93, 95, 96
Baptist Church, 86, 138
Barley, 318
Barnes Entomological Collection, 417
Barrier Canyon, 350
Barter, 77, 113, 149, 310
Bartleson-Bidwell party, 51, 126, 386
Basketmakers, 33, 34, 35, 158, 383, 401, 440, 466, 498
Basketry, 19, 21, 40, 308, 498, 504
Bateman, William, 303
Battle: Creek, 193; of Bear River, 43, 272, 273; of the Bulls, 246; of Nauvoo, 57
"Battleground, The," 348
Bauer, 392
Baxter Basin, 206
Beaches, 331
Bean, Orestes Utah, 157
Bear Dance, 41, 375
Bear Flag Rebellion, 52
Bear Lake, 24, 27, 49, 106, 143, 198, 203, 330, 331, 494: Valley, 74
Bear River, 11, 48, 76, 193, 273, 274, 275, 276, 278, 332, 352, 354, 361, 362, 363, 481, 483: Battle Monument, 272; Bay, 481, 487; Bird Refuge, 31; Canal, 109; Canal Company, 352; City, 101, 364; Gun Club, 278; Migratory Bird Refuge, 145, 198, 214, 277; Mountains, 271, 273, 275; Valley, 58, 330, 351, 352, 362
Beauregard, Donald, 165

Beaver, 25, 28, 31, 50, 143, 144, 151, 202, 265, 276, 295, 296, 304, 305, 309, 312, 374, 399, 400, 502: Canyon, 295; City, 219, 322; County, 38, 120, 125, 296; Creek, 312, 368; Dam, 309; Dam Wash, 309; dams, 310, 313; Dam Mountains, 309; Indians, 38; Mountains, 25; Ridge, 322; River, 47, 323
Beck: George, 414; Gotlieb, 414; John, 414
Becks Hot Springs, 17, 284
Beckwourth, James P., 154, 202, 272
Bee culture, 277, 333, 372
Beehive, 7, 232, 237, 241, 244, 245, 257
Beehive House, 7, 162, 183, 231, 243
Behunin family, 329
Beliefs, Mormon, 91, 92, 93, 95, 96, 171
Bell, William, 162
Bell Canyon, 18
Benson, E. T., 131, 275
Bethune, Harry, 416
Bible, 7, 19, 49, 53, 91, 135: Students, 86
Bicknell, Thomas W., 348, 434-5
Bicknell, 340, 348: Bottoms, 348
Big Bush Creek Cave, 373
"Big Chief," 432
Big Cottonwood Canyon, 13, 15, 18, 29, 70, 285, 313, 314, 315, 370
"Big Cottonwood Tree," 21, 427
Big Flat, 423
Bighorn sheep, 24, 31, 36, 39, 144, 491, 502, 521
Big Rock Candy Mountain, 339
Bingham: (town), 15, 123, 318, 319, 320, 321, 322, 392; Canyon, 112, 121, 186, 285, 316, 317, 392; Tunnel, 321
Bingham, Sanford, 120, 318
Bingham, Thomas, 120, 318
Binghams Fort, 204
Bird, Elzy J., 169
Bird Island, 27, 483, 485
Bird refuges, 283, 364, 377
Birds, 26, 27, 310, 451, 457, 467, 472, 483, 485, 486, 491, 502, 521
Birney, Hoffman, 156, 177, 308, 436, 437
Birth rate, 5, 6, 9, 89
Bishop: Gladden, 77; William W., 155
Bishop, Mormon, 5, 81, 94, 97
Bishops' courts, 3, 94
Bits, 160
Bittner ranch, 367
Black, Joseph, 522
Black and White Days, 273
Black: Butte, 365; Mesa, 433; Moun-

tains, 296; Point, 311; Rock, 262; Rock Beach, 383; Rock Cave, 383; Rock Volcano, 295; Volcanic Craters, 303
Black Hawk: Celebration, 337; Treaty, 337; War, 76, 335, 337, 341, 346, 421
Blackburn, John, 217
Blackbush, 467
Blackfoot Indians, 48, 201, 202
Blacks Fork, 51, 70
Blacks Fork Ranger Station, 494
Blacksmith Fork Canyon, 276, 312
Blanding, 37, 348, 434, 435, 501, 502, 503, 504, 506, 507
Blood, Henry H., 169, 170, 257, 281, 282
Blue Creek: 365; Reservoir, 365
Blue: Hills, 351; Knoll, 421; laws, 336; Mountains (Abajo), 10, 144, 422, 423, 431-35, 442, 496, 502; Valley, 349
Bluff, 37, 147, 160, 431, 434, 435, 436, 437, 438, 439, 440, 441, 442
Bluffdale, 287
Boating, 134, 143, 146, 224, 383, 483
Boggs, Governor Lilburn W., 55
"Bonanza City," 301
Bonneville, Captain B. L. E., 51, 50, 154, 386
Bonneville Terrace, 16
Bonny Lake, 493
Book of Mormon, 3, 7, 53, 62, 91, 92, 155, 157, 164, 235, 237, 274, 283, 288, 293, 298, 334, 335, 454
Book Cliffs, 396, 397, 401, 433, 450
Borglum: Gutzon, 524; Solon H., 207
Boulder, 340, 341, 348: Dam, 399, 441
Bountiful, 60, 135, 283: Peak, 282
Bowery, Old, 176, 230
Bowman, A. C., Archeological Collection, 344
Bowring, Harry, 176, 177
Bowring's Theater, 176
Box Elder (Brigham City), 277: Canyon, 277; County, 22, 38, 277; Lake, 361
Branch Agricultural College, 141, 156, 299
Brandebury, Lemuel G., 64, 65
Brannan, Samuel, 61, 182, 229
Brant, 364
Brian Head: Park, 297; Peak, 297, 472
Bridal Veil Falls, 224, 370
Bridge, 487: Canyon, 509; Mountain, 523
Bridger, James, 48, 50, 51, 58, 202, 229, 466, 481
Brigham City, 17, 87, 184, 277, 330, 332, 333, 354, 361

Brigham Young: Academy, 139, 219; Cemetery, 245; College, 139, 197; Monument, 233, 240; Museum, 242; Summer School, 517; University, 36, 96, 139, 140, 156, 159, 165, 166, 168, 175, 185, 216, 218, 219, 516
Brigham Young's: Gristmill, 384; Office, 243; Winter Home, 307
Bright Angel: Point, 345; Trail, 399
Brighton, 70, 146, 147, 315, 316
Brimhall, George Washington, 92, 220, 229, 291, 306, 346, 347
Brocchus, Perry D., 64, 65
Broncos, 430
Brooks, Maurice, 168
Broom, John, 208
Broom, Mrs. John, 210
Brown: Barnum, 397, 479; Benjamin, 335; Charles F., 353; Francis A., 212, 213; Frank M., 425; Captain James, 203, 204; James S., 63, 154
Brown: Cliffs, 396; Duck Lake, 369; House, The, 212
Browning: John Moses, 207, 212; Jonathan L., 207, 212; Matt, 212
Browns Hole, 51, 52, 86, 373, 402
Brownsville (Ogden), 60, 204
Brush Basin, 503
Brush Creek, 373
Bryant-Russell party, 359
Bryan, William Jennings, 207
Bryce, Ebenezer, 459
Bryce Canyon, 143: Lodge, 461; National Park, 11, 15, 117, 272, 341, 342, 456-63, 464, 472, 473
"Bryce National Bridge," 462
"Bryce Point," 462
Buchanan, James, 69, 71, 72
"Buchanan's Blunder," 71
Buckbrush, 21
Buckhorn: Flat, 403; Wash, 403
Buckskin Valley, 26
Buddhist Church, 86
Buenaventura River, 202, 203
Buffalo (bison), 24, 39, 126, 192, 331, 481, 482, 483, 484
"Buffalo Dave," 415
Bullionville, 373
Bureau of Information & Museum, 234
Burros, 147, 324
Burrows, Hal, 167
Burrville, 346
Burton, Sir Richard F., 137, 150, 156, 180, 186, 241, 244, 316, 356, 375, 481
Butcher Boy mine, 414
Butt, Parley, 431

Cable Mountain, 525
Cache: Cave, 355; County, 38;

County Relic Hall, 197; County Fair, 192; National Forest, 24, 142, 192; Valley, 16, 48, 58, 74, 191, 192, 193, 194, 195, 196, 197, 202, 272, 273, 274, 275, 352, 355
Cactus Mine, 325
Cadmium, 123, 317
Cainesville, 349
Cajon Canyon, 496, 497, 498
Calcium deposits, 275
California, 33, 39, 49, 50, 51, 56, 57, 58, 61, 62, 63, 70, 77, 97, 129, 130, 131, 151, 182, 186, 203, 204, 216, 360, 386, 387, 392, 393: emigrants, 303
California-Nevada Volunteers, 75, 113, 120, 231, 254, 272, 285, 378, 393
Callao, 388
Camp: Floyd, 72, 87, 113, 149, 176, 177, 231, 289; Floyd Mining District, 122; Killkare, 368; Scott, 70, 71, 72; Timpanoke, 517; Williams, 287, 288, 289
Camp grounds, 142, 309, 313, 345, 369, 429, 495
Campbell: Allan G., 82, 324; Canyon, 462; Malcolm, 390; Orson D., 166
Campbellites, 53
Canaan Mountain, 342
Candy manufacture, 115, 117
Cane Springs, 429
Cannel coal, 124
Canning, 99, 115, 117, 206, 274, 280, 281, 284, 289, 290, 359
Cannon: Angus, House of, 307; David, 305; Frank J., 157, 207; George Q., 82, 155, 207, 223; Lewis Telle, 262; M., 163; Tracy Y., 174, 175
Cannon, Ashley's, 49, 51, 126, 306
Cannonville, 340, 342
Canyon Road, 250
Capital, 81, 88, 89, 114, 121, 194, 378
Capitol: Gorge, 465, 467, 469; Museum, 162, 180; Reef National Monument, 11, 14, 272, 345, 349, 464-70; Wash, 468
"Capitol Dome," 468
Carbon County, 14, 116, 124, 166, 290, 401, 406
Carbon Dioxide Well, 401
Carbon Junior College, 141
Carbonville, 402
Cárdenas, Captain Garcia Lopez de, 9, 46, 47, 49
Cardston Temple, Canada, 95
Carlisle College, 308
Carnival, 212, 217
Carnotite, 403
Caroline Bridge (Kachina), 505, 506
Carr Fork Gulch, 319

Carrington, Albert, 486, 482
Carrington Island, 486
Carson, Christopher (Kit), 52, 159, 386, 443, 484
Carson Valley, 61, 70, 388
Carter, Kate B., 137, 290
Carter Creek, 374: Canyon, 374
Carvalho, S. N., 154, 163, 293, 298
Cascades, 518
Cassidy, Butch, 373, 402, 405, 406
Castle Dale, 403, 405: Rock, 356, 406, 425; Valley, 38, 425, 429
Castlegate, 376, 401, 405, 406
Castleton, 425, 429
Cataract Canyon, 399, 427
"Cataract of Lodore, The," 477
Cathedral, The, 356
Cathedral of the Madeleine, 185, 227, 257
Catholic Church, 86, 87, 138, 139, 141, 201, 257, 301, 379
Cattle, 293, 332, 334, 338, 340, 343, 345, 349, 352, 359, 365, 367, 422, 423, 424, 426, 427, 428, 429, 431, 432, 434, 496
Cattle brands, 160
Causeway, 503
Cave Lakes, 344
Caves, 342, 345, 409, 429, 512
Cedar Breaks National Mon., 11, 15, 272, 457, 471-74, 525
Cedar: City, 45, 112, 116, 141, 123; 152, 156, 196, 290, 296, 297, 298, 303, 337, 435, 472, 526; City Mormon Chapel, 299; Indians, 38; Mesa, 439; Mountain, 385, 388, 525; Valley, 72, 289
Celebrations, 201, 202, 205, 229, 291, 296, 344, 395, 402, 427, 517
"Celestial order," 95
Centerfield, 335
Centerville, 282, 283
Central, 338
Central Pacific Railroad, 77, 129, 130, 131, 346, 362
Central Utah Museum, 335
Ceramics, Indian, 33, 34, 35, 36, 37, 62, 158, 161, 162, 499, 503
Ceremonies, Indian, 41, 42, 45, 170, 375
Chain Lakes, 494
Chalk Creek Canyon, 294, 367
Chamber of Commerce, 84, 315, 316
Chapman, Robert C., 211, 213
Charleston, 369, 370, 377
Cheese factories, 336, 341
Cherry Creek, 414
Cherrypickers, 282
Chester, 334
Chesterfield mine, 397
Cheyenne Indians, 355

Cheyenne, Wyoming, 129
Children's Hospital, 96
Chimney Rock, 465
Chinatown, 358
Chinchillas, 197, 198
Chinese, 129, 362, 379, 407
Chinle formation, 342; Wash, 441
Chisholm Trail, 160
Chocolate Fountain, 515
Chairs, 97, 171, 173
Chorpenning, Major George, 412
Christensen: Casper, 403; C. C. A.,
    163; C. L., 432; W. C., 258
Christian Scientists, 86
Christy Mill, 301
Clubs, 27, 278
Church Historian's Office & Library,
    241: Island, 484; Museum, 164;
    Music Committee, 175; offices, 183;
    Train, 314; Welfare Program, 89,
    100
Cinnabar (quicksilver), 394
Circle Cliffs, 338, 340, 465
Circle Valley, 74
Circleville, 341, 405
Cirques, 518
Cisco, 396, 397, 425
City Cemetery, 251
City Creek, 58, 98, 112
City Creek Canyon, 227, 244, 283
Civil Aeronautics Authority, 133
Civil War, 73, 74, 75, 77, 87, 128,
    176, 232, 289, 362, 392
Civilian Conservation Corps, 30, 278,
    279, 282, 421
Clark: J. Reuben, 384; Samuel, 217
Clarkston, 198, 274
Clay: brothers, 318; Dan, 318; Henry,
    62
Clay, 336, 358, 365: Bar, 318; Hills,
    436, 444
Clayton, William, 126, 127, 172
Clawson: Hiram B., 177; John W.,
    165; Rudger, 83
Clear Creek, 123: Canyon, 295
Clearfield, 280
Cleveland, Grover, 85, 432
Cleveland, 402, 405
Cliff Dwellers, 9, 37, 158-9, 180-1,
    339-40, 342, 345, 348, 350, 396, 401,
    433, 440-1, 496-9, 500-1, 503-4, 507,
    509-10, 522
Cliff Ridge, 372
Climate, 8, 12, 18, 101, 103, 115, 179,
    476
Clothing, 33, 34, 39, 40, 61, 102, 115,
    206, 242, 272, 294, 343
Clyman, James, 154, 202, 355, 386,
    481
Clyman party, 358
Coal, 14, 63, 76, 116, 123, 124, 134,
    250, 290, 297, 299, 336, 367, 396,
    397, 401, 403, 404, 405
Coalville, 132, 355, 367, 379
Codman, Captain John, 286
"Cohabitation Canyon," 468
Coke, 290, 317, 401
Collinston, 15, 332, 333
Colonization, 58, 59, 60, 61, 63, 66, 67,
    74, 107, 108, 193, 203, 204, 217, 274,
    283, 297, 300, 305, 307, 338, 332,
    366, 437
Colorado, state, 8, 10, 25, 32, 33, 34,
    35, 36, 38, 43, 47, 62, 63, 86, 94,
    132, 213, 373, 375, 427, 429, 430,
    432, 435, 441, 444, 475, 496
Colorado Plateau, 8, 11, 180, 371, 372,
    423, 429, 432, 450, 498
Colorado River, 9, 11, 24, 26, 28, 30,
    37, 43, 46-9, 74-5, 86, 123, 134, 143,
    145, 147, 154, 163, 181, 271, 308,
    340, 347-350, 372, 395, 397-8, 422,
    423-9, 434-8, 441-3, 450, 455, 459,
    498, 501, 503-4, 508-9, 522
Colton, D. C., 373
Colton, 406
Columbia, 400
Columbine Falls, 518
Colville, C. A., 510
Comb Ridge, 435, 439, 504
Comb Wash, 437, 438
Commerce, 73, 77, 112-18
Como Springs, 214, 359
"Compromise level," 223
Compson, 326
Conchas, 160
Conferences, annual and semi-annual,
    7, 95, 239
Confusion Mountains, 421
Congregationalist Church, 86, 87, 138
Congress, 62, 63, 64, 75, 76, 80, 82, 83,
    84, 85, 87, 107, 149, 362, 363, 467
Connor Col. Patrick E., 75, 76, 78,
    80, 119, 120, 121, 231, 254, 272, 273,
    285, 318, 360, 363, 378, 392, 393,
    394
Consecration, 68, 80, 81
Consecration of property, 77
Conservation, 19, 20, 28, 31, 59, 100,
    102, 106, 490, 536
Consolidated-Sevier Reservoir, 106
Continental Divide, 48, 51, 203, 429
Constitutional Convention, 85, 140
Constitution Monument, 168
Converse Hall, 265
Cooke, Jay, 324, 325
"Cooks Mesa", 348
Cool Spring House, 498
Cooley Pass, 432
Cooperative, 77, 80, 81, 88, 100, 107,
    109, 114, 116, 277, 296, 334, 335,
    420

Cope, Gordon, 169, 248, 249
Copper, 88, 114, 119, 120, 121, 122,
    123, 162, 186, 246, 319, 322, 342,
    378, 390, 393, 409, 411, 488
Copperfield, 321
Copperton, 186, 317, 321
Corinne, 78, 86, 132, 151, 177, 361,
    362, 363, 393, 483
"Corkees," 347
Cormorants, 485, 486
Corn, 61, 318, 340
Cortez, Colorado, 433
Cosnina, 47
Cotton, 19, 115, 161, 302, 305, 328
Cottonwood Canyon, 412, 435
Cottonwood Creek, 437
Cottonwood trees, 21, 23, 294, 310,
    313, 357, 369
Cottonwood Wash, 503
Council: Bluffs, 52, 57; House, 246,
    247
Court of the Patriarchs, 524
Courthouse towers, 452, 453
Cove: of Caves, 453; Fort, 184, 295;
    Mountain, 346
Cow Canyon, 435
Cowboy Pass, 421
Cowdery, Oliver, 235
Cox: Coleman, 207; John, 347
Coyotes, 25, 41, 144, 310, 346, 366,
    410, 419, 451, 459, 467, 491, 502,
    506, 521
Cradlebaugh, Judge John, 73, 304,
Crafts, 21, 44, 61, 158-62, 184, 235,
    241, 242, 244, 250, 257, 262, 264,
    488, 504: Indian, 33, 158, 308, 346,
    352, 375, 391, 435, 443, 444
Craig: David, 51; Colorado, 372
Crawford, William (Galbreith), 167
Crescent Junction, 397, 422
Crickets, 27, 28, 61, 68, 92, 104, 230,
    240, 352, 486
Crooked River, 55
Crosby, Oscar, 229
Crow Indians, 355
Crystal Hot Springs, 333
Cub: Island, 486; River, 273
Culmer, H. L. S., 164, 249
Cumming, Alfred, 71, 72, 73, 205
Curlew Valley, 365
Culture, pioneer, 3, 9, 23, 161, 192,
    194, 211, 230, 274, 328, 334, 438
Cyanide process, 122, 394

Daggett County, 374
Dairying, 100, 116, 117, 203, 272, 274,
    285, 333, 336, 343, 365
Dallin, Cyrus E., 166, 167, 237, 240,
    247, 250, 291
Dandy Crossing, 349
Daniels Canyon, 377

Danites, 149
"Dark Angel," 455
Dark Canyon, 502, 503: Plateau, 503,
    504
Daughters of Utah Pioneers, 197, 211,
    222, 249, 282: Museum, 161
David Eccles Home, 186
Davis: Allen, 331; John, 459
Davis County, 282
Daynes, Joseph J., 174, 232
Deacons, duties of, 93
"Dead Man Points," 409
Dead Man's Cave, 409
Death Hollow, 340
Dead Horse Point, 423
Deadhorse Pass, 494
Dee Hospital, 96
Deer, 21, 24, 31, 36, 39, 295, 296, 310,
    337, 339-41, 346, 369, 410, 432, 472:
    Creek Canyon, 339; Creek Reser-
    voir, 29, 224, 370; Haven Forest
    Camp, 299; Hunters Dance, 296
Deep Creek, 38, 365: Canyon, 377;
    Mountains, 390
Deer Creek Railroad, 390
De Fas Park, 369
Delicate Arch, 451-53, 455
Delano Peak, 296
Dell Adams Collection, 281
Dellenbaugh, F. S., 154, 399
Delta, 410, 420
Democratic Party, 85, 87
Denominational churches, 86, 87
Denominational schools, 138, 139, 193
Denver & Rio Grande Western Rail-
    road, 86, 132, 218, 232, 320, 371,
    376, 379, 381, 396, 397, 400, 404, 416
Depredations, Indian, 43, 66, 67, 76,
    101, 193, 202, 303, 337, 355, 388,
    412, 427, 438
Depression, 55, 80, 88
Dern, George H., 393, 467
Deseret: (town), 7, 421; State of, 62-
    64, 75, 76, 78, 120, 135, 136, 218,
    229, 230, 258, 291, 314
Desert Range Experiment Station,
    101, 326
De Smet, Father Pierre J., 127, 211
Desolation Canyon, 476
Devils: Canyon, 434; Garden, 422,
    450, 452-55; Gate, 359; Slide, 358;
    Stewpots, 403
DeVoto, Bernard, 42, 53, 66, 156, 157,
    207, 360
Deweyville, 333
Diamond Gulch, 373
Diamond mine, 414
Dikes, volcanic, 345
Dilworth, Mary J., 135, 266
Dinosaurs, 9, 13, 14, 36, 250, 260,
    342, 397, 402, 450, 475, 479, 502, 522

Dinosaur National Monument, 14, 372, 475-79
Dirty Devil (Fremont) River, 348, 349, 467
Disappointment Island, 485
Disciples of Christ, 86
Diversion dams, 105, 106
Divorce, 80, 93, 282, 362: Brigham Young sued for, 80, 256
Dixie: Junior College, 141, 306; Mission, 305, 307; National Forest, 297, 299, 341; Sugar Loaf, 306
Doctrine, Mormon, 81, 91-96, 171
Dodds, Pardon, 372
Dodge, Grenville, 129, 131, 364
Dogs, 39, 103, 104, 134, 283, 336, 337, 341, 344, 418
Dollar Lake, 494
Dolores River, 426, 430
Dolphin Island, 486
Dominguez, Father Francisco Atanasio, 47, 216, 372, 497
Donner-Reed party, 52, 58, 246, 262, 356, 358, 384, 385, 387, 388
Douglas: Dr. Earl, 478; James, 442; Stephen H., 69; W. L., 510
Douglas Mesa, 443
Drainage, 11
Drama, 157, 172, 176-79, 220, 379
Draper, 132, 287
Dredges, 349, 509
Drought, 28, 88, 204
Dry farming, 88, 98, 101, 115, 132, 274, 275, 281, 289, 316, 332, 351, 352, 354, 364, 365, See also Farming
Duchesne, 146, 369, 371, 374, 376, 377, 406: County, 262; River, 47, 51, 369, 375, 376
Duck Creek, 299: Camp, 299
Duck stamp, 145
Ducks, 26, 27, 145, 278, 339, 348, 364
Dude ranches, 148, 311, 460
Dugway, 269, 329, 424, 429, 436
Dunes, 349
Dunne, Barney, 417
Dust bowl, 30, 384
Dyar, W. W., 503, 506
Dyes, 23, 161, 328

Eagle Gate, 233, 244-46, 250
Eagle Rock, 453
Eagles, 503
Earthquake, 185, 304, 364
"Earth Stones," 237
East Canyon, 359, 381
East Canyon reservoir, 359
East Fork of Smiths Fork Creek, 495
East Fork, Sevier River, 339
East Fork, Virgin River, 522
East Indian Architecture, 186
East Rim, 525

East Rim Trail, 525
East Temple, 521, 524
East Tintic Mountains, 293, 411
Eastmond, E. H., 165
Eccles, David, Home of, 186
Eccles, Marriner S., 194, 207, 274
Echo, 129, 356, 357, 368, 389
Echo: Canyon, 70, 77, 128, 180, 354-56, 358; Canyon Creek, 355; Dam and Reservoir, 366; Junction, 354, 366; Reservoir, 106, 366
Ecker Hill ski jump, 146, 381
Edgerton, Lycurgus, 324
Edmunds Act, 82, 83, 281
Edmunds-Tucker Act, 83
Education, 7, 84, 87, 89, 96, 135-41, 193, 196, 197, 206, 211, 213, 218-20, 243, 264, 306, 363, 384
Edward Rosenbaum Memorial Library, 259
Edwin Bridge (Owachomo), 505
Egg Island, 483, 486
Eighty-eighth Reconnaissance Squadron, 254
Elberta, 411
Elders, 93, 94
Elections, 83, 87, 88
Electricity, 30, 98, 114, 218, 334, 534
Elgin, 397
Elk, 24, 31, 143, 144, 346, 491, 492: Horn Campground, 369; Horn Ranger Station, 347; Mountain Mission, 424, 427; Mountains (La Sals), 426; Ridge, 431, 434, 437, 501-05
El Patio Del Rancho, 311
Elton Tunnel, 29, 391
Elsinore, 338
Elwood, 364
Emerald: Lake, 518; Pool Trail, 524; Pools, 524, 525
Emery, 403: County, 14, 124
Emigration, 51, 52, 126, 437: Canyon, 167, 254, 255, 358, 387
Emigrants, 113, 231, 354, 356, 385-87
Empey, Nelson P., 256-57
"Emperor," 444
Enabling Act, 85, 109
Endowment House, 68
Enos, 300
Ensign peak, 16, 226
Enterprise, 304
Ephraim, 36, 141, 146, 186, 334, 335, 403
Episcopal churches, 86, 87, 138, 193
Eroded boulder house, 498
Erosion, 11, 18, 30, 105
Escalante, Father Silvestre Velez de, 42, 46-9, 126, 134, 154, 216, 222, 247, 298, 340, 372, 477, 481, 497, 509, 516

Escalante, 340, 348, 437, 438: Desert, 298, 340; River, 441
Eureka, 137, 140, 411, 413-17, 419
Eutau Indians, 49
Evans, John Henry, 155, 407
Exploration, 46, 47-50, 52, 154, 192, 193, 216, 217, 354, 372, 385, 386, 397, 399, 435, 481, 482, 497, 509
Eyston, Capt. G. E. T., 346, 390

Fairbanks, Avard, 165, 167, 237, 249: John B., 165, 167
J. Leo, 165; John B., 165, 167
Fairfield, 289
Fairs, 102, 112, 165, 192, 210, 266, 375, 427
Fairview, 333, 402
"Fairy Castle," 462
"Fairyland," 460, 461, 462
Family life, Mormon, 5, 155
Famine, 60, 61, 62, 68, 204, 230
Farm: communities, 328, 329, 330, 421; Creek Mountain, 146; resettlement, 30, 339; tenantry, 100
Farming, 9, 30, 323, 327, 331, 333, 334, 336, 338, 339, 342, 344, 346, 348, 349, 352, 353, 358, 359, 361, 365, 367, 368, 439. See also dry farming
Farmington, 30, 282, 283
Farms, 313, 410, 425, 434
Farnham, Mary, 168; Thomas J., 385
Farnsworth, Philo, 218, 219
Farr, Lorin, 211, 213
Fausett, Dean, 166, 402
Fausett, Lynn, 166, 169, 402
Federal: Antiquities Act, 38; Bureau of Reclamation, 110; Emergency Relief Administration, 117, 249; Fish Hatchery, 290; Land Office, 340; land utilization project, 339; officials, conflicts with, 64, 65, 67, 69, 70, 79; Reclamation Project, 311, 366, 377; Reserve Board, 194, 207; Writers' Project (Arizona), 444
Ferries, 332, 345, 424
Fewkes, J. Walter, 497, 498, 499
Fiction, 102, 156, 157, 344, 467, 505
Fielding, 352
Fields, Dan, 416: Heber, 419
Fifth Air Base Group, 254
Fifty Mile Mountain, 340
Fillmore, 15, 18, 67, 184, 229, 246, 247, 262, 294, 420
Fillmore, Millard S., 63
First Congregational Church, 173, 265
First Methodist Episcopal Church, 185
First Presbyterian Church, 185, 265
Fish, 27, 31, 222, 278, 292, 316, 369: hatcheries, 28, 31, 290, 332; lake,

145, 346, 408, 495; Lake Treaty Marker, 346; Springs, 388, 417
Fisher, Vardis, 156
Fisher: Towers, 425; Valley, 425
Fishing, 31, 142, 143, 145, 147, 222, 224, 292, 332, 341, 346, 359, 366, 367, 368, 370, 491, 493
Fishlake National Forest, 24, 142, 294, 295, 346, 403
Fitzpatrick, Thomas, 50, 51, 201, 202
Flake, Green, 229
Flathead Lake, 48
Fletcher: Calvin, 168; Harvey, 218; Irene, 168
Floods, 29, 30, 278, 282, 307, 406, 426, 434, 442
Flora, 370, 467, 472, 488, 491, 504, 518, 526
Flour gold, 123, 349, 400, 509
Flowers, 22, 23, 310, 472, 488, 518
Folsom, William, 183, 184, 239
Folk music, 170, 172
Folklore, 41, 61, 123, 170, 181, 240, 287, 298, 305, 331, 375, 415, 417, 434, 444, 459, 465, 466, 481, 482, 499, 506, 510, 511
Forbidden Valley, 325
Forest fires, 20: Service Lodge, 146
Forests, 431: national, 24, 25, 26
Fort: Bridger, 58, 70, 71, 355, 366, 386; Buenaventura, 51, 211; Davy Crockett, 51; Deseret, 184; Douglas, 16, 113, 130, 227, 231, 254, 272, 363, 392; Duchesne, 45, 170, 295, 375, 376; Hall, Idaho, 51, 203, 351, 386; Harmony, 300; Laramie, 58, 220; Leavenworth, 204; "Misery," 51; "Nonsense," 50; Provo (Fort Utah), 297; Robidoux Monument, 375; Sutter Historical Museum, 387; Utah (Fort Provo), 63, 66, 217
Fortification, 59, 61, 67, 70, 184, 193, 204, 217, 230, 293, 295, 367, 368, 414, 421, 426, 435
"Fossilized sand dunes," 344
Fossils, 13, 14, 260, 330, 332, 342, 356, 402, 465, 475, 477, 478, 479, 513, 522
Fountain Green, 334
Four Corners, 441, 445
Four Lakes Basin, 493
Francis, 368, 369
Frazier, Dr. Russell G., 321, 399
"Free range," 340, 434
"Free Republic of Tooele," 78
Freedom, 281
Freemasonry, 87
Freighting, 113, 127, 133, 134, 257, 298, 305, 314, 360, 362, 364, 434, 483, 510
Fremont, Captain John C., 51, 52, 57,

134, 154, 247, 386, 482, 483, 484, 485, 487
Fremont: Gorge, 465; Junction, 403; Island, 360, 482, 485, 486, 487; River (Dirty Devil), 11, 348, 349, 467, 468, 469
"Frenchie," 427
Frisco, 232, 323, 324, 325
Frogtown, 289
Fruit-growing, 9, 99, 279, 302, 318, 327, 328, 335, 338, 360
Fruita, 348, 465, 466, 467, 468
Fruitland, 337, 371, 377
Fur: farms, 25, 197, 198; trade, 48, 50, 51, 202, 203, 272, 374; traders, 201, 247

Galena, 120, 312, 318, 324
Gallatin, 55
Gambling, 42, 318, 324, 357
Garcia, Lagos, 48
Garden City, 330, 331
Garden of the Gods, 440
Gardo House, 162
Garfield, 133, 224, 228, 361, 383, 392, 409; Beach, 363; County, 38, 341
Garland, 133, 353
Garnet, 125
Garrison, 326: Ranch, 326
Gartersnakes, 28, 467
Gas, manufactured, 534
Gas, natural, 206, 405, 442, 535, 537
Gates: B. Cecil, 174; Emma Lucy, 174, 307; Jed, House of, 307; Susa Young, 155
Gaudy Gardens, 425
Gemini mine, 411, 415
Gemmell, Robert C., 121, 319
Gentiles, 4, 5, 6, 55, 68, 76, 84, 92, 114, 120, 138, 151, 173, 205, 287, 296, 379
Geology, 12, 18, 340, 441, 450, 465, 475, 476, 477, 478, 481, 522
George, Brig, 308
George H. Dern House, 258
Geysers, 377, 397, 400
Geyser, Al, 429
Geyser Pass, 429
Ghiselin, Brewster, 157
"Ghost government," 75, 76
Ghost towns, 122, 285, 287, 300, 302, 312, 339, 361, 373, 390, 393, 394, 395, 407, 411, 413, 429
Giants, 36, 303
Gibson, A. E., 403, 404
Gibraltar, 356
Giles, Thomas, 175, 349
Gilsonite, 124, 376
Gisborn, Mack, 393, 394
Glaciers, 18, 491, 513, 518
Glass, 184, 306: blowing, 161

Glass Lake, 494
Glassware, 125, 161, 162
Gleason Early Elberta Peach, 281
Glen Canyon, 46, 436, 501
Glendale, 81, 343
"Glory hole," 325
Glyphs, 36, 37, 158
Godbeites, 78, 363
"Gold Bible," 53
Gold, 119, 120, 121, 122, 123, 306, 317, 318, 319, 322, 339, 349, 365, 378, 390, 391, 392, 393, 394, 395, 400, 409, 411, 432, 441, 442, 492: discovery of, 58, 63, 246; Hill, 390; rush, 63, 127, 204, 230, 231, 349, 388, 431, 432, 442, 509
Golden: Jubilee, 233, 240, 250; Pass, 381; plates, 334; Spike ceremony, 128, 130, 205, 208
Goodridge, E. L., 441, 442
Goodyear, Miles, 51, 59, 60, 157, 182, 203, 204, 211
Goosenecks of the San Juan River, 440, 442
Gorgoza, 381
Gorgozada, Rodriguez, 381
Goshen, 337, 410
Gospel Missions, 86
Goshute Indian Reservation, 391
Gosiute Indians, 38, 39, 40, 41, 42, 45, 66, 128, 133, 170, 182, 384, 385
Gould, Jay, 324, 325
Goulding, Harry, 444, 452
Goulding's Trading Post, 444, 445, 509
Governor's Mansion, 257
Grain, 293, 294, 330, 353, 357, 361, 364, 365, 434
Grand Canyon of the Colorado, 46, 75, 345, 398, 399: Lodge, 345
Grand: Central mining claim, 413; County, 424, 426, 427, 432, 450; Gorge, 465, 468; Gulch, 436, 437, 440, 502, 503; Gulch Plateau, 503, 504, 505; Junction Colorado, 132, 396, 425; River, 38, 424; River Valley, 396
"Grand Wash," 468, 469
Grandaddy Lakes, 145, 490
Granite Wash, 349
Granstaff, William (Nigger Bill), 425, 427
Grant: Heber J., 94, 178, 220, 359; Jedediah M., 68, 359; Ulysses S., 78, 79, 286
Grantsville, 30, 371, 382, 384, 389
Grass, 332, 340, 346, 365, 396, 409, 412, 431, 432, 510
Grasshoppers, 28, 39, 63, 68, 92, 204, 273, 283, 325, 332, 358, 386
Grayson, 348, 434, 435
Grazing, 102-04, 274, 318, 326, 334,

339, 340, 345, 352, 364, 372, 421, 422, 429, 430, 434, 452, 455, 487, 488, 490, 503, 534

Great: Basin, 11, 12, 13, 15, 16, 17, 19, 27, 30, 48, 51, 57, 103, 128, 185, 202, 227, 230, 271, 481; Bend, 442; Divide, 203; Medicine Road, 51; White Throne, 469, 521, 524, 525, 526

Great Salt Lake, *passim:* Base & Meridian Stone, 234; Desert, 11, 26, 49, 51, 52, 203, 254, 262, 266, 371, 382, 384, 385, 386, 387, 389, 390, 396; Valley, 51, 57, 58, 59, 63, 70, 72, 98, 107, 112, 113, 116, 135, 161, 193, 217, 229, 235, 240, 241, 246, 248, 266, 282, 284, 285, 319, 355, 358, 359, 361, 370, 382, 386, 387, 481, 482

Greek Churches, 86

Green: George, 427; Silas, 427

"Green House," 379

Green: Lake, 374; River, 11, 24, 30, 37, 38, 47-51, 74, 123, 134, 145, 147, 202, 206, 348, 349, 350, 370, 372, 374, 376, 397, 398, 423, 425, 427, 428, 476, 477, 478

Greenriver, 49, 350, 396, 397, 399, 427, 435, 470

Greenville Experiment Station Farm, 99

Gregory, Dr. Herbert E., 340, 431, 432, 434, 437, 439, 441, 496, 497, 503, 504, 522

Gregory Natural Bridge, 441

Grey, Zane, 102, 156, 344, 467, 504, 505

Groome, 488

Grotto, 524: Ranger Station, 524; Trail, 524

Grouse Creek Valley, 488

Grover, 348

Grow, Henry, 183, 239

Guano, 485

Guides, 337, 340, 344, 350, 369

"Gun shot," 342

Gunlock Indians, 38

Gunnison, Captain J. W., 43, 67, 69, 154, 335, 349, 421

Gunnisons Crossing, 349

Gunnison: Island, 27, 483, 485, 486, 488; Monument, 421

Gunsight Pass, 494

Gypsum, 125, 334, 336

Hackberry Canyon, 496, 498

Hafen, John, 165, 166, 168, 291

Haight, Isaac C., 247, 304

Hailstone, 369, 377, 378

Hale: Girard, 248; Solomon, 411

Halls Crossing, 350

Halverson, Chris, 400

Hamblin, Jacob, 304, 307, 308, 399, 435

Hammond, Francis A., 312, 439

Hammond Canal, 333

Hampton, 332

Hand cart immigration, 68, 69, 128, 168, 234, 290

Hanksville, 349, 350

Hanna, 369, 370

Hansel Valley, 233

Hansen: Martin, 514, 515; Ramm, 262; Prof. W. F., 157

Hansen Cave, 514, 516

Harbach, Otto, 157, 179

Harlan-Young party, 356, 358, 359

Harney, General W. S., 70, 71

"Harmony No. 2," 300

Harrington, Dr. John P., 444

Harris: Broughton D., 64; Llewellyn, 300; Martin, 198, 237

Harrisburg Junction, 302

Harrison: Elias L. T., 78; George (Beefsteak), 231, 290

Harvey, William Hope (Coin), 212, 312

Hastings, Lansford W., 358, 386

Hastings Cutoff, 387, 388, 389

Hatch Wash, 430

Hatchtown Reservoir, 109, 110

Hauns Mill Massacre, 55

Hawaiian Temple, 88, 95, 384

Hawthorne, 21

Hay, 333, 335, 368, 434

Haydens Peak, 490

Hayden Survey, 431, 432, 497

Hayne, Julia Dean, 178, 243

Haystack Mountain, 429

Haywood, W. D. (Bill), 157, 380

Head, Colonel F. H., 337

Health, 92, 204, 206, 335, 363, 384, 400

Hearst, William Randolph, 378, 388

Heart of Timpanogos, 515

Heber City, 371, 377, 378

Hebron, 304

Helictites, 514

Hells Backbone, 340: Bridge, 341

Helper, 169, 403-405: Art Gallery, 405

Henefer, 358

Henrieville, 337, 340, 342

Henrys Fork, 49, 202, 374, 494: Lake, 494; Park, 494

Henry Mountains, 10, 16, 340, 347, 422, 423, 429, 433, 444

Herron: Edwin, 157; Jim, 402

Hester, J. A., 183, 186

Hidden Falls Picnic Area, 314

Hidden Lake, 518

Hideout Canyon, 374

Higbee: John M., 304; John S., 217; Lorine Isabel Lamb, 327
High: Council, 59, 94; grading, 415; priests, 93, 94; Uintas Primitive Area, 18, 145, 147, 366, 369, 489-95; Uintas Highline Trail, 369; Uintas Highland Trail, 493-95; schools, 138, 140
Highline Canal, 311
Highway building, 133, 143, 389, 536
Hiking, 147, 213, 279, 283, 493-95, 513, 517, 518, 524, 525
Hill Cumorah, 53, 168
Hill Field, 280
Hinckley, 410, 421
Historic Markers, 88, 167, 208, 211, 234, 235, 237, 240, 246, 254, 256, 264, 272, 279, 289, 291, 310, 312, 316, 355, 364, 367, 368, 372, 375, 385
Hite, Cass, 349, 503, 509
Hite, 349, 350, 399
Hites Crossing, 349, 509
Hobbs party, 437
Hodgson, Leslie S., 211
Hogup, 488: Mountains, 488
Hogle Gardens Zoo, 255
Hold-Dern process, 258
Holden, 294
Hole-in-the-Rock Pioneers, 350, 431, 435, 436, 437, 438, 440
Holstein cows, 273
Homansville Canyon, 416
"Home-D" scrip, 277
Home of Truth Colony, 430
Homesteading, 108, 352, 460, 485, 492
Honey, 333
Honeyville, 333
Hooper, 279
Hoover, Herbert, 460
Hoover Lake, 492
Hope Creek, 374
Hopi Indians, 435, 466, 499, 500
Horn silver, 301
Horne, Mrs. Alice Merrill, 169, 249
Hospitals, 96, 206, 365
Hot Pots, 377: Springs, 15, 284, 333, 338, 352, 359, 377
Hotel Utah, 7, 185, 227, 241
Horse: Creek Canyon, 429; Pasture Plateau, 525; Thief Gulch, 395; Thief Pasture Mesa, 350
"Horse Jaw-Kid," 394
"Horse town," 340
Horses, 17, 39, 102, 126, 204, 210, 262, 275, 336, 344, 369, 423, 430, 432, 437, 439, 467, 484, 509, 510
Horseshoe: Canyon, 350, 374, 398; House, 498; Mountain, 146
Hovenweep: Castle, 498; House, 497;

National Monument, 37, 180, 496-500
Howe: E. D., 155; Maurice, 157, 461
Hoytsville, 367
Hudson's Bay Company, 48, 50, 201, 202, 203, 247, 374
Hulketo Wash, 444
Humboldt Wells, 129
Humbug mine, 414
Hunt, Captain Jefferson, 311
Hunting, 24, 25, 26, 31, 36, 39, 143-5, 278, 296, 299, 310, 326 339, 341, 344, 346, 348, 363, 366, 369, 492
Huntington: Dimick B., 412; Oliver B., 424; William, 424
Huntington, 402, 405
Huntsman, Orson W., 304, 305
Huntsville, 311: School, 312
Hurricane, 302
Hurricane Fault, 302, 526
Hutchings, John, archeological collection, 288
Hyde Park, 275
Hydro-electric power, 30, 114, 145, 359
Hymns, 60, 155, 170-2, 173, 211, 239, 279, 365
Hyrax, 26
Hyrum, 276: Dam and Reservoir, 276; Loop, 275
Hys Bottom, 427

Ibapah, 128, 391
Ibis, 278
Ice Cave, 299
Ichthyol, 124
Idaho, 12, 38, 42, 50, 61, 62, 63, 70, 74, 89, 97, 131, 157, 190, 192, 203, 212, 213, 219, 273, 331, 332, 364, 386
Idaho Falls, 97
Illinois, 55, 64
Immigration, Mormon, 57, 58, 67, 68, 229, 275
Independence Mountains, 488
Index of American Design, 161, 162
Indians, passim, especially, 32
Indian reservations, 45, 74, 76, 86, 294, 298, 308, 326, 346, 351, 352, 375, 384, 391, 443, 444, 503, 504
Indian paintbrush, 22, 310, 467, 518
Industry, 61, 81, 85, 89, 94, 112, 113, 115, 118, 192, 206, 207, 213, 218, 271, 274, 282, 360, 367
Inglesby, Dr. A. L., 350, 399, 467
Inglesby House, 468
Inman, Col. Henry, 481
Inns, 315
Inscriptions, 46, 355, 399
Insects, 28
Inspiration Point, 462
Intermountain Band Contest, 402

Interurban railroads, 132, 218
Iosepa Colony, 384
Iridium, 123
Iron, 63, 76, 114, 116, 123, 206, 208, 290, 297, 342, 409
Iron: County, 38, 297; County Mission, 297, 299; Mountains, 123; Springs Campground, 373
Ironton, 116, 123, 290, 413
Irrigation, 28, 29, 30, 39, 47, 61, 68, 88, 98, 99, 101, 102, 105-11, 145, 193, 204, 217, 223, 229, 230, 263, 273, 274, 276, 281, 311, 316, 322, 323, 330, 335, 339, 340, 349, 352, 357, 359, 361, 362, 370, 392, 400, 410, 411, 427, 434, 438, 439
Isaac Chase House, 265
Islands, of Great Salt Lake, 483, 486
Island Improvement Company, 24
Isom, Alice P., 328
Ivanowski, Sigismund de, 258

"Jask-ass Mail," 412
"Jack Mormons," 57
Jackling, Daniel C., 119, 121, 319, 320
Jackson County, Missouri, 54, 81
Jackson: David E., 49, 202; W. H., 432, 497
Jackson's Hole, 24, 202
Jacob Hamblin: House, 307; Monument, 344
Jacob Lake, 345
Japanese, 192, 206, 368, 400: Buddhist Cemetery, 251
Jasper, 125, 465
Jed Gates House, 307
Jenkins, Ab, 234, 389
Jenny Lind Spring, 414
Jensen, 14, 145, 372, 399, 475, 477
Jericho, 103, 293, 419
Jericho Wool Pool, 103
Jet, 124
Jewish: Churches, 86; Colony, 335
Jim Bridger Monument, 364
Johnson: Nephi, 522; S. M., 331; Zeke, 445, 502, 503, 505, 506, 507, 511
Johnson, 344, 345: Canyon, 344; Creek, 432
Johnston, Colonel Albert Sidney, 71, 72, 73, 193, 218
Johnston Expedition, 70-1, 73, 87, 113, 120, 176-7, 204, 208, 218, 231, 238, 250, 289, 291, 299, 303-4, 316, 358, 370, 415
Jones: Daniel W., 154; John Wesley, 163; Kumen, 436, 437
Jordan: Narrows, 17, 284, 287, 288; River, 11, 72, 75, 88, 217, 222, 223, 224, 226, 513
Joseph, 339

"Joseph Smith," 454
Juab County, 38, 121, 125, 292
Judd, Zodak Knapp, 231, 302
"Jughandles, the," 451, 453
"Jumping-off Place," 424
Junction, 296, 339
Juniper Jardine, 20, 332
Juniper trees, 20, 310, 326, 354, 361, 467, 491, 502

Kachina Bridge, 505, 506
Kaibab: Forest, 525; Indians, 38, 39; Plateau, 457
Kaiparowits: Indians, 38; Plateau, 38, 147, 340, 342, 344, 433, 457, 504
Kamas, 368, 378, 493
Kamuduka Indians, 38
Kanab, 337, 342, 344: Canyon, 344; River, 32
Kanarra, Chief, 299
Kanarraville, 299, 526
Kane, Colonel Thomas L., 58, 71, 156
Kane County, 38, 344
Kanosh, 295, 337: Indian Reservation, 294
Kansas, 203, 204
Kayenta, Arizona, 510
Kay's Ward, 281
Kaysville, 68, 281, 282
Kearns: Mrs. Jennie J., 257; Thomas J., 257, 378
Keeley Canyon, 496, 498
Keith, David, 378
Kelly, Charles, 156, 157, 387, 399, 405
Kelton, 364
Kemmerer, Wyoming, 331
Kemple, John, 301
Kenilworth, 404
Kenner, Scipio Africanus, 149, 150, 151
Kigalia Ranger Station, 504
Kimball: Edward P., 174; Geo., 381; Heber C., 62, 65, 72, 75, 177; Leland H., 370; William H., 367; Wm. Henry, 378
Kimball, 381: Junction, 368; Ranch, 166
Kimballs Stage Station, 367
Kimballs Station Monument, 367
King: Clarence, 373; "Little Billie," 416, 417; William H., 87, 220, 294
Kingfisher Canyon, 398
Kingdom of God, 56, 61, 63, 96, 297
Kings Peak, 10, 375, 490, 494
Kingsbury Hall, 263
Kirtland, Ohio, 53, 54, 65, 184
Kiskadden, Annie Adams, 180
Kletting, Richard K. A., 245
Klingensmith, Philip, 304
Klondike Bluffs, 450, 452, 454
Knaphus, Torlief, 168, 234

Knell family, 298
Knight, 395
Knight, Jesse, 395, 413
Knightsville, 413, 414
Knitting, 243
Knolls, 385
Knowles, Emery, 503
Kolb: Emery C., 399; Ellsworth, 399
Kolob, 526
Kolob Canyons, 11, 526: Plateau, 300, 526
Koosharem, 346: Indian Reservation, 346
Kosmo, 364
Kosunate Indians, 38
Koyle, Bishop, 292

La Plata, 312: Mountains, Colorado, 431, 433
La Sal, 429: Junction, 429; Mountains, 10, 16, 24, 25, 422-33, 450, 454, 455, 496; National Forest, 427, 429, 504
La Verkin, 302, 526: Creek, 526
Labor, 89, 117, 282, 380
Labor Day, 383
Lady Mountain, 521, 524
Lagoon Resort, 214, 283
Lake, 364: Atwood, 494; Blanche, 314; Bonneville, 16, 17, 18, 32, 50, 51, 190, 192, 196, 200, 215, 226 251, 255, 258, 271, 316, 332, 360, 371, 481, 517; Catherine, 315; Florence, 314; Fork Creek, 494; Lillian, 315; Martha, 315; Mary, 315; Mead, Nevada, 349; Mountains, 216; Point, 363, 383, 393, 483; Point Junction, 410; Salido, 242; Solitude, 315; Timpanogos, 242; Uinta, 124, 372
Lakes, prehistoric, 16, 18
Lakeside, 487, 488: Mountains, 385, 488
Laketown, 203, 312, 331
Lamanites, 42, 92, 93, 298
Lambourne, Alfred, 164, 176, 178, 179, 484, 485
Land: grants, 109, 129, 138, 139, 203; jumping, 108; tenure, 43, 59, 68, 78, 100, 107, 108, 193, 203, 340, 351, 533
Larson, Bent F., 166
Latuda, 405
Latter Day Saints: Historian's Office, 103; Hospital, 96, 97; Museum, 36, 127, 168, 255, 298; Office Building, 241; Sunday School Union, 96
Lava, 15, 316, 341, 345
Lavender skunkweed, 316
Laws: 29, 59, 66, 72, 89; on archeological digging, 37; bird, 486; game, 31; school, 136, 138, 139, 140, 141;

social, 89; water, 107, 109, 110, 111
Lay: Elza, 405; Hark, 229
Layton, 29, 281
Lead, 46, 76, 114, 119, 120, 121, 122, 123, 317, 319, 322, 378, 379, 390, 392, 393, 409, 411, 414, 488
League of Utah Writers, The, 258
Leatherworking, 113, 160, 373
Lecture Ledge, 518
Lee: Buck (William), 160, 250, 439, 440; Charles, 465; Charles D., 466; Charles W., 348; John D., 43, 155, 230, 296, 300, 303, 304, 345, 466; Luke, 388
Leeds, 150, 300, 301, 302
Lees Ferry, Arizona, 304, 350, 398, 399, 435, 441
Legends, Indian, 170, 181, 331, 459, 465, 466, 499, 506
Legends, Mormon, 240, 287, 298
Legislature, baptism of, 68, 247
Lehi, 7, 115, 288, 515
Lemar, Captain Joseph de, 319
Lester Park, Ogden, 211
Levan, 293
Levan Ridge, 293
Levy, Louis Edward, 219
Lewis and Clark expedition, 48, 201
Lewis: B. Roland, 158; Oscar, 130
Lewiston, 273, 394
Lewiston-Bear Lake Irrigation Company, 273
Liberal Party, 78, 82, 84, 85, 232, 363
Liberty, 311
Liberty Park, Salt Lake City, 183, 228, 255, 265
Libraries, 96, 196, 205, 208, 220, 241, 259, 333, 348, 365, 379, 405, 415, 434, 435
Limber Pine, 20
Lime quarrying, hydrating, 413
Lime Ridge, 439
Limerock, 317
Limestone, 310, 358, 513
Limestone: Cave, 513; Spring, 312
Lincoln, Abraham, 43, 77, 90, 375
Lincoln Mine, 120, 323
Lindon, 290
Lindsay, J. S., 176
Linwood, 374
Lion House, 81, 162, 163, 183, 241, 243
Lion hunting, 336, 337
Literature, 7, 102, 153-58, 275, 384, 387, 467, 485, 505
Little, Jesse C., 217
Little: Bear River, 276; Bridge, 505; Cottonwood Canyon, 18, 122, 132, 233, 238, 285; Grand Mining District, 123; Miracle, 254; Mountain,

212, 363, 487; Salt Lake, 296, 297; Salt Lake Valley, 63; Zion, 522
Livestock, 3, 9, 82, 86, 89, 99, 101, 102, 103, 114, 117, 193, 207, 265, 291, 326, 332, 333, 334, 335, 336 337, 338, 339, 341, 344, 345, 346, 348, 352, 358, 365, 368, 421, 423, 427, 430, 451, 452
Loa, 348, 468
Locomotive Springs, 364
Lodges, summer, 313
Lodore Canyon, 398
Log cabins, 315, 358, 368
Log hotels, 315
Log stores, 315
Logan, Ephraim, 193
Logan, 8, 97, 132, 133, 139, 143, 146, 152, 168, 184, 185, 191, 198, 232, 275, 330, 331, 332: Canyon, 20, 192, 198, 330, 331, 332; Cave, 332; Peak, 192; River, 145, 192, 193, 332; Tabernacle, 192, 194; Temple, 97, 192, 194, 196
Logging, 369, 378, 492
Lon Chaney Peak, 403
Long, Horace M., 503, 505, 506
Long Valley, 342
Long Valley Junction, 299, 343, 472
Looking Glass Rock, 429
Loper, Bert, 399
Lopez, Rafael, 320, 321
Los Angeles, 86, 198, 267
Lost Creek, 358
Low Pass, 385
Lowry, John, 337
Loyal Legion, 379
Lucin, 366, 389, 486, 488
Lucin Cutoff, 132, 134, 206, 214, 363, 484, 487, 488
Luke's Hot Pots, 377
Lumber, 20, 31, 62, 114, 367
Lumbering, 369, 378, 492
Lund, 298
Lund: Alfred, 401; Anthony C., 173; Anton, 251
Lupine, 22, 346, 472
Lutheran Church, 86, 138
Lyman, Walter C., 434
Lyne, Thomas A., 178
Lynndyl, 410, 420

Machinery, 314
Madder, 328
Madeline Collection, 256
Maeser, Karl G., 139, 140, 185, 219
Magna, 133, 224, 228, 408
Magnesium chloride, 125
Magpie Picnic Ground, 312
Magraw, R. M., 397
Maguire, Don, 256
Mail, 127, 128, 133, 412

Major Powell, 427
Malad: Creek, 151; River, 352; Valley, 351, 355
Malin, Millard F., 168, 248, 249
Mammoth, 17, 262, 413, 415, 419, 420
Manganese, 123, 342
Manila, 374
Manly Expedition, 157
Manti, 7, 63, 66, 146, 184, 329, 335, 337, 412: National Forest, 24; Temple, 95, 184, 335
Mantua, 277
Manufacturing, 61, 81, 88, 90, 112, 117, 218, 275, 285, 299, 314, 360, 382
Manwill, Vearl J., 515
Manypenny, Commissioner, 42
Manzanita, 502, 504
Margetts, "Phil," 176
Marjum Pass, 421
Markagunt Plateau, 471
Markham Gulch, 321
Marks, Mrs. Anna, 415
Marl, 358
Marriage, 65, 93, 95, 97
Marriott, 208
Marshall, James W., 63, 306
Marten, 25
Martin, Gail, 169
Mary Dilworth Hammond Monument, 312
Marysvale, 74, 123, 338, 339
Marysvale Canyon, 338, 339
Masashi Coto, 368
Masonic Temple, 257
Masonry, 87, 307
Mastodon, 262, 428
Maughan, Lieutenant Russell, 194
Maughan, Peter, 194
Maverick: Point, 505; Spring, 504
Mavericks, 430
Maxwell, General George A., 363
Maxfield Lodge, 314
Mayfield, 335
Maynard, Ed, 301
Mayo, Thomas, 308
McAllister, D. M., 238
McChrystal, Jack, 415
McClellan, John J., 173, 174
McCombs, Andrew, 274
McCune School of Music and Fine Arts, 175
McElmo Creek, 496, 497
McGinley, Phyllis, 157, 207
McHenry, Gulch, 378
McIntosh, William, 414
McIntyre: Samuel, 414; William, 414
McKean, James B., 79, 80
McLaughlin, John B., 50, 203
McNally, Thomas, 301
MacNeill, Charles, 319
Meadow, 294

Meadow Picnic Grounds, 312
Meat packing, 116, 117, 284
Medicine, Indian, 41, 42, 124, 375
Medicine, pioneer, 23, 61, 243, 303, 312, 402
Medicine man, 41, 44
Meeker Massacre, 248
Meeks, Dr. Priddy, 230, 241, 297, 302, 491, 492
Meeting house, 5, 95, 138, 184
Melchizedek Priesthood, 93, 237
Memorial House, 250
Memory Grove Park, 250
Mendon, 276, 332
Mercur, 122, 258, 289, 319, 393, 394, 395: Pioneer Reunion, 395
Mercury sulphide, 122
Mericate, 42, 293, 346
Merrick Butte, 445
Merrill, Harrison R., 518
Mertensia, 22
Mesa Temple, 95
Mesa Verde, 35
Messa, Matteo, 415
Mestas, Manuel, 48
Metates, 37
Meteorite, 262
Methodist Church, 86, 87, 138
Methodist exhorters, 52
Metropolitan Opera, 207
Mexican Hat, 37, 147, 439, 441, 442, 509: Bridge, 443; Butte, 441; Lodge, 441
Mexican Land Grants, 203
Mice, 340
Middle: Cave, 514; Section, 430
Midgley, Waldo, 166
Midlake, 487
Midvale, 224, 316, 317
Midvale Junction, 316
Midway, 377
Midway Hot Pots, 224, 370
Migration from Utah, 9, 89
Migratory birds, 26, 278, 346, 348
Milford, 18, 85, 132, 232, 322, 323, 325
Milford Military Hospital, 323
Military: Cemetery, 289; reservation, 227
Militia, territorial, 412
Mill Creek, 112, 426, 427, 428
Millard County, 38, 145, 294
Millennium, The, 53, 60, 360, 430
Miller, "Broncho Charlie," 412
Millerites, 60
Milling, 112, 115, 117, 193, 217, 314, 323, 368
"Million dollar bell," 235
Mills, C. C., 163
Mills, John M., 140, 206, 476
Mills Junction, 303, 384, 391
Millville, 276

Milner, H. O., 394
Mine disasters, 406, 407, 536
Mine production, 121, 122, 285, 286, 301, 318, 319, 322, 324, 378, 393, 407, 413, 414, 418
Mineral Mountains, 295, 322
Minersville, 112, 323
Minidoka National Forest, 142
Mining, 9, 29, 31, 46, 63, 76, 78, 82, 85, 88, 90, 100, 114, 116, 117, 118-25, 184, 212, 257, 285-87, 296, 300, 305, 318, 319, 334, 335, 338, 339, 341, 343, 362, 365, 367, 378, 379-81, 390, 391, 392, 393, 394, 395, 400-07, 418, 431, 432, 441, 442, 483, 490, 493
Mining district, 76, 121, 122, 123
Mink, 144
Minnows, 28, 145, 278
Mirages, 365, 382, 385, 487, 488
Mirror Lake, 145, 368, 490, 493
Mirror Lake Lodge, 368
Miser, Hugh D., 422
Missionaries, 6, 60, 61, 74, 93, 97, 101, 172-73, 178, 235, 245, 277, 298, 305, 391, 424
Missionary system, 95
Mississippi River, 57, 115, 480
Mississippi Saints, 58
Missouri, 54, 55, 60, 64, 68, 81; River, 48, 57, 127, 129, 130, 201
Moab, 21, 147, 160, 424, 425, 426, 427, 428, 434, 435, 450, 451, 453: Canyon, 424; Valley, 425, 426, 453
Modena, 298
Mohave Indians, 49
Moki Canyon, 501, 504
Molybdenum, 121
Mona, 292
Monday Town, 359
Monette, E. R., 399
Monroe, 74, 338
Monroe Hot Springs, 338
Montana, 76, 131, 132, 201, 332
Monte Cristo: Peak, 312; Recreation Area, 214, 313
Monterey, California, 47, 154, 216
Montezuma, 437: Creek, 432, 435, 437, 496, 497
Monticello, 430, 431, 432, 433, 438, 439
Monument: Pass, 444; Valley, 439, 443, 444, 445, 452, 504
Monuments, 88, 167, 208, 211, 234, 235, 237, 240, 246, 254, 255, 264, 272, 279, 289, 291, 299, 344, 346, 355, 364, 367, 368, 372, 375, 385
Moon Lake, 145, 490, 494
Moore: L. C., 403; Mason, 390; Walter, 427
Moore, 403
Moose, 24
Morals, 3, 6, 55, 56, 59, 60, 62, 64, 65,

67, 73, 92, 178, 282, 317, 321, 324,
338, 356, 374, 378, 379-81, 393, 414,
417, 418
Moran, Thomas, 164
Morgan, 359
Mormon: architecture, 210; Battalion,
57, 58, 61, 63, 203, 246, 306; Bat-
talion Monument, 246; Church, 4,
52, 53, 54, 55, 56, 59, 62, 64, 65, 67,
68, 72, 73, 74, 76, 77, 78, 81, 82, 83,
84, 85, 88, 89, 91, 97, 100, 108, 114,
139, 141, 162, 175, 177, 183, 194, 223,
241, 276, 287, 325, 328, 384; crafts,
160-62; doctrine, 171; literature,
155; Missionary Home, 245
"Mormon buckskin," 507
"Mormonee," 42, 293
"Mormonesque architecture," 184
Moroni, Angel, 3, 237, 334
Morphine, 379
Morrill Act, 139
Morris, Joseph, 360
Morrisites, 77, 360
Morrisite War, 360
Moser, Henri, 167
Moshoquop, 43
Mosida, 411
Moss Ledge Falls, 315
Moss Ledge Falls Picnic Area, 315
Moss Falls, 518
Mouk, Eunice, 329
Mound Fort, 204
Mount: Agassiz, 493; Baldy, 296;
Belnap, 296; Carmel, 344; Carmel
Highway, 523; Carmel Junction,
327; Carmel Tunnel, 523; Joseph,
385; Lovenia, 494; Majestic, 315;
Mellenthin, 429; Milicent, 315;
Nebo, 147, 292; Ogden, 200, 213;
Ogden Game Preserve, 310; Peale,
428, 429; Pisgah, 277; Pleasant,
151, 333, 334; Timpanogos, 10, 146,
147, 216, 220, 224, 289, 371, 395,
513, 515, 516, 517, 518; Tukuhniki-
vatz, 429; Wolverine, 315
Mountain: Alder, 21; Ash, 491; Dell
Reservoir, 381; Home, 369; lions,
25, 144, 299, 336, 337, 341, 344, 346,
491, 502, 521; Meadows Massacre,
70, 71, 73, 155, 296, 300, 304, 345;
Men, 27, 28, 48, 49, 50, 51, 58, 192,
193, 201, 203, 204, 229, 272, 279,
355, 358, 375, 385, 386, 397, 477,
481; of the Sun, 524; Park Camp,
315; States Conference, 197, 220,
260
Mountains, 10, 12
Mourning doves, 334, 502
"The Move," 72, 74, 204, 218
Moving pictures, 179, 298, 318, 326,
344, 443

Mud Island, 486
Muddy Creek, 403
Mueller, George, 278
Mueller Park, 283
Muir, John, 27
Mukuntuweap, 522: National Monu-
ment, 522
Mule deer, 24, 143, 144, 491, 502, 521
Municipal light and power, 194, 208,
218, 283, 294
Municipal power, 276
Murals, 163, 166, 169, 247, 248, 249
Murdock, Abe, 296
Murphy, "Metalliferous," 300, 301
Murray, 227, 285, 319
Museum of American Art, New York,
350
Museums, 36, 158, 162, 163, 165, 168,
180, 211, 220, 234, 242, 249, 250, 255,
256, 260, 262, 264, 281, 282, 288, 294,
298, 335, 344, 348, 373, 384, 387, 461,
466, 467, 473, 475, 517, 524
Music, 7, 60, 170, 175, 220, 239, 264,
279
Myers, L. B., 217
Myton, 260, 375, 376

Napoleon, Louis, 127
Narrows Trail, 526
National: forests, 24, 31, 142, 147, 218,
368; Guard, 320; parks, 117, 208,
267, 450, 452, 454, 475, 479; Park
Service, 450, 452, 454, 475, 479;
Reclamation Act, 110; Women's Re-
lief Society, 96; Youth Administra-
tion, 162
Natural bridges, 9, 11, 18, 433, 441,
445, 467, 468, 469, 470, 501-10, 523
Natural Bridges National Monument,
11, 445, 501-07
Natural gas, 206, 396, 405, 536, 537
Natural resources, 20, 21, 28-31, 59,
100, 117, 118, 123, 490
Navaho Hill, 439
Navaho: Indians, 41, 43, 45, 159, 160,
181, 182, 427, 435, 438, 443, 452, 499,
509, 510; Lake, 146, 299; Moun-
tain, 340, 349, 433, 445, 457, 509;
Springs, 439
Nauvoo, Illinois, 55, 56, 57, 65, 87,
163, 212, 287
Nauvoo: Legion, 55, 70; Temple, 56,
235
Nay, Arm, 421
Nazarene Church, 86
Nebo Loop road, 292, 334
Neff, A. L., 158
Negroes, 92-3, 229, 400
Nelson: Joseph, 222; Lowery, 117
Nephi, 7, 15, 101, 125, 140, 271, 272,
292, 293, 334, 337, 420

Nephi-Levan Ridge Experimental Station, 293
Nephites, 91, 298
Nesbitt, Watson N., 301
Nevada, 17, 32, 33, 61, 70, 74, 129, 131, 190, 363
Nevills, Norman D., 441
New Harmony, 300
"New Jerusalem," 231
New Mexico, 10, 32, 33, 34, 35, 38, 47, 62, 63, 67, 159, 441, 443, 444, 449
"New Movement," 78
Newcastle, 298
Newfoundland Mountains, 488
Newhouse, 323, 325: Building, 325; Hotel, 325; Junction, 326
Newhouse, Samuel, 319, 325
Newman, Rev. J. P., 79
Newspapers, 73, 96, 149-52, 143, 205, 331, 430
Newton, 275
Newton Brothers Leather plant, 373
Newton, William B., 373
Nibley, Preston, 155
Nicholsen, John, 394
Nickel, 342
Nielson, Jens, 341
Nigger Bill Canyon, 425
"Niggerhead," 310
Nine Mile Canyon, 37, 159, 401
"No-You-Don't Mine," 318
Non-Mormon churches, 86, 87, 201, 210
North: Canyon, 432; Fork Canyon, 522; Duchesne River, 369, 493; Uinta River, 494; Virgin River, 522; Horn Mountain, 402; Ogden, 279, 311; Rim of Grand Canyon, 525; Star Lake, 494
"North Window," 453
Northern Pacific Railroad, 324
Northwestern turkey growers, 100
"Not Zion," 522
Notom, 349

Oakley, 368, 370
Oak City, 420
Oasis, 509
Observatory Peak, 213
Observation Point, 524, 525
O'Connell, Dan, 127
Odlum, Harriet McQuarrie, 157
O'Donnell, Patrick, 431
Ogden: Mrs. Marie M., 430; Peter Skene, 48, 154, 201, 204, 247
Ogden City, 8, 77, 84, 85, 96, 114, 131, 132, 133, 135, 139-41, 143, 150-52, 156, 173-75, 177, 182, 183, 185, 186, 199-214, 232, 275, 279, 286, 310, 360-62, 486, 487

Ogden Bay Migratory Bird Refuge and Hunting Grounds, 279
Ogden Buddhist temple, 210
Ogden Canyon, 147, 200, 213, 214, 279, 309-11
Ogden: Carnegie Free Library, 208; Horse Show, 213; Livestock Coliseum, 210; Livestock Show, 210; Oratorio Society, 173; Ordnance Depot, 280; River, 12, 48, 200, 310; Stadium, 213; Tabernacle, 185, 210; Tabernacle Choir, 174; Valley (Ogden Hole), 48, 206, 310, 366; Waterworks Conduit, 310
Ogdens Hole (Ogden Valley), 48, 206, 310, 366
Ogilvie, George, 121, 318
Oil, 124, 284, 328, 364, 403, 406, 422, 441, 442; lamps, 430; refining, 284
"Oil boom," 439
Old: Chase Mill, 265; Courthouse, 247; Irrigation Canal Arroyo, 427; Juniper Camp, 332; Kentucky, 127; La Sal, 429; Mill, 213; Mill Club, 313, 314; Mormon Breastworks, 356; Mormon Trail, 358, 367; Spanish Trail, 47; Spring, 421; State House, 184, 246, 247, 250, 294
"Old Crow," 318
"Old Jack," 326
"Old Joe Mountain," 339
"Old Posey," 43
Oldfield, Barney, 233
"Ole Ephraim," 24
Olsen, Cuthbert L., 207
Olson, Moroni, 207
Oliver, Rev. French, 380
Omaha, Neb., 129, 131
Onion Creek, 425: Creek road, 425; celebration, 292
Ontario Mine, 121, 378, 380
Onaqui Mountains, 392
O'Neil, Mike, 428
Oolitic limestone, 186
Opals, 125
Open pit mining, 121, 123, 125, 295, 399
"Opera houses," 177
Ophir, 324, 393, 415: Junction, 394
Oquirrh Mountains, 16, 29, 217, 226, 228, 258, 316, 361, 383, 391, 392, 394, 408
Orange Cliffs, 350
Orangeville, 402
Oratorios, 173
Orchards, 307, 313, 328, 342, 343, 364, 422
Orchestras, 174, 175
Orderville, 81, 343
Ore roasting process, 258
Ore-sampling, 285

Oregon, 8, 21, 50, 56, 57, 62, 63, 203, 360, 386
Oregon Trail, 9, 51, 58, 386
Oregon Short Line Railroad, 132
Orem, 29, 290
"Organ, The," 454, 525
Osmium, 123
Ottinger, George Martin, 163-65, 262
Ouray (Ute chief), 41, 43
Ouray, 375
Ouray, Colorado, 400
Outdoor summer school, 513
Outdoor Theater, 341
Outer Portal, 430
Outermost Point, 430
"Outlaw tamer," 361, 362
Outlaws, 86, 326, 341, 350, 355, 356, 362, 373, 388, 402-06, 421
Overland Stage, 354, 357, 358, 366, 381, 388, 392
Overland Telegraph, 74, 128
Overgrazing, 30, 143, 144, 282, 384
Owachomo Bridge, 502, 505, 507
Ox-team transportation, 29
Ozokerite, 124, 407
Ozokerite mines, 407

Pack Creek, 426, 428
Pack Creek Campground, 429
Pack: Dr. Frederick J., 479; John, 136, 230
Pack trips, 340, 348, 369, 440, 441, 444, 493-95, 509, 526
Packard, John Q., 414, 415
Padre Creek, 47
Pahvant: Indians, 38, 43, 67, 294, 421; Mountains, 144, 271; Plateau, 10; Valley, 420
Painted Desert: Arizona, 46; Utah, 347
Painting, 162, 163-70, 235, 247, 249, 291
Paiute Indians, 7, 38-41, 43, 45, 66, 170, 182, 297, 299, 303, 316, 326, 346, 427, 438, 457, 459, 465, 503, 504, 509, 510, 516
Palisade Park Forest Camp, 374
Palladium, 123
Palmer, Loeffler: 390, 391; William R., 42, 43, 465
Palmyra, N. Y., 52
Panguitch, 74, 304, 337, 338, 341, 436: Indians, 38; Lake, 146, 341; Plateau, 12
"Panhandle style grazing," 503
Panthers, 25, 336
"Parade of Elephants," 453
Paradise, 276
Paragonah, 296, 297
Paria River, 32
"Paria View," 462

"Park Avenue," 453, 454
Park City, 15, 123, 132, 146, 257, 315, 371, 378-81, 412, 492; Mining District, 121
Park, John R., 139, 259, 287
Park Utah Consolidated Mining Company, 378
Park Valley, 365
Parker: George Le Roy, 341, 405; N. S., 156
Parkinson, William J., 170
Parley's Canyon, 255, 358, 368, 382
Parowan, 177, 229, 239, 297: Canyon, 297; Mountains, 25; Valley, 296
Parry, Caroline, 166
Parunuweap, 522: Canyon, 522
Pastor, Tony, 179
Passion play, 179
Pasture lands, 294, 327
Patio Springs, 311
Paunsaugunt Plateau, 342, 457
Pavogogwunsing Indians, 38
Payson, 133, 262, 292, 338, 515: Canyon, 292
Payton, Frank, 393
Peace commissioners, 72
Peace treaties, 293, 337, 346, 352
Peach Day, 277
Peaches, 277, 327, 328, 411
Pearson, Henry A., 287
Peas, 359
Pectol, Ephraim P., 348, 466, 467
Pederson, Anton, 174
"Peek-a-boo Canyon," 462
Peery, Harman, 207
Peerless, 405
Pendleton, Mark, 301, 343
Penitentiary, State, 266
Penrose: Charles W., 151, 171, 211, 282, 365; Spencer, 319
Pentecostal churches, 86
Pentstemon, 22, 472, 518
Peoa, 368
People's Political Party, 78, 82, 84, 85, 363
Perkins, Tom, 428
Perpetual Emigration Fund Company, 83, 532
Perry, 278
Peruvian Gulch, 287
Peterson, 359
"Petrified" beaver dams, 276
Petrified forests, 14, 262, 301, 330, 338, 344, 465, 466, 468, 469
Petroglyphs, 37, 158, 234, 292, 356, 397, 401, 403, 428, 466, 505, 509
Petroleum, 124, 284
Petty, Mrs. Julia Wright, 274
Peyton Home, the, 186
Peasants, 26, 27
Philippine Islands, 87, 88

Phosphate, 98, 99, 311
Photograph: Gap, 430; Rock, 345
Photography, 130, 162, 163, 193, 399, 453, 467, 525
Picnic grounds, 143, 310, 311, 313
Pictographs, 158, 397, 466, 509
Pierce, R. C., 442
Pierre's Hole, 50
Pig iron, 123, 290
"Pigeon express," 133
Pigeon Hollow Junction, 334
Pilot Peak, 213, 386, 387
Pine Canyon, 319
Pine Valley, 326; Mountains, 144, 271, 300; Reservoir, 146
Pine View Reservoir, 147, 206, 214, 311
"Pine Tree Arch," 455
Pinedo, Arie, 122, 394
Pines, 20, 21, 310, 313, 326, 346, 428, 432, 491, 502, 513
Pink Cliffs, 342, 457, 459, 472
Pioche, Nevada, 298, 300, 301, 304
"Pioneer Day," 58, 70
Pioneer Day Celebration, 201, 207
Pioneer: Fort, 182; Memorial Building, 222; Park, 222, 234, 266
Pipe lines, 134, 284
Pit houses, 33, 35
Piute: County, 38, 339; Reservoir, 106, 109, 110, 296, 339
Plant zones, 18, 19, 491, 517
Platinum, 123, 292
Platte River, 48
Playgrounds, 341
Playwrights, 157, 179
Pleasant Creek, 465, 469
Pleasant Grove, 184, 289, 517-19
Plebiscites, 78
Plum Creek, 206
Plymouth, 352
"Pocatello Mine," 393
Pocketville, 328
Poetry, 157
"Poikneapsy the bishop," 347
Point of the Mountain, 288
"Point Supreme," 473, 474
Polehaven, 146
Politics, 6, 55, 69, 78, 82, 84, 85, 87, 88, 363
Pollock, Channing, 157, 179
Polygamy, 3, 5, 6, 41, 56, 64-66, 69, 75, 77-80, 82-85, 87, 88, 114, 205, 232, 241, 251, 265, 281, 288, 301, 305, 306, 307, 327, 363, 379, 420, 468
"Polyg hunts," 83, 301, 308, 327
Polysophical Society, 138
Poncho House, 37, 441
Pond Town, 292
Pony Express, 74, 128, 231, 264, 354, 357, 358, 388, 412

Population distribution, 42, 97, 106, 117
Porcupines, 26, 340, 491, 521
Porcupine: Draw, 429; Pass, 494
Portage, 352
Potash, 123, 339
Potato: Hollow, 525; Valley, 340
Pothole, 505
Potter, Isaac, 355
Pottery, 33-36, 62, 112, 158, 161, 162, 262, 335, 344, 499, 503
Poultry industry, 99, 335, 343, 368
Powder River, 203
Powell, Major John W., 43, 147, 154, 163, 308, 348, 374, 398, 428, 467, 477, 522
Powell National Forest, 144
Powell, William Clement, 163, 398
Pratt, Orson, 58, 62, 79, 127, 138, 155, 229, 230, 234, 355, 356
Pratt, Parley P., 54, 55, 58, 62, 153, 155, 381, 382
Pratt, Teancum, 404
Precipitation, 12, 405
Predators, 25-27, 103, 104, 143
Presbyterian churches, 86, 87, 138, 139, 141, 193, 265
Preston, Idaho, 133, 272
Price, 141, 152, 159, 169, 373, 396, 401-03; Art Gallery, 402; River, 401, 403, 406; River Canyon, 403, 406
Priesthood, Mormon, 93, 94
Primary Organization, 96
Printing, 116, 117
Proctor, A. Phimister, 264
Prohibition, 5, 36, 88
Promontory, 77, 128, 130, 131, 163, 364, 487; Mountains, 132, 360: Point, 37, 262, 363, 482, 487; Point Station, 487
Property, Mormon viewpoint on, 59, 68, 81
Prosecution of polygamists, 80, 82, 83
Prospectors, 323, 324, 349, 427, 431, 432
Providence, 275: Canyon, 275; Limestone Quarry, 275
Provo, 8, 25, 29, 36, 63, 96, 114, 133, 139, 140, 143, 152, 159, 162, 167, 169, 175, 177, 185, 202, 204, 215-24, 232, 262, 289, 290, 342, 370, 371, 517, 518
Provo: Canyon, 29, 145, 224, 290, 366, 370, 371; Peak, 216; River, 12, 29, 145, 215-17, 224, 357, 368-70, 377, 516, 517; Tabernacle, 185; Terrace, 16; Valley, 74
Provot, Etienne, 48, 202, 216, 355
Prudden, T. M., 440
Public shooting grounds, 145
Public Works Administration, 208, 213

Public Works of Art Project, 249
Pueblo Bonito, 35
Pueblo Indians, 33-37, 262, 409, 443, 466, 497-99
Puffer Lake, 145, 296: Lake Resort, 295
Pygmies, 35, 36
Pyle, Ernie, 197, 431, 445
Pyper, George D., 177-79

Quantrill, William, 289, 349
Quartzite, 310, 513
Quorum of the Twelve Apostles, 54, 56, 59, 83, 94

Race and Stampede Celebration, 273
Racial distribution, 228
Racial groups, 201, 393, 403
"Racket Gang," 357
Radcliffe, T., 173
Raddatz, E. J., 415
Raddon, S. L., 152
Radio, 149, 152, 174, 239, 382
Radio-active ores, 403
Raft River, 11: Mountains, 488
Railroads, 7, 64, 67, 76, 77, 85, 86, 113, 114, 121, 128, 129, 134, 138, 151, 187, 194, 200, 206, 208, 218, 233, 286, 305, 320, 324, 325, 354, 358, 361, 362, 376, 379, 381, 388, 390, 394, 400, 404, 416, 435, 487, 536
Rail tour, 486, 488
Rainbow Bridge National Monument, 11, 441, 508-511
Rainbow: Natural Bridge, 148, 445; Lake, 493; Lodge, 509
"Rainbow Mountain," 457
"Rainbow Park," 478
"Rainbow Point," 462
Ralston, William, 373, 374
Ramsey, Ralph, 162, 164, 244, 250
Randolph, 331
Range, use of, 19, 24, 30, 31, 101, 102, 143, 144, 488
Raplee Anticline, 441
Rasmussen, Henry N., 168, 248, 249
Rawlins, Joseph, 424
Rawlins, Joseph L., 85
Recapture Canyon, 434, 435
Reclamation, 29, 88, 105, 106, 109, 110, 276, 366, 370, 377
Recreation, 31, 50, 90, 95, 96, 97, 117, 142, 148, 211, 285, 299, 370, 379, 490, 517: Indian, 42, 170
Red: Butte Canyon, 254; Canyon, 341, 374; Fork Canyon, 356; House Cliffs, 504; Knob Pass, 494; Mountain, 373; Plateau, 402; Rock Pass, 16; Spring Camps, 374
Redford, Grant H., 156
Redmond, 335

Reed, Harry, 452, 455
Reese, 487
Reforestation, 20, 30, 31, 282
Refrigeration Canyon, 525
Reid, William K., 139
Relief, 88, 230: Society, 96
Remy, Jules, 297
Rendezvous, trappers, 48, 49, 51, 201-03, 374
Republican Party, 85, 87
Reservations, see Indian reservations
Reservoir Hill, 277
Resorts, 268, 283, 285, 287, 288, 315, 383
"Revelations," 53, 57, 65, 80, 91, 360, 420, 430
Reynolds: H. Reuben, 168; Henry, 368
Rhodes, Caleb, 401, 493
Rhodes, Thomas, 367, 368
Rhodes Valley, 368
Rich, Charles Coulson, 74, 230, 240, 330
Rich County, 38, 331
Richards: Lee Greene, 166, 248; Lela Horne, 156; Willard, 62, 65
Richardson, Frank, 399
Richens, Lucile, 400
Richfield, 74, 81, 333, 336, 337, 338, 341: Park, 338
Richmond, 273: Holstein Show, 273; Tabernacle, 273
Ricks, Joel, 193
Ridges, Joseph H., 239
Riding, 147, 148, 313, 523, 524, 526
Rigby, Idaho, 219
Rigdon, Sidney, 53, 54, 55
Rim of the Great Basin, 296
Rim Road, 457, 460, 461, 462
"Rimrock" Annie, 430
Ringhoffer, Alexander, 451
Rio Grande: River, 160, 498; Valley, 106; Western Railroad, 416
Rishel, William D., 389
Riswold, Gilbert, 234
Ritchie, J. M., 369
River Gorge, 468
River running, 134, 143, 146, 147, 397, 399, 427, 441, 442
Riverdale, 204
Riverside, 332, 352
Riverton, 287
Roadometer, 126, 127, 235
Robbers Roost, 86, 349, 350, 402, 403, 421, 467
Roberts, Brigham H., 65, 87
Robertson, Frank G., 156
Robertson, LeRoy J., 175
Robidoux, Antoine, 51, 375
Robinson: J. Will, 367; Mark, 175
Robinson Ranch, 345

Robinson's Ranch, 422
Rochester, 403
Rock: asphalt, 124, 401; Creek, 369, 492, 493; crystal, 125; dust, 404; wool, 285
"Rockfort," 368
Rockport, 368
Rockville, 328
Rockwell, Orrin Porter, 287, 288
Rocky Ford Reservoir, 322
Rocky Sea Pass, 493
Rodeos, 213, 229, 353, 402, 427
Roger Peak, 340
Rollins, James A., 323
Roman Catholic Church, see Catholic Church
Rookeries, 27, 485
Roosevelt, 376
Roosevelt, Franklin D., 87, 258, 475
Roosevelt, Theodore, 511
Rosenbaum, Howell, 170
Rosette, 366
Ross, Harold, 157
Round Valley, 276
Roundups, 102, 345
Royal, 406
Royle, Edwin Milton, 157, 179
Rozel, 124, 364
Ruby, Glen M., 397
"Ruby Mine," 390
Rubys Inn, 460
Ruin Canyon, 496-99
Rush Lake, 17
Rush Valley, 17, 392
Russell, Majors, and Waddell, 127, 128
Russell: Charles S., 399; Osborne, 154, 483
Russian Colony, 365, 366
Rust, George, 122, 412
Rustler Mountain, 286
Rustling, 307, 326, 337, 349, 403, 406, 428
Ryan: Daniel, 362; Dennis, 324; James, 323

Sabueganas Indians, 222
Sacramento, California, 127, 128, 131, 231, 306, 387
Sage Creek Junction, 331
Sage Plain, 430, 431, 433, 434, 435, 496, 497, 503, 504
Sage, Rufus B., 229
Sagebrush, 19, 22, 182, 294, 355, 396, 412, 428-9, 435, 467, 488, 491, 504
Sager, Merel S., 425
St. George, 47, 128, 141, 161, 182, 184, 250, 301, 302, 304, 305, 306, 307, 308, 525: Tabernacle, 301, 306; Tabernacle Choir, 301; Temple, 95, 184, 304, 306

St. Joseph, Missouri, 127, 128, 231
St. Charles, Idaho, 331
St. Marks' Episcopal Cathedral, 265
St. Mary's Academy, 139
St. Mary's of the Wasatch, 141, 256
Salem, 292
Salina, 74, 144, 336, 337, 400, 403, 435
Salt Palace, 233
Salt Lake: Chamber of Commerce, 114; Choral Society, 173; City, passim; esp. 225; City Municipal Airport, 254, 267; Collegiate Institute, 139, 266; County, 223, 286; and Park City Railroad, 379; Philharmonic Orchestra, 174; Symphony Orchestra, 174; Tabernacle, 79, 97, 183, 184, 232, 234, 238, 239; Tabernacle Choir, 172, 173, 174, 239; Temple, 94, 162, 183, 184, 226, 230, 232, 233, 234, 237, 238, 285; Theater 163, 164, 172, 173, 174, 176, 177, 178, 179, 180, 232, 250; Yacht Basin, 147; Yacht Club Harbor, 147, 383
Salt manufacturing, 115, 382
Salt Valley, 454, 455
Saltair Resort, 16, 373, 480
San: Buenaventura River, 47, 49; Diego, California, 246; Diego Fair, 334; Francisco, 130, 131, 149, 208, 219, 267, 334; Francisco Mountains, 322, 324; Gabriel Mission, 49
San Juan: Basin, 33, 34, 43; Canyon, 442; County, 38, 101, 348, 431, 432, 434, 435, 438, 439, 445, 497, 502, 503; Mountains, Colorado, 441; River, 11, 32, 37, 134, 145, 147, 431, 432, 434, 435, 437, 438, 439, 440, 441, 442, 443, 496, 497, 498, 499, 502, 508; Stake, 439; Valley, 35, 262, 435, 497
San Miguel Mountains, Colorado, 431, 432
San Pedro, 86
Sanpete Counties, 125, 139, 335
San Rafael: Bridge, 403; Mountains, 123; River, 350; Swell, 160, 345, 396, 400, 402
Sand Creek Canyon, 340
Sand: dunes, 18, 338, 342; ridge, 281
Sandstone, silver in, 122
Sandy, 285
Sanpete Valley, 38, 63, 67, 74
Sapir, Dr. Edward, 308
Sanpitch Mountains, 271, 334
Sanpitch plateau, 10
Santa Clara: 307; Valley, 12, 303
Santa Fe, New Mexico, 47, 50, 154, 216, 246, 385
Santa Fe Museum, 165
Santaquin, 17, 292, 338, 410

Sardine Canyon, 275, 277, 332
Saratoga Springs Resort, 288
Savage, Charles R., 130, 163
Savage's Ranch, 369
Sawmill Canyon, 356
Sawmills, 318, 330, 341, 368
Scanlan, Lawrence, 86, 301
Schaefer, Jack, 394
Schettle, Louis, 248
Schettler, Paul, 414
Schisms, 77, 78, 360
Schick, Murray, 324, 325
Schieder, "Dutch," 255
Schneitter's Hot Pots, 377
Schools, 5, 84, 87, 96, 135-41, 168, 193, 196, 206, 211, 218, 219, 233, 245, 306, 308, 363
School teachers, 137, 140, 306, 312
Schreiner, Alexander, 173, 174
Scipio, 293, 294
Scofield: 218, 407; Reservoir, 106, 407
Scorup, James, 503, 505, 506
Scott, Donald, 401
Scrip, 77, 113, 250, 277
Sculpture, 163, 167-68, 207, 234-37, 240, 246-50, 255, 256, 291, 475
Scutter Lake, 493
Sea Gull Monument, 167, 240
Seagulls, 27, 61, 227, 230, 383, 483, 485, 486
Seely, John Henry, 334
Seely, Orange, 402, 403
Silverman, Samuel M., 302
Seminaries, 96, 141, 218
Senecio, 23
Sentinel Peak, 403
Service berries, 21, 22, 23, 39
Sessions, Peregrine, 60, 283
Session's Settlement, 283
Settlement (see Colonization)
Seuvarit Indians, 38
Sevier, 338: Bridge Reservoir, 293; County, 38, 125, 336; Desert, 12, 420; Lake, 67; River, 12, 26, 67, 146, 338, 339, 420; River Reservoir, 420; Stake Mormon Tabernacle, 337; Valley, 61, 74, 293, 296, 335, 338, 379
Sevenmile Creek, 346
"Seventh Angel," 360
Seventh Bombardment Group, 254
Seventh Day Adventists, 86
Seventies, 93, 94
Shamanism, 421
Sharp, John, 130
Shay Mountain, 430
Sheep, 27, 103, 104, 293, 309, 333, 334, 338, 340, 343, 344, 345, 346, 352, 365, 367, 412, 422, 423, 426, 427, 428, 429, 431, 434, 496, 534
Sheep, shearing, 103, 419

Sheep Creek, 374
"Sheep Rock," 454
Sheeprock Mountains, 395
Sheets Gulch, 465
Shepherd: Arthur, 174; Charles, 174
"Shirt Tail Factory," 379
Shirts, Peter, 434, 497
Shivwit Indians, 43, 398
Shivwits-Shebit Indian reservation, 308
Shoal Creek, 304
Shoshoni Indians, 36, 38, 39, 40, 41, 42, 43, 45, 76, 159, 170, 201, 202, 213, 274, 311, 331, 351, 352, 355, 356, 384
Shurtliff, Lewis W., 204
Shurtliff, W. H., 170
Sigurd, 125, 336, 346, 468
Silica, 125, 317
Silk culture, 115, 161, 213, 222, 250, 328
Silver, 100, 114, 119, 120, 121, 122, 287, 301, 317, 318, 319, 322, 323, 339, 378, 379, 381, 390, 392, 393, 394, 409, 411, 414: City, 413, 419; Creek, 368; Creek Canyon, 367; Fork Canyon, 315; Horn, 414; Lake, 70, 146, 315; Reef, 122, 300, 301, 302, 304, 305
Simpson, J. H., 388
Sinbad area, 403
Sinclair, Charles E., 73
"Singing Rock," 469
Sioux Indians, 76, 129, 355
Sipapu Bridge, 502, 506, 507
Skating, 143, 146, 370
Skiing, 143, 146, 287, 313, 315, 370, 381
Skull Valley, 38, 385, 386
Skull Valley Indian Reservation, 384
Skutumpah Ranch, 345
Skyline Drive, 408
Slack: John, 373; Louise, 327, 328
Slade, Jack, 357
Slag, 285, 292, 358, 394, 409, 410
Slavery, 69
Slavery Indian, 41, 48, 66, 67, 385, 500
"Sleeping Ute," 468
Sleighing, 146
Slick Rocks, 436, 437, 454, 455, 497, 505, 509
Slight, Thomas, 331
Smelting, 112, 116, 118, 119, 121, 123, 285, 292, 299, 316, 317, 320, 390, 409, 413
Smith: Elmer, 409; George A., 58, 63, 297; Hyrum, 55, 56, 167, 276; Jedediah Strong, 48-50, 154, 201-203, 208, 385; Joseph, 394; Joseph (the prophet), 3, 52-60, 65, 75, 79, 91,

155, 167, 235, 243, 283, 334; Joseph Fielding, 155, 251, 352; Lot, 70, 282; Mary Weathman, 312; Paul, 170; Silas S., 435, 436; William G., 273; William H., 367
Smithfield, 116, 198, 275
Smiths Fork Creek, 495
Smithsonian Institution, 163, 403, 421, 444, 479, 497
Smoking Mountain, 338, 342
Smoot, Reed, 87, 88, 207, 220
Smyth, A. C., 173
Snake: Canyon, 439; Creek, 38; Indians, 412; Mountains, 422; River, 11, 16, 48, 190; Valley, 422
Snakes, 28, 467, 502
Snell, George Dixon, 157
Snipe, 364
Snow: Basin, 311; College, 36, 141, 335
Snow: Edgar, 157; Eliza R., 171, 243; Erastus, 58, 301, 305, 307; Lorenzo, 277, 365; Zerubabbel, 65, 291
Snowberry, 502
Snowshoe rabbit, 25, 346
Snowslides, 287, 315, 321
Snowville, 365
Soap Creek Rapids, 425
Social Hall, 176, 177, 178
Society, Indian, 40, 41, 44
Society, Mormon, 58, 59, 60, 62
Soda ash, 125
"Soda Water Fred," 394
Sodium bicarbonate, 125
Sodium sulphate, 125, 383
Soil destruction, 30, 282, 353
Soldier Summit, 396, 404, 408
South: Eden, 331; Hecla Mine, 286; Pass, 48, 70, 201; Rim of the Great Basin, 299; Salt Lake, 284; Weber, 360
South Fork: Ogden River, 311; Provo River, 368; Sevier River, 339; Picnic Ground, 312; Ranger Station, 516
"South Window," 453
Southern Pacific Railroad, 132, 208, 363, 364, 373, 389, 481
Sowiette, 43: Park, 220
Spalding, Tom, 417
Spanish-American War, 87
Spanish: explorations, 47, 48; mariposa, 22; mine, 323; trail, 50
Spanish Fork, 92, 262, 284, 291, 292, 333, 347, 396, 408: Canyon, 47, 52, 403; River, 12
"Spanish River," 49
Spaulding, Solomon, 53
Spearhead Point, 524
Speedboat races, 311
Spencer, Clarissa Young, 155, 243

Spendlove, Beatrice, 320, 321
Sphinx, 356
Spiritualist Church, 87
Spring: Canyon, 405; City, 334; Lake Villa, 338
Springdale, 329, 523
Springville, 67, 165-9, 218, 224, 290-1
Split Mountain, 476: Canyon, 372, 478
Split Rock Canyon, 398
Spruces Camp, 315
Spry, Governor William, 247
Square Tower, 497: Canyon, 497
"Squatters," 340
Squaw Basin, 494
"Squaw Springs," 324
Squires, Lawrence, 165
Stage coaches, 177, 323, 332, 356, 367, 379, 412
Stagecoach, 443
Stage lines, 74, 76, 332, 364
Stairs Power Plant Reservoir, 314
Stake of Zion, 59, 94
Stamp mill, 365
Standard Oil Company, 284, 319
Standardville, 405
Stanford, Leland, 131
Stanislaus River, 49
Stansbury Expedition, 351
Stansbury, Captain Howard, 25, 66, 112, 154, 217, 230, 235, 387, 388, 482, 484-86
Stansbury Island, 483, 486
Stansbury Mountains, 226, 384, 391
Stansbury Terrace, 17
Stansfield, John H., 167
State Capitol, 144, 165-69, 185, 226-28, 232, 233, 245, 246, 248, 249
State Capitol Relic Hall, 249
State Fair, 165, 229
State Flower, 22
State Tree, 19
Statehood, 62, 69, 75, 76, 80, 83-85
Statistics: agricultural, 99-101, 103, 105, 106, 109, 110, 117, 311, 366, 370; animal life, 24-6, 278; art, 169, 175; Indian, 45, 375; industrial, 31, 115-18, 284, 418; irrigation, 105, 106; livestock, 101-04, 127, 372; mining, 119, 121-24, 393; recreation, 142, 143, 287; smelter production, 121, 285, 316, 409; water resource and power, 29, 30
Steamboat Rock, 356
Steamboats, 361, 363, 364, 483
Steel, 358
Steele, John, 61
Steen, Rector, 121, 378
Stegner, Wallace, 157
Stenhouse, T. B. H., 131, 151, 156, 231

Stephens: Evan, 173, 279; Wade N., 174; William, 368
Steptoe, E. J., 67
Steward, Julian H., 383
Stewardship, 80, 81
Stewart, Jackson, 424; Le Conte, 166; Randolph H., 331; Robert, 99; William M. School, 259
Stiles, George P., 69
Stillwater Canyon, 398
Stock breeding, 102, 273, 334, 369
Stockmore Ranger Station, 369
Stockton, 363, 391-93
Stockton Bar, 17
Stokes: Jeremiah, 156; Lee, 402
Stone: George, 399; Julius F., 399
Stookey, Dr. W. W., 387
Storm Mountain Picnic Area, 314
Stowell, Heber J., 404
Strang, James J., 56
"Stranger's Plat," 251
Strawberry: Day, 275; Reservoir, 106, 145, 377; River, 47; Valley, 337, 346, 377
Street cars, 206, 233, 245, 534
Stronghold House, 498
Strongknob Mountains, 486
Strongs Knob, 486
Sublette: Milton G., 50; William, 48, 49, 202
Suckers, 27, 145, 222, 278
Sugar beets, 9, 19, 30, 88, 99, 100, 112, 115, 275, 288, 330, 335, 338, 353, 354, 361, 364, 365
Sugar Loaf, 430
Sugar manufacturing, 88, 117, 273, 338, 353
Sugarhouse, 314
Sugarhouse Monument, 168
Sullivan, Jake, 416
Sulphide ores, 123, 317
Sulphur Springs, 363
Sulphurdale, 125, 295
Summer-fallowing, 101
Summit Creek, 367
"Sun Beam" mine, 412
"Sun Stones," 237
Sunnyside, 400
Sunrise Peak, 292
"Sunrise Point," 461, 462
Sunset: 280; Beach, 383; Mine, 312; Peak, 315
"Sunset Point," 460, 462
"Sunset View," 474
Surface mining, 319
"Surrounds," 39
Sutherland, George, 220, 419
Sutter's Fort, 63, 306, 387
Sutter's Mill, 58, 246
Swallows, 355, 356, 502
Swazey Peak, 421

"Swede, the," 492
"Sweet Singer of Israel, The," 242
Sweetwater River, 48, 69
Sweet-william, 22, 23
Swimming, 143, 260, 280, 284, 288, 333, 370, 482
Symbolisms, 7, 36, 237, 238
Syracuse, 281
Syrett, Ruben C., 460

Tabbyville, 369
Tabby, Ute chief, 369
Tabernacle Park, Ogden, 210
Tabiona, 369
Table Mountain, 217
Taft, Howard, 522
Tailings, dumps, 318
Talmadge, 369
Talmadge, James E., 238
Tamarix, 19
Tammen, Harry, 254
"Tanks," natural water, 465, 505
Tanner, Faun McConkie, 424
Tanning, 113, 114
"Tapideros," 160
Tarantulas, 300
Tavaputs Plateau, 450
Taylor: Canyon, 213; Field, 146
Taylor: John, 58, 81, 84, 101, 196, 223, 281, 435; L. T., 451; Norman, 424
Teal, 26, 278
Teasdale, 348, 468
Teasdale, Mary, 165, 166
Tecumseh Ridges, 301
Telegraph, 7, 64, 74, 128, 193, 231
Telephone, 206, 367, 435
"Temple of Osiris," 463
"Temple of Sinawava," 523, 524, 526
Temple Square, 4, 36, 115, 167, 176, 183, 226, 227, 228, 230, 232, 234, 314
Temples, 94, 95, 184, 335
Tepees, 39, 40, 182
Territorial Legislature, 107, 109, 135, 196, 294, 362
Territory of Utah, 63, 64, 67, 70, 123, 229
Tesora mine, 414
Tetzleff, Teddy, 389
Textiles, 115, 117, 161, 276
Thatcher, Hezekiah, 193, 197
Theater, 176, 179, 379
"Theater," 513
"This Is The Place" Monument, 255
Thistle, 330, 333, 408
Thomas: Charles J., 173; Elbert D., 157; Elijah, 301; George, 275; Preston, 488
Thompson, Philip, 51
Thompsons, 158, 397
Thomson, Ross, 428

Thorne's Museum, 373
Thornley, John, 281
"Thor's Hammer," 462
Thousand Lake Mountain, 146, 347
"Three Gossips," 454
Three Lakes Canyon, 344
Three Mile Canyon, 278
"Three Patriarchs," 524
"Three Wise Owls," 469
Three Witnesses Monument, 235, 237
Thurber, 348, 434
Thurber, A. K., 347
Tibbetts, William, 428
Tidwell, Jefferson, 400
Tillohash, Tony, 308
Timbimboo: Moroni, 352; Yeagah, 352
Timber, 20, 21, 29, 31, 59, 114
Timpanogos: Camp, 516; Cave National Monument, 224, 288, 289, 512, 519; Loop, 513, 518, 519; Theater, 517
Timpanogats Indians, 38
Timpanois Indians, 481
Timpie Junction, 384, 385
Tintic, 123, 137, 363, 411, 413, 416, 417
Tintic mining district, 121, 122, 395
Tintic Mountains, 412
Tippett, 391
Tithing, 81, 97
Tithing House, 177
Titmouse, gray, 27
Toab, Foster Charles, 308
Tolls, 128, 310, 381
Tomatoes, 280
Tompkins, Harvey, 415
Tongue River, Montana, 76
Tony Grove, 146
Tooele, 116, 319, 391, 392: County, 17, 38, 78, 122, 392; Valley, 29, 58, 388
Topaz, 125
Topography, 8, 18, 133
Toquerville, 327
Torrey, 348, 466-68
Totem Pole, 425
Totem Pole Park, 358
Tourism, 89, 117, 118, 143
Tout: Erwin F., 207; Margaret, 207; Nannie, 207; Romaine, 207
"Tower Arch," 454
Tracy: Russell L., 265; Mrs. Russell L., 265
Tracy's Aviaries, 265
Trade: emigrant, 63, 277; Indian, 48, 274, 277
Trading posts, 162, 444, 510
Trails, 313, 315, 332, 517, 518, 525, 350, 423
"Train Rock," 444
"Transportation," passim, esp. 126.

Trappers, 25, 48, 52, 153, 154, 192, 193, 201, 203, 272, 354, 355, 358, 385, 386, 397, 399, 481, 491, 497, 503
Traverse Mountains, 16
Travertine, 334
"Travois," 126, 134
Treaty of Guadaloupe Hidalgo, 59
Tremonton, 133, 353, 364, 365
Trenton, 274
Trimble, K. W., 442
Troops, 70, 73, 120, 176, 296
Tropic, 340, 341, 459
Trout, 27, 145, 316, 359
Trout Creek, 38: Ranger Station, 373
Trucking, 88, 116, 133, 289
Trumbull Mountain, 457
Tuba City, Arizona, 435, 445
Tubaduka Indians, 38
Tucker, 408
Tuilla, Indian Chief, 392
Tukuhnikivatz Peak, 450, 455
Tullidge, John, 163, 164, 262
Tungston, 390
Tunnel, Mt. Carmel, 327
Turkey Day, 334
Turnbow, 451
Turnbow's Cabin, 455
"Turret Arch," 453
Turtle Mountain, 342
Tushar Mountains, 144, 271, 295, 296, 338
Tushar Plateau, 10
Twain, Mark, 113, 355, 391
Twelve Milk Creek, 335
Twentieth Wing Headquarters, 254
"Twin Brothers," 524
Twin: Lakes, 315; Peaks, 228; Towers, 498
Tyner, Dick, 417

Udy Hot Springs, 352
Uinkaret Indians, 38
Uinta: Indians, 38; Lakes, 491; Mountains, 8, 10, 11, 12, 15, 18, 25, 26, 47, 49, 144, 145, 313, 361, 366, 369, 371, 372, 373, 375, 376, 478, 489, 490, 491, 492, 493, 495; National Forest, 24, 218, 368; River, 51, 398, 494
Uintah-Ouray Indian reservation, 45, 248, 294, 375, 376
Uintah Basin, 10, 14, 35, 38, 43, 48, 51, 52, 74, 76, 86, 124, 145, 170, 260, 360, 371, 372, 375, 376, 377, 478, 490: Industrial Convention, 375
Umpqua Indians, 50
Uncle Sam Mine, 414
Unemployment insurance, 89
Ungustroup, Indian chief, 346
"Unjoined Rock," 454

Unlawful cohabitation, 80, 82, 83
Union Pacific Railroad, 77, 88, 103, 129, 130, 131, 132, 208, 218, 299, 323, 358, 360, 361, 364, 379, 391, 395, 416, 420, 460
Union Stock Yards, Ogden, 207
Unitarians, 86
United Order, 80, 81, 82, 85, 114, 193, 250, 343
U. S. Army, 149, 159, 282, 356: Munitions Station, 280
U. S. Biological Survey, 25, 278, 337, 278
U. S. Bureau: of Fisheries, 290; of Mines, 119, 362, 378; of Public Roads, 206; of Reclamation, 105
U. S. Coast Geodetic Survey, 234
U. S. Department of Agriculture, 103, 282, 326, 353
U. S. Deputies, 305, 327
U. S. Forest Service, 24, 26, 101, 102, 103, 206, 211, 283, 287, 297, 312, 313, 314, 315, 337, 339, 369, 374, 377, 429, 490, 495, 515, 516, 617; Camp, 369; Campgrounds, 294
U. S. General Land Office, 510
U. S. Geological Survey, 124, 431, 442, 477, 502
U. S. Grazing Service, 101, 423
U. S. Gypsum Plant, 334
U. S. Land Laws, 107
U. S. Land Office, 108
U. S. Mine, 319
U. S. National Park Service, 425, 496, 452, 513, 516
U. S. Rock Wool Plant, 285
U. S. Senate, 79, 220, 257, 432
U. S. Soil Conservation Service, 30, 196, 384
U. S. Supreme Court, 79, 83, 220
U. S. Veterans Hospital, 251
Unionville, 367
University Hill, Provo, 216, 219
University Mine, U. of U., 263
University of the City of Nauvoo, 55
University of Deseret, 136-37, 139, 259
University of Utah, 36, 139, 140, 157, 164, 166, 168, 175, 177, 227, 258, 259, 339, 355, 409, 479, 481, 510
University of Utah Archeological Museum, 409
University of Utah, Biological Survey, 260
University of Wyoming, 169
University Ward Chapel, 258
Untermyer, Samuel, 319
Upjohn, Hobart B., 265
Upper Bingham, 321
Upper Campus, B.Y.U., 219, 220

Upper Grand Canyon of the Colorado, 423
Upper Rocky Creek Valley, 493
Upper Spanish Fork Canyon, 408
Upper Stillwater, 369
Uranium, 123, 396, 403
"Urim and Thumminn," 53
Ursenbeck, Octavius, 161
Utah and Pleasant Valley Railroad, 218
Utah Art Project, 264, 350, 402, 405
Utah Central Railroad, 85, 132, 232, 360, 379
Utah Commission, 83
Utah County, 121, 222, 223, 339
Utah Copper Company, 317, 319, 321, 322
"Utah's Dixie," 12, 19, 61, 74, 85, 271, 296, 300, 302, 305, 307, 328, 525
Utah Emergency Relief Administration, 106
Utah Engineering Experiment Station, 263
Utah Farm Bureau, 88
Utah Fish and Game Commission, 24, 26, 144, 224, 337
Utah Historical Records Survey, 264, 400, 402, 491
Utah Historical Quarterly, 43, 204 229, 343, 436, 465
Utah Horse and Cattle Growers Association, 100
Utah Hot Springs, 214, 279
Utah Jubilee (see Golden Jubilee)
Utah Lake, 11, 12, 17, 27, 29, 38, 47, 51, 72, 106, 143, 162, 216, 217, 222, 223, 224, 271, 288, 289, 320, 330, 408, 411, 481
Utah Music Project, 264
Utah National Guard, 287
Utah Northern R.R., 132, 194, 232, 333
Utah Parks Company, 460
Utah Poultry Co-operative Association, 335
Utah Power and Light Company, 224
Utah Southern Extension Railroad, 85, 232
Utah Southern Railroad, 85, 132, 218, 232, 416
Utah State Agricultural College, 99, 139, 141, 168, 175, 185, 192, 194, 196
Utah State Agricultural Extension Service, 100
Utah State Art Center, 141, 169, 175, 264
Utah State Art Collection, 249
Utah State Department of Public Instruction, 335
Utah State Engineer, 110

Utah State Fair Association, 169, 249
Utah State Fairgrounds, 266
Utah State Historical Society, 149, 240
Utah State Institute of Fine Arts, 168, 169, 175, 249
Utah State Legislature, 109, 245, 248, 249
Utah State Mental Hospital, 222
Utah State Militia, 70, 432
Utah State Park Commission, 38
Utah State Planning Board, 24, 89, 117, 143, 192
Utah State Road Commission, 372
Utah State Supreme Court, 245, 249
Utah State Symphony Orchestra Association, 175
Utah State Trout Hatchery and Game Farm, 290, 341
Utah Territory, 63, 64, 137
Utah Valley, 47, 58, 66, 67, 72, 215, 216, 222, 284, 288, 370, 377, 403, 408, 513, 517
Utah War, 69, 72, 193, 204, 208, 218, 231, 238, 282, 356
Utah Wool Growers Association, 100
Utah Wool Pulling, 384
Utah Writers' Project, 264, 328
Ute Indians, 7, 38, 39, 40, 41, 42, 43, 63, 66, 76, 160, 170, 182, 213, 217, 220, 248, 337, 346, 355, 367, 375, 412, 432, 450, 482, 491, 503
Ute Mountains, Colorado, 431, 433
Uvada, 298

Valdez, Juan, 320
Valley Mountains, 271
Valley Tan, 113, 276
Vanadium, 123, 396
Vancouver Island, 57
Van Vliet, Captain Maurice, 70, 71
Vaudeville, 179, 318
Vegetables, 9, 318
Velocipede Mine, 393
Vermilion: Castles, 297; Cliffs, 342
Vermont, 52, 56
Vernal, 36, 37, 371, 372-74
Vernon, 392, 395
Victorian architecture, 183, 185, 228, 257, 258
View Point, 331
Vigilantes, 357
Vinery, Toquerville, 327
Vineyard, 289
Vineyards, 327, 328
Virgin City, 328, 526
Virgin River, 11, 18, 24, 46, 47, 309, 349, 522, 525
Virgin River Valley, 12, 32, 525
Virginia, 431
Vivian Park, 370

Vivarium, 260
Volcanic craters, 15, 295, 302, 345

W-Bar-L Ranch, 160, 439
Wage-and-hour law, 89
Wagoners, 127
Wah Wah Mountains, 326
Wah Wah Valley, 326
Wahweep Creek, 160
'Waiva,' 340
Wakara (Walker), 293
Wales, 123
Wales, Nym, 157
Walker: Charles, 305; Joseph, 386, 50; Brothers, 286, 301
Walker Brothers Bank, 114, 393
Walker: Gulch, 378; Opera House, 179; War, 300
Wall, Colonel Enos, 119, 121, 319
Wall's Rocks, 121, 319
"Wall Street," 462, 463
Wall of Windows, 458, 462
Walton, Isaac, 369
Walton Canyon, 313
Wampanoags Indians, 247
Wanship, 366-68, 381
Ward: Captain E. B., 414; William, 163, 183, 241; Mormon, 5, 94, 138
Ware, Florence, 166
Warner Campground, 429
Warner, Glenn S. (Pop.), 308; Matt, 402; Ranger Station, 429
Wars, Indian, see Depredations
Wasatch: 354; Fault, 15; Mountains, passim; National Forest, 142, 289, 314, 368, 490
Wash basin, 329
Washakie, 41, 311, 351, 352
Washakie Indians, 353
"Washes," 429, 439
Washington, 21, 302: County, 38, 145, 300, 305; Monument, 62; Giant, 303
Washington, D. C., 73, 100, 432, 465, 506, 507, 511
Wassmer, Milton, 167
Watchman, The, 523
Water, 8, 59, 314, 315, 323-25, 394, 409, 414, 430, 510: conservation, 28, 29, 106; holes, 432, 439; rights, 107-10, 223; storage, 102, 200, 223, 314, 340, 341, 381; supply, 340; transportation, 134
Water Pocket Fold, 340, 465
"Water running over rocks," 516
Water Ute Indians, 38
Waterfalls, 310, 370, 517, 518, 524, 525
Watering place, 429
Watersheds, 31
Watson, George H., 286, 287

Watson, 376
Wattis, 402
Wayne County, 348
Wayne Wonderland, 467
Weaber River, 358
Weaver, Pauline, 358
Weaver River, 358
Weber, Capt. John G., 357
Weber Canyon, 48, 77, 128, 200, 213, 214, 333, 354, 358-360, 368, 386
Weber College, 141, 211
Weber: Mountain, 359; River, 12, 49, 59, 145, 200, 204, 211, 280, 354, 356-58, 367, 368, 370; Stake Academy, 211; Station, 357; Utes, 38; Valley, 357, 360, 366
Webster: Gulch, 378; Junction, 273
Weeds, E. H., 417
Weeping Rock, 525
Weggeland, Daniel, 163-65, 262, 283
Weir, Thomas, 193, 319
Wellington, 400
Wells: Dan. H., 72, 232; Heber M., 85, 179
Wellsville, 193, 276, 277, 332: Cone, 276; Grouse Refuge, 276; Mountains, 330
Welsh, 380
Welti, Walter, 175
Wendover, 17, 262, 371, 382, 385, 386, 390
Werner, Merton R., 155
West Cache Canal, 274
West: Caleb W., 85, 432; Ray B., 156
West Canyon, 525
West Fork, Blacks Fork Creek, 494
West Mountain District, 322
West Rim Trail, 524, 525
West Temple, 521, 523
West Tintic Agricultural Cooperative Colony, 420
West Tintic Mountains, 395
Western Federation of Miners, 320, 380
"Western Jordan" River, 288
Western Pacific Railroad, 86, 132, 371
Western Union, 128
Westminster College, 139, 141, 265
Wetherill: John, 510, 511; Mrs. John, 510
Wheat, 9, 61, 246, 318, 335, 354, 361, 364, 367
Wheat & Beet Day, 353
Wheeler Basin, 311
Wheeler Canyon, 311
Wheelwright, Lorin F., 175
Whipple, Maurine, 156
Whirlpool Canyon, 478
Whisky, 50, 113, 276, 287, 372, 381

Whisky Street, 73, 231
White, A. F., 417
White: Sergeant R. C., 176; Richard, 248
White: Canyon, 503, 504, 506, 507, 510; Cliffs, 342; Creek Canyon, 350; Indians, 388; Mesa, 434; Mountain, 294; River, 47, 478; River Agency, 43; Rock Island, 483, 486; top, 410
"White Water" boatman, 441
Whiterocks, 41, 42, 170, 248, 372, 375, 376, 398, 494
Whiterocks Indian School, 376
Whitesage, 300
Whiting Brothers, 369
Whitingham, Vermont, 56
Whitman, Dr. Marcus, 51
Whitman Party, 203
Whitmer, David, 235
Whitney: Asa, 128; John L., 414; Orson F., 120, 157, 179
Widtsoe: Dr. John A., 155, 339; Leah, 155, 339
Widtsoe, 341
Widtsoe Project, 31
"Wife Sacrifice," 420
Wight, Lyman, 55
Wigons, John, 294
Wild Bunch, 373, 467
"Wild Delirium Mine," 393
Wild: horses, 102, 103, 364, 467, 484; life refuges, 31, 283, 310, 377; mustard, 310; pansies, 310; rose, 22
"Wild West Division," 88
Wildcat, 451
Wildwood, 370, 518
Willard, 30, 206, 278, 279
Willard Peak, 276
Willamette Valley, 50, 51
Williams: Benjamin, 193; J. W., 451
Willow Creek Canyon, 406
Willow Springs Cabin, 452
"Willow Valley," 192
Wilson: A. G., 427; Charley, 355; Elijah Nicholas, 154, 384; Harry Leon, 156; Woodrow, 326, 522
Wilson: Lane, 210; Peak, 494
Wind erosion, 30, 384, 451, 452, 454, 455, 497
Wind River, 203: Mountains, 51
Windmills, 326
Windows, The, 424, 452
Windows Reef, 453
Winkleman Resort, 339
Winnamuck Smelter, 318
Winsor, L. M., 100
Winter Quarters, 58, 59
Winter sports, 143, 146, 285, 315, 370
Winterton Bros., 369
The Witches, 357

Wolf Creek Pass Campground, 369
Wolf Ranch, 451
Wolfskill, Wm., 50
"Woman's Lode, The," 318
Women in Mormon theology, 94
Woodbury, Dr. A. M., 329, 481
Woodman: J. B., 122, 285; Jean, 156
Woodruff, 309, 313, 331: W. W., 135;
  Wilford, 84, 196, 251, 255; William,
  229
Woodruff Manifesto, 114
Woods Cross, 284
Woodside, 396, 400
Word of Wisdom, 92
Work Projects Administration, 141,
  161, 168, 175, 280, 291, 402, 405,
  479
W P A Art Program, 169, 264
Work relief, 230
Workmen's compensation law, 89
Workmen's lien law, 89
Workmen's safety appliance laws, 89
World War, 88, 116, 197, 250, 334,
  381
Worm Creek, 273
Wright, Alma B., 166
Writers, 154-58
Wyoming, 11, 12, 24, 25, 38, 41, 42,
  50, 51, 62, 63, 69, 75, 86, 201, 203,
  206, 207, 212, 213, 282, 331, 361,
  373, 415

Yachting, 134, 147, 383, 483
Yampa Indians, 38
Yampa River, 477
Yellowstone National Park, 267, 466
Yosemite No. 1, 318
Young, Ann Eliza Webb, 80, 155, 256
Young, Brigham, 4, 29, 42, 52, 55, 56,
  57, 58, 59, 60, 61, 62, 63, 64, 65, 67,
  69, 70, 71, 72, 75, 76, 77, 80, 81,
  82, 89, 92, 113, 120, 131, 132, 136,
  151, 155, 161, 162, 163, 167, 172,
  173, 174, 177, 178, 179, 183, 192,
  194, 196, 204, 217, 218, 219, 229,
  230, 231, 232, 235, 237, 238, 239,
  240, 241, 242, 243, 244, 245, 246,
  247, 250, 255, 256, 257, 264, 266,
  277, 281, 287, 288, 293, 294, 302,
  307, 311, 314, 318, 331, 352, 356,
  358, 362, 368, 370, 381, 383, 384,
  388, 411, 421, 483, 484, 522
Young John W., 381
Young, Levi Edgar, 66, 157
Young, Mahonri, 166, 167, 237, 240,
  256
Young, Phineas, 164
Young, Samuel G., 386
Young, Franklin B., 348
Young, Franklin D., 467
Young, John R., 229
Yucca, 19, 39, 467, 502
Yuta Indians, 47

Zane, Charles S., 83, 84
Z C M I, see Zion's Cooperative
  Mercantile Institution
"Zero level," 483
"Zeke's bathtub," 505
"Zeke Johnson's Last Half Mile," 505
Zinc, 119, 120, 122, 123, 317, 322, 378,
  393
Zion, 54, 60, 68, 70, 75, 92
Zion Canyon, 328
Zion Canyon Easter Pageant, 179
Zion lodge, 521, 523, 524
Zion-Mt. Carmel Highway, 329, 523
Zion Museum, 524
Zion National Monument, 11, 526
Zion National Park, 11, 14, 15, 24,
  36, 117, 124, 143, 272, 300, 327,
  329, 457, 460, 465, 469, 472, 520-27
Zion Stadium, 522, 526
Zion's Cooperative Mercantile In-
  stitution, 77, 282
Zions Park public campgrounds, 523-
  25
"Zion, Stake of," 59
Zoological museum, 260
Zoos, 254, 265, 290
Zuni, 35, 46, 47
Zuni Indians, 499

Wolf Creek Pass Campground, 792
Wolf Ranch, 437
Wolfskill, Wm., 40
Women in Mormon theology,
Woodbury, Dr. A. M., 350, 381
Woodmans,
Woodruff, 302, 313, 351; W. W., 116
Wilford W., 253, 255; William,
Woodward Manifesto, 114
Woods Cross, 582
Woodside, 259, 500
Wood of Wisdom, 92
Work Projects Administration, 117,
  162, 254, 290, 291, 292, 296,
  379
W. P. A. Art Project, 162, 254
Work relief, 290
Workmen's compensation laws, 89
Workmen's state injurance laws, 89
World War, 116, 295,

Worm Creek, 479
Wright, Alma B., 304
Wyoming, 41, 42, 44, 45, 46, 47, 48,
  49, 52, 55, 64, 65, 66, 70, 200,
  206, 207, 272, 315, 343, 351, 352,
  353, 355

Yachting, 329, 330, 383, 385
Yampa Indians, 65
Yampa River, 177
Yellowstone National Park, 267, 269
Yosemite Nat'l Park, 334
Young, Ann Eliza, Wife, 93, 153, 225
Young, Brigham, 39, 40, 41, 43, 51,
  56, 58, 60, 61, 62, 63, 64, 67, 69,
  70, 71, 75, 76, 78, 80, 81, 82,
  113, 114, 115, 116, 119, 135, 136,
  137, 176, 177, 178, 179, 181, 192,
  193, 206, 207, 217, 253, 254,
  287, 313, 334, 352, 355, 357, 393

220, 221, 222, 223, 224, 225, 242,
247, 250, 255, 256, 257, 258, 259,
277, 281, 285, 288, 292, 293, 294,
295, 304, 313, 314, 325, 331, 357,
358, 413, 457, 462, 481, 512,
Young, John W., 62
Young, Levi Edgar, 63
Young, Mahonri, 160, 162, 253, 254,
  255
Young, Phineas, 154
Young, Samuel C., 98
Young, Franklin S., 235
Young—Franklin D., 162
Young, John R., 224
Young—Lorenzo, 162, 192
Yuta Indians, 65

Zane, Charles S., 81, 135
Z. C. M. I., 100, Zion's Cooperative
  Mercantile Institution
"Zero level," 394
Zest balloon, 394
Zeke Johnson's Bent Hall Mine, 504,
  595
Zinc, 219, 220, 222, 223, 313, 351
Zion, 41, 80, 68, 70, 71, 93
Zion Canyon, 228
Zion Canyon Easter Pageant, 179
Zion Lodge, 191, 193, 194
Zion—Mt. Carmel Highway, 190, 193
Zion Museum, 383
Zion National Monument, 213, 230
Zion National Park, 10, 11, 12, 184,
  187, 188, 189, 190, 191, 193, 197,
  213, 228, 229, 230, 231, 232, 233,
  234, Zion public campgrounds, 193
"Zion, Stake of," 40
Zoological museum, 160
Knox, 251, 265, 270
Zigi, 33, 36, 37
Zuni Indians, 304

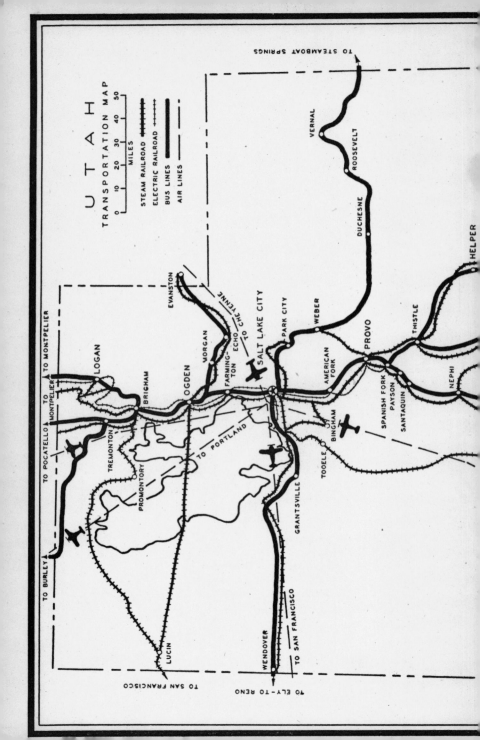